Economy	Population thousands 1998	Population growth rate % per year 1990–98	Private consumption per capita average annual % growth 1990–98	Safe water % of population with access 1990–96[a]	Life expectancy at birth years 1998	Infant mortality rate per 1,000 live births 1998	Child malnutrition % underweight 1992–98[a]	Net female primary enrollment % 1997	Female labor force % of total 1998
[illegible]n	25,051	5.0	..	12	46	149	49	33	35
[illegible]	3,339	0.2	5.9	76	72	25	8	..	41
[illegible]	29,922	2.6	–3.5	..	71	35	13	93	26
[illegible]amoa	63	4.2	..	..	..	..	..	..	..
[illegible]	65	..	..	..	..	..	..	..	..
[illegible]	12,001	3.8	–6.3	32	47	124	..	34	46
[illegible] Barbuda	67	0.6	..	95	75	17	..	..	..
[illegible]	36,125	1.5	2.7	65	73	19	2	100	32
[illegible]	3,795	1.0	–8.2	..	74	15	3	..	48
[illegible]	94	..	..	..	..	..	..	..	..
[illegible]	18,751	1.3	2.5	99	79	5	..	100	43
[illegible]	8,078	0.6	1.4	..	78	5	..	100	40
[illegible]	7,910	1.4	..	..	71	17	10	..	44
Bahamas, The	294	2.0	..	97	74	17	..	100	47
Bahrain	643	3.5	..	100	73	9	..	99	20
Bangladesh	125,629	1.9	2.1	84	59	73	56	70	42
Barbados	266	0.4	0.8	100	76	14	..	95	46
Belarus	10,239	0.0	–3.4	..	68	11	..	84	49
Belgium	10,204	0.3	0.9	..	78	6	..	100	41
Belize	239	3.3	1.9	73	75	28	6	100	24
Benin	5,948	3.3	0.6	50	53	87	29	50	48
Bermuda	63	0.6	..	..	..	..	..	..	..
Bhutan	759	3.4	..	64	61	61	..	..	40
Bolivia	7,950	2.7	0.9	55	62	60	8	95	38
Bosnia and Herzegovina	3,768	–2.4	..	..	73	13	..	..	38
Botswana	1,562	2.9	0.8	70	46	62	..	83	46
Brazil	165,874	1.6	3.3	72	67	33	6	94	35
Brunei	315	2.9	..	..	76	9	..	89	35
Bulgaria	8,257	–0.8	–1.5	..	71	14	..	99	48
Burkina Faso	10,730	2.7	0.6	..	44	104	33	25	47
Burundi	6,548	2.6	–4.0	52	42	118	..	33	49
Cambodia	11,498	3.3	..	13	54	102	..	100	52
Cameroon	14,303	3.2	0.0	41	54	77	22	59	38
Canada	30,301	1.2	0.9	99	79	5	..	100	45
Cape Verde	416	2.8	0.1	51	68	55	..	100	39
Cayman Islands	36	..	..	..	..	..	..	..	..
Central African Republic	3,480	2.4	–2.1	19	44	98	23	38	..
Chad	7,283	3.4	..	24	48	99	39	35	45
Channel Islands	149	0.6	..	..	79	6	..	..	..
Chile	14,822	1.8	7.0	85	75	10	1	89	33
China	1,238,599	1.2	8.0	90	70	31	16	100	45
Hong Kong, China	6,687	2.3	2.9	..	79	3	..	93	37
Macao, China	459	3.0	2.2	..	78	6	..	81	42
Colombia	40,804	2.2	1.9	78	70	23	8	89	38
Comoros	531	2.9	–4.9	48	60	63	26	45	42
Congo, Dem. Rep.	48,216	3.6	–9.2	27	51	90	34	48	43
Congo, Rep.	2,783	3.2	–1.6	47	48	90	..	76	43
Costa Rica	3,526	2.3	1.0	92	77	13	5	89	31
Côte d'Ivoire	14,492	3.1	–1.8	72	46	88	24	50	33
Croatia	4,501	–0.9	..	63	73	8	1	100	44
Cuba	11,103	0.6	..	93	76	7	..	100	39
Cyprus	753	1.4	..	100	78	8	..	96	39
Czech Republic	10,295	–0.1	2.8	..	75	5	1	100	47
Denmark	5,301	0.4	3.0	..	76	5	..	100	46
Djibouti	636	3.0	..	24	50	106	..	27	..
Dominica	73	0.1	0.4	..	76	15	..	..	..

Economy	Population thousands 1998	Population growth rate % per year 1990–98	Private consumption per capita average annual % growth 1990–98	Safe water % of population with access 1990–96[a]	Life expectancy at birth years 1998	Infant mortality rate per 1,000 live births 1998	Child malnutrition % underweight 1992–98[a]	Net female primary enrollment % 1997	Female labor force % of total 1998
Dominican Republic	8,254	2.1	2.4	71	71	40	6	94	30
Ecuador	12,175	2.4	0.2	70	70	32	..	100	27
Egypt, Arab Rep.	61,401	2.3	2.1	64	67	49	12	91	30
El Salvador	6,058	2.4	3.7	55	69	31	11	89	36
Equatorial Guinea	431	2.9	–5.3	95	50	106	..	80	35
Eritrea	3,879	3.0	..	7	51	61	44	28	47
Estonia	1,450	–1.1	0.0	..	70	9	..	100	49
Ethiopia	61,266	2.6	1.0	27	43	107	48	27	41
Faeroe Islands	44	..	..	..	..	..	..	..	..
Fiji	790	1.0	..	100	73	19	8	100	29
Finland	5,153	0.5	–0.1	98	77	4	..	100	48
France	58,847	0.5	0.8	100	78	5	..	100	45
French Polynesia	227	2.0	..	..	72	11	..	..	..
Gabon	1,180	3.0	–4.1	67	53	86	..	..	45
Gambia, The	1,216	4.0	–0.2	76	53	76	26	58	45
Georgia	5,442	0.0	..	..	73	15	..	89	47
Germany	82,047	0.5	0.9	..	77	5	..	100	42
Ghana	18,460	3.1	1.2	56	60	65	27	..	51
Greece	10,515	0.5	1.3	..	78	6	..	100	37
Greenland	56	0.1	..	..	68	18	..	..	..
Grenada	96	0.4	2.5	85	72	14	..	..	..
Guam	149	1.5	..	..	77	8	..	..	..
Guatemala	10,799	3.0	1.7	67	64	42	27	70	28
Guinea	7,082	3.0	1.6	62	47	118	..	33	47
Guinea-Bissau	1,161	2.5	2.3	53	44	128	..	39	40
Guyana	849	0.9	5.6	81	64	57	18	93	34
Haiti	7,647	2.4	..	28	54	71	28	..	43
Honduras	6,156	3.3	0.3	65	69	36	25	89	31
Hungary	10,114	–0.4	–1.0	..	71	10	..	97	45
Iceland	274	1.0	0.4	100	79	3	..	100	45
India	979,673	2.0	4.0	81	63	70	53	71	32
Indonesia	203,678	1.9	5.9	62	65	43	34	99	40
Iran, Islamic Rep.	61,947	1.9	1.2	83	71	26	16	89	26
Iraq	22,328	3.0	..	44	59	103	12	70	19
Ireland	3,705	0.8	3.9	..	76	6	..	100	34
Isle of Man	76	..	..	..	..	..	..	..	..
Israel	5,963	3.5	3.4	99	78	6	..	..	41
Italy	57,589	0.2	0.4	..	78	5	..	100	38
Jamaica	2,576	1.0	–1.1	70	75	21	10	96	46
Japan	126,410	0.3	1.6	96	81	4	..	100	41
Jordan	4,563	5.2	0.2	89	71	27	5	68	23
Kazakhstan	15,593	–0.7	..	..	65	22	8	..	47
Kenya	29,295	3.1	–0.2	53	51	76	23	67	46
Kiribati	86	2.5	..	100	61	58	..	..	..
Korea, Dem. Rep.	23,171	1.8	..	..	63	54	32	..	43
Korea, Rep.	46,430	1.1	4.6	83	73	9	..	100	41
Kuwait	1,866	–1.9	..	100	77	12	2	64	31
Kyrgyz Republic	4,699	1.0	–5.2	81	67	26	11	99	47
Lao PDR	4,974	3.0	..	39	54	96	40	69	..
Latvia	2,449	–1.2	..	..	70	15	..	100	50
Lebanon	4,210	2.1	5.3	100	70	27	3	..	29
Lesotho	2,058	2.5	–3.9	52	55	93	16	74	37
Liberia	2,962	2.8	..	30	47	114	..	..	40
Libya	5,302	2.6	..	90	70	23	5	100	22
Liechtenstein	32	..	..	..	..	..	..	..	..
Lithuania	3,703	–0.1	–2.0	..	72	9	..	..	48

Global Marketing Strategies

Global Marketing Strategies

Fifth Edition

Jean-Pierre Jeannet

F. W. Olin Distinguished Professor of Global Business
Babson College, Wellesley, Massachusetts

Professor of Global Marketing and Strategy
International Institute for Management Development (IMD)
Lausanne, Switzerland

H. David Hennessey

Associate Professor of Marketing and International Business
Babson College, Wellesley, Massachusetts

Associate, Ashridge Management College
Berkhamsted, United Kingdom

Houghton Mifflin Company Boston New York

Associate Sponsoring Editor: *Joanne Dauksewicz*
Senior Project Editor: *Maria Morelli*
Editorial Assistants: *Cecilia Molinari, Tanius Stamper*
Senior Production/Design Coordinator: *Jill Haber*
Senior Manufacturing Coordinator: *Marie Barnes*

Printed in the U.S.A.

Library of Congress Catalog Card Number: 00-133788

ISBN: 0-618-07188-1

123456789-FFG-04 03 02 01 00

Brief Contents

Contents

Preface

As the fifth edition of *Global Marketing Strategies* goes to press, we face a new environment where global marketing has become the norm—rather than the exception—for most businesses big and small. Within the span of three years since the publication of our previous edition, the global business environment has been subject to enormous changes. First and foremost, the face of global marketing has been changed forever by the emergence of the networked economy through the rapid development of the Internet and the related electronic business activities. Regionally, the economies of Asia have returned to aggressive growth and China is about to join the World Trade Organization (WTO). Latin American economies have become more attractive to global firms resulting in renewed investments in that area. In Europe, we have witnessed the transition to a common currency, the Euro. Throughout this period, global companies have continued to be involved in business transformations often witnessed through a spate of large, global mergers.

To students of business, these recent developments have important implications. In particular the development of the Internet has allowed many small firms to have a global presence, to reach customers in many different countries, all at a much smaller cost than was the case in the pre-Internet era. A senior World Bank executive recently documented that this is reaching into even the most unexpected regions of the world. In Ethiopia, one local businessman has already built a prosperous e-commerce-based business. Since it is traditional for emigrated Ethiopians to offer their families a goat on certain occasions, the local executive built his web business by offering the opportunity to order a goat, pay by credit card, and arrange for the transport and delivery of the goat to local families.

While the globalization of the world economy is expanding at a rapid pace, in the past few years we have seen the first strong challenges to this trend. Actions taken by protesters at the meeting of the World Trade Organization in Seattle in 1999 has demonstrated that there are several constituencies who do not consider themselves to be gaining from the general globalization trend. Some of these protesting organizations are expected to play a growing role in the near future—posing a constant challenge to the unbridled globalization process.

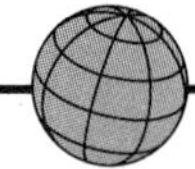

Major Features Retained

We have retained a number of features from the previous editions. *Global Marketing Strategies* continues to target the manager and student with a global marketing vision, regardless of nationality, industry, or location. Our approach is largely managerial. We look at the global marketing task through the eyes of the marketing manager. As in previous editions, we maintain our strategic focus throughout. We believe that success in global marketing today is not only a function of broad cultural understanding but also modern global strategic thinking, which we refer to as a global mindset. We have also retained our emphasis on the practical aspects of global marketing by including numerous current examples from well-known companies in Europe, Asia, and the Americas. Finally we continue to offer full-length cases that explore global marketing issues in depth.

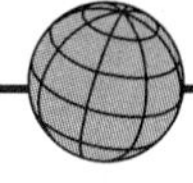

Major Changes in the Fifth Edition

We have updated the text material in the fifth edition by using examples from the late 1990s, with a particular concentration on the period 1997 to 1999. Given that our final completion of most revisions was in early 2000, most chapters have several 2000 sources, which will make the text more updated than in the past.

While the forth edition had a substantial amount of material focused on regional economic developments in Asia (ASEAN), and China in particular, the impending changes in Europe (with the EU and EMU), in North America (NAFTA), in Latin America with Mercossur, the fifth edition has a substantial amount of new material dealing with the new economy or e-business and its impact on global marketing.

Philosophically, we have moved more strongly in the direction of global marketing having adopted a global mindset throughout the text. This is sometimes a reflection of language only, but is often reflected in material and content. Some of the chapter headings have also been adjusted accordingly.

Structurally the text has undergone some changes. Cases have been moved to a separate casebook so that they can be revised and updated on an annual basis. In addition, the text design has been completely revised and enhanced through the introduction of color. Some chapters appear in the fifth edition in a different sequence that they did in the forth, although the number of chapters and sections has remained constant. All chapters have been updated, and some have undergone substantial changes as detailed below.

Chapter 1, "Global Marketing: An Overview," has been extensively updated with new examples. Structurally, the chapter remains unchanged.

Part 1, "Understanding the Global Marketing Environment," has not been structurally changed, but has been revised to reflect the realities of groups like EU, NAFTA, ASEAN, and the World Trade Organization. Chapter 2, "The Global Economy," has been updated to include the latest available statistics on world trade and growth rates. The chapter also includes recent examples of the impact of exchange rates on companies and an update on the launch of the Euro in Europe. Chapter 3, "Cultural and Social Forces," includes a number of new examples of how companies are successfully responding to issues such as language and cultural differences from country to country. Chapter 4, "Political and Legal Forces," has been updated to illustrate how countries use their political and legal systems to defend and support their local economy. The chapter also includes a number of recent examples of actions global companies have taken to respond to host and home country pressures. The latest political risk statistics are included in the revised chapter.

In Part 2, Chapter 5, "Global Markets and Buyers," includes a large volume of information that has been updated. Chapter 5, renamed to "Analyzing Global Marketing Opportunities," includes the recent revisions to the regional trade groups as well as a review of these groups importance relative to the WTO. We have also updated the country statistics inside the back cover of the text and updated the 8 pages of color summaries of world statistics. Chapter 6, renamed "Global Marketing Research," has been updated with the latest statistics as well as new resources now available on-line.

In Part 3, Chapter 7, "Developing a Global Marketing Mindset," has been adapted to reflect the latest conceptual developments in this area and furnished with new visuals and examples. Chapter 8, "Global Marketing Strategies" has been completely revised. The order of topics has been changed and expanded, with an enhanced discussion of global marketing strategies, with many new references and examples. Chapter 9, "Global Market Entry Strategies," has been expanded to include of the impact of electronic commerce (Internet, Web sites) on global marketing in the form of portal strategy as a separate entry strategy.

The revision emphasis in Part 4, "Designing Global Marketing Programs," focused on updating examples and references, and maximizing new company examples from the period 1997 to 2000. Most importantly, the sequence and some of the names of chapters were changed. The section begins with treatment of pricing, promotion, and advertising. Product strategies and distribution are at the end of this section, reversing the order from the previous edition. Chapter 10 (formerly chapter 13) and has been renamed to "Pricing for Global Markets." This chapter has been updated with recent examples of how companies develop global pricing strategies. Chapter 11 (previously chapter 14) has been renamed "Global Promotional Strategies". The chapter has been improved with new examples of companies' promotional programs using sales promotion, direct mail and sports sponsorship, as well as the rapid growth of the Internet. Chapter 12 (formerly chapter 15) includes over 30 new references, primarily providing information on how companies are successfully using global advertising.

Chapter 13, (previously chapter 10) was renamed "International and Global Product and Service Strategies," and includes a revised branding section. Chapter 14 (previously chapter 11), "Developing New Products for Global Markets," has been revised with examples to illustrate how companies are developing new products in a global context. We have also added discussions of new techniques, such as modularity in product development. In Chapter 15, "Managing Global Distribution Channels," we expanded the section dealing with the use of the Internet as a distribution channel.

"Managing the Global Marketing Effort," Part 5 of the book; has been updated with new examples. We placed greater emphasis on global organizations and their impact on global marketing. Chapter 16, "Organizing for Global Marketing," reflects the strengthening of the role of the global marketing organization with enhanced concepts like global mandates. Chapter 17, "Planning and Controlling Global Marketing," maintains the same organizational structure. New examples were included and references updated. Chapter 18, "The Export and Import Trade Process," was updated with some of the new Internet based tools that can be used to expedite the import/export processes. Also, the obstacles to foreign imports have been updated as well with current examples.

Complete Teaching Package

The teaching package for the fifth edition includes the *Instructor's Resource Manual with Test Questions*, *Case Teaching Guide*, a computerized test bank, a videotape with instructor's guide, PowerPoint slides, and student and instructor web sites, which are new to this edition.

- The *Instructor's Resource Manual* contains suggestions on how to design a global marketing course, student projects, answers to text questions, brief chapter outlines, and a completely revised test bank.
- Complete case teaching notes appear in the *Case Teaching Guide*.
- The PowerPoint slides, including over 25 slides per chapter plus additional slides for the cases, combine clear, concise text and art.
- The videos highlight well-known companies and up-to-date global issues. The video guide provides complete teaching notes to set the stage for each video and stimulate discussion.
- The student site includes Internet exercises with hyperlinks to key web resources and companies, suggested applications of course content for applied projects and research papers, and recommended Internet sites for research on many global marketing topics.

- The instructor site provides lecture notes, PowerPoint slides, comments on the Internet exercises, as well as additional mini-cases, scenarios, and/or critical thinking incidents that can be used for testing purposes to provide additional examples of course concepts.

Acknowledgments

Writing a new edition of a textbook on global marketing is a major undertaking that could not have been completed without the active support of a great many people.

We are indebted to our home institution, Babson College, for generously supporting us in the manuscript stage and allowing us the flexibility to spend time overseas to develop the material for this book. To International Management Development Institute (IMD), we are indebted for their support of our case research and for allowing us to publish IMD cases in the casebook. To Ashridge Management College, we are thankful for providing access to its extensive database, which proved helpful in updating this new edition. And finally, we would like to express our gratitude to our colleagues at Babson, IMD, and Ashridge for their support and willingness to discuss global marketing issues, which has helped us clarify many of our concepts.

To turn the collected material and data into readable form, we could always count on a number of students, graduate assistants, and research associates. Two of our Babson MBA students, Xiaolin Liu and Suonan Zheng , were instrumental in our data search for new examples for our fifth edition.

For their assistance with the supplements package, we would like to thank Jacob Chacko (Clayton College & State University and Milton Pressley (University of New Orleans).

Throughout the development of this edition and the previous edition, a number of reviewers have made important contributions. These reviews were extremely important in the revision and improvement of the text. We especially thank the following people:

B. G. Bizzell
Stephen F. Austin University

Jean Boddewyn
CUNY-Bernard M. Baruch College

Sharon Browning
Northwest Missouri State University

Roger J. Calantone
Michigan State University

Jacob Chacko
Clayton College & State University

Alex Christofides
Ohio State University

John Chyzyk
Brandon University

William Cunningham
Southwest Missouri State

Charles P. de Mortanges
University of Limburg

Dharma deSilva
Wichita State University

Susan P. Douglas
New York University

Adel I. El-Ansary
The George Washington University

Jeffrey A. Fadiman
San Jose State University

Ying Fan
University of Lincolnshire

Kate Gillespie
University of Texas at Austin

John L. Hazard
Michigan State University

Joby John
Bentley College

H. Ralph Jones
Miami University

W. Wossen Kassaye
Bentley College

A. H. Kizilbash
Northern Illinois University

Saul Klein
Northeastern University

G.P. Lauter
The George Washington University

Monle Lee
Indiana University South Bend

Sarah Maddock
University of Birmingham

Joseph L. Massie
University of Kentucky

James McCullough
The University of Arizona

Taylor W. Meloan
University of Southern California

Aubrey Mendelow
Duquesne University

Joseph C. Miller
Kelley School of Business, Indiana University

Avvari V. Mohan
Universiti Telekom, Malyasia

Thomas Ponzurick
West Virginia University

Zahir A. Quraeshi
Western Michigan University

Samuel Rabino
Northeastern University

Daniel Rajaratnam
Baylor University

Pradeep Rau
University of Delaware

F. J. Sarknas
University of Pittsburgh

Chris Simango
University of Northumbria

J. Steenkamp
University of Leuven

Michael Steiner
University of Wisconsin-Eau Claire

Gordon P. Stiegler
University of Southern California

Ruth Lesher Taylor
Southwest Texas State University

L. Trankiem
California State University at Los Angeles

Arturo Vasquez
Florida International University

Phillip D. White
University of Colorado at Boulder

Van R. Wood
Texas Tech University

Yoo S. Yang
Chung Ang University, Seoul

Attila Yaprak
Wayne State University

Poh-Lin Yeoh
University of South Carolina, Columbia

We are grateful to our publisher, Houghton Mifflin Company. Throughout the revision, we have had the pleasure of working with a number of their editors who have seen this project through to its completion. We thank them for their patience, encouragement, and professionalism in supporting our writing efforts. The marketing, production, art, editorial, permissions, and manufacturing staffs have substantially added to the quality of this finished book. Houghton Mifflin has also accommodated the need to include the latest statistics, visuals, and references in this edition.

This edition has benefited from our work with numerous executives who face the challenges of global marketing daily. Our work on executive programs with Ares-Serono, Siemens, Deloitte Touche Tohmatsu, Bausch & Lomb, Medtronic, Jardine Matheson, DSM, Novartis, ICI, Zeneca, and many others has shaped our thinking for this revision.

We also extend our greatest gratitude to our students at Babson College and IMD Institute for their constant help and inspiration. Their interest in global marketing issues inspired us to undertake and complete this project.

Finally, we thank our families for their support through the revisions, page proofs, artwork, and e-mails. We are pleased to dedicate this version to Pat, Anne-Marie, and Liz.

Jean-Pierre Jeannet
H. David Hennessey

Introduction

1 *Global Marketing: An Overview*

In this first chapter of the text, we introduce the field of global marketing. An overview of the most important global marketing decisions is given, and the major problems likely to be encountered by international firms are highlighted. This introduction to the text also explains the conceptual framework we used to develop the book. Understanding this underlying plan will help you to quickly integrate these concepts into an overall framework for global marketing. It should also make it easier for you to appreciate the complexities of global marketing.

1

Introduction to Global Marketing

THIS FIRST CHAPTER IS INTENDED TO INTRODUCE YOU TO THE FIELD OF GLOBAL marketing. Initially, we concentrate on the scope of global marketing, using several examples to illustrate that it is a broad-based process encompassing many types of participating firms and a wide range of activities. We next present definitions that relate global marketing to other fields of study. We examine the differences between domestic, international, and global marketing and explain why companies often have difficulty marketing abroad. The chapter continues with a description of the major participants in global marketing. We also provide an explanation of why mastering global marketing skills can be valuable to your future career. A conceptual outline of the book concludes the chapter.

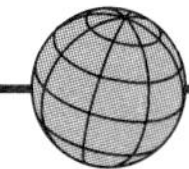

The Development of Global Marketing

The term *global marketing* has been in use only since the early 1980s. It began to assume widespread use in 1983 with the seminal article by Ted Levitt.[1] Prior to that, *international marketing*, or *multinational marketing*, was the term used most often to describe international marketing activities. However, global marketing is not just a new term for an old phenomenon; there are real differences between international marketing and global marketing. In many ways, global marketing is a subcategory of international marketing with special importance in our present world. It has captured the attention of marketing academics and business practitioners alike, and as indicated by the title of our book, we attach considerable importance to this latest type of international marketing. However, before we explain global marketing in detail, let us first look at the historical development of international marketing as a field and gain a better understanding of the phases through which it has passed.

Domestic Marketing

Marketing that is aimed at a single market, the firm's domestic market, is referred to as domestic marketing. In domestic marketing, the firm faces only one set of competitive, economic, and market issues and essentially must deal with only one set of customers, although the company may serve several segments in this one market. The marketing concepts that apply to domestic, or single-country, marketing are those we expect our readers are well versed in; they will not be covered further in this book.[2]

Export Marketing

The field of export marketing covers all those marketing activities involved when a firm markets its products outside its main (domestic) base of operation and when products are physically shipped from one market or country to another. Although the domestic marketing operation remains of primary importance, the major challenges of export marketing are the selection of appropriate markets or countries through marketing research, the determination of appropriate product modifications to meet the demand requirements of export markets, and the development of export channels through which the company can market its products abroad. In this phase, the firm may concentrate mostly on the product modifications and run the export operations as a welcome and profitable by-product of its

1. Theodore Levitt, "The Globalization of Markets," *Harvard Business Review*, May-June 1983, pp. 92–102.
2. Philip Kotler and Gary Armstrong, *Principles of Marketing*, 8th ed. (Englewood Cliffs, N.J.: Prentice Hall, 1996).

domestic strategy. Because the movement of goods across national borders is a major part of an exporting strategy, the required skills include knowledge of shipping and export documentation.[3] Although export marketing probably represents the most traditional and least complicated form of international marketing, it remains an important aspect for many firms. As a result, we devote Chapter 18 exclusively to this topic.

International Marketing

When practicing international marketing, a company goes beyond exporting and becomes much more directly involved in the local marketing environment within a given country or market. The international marketer is likely to have its own sales subsidiaries and will participate in and develop entire marketing strategies for foreign markets. At this point, the necessary adaptations to the firm's domestic marketing strategies become a main concern. Companies going international now will have to find out how they must adjust an entire marketing strategy—including how they sell, advertise, and distribute—in order to fit new market demands.

An important challenge for the international marketing phase of a firm becomes the need to understand the different environments the company needs to operate in. Understanding different cultural, economic, and political environments becomes necessary for success. This is generally described as part of a company's internationalization process, whereby a firm becomes more experienced in operating in various foreign markets. It is typical to find a considerable emphasis on the environmental component at this stage. Typically, much of the field of international marketing has been devoted to making the environment understandable and to assisting managers in navigating through the differences. The development of the cultural/environmental approach to international marketing is an expression of this particular phase.

Multinational Marketing

The focus on multinational marketing came as a result of the development of the multinational corporation. These companies, characterized by extensive development of assets abroad, operate in a number of foreign countries or markets as if the firms were local companies. Such development led to the creation of many domestic strategies—thus the name *multidomestic strategy*—whereby a multinational firm competes with many strategies, each one tailored to a particular local market. The major challenge of the multinational marketer is to find the best possible adaptation of a complete marketing strategy to an individual country. This

3. Gerald Albaum, Jesper Strandskov, Edwin Duerr, and Laurence Dowd, *International Marketing and Export Management* (Reading, Mass.: Addison-Wesley, 1989).

approach to international marketing leads to a maximum amount of localization and to a large variety of marketing strategies. Often, the attempt of multinational corporations to appear "local" wherever they compete results in the duplication of some key resources. The major benefit is the ability to completely tailor a marketing strategy to the local requirements.

Pan-Regional Marketing

Given the diseconomies of scale of individualized marketing strategies, each tailored to a specific local environment, companies have begun to emphasize strategies for larger regions. These regional strategies encompass a number of markets, such as pan-European strategies for Europe, and have come about as a result of regional economic and political integration. Such integration is also apparent in North America, where in 1993 the United States, Canada, and Mexico committed themselves to a far-reaching trade pact in the form of the North American Free Trade Agreement (NAFTA). In the Pacific Rim area, regional integration took a step forward with the first Pacific Rim country summit, held in Seattle in 1993, following a decade of rapid economic progress in that part of the world. Clearly, progress toward integration has been most pronounced in Europe, with the passing of the Maastricht Treaty to form the European Union (EU) and the impending implementation of the European Monetary Union (EMU).

Companies considering regional strategies look to tie together operations in one region rather than around the globe, the aim being increased efficiency. Many firms are presently working on such solutions, moving from many multidomestic strategies toward selected pan-regional strategies.

Global Marketing

Over the years, academics and international companies alike have become aware that opportunities for economies of scale and enhanced competitiveness are greater if they can manage to integrate and create marketing strategies on a global scale. A global marketing strategy involves the creation of a single strategy for a product, service, or company for the entire global market, encompassing many countries simultaneously and aimed at leveraging the commonalties across many markets. Rather than tailor a strategy perfectly to any individual market, in global marketing the company aims at settling on one general strategy that can be applied throughout the world market while maintaining at the same time flexibility to adapt that strategy to local market requirements where necessary. The management challenge is to design marketing strategies that work well across multiple markets. It is driven not only by the fact that markets appear increasingly similar in environmental and customer requirements but even more so by the fact that large investments in technology, logistics, or other key functions force the companies to expand their market coverage.

Thus, global marketing is the last stage in the development of the field of international marketing. Although global marketers face their own unique challenges that stem from finding marketing strategies that fit many countries, the skills and concepts of the earlier stages remain important and continue to be needed. In fact, companies that take a global marketing approach will be good exporters because they will include some exporting in their strategies. Such firms will also have to be good at international marketing because designing one global strategy requires a sound understanding of the cultural, economic, and political environment of many countries. Furthermore, few global marketing strategies can exist without some local tailoring, which is the hallmark of multinational marketing. As a result, global marketing is but the last of a series of skills, all included under the umbrella of international marketing.

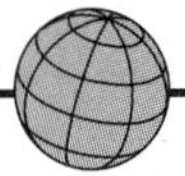

The Scope of Global Marketing

A company such as Boeing, the world's largest commercial airline manufacturer and one of the leading exporters from the United States, obviously engages in global marketing when it sells its aircraft to airlines across the world. Likewise, Ford Motor Company, which operates automobile manufacturing plants in many countries, engages in international marketing even though a major part of Ford's output is sold in the country where it is manufactured.[4]

Today, however, the scope of global marketing is broader and includes many other business activities. Those of large U.S. store chains, such as Kmart and Wal-Mart, include a substantial amount of importing. When these stores search for new products abroad to sell in the United States, they practice another form of global marketing. A whole range of service industries are involved in global marketing; major advertising agencies, banks, investment bankers, accounting firms, consulting companies, hotel chains, airlines, and even law firms now market their services worldwide.

Entertainment is another important product category with large global potential. The worldwide recorded music retail market was estimated at $38.7 billion in 1998. North America, which includes the United States and Canada, accounted for 34 percent of the world market, with the European Union accounting for 30 percent and Japan 17 percent.[5] This entire market was dominated by "the Big Five," a few large firms from the United States and Europe that claimed a large share of the world market.[6] PolyGram of the Netherlands (recently acquired by Seagram) leads with 22 percent share of market, followed by Sony of Japan with 15 percent, EMI of the United Kingdom with 15 percent, Time Warner of the

4. "Remaking Ford," *Business Week*, October 11, 1999, p. 132.
5. *Economist*, May 15, 1999, p. 114.
6. "Study Sees 7 Percent Annual Rise in Music Sales," *Financial Times*, January 21, 1997, p. 20.

United States, and Bertelsmann of Germany. All of these firms are heavily engaged in global marketing.

International marketing is even engulfing symphonic orchestras. Leading orchestras command as much as $150,000 per concert and are booking performances all over the world. Japan and London are viewed as key destinations, whereas the fees for the U.S. market have fallen because of an oversupply of events. Leading orchestras from Vienna, Berlin, New York, and Philadelphia are receiving competition from those in St. Petersburg and Moscow, whose fees are lower than those from more established locations.[7]

Defining Global Marketing Management

Although much conceptual work has been accomplished in global marketing, the use of the word *global* remains unclear among many marketing academics and executives. For many, *global* is just a new or replacement term for *international.* Since we take it to mean something new and different, we plan to make use of the term in a judicious way. For us, global marketing is a subset, albeit different and distinct, of international marketing. In general, we still occasionally use the term *international* to describe factors that relate to the entire field and use *global* mainly when it refers to the specific new phenomena of marketing globally. The term *global* was selected as the title for this book to indicate that a significant portion of this text will deal specifically with new concepts and strategies without neglecting the standard conventions of export, international, or multinational marketing.

Having examined the scope of international and global marketing, we are now able to define it more accurately. Any definition has to be built, however, on basic definitions of marketing and marketing management, with an added explanation of the international dimension. We understand *marketing* as the performance of business activities directing the flow of products and services from producer to consumer. A successful performance of the marketing function by a firm is contingent upon the adoption of the *marketing concept. Marketing management* is the execution of a company's marketing operation. Management responsibilities consist of planning, organizing, and controlling the marketing program of the firm.[8] To accomplish this job, marketing management is assigned decision-making authority over product strategy, communication strategy, distribution strategy, and pricing strategy. The combination of these four aspects of marketing is referred to as the *marketing mix.*

For global marketing management, the basic goals of marketing and the responsibilities described above remained unchanged. What is different is the execution of

7. "When Capitalism Calls the Tune," *Financial Times*, September 25, 1995, p. 13.
8. Ibid.

these activities across more than one country. Consequently, we define *global marketing management* as a process to craft a coherent, integrated, and unified marketing strategy for a product or service against the entire global opportunity. A marketing strategy to be global does not require absolute standardization. Rather, it suffices if core elements are applied consistently across multiple markets and with varying degrees of customization as the situation requires. Under global opportunity we imply that the strategy is built around a full and complete understanding of all relevant markets, but need not include all countries. A coherent strategy around a number of key markets suffices to meet the requirements for a global strategy. Global marketing thus requires moving from a single-country to a multicountry focus. As we see in Figure 1.1, many countries or markets are involved simultaneously when we speak of global marketing activities.

A U.S. firm exporting products to Japan is engaged in a marketing effort across two countries: the United States and Japan. Another U.S. firm operating a sub-

FIGURE 1.1

International and Global Marketing

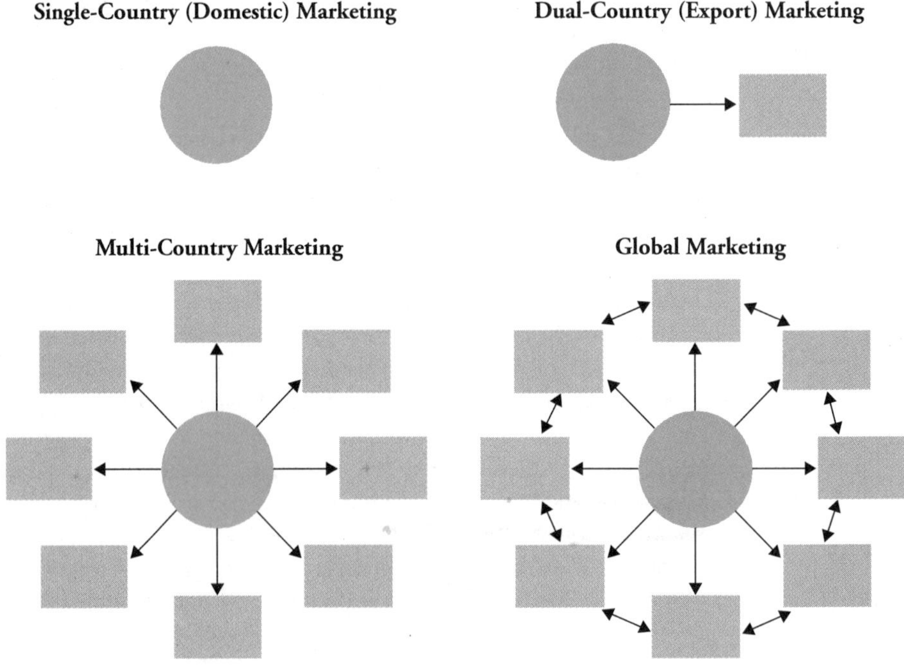

sidiary in Japan that manufactures and markets locally under the direction of the head office in the United States is also engaged in global marketing to the extent that the head office staff directs and supervises this effort. Consequently, global marketing does not always require the physical movement of products across national borders. Global marketing occurs whenever marketing decisions are made that encompass several countries.

Relationships with Other Fields of Study

The field of global marketing is related to other fields of study. In its broadest terms, global marketing is a subset of *international business*, which is defined as the performance of all business functions across national boundaries. International business includes all functional areas, such as international production, international financial management, and international marketing (see Figure 1.2).[9]

FIGURE 1.2

International and Global Marketing and Related Fields of Study

9. Henry W. Lane and Joseph J. DiStefano, *International Management Behavior: From Policy to Practice*, 2nd ed. (Boston: PWS-Kent, 1992); Paul W. Beamish et al., *International Management: Text and Cases* (Homewood, Ill.: Irwin, 1991); David K. Eiteman, Arthur I. Stonehill, and Michael H. Moffet, *Multinational Business Finance*, 6th ed. (Reading, Mass.: Addison-Wesley, 1992); Alan C. Shapiro, *Multinational Financial Management*, 4th ed. (Boston: Allyn & Bacon, 1992).

International trade theory, which explains why nations trade with each other, is a related concept. This theory is aimed at understanding product flows between countries, in the form of either exports or imports. A U.S. corporation exporting machinery to China would find its transactions recorded as an export in the United States, whereas the same transaction is treated as an import in China. In this situation, global marketing and international trade are concerned with the same phenomenon.[10]

Should the U.S. company produce its machinery in China and sell locally, however, there would be no exchange of goods between the two countries. Consequently, there would be no recognized trading activity. However, as we have seen earlier, the U.S. company's decision to build machinery in China and sell it there is still considered a global marketing decision. Therefore, we can conclude that global marketing goes beyond strict definitions of international trading and includes a wider range of activities.

Global marketing should not be confused with *foreign marketing*, which consists of marketing activities carried out by foreign firms within their own countries. Marketing by Mexican firms in Mexico is, therefore, defined as foreign marketing and is not the principal focus of this book. However, Mexican firms engaged in marketing their products in the United States are engaged in global marketing and are subject to the same concepts and principles that govern U.S. firms marketing in Mexico.

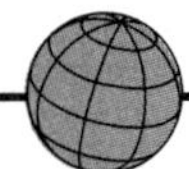

Exploring the Challenge of Global Marketing

Companies that market products or services globally have always had to deal with a wider range of issues than those encountered by domestic firms. The following example gives some insight into the special difficulties encountered in the international market.

When a company uses an initial marketing strategy abroad, success or failure depends greatly on the market where it is used. In 1977, Apple Computer Company began distribution of its personal computer in Japan. By 1985, Apple still had only a very small market share. Japanese competitors and IBM had begun to market Japanese-language machines. Apple computers could be used only by Japanese who understood English very well. It wasn't until years later that Apple brought in a team of technicians from its head office to adapt its products to the

10. Paul R. Krugman and Maurice Obstfeld, *International Economics: Theory and Policy*, 2nd ed. (New York: HarperCollins, 1991); Francisco L. Rivera-Batiz and Luis A. Rivera-Batiz, *International Finance and Open Economy Macroeconomics*, 2nd ed (New York: Macmillan, 1994); Jeffrey D. Sachs and B. Felipe Larrain, *Macroeconomics in the Global Economy* (Englewood Cliffs, N.J.: Prentice Hall, 1993); Beth V. Yarbrough and Robert M. Yarbrough, *The World Economy: Trade and Finance* (New York: Harcourt Brace, 1994).

Japanese language and built a subsidiary staff with local managers.[11] Eventually, Apple calibrated its marketing strategy for Japan, targeting the school and home markets.[12] Apple's market share in Japan stood at 14.2 percent in 1995, and sales in Japan represented about 17 percent of Apple's total worldwide sales, up from just 6 percent in 1991.[13] Apple continued strongly in Japan and remains in fourth position with a share of 12 percent.[14] Despite Apple's difficulties in the United States over the years, the company has been able to maintain its relatively high share in Japan and is now reaping the benefit through high sales of its newer iMac and G3 computers.[15]

In marketing its computers abroad, Apple tried to duplicate a marketing strategy that had been successful in its home market. It failed initially in Japan, whereas in Europe it succeeded, with Apple achieving a higher market share than in its home market. The success in its European markets also caused the company to bring the lessons learned abroad back to the United States by transferring executives from abroad. Apple's example shows that success in international markets does not always require the complete transformation of a company's strategy, but that doesn't mean one will never have to change anything. The Apple situation supports a pattern in which managers have to evaluate situations and sometimes change, sometimes adapt, and other times extend the same strategy abroad. The reasons for these patterns are explained in the next section.

Factors Limiting Standardization of Global Marketing Strategies

From an global marketing manager's point of view, the most cost-effective method to market products or services worldwide is to use the same program in every country, provided environmental conditions favor such an approach. However, invariably (as we have seen in the previous section), local market characteristics exist that may require some form of adaptation to local conditions. One of the challenges of global marketing is to be able to determine the extent to which a standardized approach may be used for any given local market. To do this, the global marketing manager must become aware of any factors that limit standardization. Such factors can be categorized into four major groups: market

11. "Apple Loser in Japan Computer Market, Tries to Recoup by Redesigning Its Models," *Wall Street Journal*, June 21, 1985, p. 30.
12. Ibid.
13. "Apple Japan Rides Crest of PC Wave," *Nikkei Weekly*, February 5, 1996, p. 8.
14. Comline Pacific Research Consulting, June 9, 1999.
15. "Mac's Success Helps Apple Again Beat Profit Prospects," *Asian Wall Street Journal*, April 16, 1999, p. 14.

characteristics, competitive conditions, marketing infrastructure, and regulatory conditions.[16]

The debate over the amount or extent of standardization is one of the longest in the field of international marketing. Some see markets as becoming more similar and increasingly more global, such as those markets espoused by Levitt.[17] Others point out the difficulties in using a standardized approach, as experienced by many companies and the research of many academics.[18]

Market Characteristics

Market characteristics can have a profound effect on a global marketing strategy. The *physical environmental conditions* of any country—determined by climate, product use conditions, and population size—often force marketers to make adjustments to products to fit local conditions. Many cars in Canada come equipped with a built-in heating system that is connected to an electrical outlet to keep the engine from freezing while turned off. Cars manufactured for warmer climates are not equipped with such a heating unit but are likely to feature air conditioning. The product use conditions for lawn mowers differ considerably from one country to another. This was experienced by Flymo, a British company. Flymo had pioneered the flying mower, which hovers above the lawn without use of wheels. Very popular in the United Kingdom, the product failed in continental Europe, where lawns were much larger and mowers on wheels were preferred.[19] Likewise, Procter & Gamble, marketing its Cheer all-temperature brand in Japan, soon learned that cold washing was required in Japan and that the product therefore had to be reformulated to allow for the addition of fabric softener with cold water. The original Cheer formula produced insufficient suds in cold water to satisfy the Japanese consumer.[20]

A country's *population* affects the market size in terms of volume, allowing for lower prices in larger markets. Market size, or expected sales volume, greatly affects channel strategy. Company-owned manufacturing and sales subsidiaries are often possible in larger markets, whereas independent distributors are often used in smaller countries.

16. This section draws heavily on Robert D. Buzzell's classic article "Can You Standardize Multinational Marketing?" See *Harvard Business Review*, November–December 1968, pp. 102–103.
17. Theodore Levitt, "The Globalization of Markets," *Harvard Business Review*, May–June 1983, pp. 92–102.
18. See Kamran Kashani, "Beware of the Pitfalls of Global Marketing," *Harvard Business Review*, September–October 1989, pp. 91–98; "Marketers Turn Sour on Global Sales Pitch Harvard Guru Makes," *Wall Street Journal*, May 12, 1988, p. 1.
19. "Flymo Finds a Fresh Cutting Edge," *Financial Times*, November 2, 1988, p. 16.
20. "After Early Stumbles, P&G Is Making Inroads Overseas," *Wall Street Journal*, February 6, 1989, p. B1.

Macroeconomic factors also greatly affect international marketing strategy. Income level, or gross national product (GNP) per capita, varies widely among nations—from below $100 per year for some of the world's poorest nations to above $20,000 per year for rich countries such as Kuwait, Sweden, and the United States. As can be expected, marketing environments will differ considerably according to income level. If the population's level of technical skill is low, a marketer may be forced to simplify product design to suit the local market. Pricing may be affected to the extent that countries with lower income levels show a higher price elasticity for many products, compared with more developed countries. Furthermore, convenient access to credit is often required of buyers in developing countries. This has negative impact on the sale of capital goods and consumer durables.

To accommodate the lower income level in China, McDonald's typically resorted to introductory pricing, which sometimes fails to cover the cost of the burger. Lower prices attract more customers, though, and a restaurant can then become profitable quickly. Half of China's seventy-three McDonald's restaurants were profitable by mid-1996, although at the country level the company was not yet profitable.[21] When burgers cost 8 yuan and a value meal 20 yuan, a Chinese family of three would pay about 100 yuan, or about 10 percent of a typical monthly urban salary, to eat one meal out at McDonald's. Despite these prices, eating habits quickly adjusted, and the company expected to double its restaurants to 150 by the end of 1997, and to 300 by the end of 1998.[22] By 1999, McDonald's operated 34 restaurants in Bejing alone, and planned to expand to more than 100 by the year 2000.[23]

Cultural and social factors are less predictable influences on the marketing environment, and they have frustrated many international marketers. Customs and traditions have the greatest effect on product categories when a country's population has had prior experience with a given product category. Although Coca-Cola has been very successful transferring its Coke brand into many countries, it has also run into difficulties with other products. Its canned coffee drink, Georgia Coffee, which met with success in Japan, did not find any acceptance elsewhere. And a soy drink that did very well in Hong Kong did not take off in the United States.[24] Nestlé, which wanted to capitalize on the cold-coffee-drink opportunity in the United States, stopped marketing its Nescafé blended cold-coffee drinks because the size of the iced-coffee category in the United States had not met its expectation.[25]

21. "Macworld," *Economist*, June 29, 1996, p. 61.
22. "Houses, Cars Become All-Consuming Passion," *Nikkei Weekly*, January 20, 1997, p. 18.
23. "Fast Food, Western Colas Highlight China Growth," *National Catholic Reporter*, January 29, 1999, p. 15.
24. Kashani, "Marketers Turn Sour," p. 1.
25. "Soda Pop Shakes Awake Dozing Coffee Companies," *Wall Street Journal Europe*, June 9, 1999, p. 4.

Language can be another hurdle for international marketing, and international marketers are focusing their attention on this problem. Few areas have been as affected by language as the software industry. One of the most daunting tasks for western software companies was to enter the Asian markets with products using Chinese characters. Neither IBM nor IBM-compatible PCs could make a major dent in the Japanese PC market until 1991, when IBM developed DOS/V, a bilingual operating system for use with the Japanese language. A different challenge faced Microsoft. A pair of Chinese-language characters in Microsoft's translation of its Windows 95 operating system resulted in unexpected difficulties. Among the large selection of available characters were two that could form the term "communist bandit," which was clearly unacceptable to the Chinese government. These characters came up as suggestions a seventy-thousand-phrase dictionary offered up on demand. The problem stemmed in part from programs written for the more complex characters in Taiwan and Hong Kong that had also found their way onto the mainland. Microsoft, eager to meet local market requirements, had to promise to exchange all disks and to eliminate offensive terms.[26] Such a move is definitely worthwhile: it is expected that the Chinese market for PCs will become the world's third-largest market behind the United States and Japan.[27] With China's PC penetration rate at about 10 percent of households in major cities such as Beijing, and as low as 2 percent in smaller cities, there is still considerable room for growth in that market.[28]

Different language environments affect even the Internet. Although most people consider English to be the language of the Internet community, when it comes to on-line shopping, data show that the majority of consumers may browse the web in more than one language, such as speakers of English as a second language. Consumers also prefer to buy products and services in their own native tongue. With some 60 percent or more of Internet users and 40 percent of e-commerce users coming from outside the United States within the next few years, many e-commerce merchants will be forced to maintain multiple sites for different languages.[29]

Industry Conditions

Industry conditions often vary by country because products frequently are in varying stages of the product life cycle in different markets. Also, a company may find that one country's limited awareness of or prior experience with a product requires a considerable missionary sales effort and primary demand stimulation, whereas in more mature markets the promotional strategy is likely to concentrate

26. "A Matter of Wording," *Far Eastern Economic Review*, October 10, 1996, p. 72.
27. "China Goes PC," *UPSIDE Today*, June 17, 1999.
28. Ibid.
29. "Idiom App Speaks Your Language," *Computerworld*, May 31, 1999, p. 66.

on brand differentiation. The level of local competition can be expected to vary substantially by country. The higher the technological level of the competition, the more an international company must improve the quality level of its products. In countries where competitors control distribution channels and maintain a strong sales force, the strategy of a multinational company may differ significantly from that in a country where the company holds a competitive advantage.

The telecommunications industry is typical of widely differing industry conditions. Only a few years ago, the industry was very fragmented, with operators and suppliers restricted to their domestic markets only. Today the industry in most countries is experiencing a major push toward liberalization. However, the process has unfolded differently, having reached the most advanced stage in the United States. In Japan, the market power is still much more concentrated in the hands of a single or a few companies than is the case in the United States or Europe.[30] To compete in such differently structured markets requires a substantial adjustment in the strategy of a firm such as AT&T. The company has therefore engaged in a series of alliances and joint ventures to help it navigate the different local competitive structures, among them a joint venture with CANTV in Venezuela; a minority stake in Unitel in Canada; a stake in Unisource, a consortium of several European telephone companies for corporate customers; and a venture in Ukraine in a long-distance company.[31] More recently, AT&T added a venture with NTT, the leading Japanese telecommunications company, as well as stakes in the Philippines and Sri Lanka.[32]

Marketing Infrastructure

For historical and economic reasons, the marketing infrastructure assumes different forms in different countries. Practices in distribution systems often entail different margins for the same product, requiring a change in company pricing strategy. Availability of outlets is also likely to vary by country. Mass merchandisers such as supermarkets, discount stores, and department stores are widely available in the United States and other industrialized countries but are largely absent in less developed nations in southern Europe, Latin America, and other parts of the world. Such variations may lead to considerably different distribution strategies. Likewise, advertising agencies and the media are not equally accessible in all countries, and the absence of mass media channels in some countries makes a "pull" strategy less effective.

Eastern Europe is an area where many companies found they had to adapt to a much less developed marketing infrastructure. Xerox, in expanding its business in Czechoslovakia following the economic and political liberalization, found

30. "Telecom Bureaucracy Eyed for Breakup," *Nikkei Weekly*, December 5, 1995, p. 8.
31. "Who'll Be the First Global Phone Company?" *Business Week*, March 27, 1995, p. 176.
32. "It's Test Time for NTT's Global Ambitions," *New York Times*, July 6, 1999, p. C4.

it difficult to increase its sales to independent copy shops. All copying was previously done by government-owned shops, where customers had to show identification. Sales were transacted through only three government-owned sales outlets. Although a sufficient number of government-employed service technicians existed in the country, the company found it very difficult to find independent people willing to start copy shops, or even independent dealers for local sales.[33] The opening of eastern Europe during 1991 completely changed this situation, resulting in opportunities for numerous independent dealers.

Regulatory Environment

The regulatory environment also requires consideration for the development of a global marketing strategy. Product standards issued by local governments must be observed. To the extent that they differ from one country to another, unified product design often becomes a challenge. Tariffs and taxes may require such adjustments in pricing that a product can no longer be sold on a high-volume basis. Specific restrictions may also be problematic. In Europe, restrictions on advertising prohibit the mention of a competitor's name, despite the fact that such an approach may be an integral part of the advertising strategy in the United States.

Under the auspices of the World Trade Organization (WTO), the international trade body based in Geneva, efforts are under way to deal with the multitudes of patent law interpretations. Indonesia and India were traditionally two countries that had adhered to the rule of patenting processes for pharmaceutical drugs, rather than the products themselves. As a result, a local firm could copy the products of international pharmaceutical firms as long as it used a different manufacturing process to arrive at the final product. With India now joining the WTO, its old patent rules will have to change by the year 2005, and its local firms will also have to apply for product patents, substantially impacting India's twenty-four thousand local pharmaceutical firms.[34] In Jordan, another country where patents for drugs are issued on the process, U.S. pharmaceutical firms estimate that they are losing substantial sums to the lack of patent protection, with some 70 percent of the Jordanian firms' output sold on export markets. Again, Jordan aspires to join the WTO, which will force an eventual change in this country's patent practices.[35]

To carry out the international marketing task successfully, international managers have to be cognizant of all the factors that influence the local marketing environment. Frequently, they need to target special marketing programs for each country. With newly emerging institutions such as the WTO, however, the world is moving closer to a level playing field with fewer differences in regulations, and

33. "Dilemma of a Salesman in Prague," *New York Times*, December 27, 1990, p. D1.
34. "Patents of EMR: The Choice Between Two Evils," *Statesman* (India), January 18, 1999.
35. "WTO Patent Law Effects on Pharmaceuticals," *World News Connection*, May 13, 1999.

the opportunity for firms and governments to bring a lawsuit if they believe they have suffered under undue protection or unfair trade practices.

Participants in Global Marketing

Several types of companies participate in global marketing. Among the leaders are multinational corporations (MNCs), global corporations, exporters, importers, and many different service companies. These firms may be engaged in manufacturing consumer or industrial goods, in trading, or in the performance of a range of services. What all participants have in common is a need to deal with the complexities of the global marketplace.

Multinational Corporations' Role in Global Marketing

Multinational corporations (MNCs) are companies that manufacture and market products or services in several countries. Typically, an MNC operates a number of plants abroad and markets products through a large network of fully owned subsidiaries. Although no clearly acceptable definition exists, MNCs are also referred to as global companies, transnational firms, or stateless corporations. For the purpose of this text, we have chosen the terms *international*, *multinational*, and *global* corporations. We use the term *international* to indicate a company with some international activities. The term *MNC* is reserved for a company with extensive overseas operations, including overseas manufacturing in several countries. We would call a company global if its operations span the globe and follow a coherent and integrated strategy for the entire world. Although *multinational (MNC)* and *global* tend to be more specific terms, we have chosen to increasingly use the term *global firm* since this is the preferred terminology of many researchers and executives.

The United Nations Conference on Trade and Development (UNCTAD) listed some 53,600 active MNCs in 1997, with a total of 449,000 recorded affiliates worldwide, up from 37,000 MNCs and 190,000 affiliates six years earlier. These companies undertook some $425 billion in investments; some of these investments abroad served to overcome trade barriers, but increasingly the investment goal has been to locate operations in countries where they could operate most efficiently. Sales of foreign affiliates were estimated at $9.5 trillion alone.[36]

Fortune's list of the world's largest 500 companies shows how much international business has been developed outside the United States by huge, growing firms around the world. *Fortune*'s ranking includes service companies as well as industrial firms and is based on revenue. In 1998, 185 of the top 500 firms were

36. *UNCTAD World Investment Report 1998* (New York: 1998), pp. 2–4.

U.S. based; Japan followed with 100 firms, and European firms numbered 170 in the list. Other countries were represented by smaller numbers, such as South Korea with 9 and China with 6.[37]

At the same time, foreign investment increased rapidly. Of the more than $400 billion in foreign direct investments in 1996, the largest share was invested into the United States ($76 billion), China ($41 billion), the United Kingdom ($26 billion), and France ($22 billion). Among the sources of this capital, the United States contributed $75 billion and presented a balanced account. The United Kingdom ($34 billion), the Netherlands ($23 billion), and Switzerland ($12 billion) were net contributors of investment funds, whereas China, with an outward investment of only $2 billion, was a net recipient of investment funds.[38]

With foreign firms entering into many countries, foreign direct investment in the United States increased rapidly. Great Britain accounted for the largest portion of foreign direct investments in the United States. For several large British firms, U.S. sales accounted for a large portion of global sales. For ICI (chemicals) and for Grand Met (acquired Pillsbury and Burger King), U.S. sales amounted to about 30 percent. For the two large German chemical firms, BASF and Hoechst, U.S. sales accounted for some 25 percent of corporate volume. For Swedish Electrolux, the U.S. volume rose to 30 percent through the acquisition of White-Westinghouse. Pechiney of France has 40 percent of its corporate sales in the United States. Even some Japanese firms, such as Honda (50 percent), Mitsubishi Electric (50 percent), and Nissan (25 percent) have become dependent to a large degree on U.S. sales.[39]

Global Companies' Role in Global Marketing

True global companies differ from MNCs in that they pursue integrated strategies on a worldwide scale rather than separate strategies on a country-by-country basis. They tend to look at the whole world as one market and move products, manufacturing, capital, or even personnel wherever they can gain an advantage. Global firms also tend to have a strong base in all of the major economic regions of North America, Europe, and Asia's Pacific Rim countries. Products are developed for the entire world market, and the organization has undergone changes in order to be able to move from regional to product line–based profit centers. Many of the senior executives come from foreign countries.

Bartlett and Ghoshal differentiate among several types of internationally active firms. In their view, global firms operate on a world scale and tend to be heavily centralized; strategies tend to be controlled closely from the head office. In the multinational firm, each country is treated as a separate market. Multinational firms develop fairly independent clones of the parent firm in each market, with a

37. "The Fortune Global 500," *Fortune*, August 1999 (web site).
38. *UNCTAD World Investment Report 1998* (New York: 1998) pp. 2–4.
39. "Nice View from Up Here," *Economist*, November 24, 1990, p. 68.

focus on mostly local business. International firms, by contrast, have a pattern of more decentralization than global ones do, but the source of their strength is the exploitation of developments from their home market.[40]

General Electric, one of the largest U.S. corporations, is pursuing its own particular global strategy. Each of the company's business units is expected to reach the number one or number two position worldwide in its respective area.[41] However, GE from its origin has been more of an international company, based in the United States with most of its international business concentrated in Europe and Japan. In 1980, only two of its major divisions (plastics and jet engines) were true global players. Since 1987, international revenues have risen faster than U.S. sales and accounted for 43 percent in 1998, up from just 29 percent in 1987. Of total international sales of $43 billion in 1998, $8.7 billion were exports from the United States alone.[42]

Texas Instruments is pursing globalization to compete in the very tough market for memory chips. The company designated a single design center and factory worldwide for each type of memory chip; it built two of its four new memory chip plants in Taiwan and Japan to take advantage of lower capital costs. An alliance with Hitachi of Japan helps share research costs. The global responsibility for TI's memory business is assigned to its country manager for Japan, a Japanese executive.[43] The international side of TI's business has now grown to 67 percent, with the bulk coming from Asia.[44]

Firms Based in Emerging Economies Participate in Global Marketing

A recent development in international business with important implications for global marketing is the rise of international firms based in emerging countries or in smaller countries not typically hosts to global firms. As these firms have entered the global markets, not only have they begun to compete locally or regionally, some have even achieved global status in their own right.

South Korea has spawned an increasing number of multinational and global firms. Leaders are the large conglomerates, or *chaebol*, that get involved in a number of different types of businesses. Names such as Daewoo (1998 sales of $33.5 billion), Hyundai ($27.8 billion), Samsung Corporation ($36.3 billion), and LG Electronics ($14 billion) have become widely known on world markets.[45]

40. Christopher Bartlett and Sumantra Ghoshal, *Managing Across Borders* (Boston: Harvard Business School Press, 1989).
41. "Business Leaders Discuss Formulas for 21st Century," *Nikkei Weekly*, October 11, p. 1.
42. General Electric, *Annual Report, 1998*.
43. "How to Go Global—and Why," *Fortune*, August 28, 1989, p. 72.
44. Texas Instruments, *Annual Report, 1998*.
45. Asiaweek, "The Asiaweek 1000, 1999" (Asia's largest companies) (*Asiaweek* web site).

Although recent economic developments in Korea have reduced the growth of these firms, they remain among the most notable global competitors from emerging countries.

One of the most aggressive and successful Korean firms is Samsung Group. With employment of 267,000 worldwide and global group sales of $96.1 billion in 1998, this group operates some 26 core affiliates and 390 overseas facilities in sixty-three different countries. Its main activities include electronics, machinery, automotive, chemicals, and financial services.[46] Its main operating unit in the electronics industry, Samsung Electronics, had sales of $20 billion in 1998, almost 70 percent of those going into exports. The company is active in semiconductors, telecommunications, PCs, notebook computers, TVs, home appliances, and many other products.[47] The company has reached the number one position, with a global market share of 20 percent in DRAM (dynamic random access memory chips), the most common kind of PC memory chips.[48]

New firms have edged into the global market from a number of other Asian countries. Acer Inc., founded in 1976 in Taiwan, already ranks as an international firm with sales of $6.7 billion in 1998. Known for making PCs, monitors, fax machines, notebook computers, servers, and custom chips, the company has become a major producer of key components for PCs, supplying well-known PC firms in Japan and the United States. The company has developed a global distribution network and has 42 percent of its sales in North America, 24 percent in Europe, 4 percent in Latin America, and 24 percent in the Asia Pacific area. Domestic sales account for only 10 percent of volume. As part of its global expansion, Acer has bought out the stake of Texas Instruments in its joint venture making memory chips in Taiwan.[49] Acer has intensified its cooperation with IBM of the United States. IBM accounts for more than one-third of Acer's computer equipment sales already.[50] And to expand its position in Europe, Acer has acquired plants from Siemens of Germany as that company began to exit the PC business. Acer plans to use the plant to supply its own brand of PCs as well as to continue supplying equipment for Siemens under the German company's brand name.[51]

Thailand is the home base of another rapidly growing firm with regional impact and global ambitions. Charoen Pokphand, typically referred to as CP Group, has grown in just twenty years into a firm employing 100,000 people in some 250 firms and reaping revenues of $7.6 billion in 1994. The company's origins were in chicken farming, with a weekly output of some 25 million chickens. Later, CP

46. Samsung Corporate web site (www.samsung.com).
47. Samsung Electronics, *Annual Report, 1998.*
48. "Chip Wars," *Far Eastern Economic Review*, September 23, 1999, pp. 40–42.
49. "Taiwan's Acer Moves to Buy Out TI Stake in Chip Venture," *Dow Jones Online News*, March 4, 1998.
50. "IBM, Taiwan's Acer Will Announce Pact to Deepen Their Ties," *Wall Street Journal,* June 7, 1999, p. C17.
51. "Siemens to Quit PC Market, Sell Plants to Acer," *Wall Street Journal*, April 24, 1998, p. A13.

branched out into motorcycles, telecommunications, and semiconductor manufacturing.[52] The firm has signed joint venture agreements with NYNEX and Wal-Mart.[53] In China, CP is considered the largest foreign investor, with 170 ventures operating various types of agrobusinesses and animal-feed mills. The ventures are spread across most of China's thirty provinces, represent total assets of more than $4 billion, and with more than 60,000 employees generate revenues of about $3.6 billion (1998).[54] Despite some recent setbacks due to the economic recession in Thailand, the company continues on its expansion course, focusing its agrobusiness on the major countries of Thailand, Indonesia, India, and Vietnam and new ventures in retailing and telecommunications.

Indofood, the world's largest producer of instant noodles, with an annual output of about 7 billion packages, has become a major international firm, surpassing Nissin Food of Japan in the process. Part of the Salim Group, an Indonesia-based conglomerate, Indofood has an important position in oleochemicals—oil- and fat-based chemicals used for the manufacture of detergents, cosmetics, soaps, food additives, and similar products—as well as in plantations to supply palm oil for processing and flour mills.[55]

Malaysia is home to a local car company, Perusahaan Otomobil Nasional, or Proton, founded in 1985. Expanding its capacity from 7,500 units annually to 180,000 by 1996, the company had its origin in a venture with Mitsubishi Motors of Japan. In 1996 Proton introduced a new model, the Tiara, which was its first car built without Mitsubishi's assistance. Proton sells most of its cars domestically, where it had a market share of about 60 percent.[56] With corporate revenue in excess of $2.4 billion (1998), the company is building an international distribution network and aims for sales of up to 1 million units by the year 2010.

Even from mainland China, firms have begun to expand overseas. By the end of 1998, some 5,700 Chinese companies were estimated to have invested $6.3 billion overseas, but only about 1,400 firms were involved in manufacturing operations. Jinan Qingqi Motorcycle, a Chinese state-owned company, set up its first assembly plants in Pakistan and in Lithuania in 1995. Other ventures in Sri Lanka and Argentina followed, producing the 50–100 cc brand-name motorcycles. Konka Group, China's second-largest TV producer, set up its first overseas plant in India in 1999. Konka holds a 51 percent ownership and plans to move production from an initial 300,000 sets to 1 million sets a year, with sales going to both India and Pakistan. A second venture in Mexico will ship to Canada, the United States, and Argentina, reaching a planned volume of 1 million units by 2001.[57]

52. "From Chickens to Microchips," *Far Eastern Economic Review*, January 23, 1997, pp. 38–45.
53. "Asia's New Giants," *Business Week*, November 27, 1995, pp. 64–80.
54. "CP Committed to Business in China," *Bangkok Post*, July 1, 1999, p. 2.
55. "Sales of 60 Percent in Indofood Planned," *Wall Street Journal*, December 16, 1998, p. A19.
56. "Pedal to the Metal," *Far Eastern Economic Review*, May 2, 1996, pp. 64–66.
57. "China Encourages Manufacturers to Invest Overseas," *Far Eastern Economic Review*, April 15, 1999, p. 82.

Latin America has also been the home of many newly emerging global firms. Vitro, a Mexico-based glass-making company with sales of $2.5 billion (1998), made its first large acquisition in the United States in 1989. The company has since grown its international business to a volume of $685 million in 1998, exporting to seventy countries, and operates some fifteen international subsidiaries with one-hundred facilities. About 80 percent of its exports go to the United States, where the firm employs 2,500 people.[58] Vitro has entered into a number of alliances with global firms, including Ford Motor, Solutia, Pilkington, Whirlpool, General Electric, and Owens Corning.[59]

CCU, Chile's leading brewery, with a domestic market share of more than 80 percent, found itself attacked in its home market by Quilmes, Argentina's largest brewery. After defending its home market, CCU acquired two smaller breweries in Argentina. CCU, partially owned by the Chilean Luksic family and the German brewery Paulaner, began expanding its Argentinian base.[60] Recent investments allow CCU to expand its Budweiser product line throughout Latin America.[61] Other emerging international groups based in Latin America include PDVSA of Venezuela, in oil and refining; Petrobras, the Brazilian oil company; Cemex, a Mexican cement producer; and many family-owned firms not listed on the stock market but of important economic impact.

New global firms are also born in traditional but small industrialized countries. Finland, despite its small domestic market, is home to Nokia, a company that had its origins in paper and forestry products but which has now changed completely to telecommunications. Nokia had sales of about $11 billion in 1998 and more than 52,000 employees by mid-1999. Its global operations span some 130 countries, with only 2.5 percent in its home market. Largest markets are the United States with 12 percent and China with 11 percent. The company concentrates on mobile telecommunications infrastructure systems and mobile phone handsets. Nokia is the global leader in handsets, with a market share of 23 percent and a volume of about 41 million handsets shipped.[62] Its success has also driven up the value of its brand name, which was ranked eleventh among a list of global firms led by such names as Coca-Cola, Microsoft, and Intel.[63] At present growth rates, Nokia is expected to reach sales of $19 billion by the end of 1999.[64]

The summaries of the strategies of these recently emerging global firms clearly demonstrate that global marketing is not only practiced by firms from the major industrial nations of Europe, the United States, and Japan. Increasingly, compa-

58. "Vitro Plans Expansion in U.S.," *Mexico Business Monthly*, May 1, 1999.
59. Groupo Vitro, *Annual Report 1998*.
60. "Chilean Brewery Prepares for War," *Financial Times*, November 29, 1995, p. 22.
61. "CCU of Chile to Expand Plant in Santa Fe," *El Cronista*, November 19, 1998, p. 14.
62. "Nokia Takes the Lead as Wireless Makers Sell 162.9 Million Phones in '98," *Wall Street Journal*, February 2, 1999.
63. "Nokia Is Europe's Most Valuable Brand," *M2 Presswire*, July 13, 1999.
64. "Next Up for Cell Phones: Weaving a Wireless Web," *Fortune*, October 25, 1999, p. 225.

nies from many different countries are entering the world of global marketing, making the need to understand global marketing practices universal.

Service Companies as Participants in Global Marketing

Early global companies were largely manufacturers of industrial equipment and consumer products. Many of the newer global firms are service companies. Banks, investment bankers, and brokers have turned themselves into global service networks; airlines and hotel companies have gained global status. Less noticeable are the global networks of accounting and professional service firms, consulting companies, advertising agencies, and a host of other service-related industries. This globalization of the service sector has not been restricted to the United States alone but has been mirrored in other countries as well.

Among the service companies pursuing international marketing strategies, retailers stand out. Although in the past they have seen themselves as domestic business, retailers have begun a massive move to globalize. In Europe alone, some fifty U.S. retailers have operations, compared with less than fifteen just a few years ago. The Gap, Pier 1, Foot Locker, and Toys "R" Us are but a few of the major stores. Other U.S.-based retailing chains have expanded in Latin America. J.C. Penney started in Mexico, and Wal-Mart already operates scores of stores there through a joint venture with Cifra, a Mexican firm. Other Wal-Mart operations have been undertaken in Argentina, Brazil, Hong Kong, and China.[65] Wal-Mart's largest move to date is the acquisition of Asda, a U.K.-based retailer with sales of $10.8 billion and 229 stores, which will come in addition to international sales of $12.2 billion from the previous year. The retailer's global expansion is expected to continue and to reach as much as 30 percent of Wal-Mart sales over the next five years.[66]

Non-U.S.-based retailers are globalizing as well. Marks & Spencer of Britain acquired Brooks Brothers of the United States in 1988 and is establishing a string of smaller stores around the world. Benetton of Italy, although not a store owner, has had its retailing concept adopted by independent retailers around the world in some 120 countries. Carrefour of France, a major operator of hypermarkets, has become a leading retailer in Argentina and Brazil.[67] Ahold, a Dutch supermarket chain, expanded into the United States through acquisitions of Stop & Shop, BI-LO, Finast, Giant Carlisle, and Pathmark.[68] And finally, IKEA, a Sweden-based furniture retailer, has expanded, first throughout Europe, then into the United States, to become the world's largest furniture retailer. With 142 stores worldwide IKEA had sales of $5.8 billion in 1996. IKEA'S 13 U.S. stores had combined

65. "Retailers Go Global," *Fortune*, February 20, 1995, pp. 102–108.
66. "Wal-Mart Seeks U.K. Supermarket Firm," *Wall Street Journal*, June 15, 1999, p. A3.
67. "Retailers Go Global," *Fortune*, February 20, 1995, pp. 102–108.
68. "Global Corporate Report: Business Diary," *Wall Street Journal Europe*, June 11, 1999, p. 7.

sales of $530 million in 1996.[69] All of these retailing stores demonstrate that global marketing has become important even for a traditional and formerly domestic industry.

Financial service firms are also expanding globally. U.S.-based investment banks are leaders in raising capital for clients worldwide, not just in the United States. Merrill Lynch has made acquisitions in the United Kingdom and Canada and recently began retail brokerage operations in Japan, adding some 4,500 new staff in the process. Likewise, Morgan Stanley Dean Witter expanded its European staff faster than its domestic staff, to 3,800 to tap a market that was viewed as becoming as large as the U.S. market for mergers and acquisitions.[70]

International financial services institutions have also undertaken a path of rapid globalization. HSBC operates in Asia through the Hongkong and Shanghai Banking Corporation and has acquired Marine Midland Bank in the United States and Midland Bank in the United Kingdom.[71] ING Group and ABN Amro, both Dutch-based firms, have expanded their networks in Europe and the United States. Banco Santander, the largest Spanish bank, has expanded its operations throughout Latin America. Deutsche Bank acquired Bankers Trust of the United States to become one of the world's largest banks. And Credit Suisse and UBS, two Swiss-based banks, have expanded asset management and investment banking around the world.[72] This drive to globalize service industries has led to global marketing activities in many new sectors that previously had been viewed as domestic only.

Exporters as Global Marketers

Exporters are important participants in global marketing. In 1998, total merchandise exports amounted to $717 billion, up from $393 billion in 1990. U.S. manufacturers saw their export rise 82 percent between 1990 and 1998. As a contributor to the overall economy, the role of export trade has been growing. In 1990, exports and imports combined equaled 13 percent of the U.S. gross domestic product (GDP). In 1999, they amounted to well over 30 percent. For 1999, it was estimated that more than 11 million jobs depended on exports.[73]

Among the leading U.S. exporters we find many global corporations. Their exports from the United States alone added up to substantial amounts. Boeing, the world's largest aerospace company, had export sales in 1998 of $26.5 billion, or 47 percent of corporate revenue. Boeing exports are high because the company

69. "IKEA Weighs Opening Store Near Boston," *Wall Street Journal*, April 15, 1998, p. NE1.
70. "The Deal Machine," *Business Week*, November 1, 1999, p. 70.
71. "As a Global Behemoth, New Citigroup Won't Be Alone," *Wall Street Journal*, April 7, 1998, p. A13.
72. "European Banks Rethink Globalization," *Wall Street Journal*, October 5, 1998, p. A23.
73. "United States Trade," *Cambridge International Forecast Country Report*, April 1, 1999, p. 1.

sells to customers in more than 145 countries, from a largely U.S. manufacturing base.[74] Other major exporters include General Motors (cars, locomotives), Ford (cars and parts), DaimlerChrysler (cars and parts), General Electric (jet engines, turbines, plastics, medical systems, and locomotives), and Motorola (communications equipment and semiconductors). Global companies with production sites located around the world have naturally a smaller percentage of exports. However, global firms, even those with extensive networks of manufacturing sites around the world, supply some of their markets on an export basis because few firms in today's competitive environment could supply each market from local sources only.

Smaller and medium-sized firms are also exporters, although the extent of their involvement differs by geographic region. Some 51,000 U.S. firms export regularly, and about 87 percent of those employ fewer than five hundred. As a whole, exporting accounts for about 12 percent of U.S. GNP, up from 7.5 percent in 1987. Smaller firms have a bigger chance today because of new communications technology. One such example is Cardiac Science Inc., a small manufacturer and distributor of cardiac medical devices. The company used some help from the U.S. Department of Commerce. Its most potent weapon, however, turned out the opening of its own web site. The company, with sales of under $1 million in 1997, began to open up international business and shipped to customers in forty-six countries in 1998.[75]

The record of European small to medium-sized exporters is quite different. In Germany, medium-sized firms are called *Mittelstände*. These firms, with sales of under U.S. $250 million, account for a large share of Germany's exports. These firms typically market industrial products, which means they are little known to the average consumer. In their chosen market niche, however, they have become worldwide leaders with a clear number one position. They focus on a technical niche and a narrow product assortment but sell worldwide. Typically, they have about a dozen sales subsidiaries abroad. Most of them maintain their own presence in the U.S. market. Although less well known than such large German firms as BMW or Siemens, they have been able to do extremely well in the role of exporter.[76]

Recent research by UNCTAD, a United Nations–affiliated trade organization, has shown that investments in international business do not have to be large to be effective. For Asia, UNCTAD estimates that the annual investment by smaller firms in other smaller Asian firms averages $1 million. Because these small firms account for as much as 95 percent of all Asian companies and, depending on the

74. Boeing Co., *Annual Report 1998*.
75. "Small Business and International Trade Going Global by Online Growth," *Los Angeles Times*, February 11, 1998, p. D1.
76. Hermann Simon, "Lessons from Germany's Midsize Giants," *Harvard Business Review*, March–April, pp. 115–123.

country, account for 30 to 60 percent of the economy, these small-package international investments represent a substantial portion of all foreign investments received by these countries.[77]

Importers as Participants in Global Marketing

Importing is as much an international marketing activity as exporting. Companies that neither export nor have multinational status may well participate in global marketing through their importing operations. Many of the largest U.S. retail chains maintain import departments that are in contact with suppliers in many overseas countries. Other major importers are global firms that obtain products from their plants abroad or from other clients. Among the largest U.S. importers are oil companies and subsidiaries of foreign-based firms, particularly those of European and Japanese origin.

A classic importer-only firm is Schwinn Bicycle Company. Having shifted its production over the years from the United States to the Far East, the company now sources virtually all of its bicycles from Taiwan and China. However, Schwinn markets almost none of its products outside of the United States. Although this strategy allows the company to market in a known, or domestic, market, Schwinn encounters many of the same problems faced by exporters, particularly issues related to logistics, supply, and international trade financing.[78] These aspects are primarily treated in Chapter 18.

As we have seen from this section, global marketing includes many different types of players. Rather than specifying a particular type of participant each time, for the purpose of this text we will use *international company* or *global company* as umbrella terms that may include MNCs, global firms, exporters, importers, or global service companies.

Start-Up Firms and Entrepreneurial Ventures in Global Marketing

There is growing evidence among new ventures, particularly in the high-technology field, that an early involvement in global marketing can actually be a requirement for later success. Traditionally, managers believed that expansion into international markets came as a logical extension of a domestic strategy, and that the domestic market had to be secured first. For many industries, however, leaving international markets uncovered can have substantial strategic risks: competitors elsewhere might occupy important segments first, thus preventing later interna-

77. "The UN's Small Business Global Edge," *World Trade*, September 1, 1998, p. 14.
78. Robert Howard and Jean-Pierre Jeannet, "Schwinn Bicycle Company" (case available through the European Case Clearing House at Babson, Ltd., 1993).

tional market expansion. Logitech, a maker of computer input devices, was founded with a global marketing approach from its outset. Located in both Europe and the United States from the start, the company never had a "domestic" market but from day one considered the global market as the only relevant one.[79] Similarly, many upstart companies in the United States, Europe, and Asia are intending to become immediate global marketers.

E-Commerce Companies Enter Global Marketing

Few sectors of the economy have been growing faster than e-commerce. These Internet, or web-based, firms have grown everywhere. With access from any computer in the world guaranteed to reach e-commerce firms wherever they are, these companies have achieved a global reach from the moment they first opened for business. Yahoo, the U.S.-based portal company, has grown overseas even faster than in the United States. AOL concluded a joint venture with Bertelsmann of Germany in 1995 to tap into the European market and entered into another deal with Cisneros, a Venezuela-based group, to penetrate Latin America.[80] Charles Schwab, the U.S.-based discount brokerage company, has seen its Asian business grow substantially. This has resulted in a decision to enter the Japanese market with its on-line trading technology for individual investors, with Tokyo Marine Securities as a partner. Schwab and other e-commerce-based brokerage firms, such as DLJ*direct* and E*Trade, could enter the Japanese market with their new technology. Smaller firms without major international infrastructure are thus in a position to compete for markets far way.[81] Although an e-commerce web site was estimated to require an investment of about $1 million in development and investment costs, many smaller firms were expected to avail themselves of e-commerce as their ticket into the global economy. Some experts believe that e-commerce will become the new growth engine for the entire global economy.[82]

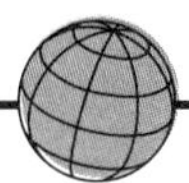

The Importance of Global Marketing

The globalization of markets is one of the major forces impacting on companies worldwide. Although it once meant forays abroad from a strong domestic market base, it has now assumed the meaning of open trade, in which a company can be attacked anywhere, including in its home markets. "Sanctuaries," or protected

79. Vijay Jolly, *Logitech International S.A. (A) and (B)* (case series) (Lausanne: IMD Institute, 1991).
80. "U.S. Service Firms Find the World's a Stage," *Knight-Ridder Business News*, July 9, 1999.
81. "Schwab to Go to Japan," *Financial Times*, October 21, 1999, p. 21.
82. "The Internet Age," *Business Week*, October 4, 1999, p. 70.

domestic markets, are rapidly disappearing. This change has increased the importance of global marketing to many firms and made it into the broad and pervasive activity it is today.

Global marketing is a very broad activity and is expanding rapidly. The combined value of world exports (in the form of physical goods or merchandise) and services (also sometimes referred to as invisibles, such as financial services) exceeded $6 trillion in 1998. Merchandise exports amounted to $5,225 billion in 1998, and international trade in services reached $1,290 billion in the same year. For the period of 1990–1998, world merchandise exports grew 4 percent or more in most years, and exceeded world GDP growth every year. This indicates that the global aspect of the world economy was growing faster than the domestic segments, further contributing to an ever more globalizing pace of the economy.[83]

World services exports, or earnings, reached an amount of $1,290 billion in 1998 and took many forms. The role of banks, insurance companies, accounting firms, and consulting companies has already been well documented. A recent effort in this field comes from medical institutions. Several leading U.S. medical centers have begun to market their services abroad. In 1997, an estimated 385,000 international patients were treated at U.S. hospitals on an outpatient basis, and another 66,000 received inpatient care. In the Philadelphia region, ten local hospitals formed a venture, "Philadelphia International Medicine," with the goal of bringing 6,000 foreign patients to those hospitals every year. The spending on medical services was believed to amount to $60 million, with another $140 million to be spent in the region for travel, hotels, and food for patient families.[84] Johns Hopkins in Baltimore was estimated to treat 7,000 international patients annually, generating an annual $30 million in revenue. Other leading hospitals included the Cleveland Clinic, and the Mayo Clinic in Rochester, Minnesota.[85] This is not solely a U.S. phenomenon: in Thailand, many privately held local clinics have started to attract Japanese patients. Thai medical costs are said to be among the lowest in the world and are only 25 percent of corresponding costs in Japan.[86]

A substantial portion of global marketing operations does not get recorded in international trade statistics. In particular, overseas sales of locally manufactured and locally sold products are not included in world trade figures as the products did not cross any borders. Consequently, total volume in global marketing far exceeds the volume for total world trade. Sales of overseas sub-

83. "World Trade Growth Slower in 1998," press release, World Trade Organization (WTO), Geneva, April 16, 1999.
84. "Hospitals Seek Foreign Patients," *Philadelphia Business Journal*, November 13, 1998, p. 1.
85. "Medical Globe-Trotting," *Pittsburgh Business Times & Journal*, January 15, 1999, p. 1.
86. "Hospitals Seek Foreigners as Poor Economy Prices Locals Out," *South China Morning Post*, May 30, 1999, p. 4.

sidiaries of U.S. companies are estimated at three times the value of these companies' exports.[87] Although no detailed statistics are available, this pattern suggests that the overall volume of international marketing amounts to a multiple of world trade volume.

As we pointed out earlier, global marketing activities of firms go beyond mere exports of products and services. The volume of this trade, however, can be a good gauge as to the pervasiveness of global marketing activities. When Procter & Gamble of the United States, which pioneered the "everyday low pricing" strategy in the U.S. market to combat traditional high rebates to retailers, adopted this strategy for its European operations as well, the company did not engage in traditional exporting of goods but instead in "concept exports" or "conceptual global marketing."[88] A considerable amount of global marketing takes the shape of just such conceptual approaches. Data measuring the extent of these approaches are not available, however.

The Logic for Involvement in Global Marketing

Companies become involved in international markets for a variety of reasons. Some firms simply respond to orders from abroad without any organized efforts of their own, but most companies take a more active role because they have determined that it is to their advantage to pursue export business on an incremental basis. The profitability of a company can increase when fixed manufacturing costs are already committed and additional economies of scale are achieved.

For some firms, the impetus to globalize comes from a domestic competitive shock. General Electric Lighting (a division of GE) was the traditional market leader in the United States and had been in the business since 1878. In 1983, Westinghouse, its largest U.S. competitor, sold its lighting division to Philips of the Netherlands. This brought a strong foreign competitor right into GE's own backyard; yet GE was not competing in Philips's own territory in Europe. As a result, GE Lighting expanded by buying Tungsram, a Hungarian lighting company, in its first big move into eastern Europe. This was followed by the acquisition of Thorn-EMI's lighting interest, a U.K.-based unit. And in Asia, GE Lighting concluded a joint venture with Hitachi of Japan. This gave GE's international sales a boost from just 20 percent in 1988 to above 40 percent in 1993—and more than 50 percent for 1996. In Europe alone, GE Lighting's share rose to 15 percent. In the space of just a few years, the nature of the GE lighting business thus changed from a predominantly domestic into a global business.[89]

87. "Welcome to the Revolution," *Fortune*, December 13, 1993, pp. 66–80.
88. "Old World, New Investment," *Business Week*, October 7, 1996, pp. 50–51.
89. Ibid., pp. 66–67.

Some companies pursue growth in other countries after their domestic market has reach maturity. Coca-Cola, a market leader worldwide in the soft-drink business, finds that on a per capita basis, foreign consumers drink only a fraction of the amount of soft drinks consumed by Americans. However, the company, which still sees enormous additional potential in international markets, already earns 75 percent of its total profits overseas.[90] Of its total sales of $18.8 billion, $12.5 billion are accounted for by international markets.[91]

The Swiss-based food company Nestlé, with five hundred factories in seventy-seven countries employing 225,000 workers and sales of $52 billion in 1998, is one of the world's oldest and most established global firms.[92] Facing maturing markets in Europe, Nestlé is aiming at Asia as a major source of growth and new revenue. Developing and emerging countries accounted for just 20 percent of sales in 1992; because of above-average growth, those regions were expected to contribute some one-third of Nestlé's worldwide growth by the year 2000. Nestlé has targeted China as a key market, opening joint ventures in China for marketing Nescafé, Coffee-Mate creamer, and milk powder. A recent entry was an ice cream plant in southern China through the acquisition of a Hong Kong firm's interest in the dairy business.[93] Since 1980, Nestlé has invested about $500 million into the Chinese market, building fifteen modern factories and hiring some 5,000 employees.[94] Clearly, the company expects emerging markets such as China to play a much larger role in its strategy in the future.

Customers moving abroad provide reasons for many firms to follow. Major U.S. banks have shifted to serve their U.S. clients in key financial centers around the world by opening branches. Advertising agencies in the United States have created networks to serve the interests of their multinational clients. As some Japanese automobile manufacturers opened plants in the United States, many of their component suppliers followed and built operations nearby. Not following these clients would have meant a loss of business.

For some firms, however, the reason to become involved in global marketing has its roots in pure economics. Producers of television shows in Hollywood spend about $1.5 million to produce a single show for a typical series. However, U.S. networks only pay about $1 million to air a single show. As a result, the series producers rely on international markets for the difference. Without the opportunity to market globally, they would not even be able to produce the shows for the U.S. market.[95]

90. "All-Star Analysts 1999 Survey: Beverages," *Wall Street Journal*, June 29, 1999, p. R2.
91. "Future Damage Hard to Assess," *Marketing News*, September 27, 1999, p. 12.
92. "Nestlé Operating Profitably in China," *Asia Pulse*, April 22, 1999.
93. "Old World, New Investment," *Business Week*, October 7, 1996, pp. 50–51.
94. "Nestlé Operating Profitably in China," *Asia Pulse*, April 22, 1999.
95. "Think Globally, Script Locally," *Fortune*, November 8, 1999, p. 157.

In Chapter 7 we revisit these reasons for becoming involved in global marketing, devoting a section of Chapter 7 to global logics and the underlying causes of the global marketing "imperative."

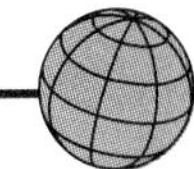

Why Study Global Marketing?

You have probably asked yourself why you should study global marketing. You also may have wondered about the value of this knowledge to your future career. While it is not very likely that many university graduates can find an entry-level position in international or global marketing, it is nevertheless a fact that each year U.S.-based international companies hire large numbers of marketing professionals. Since many of these firms are becoming increasingly globalized, competence in global marketing will become even more important in the future—and many marketing executives will be pursuing global marketing as a career. Other career opportunities exist with a large number of exporters, and candidates will require international marketing skills. Furthermore, many university graduates are hired each year for the marketing efforts of foreign-based companies in the United States. These companies are also looking for international and global competence within their managerial ranks.

With the U.S. service sector becoming increasingly globalized, many graduates joining service industries have found themselves confronted with international opportunities at early stages of their careers. Today, consulting engineers, bankers, brokers, public accountants, medical services executives, and e-commerce specialists are all in need of global marketing skills to compete in a rapidly changing environment. Consequently, a solid understanding and appreciation of global marketing will benefit the careers of most business students, regardless of the field or industry they choose to enter.

However, as we have seen from the many examples cited in this first chapter, global marketing concepts are not limited to U.S. firms expanding abroad. Companies from all countries are affected by the globalization of markets. Global firms can be headquartered just as easily in Japan, the United Kingdom, Germany, the Netherlands, India, China, or Canada. Consequently, the concepts described in this text are meant for any aspiring global marketer, whether the person intends to start a career in the United States or elsewhere. This includes even such emerging regions as Asia, Latin America, and eastern Europe, where more and more global marketing executives will be needed to ensure the survival of firms based there.

A Need for More Global Marketers

Compared with other industrialized nations, the United States severely lacks a sufficient number of global marketing professionals. As active participants in global marketing, global marketers play a key role in the success of international firms.

In this competitive business, the United States has seen its share of world exports steadily decline. In 1953, the United States accounted for 19 percent of total world exports, more than twice the share of the second-ranked United Kingdom, which claimed about 8 percent. At that time, Japan accounted for only 2 percent of world exports. The U.S. share of world exports was down to 12 percent in 1998, still ahead of Japan (7 percent), the United Kingdom (4.8 percent), and China (3.8 percent). In 1999, the European countries that are part of the Euro-zone accounted for 15.9 percent of world exports.[96]

There are further indications that the United States is lagging behind other countries in global marketing. From 1870 to 1970, the United States almost always reported a positive trade balance, exporting more goods than importing. This began to change in the 1970s, and despite the large increase in earnings of the service industry, the overall balance of trade has turned negative. It has been estimated that its large trade deficit has cost the United States several million jobs. Although many reasons for this lagging performance lie beyond the control of individual companies, company management can do much to redress the imbalance. Foreign companies fight much harder than U.S. firms to retain foreign markets. Because the foreign firms' domestic markets are usually smaller than the U.S. market, foreign firms are more motivated than U.S. firms to succeed abroad.

Union Switch, a manufacturer of railroad signaling systems based in Pittsburgh, had a traditional export volume of only about 10 percent. Acquired in 1996 by Ansoldo Trasporti of Italy, the company's international business expanded rapidly to about one-third of total volume. One of its marketing managers, John Aliberti, spent a considerable amount of time developing the market in China and won three contracts worth $37 million in just a few years. This demonstrates that firms with little international experience can do well abroad if they employ capable managers willing to travel to potential markets and invest time and effort into business development.[97]

Despite the alarming unbalance of trade, foreign trade, or international marketing, is still not given enough attention by large sectors of U.S. society. Whereas university graduates in other countries have learned one or more foreign languages as a matter of course, U.S. graduates usually have limited foreign language competency. About 50,000 Japanese business professionals work in New York, all with a good understanding of English; only about 1,000 U.S. business professionals working in Tokyo have a solid command of the Japanese language. Although it is too simplistic to associate foreign-language capabilities with effectiveness in global marketing, this comparison nevertheless serves as an indicator of interest in international business.

96. "America's Place in World Competition," *Fortune*, November 6, 1989, p. 83; "Euro Makes a Useful Contribution," *Accountancy*, June 7, 1999, p. 66.
97. "Tethered to Pittsburgh for Years, an Engineer Thrives on Trips to Asia," *Wall Street Journal*, November 19, 1996, pp. 1, 5.

During the 1980s, many U.S.-based firms reduced the posting of executives overseas. Non-U.S. firms expanded at the same time. Mitsubishi, the $160 billion Japanese trading company, has half of its revenue based abroad and maintains 1,000 of its 9,900 Japanese employees overseas. Many of these executives have had more than one tour of service overseas. Some U.S.-based firms have reversed the earlier trend and are rapidly expanding opportunities for their staff overseas.[98]

Although the concepts introduced in this text are certainly important to anyone posted overseas in a global marketing assignment, the following section will demonstrate that these concepts have just as much validity for those of us who "stay home."

A Need for Global Mindsets

Few of us can avoid the impact of global competition today. Many of our domestic industries have been greatly affected by foreign competition, which has made enormous inroads in the manufacture of apparel, textiles, shoes, electronic equipment, and steel. As a result, these industries have become globalized and pulled into the global economy. Although foreign competition for many consumer goods has been evident for years, inroads by foreign firms in investment goods industries have been equally spectacular. Management of companies competing with foreign firms requires global minds: an ability to judge the next move of foreign competitors by observing them abroad in order to be better prepared to compete at home.

Import competition has been rising even in industries that used to be reserved largely for domestic companies. Nissin, a Japanese maker of instant noodles, started to make a dry soup called "Oodles of Noodles" in 1976 and, by expanding its manufacturing to a plant on each coast, accounts for a 4 percent share of the U.S. soup market, estimated at $2.3 billion. The company competes with Lipton, a traditional supplier of dry soups, by shipping smaller quantities to retailers. This results in faster product turnover at the retail level and a fresher product. Although the initial results were not successful, Nissin stayed in for the long haul and is now a successful competitor in the United States.[99]

Foreign competition has also reached U.S. retailers. IKEA, based in Sweden and the world's largest furniture retailing chain, came to the United States in 1985. From a small beginning in New Jersey, the company grew the business, sometimes by acquisitions, to almost $500 million of sales in the United States and Canada, or some 14 percent of IKEA's total revenue. IKEA brought with it a concept new to the United States: large stores where consumers could browse, buy,

98. "The Fast Track Leads Overseas," *Business Week*, November 1, 1993, pp. 64–68.
99. "Japan's Next Push in U.S. Markets," *Fortune*, September 26, 1988, p. 135.

and take furniture home in disassembled form at the end of their visit. Although successful and profitable now, IKEA had to struggle in the early years and made several changes to its retailing formula to adapt to U.S. requirements.[100] IKEA is but one example of an international global competitor entering a previously "safe" market with new ideas, thus bringing global competition to the doorstep of strictly domestic companies.

The need to become more competitive in a global economy will force many changes on the typical company. Companies will have to become international and compete in global markets to defend their own domestic markets and to keep up with global competitors based in other countries. These firms will need an increasing cadre of managers who can think with a global perspective.[101] This perspective requires not only a knowledge of other countries, economies, and cultures but a clear understanding of how the global economy works. Managers with a global perspective will also have to integrate developments in one part of the world with actions somewhere else. This means that a U.S. executive will be required to use input, facts, or ideas from a number of other countries for decisions on United States markets so that the best products may be marketed most efficiently and effectively.

Managers with a global perspective will also be challenged to deal with new strategies that were not part of the domestic or older international business scenes. These concepts, created and developed as of today, have been included in our text and will become apparent to the reader on a chapter-by-chapter basis. As a result, the reader will come to appreciate that the term *global* is more than just a replacement for *international*. It is a combination of a new perspective on the world and a series of new strategic concepts that add to the competitiveness of global marketing strategies. Mastering both this new outlook and the new concepts will become a requirement for firms that aspire to a position of global player in their chosen industries or market segments. Because this global mindset is so important to marketers, we have devoted much of Chapter 7 to covering the concept in depth.

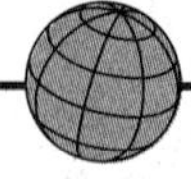

Organization of This Book

This text is structured around the basic requirements for making sound global marketing decisions. It takes into account the need to develop several types of competencies to analyze global marketing issues. The global marketer must be able to deal with decision areas on various levels of complexity. We will discuss

100. "Furnishing the World," *Economist*, November 19, 1994, pp. 79–80.
101. Jean-Pierre Jeannet, *Managing with a Global Mindset* (London: Pitman, Financial Times Management, 2000).

each of these dimensions of the global marketing task before we discuss the outline for this text.

Competencies

To compete successfully in today's global marketplace, companies and their management must master certain areas. *Environment competence*, needed to navigate the global economy, includes a knowledge of the dynamics of world economy, of major national markets, and of political, social, and cultural environments. *Analytic competence* is needed to pull together a vast array of information and data and to assemble relevant facts. *Strategic competence* helps executives focus on the strategic or long-term requirements of their firms, as opposed to short-term, opportunistic decisions. A global marketer must also possess *functional competence*, or a thorough background in all areas of marketing. Finally, *managerial competence* is the ability to implement programs and organize effectively on a global scale.

Managers with domestic responsibility also need analytic, strategic, functional, and managerial competence. They do not need global competence. Consequently, we will concentrate on those areas that set global marketing executives apart from their domestic counterparts.

Decision Areas

Successful global marketing requires the ability to make decisions not typically faced by single-country firms. These decision groupings include environmental analysis, global opportunity analysis, global marketing strategies, global marketing programs, and marketing management. Managers continuously must assess foreign environments and perform *environmental analyses* relevant to their businesses. In a second step, managers need to do an *opportunity analysis* that will tell them which products to pursue in which markets. Once opportunities have been identified, *global marketing strategies* are designed to define long-term efforts of the firm. The company then may design *global marketing programs* to determine the marketing mix. Finally, international marketing must *manage the global marketing effort*, which requires attention to planning, personnel, and organization.

Our five competence levels are closely related to the five major global marketing decision areas described above. Environmental competence is needed to perform an analysis of the global economic environment. Analytic competence is the basis for global opportunity analysis. Sound global marketing strategies are based on strategic competence. To design global marketing programs, one needs functional competence. Finally, managerial competence is needed for managing a global marketing effort.

FIGURE 1.3

International Marketing Management

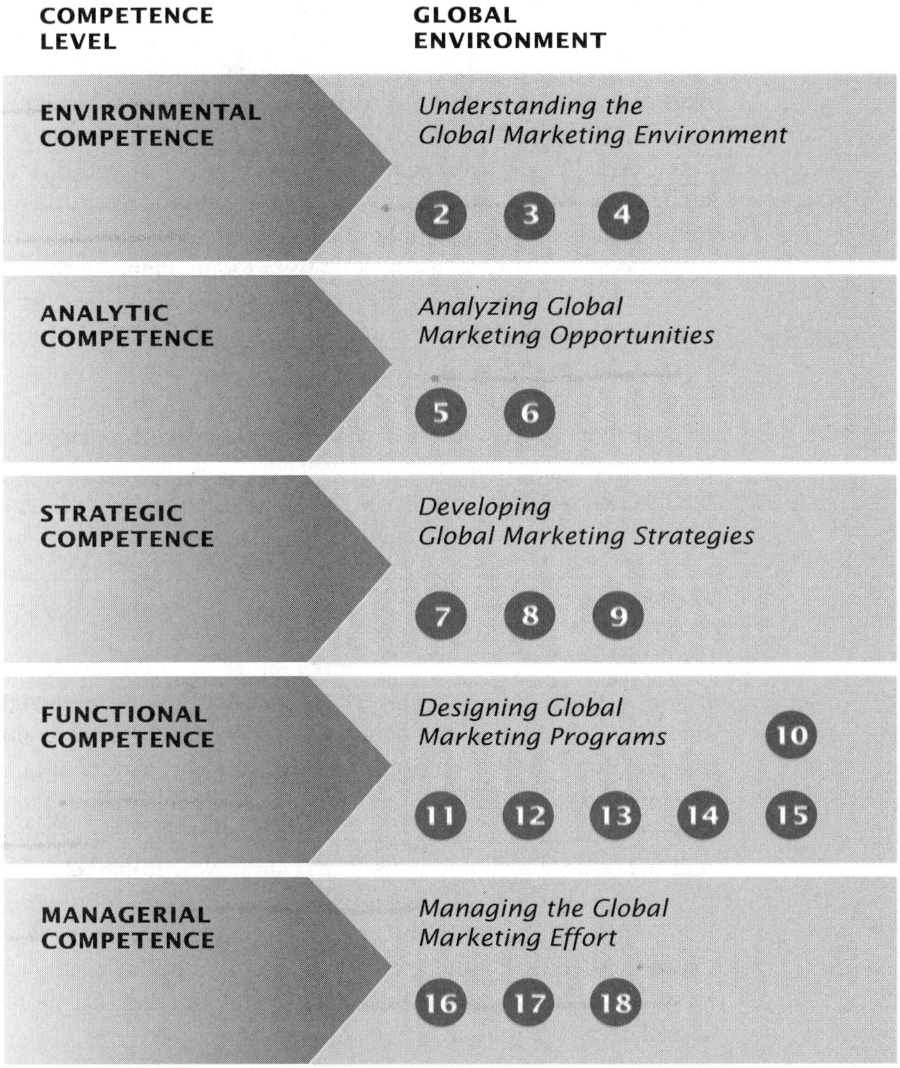

Chapter Organization

This text is organized around the flow of decisions, as depicted in Figure 1.3. The five decision areas are treated in several chapters that delineate the respective competence levels most appropriate for each decision area.

Chapter 1 provided an introduction and overview of global marketing and its challenges today.

Part 1, Chapters 2 through 4, is concerned with the global marketing environment. In order to build environmental competence, special emphasis is given to the economic, cultural, social, political, and legal forces companies must navigate in order to be successful.

Part 2, Chapters 5 and 6, concentrates on the global market opportunity analysis. Chapters in this section highlight international markets or countries, international buyers, and the research or analysis necessary to pinpoint marketing opportunities globally.

Chapters 7, 8, and 9, which make up Part 3, deal with strategic issues. Chapter 7 deals primarily with the mindset of the global marketer. Chapter 8 introduces the elements of global marketing strategy. Chapter 9 describes how companies can enter markets they have decided to target.

Part 4, Chapters 10 through 15, aims at developing the competence to design global marketing programs consistent with a global strategy. The chapters in this section cover product strategies, product development, channel management, pricing, promotion and communications, and advertising.

The text concludes with Part 5, Chapters 16 through 18. Here the emphasis is on building managerial competence in a global environment. Chapters 16, 17, and 18 deal with organizational and controlling issues and also with the technical aspects of the export and import trade process.

Finally, the cases at the back of the book address global marketing issues and give you an opportunity to practice the concepts developed in the text. These cases feature a range of complexity levels and address different decision areas of the global marketing process. They are all based on real situations, although the names of some of the companies are disguised.

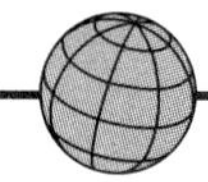

Conclusions

As a separate activity of business, global marketing is of great importance to nations, to individual companies, and to prospective managers. With markets and industries becoming increasingly globalized, most companies must become active participants in global marketing. The competitive positions of most companies, both abroad and in their domestic markets, rests on their ability to succeed in global markets. At the same time, the economies of entire countries rest on the global marketing skills of managers. The standard of living of many people will depend on how well local industry does in the global marketplace. These forces will place a premium on executive talent that is able to direct marketing operations from a global perspective. Clearly, many business professionals will need to understand the global dimension as it pertains to the marketing function if they are to progress in their careers.

In assembling a trained cadre of professional global marketing executives, the United States has typically lagged behind other countries. The U.S. market is so large that domestic problems tend to overshadow global marketing opportunities. As a result, most U.S. executives develop their careers largely in a domestic setting and have little direct exposure to foreign markets. Executives in foreign countries are more apt to have traveled abroad and tend to speak one or two foreign languages. Thus, their ability to understand global complexities is more developed than is that of their U.S. counterparts. All of this gives many foreign firms a considerable edge in competing for global dominance.

Although the need to develop a global competence may be clear, the circumstances that determine successful marketing practices for foreign markets are far less clear. The foreign marketing environment is characterized by a wide range of variables not typically encountered by domestic firms. This makes the job of global marketing extremely difficult. However, despite the complexities involved, there are concepts and analytic tools that can help global marketers. By learning to use these concepts and tools, you can enhance your own global marketing competence. You will be able to contribute to the marketing operations of a wide range of firms, both domestic and foreign.

QUESTIONS FOR DISCUSSION

1. Explain the scope of global marketing.
2. How and why does global marketing differ from domestic marketing?
3. Which do you think would be the most relevant factors limiting international marketing standardization of yogurts, automobiles, and desktop personal computers?
4. How does global marketing as a field relate to your future career in business? How would you expect to come into contact with global marketing activities?
5. Why are so many U.S. industries facing import competition?
6. Investigate one or two U.S. firms that do well abroad and analyze why they are successful.
7. Explain the major roles of multinationals (MNCs) and global corporations, as well as other types of firms in international marketing, and how they participate in this activity.
8. What do you think are the essential skills of a successful "global marketer"?
9. Which are the important skills for successful global minds?
10. List ten items important to you that you hope to be able to understand or accomplish after studying this book.

FOR FURTHER READING

Bartlett, Christopher, and Yves Doz. *Managing the Global Firm.* Thompson Business Press, 1990.

Bartlett, Christopher, and Sumantra Ghoshal. *Managing Across Borders*. Boston: HBS Press, 1989.

Buzzell, Robert D. "Can You Standardize Multinational Marketing?" *Harvard Business Review*, November-December 1968, pp. 102-113.

Gingrich, James A. "Five Rules for Winning Emerging Market Consumers," *Strategy & Business*, Second Quarter 1999, no. 15, pp. 19-33.

Govindarajan, Vijay, and Anil K. Gupta. "Taking Wal-Mart Global: Lessons from Retailing's Giant," *Strategy & Business*, Fourth Quarter 1999, no. 17, pp. 14-25.

Hamel, Gary, and C. K. Prahalad, *Competing for the Future*. Boston: Harvard Business School Press, 1994.

Jeannet, Jean-Pierre. *Managing with a Global Mindset*. London: Pitman, Financial Times Management, 2000.

Jolly, Vijay K., Matti Alahuhta, and Jean-Pierre Jeannet. "Challenging the Incumbents: How High Technology Start-Ups Compete Globally." *Journal of Strategic Change*, January 1992, vol. 1.00-00, pp. 11-1-11-12.

Kashani, Kamran. "Beware of Pitfalls in Global Marketing." *Harvard Business Review*, September-October 1989, pp. 91-98.

Levitt, Theodore. "The Globalization of Markets." *Harvard Business Review*, May-June 1983, pp. 92-102.

Ohmae, Kenichi. *The Borderless World*. New York: Harper & Row, 1990.

———. "Managing in a Borderless World." *Harvard Business Review*, May-June 1989, pp. 152-161.

———. *Triad Power*. New York: Free Press, 1985.

Porter, Michael E. "The Strategic Role of International Marketing." *Journal of Consumer Marketing*, Spring 1986, pp. 17-21.

Prahalad, C. K., and Yves L. Doz. *The Multinational Mission*. New York: Free Press, 1987.

Reich, Robert B. *The World of Nations*. New York: Knopf, 1991.

Taylor, William. "The Logic of Global Business: An Interview with ABB's Percy Barnevik." *Harvard Business Review*, March-April 1991, pp. 91-105.

Unctad World Investment Report 1998. New York: United Nations, 1998.

I Understanding the Global Marketing Environment

This part of the book introduces you to the environmental factors that influence global marketing decisions. Throughout Part 2 we maintain an analytical emphasis so that general concepts can be applied from country to country. Rather than describe a large number of environmental differences, we focus on several approaches companies adopt to cope with these differences. Our aim is to maintain a managerial point of view throughout.

In Chapter 2 we explain the nature of the various global economic forces that shape developments within individual countries as well as within the global economy. In Chapter 3 we describe the social and cultural influences that shape the local marketing environment, and in Chapter 4 we discuss the political and legal forces that affect international firms, focusing on how companies cope with these forces.

2

The Global Economy

BILLIONS OF DOLLARS IN GOODS AND SERVICES ARE TRADED BETWEEN NATIONS each day. Businesses establish operations and borrow funds in locations throughout the world. Financial investors expeditiously purchase stocks and bonds on U.S., European, and Asian markets. Banks lend and arbitrage currencies worldwide. It is only when these transactions are interrupted or threatened that the scope and significance of the international economy are appreciated.

The nations of the world are linked by a multidimensional network of economic, social, cultural, and political ties. As these connections become more important and complex, countries will find themselves richer but more vulnerable to foreign disturbances, and this vulnerability increasingly will move the issues surrounding international trade and finance into the political arena.

This chapter introduces the important aspects of world trade and finance. We begin by explaining comparative advantage, which is the basis for international trade. We then explain the international system to monitor world trade, particularly the balance of payments measurement system. From this base, we describe the workings of the foreign exchange market and the cause of exchange rate movements. Finally, we discuss the international agencies that promote economic and monetary stability, as well as the strategies that countries use to protect their own economies.

International Trade: An Overview

Few individuals in the world are totally self-sufficient. Why should they be? Restricting consumption to self-made goods lowers living standards by narrowing the range and reducing the quality of goods we consume. For this reason, few nations have economies independent from the rest of the world, and it would be difficult to find a national leader willing or able to impose such an economic hardship on a country.

Foreign goods are central to the living standards of all nations. But, as seen in Table 2.1, there is considerable variation among countries concerning their reliance on foreign trade. In 1998, imports were less than 12 percent of the gross domestic product (GDP) of Japan and the United States, whereas Belgium had an import-to-GDP ratio of 70 percent.

Even in countries that seemingly do not have a great reliance on imports, such as the United States, where imports were 12 percent of the 1998 GDP and exports were 11 percent, world trade in goods and services plays an important role. In 1998, the U.S. trade in import and exports was $1.8 trillion, making it the largest trading country in the world. Also the volume of U.S. trade has increased, from 17 percent of GDP in 1985, to 21 percent in 1993, to 25 percent in 1997. In addition, most of the U.S. *Fortune* 500 receive over 50 percent of their profits from overseas.[1]

> Peter Johnson, a student, is awakened in the morning by his Sony clock radio. After showering, he puts on an Italian-made jacket while listening to the latest release by Tears for Fears, a British singing group. At breakfast, he has a cup of Brazilian coffee, a bowl of cereal made from U.S.-grown wheat, and a Colombian banana. A quick glance at his Swiss watch shows him that he will have to hurry if he wants to be on time for his first class. He drives to campus in a Toyota, stopping on the way to fill the tank with gas from Saudi Arabian oil. Once in class, he rushes to take a seat with the other students, 30 percent of whom hold non-U.S. passports.

1. "American Trade Policy," *Economist*, January 30, 1999, p. 65.

TABLE 2.1

Imports and Exports as a Percentage of GDP, 1998 Estimates (in Billions of Dollars)

	GDP	Imports	Imports/ GDP	Exports	Exports/ GDP
INDUSTRIAL					
Australia	394	80	20%	82	21%
Belgium	243	171	70	184	76
Canada	608	211	35	234	39
Germany	2092	541	26	570	27
Japan	4190	432	10	457	11
Netherlands	360	187	52	212	59
New Zealand	65	18	28	19	29
Norway	153	51	33	64	42
Switzerland	255	94	37	106	42
United Kingdom	1286	350	27	341	27
United States	7834	966	12	856	11
DEVELOPING					
China	902	167	19%	207	23%
Greece	123	29	24	19	15
Hong Kong	171	232	135	225	132
India	382	59	16	44	12
Mexico	403	122	30	122	30
Romania	35	13	37	10	30
Saudi Arabia	140	43	31	63	45
South Korea	443	172	39	169	38

Source: Adapted from *World Outlook 1999*. (London: *Economist Intelligence Unit*, January 1999).

The figures given in Table 2.1 are useful for identifying the international dependence of nations, but they should be viewed only as rough indicators. In a disruption of international trade, there is little doubt that the United States would be harmed much less than the Netherlands. But this is not to say that a disruption of trade would not also be harmful to the United States and Japan as well, both of which have large domestic markets but depend heavily on world trade for growth.

So far, the focus has been on world trade for goods. Services also are an important and growing part of the world's economy. Services make up approximately 20 percent of the world's exports, totaling $1.29 trillion in 1998. Industries such as banking, telecommunications, insurance, construction, transportation, tourism, and consulting make up over half the national income of many rich economies. A country's invisible exports include export of services, transfers from workers abroad, and income earned on overseas investments. In volume, the top four countries in service exports were the United States ($234 billion), the United Kingdom ($100 billion), France ($79 billion), Germany ($76 billion), and Italy ($70 billion).[2]

The Growth in World Trade

World trade has grown sixteenfold since 1950, far outstripping the growth in GDP.[3] This growth has been fueled by the opening of world markets. The Bretton Woods conference of world leaders in 1944 led to the establishment of the General Agreement on Tariffs and Trade (GATT) in 1948, which will be discussed in detail later. The original group of twenty-three countries expanded to almost one hundred. GATT, and now the World Trade Organization (WTO), have helped to reduce tariffs from 40 percent in 1947 to an estimated 4 percent in 2000.[4] A recent study showed that open economies with limited duties and government restrictions grew 1.2 percent faster per year than closed economies.[5] The WTO reports that tariffs are down to an average of 3.8 percent in developed countries. The WTO has 135 members, and another 30 countries, including Jordan, Saudi Arabia, Vietnam, and China, have petitioned to join.[6] The principle of free trade has led to the building of market interdependencies. As shown in Figure 2.1, international trade has grown much faster than world GDP output, showing that national economies are becoming much more closely linked and interdependent by means of their exports and imports. Foreign direct investment, another indication of global integration, grew by 100 percent between 1990 and 1997.[7]

2. "Export of Commercial Services, 1998," *Economist*, May 8, 1999, p. 109.
3. "The World's Current Economic Troubles Strengthen the Case for a New Round of Trade Talks," *Economist*, March 10, 1998, Survey p. 3.
4. "Border Battles," *Economist*, October 3, 1998, Survey p. 6.
5. Jeffrey Sachs, "The Limits of Convergence," *Economist*, June 14, 1997, p. 20.
6. "Estonia to Become 135th Member of WTO," WTO *press release*, May 21, 1999 (www.wto.org/new/pressest).
7. "Does the WTO Need Rules for Foreign Direct Investment?" *Economist*, March 10, 1998, Survey p. 10.

FIGURE 2.1

Growth of World Trade and GNP (1950 = 100)

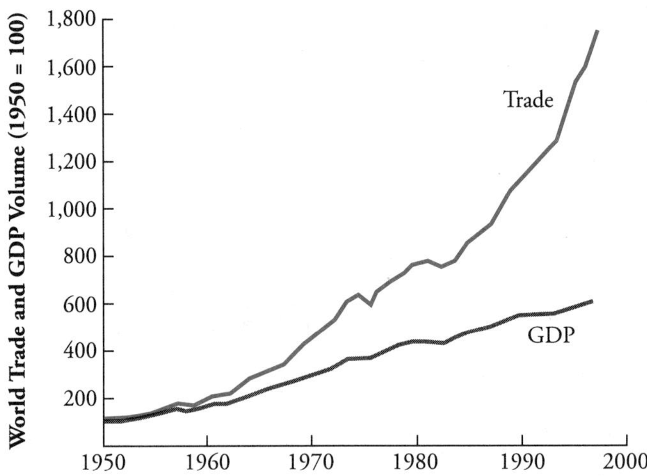

Source: "World Trade: Runaway Success," *Economist,* October 3, 1998, Survey p. 4. © 1998 The Economist Newspaper Group, Inc. Reprinted with permission, further reproduction prohibited. www.economist.com

Owing to the lengthy (seven years) Uruguay Round of GATT talks and agreements that ended in 1993, world trade has grown 6 percent per year since 1993, versus 4 percent for the 1980s.[8] In fact, in 1997 the WTO estimated that world trade of goods grew by 10 percent, three times the world GDP growth. In 1998, world trade only grew by 3.5 percent owing to the economic contraction in Asia.[9] As the WTO replaced GATT in 1996, the major challenge was to assure compliance and to assert the authority of the WTO over powerful regional trade agreements like the European Union (EU), the North American Free Trade Agreement (NAFTA), the Common Market of the South (MERCOSUR), and the Asian-Pacific Economic Cooperation (APEC). There are over eighty regional agreements between countries granting preferential access to each other's markets. All but 3 of the 135 members of the WTO belong to at least one of these regional pacts.[10] Understanding the economics of trade is critical to understanding that the need for free trade flows from country to country.

8. "Spoiling World Trade," *Economist,* December 7, 1996, p. 15.
9. "World Trade Growth Slower in 1998 After Unusually Strong Growth in 1997," WTO press release, April 16, 1999 (www.wto.org/intltrade/internat).
10. "A Question of Preference: Do Regional Trade Agreements Encourage Free Trade?" *Economist,* August 22, 1998.

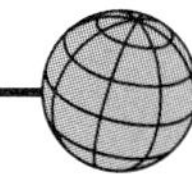

The Basis for Trade: Absolute Versus Comparative Advantage

Internationally traded goods and services are important to most countries, as is shown in Table 2.1. Because jobs and standard of living seem to be so closely tied to these inflows and outflows, there is much debate about why particular countries find their comparative advantages in certain goods and services and not in others, whereas other countries have different advantages and disadvantages.

Over the past twenty years, not only has there been a dramatic rise in the volume of trade, but numerous changes have occurred in the patterns of trade as well. Countries that once exported vast amounts of steel, such as the United States, are now net importers of the metal. Other nations, such as Japan, once known for inexpensive, handmade products, now compete globally in high-tech products. What caused these trade pattern changes? Why do countries that are able to produce virtually any product choose to specialize in only certain goods? Where do international cost advantages originate? In the twenty-first century, will we still think of Indonesia and China as having the greatest advantage in handmade goods, or in the future will they be as Japan and Taiwan are today?

The early work of Adam Smith provides the foundation for understanding trade today. Smith saw trade as a way to promote efficiency because it fostered competition, led to specialization, and resulted in economies of scale. Specialization supports the concept of absolute advantages—that is, sell to other countries the goods that utilize your special skills and resources, and buy the rest from those who have some advantage. This theory of selling what you are best at is known as *absolute advantage.* But what if you have no advantages? Will all your manufacturers be driven out of business? David Ricardo in his 1817 publication *Principles of Political Economy* offered his theory of comparative advantage.[11] This theory maintains that it is still possible to produce profitably what one is best at even if someone else is better. The following sections further develop the concepts of absolute and comparative advantage—the economic basis of free trade and hence all global trade.

Absolute Advantage

Although many variables may be listed as the primary determinants of international trade, productivity differences rank high on the list. Take, for example, two countries—Vietnam and Germany. Suppose the average Vietnamese worker can produce either 400 machines or 1,600 pounds of tomatoes in one year. Over the same time period, the average German worker can produce either 500 machines or 500 pounds of tomatoes. (See example 1 in Table 2.2.) In this case, German

11. "The Economies of Free Trade," *Economist,* September 22, 1990, p. 12.

TABLE 2.2

Absolute Versus Comparative Advantage: Worker Productivity Examples

	Vietnam	**Germany**
EXAMPLE 1		
Yearly output per worker		
Machinery	400	500
Tomatoes	1,600	500
Absolute advantage	Tomatoes	Machinery
EXAMPLE 2		
Yearly output per worker		
Machinery	200	500
Tomatoes	800	1,000
Opportunity costs of production	1 machine costs 4 lb tomatoes	1 machine costs 2 lb tomatoes
	or	*or*
	1 lb tomatoes costs 0.25 machines	1 lb tomatoes costs 0.50 machines
Absolute advantage	None	Tomatoes
		Machinery
Comparative advantage	Tomatoes	Machinery

workers can produce more machinery, ***absolutely,*** than Vietnamese workers can; whereas Vietnamese workers can produce more tomatoes, ***absolutely,*** than can their German counterparts.

Given these figures, Vietnam is the obvious low-cost producer of tomatoes and should export them to Germany. Similarly, Germany is the low-cost producer of machines and should export them to Vietnam.[12]

12. The concept of absolute advantage can be found in Adam Smith, *The Wealth of Nations* (New York: Prometheus Books, 1999). Originally published in 1776.

Comparative Advantage

We should not conclude from the previous example that absolute differences in production capabilities are necessary for trade to occur. Consider the same two countries—Vietnam and Germany. Now assume that the average Vietnamese worker can produce either 200 machines or 800 pounds of tomatoes each year, whereas the average German worker can produce either 500 machines or 1,000 pounds of tomatoes (see example 2 in Table 2.2). Germany has an absolute advantage in both goods, and it appears as though Vietnam will benefit from trade because it can buy from Germany cheaper goods than Vietnam can make for itself. However, the basis for mutually advantageous trade is present, even here. The reason lies in the concept of comparative advantage.

Comparative advantage measures a product's cost of production, not in monetary terms but in terms of the forgone opportunity to produce something else. It focuses on tradeoffs. To illustrate, the production of machines means that resources cannot be devoted to the production of tomatoes. In Germany, the worker who produces 500 machines will not be able to grow 1,000 pounds of tomatoes. If we standardize, the cost can be stated as follows: each pound of tomatoes costs 0.5 machines, or 1 machine costs 2 pounds of tomatoes. In Vietnam, producing 200 machines forces the sacrifice of 800 pounds of tomatoes. Alternatively, this means that 1 pound of tomatoes costs 0.25 machines, or 1 machine costs 4 pounds of tomatoes.[13]

From the example above, we see that even though Vietnam has an absolute disadvantage in both commodities, it still has a comparative advantage in tomatoes. For Vietnam, the cost of producing a pound of tomatoes is 0.25 machines, whereas for Germany the cost is 0.5 machines. Similarly, even though Germany has an absolute advantage in both products, it has a comparative cost advantage only in machines. It costs Germany only 2 pounds of tomatoes to produce a single machine, whereas in Vietnam the cost is 4 pounds of tomatoes.

The last step in the discussion of the comparative advantage concept is to choose a mutually advantageous trading ratio and to show how it can benefit both countries. Any trading ratio between 1 machine = 2 pounds of tomatoes (Germany's domestic trading ratio) and 1 machine = 4 pounds of tomatoes (Vietnam's domestic trading ratio) will benefit both nations (see Table 2.3). Suppose we choose 1 machine = 3 pounds of tomatoes. Since Germany will be exporting machinery, it gains by getting 3 pounds of tomatoes rather than the 2 pounds it would have produced domestically. Likewise, because Vietnam will be exporting tomatoes, it gains because 1 machine can be imported for the sacrifice of only 3 pounds of tomatoes, rather than 4 pounds of tomatoes if Vietnam made the machine itself.

13. David Ricardo, "Principles of Political Economy and Taxation," Ch. 7 in *The Works and Correspondence of David Ricardo,* ed. Pierro Sraffa and Maurice H. Dobb (Cambridge: Cambridge University Press, 1951–1955).

TABLE 2.3

Mutually Advantageous Trading Ratios

Tomatoes	*Machines*
Germany, 1 pound tomatoes = 0.50 machines	Vietnam, 1 machine = 4 pounds tomatoes
Vietnam, 1 pound tomatoes = 0.20 machines	Germany, 1 machine = 2 pounds tomatoes

Another way to think of comparative advantage is in terms of the value of labor. If workers are paid relative to their output, at the end of a year a German worker could have 500 machines or 1,000 pounds of tomatoes, and a Vietnamese worker 200 machines or 800 pounds of tomatoes. Given the relative output of each, a German worker could trade 1 machine for 2 pounds of tomatoes in Germany or 4 pounds of tomatoes in Vietnam. The Vietnamese worker could trade 1 pound of tomatoes for 0.25 machines in Vietnam or 0.5 machines in Germany. In the end, the Vietnamese worker will end up with fewer goods because productivity is less, which means he or she will be paid less, so the goods will be cheaper than in Germany, where the output per worker is higher and therefore more expensive.

The discussion of comparative advantage illustrates that relative rather than absolute differences in productivity can form a determining basis for international trade. Although the concept of comparative advantage provides a powerful tool for explaining the rationale for mutually advantageous trade, it gives little insight into the source of the relative productivity differences. Specifically, why does a country find its comparative advantage in one particular good or service rather than in another? Is it by chance that the United States is a net exporter of aircraft, machinery, and chemicals but a net importer of steel, textiles, and consumer electronic products? Or can we find some systematic explanations for this pattern?

The answers to these questions are of more than just academic concern; they have an impact on the standard of living and livelihood of millions of people. The importance of understanding productivity differences is especially apparent in countries where trade barriers (for example, tariffs and quotas) are about to be either erected or dismantled. For instance, during the formative years of the European Common Market, discussions centered on the economic disruptions that would occur when Germany, Italy, and France dropped their tariff barriers and permitted free trade among themselves. These issues have resurfaced each time a new country (such as Greece, Spain, or Portugal) has applied for membership to the European Community (now the European Union). They were hotly debated in 1982, when the U.S. government proposed trade liberalization measures for Latin American countries in the Caribbean Basin Initiative. Similarly, they were at the center during the Uruguay Round of GATT trade talks, which ran into difficulty over the elimination of farm subsidies by member countries.

The notion of comparative advantage requires that nations make intensive use of those factors they possess in abundance. They export *these* goods and import *those* goods for which they have a comparative disadvantage. So Hungary, with its low labor cost of one dollar per hour, will export labor-intensive goods, such as unsophisticated chest freezers and table linen, while Sweden, with its high-quality iron ore deposits will export high-grade steel. In essence, the theory of comparative advantage says it pays for countries to engage in international trade exporting in which they are efficient and to import goods that they are relatively inefficient at producing.[14]

Michael Porter argues that although the theory of comparative advantage has appeal, it is limited just to the factors of production, which include land, labor, natural resources, and capital. Porter's study of ten trading nations that account for 50 percent of world exports and one hundred industries resulted in a new theory. This theory postulates that the country will have a significant impact on the competitive advantage of an industry depending on the following factors:

1. The elements of production
2. The nature of domestic demand
3. The presence of appropriate suppliers or related industry
4. The conditions in the country that govern how companies are created, organized, and managed, as well as the nature of domestic rivalry[15]

This view of competitive advantage does not refute the theory of comparative advantage; rather it helps explain why industries have a comparative advantage.

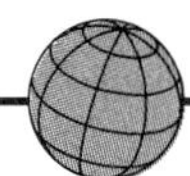

Balance of Payments

Newspapers, magazines, and nightly TV news programs are filled with stories relating to aspects of international business. Often, media coverage centers on the implications of a nation's trade deficit or surplus or on the economic consequences of an undervalued or overvalued currency. What are trade deficits? What factors will cause a currency's international value to change? The first step in answering these questions is to gain a clear understanding of the contents and meaning of a nation's balance of payments.

14. "A Short Tour of Economic Theory: Why Trade Is Good for You," *Economist*, March 10, 1998, Survey p. 4.
15. Michael E. Porter, *The Competitive Advantage of Nations* (New York: Macmillan, 1990), pp. 69–175.

The balance of payments is an accounting record of the transactions between the residents of one country and the residents of the rest of the world over a given period of time.[16] It resembles a company's statement of sources and uses of funds. Transactions in which domestic residents either purchase assets (goods and services) from abroad or reduce foreign liabilities are considered uses (outflows) of funds because payments abroad must be made. Similarly, transactions in which domestic residents either sell assets to foreign residents or increase their liabilities to foreigners are sources (inflows) of funds because payments from abroad are received.

Listed in Table 2.4 are the principal parts of the balance of payments statement: the current account, the capital account, and the official transactions account. There are three items under the current account. The goods category states the monetary values of a nation's international transactions in physical goods. The services category shows the values of a wide variety of transactions,

TABLE 2.4

Balance of Payments

	Uses of Funds	*Sources of Funds*
CURRENT ACCOUNT		
1. Goods	Imports	Exports
2. Services	Imports	Exports
3. Unilateral transfers	Paid abroad	From abroad
CAPITAL ACCOUNT		
1. Short-term investment	Made abroad	From abroad
2. Long-term investments	Made abroad	From abroad
a. Portfolio investment		
b. Direct investment		
OFFICIAL TRANSACTIONS ACCOUNT		
Official reserve changes	Gained	Lost

16. An excellent source of historical and internationally comparable data can be found in the *Balance of Payments Yearbook*, published yearly by the International Monetary Fund (Washington, D.C.).

such as transportation services, consulting, travel, passenger fares, fees, royalties, rent, and investment income. Finally, unilateral transfers include all transactions for which there is no quid pro quo (that is, gifts). Private remittances, personal gifts, philanthropic donations, relief, and aid are included within this account.

The capital account category is divided into two parts on the basis of time. Short-term transactions refer to maturities less than or equal to one year, and long-term transactions refer to maturities longer than one year. Purchases of treasury bills, certificates of deposit, foreign exchange, and commercial paper are typical short-term investments. Long-term investments are separated further into portfolio investments and direct investments.

In general, portfolio investments imply that no ownership rights are held by the purchaser over the foreign investment. Debt securities such as notes and bonds would be included under this heading. Direct investments are long-term ownership interests, such as business capital outlays in foreign subsidiaries and branches. Stock purchases are included as well, but only if such ownership entails substantial control over the foreign company. Countries differ in the percentage of total outstanding stock an individual must hold for an investment to be considered a direct investment in the balance of payments statements. The International Monetary Fund reports that these values range from 10 percent for widely dispersed holdings to 25 percent.[17]

Because it is recorded in double-entry bookkeeping form, the balance of payments as a whole must always have its inflows (sources of funds) equal to its outflows (uses of funds). Therefore, the concept of a deficit or surplus refers only to selected parts of the entire statement. A deficit occurs when the particular outflows (uses of funds) exceed the particular inflows (sources of funds). A surplus occurs when the inflows considered exceed the corresponding outflows. In this sense, a nation's surplus or deficit is similar to that of individuals or businesses. If we spend more than we earn, we are in a deficit position. If we earn more than we spend, we are running a surplus.

Balance of Payments Measures

Three balance of payments measures are considered to be important by many businesspeople, government officials, and economists. These are the balance on merchandise trade, the balance on goods and services, and the balance on current account.[18] The balance on merchandise trade is the narrowest measure because it considers only internationally traded goods. For this reason, critics feel that it is of the least practical value. They argue that the balance on merchandise

17. International Monetary Fund, *Balance of Payments Manual,* 4th ed. (Washington, D.C.: International Monetary Fund, 1977), pp. 137–138.
18. The classic discussion of balance of payments is found in James Meade, *The Balance of Payments* (London: Oxford University Press, 1951).

trade is a vestigial remnant of the seventeenth-century mercantilist conviction that if one country gained from trade, the other lost.[19] In those war-torn times, domestic economic policies were geared toward ensuring that exports exceeded imports. In so doing, domestic jobs were provided, and the excess funds (usually precious metals) earned through the surpluses could be used to support armies and navies for imperialist expansions—or to defend against them. However, if jobs are the goal, there seems to be little point in separating goods from services. Both activities give jobs to willing workers.

Defenders of the balance on merchandise trade measure feel that jobs connected to physical goods are more important than service-oriented jobs, and therefore the balance on merchandise trade is a useful economic indicator. They contend that if an international disruption occurred, it would be better to live in a country with textile factories, steel mills, farms, and electronics firms rather than to live in a country with a labor force of insurance clerks, computer consultants, and tourist guides.

The balance on goods and services has a direct link to most national income accounting systems. It is reported in the national income and national product statements as "net exports." If this figure is positive, a net transfer of resources is taking place from the surplus nation to the debtor nations. Many analysts feel that a negative balance is an indication that a nation is not living within its means. To have such a deficit position, the country would have to be a net borrower of foreign funds or a net recipient of foreign aid.

The most widely used measure of a nation's international payments position is the statement of balance on current account. As with the balance on goods and services statement, it shows whether a nation is living within or beyond its means. Because it includes unilateral transfers, deficits (in the absence of government intervention) must be financed by international borrowing or by selling foreign investments. Therefore, the measure is considered to be a reflection of a nation's financial claims on other countries.

Exchange Rates

The purchase of a foreign good or service can be thought of as involving two sequential transactions: the purchase of the foreign currency, followed by the purchase of the foreign item itself. If the cost of buying either the foreign currency or the foreign item rises, the price to the importer increases. A ratio that measures the value of one currency in terms of another currency is called an *exchange rate.* With it, one is able to compare domestic and foreign prices.

19. Examples of mercantilist thought can be found in Thomas Mun, "England's Treasure by Foreign Trade," in *Early English Tracts in Commerce,* ed. John McCullock (Norwich, England: Jarrold and Sons, 1952). See also Joseph Schumpeter, *History of Economic Analysis* (New York: Oxford University Press, 1954).

When a currency rises in value, it is said to *appreciate.* If it falls in value, it is said to *depreciate.* Therefore, a change in the value of the U.S. dollar exchange rate from 0.50 British pounds to 0.65 British pounds is an appreciation of the dollar and a depreciation of the pound. After all, the dollar now commands more pounds while a greater number of pounds must be spent to purchase one dollar.

The strength of a domestic currency against the currency of your trading partners can have a negative effect. For example, the yen rose 18 percent against the pound in the last quarter of 1998, which was a major factor in British Airways reporting a third-quarter loss of $123 million.[20]

As the yen dropped in value from 110 yen per dollar in 1997 to 145 yen to the dollar in mid-1998, the Japanese car companies earned more yen for every car sold overseas. Every yen that the dollar rises against the Japanese currency adds about 6 billion yen ($41.9 million) to Honda's profits and about 10 billion yen ($69.8 million) to Toyota's.[21] The falling yen created the opposite problem for U.S. manufacturers exporting to Japan. For example, Eddie Bauer had to lower dollar prices on clothes in its twenty-six Japanese stores to keep the yen prices down. Recreational Equipment Inc., which sells outdoor clothing in Japan via catalogue and the Internet, saw the yen price of a $375 North Face mountaineering jacket go from 42,000 yen in 1997 to 55,000 yen in mid-1998.[22]

The Foreign Exchange Market Unlike major stock markets, where trading is done on central exchanges (for example, the New York Stock Exchange and the London Stock Exchange), foreign exchange transactions are handled on an over-the-counter market, largely by phone, fax, and email. Private and commercial customers as well as banks, brokers, and central banks conduct millions of transactions on this worldwide market daily.

As Figure 2.2 shows, the foreign exchange market has a hierarchical structure. Private customers deal mainly with banks in the retail market, and banks stand ready to either buy or sell foreign exchange as long as a free and active market for the currency exists.

Not all banks participate directly in the foreign exchange market. In the United States, a bank must have a substantial volume of international business to justify setting up a foreign exchange department. Thus, most small financial intermediaries handle customers' business through correspondent banks.

Banks that have foreign exchange departments trade with private commercial customers on the retail market, but they also deal with other banks (domestic or

20. "British Air Posts Quarterly Loss on More Competition, Strong Yen," *Wall Street Journal,* February 10, 1999, p. A17.
21. Lisa Shuchman and Gregory White, "Japanese Car Makers to Hold U.S. Prices," *Wall Street Journal,* June 18, 1998, p. A15.
22. Khanh T. L. Tran, "Falling Yen Creates Painful Dilemma for U.S. Marketers in Japan," *Wall Street Journal,* June 30, 1998, p. A13.

FIGURE 2.2

Structure of the Foreign Exchange Market

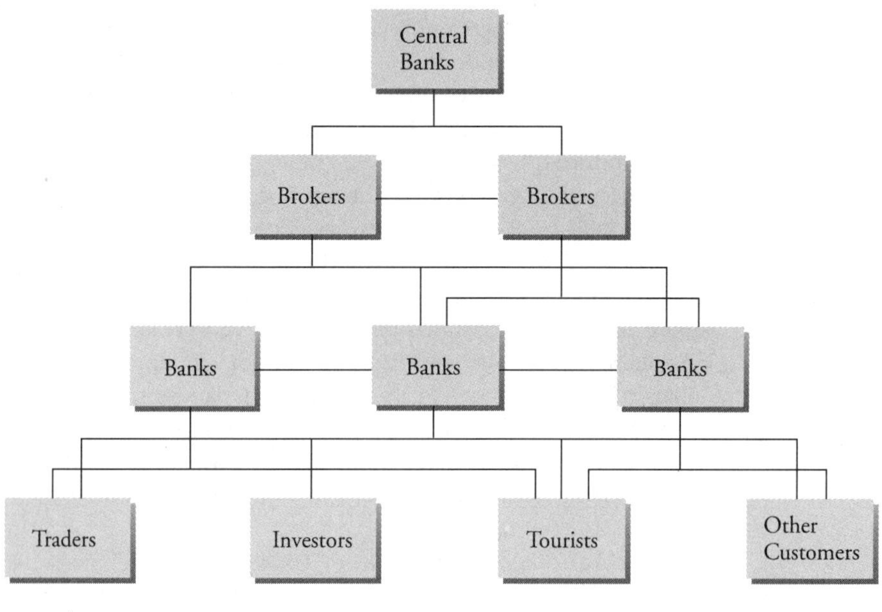

foreign) and brokers on the wholesale market. Generally, these wholesale transactions are for amounts of $1 million or more. Many of these trades are made on the basis of verbal agreements, and only some days later is written documentation formally exchanged.

The foreign exchange market is probably as close as one can get to the economist's proverbial ideal of pure competition. There are many buyers and sellers, no one buyer or seller can influence the price, the product is homogeneous, there is relatively free entry into and exit from the market, and there is virtually perfect worldwide information. If prices among banks differed by even a fraction of a cent, arbitrageurs would immediately step in for the profits they could earn risk-free. Through telex machines, telephone calls, and voice boxes that lead directly into the trading rooms of other banks and brokers, participants keep abreast of the market. Positions are opened and closed minute by minute, and the pace of activity in a foreign exchange dealing room can be quite frantic.

Central banks play a key role in the foreign exchange markets because they are the ultimate controllers of domestic money supplies. When they enter the market to directly influence the exchange rate value, they deal mainly with brokers and large money market banks. Their trading is not done to make a profit but to attain some macroeconomic goal, such as altering the exchange rate value, reducing inflation, or changing domestic interest rates. In general, even if central banks do not intervene in the foreign exchange markets, their actions influence exchange rate values because large increases in a nation's money supply will increase its inflation rate and lower the international value of its currency.

Causes of Exchange Rate Movements Exchange rates are among the most closely watched and politically sensitive economic variables. Regardless of which way the rates move, some groups are hurt while other groups are helped. If a currency's value rises, domestic businesses will find it more difficult to compete internationally, and the domestic unemployment rate may rise. For example, the weakening of the yen in 1998 to 130 yen to the dollar meant that Ford was losing money on every car it made in the United States and sold in Japan. Ford therefore expanded its production in Japan, using the excess capacity at the Mazda Motor Corp., of which Ford owns 33.4 percent.[23]

If the value of the currency falls, foreign goods become more expensive, the cost of living increases, and goods become cheaper to foreign buyers. What are the causes of these exchange rate movements, and to what extent caan governments influence them? Market exchange rates are determined by the forces of supply and demand. The greater the supply of a currency to the foreign exchange market or the lesser its demand, the lower will be its international value. Similarly, the greater the demand for a currency in the foreign exchange market or the lower its supply, the higher will be its international value. Therefore, to predict movements in a currency's international value, one must identify the participants whose transactions affect these supply and demand forces and determine which factors will cause them to change their behavior.

Identifying the international participants is a relatively easy matter because they have already been implicitly mentioned in the discussion of the balance of payments. Recall that the balance of payments is nothing more than a summary of a nation's international transactions. In the current account and the capital account, traders, speculators, and investors are the major players. To this list, we will add government participants. The following sections will show how these groups act and react to overlapping market signals.

Traders. International trade in goods and services is influenced mainly by changes in relative international prices and relative income levels. If, for example, the U.S. inflation rate exceeds that of Germany, then U.S. goods will become progressively more expensive than German goods. Consequently, U.S. consumers will begin to demand more of these foreign goods, thereby increasing the supply of dollars to the foreign exchange market (that is, increasing the

23. Valerie Reitman, "Ford Might Build Its Vehicles in Japan," *Wall Street Journal,* January 7, 1998, p. A1.

demand for German marks). For the same reason, German consumers will reduce their demand for dollars (that is, reduce their supply of marks) as they purchase fewer U.S. goods. Therefore, relatively high inflation in the United States will cause the international value of the dollar to fall and the value of other currencies to rise.

Consumption is constrained by income, the ability to borrow, and the availability of credit. This is true both for individuals and nations. However, when speaking of a country's income, gross domestic product (GDP) is the most widely used measure. An increase in GDP will give the citizens of a nation the wherewithal to purchase more goods and services. Since many of the newly purchased goods are likely to be foreign, increases in GDP will raise the demand for foreign products and therefore raise the demand for foreign currencies. If, for example, the U.S. growth rate exceeds that of Germany, there will be a net increase in the demand for German marks and a lowering of the dollar's international value.[24]

Speculators. Speculators buy and sell currencies in anticipation of changing future values. If there were a widespread expectation that the Japanese yen would rise in relative value to the dollar, speculators would try to purchase yen (that is, sell dollars) in anticipation of that change. As the demand for yen increased in the spot market and the supply of yen for dollars fell, the yen's exchange rate value would rise. (A spot market is for the immediate delivery of currency within two days of the transaction.) Similarly, as the supply of dollars increased and the demand for them decreased, the international value of the dollar relative to yen would fall. Consequently, spot market rates are very much influenced by future expectations.

Investors. One of the main factors influencing investors' decisions is the differential between international interest rates. If, for example, Italian interest rates were greater than U.S. interest rates (adjusted for such things as risk, taxability, and maturity), then investors would have an incentive to place their funds where they earned the highest return—in Italy. The supply of dollars in the foreign exchange market would rise (as U.S. investors purchased Italian securities), and the demand for dollars would fall (as Italians purchased domestic rather than U.S. securities). The effect of these investments would be to lower the value of the dollar relative to the lira.

As important as relative interest rates are to the international investment decision, expected changes in exchange rates are equally important. There can be a substantial difference between the interest rate at which funds are placed in foreign investments and the net return after repatriation. The gains made on higher foreign interest rates can be partially or fully offset by changes in a currency's value. This risk may be eliminated by contracting on the forward exchange market, but in general the forward rates are arbitraged to the point where these rates completely offset the interest rate advantage. This is why relative inflation rates

24. For an alternative point of view, see Jacob A. Frenkel and Harry Johnson, "The Monetary Approach to the Balance of Payments: Essential Concepts and Historical Origins," in *The Monetary Approach to the Balance of Payments,* ed. J. A. Frenkel and H. G. Johnson (Toronto: University of Toronto Press, 1976).

reappear as an important determinant of international transactions. A relatively high domestic inflation rate is one of the major causes of a depreciation in the exchange value of a currency.[25] Therefore, a high inflation rate implies that the currency carries high nominal interest rates, an expensive spot exchange value, and a relatively cheap forward exchange rate value.

Governments. Governments enter foreign exchange markets in a variety of ways, ranging from the international purchase of goods and services to the granting of foreign aid. Perhaps the most pronounced impact governments have is as discretionary interveners in foreign exchange markets. Suppose the United States and Japan agreed to lower the dollar's value relative to the yen. To do so, dollars would have to be supplied—and yen demanded—in the foreign exchange markets.

For the United States, this would mean putting upward pressure on the domestic money supply as newly created dollars were exchanged for circulating Japanese yen. For Japan, this type of intervention would mean putting downward pressure on its money supply as dollar reserves were used to take yen off the market. Because governments have such strong and direct controls over domestic money supplies, subsequent changes in other economic variables (for example, inflation rates or interest rates) will result from this activity.

International Agencies for Promoting Economic and Monetary Stability

Stability in the international economy is a prerequisite for worldwide peace and prosperity. It was for this reason that at the end of World War II, representatives from several countries met at Bretton Woods, a small ski resort in New Hampshire, and formed both the International Monetary Fund and the World Bank (the International Bank for Reconstruction and Development). With headquarters in Washington, D.C., these two agencies continue to play major roles in the international scene. Although they have many notable achievements, perhaps their most important contribution has been to initiate forums for summit discussions of controversial financial topics.

International Monetary Fund

The major goals of the International Monetary Fund (IMF) are to promote orderly and stable foreign exchange markets, maintain free convertibility among the currencies of member nations, reduce international impediments to trade, and pro-

25. The purchasing power parity theory explains that exchange rates can be predicted by estimating relative international inflation rates. See Gustav Cassel, *The World's Monetary Problems* (London: Constable, 1921); Jacob A. Frenkel, "Purchasing Power Parity: Doctrinal Perspective and Evidence from the 1920s," *Journal of International Economics,* 8 (May 1978); and Jacob A. Frenkel, "The Collapse of Purchasing Power Parity During the 1970s," *European Economic Review,* 16 (May 1981).

vide liquidity to counteract temporary balance of payments disequilibria. Although the IMF has no legal powers to enforce its decisions, strong and subtle pressures can be brought to bear on noncomplying nations.

In the early years following its creation, the IMF focused its attention on restoring currency convertibility among members and ensuring that adequate liquidity existed for countries experiencing balance of payments difficulties. Free convertibility was regained by 1958, but the liquidity issue was a much more difficult problem to solve. International trade expanded rapidly over the postwar period, but international reserves in both dollars and gold grew less rapidly. To increase the amount of international liquidity and to take some of the pressure off these reserve assets, the IMF in 1970 began issuing special drawing rights (SDRs) to member nations. These SDRs (mutual book credits) gave nations the right to purchase foreign currencies, and with these currencies they could finance temporary balance of payments deficits.

In 1973, major trading nations abandoned the fixed exchange rate system set up at Bretton Woods in 1944. As a result, the need for increases in world liquidity to finance balance of payments deficits was reduced substantially. Prior to the 1970s, the agency funded operations with contributions from member nations, but this changed as the IMF began selling some of its gold reserves and banking part of the capital gain.

The IMF's core mission is to help stabilize an increasingly global economy. The IMF has shifted its focus over the years from exchange rate relations among industrialized countries to the prevention and rescue of economic instability in developing countries and countries in transition. For example, in 1998 and 1999, the IMF led a $17.2 billion rescue for Thailand, a $42 billion package for Indonesia, and a $41.5 billion deal for Brazil. South Korea got a whopping $58.4 billion when it was on the verge of bankruptcy.[26] Such rescue packages stabilize the economy and avoid the total economic collapse of developing countries.

Over the past decade, the IMF has begun to extend longer-term credits to developing nations, rather than only short-term balance of payments aid. To qualify such loans, the fund may require that countries take drastic economic steps, such as reducing tariff barriers, making businesses independent, curbing domestic inflation, and cutting government expenditures. For example, since 1997 the IMF has delayed a $170 million financial agreement for Kenya until Kenyans name new leadership to the Kenya Anti-Corruption Authority.[27] Although many nations have resented such intervention, banks worldwide have used the IMF as a screening device for their private loans to many developing countries. If countries qualify for IMF loans, they are considered for private credit.

26. Michael Phillips, "A Look at How the Global Finance Crisis Began and How It Spread," *Wall Street Journal,* April 4, 1999, p. R4.

27. Michael Phillips, "IMF Makes a Push for Good Government," *Wall Street Journal,* April 19, 1999, p. A2.

World Bank (International Bank for Reconstruction and Development)

The World Bank gives long-term loans mainly to developing nations. In this sense, it functions like a merchant banker (that is, supplier of capital) for the developing nations.

The World Bank acts as an intermediary between the private capital markets and the developing nations. It makes long-term loans (usually for fifteen or twenty-five years), carrying rates that reflect prevailing market conditions. By virtue of its AAA credit rating, the bank is able to borrow private funds at relatively low market rates and pass the savings to the developing nations. However, because it must borrow to obtain capital and is not funded by members' contributions, the World Bank must raise lending rates when its costs (that is, market interest rates) rise.

In 1997, when private funds were pouring into developing economies, some critics questioned the future role of the World Bank. However, with the Asian crisis, the flow of private funds to developing countries dropped by more than $100 billion in 1998. The World Bank has expanded its role from mostly loans to partial guarantees of government bonds for investment projects. In Thailand, the World Bank partially guaranteed the Electricity Generating Authority of Thailand. The guarantee attracted investors and spawned interest for similar programs in South Korea and the Philippines.[28] The World Bank and four regional development banks in the Americas, Africa, Asia, and Europe have been encouraged to focus more on people development and environmental projects in addition to traditional infrastructure projects. The development banks are being encouraged by the Group of Seven (see below) to sharply reduce funding to those countries that do not demonstrate commitment to poverty reduction. Also, the banks are focusing more on trying to get governments to improve financial supervision, strengthen bankruptcy laws, and reduce red tape.[29]

Group of Seven

The world's leading industrial nations have established a Group of Seven, which meets regularly to discuss the world economy. Finance ministers and central bank governors from the United States, Japan, Germany, France, Britain, Italy, and Canada make up this group, referred to as the G7. The group works together informally to help stabilize the world economy and reduce extreme disruptions. For example, the G7 met in June 1999 and developed proposals to reduce the debt of thirty-three impoverished nations, mostly in Africa, by 70 percent. When former Russian president Boris Yeltsin joined the meeting for one day (when Russia joins the talks, the group calls itself the G8), the G8 agreed to rebuild Kosovo and the

28. "The World Bank: Back in the Driving Seat," *Economist,* February 13, 1999, p. 71.
29. "Europe's Bank Rethinks Development," *Economist,* April 17, 1999, p. 76.

Balkan countries, including Serbia, if the latter demonstrates a full commitment to economic and democratic reforms.[30]

European Monetary System

In the early 1970s, a group of European countries established the European Joint Float agreement. The values of the currencies were fixed against one another in a narrow range of plus or minus 2.25 percent. The movement of these currencies back and forth within this range became known as the snake. This early system was later replaced by the European Monetary System (EMS), which included the fifteen members of the European Union (EU). Britain was the last to join, in late 1990. The EMS included a set of features to force member countries to regulate their economies so that their currency stays within 2.25 percent of the central rates. If a currency slips out of this band, it may be required to increase or lower interest rates to stay in line with the other currencies. The EU countries had all contributed to the European Monetary Cooperation Fund, which had a pool of over $30 billion to buy or sell currency in order to keep all currencies within their acceptable band. The EMS also developed a new currency called the European Currency Unit (ECU), made up of a weighted average of fifteen currencies from the EU countries. The EMS tended to produce abnormal results because of the dominance of the German mark and therefore the German Bundesbank. This led the French and German finance ministers to recommend a monetary union for Europe. With the support of German chancellor Helmut Kohl and French president François Mitterrand, a proposal was made for a European currency area and a European central bank. After study, the European leaders produced the Maastricht Treaty in 1991.[31]

The Maastricht Treaty established the European Monetary Institute (EMI) in 1993 as a precursor to a European central bank. The EMI worked with the European central banks to evaluate each country's performance on the convergence criteria agreed to at Maastricht.[32] To be part of the new European Monetary System, countries had to have a budget deficit of less than 3 percent of GDP and a total government debt of less than 60 percent of GDP by 1997. The United Kingdom, Sweden, and Denmark opted out of the European Monetary Union (EMU). Greece wanted to join but did not meet the convergence criteria. The remaining eleven EU countries of Austria, Belgium, Finland, France, Germany, Ireland, Italy, Luxembourg, the Netherlands, Portugal, and Spain all became part of the EMU.[33]

30. Bob Davis, "G-7 Moves to Revamp Financial Systems," *Wall Street Journal*, June 21, 1999, pp. A18, A23.

31. "EURO BRIEF: Eleven into One May Go," *Economist*, October 17, 1998, p. 81.

32. Andrew Fisher, "EMI: Technicians Look to 1999," *Financial Times*, September 27, 1996, World Economy and Finance section, p. 27.

33. "Europe's Adventure Begins," *Economist*, January 2, 1999, p. 15.

Beginning in January 1999, the new European Union single currency, the euro, replaced these eleven countries' national currencies. From 1999 until 2002, these EMU countries will use national currencies for notes and coins, but most prices will also be quoted in euros. The European Central Bank (ECB), established in 1998, has complete control over the euro and is obliged to maintain price stability and avoid inflation or deflation.[34] The national central bank governors from the eleven EMU countries sit on the ECB council and use interest rates to control inflation at less than 2 percent.

The supporters of the euro think it will reduce transaction costs and foreign exchange risk within Europe and provide a strong viable currency alternative to the dollar. The dollar accounts for over 50 percent of official reserves around the globe, which is more than twice its share of global output. The euro may also unite European capital markets and improve the liquidity of Europe's financial markets as private investors switch dollar assets into euros. The critics argue that the ECB must deal with eleven economies that may not be going in the same direction. For example, in 1999, the German and Italian economies slowed down, the French economy was flat, and the other EMU economies were expanding. Also, local politicians may favor local over regional concerns. Wim Duisenberg, the president of the ECB, blamed the weakness of the euro in 1999 on Oskar Lafontaine, Germany's finance minister, who had pressed local banks to reduce interest rates.[35] At the same time, the ECB did not reduce interest rates because IG Metall, Germany's largest trade union, won a 4 percent pay raise, while Germany's inflation rate was only 0.2 percent. Finally, critics say the future of the euro is unclear since it is uncertain when and how the United Kingdom, Greece, and Sweden will join the EMU, as well as the other potential new members of the European Community.[36]

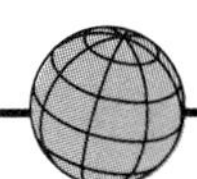

International Trade: Does It Deserve Special Treatment?

The principles of comparative advantage can be applied to any type of trade—international, intranational, or interpersonal. But if this is true, why is there so much concern about the international sector? Few residents of Massachusetts complain about the jobs that Pennsylvania, California, or Michigan factories take away from the New England area. Is the problem that people perceive international trade as an "us against them" situation whereas they perceive domestic trade as "us against us"? Or are there legitimate differences when one goes beyond national borders?[37]

34. "EURO BRIEF: Eleven into One May Go," *Economist,* October 17, 1998, p. 81.
35. "The Euro: Neurosis," *Economist,* February 27, 1999, p. 73.
36. "Ins and Outs," *Economist,* January 2, 1999, p. 21.
37. See Lester Thurow, *The Zero Sum Society: Distribution and the Possibilities for Economic Change* (New York: Basic Books, 1980).

One can point to some obvious factors in differentiating international from intranational trade. Varying currencies, languages, traditions, and cultures are just a few examples. But how significant are they? Switzerland, a developed but relatively small European country, has four official languages (German, French, Italian, and Romansch) and an assortment of widely differing dialects. The country is divided into twenty-six cantons, and in most respects each canton wields more authority than does the national government. The result is a nation in which rules and regulations vary canton by canton. Switzerland is bordered by Germany, France, Austria, Italy, and Liechtenstein. Although the Swiss franc is the national currency, many merchants throughout the country accept payment in any of the neighboring countries' currencies. What factors distinguish foreign from domestic trade in Switzerland? It seems that there are few, if any, distinguishing characteristics. Certainly, the ones listed above are more apparent than real. If, in general, this is true, then international trade becomes nothing more than a simple subset of broader trade issues.

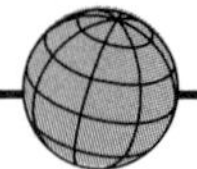

Protectionism and Trade Restrictions

Economists have spent considerable time identifying and quantifying the net gains from free international trade. In large part, the benefits are obvious. After all, trade by its very nature involves a voluntary exchange of assets between two parties. In the absence of coercion, the motives behind this exchange must be for mutual benefit. The controversy surfaces when domestic producers are considered. Foreign imports seem to take business away from domestic firms and to increase the domestic unemployment rate.[38]

Free trade, like all competitive or technological changes, creates and destroys; it gives and it takes away. By increasing competition, free trade lowers the price of the imported goods and raises the demand for efficiently produced domestic goods. In these newly stimulated export industries, sales will increase, profits will rise, and stock prices will climb. Clearly, consumers of the imported good and producers of the exported good benefit by these new conditions. However, it is equally clear that there are groups that are harmed as well. Domestic producers of the import-competing good are one of the most visible groups. They experience noticeable declines in market share, falling profits, and deteriorating stock prices.

It is a fact of life that there are both beneficiaries and victims from free trade, just as there are when virtually any change is made. For instance, if someone were to discover a way for people to grow three or four sets of teeth in a lifetime, most people would benefit from this discovery. Nevertheless, there exists a group

38. For details on the arguments against protectionism, see Robert Z. Lawrence and Robert E. Litan, "Why Protectionism Doesn't Pay," *Harvard Business Review,* May–June 1987, pp. 60–67.

of people—dentists, oral surgeons, and periodontists—who would be hurt. Should this invention be withheld from the market because this group is hurt? The true test of a discovery is not whether or not victims exist but whether the benefits outweigh the inevitable losses.[39]

Herein lies the major reason for protectionist legislation. The victims of free trade are highly visible and their losses quantifiable; governments use protectionism as a means of lessening the harm done to this easily identified group. Conversely, the individuals who are helped by free trade tend to be dispersed throughout the nation rather than concentrated in one particular region. Moreover, their monetary gain is only a fraction of the total purchase price of the commodity.

A study by Australia's Center for International Economies (CIE) prepared a detailed model of the international trading system in order to measure the impact of reduced protectionism on world trade. If the countries in GATT reduced their tariff and nontariff barriers by 50 percent, CIE estimates that trade would increase $750 billion: $208 billion in the United States, $245 billion in Europe, and $287 billion in Asia/Pacific.[40] The GATT agreements reached in 1993 reduced prices U.S. consumers paid by $32.8 billion per year. For example, $17 billion came from liberation of the textile and apparel industry, and $1.2 billion came from reduced agricultural production.[41]

Protectionist legislation tends to be in the form of either tariffs, quotas, or qualitative trade restrictions. This section describes these barriers and their economic effects.

Tariffs

Tariffs are taxes on goods moving across an economic or political boundary. They can be imposed on imports, exports, or goods in transit through a country on their way to some other destination. In the United States, export tariffs are constitutionally prohibited, but in other parts of the world they are quite common. Of course, the most common type of tariff is the import tariff, and it is on this tariff that we focus our attention.

Import tariffs have a dual economic effect. First, they tend to raise the price of imported goods and thereby protect domestic industries from foreign competition. Second, they generate tax revenues for the governments imposing them. It is important to recognize this duality because, often, the situations resulting from the tariffs are quite different from what was originally intended. Moreover, regardless of what the goals are (for example, increasing tax revenue or raising employment), tariffs may not be the most direct or effective means of attaining them.

39. Leland Yeager and David G. Tuerck, *Foreign Trade and U.S. Policy* (New York: Praeger, 1976), pp. 1–11, 40–88.
40. "Once and Future GATT," *Economist,* September 22, 1990, p. 39.
41. "GATT's Payoff," *Fortune,* February 7, 1994, p. 28.

Today, most nations impose import duties for the purpose of protecting domestic manufacturers. In some cases (as when they are imposed on expensive-to-store agricultural products), foreign sellers will lower their prices to offset any tariff increase. The net effect is for the consumer-paid price to differ only slightly, if at all, from the pretariff level. Consequently, the nation has greater tariff revenues but little additional protection for the domestic producers.

When tariffs do raise the price of the imported good, consumers of the imported good develop a disadvantage, whereas the import-competing industries are helped. Quite often, another unintended group is hampered as well. For example, the U.S. Department of Commerce raised duties from 27 percent to 36.5 percent on imported steel in response to foreign manufacturers' dumping of steel in the United States. Although higher duties helped U.S. steel manufacturers, U.S. purchasers complained that the increased duties increased the price of steel by over 20 percent, making U.S. steelmakers less competitive in the global marketplace.[42] In another case, the Department of Commerce revoked the 63 percent import duties on advanced flat screens used on laptops, because although the duty helped some small U.S. screen manufacturers, it hurt computer companies such as Apple, Compaq, and IBM. These companies argued that the high duty inflated the cost of their products, harmed their ability to compete abroad, and would force them to shift production to other countries.[43] In yet another case the U.S. government put a 33 percent tariff on Mexican brooms imported into the United States, owing to alleged dumping of the brooms below market prices; however, critics argue the tariff is to protect U.S. broom manufacturers, who have a strong lobby in Illinois.[44]

Quotas

Quotas are physical limits on the *amount* of goods that can be imported into a country. Unlike tariffs, which restrict trade by directly increasing prices, quotas increase prices by directly restricting trade. Naturally, to have such an effect, imports must be restricted to levels below the free trade level.

For domestic producers, quotas are a much surer means of protection. Once the limit has been reached, imports cease to enter the domestic market, regardless of whether foreign exporters lower their prices. Consumers have the most to lose with the imposition of quotas. Not only are their product choices limited and the prices increased, but the goods that are imported carry the highest profit margins. Restrictions on imported automobiles, for instance, will bring in more luxury models with high-cost accessories.

Like tariffs, quotas have both revenue and protection effects. The protection effects are the most apparent because trade is unequivocally being curtailed. The

42. "Punitive Tariffs Raised Against Foreign Steel," *New York Times,* June 23, 1993, pp. D1, D20.
43. "Steel Users Condemn U.S. Trade Cases," *Financial Times,* June 7, 1993, p. 4; "Duties Ended on Computer Flat Screens," *New York Times,* June 23, 1993, pp. D1, D18.
44. "One Bad Apple Agreement," *Wall Street Journal,* March 30, 1998, p. 18.

revenue effects are less obvious. When a government imposes arbitrary restrictions on imported goods, companies vie for the right to conduct this limited trade. The net effect is that consumers pay more for the goods in terms of higher prices.

Orderly Marketing Arrangements and Voluntary Export Restrictions

The word *quota* has come to be associated with the most selfish of protectionist legislation. There can be strong political and economic repercussions associated with such unilateral, beggar-thy-neighbor policies. To avoid these problems, the new terms *orderly marketing arrangement* and *voluntary export restriction* have been invented.[45] In general, an orderly marketing arrangement is an agreement between countries to share markets by limiting foreign export sales. Usually these arrangements have a set duration and provide for some annual increase in foreign sales to the domestic market. In 1999, the U.S. Department of Commerce reached an agreement with Russia to voluntarily limit Russian steel imports into the United States to 750,000 tons per year, compared with 3,500,000 tons imported in 1998. If Russia had not agreed to the limits, the Commerce Department was prepared to announce duties of 71 to 218 percent on Russian steel as a punishment for Russia's allegedly selling steel in the United States below market prices.[46] Voluntary restraints can also take a funny twist. Mazak, a Japanese toolmaker with a factory in Kentucky, has used the voluntary restraint agreement to limit Japanese imports into the United States. In fact, Mazak prepared a video of Japanese screwdriver (assembly only) factories to show how his Tokyo competitors were circumventing the agreement.[47]

The euphemistic terms are intended to give the impression of fairness. After all, who can be against anything that is orderly or voluntary? But when one scratches beneath the surface of these so-called negotiated settlements, a different image appears. First, the negotiations are initiated by the importing country with the implicit threat that, unless concessions are made, stronger unilateral sanctions will be imposed. They are really neither orderly nor voluntary. They are quotas in the guise of negotiated agreements.

The Omnibus Trade and Competitiveness Act of 1988 gave presidents of the United States the right to negotiate orderly marketing arrangements and set countervailing duties to deal with the problems of trade deficits, protected markets, and dumping. The use of these voluntary export restraints (VERs) has spread to textiles, clothing, steel, cars, shoes, machinery, and consumer electronics. There

45. See Kent Jones, *Politics Versus Economics in World Steel Trade* (London: George Allen & Unwin, 1986).
46. Helene Cooper, "Russia Agrees to Limit Steel Shipments," *Wall Street Journal,* February 23, 1999, p. A8.
47. "Look Who's Taking Japan to Task," *Business Week,* June 4, 1990, p. 26.

are approximately three hundred VERs worldwide, most protecting the United States and Europe. Over fifty agreements affect exports from Japan, and another thirty-five affect South Korea.[48] A study conducted by the Institute for International Economics in Washington, D.C., found that the import restrictions, tariffs, and voluntary restraints in Europe cost the European consumer dearly. For example, banana import restrictions cost European consumers $2.0 billion or $0.55 per kilo; beef tariffs, local subsidies, and bans on hormone-treated beef cost consumers $14.6 billion, or $1.60 per kilo. The total cost of all this protection in Europe on fruits, cars, steel, textiles, video recorders, beef, milk, cheese, telecoms, airlines, and more is estimated to be $43 billion. According to the research by the Institute for International Economics, these restrictions save approximately 200,000 jobs in Europe at a cost of $215,000 per job saved—enough to buy each lucky worker a new Rolls Royce each year.[49]

The use of quotas and voluntary export restrictions is declining with the strengthening of the WTO and increased compliance by the 135 member countries. In its first three years (1995–1998), the WTO dealt with 132 complaints, with the dispute panels having complete power to force countries found in the wrong to change their ways, offer compensation, and/or face sanctions by all 135 member countries. The WTO has not been used by the big countries to control the smaller ones, as some feared. For example, Costa Rica asked the WTO to rule against American barriers to its export of men's underwear and won the case, forcing America to change its import rules.[50]

The United Nations Trade and Development (UNCTAD), which represents the interests of the 48 percent poorest nations, is working with the WTO to bring the nations into the mainstream of world trade.[51]

Formal and Administrative Nontariff Trade Barriers

The final category of trade restrictions is perhaps the most problematic and certainly the least quantifiable. Nontariff barriers include a wide range of charges, requirements, and restrictions, such as surcharges at border crossings, licensing regulations, performance requirements, government subsidies, health and safety regulations, packaging and labeling regulations, and size and weight requirements. Not all of these barriers are discriminatory and protectionist. Restrictions dealing with public health and safety are certainly legitimate, but the line between social well-being and protection is a fine one.

At what point do consular fees, import restrictions, packaging regulations, performance requirements, licensing rules, and government procurement proce-

48. "A Survey of World Trade," *Economist,* September 22, 1990, p. 8.
49. "Trade: Europe's Burden," *Economist,* May 22, 1999, p. 12.
50. "Fifty Years On," *Economist,* May 16, 1998, p.21.
51. William Barnes, "Poor Nations Assert Place in Global Trade," *Financial Times,* February 21, 2000, p. 6.

dures discriminate against foreign producers? Is a French tax on automobile horsepower targeted against powerful U.S. cars, or is it simply a tax on inefficiency and pollution? Are U.S. automobile safety standards unfair to German, Japanese, and other foreign car manufacturers? Does a French ban on advertising bourbon and Scotch (but not cognac) serve the public's best interest? Are chickens slaughtered in the United States not fit to grace the tables of Europeans, as claimed by EU officials, because Americans use a different process to clean their fowl?[52]

Sometimes, nontariff barriers can have considerable impact on foreign competition. For decades, West German authorities forbade the sale of beer in Germany unless it was brewed from barley malt, hops, yeast, and water. If any other additives were used—a common practice elsewhere—German authorities denied foreign brewers the right to label their products as beer. In 1987, the law was struck down by the European Court of Justice.[53] In the EU, Japan agreed to a voluntary restraint agreement limiting automobile exports to 15 percent of the EU market by 1999. What is interesting is that the nontariff trade barriers significantly affected the share of Japanese automobiles imported into Europe: 2 percent in Italy and Spain, 3 percent in France, 12 percent in the United Kingdom, 16 percent in Germany, 29 percent in Switzerland, 36 percent in Denmark, and 39 percent in Finland.[54]

General Agreement on Tariffs and Trade (GATT)

Because of the harmful effects of protectionism, which were most painfully felt during the Great Depression of the 1930s, twenty-three nations banded together in 1948 to form the General Agreement on Tariffs and Trade (GATT). Over its lifetime, through periodic trade rounds, or negotiations, GATT served as a major forum for the liberalization and promotion of nondiscriminatory international trade between participating nations.

The principles of a world economy embodied in the articles of GATT were *reciprocity, nondiscrimination,* and *transparency.* The idea of reciprocity is simple. If one country lowers its tariffs against another's exports, then it can expect the other country to do the same. This practice of reciprocity has been important in the bargaining process to reduce tariffs. Nondiscrimination means that one country should not give one member or group of members preferential treatment over other members of the group. Referred to as the "most favored nation" (MFN) status, the designation does not mean that one nation is the *most* favored but rather that the nation is favored to the same degree as other nations. Trans-

52. "Trade: Standard Fare," *Economist,* May 24, 1997, p. 72.
53. "EC Claims Victory as Court Overturns Germany's Age-Old Ban on Beer Imports," *Wall Street Journal,* March 13, 1987, p. 29.
54. "Car Sales Charter for a Good Citizen," *Financial Times,* August 2, 1991, p. 11.

parency refers to the GATT policy that nations replace nontariff barriers (such as quotas) with tariffs and then bind the tariff, which means to agree not to raise it. Nontariff barriers do much more harm to trade than tariffs, especially bound tariffs. Tariffs reduce uncertainty and are out in the open, so they are easier to negotiate down in the future.[55] Through these principles, GATT effectively reduced trade restrictions and minimized price distortions.

Although its most notable gains were in reducing tariff and quota barriers on certain goods, GATT also helped to simplify and homogenize trade documentation procedures, reduce qualitative trade barriers, curtail dumping (that is, selling abroad at a cost lower than the cost of production),[56] and discourage government subsidies. GATT reduced tariffs from 40 percent in 1947 to fewer than 5 percent in 1990.

The Uruguay Round of GATT talks, which lasted from 1986 to 1994, ended in agreements covering the following areas:

- *Agriculture:* Europe will gradually reduce farm subsidies. Japan and Korea will start to import rice. The United States will reduce subsidies to growers of sugar, citrus fruit, and peanuts.
- *Entertainment, pharmaceuticals, and software:* New rules will protect copyrights, patents, and trademarks. Developing nations will have a decade to implement patent protection for drugs. France refused to liberalize access for the U.S. film industry.
- *Financial, legal, and accounting services:* For the first time, these services come under the rules of international trade.
- *Textiles and apparel:* The strict quotas limiting imports into the United States will be phased out over ten years.[57]

The final act of GATT was to replace itself with the World Trade Organization.

World Trade Organization

The World Trade Organization (WTO), which replaced GATT in 1995, continues to pursue reductions in tariffs on manufactured goods as well as liberalization of trade in agriculture and services. The major benefit of the WTO over GATT is the resolution of disputes. Under GATT, any member could veto the outcome of a panel ruling on a dispute. WTO panels are stricter. They must report their decisions in nine months and can be overturned only by consensus. Countries that break the rules must pay compensation, mend their ways, or face trade sanctions.

55. "The ITO That Never Was," *Economist,* September 22, 1990, pp. 7–8.
56. Economists prefer to define *dumping* as selling below the variable cost per unit, because only in such cases is the decision uneconomical.
57. "What's Next After GATT's Victory?" *Fortune,* January 10, 1994, pp. 66–70.

With 135 member countries as of 2000 and 30 more who want to join, the WTO is the global watchdog for free trade. The major role of the WTO is completing the unfinished business of GATT. WTO's efforts are in four areas. First, WTO will continue to push for liberalization of trade of goods and services, especially in the areas of agricultural trade and services. Agriculture is always difficult, as every country wants to protect its farmers. Information technology is another item on the liberalization agenda for the WTO, as the United States wants reduced tariffs on computers, semiconductors, and software. Second, the WTO must decide how to integrate China. As the world's second largest economy and tenth biggest exporter, China needs to become part of the WTO, but its vast semi-planned economy, with its formidable array of import quotas, trade licenses, and import inspections, hinders access to the WTO. Also, Chinese emigration policy and human rights policies have strained the U.S.-China relationship, which may restrict admittance to the WTO. The third challenge facing the WTO comprises the "new issues" of trade policy concerning foreign investment, competition policy, and labor standards. Although most countries want foreign investment, developing countries such as India, Malaysia, and Tanzania still want to set the terms of entry for foreigners. The United States and Europe insist on some core labor standards, such as a ban on child labor and trade union freedom. Although many countries are in favor of labor standards, the developing countries argue that low labor costs are the basis of most of their exports. The fourth issue facing the WTO is the spread of regional trading agreements. The WTO acknowledges eighty regional agreements. Given the seven years it took to resolve many of the issues in the Uruguay Round of trade talks, it seems many governments are favoring regional agreements to establish some collective trade power. Also, the ratification of NAFTA in the 1990s along with the strengthening of the EU may prompt other countries to form similar alliances. As these regional groups tend to favor regional trade over global trade, the WTO will need to address potential conflicts between regional versus global needs.[58]

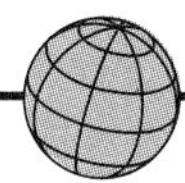

Economic Integration as a Means of Promoting Trade

For years public policymakers, economists, and academics have argued over the linkage between economic freedom and economic growth. Through a study of 102 countries from 1975 to 1995, economists James Gwartney, Robert Lawson, and Walter Block classified countries based on concrete measures of economic liberty and compared these ratings with GDP per person and GDP growth per person. Countries with high levels of economic freedom like Hong Kong, Singapore, New Zealand, the United States, and Switzerland had a GDP of $16,000 per person and GDP growth per person of over 3 percent per year, whereas coun-

58. "World Trade: All Free Traders Now," *Economist,* December 7, 1996, pp. 21–23.

tries with low levels of economic freedom like Zaire, Algeria, Iran, Syria, Haiti, and Romania had a GDP of less than $2,000 per person and GDP growth per person of 11 percent per year.[59]

There is little argument that free trade bestows net gains on trading nations—especially in the long run. The problem is that with so many entrenched vested interest groups, it is difficult to update existing trading rules. A reduction of protectionist legislation causes considerable short-term dislocations, putting much economic and political pressure on a nation's power structure.

As a partial step in the trade liberalization process, countries have begun to move toward limited forms of economic integration. Although the degree of economic integration can vary considerably from one organization to another, four major types of integration can be identified: free trade areas, customs unions, common markets, and monetary unions. Some of these concepts will be covered in greater detail in Chapter 5.

Free Trade Areas

The simplest form of integration is a free trade area. Within a free trade area, nations agree to drop trade barriers among themselves, but each nation is permitted to maintain independent trade relations with nongroup countries. There is little attempt at this level to coordinate such things as domestic tax rates, environmental regulations, and commercial codes, and generally such areas do not permit resources (that is, labor and capital) to flow freely across national borders. Moreover, because each country has autonomy over its money supply, exchange rates can fluctuate relative to both member and nonmember countries. Examples of free trade areas are the Latin American Free Trade Area and the European Free Trade Area.

Customs Unions

Customs unions, a more advanced form of economic integration, possess the characteristics of a free trade area but with the added feature of a common external tariff/trade barrier for the member nations. Individual countries relinquish the right to set their nongroup trade agreements independently. Rather, a supranational policymaking committee makes these decisions.

Common Markets

The third level of economic integration is the common market. Here, countries have all the characteristics of a customs union, but the organization also encourages resources (labor and capital) to flow freely among the member nations. For

59. "Economic Freedom: Of Liberty and Prosperity," *Economist,* January 13, 1996, pp. 21–23 .

example, if jobs are plentiful in Germany but scarce in Italy, workers can move from Italy to Germany without having to worry about severe immigration restrictions. In a common market, there is usually an attempt to coordinate tax codes, social welfare systems, and other legislation that influences resource allocation. Finally, although each nation still has the right to print and coin its own money, exchange rates among nations are often fixed or permitted to fluctuate only within a narrow range. The most notable example of a common market is the European Union (EU). It was established in 1958 as the European Economic Community; in 1968 it became the European Community and finally the European Union in 1992. The EU has been an active organization for trade liberalization and continues to increase its membership size.

Monetary Unions

The highest form of economic integration is a monetary union. A monetary union is a common market in which member countries no longer regulate their own currencies. Rather, member-country currencies are replaced by a common currency regulated by a supranational central bank. With the ratification of the Maastricht Treaty by EU members, the European Union became the first monetary union in January 1999.[60]

The Global Economy

The global economy is in a state of transition from a set of strong national economies to a set of interlinked trading groups. This transition has accelerated over the past few years with the fall of the Berlin Wall, the collapse of Communism, and the coalescing of the European trading nations into a single market. The investment by Europeans, Japanese, and Americans in one another's economies is unprecedented. U.S. companies create and sell over $80 billion per year in goods and services in Japan. The flow of British direct investment abroad was $58.2 billion in 1997, of which 30 percent went to the United States, making Britain the biggest foreign owner of business, followed by the Dutch and Japanese.[61] Foreign direct investment of private funds into emerging economies peaked in 1996 at $212 billion, and is estimated to be $145 billion in 2000. China is one of the largest benificiaries, receiving $20 billion in 1998.[62] As companies globalize, manufacturing becomes more flexible, and engineers have instant access to the latest technology, we see microchips designed in California, sent to Scotland to be fabricated, shipped to the Far East to be tested and assembled, and returned to the United States to be sold.[63]

60. "The Euro: Neurosis," *Economist,* February 27, 1999, p. 73.
61. "Foreign Investment: Ruling the Merger Wave," *Economist,* January 23, 1999, p. 53.
62. Kevin "Uncertain Prospects," *Economist,* April 24, 1999, p. 23.
63. William Van Dusen Wishard, "The 21st Century Economy," *Futurist,* May-June 1987, p. 23.

The physical shipment of goods is increasingly being replaced by local manufacturing as global companies bypass trade business and take advantage of local labor and market knowledge. So, while world trade of goods and services was $4.8 trillion, sales of foreign affiliates of transnational companies was $5.2 trillion. Foreign direct investment is coming from industrial countries, especially the United States, Japan, Germany, France, and the United Kingdom, with approximately 60 percent of the funds going to developed economies. The growth of foreign investment, especially in China, will boost sales by foreign affiliates over the next ten years.[64]

There is no doubt the world is moving toward a single global economy. Of course there are major difficulties on the horizon, such as the development of a market-based economy in Eastern Europe, a reduction of hostilities and the establishment of political stability in the Middle East and parts of Eastern Europe, and stabilization and growth in the former Soviet Union. The global marketer needs to understand the interdependencies that make up the world economy in order to understand how a drop in the U.S. discount rate will affect business in Stockholm or how Britain's joining the European Monetary System will affect sales in London.

Clearly the economies of the world are becoming more and more interlinked, with small changes in markets being felt in many places around the world. For example, the world equity markets rose in Europe, China, and Tokyo in June 1999 as traders around the world anticipated that U.S. Federal Reserve chairman Alan Greenspan would raise interest rates on June 30, 1999, by 0.25 percent.[65] Information technology, telecommunications, and the Internet have made worldwide information on prices, products, and profits available globally and instantaneously. With markets thus more transparent, buyers, sellers, and investors can access the best opportunities, lowering costs and ensuring that resources are allocated to their most efficient use. The focus of monetary policy from Britain to Brazil has been to control inflation, with great success—only 1 percent in the G7 economies, the lowest in half a century.[66] These changes are fundamentally changing national, regional, and the global economic systems.[67] As the speed of change accelerates, successful companies will be able to anticipate the trends and either take advantage of them or respond to them quickly. Other companies will watch the changes going on around them and wake up one day to a different marketplace with new rules.

64. "FDI Shifts with Global Growth," *Crossborder Monitor, Economist Intelligence Unit,* June 12, 1996, p. 12.
65. "Mood Lifts on Likelihood of U.S. Rate Rise," *Financial Times,* June 29, 1999, p. 36.
66. "The New Danger," *Economist,* February 20, 1999, p. 15.
67. "Stop the World, I Want to Get Off," *The Economist,* September 18, 1996, Survey of the World, Economy, p. 46.

Conclusions

We learn from the study of economics that changes in rules or in financial circumstances help some groups and hurt others. Therefore, it is important to understand that papers and speeches have particular points of view. Exchange rate movements, tariffs, quotas, and customs unions can be viewed as alternative ways to achieve economic goals. The issue is not whether a change will take place but rather *which* change will provide the most benefit to the greatest number with the least cost.

This chapter has described the fundamentals of international trade and finance. An understanding of the fundamentals will enable you to comprehend the technical issues raised by the media and to formulate your own views. It is particularly important to understand how actions or events in one part of the world can impact a business in another part of the world.

QUESTIONS FOR DISCUSSION

1. If a nation has a balance on merchandise trade deficit, can it be said that the nation has a weak currency in the international markets as well?
2. Regarding question 1, examine both the balance of payments statistics and the foreign exchange rate statistics presented in the International Monetary Fund's *International Financial Statistics.* What link, if any, do you see between Switzerland's balance on merchandise trade and the value of the Swiss franc over the past five years?
3. Calculate your individual balance of payments over the past month. What were your balance on merchandise trade, balance on goods and services, and current account balance?
4. Exchange rate changes have been called a "double-edged sword" because they hurt some sectors of the nation while helping other sectors. Explain why this is true.
5. If interest rates in the United Kingdom rise while those in Germany remain unchanged, explain what pressure this will put on the British pound per the German mark exchange rate.
6. Suppose the U.S. Federal Reserve reduces the rate of growth of the money supply, causing the U.S. inflation rate to fall, interest rates to rise, and economic growth to decline. What impact will these economic changes have on the actions of the participants in the foreign exchange market?
7. The concept of *comparative advantage* is one of the most powerful in all of economic theory (both at the domestic level and the international level). Explain why this is true. What does the concept show? What are its implications for international and intranational trade?
8. Suppose Brazil can produce with an equal amount of resources either 100 units of steel or 10 computers. At the same time, Germany can produce either 150 units of steel or 10 computers. Explain which nation has a comparative advantage in the production of computers. Choose a mutually advantageous trading ratio and explain why this ratio increases the welfare of both nations.

9. In April 1987, President Reagan imposed a tariff on goods made with Japanese semiconductors and imported into the United States. Explain which groups in the United States were helped by this action and which groups were hurt by it. Do you believe this action is evidence of good economic thinking? Why?
10. In terms of their economic effects on a nation's economy, explain the similarities and differences between tariffs and quotas.
11. For each of the following distinct and separate cases, explain which trade theory best describes the trading pattern cited. Briefly explain why you chose the theory you did.
    (a) The opening of trade between the United States and China has resulted in U.S. importation of textiles and other handmade craftwork from China and the exportation of machinery and steel from the United States to China.
    (b) Currently, the United States is a major importer of televisions from Japan. It once was a major exporter of televisions to Japan.

FOR FURTHER READING

Adelman, M.A. "Globalization of the World Economy." *Energy Policy,* December 1996, pp. 1021–1024.

Aggarwal, Raj. "The Strategic Challenge of the Evolving Global Economy." *Business Horizons,* July-August 1987, pp. 38–44.

Baldwin, Richard, et al., *Market Integration, Regionalism and the Global Economy.* Cambridge: University Press, 1999.

"Getting a Grip on the GATT." *Financial Times,* February 5, 1991, p. 18.

Hollerman, Leon. *Japan Disincorporated: The Economic Liberalization Process.* Stanford, Calif.: Hoover Institution Press, 1988.

Hufbauer, Gary. "U.S. Trade Policy and Global Growth: New Directions in International Economy." *Journal of Economic Literature,* March 1997, pp. 138–140.

Irwin, Douglas A. "The United States in a New Global Economy? A Century's Perspective." *American Economic Review,* May 1996, pp. 41–46.

Marriott, Cherie. "How Companies Fare in a Really Liberated Economy." *Global Finance,* January 1997, pp. 22–26.

The Omnibus Trade and Competitiveness Act of 1988. Washington, D.C.: U.S. Department of Commerce, International Division, 1988.

Porter, Michael E. *The Competitive Advantage of Nations.* New York: Macmillan, 1990.

Root, Franklin R. *International Trade and Investment.* 6th ed. Cincinnati: South-Western, 1990.

Rostow, W. W. *The Stages of Economic Growth.* 2nd ed. Cambridge, U.K.: Cambridge University Press, 1971.

Schuknecht, Ludger, "A Trade Policy Perspective on Capital Controls," *IMF Publications Services,* March 1999, vol. 36, no. 1, p. 1.

Tolchin, Martin. *Buying into America: How Foreign Money Is Changing the Face of Our Nation.* New York: Times Books, 1988.

Vernon, Raymond. "Can the U.S. Negotiate Trade Equality?" *Harvard Business Review,* May-June 1989, pp. 96–101.

Vernon, Raymond, and Debora L. Spar. *Beyond Globalism: Remaking American Foreign Policy.* New York: Free Press, 1989.

Wells, Louis T. Jr. "A Product Life Cycle for International Trade?" *Journal of Marketing,* July 1968, pp. 1–6.

"World Industrial Survey." *Financial Times,* January 15, 1991, sec. 3, pp. 1–4.

3

Cultural and Social Forces

IN CHAPTER 1 WE EXPLAINED THAT THE COMPLEXITIES OF GLOBAL MARKETING ARE partially caused by societal and cultural forces. In Chapter 3 we describe some of these cultural and societal influences in more detail. However, since it is not possible to list all of them—or even to fully describe the major cultures of the world—only the more salient forces are highlighted. Figure 3.1 shows the components of culture that are described in this chapter. We also provide an analytical framework that suggests to the global marketing practitioner what to look for. Thus, rather than suggesting all the possible cultural or societal factors that may affect global marketers, we concentrate on the analytical processes marketers can use to identify and monitor any of the numerous cultural influences they will encounter around the globe.

FIGURE 3.1

Cultural Analysis

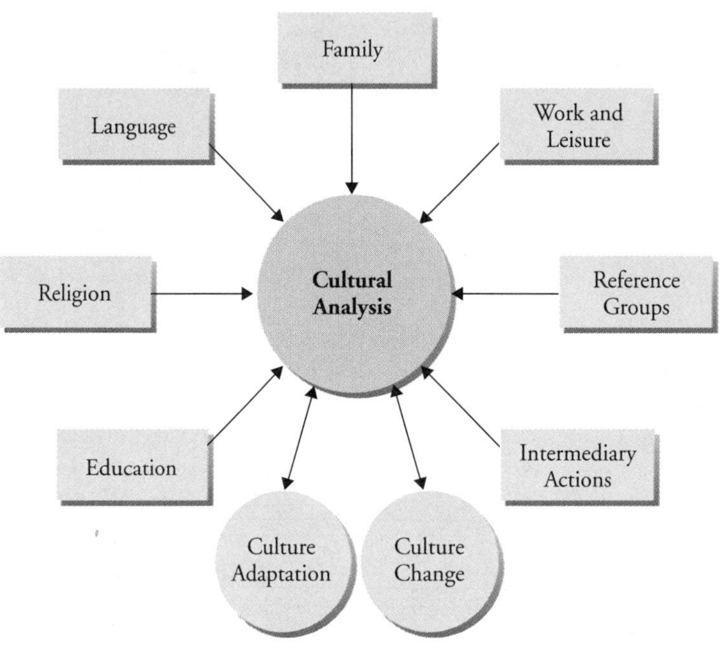

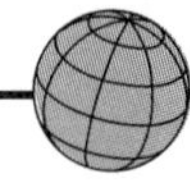

A Definition of Culture

Anthropology, the study of humans, is a discipline that focuses on the understanding of human behavior. Cultural anthropology examines all human behaviors that have been learned, including social, linguistic, and family behaviors.[1] *Culture* includes the entire heritage of a society transmitted by word, literature, or any other form. It includes all traditions, habits, religion, art, and language. Children born anywhere in the world have the same essential needs for food, shelter, and clothing. But as they grow, children will develop desires for nonessential things. The development and priority of these *wants* are based on messages from families and peers and is the socialization process that reflects each person's culture. Culture reflects the human aspect of a person's environment; it consists of beliefs, morals, customs, and habits learned from others. The role of culture in modern society is evolving as more and more economies are be-

1. Charles Winick, "Anthropology's Contributions to Marketing," *Journal of Marketing,* July 1961, p. 54.

coming interlinked; as trade grows, heritage and traditions also become shared. Samuel Huntington argues that with the fall of communism, conflict in the post-Cold War era will be between the major cultures of the world rather than between nations. Huntington identifies the cultures of the world as western (United States, western Europe, Australia), Orthodox (former Soviet republics, central Europe), Confucian (China, Southeast Asia), Islamic (Middle East), Buddhist (Thailand), Hindu (India), Latin American, African, and Japanese.[2]

Cultural Influences on Marketing

The function of marketing is to earn profits from the satisfaction of human wants and needs. In order to understand and influence the consumer's wants and needs, marketers must understand the culture, especially in an international environment. Figure 3.2 illustrates how culture affects buyer behavior. As the figure shows, culture is embedded in elements of the society such as religion, language, history, and education. These elements send direct and indirect messages to consumers regarding the selection of goods and services. The culture we live in answers such questions as, Is tea or coffee the preferred drink? Is black or white worn at a funeral? What type of food is eaten for breakfast?

Isolating Cultural Influences

One of the most difficult tasks for global marketers is assessing the cultural influences that affect their operations. In the actual marketplace there are always several factors working simultaneously, and it is extremely difficult to isolate any one factor. Frequently, *cultural differences* have been held accountable for any noticeable differences between countries. However, when environmental factors differ, what is thought to be *cultural* may in fact be attributable to other factors.

FIGURE 3.2

Cultural Influences on Buyer Behavior

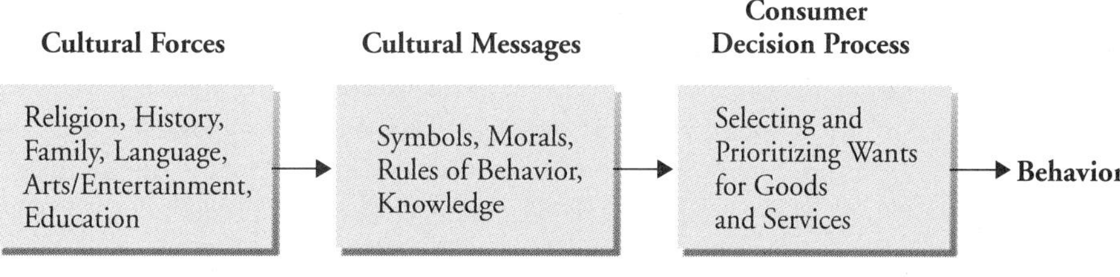

2. "Cultural Explanations: The Man in the Baghdad Café," *Economist,* November 9, 1996, pp. 23–26.

Quite often, when countries with both economic and cultural differences are compared, the differences are credited solely to the varying cultural systems. The analyst should be aware that although many of the differences are culturally based, other environmental factors, such as level of economic development, political system, or legal system, may be responsible for these differences. (These other aspects of the environment are discussed in Chapters 2 and 4.)

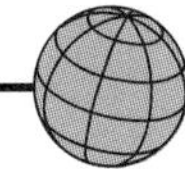

Language

Language is a key component of culture because most of a society's culture finds its way into the spoken language. Thus, in many ways, language embodies the culture of the society. Knowing the language of a society can become the key to understanding its culture. But language is not merely a collection of words or terms. Language expresses the thinking pattern of a culture—and to some extent even forms the thinking. Linguists have found that cultures with more primitive languages or a limited range of expression are more likely to be limited in their thought patterns. Many languages cannot accommodate modern technological or business concepts, forcing the cultural elite to work in a different language. The French are particularly sensitive about their language and culture, so much so that the French government has proposed legal action to limit further incursions of other languages, especially English. For example, *le airbag* is called *coussin gonflable de protection,* and *fast food* is *restauration rapide.* France persuaded the European Community that 40 percent of TV programming should be domestic. Cinema tickets in France are taxed and the funds used to support the French film industry, as protection against the U.S. film industry, which has a 70 percent share of the European film market.[3]

Forms of Address

The English language has one form of address: all persons are addressed with the pronoun *you.* Not so in many other languages. In the Germanic, Romance, and Slavic languages, there are always two forms of address, the personal and the formal. In Japanese, there are three forms. Depending on status, a Japanese person will speak differently to a superior, a colleague, or a subordinate, and there are different forms for male and female in many expressions. These differences in language represent different ways of interacting. English, particularly as it is spoken in the United States, is much less formal than Japanese. Japanese traveling to the United States will sometimes adopt Americanized nicknames. As it turns out, most Japanese prefer to be called with a combination of their last name with *san* attached—for example, Endo-san for Mr. Endo. Knowing the Japanese language gives a foreigner a better understanding of the cultural mores regarding social

3. "Cultural Wars," *Economist*, September 12, 1998, p. 97.

status and authority. Of course, one can develop a cultural understanding or empathy by learning about a culture directly. However, just learning a foreign language can substantially help develop cultural empathy. Forms of address can be found to vary even within the same language. For example, in Australia, English immigrants are referred to as "poms," short for pomegranate, referring to their ruddy complexion.[4] As Australians often use "pom" along with other derogatory words like "bloody," "bastard," or "whingeing," it may be in poor taste to use "pom" in a business meeting.

Overcoming the Language Barrier

Global marketing communications are heavily affected by the existence of different languages. Advertising has to be adjusted to each language, and personal contacts are made difficult by a widely existing language barrier. To overcome this language barrier, businesspeople all over the world have relied on three approaches: the direct translation of written material, interpreters, and the acquisition of foreign language skills.

Translations are made for a wide range of documents, including sales literature, catalogs, advertising, and contracts. Though this increases the initial costs of entering a market, few companies can conduct their business over the long run without translating material into the language of their customers. If a company does not have a local subsidiary, competent translation agencies are available in most countries. Some companies even route their foreign correspondence through a translation firm, thus communicating with foreign clients on all matters in the client's own language. This often increases the likelihood of concluding a deal. It is important when traveling in Asia not to use your senior management, who are usually bilingual, as translators. Translators are considered low-level staff positions, and your senior manager would therefore be looked down upon by others after your departure.

The use of translators is usually restricted to higher-level executives because of the higher cost. Traveling with executives and attending meetings, translators perform a very useful function when a complete language barrier exists. They are best used for a limited time only, however, and realistically cannot overcome long-term communication problems. The largest translation staff in the world belongs to the European Community (EC), which has 1,500 people translating 1.2 million pages of text per year into the three working languages of English, French, and German. EC bureaucrats also use machine translation to get a rough translation that can be used for email and other less official communications.[5]

Both translation services and translators depend on translating one language into another. In many situations, it is almost impossible to fully translate a given

4. "Those Whingeing Poms," *Economist*, May 24, 1997, p. 40.
5. "Europe's Languages: Service Compris," *Economist*, August 29, 1998, p. 47.

meaning into a second language. When the original idea, or thought, is not part of the second culture, the translation may be meaningless. Brand names have been particularly affected by this problem because they are not normally translated. Consequently, a company may get into difficulty with the use of a product name in a foreign country, even though its advertising message is fully translated. For example, General Motors' Chevy Nova in Spanish translates as "does not go"—certainly not the right name for a car, and Coca-Cola translated into Chinese means "bite the wax tadpole."[6]

In contrast, a soft drink was launched in Japan with the brand name Pocari Sweat. To Japanese consumers, this name conveyed a positive, healthy, thirst-quenching image, and the drink became a market leader. Japanese consumers reacted to the brand name strictly because of its modern- (foreign-) sounding name, not its content or meaning. Needless to say, this success was credited to a local firm.[7]

Today, companies tend to choose product names carefully and test them in advance to ensure that the meaning in all major languages is neutral and positive. They also want to make sure that the name can be easily pronounced. Language differences may have caused many blunders, but careful translations have now reduced the number of international marketing mistakes. However, the language barrier still remains, and companies that do more to overcome this barrier frequently achieve better results.

If one considers the value of developing cultural empathy through learning a foreign language, an argument can be made that learning any language will develop such cultural skills. Looking at foreign languages from that point of view allows the student to approach learning as a developmental skill that can be applied in many ways. In a sense, by learning one foreign language, the student can learn to appreciate many different cultures. Whenever two executives get together and speak their respective languages to some extent, the chosen language is frequently the one that is better spoken. If an U.S. executive meets an Italian executive, and the Italian speaks better English than the American speaks Italian, it would be normal for the two to speak in English. There is strong evidence that English is becoming the global business language. According to a study by the Organization for Economic Cooperation and Development (OECD) in Paris, 78 percent of all web sites and 91 percent of secure web sites are in English.[8] Although English is becoming the language of commerce and electronic communications, personal relationships will often benefit from language skill in a customer's native tongue.

Even when executives understand each other's language, there can still be plenty of room for misunderstanding. When an American executive says yes in a ne-

6. Sherrie E. Zhan, "Marketing Across Cultures," *World Trade*, February 1999, vol. 12, no. 2, p. 80.
7. Allyson L. Stewart-Allen, "Cultural Quandaries Can Lead to Misnomers," *Marketing News*, November 23, 1998, p. 9.
8. "English and Electronic Commerce: The Default Language," *Economist*, May 15, 1999, p. 67.

gotiation, this usually means, "yes, I accept the terms." However, yes in Asian countries may mean four different things. First, it may mean that the other side recognizes that you are talking to them but not necessarily that they understand what is said. Second, it could mean that what was said was understood and was clear but not that it was agreed to. Third, it may mean that the other party has understood the proposal and will consult with others about it. And finally, yes may mean total agreement. It takes skill to understand just what yes means in any type of negotiation.[9]

However, achieving some fluency in a foreign language is not the only cultural barrier to cross. At least as important is the use of nonverbal communication, or *body language.* Sometimes referred to as the "silent language," this includes such elements as touching, the distance between speakers, facial expressions, and speech inflection, as well as arm and hand gestures. Former U.S. president George Bush during a visit to Australia gave the "V for Victory" sign with his palm turned inward, not realizing this was equivalent to the middle finger salute in the United States.[10] Mexicans happily come within a half-meter of a stranger for a business discussion, whereas Asians, Nordics, Anglo-Saxons, and Germanic peoples consider space within one meter as personal space. So when a Mexican moves closer than 16 to 18 inches to an English person, the English person feels invaded and steps back, giving the Mexican the message that he or she does not want to do business. For Latins, Arabs, and Africans, proximity is a sign of confidence. Obviously, understanding cultural space differences is important to overall communication.[11]

One can draw two major conclusions about the impact of language on global marketing. First, a firm must adjust its communication program and design communications to include the languages used by its customers. Second, the firm must be aware that a foreign language may contain different thinking patterns or indicate varying motivations on the part of prospective clients. These nuances are much more difficult to grasp. To the extent that such differences occur, the simple mechanical translation of messages will not suffice. Instead, the company may have to change the entire marketing message to reflect the different cultural patterns.

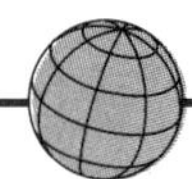

Religion

Many businesspeople ignore the influence religion may have on the marketing environment. Even in the United States, religion has had a profound impact, though people are not aware of it on a daily basis. Historically, the religious tradition in

9. Iris Kapustein, "Selling and Exhibiting Across the Globe," *Doors and Hardware*, September 1, 1998, p. 34.
10. James L. Grayson, "Gestures: The DO's and TABOOs of Body Language Around the World," *Security Management*, March 1999, p. 122.
11. Judith Bowman, "Before Going Overseas, Be Ready: Know the Protocol," *Mass High Tech*, April 26, 1999, p. 31.

the United States, based on Christianity and Judaism, emphasizes hard work, thriftiness, and a simple lifestyle. These religious values have certainly altered over time; many of our modern marketing activities would not exist if these older values persisted. Thrift, for instance, presumes that a person will save hard-earned wages and use these savings for purchases later on. Today, ample credit facilities exist to supplement or even supplant savings.

Christian Traditions

There still are, however, religious customs that remain a major factor in global marketing today. Christmas is one Christian tradition that, at least in respect to consumption, remains an important event for many consumer goods industries. Retailers traditionally have their largest sales around that time. However, Christmas can be used as an illustration of the substantial differences in customs among even largely Christian societies. A large U.S.-based retailer of consumer electronics found out about these differences the hard way when it opened its first retail outlet in the Netherlands. The company planned the opening to coincide with the start of the Christmas selling season, as this would allow the firm to show a profit in the first year, and advertising space was bought accordingly in late November and December. The results were less than satisfactory, however, because major gift giving in Holland takes place not on December 25, Christmas Day, but on St. Nicholas Day, December 6, the Dutch traditional day of gift giving. Thus, the opening of the company's retail operation was late and missed the major buying season.

Many other variations surrounding Christmas gift giving can be found. In France, it is traditional to exchange gifts on January 6, often called "Little Christmas." Also different are the personifications who bring the gifts. In the United States, Santa Claus brings Christmas gifts; in the United Kingdom, Father Christmas brings them; and in German-speaking countries, gifts are brought by an angel representing the Christ Child. In German areas, Santa Claus or St. Nicholas comes on December 6 to bring small gifts and food to children who have behaved well. All of these examples show that local variations of religious traditions can have a substantial impact on global marketing activities.

Islam

Religion's impact on global marketing becomes more apparent when the observer compares one religion to another. It is beyond the scope of this text to give a complete description of all world religions with specific implications for marketing. However, by using one non-Christian religion, Islam, we can document some of the potential impact. We chose Islam in view of its growing influence in many countries.

Islam is the religion of 20 percent of the world's population.[12] Islam was established by the prophet Mohammed in Mecca in A.D. 610. Thirteen years later, when Mohammed had to flee to nearby Medina, he established the first Islamic city-state.[13] By his death in 632, the holy book of Islam, the Koran, had been completely revealed. Muslims believe it contains God's own words. The Koran was supplemented by the Hadith and the Sunna, which contain the reported words and actions of the prophet Mohammed. These works are the primary sources of guidance for all Muslims on all aspects of life.

With the expansion of the Islamic state, additional guidance was needed; as a result, the *shari'a,* or legal system, emerged. Based on the Koran, the *shari'a* gives details of required duties and outlines all types of human interactions. It essentially constitutes what elsewhere would be considered criminal, personal, and commercial law. These Islamic guidelines cover all aspects of human life and categorize human behavior as obligatory, merely desirable, neutral, merely undesirable, or forbidden. The principal goal is to guide human beings in their quest for salvation, because the basic purpose of human existence is to serve God. Divine guidance is to be accepted as given, and it is believed to meet both the spiritual and psychological needs of individuals, making them better social beings. The nonritual divine guidance covers, among other areas, the economic activities of society. This latter guidance offers people a wide range of choices while protecting them from evil. A set of basic values restricts economic action and should not be violated or transgressed.

The Islamic value system, as it relates to economic activities, requires a commitment to God and a constant awareness of God's presence even while the person is engaged in material work. Wealth is considered a favor of God to be appreciated; it cannot be regarded as a final goal. Wealth is to be used to satisfy basic needs in moderation. With the real ownership of wealth belonging to God, man is considered only a temporary trustee. Thus, material advancement does not entail higher status or merit. In Islam, all people are created equal and have the right of life, the right of liberty, the right of ownership, the right of dignity, and the right of education. For the true Muslim, the achievement of goals is both a result of individual efforts and a blessing from God. A Muslim should therefore not neglect the duty of working hard to earn a living.

In their work, Muslims are required to uphold the Islamic virtues of truth, honesty, respect for the rights of others, pursuit of moderation, sacrifice, and hard work. Moderation applies to virtually all situations. The resulting Islamic welfare economy is based on the bond of universal brotherhood in which the individuals, while pursuing their own good, avoid wrongdoing to others. In their

12. Mushtaq Luqmani, Zahir Quraeshi, and Linda Delene, "Marketing in Islamic Countries: A Viewpoint," *MSU Business Topics,* Summer 1980, p. 17.
13. Muhammad Abdul-Rauf, "The Ten Commandments of Islamic Economics," *Across the Board,* August 1979, p. 7.

economic pursuits, true Muslims not only have their own material needs in mind but accept their social obligations and thereby improve their own position with God. The Islamic culture has many specific implications for global marketers. A summary of these implications is given in Table 3.1.

The prohibition of usury has led to quite different practices with respect to lending in Arab societies.[14] Since this law prohibits interest payments, special Islamic banks were formed. These banks maintain three types of accounts: nonprofit accounts with a very small minimum deposit and the right of immediate withdrawal without notice, profit-sharing deposit accounts, and social services funds. These banks do not charge a fixed rate of interest on loans. Instead, the "interest payment" is levied according to the profits derived from the funds employed. Thus, the depositors get earnings on their deposits, depending on the amount of profits earned by the bank. Such Islamic banks now exist in many countries, particularly Egypt, Saudi Arabia, Kuwait, Sudan, Dubai, and Jordan.

The influence of Islam is also felt in Southeast Asia. Malaysia, a country with about 53 percent of the area's population, is Muslim.[15] In that country, several business laws in banking and other areas have been made consistent with Islamic law, although in many respects a dual system exists with British law. Greater awareness of Islamic traditions also creates new business opportunities. Kohilal is a small business catering to traditional Muslims in Malaysia. The company markets, among other items, a soap that is made of palm oil and is free of animal fats. Its products are *halal* (acceptable under Islamic teaching) and typically avoid pork, pork products, and alcohol. The company also emphasizes the fact that its products are handled and distributed by devout Muslims only.[16] The world market for Muslim *halal* food is $81 billion, and fast-food companies such as McDonald's and Kentucky Fried Chicken have obtained *halal* certificates to serve the Muslim market.[17]

Another marketing challenge related to Islam was faced by Gillette when it wanted to introduce its shaving products in Iran. Islam discourages its followers from shaving, which made it difficult for Gillette's local distributor to secure advertising space. In the end, the distributor visited one local newspaper after another until he finally met an advertising manager without a beard. The distributor convinced the advertising manager that shaving sometimes was unavoidable, such as when a person had a head injury as a result of an accident, and that Gillette blades would be best. The advertising manager consulted with his clergyman and, having obtained the latter's permission, accepted the ad. As a result, other newspapers

14. Ibid., pp. 15–16.
15. "Malaysia: Country Profile," *Asia & Pacific Review World of Information* (Walden Publishing Ltd.: London, 1998), p. 1.
16. "Strong Fundamentals: In Malaysia, Islam Is a Basis for Business," *Far Eastern Economic Review*, September 16, 1993, p. 74.
17. M. M. Nazri, "An Introduction to Islamic Food Laws," *Economic Review*, August 1, 1998, p. 33.

TABLE 3.1

Marketing in an Islamic Framework

Elements	*Implications for Marketing*
FUNDAMENTAL ISLAMIC CONCEPTS	
A. *Unity*—Concept of centrality, oneness of God, harmony in life.	Product standardization, mass media techniques, central balance, unity in advertising copy and layout, strong brand loyalties, a smaller evoked size set, loyalty to company, opportunities for brand extension strategies.
B. *Legitimacy*—Fair dealings, reasonable level of profits.	Less formal product warranties, need for institutional advertising and/or advocacy advertising, especially by foreign firms, and a switch from profit-maximizing to a profit-satisficing strategy.
C. *Zakat*—2.5 percent per annum compulsory tax binding on all classified as "not poor."	Use of "excessive" profits, if any, for charitable acts; corporate donations for charity, institutional advertising.
D. *Usury*—Cannot charge interest on loans. A general interpretation of this law defines "excessive interest" charged on loans as not permissible.	Avoid direct use of credit as a marketing tool; establish a consumer policy of paying cash for low-value products; for high-value products, offer discounts for cash payments and raise prices of products on an installment basis; sometimes possible to conduct interest transactions between local/foreign firm in other non-Islamic countries; banks in some Islamic countries take equity in financing ventures, sharing resultant profits (and losses).
E. *Supremacy of human life*—Compared with other forms of life, objects, human life is of supreme importance.	Pet food and/or products less important; avoid use of statues, busts—interpreted as forms of idolatry; symbols in advertising and/or promotion should reflect high human values; use floral designs and artwork in advertising as representation of aesthetic values.
F. *Community*—All Muslims should strive to achieve universal brotherhood—with allegiance to the "one God." One way of expressing community is the required pilgrimage to Mecca for all Muslims at least once in their lifetime, if able to do so.	Formation of an Islamic economic community—development of an "Islamic consumer" served with Islamic-oriented products and services ("kosher" meat packages, gifts exchanged at Muslim festivals, and so forth); development of community services—need for marketing or nonprofit organizations and skills.

(continued)

TABLE 3.1 (Continued)

Marketing in an Islamic Framework

Elements	Implications for Marketing
G. *Equality of peoples*	Participative communication systems; roles and authority structures may be rigidly defined, but accessibility at any level relatively easy.
H. *Abstinence*—During the month of Ramadan, Muslims are required to fast without food or drink from the first streak of dawn to sunset—a reminder to those who are more fortunate to be kind to the less fortunate and as an exercise in self-control.	Products that are nutritious, cool, and digested easily can be formulated for Sehr and Iftar (beginning and end of the fast).
Consumption of alcohol and pork is forbidden; so is gambling.	Opportunities for developing nonalcoholic items and beverages (for example, soft drinks, ice cream, milk shakes, fruit juices) and nonchance social games, such as Scrabble; food products should use vegetable or beef shortening.
I. *Environmentalism*—The universe created by God was pure. Consequently, the land, air, and water should be held as sacred elements.	Anticipate environmental, antipollution acts; opportunities for companies involved in maintaining a clean environment; easier acceptance of pollution control devices in the community (for example, recent efforts in Turkey have been well received by the local communities).
J. *Worship*—Five times a day; timing of prayers varies.	Need to take into account the variability and shift in prayer timings in planning sales calls, work schedules, business hours, customer traffic, and so forth.
ISLAMIC CULTURE	
A. *Obligation to family and tribal traditions*	Importance of respected members in the family or tribe as opinion leaders; word-of-mouth communication, customer referrals may be critical; social or clan allegiances, affiliations, and associations may be possible surrogates for reference groups; advertising home-oriented products stressing family roles may be highly effective—for example, electronic games.

Elements	Implications for Marketing
B. *Obligations toward parents are sacred*	The image of functional products should be enhanced with advertisements that stress parental advice or approval; even with children's products, there should be less emphasis on children as decision makers.
C. *Obligation to extend hospitality to both insiders and outsiders*	Product designs that are symbols of hospitality, outwardly open in expression; rate of new product acceptance may be accelerated and eased by appeals based on community.
D. *Obligation to conform to codes of sexual conduct and social interaction*—These may include the following:	
1. Modest dress for women in public.	More colorful clothing and accessories are worn by women at home; so promotion of products for use in private homes could be more intimate—such audiences could be reached effectively through women's magazines; avoid use of immodest exposure and sexual implications in public settings.
2. Separation of male and female audiences (in some cases).	Access to female consumers can often be gained only through women as selling agents, salespersons, catalogs, home demonstrations, and women's specialty shops.
E. *Obligations to religious occasions*—For example, two major religious observances are celebrated—Eid-ul-Fitr, Eid-ul-Adha.	Tied to purchase of new shoes, clothing, and sweets and preparation of food items for family reunions, Muslim gatherings. There has been a practice of giving money in place of gifts. Increasingly, however, a shift is taking place to more gift giving; due to lunar calendar, dates are not fixed.

Source: Mushtaq Luqmani, Zahir A. Quraeshi, and Linda Delene, "Marketing in Islamic Countries: A Viewpoint," *MSU Business Topics,* Summer 1980, pp. 20–21. Reprinted by permission.

followed, and Gillette Blue was launched. The company is now working on TV advertising, which is permitted only for domestically made products.[18]

Coca-Cola developed a global advertisement for Ramadhan (the Muslim fasting month), which was run in twenty countries. Developed by McCann-Erickson Malaysia, the commercial included a small boy and his mother going with gifts to an orphanage, the mother with a rug and basket of food, the boy with his cherished bottle of Coca-Cola. After sunset the little boy leaves his house to go back to

18. "Smooth Talk Wins Gillette Ad Space in Iran," *Advertising Age International,* April 27, 1992, pp. 1–40.

the orphanage to break fast and share the Coca-Cola with his new friends. The ad ends with "Always in good spirit. Always Coca-Cola."[19]

Certainly, global marketers require a keen awareness of how religion can influence business. They need to search actively for any such possible influences, even when the influences are not very apparent. Developing an initial awareness of the impact religion has on one's own culture is often very helpful in developing cultural sensitivity.

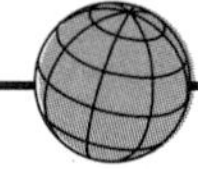

Education

Though the educational system of a country largely reflects its own culture and heritage, education can have a major impact on how receptive consumers are to foreign marketing techniques. Education shapes people's outlooks, desires, and motivation. To the extent that educational systems differ by country, we can expect differences among consumers. However, education not only affects potential consumers, it also shapes potential employees for foreign companies and for the business community overall. This will influence business practices and competitive behavior.

Executives who have been educated in one country are frequently poorly informed about educational systems elsewhere. In this section, we will indicate some of the major differences in educational systems throughout the world and explain their impact on global marketing.

Levels of Participation

The level of education and participation of young people in educational systems drives a country's level of literacy and knowledge. Table 3.2 shows the participation of the population in secondary and higher education. In the United States where education is compulsory until age sixteen, 89 percent of the relevant population attends school.

This pattern is not shared by all countries. The large majority of students in Europe go to school only until age sixteen; then they join an apprenticeship program. This is particularly the case in Germany, where formal apprenticeship programs exist for about 450 job categories. These programs are under tight government supervision and typically last three years. They include on-the-job training, with one day a week of full-time school. About 70 percent of young Germans enter such a program after compulsory full-time education.[20] During the first year, they can expect to earn about 25 percent of the wages earned by a fully trained craftsman in their field. Only about 30 percent of young Germans finish university

19. Kang Siew Li, "Coca-Cola's Global Ramadhan Commercial," *Business Times, New Straits Times Press*, January 14, 1998, p. 17.
20. "Teaching Business How to Train," *Business Week/Reinvesting America,* 1992, p. 90.

TABLE 3.2

Educational Statistics of Selected Countries (in Percentages)

Country	Participation in Secondary Education[a]	Participation in Higher Education[b]	Illiteracy Rates[c]
Argentina	NA	12.3	3.8
Australia	90	14.9	1.0
Austria	90%	9.7%	2.0%
Belgium	98	12.3	2.0
Brazil	19	3.6	15.9
Canada	92	16.9	2.0
Chile	55	NA	4.8
Denmark	86	11.1	1.0
Finland	93	14.6	1.0
France	88	13.9	1.0
Germany	88	9.4	1.0
Greece	85	11.5	4.8
Hungary	73	7.4	2.0
Indonesia	42	NA	16.2
Ireland	85	38.00	1.0
Japan	96	NA	0
Malaysia	NA	5.2	15.4
Mexico	NA	4.1	10.4
Netherlands	97	10.7	2.0
New Zealand	93	12.6	1.5
Norway	94	13.4	0
Philippines	NA	9.6	5.4

(continued)

TABLE 3.2 (Continued)

Educational Statistics of Selected Countries (in Percentages)

Country	Participation in Secondary Education[a]	Participation in Higher Education[b]	Illiteracy Rates[c]
Portugal	68	10.5	15.0
Poland	78	11.3	2.0
South Africa	52	NA	18.2
South Korea	96	13.7	2.0
Spain	94	12.8	3.5
Sweden	96	9.9	1.0
Switzerland	92	8.0	0
Turkey	50	NA	29.8
United Kingdom	92	9.4	1.0
United States	89	16.2	.5
Venezuela	20	NA	6.5

a. Percentage of relevant age group receiving full-time education.
b. Percentage of population twenty to twenty-four years old enrolled in higher education.
c. Adult (over fifteen years) illiteracy rate as a percentage of population.
Source: The World Competitiveness Report 1999 (Lausanne: IMD, 1999), pp. 499, 500, 502, 567.

schooling. In Great Britain, the majority of young people take a job directly in industry and receive only informal on-the-job training. In the United States, about 56 percent of the work force stops at a high school education (or earlier). However, in a study of employees, who have direct contact with customers in German, Japanese, and U.S. companies, the U.S. employees received the least training once employed.[21]

Participation in secondary education affects literacy levels and economic development. Even with similar levels of participation in secondary education, the attitudes of some countries about the quantity and quality of education differ. For example, Japanese high school students attend class more days than students in

21. Paul Osterman, "Reforming Employment and Training Programs," *USA Today*, January 1, 1999, p. 20.

the United States, where the school year is only 180 days long. Since students in other countries also spend a higher percentage of their school day on core academic subjects, the differences in mathematics, science, and history are 1,460 total hours for high school students in the United States; 3,170 in Japan, 3,280 in France, and 3,528 in Germany.[22] Therefore, it was not surprising that in a 1998 study, high school seniors in the United States ranked near the bottom of the twenty-one countries surveyed, behind all their European counterparts and 6 percent below the international average.[23] These differences may explain why a OECD study of reading comprehension in eight countries found that the United States outperformed only Poland. One out of five Americans surveyed did not understand the directions on an aspirin bottle. Why then is the United States economy so much more productive? A study by McKinsey Consulting found that differences in basic skills were not a large factor in productivity. Management talent, labor rules, and regulatory environment were more important—all areas the United States does well in![24]

Literacy and Economic Development

The extent of education affects marketing on two levels. First, there is the problem of literacy. In societies in which the average level of participation in the educational process is low, one typically finds a low level of literacy (see Table 3.2). A low literacy level not only affects earning potential, and thus the level of consumption, but it determines the communication options for marketing programs, as we will see in Chapters 11 and 12. A second concern is for how much young people earn. In countries such as Germany, where many of the youth have considerable earnings by age twenty, the value, or potential, of the youth market is quite different from that in the United States, where a substantial number of youths do not enter the job market until age twenty-one or twenty-two.

Recent studies by the OECD have found a definite link between the percentage of sixteen-year-olds staying in school beyond the minimum leaving age and a country's economic well-being. Countries such as Japan, Holland, Germany, Austria, and the United States get a high return on their educational expenses because so many young people stay in school, either in traditional or vocational schools. Portugal, Spain, Britain, and New Zealand get a poor return on their educational expenses because so few young people continue their education. On average, each addition year of formal schooling results in a return of 5 to 15 percent per year in additional earning.[25]

22. "U.S. Pupils Short on Basics, Study Finds," *International Herald Tribune,* May 6, 1994, p. 3.
23. "Math, Physics Scores in U.S. Come Up Short," *Pittsburgh Post-Gazette*, February 25, 1998, p. A-1.
24. "Baffled: Reading Comprehension," *Economist,* December 9, 1995, p. 27.
25. Joop Hartog, "Behind the Veil of Human Capital," *OECD Observer*, January 1999, p. 38.

The educational system also affects the type of employees and executive talent. The typical career path of a U.S. executive involves a four-year-college program and, in many cases, a master's degree in business administration (M.B.A.) program. This type of executive education is becoming more popular in Europe and Asia. Top management talent may have university degrees in other fields. For example, law is among the more popular degrees. In many areas of the world, it may be impossible to hire university graduates. In the United States, the sales organizations of many large companies are staffed strictly with university graduates. In many other countries, sales as a profession has a lower status, and it can be difficult to attract university graduates.

Different countries have substantially different ideas about education in general, and management education in particular. Overall, though differences exist between countries, traditional European education emphasizes the mastery of a subject through acquisition of knowledge. In contrast, the U.S. approach emphasizes analytic ability and an understanding of concepts. Students passing through these two different educational systems will probably develop different thinking patterns and attitudes. It requires a considerable amount of cultural sensitivity for a global manager to understand these differences and to make the best use of the human resources that are available.

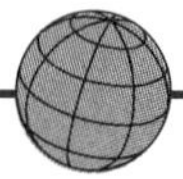

The Family

The role of the family varies greatly between cultures, as do the roles that the various family members play. Across cultures, we find differences in family sizes, in the employment of women, and in many other factors of great interest to marketers. Particularly since the family is a primary reference group and has always been considered an important determinant of purchasing behavior, these differences are of interest.[26] Companies familiar with family interactions in western society cannot assume that they will find the same patterns elsewhere. For example, the Chinese value family above individuals or even country. People have strong ties with family members. In China, 67 percent of parents with children live with one of their children, and 80 percent of parents have contact with their children at least once a week. Within a family, an individual has no rights or property—expenses are shared.[27] Therefore, product advertising appeals must focus on family benefits, not individual benefits.

Another factor to be taken into consideration in global marketing is family structure. The term *nuclear family* is used to refer to the immediate family group: father, mother, and children living together.[28] In the United States, and to some de-

26. J. Barry Mason and Hazel F. Ezell, *Marketing Principles and Strategy* (Plano, Tex.: Business Publications, 1987), p. 266.
27. Fuqin Bian, John R. Logan, and Yanjie Bian, "Intergenerational Relations in Urban China," *Demography*, February 1998, pp. 119–122.
28. John C. Mowen, *Consumer Behavior* (New York: Macmillan, 1987), p. 399.

gree in western Europe as well, we have found strong trends toward the dissolution of the traditional nuclear family.[29] As a result of an increasing divorce rate, the "typical" family of father, mother, and children living in one dwelling is rapidly becoming a thing of the past, or "atypical." Furthermore, families are smaller than they used to be, owing to a drop in fertility rates. Also, an increasing number of women are working outside the home (see Table 3.3). These circumstances have substantially changed purchasing patterns, especially among U.S. families.

Marketers who have dealt only with U.S. consumers should not expect to find the same type of family structure elsewhere. In many societies, the role of the male as head of household is more pronounced, and in some cultures (as in Asia or Latin America) the differences tend to be substantial. Some cultures still encourage male versus female children. In most cultures there are 105 boys born per every 100 girls, but in China the figure is 118.5 boys and in South Korea, 116. In some areas of South Korea, boy births outnumber girls 125 to 100, indicating that female fetuses may be being aborted.[30] This male dominance coincides with a lower rate of participation by women in the labor force outside the home. On the average, this results in a lower family income, since double wage earners increase the average family income. The number of children per family also shows substantial variations by country or culture. In many eastern European countries and in Germany, one child per family is fast becoming the rule, whereas families in many developing countries are still large by western standards.

So far we have discussed only the nuclear family. However, for many cultures, the extended family—including grandparents, in-laws, aunts, uncles, and so on—is of considerable importance. In the United States, older parents usually live alone, either in individually owned housing, in special housing for the elderly, or in nursing homes (for those who can no longer care for themselves). In countries with lower income levels and in rural areas, the extended family still plays a major role, further increasing the size of the average household.

Because the family plays such an important role as a consumption unit, marketers need to understand family roles and composition as they differ from country to country. At this point we are not so much concerned with the demographic aspects, though they will concern us as we discuss the various market opportunities in Chapters 5 and 6. Here, the primary emphasis is on the roles the individual family members play, their respective influences on each other, and the society's expectation as to what role each family member ought to play. Such an understanding is crucial for the marketing of consumer products and tends to affect both communication policy and product policy.

Families are especially important in Asia, where overseas Chinese families make up a phenomenal Chinese business network. Driven by poverty and

29. Fabian Linder, "The Nuclear Family Is Splitting," *Across the Board,* July 1980, p. 52.
30. Sheryl Wu Dunn, "Korean Women Still Feel Demands to Bear a Son," *New York Times International,* January 14, 1997, p. A3.

TABLE 3.3

Family Statistics of Selected Countries (in Percentages)

Country	*Population Growth Rates*[a]	*Female Participation in Labor Force*[b]
Australia	1.3%	43%
Austria	0.6	40
Belgium	0.3	41
Brazil	1.6	35
Canada	1.2	45
Chile	1.6	33
China	1.2	45
Denmark	0.4	46
Finland	0.5	48
France	0.5	45
Germany	0.5	42
Greece	0.5	37
Hungary	−0.4	45
India	2.0	32
Indonesia	1.9	40
Ireland	0.8	34
Italy	0.2	38
Japan	0.3	41
Malaysia	2.8	37
Mexico	2.0	33
Netherlands	0.7	40
New Zealand	1.4	45

Country	Population Growth Rates[a]	Female Participation in Labor Force[b]
Norway	0.6	46
Pakistan	2.8	28
Portugal	0.1	44
Singapore	2.2	39
South Africa	2.3	38
Spain	0.2	37
Sweden	0.5	48
Switzerland	0.8	40
Thailand	1.4	46
Turkey	1.8	37
United Kingdom	0.4	44
United States	1.1	46
Venezuela	2.5	34

a. Percentage per year 1990–97.
b. Percentage of total labor force, 1997.
Source: 2000 World Bank Atlas, Washington, D.C.: World Bank, 2000, pp. 24–25.

political upheaval, waves of families fled China to other countries in Asia. They developed dense networks of thrifty, self-reliant, business groups that distrusted outsiders. The groups were driven by insecurity to accumulate assets. These Chinese networks have flourished. For example, ethnic Chinese make up 1 percent of the population and 20 percent of the economy in Vietnam, 1 percent and 40 percent in the Philippines, 4 percent and 50 percent in Indonesia, and 32 percent and 60 percent in Malaysia.[31] As many of these families, now in their third generation, are large and complex, some question whether they will be able to maintain tight family ownership and control of their business assets.[32]

31. Simon Saulkin, "Chinese Walls," *Management Today,* September 1996, pp. 62–68.
32. "Fissiparous Fortunes and Family Feuds," *Economist,* November 30, 1996, pp. 63–64.

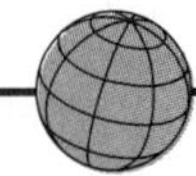

Work and Leisure

The attitudes a society holds toward work have been documented to have a substantial impact on a society's or culture's economic performance. David McClelland has maintained that it is not a country's external resources that determine its economic rise but its level of entrepreneurial spirit in exploiting existing resources.[33] What was found to be crucial was the orientation, or attitudes, toward achievement and work. Cultures with a high level of achievement motivation were found to show a faster rise in economic development than those with low achievement motivation.

Well-known German sociologist Max Weber investigated the relationship between attitudes toward work and those toward religion. In his famous work published in 1904, *The Protestant Ethic and the Spirit of Capitalism,* Weber was one of the first to speculate on the influence of religion on the work ethic by demonstrating differences between Protestant and Catholic attitudes toward work. McClelland later expanded Weber's theory to cover all religions and found that economies with a more Protestant orientation exceeded economies with a Catholic orientation in per capita income. McClelland ascribed this difference to the Protestant (particularly Calvinist) belief that man did not necessarily receive salvation from God through work but that success in work could be viewed as an indication of God's grace. Consequently, accumulating wealth was not viewed as a shameful activity that needed to be hidden. Traditional Catholic doctrine viewed moneymaking in more negative terms. It was Weber's theory that this difference in attitude toward wealth caused Protestant societies to outperform Catholic societies in economic terms.

Thus, religion appears to be a primary influence on attitudes toward work. Observers have theorized that the Shinto religion encourages the Japanese people to have a strong patriotic attitude, which is in part responsible for Japan's excellent economic performance.[34] The low rate of economic performance in some developing countries can be attributed in part to their different attitudes toward work as dictated by their religions.

A discussion on work will usually lead to a discussion of its opposite—leisure. Different societies have different views about the amount of leisure time that is acceptable. In most economically developed countries, particularly where work has become a routine activity, leisure has become a major aspect of life. In such countries, the development of leisure industries is an indication that leisure can be as intensely consumed as any other product. Society significantly influences work and leisure through statutory holiday allowances and public holidays. As shown in Figure 3.3, European statutes require companies

33. David C. McClelland and David G. Winter, *Motivating Economic Achievement* (New York: Free Press, 1969).
34. Vern Terpstra, *International Marketing* (New York: Dryden Press, 1987), p. 101.

FIGURE 3.3

Time Out: Statutory Holiday Allowances, Working Days 1994

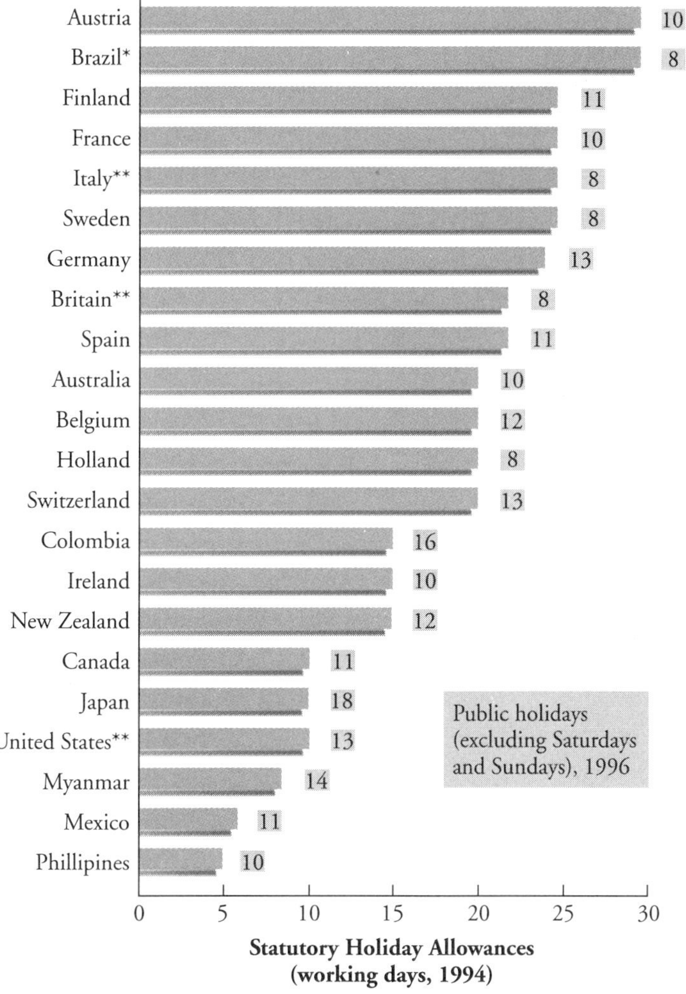

*Based on seven-day work week.
**Typical allowance (no statutory minimum)

Source: "Time Out: Statutory Holiday Allowances, Working Days," *The Economist*, December 23, 1995. © 1995 The Economist Newspaper Group, Inc. Reprinted with permission, further reproduction prohibited.

TABLE 3.4

Values of Selected Countries

	Average Number of Working Hours per Year[a]	Value of Society to Support Hard Work[b]	Managers' Sense of Entrepreneurship[c]
Australia	1,777	6.29	5.82
Austria	1,728	6.54	5.92
Belgium	1,739	6.99	6.09
Brazil	1,899	6.00	6.64
Canada	1,863	7.22	6.40
Chile	2,256	6.92	7.09
China	2,024	7.03	6.24
Denmark	1,689	5.87	5.82
Finland	1,757	8.00	7.16
France	1,742	5.58	5.41
Germany	1,699	6.36	5.69
Greece	1,815	5.22	6.65
Hong Kong	2,312	8.70	7.61
Hungary	1,830	6.78	6.29
India	2,254	5.75	5.14
Indonesia	2,121	4.54	4.32
Ireland	1.782	7.19	6.24
Italy	1,821	5.73	5.89
Japan	1,799	7.23	3.49
Malaysia	2,157	7.49	5.80
Mexico	2,302	5.66	5.72
Netherlands	1,721	7.35	6.85
New Zealand	1,880	6.81	6.43
Norway	1,748	5.73	5.65
Philippines	2,238	6.60	5.71
Portugal	1,806	6.28	5.66
Singapore	2,028	8.86	6.09

	Average Number of Working Hours per Year[a]	Value of Society to Support Hard Work[b]	Managers' Sense of Entrepreneurship[c]
South Africa	2,033	3.49	5.66
South Korea	2,253	7.93	3.96
Spain	1,798	6.03	6.17
Sweden	1,824	5.70	6.30
Switzerland	1,861	7.51	6.14
Taiwan	2,330	7.44	7.11
Thailand	2,245	6.09	5.23
Turkey	2,263	6.90	6.11
U.S.A.	1,916	7.63	6.20
U.K.	1,839	6.38	5.17
Venezuela	2,001	3.48	5.02

a. Average number of working hours per year.
b. Values of the Society Support Competitiveness, where 0 equals "do not support competitiveness" and 10 equals "supports competitiveness." Average reported from 4,160 executives from 47 countries.
c. Managers' Sense of Entrepreneurship, where 0 equals "a lack of extrepreneurship" and 10 equals "a sense of entrepreneurship." Average reported from 4,160 executives from 47 countries.
Source: The World Competitiveness Report 1999 (Lausanne: IMD, 1999), pp. 470, 497, 509.

to give employees 25 to 40 days of vacation annually, whereas the United States, Japan, Mexico, and the Philippines require only 5 to 10 vacation days.[35] These differences are reflected in Table 3.4, which shows fewer working hours per year in Europe than in the United States, Japan, or Mexico. In the United States, vacations are shorter, so people tend to use up their allotted time off. These differences in the use of leisure time reflect, to some degree, differences in attitudes toward work (see Table 3.4). A study of 25,000 people from 23 countries found a wide variance in the attitudes toward self-employment. People from Poland (80 percent), Portugal (73 percent), and the United States (71 percent) preferred to be self-employed.[36]

35. "Why Jack Is a Dull Boy," *Economist,* January 5, 1996, p. 112.
36. "Countries with the Spirit of Enterprise," *Financial Times,* February 17, 2000, p. 27.

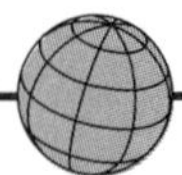

Reference Groups

Reference groups are people such as family, friends, experts that consumers turn to for advice on product purchases. The impact of reference groups on buying behavior has been documented by many writers in marketing.[37] Past experience clearly indicates that the concept of reference group influence applies to many cultures. Differences can be found in the types of relevant reference groups and in the nature of their influence on individual consumers.

Role Models

Famous sports celebrities traditionally have been used to exploit the reference group concept. The idea is to tap the prestige of accomplished athletes to promote certain products. However, not all sports are equally popular in all parts of the world. The enormous interest in baseball in the United States is shared only by certain Latin American and Asian nations and not at all by Europeans. On the other hand, soccer dominates in Europe and Latin America and not in the United States. Some sports, such as tennis or golf, have an international following, but these sports do not attract large segments of the population. Consequently, finding a sports personality that people around the world will recognize equally is difficult.

There are some reference groups of U.S. origin that appear to have substantial universal appeal. The "American way of life" is one phenomenon that may explain the success of many U.S. consumer products elsewhere. Though not always clearly defined, it does represent an attraction to large groups of people in most countries. What is considered American may in fact only be a cover for a modern or high-income lifestyle. Consequently, foreign consumers aspire to a high level of economic status as exemplified by the U.S. lifestyle, or the commonly held image of such a life. In any case, some companies have successfully capitalized on this lifestyle, and Americans have become a reference group for numerous products in markets abroad.

Another U.S. symbol with international appeal is the American cowboy of the Wild West. The image of a cowboy on horseback triggers substantially similar reactions in most countries, even where the cultural background is otherwise diverse. The cowboy may very well be one of the few commonly shared symbols around the world, and this may account for the success of Philip Morris's well-known Marlboro campaign featuring rugged western scenes.

Country Image

The success of the U.S. company Levi Strauss in foreign markets can be partially credited to the penchant of foreign consumers for western-style clothing. Several

37. Leon G. Schiffman and Leslie Lazar Kanuk, *Consumer Behavior*, 3rd ed. (Englewood Cliffs, N.J.: Prentice Hall, 1987), p. 374.

U.S. manufacturers of shoes, such as the Timberland and Sperry brands, have enjoyed strong sales in Europe. Other U.S. firms have had more difficulty, partially because of the image foreign consumers have of shoes manufactured in the United States. Market research revealed that French manufacturers were viewed as leading in high-fashion women's shoes, whereas Italian companies dominated the market for lightweight men's shoes. Europeans viewed shoes manufactured in the United States as stiff, heavy, boxy, and lacking variety in style; manufacturers in the United States took the lead only with western boots. Once a strong image exists, it is extremely difficult to change a prevailing view.

On an international level, countries can assume the position of a reference group. Over time, various countries, or the residents of various countries, have become known for achievements in some aspects of life, culture, or industry. Other countries may therefore attach a special quality to the behavior of these consumers or to products that originate in these countries. When the German beer Beck was touted in the United States as "the German beer that is number one in Germany," the idea was to capitalize on the image of German beer drinkers as being the most discriminating. BSN Gervais-Danone, the French company that brewed Kronenbourg, attempted to take on Heineken, the leading exporter to the United States, by claiming "Europeans like Heineken, but they love Kronenbourg." This campaign tried to take advantage of the fact that Kronenbourg was the largest-selling bottled beer in Europe. BSN decided not to emphasize French Alsace as the origin of the beer. Since the brand name Kronenbourg sounded German to most U.S. consumers, the company was banking on the positive image of German beers in general.[38]

The U.S. brewer Anheuser-Busch faced a different problem when entering the European market. Anheuser-Busch marketed its beer as the beer brewed with "high-country barley" from Wyoming, using the German voice used in John Wayne films as the narrator. The same western theme was used in France, where Busch beer was advertised as "the beer of the men of the West." Because the United States was not recognized by Europeans as a major beer-brewing country, the company took advantage of already existing American Western-hero images familiar to European consumers.[39]

A survey of European consumers showed that, after their own country, they tended to prefer products made in the United States. European consumers often referred to U.S. products as innovative, fashionable, and of high quality. French consumers in the survey contradicted an often-held stereotype of being anti-American, with some 40 percent viewing U.S. products as both fashionable and innovative. Other countries surveyed were the United Kingdom, Spain, Germany, Italy, and the Netherlands.[40]

38. "Big Battle Is Brewing as French Beer Aims to Topple Heineken," *Wall Street Journal,* February 22, 1980, p. 24.
39. Anheuser Tries Light Beer Again," *Business Week,* June 29, 1981, p. 140.
40. "Poll: Europe Favors U.S. Products," *Advertising Age,* September 23, 1991, p. 16.

The perfume industry, for decades dominated by French firms, has been greatly affected by the "made in Paris" phenomenon. Consumers all over the world have come to admire and expect more of perfumes made by French companies. U.S. firms have tried to overcome this handicap with aggressive marketing policies and the creation of new products based on market research and new insights into perfume-making chemistry. Still, it has proved to be very difficult to enter this high-prestige market, and some U.S. cosmetic leaders have not been able to duplicate their domestic success abroad. To overcome the "made in Paris" mystique, foreign companies have acquired French cosmetic firms.

The impact of the origin of products has interested researchers for years. Numerous studies have been conducted, and the general agreement is that there is a strong correlation between country of origin and perceived product quality.[41] For reasons of tradition, consumers tend to attach some expertise to a certain country. For products originating in that particular country, the image tends to be higher. A study in China about country of origin found that while perceived product quality may be high, it will not counterbalance high animosity toward a country.[42] The study was done using Japan, which occupied China in the 1930s and massacred thousands; however, the U.S. bombing of the Chinese embassy in Belgrade in 1999 could cause similar negative animosity. This strongly suggests that marketing managers must carefully consider the "made in . . ." implications of their products. If the country has a positive image, the origin of the product or company can be exploited. In other cases, the global firm may be advised to select a strategy that plays down the origin of the product. As global cosmetic firms have demonstrated in France, a positive country label can be obtained by opening operations in a particular country known for its achievements in a certain industry.

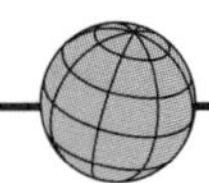

The Challenge of Cultural Change

Sometimes, what may appear to be a cultural difference may in fact be due to other influences, particularly economic ones. These other influences are subject to considerable change over short periods of time. Some examples follow.

Although Kellogg has sold Kellogg's Corn Flakes in France since 1935, it has penetrated the breakfast market in only the last 15 years. The slow growth of demand for corn flakes was related to two aspects of French culinary habits. First, the French did not eat corn; 80 percent of the corn harvested in France was fed

41. M. Thakor, V. Katsanis, and Lea Prevel, "A Model of Brand and Country Effects on Quality Dimensions: Issues and Implications," *Journal of International Consumer Marketing*, 1997, vol. 9, no. 3, pp. 79–100.
42. Jill Gabrielle Klien, Richard Ettenson, and Marlene D. Morris, "The Animosity Model of Foreign Product Purchase: An Empirical Test in the People's Republic of China," *Journal of Marketing*, January 1, 1998, p. 89.

to pigs and chickens.[43] Second, of those who ate cereal for breakfast, 40 percent poured on warm milk, which didn't do much for the crunchiness or taste of corn flakes. To overcome these cultural biases, Kellogg put instructions on its cereal boxes and radically boosted television advertising with "Tony le Tigre." The average French person ate ten ounces of cereal in 1985, and Kellogg expected consumption to increase by 25 percent each year until 1990. However, the consumption of corn flakes in France had a long way to go to reach the average consumption of nine pounds in the United States, twelve pounds in England, and thirteen pounds in Australia.[44]

Kao, Japan's largest consumer marketing company, dominates the bleach, laundry detergent, household cleaning, and shampoo markets in Japan. Although Kao has expanded outside of Japan, it has had difficulty in many markets. Kao's brand of facial care products, Biore, does well in Hong Kong, Taiwan, China, Singapore, Malaysia, and Indonesia, but is second place to Unilever's Pond brand in Thailand. After an extensive consumer research study, Kao found Thai women eighteen to twenty-nine years old did not understand proper face cleaning methods. Based on this research Kao plans to expand its product line and change its marketing techniques, and expects to double its market share in Thailand in two years.[45]

Nowhere is the influence of culture on marketing as prevalent as with food products. However, quite a few firms have overcome cultural barriers. One such celebrated case is McDonald's, the U.S. fast-food franchise operator. The first year that McDonald's opened more restaurants abroad than in the United States was 1991. All of its top ten restaurants, measured in terms of sales and profits, are located overseas. Leading stores are in Moscow, Paris, and Rome, hardly places where one would expect a typical fare of U.S.-style hamburgers to do well. However, in general, McDonald's restaurants overseas have sales about 25 percent higher than the average U.S. outlet.[46] In fact, one of the company's stores in Poland holds the world record for first-day sales, having served 33,000 customers on its opening day.[47] Still, there are some countries where McDonald's, with its hamburger menu, does not do well or is not represented. One of them is India, many of whose people avoid eating beef for religious reasons.[48]

More difficulties with marketing food globally have been experienced by Campbell Soup. The company's overseas sales are only about 25 percent of total volume; its brands are not easily transplanted. Italians are not interested in buying canned pasta, making Franco-American SpaghettiOs a poor performer. In Argentina, where rival CPC's Knorr brand dehydrated soup has dominated the

43. "While Americans Take to Croissants, Kellogg Pushes Corn Flakes on France," *Wall Street Journal,* November 11, 1986, p. 40.
44. Ibid.
45. "Kao Sets Bold Steps for Leadership in Facial-Care," *Nation*, June 24, 1999, p. 1.
46. "Overseas Sizzle for McDonald's," *New York Times,* April 17, 1993, p. D1.
47. "Big Mac's Counter Attack," *Economist,* November 13, 1993, p. 71.
48. "Overseas Sizzle," p. D1.

market with an 80 percent share, Campbell is the outsider with its wet or canned soup. The challenge is even greater in Asia, where Campbell and other western food companies must find ways to sell food in exotic markets.[49]

Few companies have recently struggled as much with cultural differences as Disney. The U.S.-based entertainment company owns 49 percent of Euro Disney, a large theme park built outside Paris with a $4 billion investment. The park, designed as a carbon copy of Disney World in Orlando, Florida, opened in 1992 to much fanfare and a $10 million advertising campaign aimed at some thirty European countries.[50] Euro Disney was rescued by its bankers, who restructured the debt and negotiated a five-year moratorium on royalties and management fees to the U.S. parent. In 1998, Euro Disney made 290 million francs, with 12 million visitors. The difficulty in Europe is that people visit theme parks 0.23 times per person per year as compared with 0.60 times per person-year in the United States and Japan.[51] This experience contrasts sharply with Disney's success in Japan. Its theme park there was expected to attract 10 million visitors a year but achieved 16 million in 1991, more than 90 percent of them repeat visitors. One observer indicated that the Japanese have a strong affinity for fantasy and were not intimidated by the U.S.-manufactured icons. In fact, they wanted the undiluted American Disney. Coming to the Disney Park was linked to the Japanese tea ceremony, with its rules, roles, and symbolism. Japanese attending the Disney Park knew that they were "in" the United States and played that role during their visit.[52] Disney plans additional parks in Tokyo, China, and Latin America.[53]

Cultural Challenges to Marketing in Eastern Europe

The opening of eastern Europe to western businesses has created many cultural challenges. In the years following World War II, eastern European countries had little exposure to western-style marketing. As a result, consumption habits remained at levels more typical to western Europe thirty-five years ago. Several U.S. companies have now made their first entry into Poland, where consumers have to learn how to deal with western-style consumer goods. Gerber, a U.S.-based baby-food maker, moved into Poland by acquiring a local company in 1991. The company needed to educate consumers in the value and use of prepared baby foods. In the United States, about 630 jars of baby food are sold for each birth; the corresponding figure is 116 in Mexico and 624 in

49. "Campbell: Now It's M-M-Global," *Business Week*, March 15, 1993, p. 15.
50. "Mr. Grumpy at the Door," *Financial Times*, September 1, 1993, p. 15.
51. Charles Fleming, "Euro Disney Reports 34% Profit Surge," *Wall Street Journal*, November 19, 1998, p. A19; ibid., "Euro Disney Grows but Europe Continues to Lag," *Travel Trade Gazette Europa*, November 29, 1998, p. 16.
52. "Japan Enters the World of Fantasy," *Financial Times*, May 6, 1993, p. 8.
53. Bruce Orwell, 'Disney Reorganizes Its Park Operations in Aggressive Plan to Expand Overseas," *Wall Street Journal*, December 14, 1998, p. B4.

France. In Poland, it reached just 12 in 1993. Tradition in Poland calls for the mother to cook the baby's food. And although some mothers are now aware of the convenience of Gerber's product, only a few can yet afford it. The company is certain, however, that the market will grow substantially in the next few years.[54]

Retailers and franchise store operators have also had experience in eastern Europe. Kmart purchased thirteen stores in the Czech Republic and Slovakia. Its largest store in Bratislava, the capital of Slovakia, had sales of $40 million in the first year, surpassing all of the company's 2,400 stores in the United States. Despite this volume, the store was unprofitable because of inefficiencies, high costs, and low margins. Kmart found changing the relationship between sales clerk and consumer particularly challenging. Although the company's sales staff understand the customer concept, after forty years of communist rule, its implementation is still not natural to them.[55] According to a study of five hundred business executives traveling to eastern Europe, the cultural challenges are numerous. For example, Poles often expect on-the-spot decisions; in Kazakhstan, canceling a meeting at the last minute is common; punctuality is strictly observed in Romania; and to a Bulgarian, a nod of the head means no and a shake of the head means yes![56] Kmart exited the Czech Republic in 1996 because of low profitability.

The few examples reviewed in this section give a glimpse of the challenges faced by global marketers. As is evident from their experience, it is not easy to predict a product's future success or failure. Chapters 5 and 6 will provide some models to analyze different strategies for countering cultural differences. However, these examples also show that over time, with economic development, many traits or habits will disappear and other, more advanced ones will emerge. A marketer who faces differences between two countries must answer the question of whether these differences are cultural or simply influenced by economic development. True cultural differences are likely to survive economic development, whereas differences driven by different income levels and living standards will rapidly disappear once economic development takes off.

Adapting to Cultural Differences

Some companies have made special efforts to adapt their products or services to various cultural environments. Nowhere are these strategies more apparent than in Japan, where foreign companies have to compete in an economically developed market with greatly differing cultural patterns.

54. "In Poland, Gerber Learns Lessons of Tradition," *New York Times,* November 8, 1993, p. 1.
55. "In East Europe, Kmart Faces an Attitude Problem," *New York Times,* July 7, 1993, p. D1.
56. Scheherazade Daneshkhu, "Poor Communication and Bureaucracy Make Eastern Europe Frustrating," *Financial Times,* September 9, 1996, p. 12.

Japan has long been known for its thrifty, credit-adverse consumers. However, Visa and MasterCard have benefited from Japan's flourishing travel industry by promoting the use of credit cards for travel. Long before the 2000 Olympis in Sydney, Australia, Visa offered Japanese consumers special travel and entertainment deals to attend the olympics.[57] Also, Japanese consumers have quickly taken to cards cobranded with groups, associations, and clubs, as the typical Japanese is proud to belong to groups or associations.[58]

After years of marketing attempts, Japanese appear finally to be warming up to credit cards. Particularly younger consumers are now becoming frequent users of credit cards. Nippon Telegraph & Telephone (NTT) has developed a "smart card" containing a microchip that allows consumers to load funds from their bank account onto their card by the Internet, telephone, or vending machines and then use the card as electronic cash for retail transactions. NTT thinks the smart card will be preferred over credit cards. MasterCard International Japan is converting its entire portfolio of credit cards to multiapplication smart cards. MYCAL, the fourth largest retailer in Japan, owns supermarkets, department stores, clothing outlets, cinemas, and restaurants. The MYCAL Card Company was established in 1982 as a credit business for MYCAL. It expects to issue 5.4 million smart cards by 2002. It is projected that consumers will have one or two smart cards that will include loyalty programs, stored funds, credit access, and health information. Japan is expected to lead the world in smart cards.[59]

Even McDonald's, which started out in Japan decades ago with what is essentially a U.S.-style menu, came to the conclusion that for further growth it had to adapt its menu to the Japanese culture. It introduced McChao, a Chinese fried rice. Rice was an obvious first try in a country where 90 percent of the population eat rice daily. The results have been astounding. Sales have climbed 30 percent during the time McChao has been served. Even more important is the fact that 70 percent of McChao sales have been in the form of take-out food bought by single businesspeople. McDonald's continues to innovate in Japan with the Teriyaki McBurger and Chicken Tatsuta. Also in 1998, as Japan experienced its eighth year of recession, McDonald's cut the price of its hamburgers to 57 cents and increased sales by 30 percent during its summer promotion.[60]

Similar adjustments were needed for Domino's Pizza, one of the many pizza franchises active in Japan. The types of pizza favored by Japanese consumers are quite different from those favored in the United States. Although Domino's adver-

57. "Global Tie-Ins," *Credit Card Management*, January 1, 1999, p. 56.
58. "Japan's Growing Credit Card Culture," *Credit Card Management*, September 1998, p. 140.
59. "Japanese MYCAL Program on Track for Five Million Multi-Application MULTOS Cards," *Business Wire-Singapore*, May 11, 1999, p. 1.
60. Elizabeth Brent, "Japan's Deep Recession Spells Big Changes for Branches of U.S. Brands," *Nation's Restaurant News*, February 15, 1999, pp. 1–5.

tises its pizza as "from the U.S.A.," it offers such toppings as teriyaki gourmet, consisting of Japanese-style grilled chicken, spinach, onion, and corn. In addition, Domino offers squid and tuna toppings, as well as corn salad.[61]

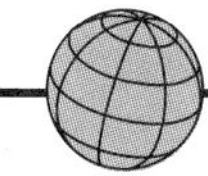

Cultural Analysis for International Marketing

It is not sufficient to describe cultural differences by citing only past experiences of companies. Clearly, one could never cover all of the possible mistakes or cultural differences that international firms may experience abroad. Consequently, this text is restricted to a few examples indicating the kinds of problems international firms face. However, because it is impossible to predict all the possible problems that can be encountered abroad, it becomes necessary to provide some analytical framework to deal with cultural differences.

In a classic article, James E. Lee exposed the natural tendency among executives to fall prey to a *self-reference criterion.* Lee defines the self-reference criterion as an "unconscious reference to one's own cultural values."[62] How does this work? Within each culture, we have come to accept certain "truths," or basic facts. These facts have become part of our experience and are, therefore, rarely challenged. As we continue our experience in one culture only, there are few occasions when such inherent beliefs can be exposed. The self-reference criterion also helps us under new circumstances. Whenever we face an unknown situation, we have an inherent tendency to fall back on prior experience to solve the new problem. There is one substantial handicap to this automatic reflex: if the new situation takes place in a different cultural environment, then the self-reference criterion may invoke past experience that is not applicable.

Lee suggests that executives, to avoid the trap of the self-reference criterion habit, approach problems using a four-step analysis. In the first step, the problem is to be defined in terms of the executive's home cultural traits, habits, or norms. Here the analyst *can* invoke the self-reference criterion. In a second step, the problem is to be defined in terms of the foreign cultural traits, habits, or norms. Value judgments should be avoided at this step. In the third step, the executive is to isolate the personal biases relating to the problem and determine if or how they complicate the problem. Finally, in the fourth step, the problem is to be redefined without the self-reference criterion influence in a search for the optimum solution. Consequently, the four-step approach is designed to avoid culture-bound thinking on the part of executives or companies. (We will further develop this approach in Chapter 6, where we present a model for analyzing the entire international environment.)

61. Prasanna Raman, "Ang Works Hard to Build Domino's," *New Straits Times Press*, March 8, 1999, p. 30.
62. James E. Lee, "Cultural Analysis in Overseas Operations," *Harvard Business Review,* March–April 1966, pp. 106–114.

Cultural Dimensions

Detailed studies of IBM managers around the world by Geert Hofstede identified four basic cultural dimensions. The first dimension is individualism versus collectivism. In a collectivist society, the identity or worth of persons as part of a social system outweighs their value as individuals. The second dimension is small versus large power distance. Large power distance cultures are more authoritarian, with subordinates dependent upon bosses. The third dimension is masculinity versus femininity, which reflects cultures dominated by males versus nurtured by females. The last cultural dimension is weak versus strong uncertainty avoidance, which is a measure of risk tolerance versus risk aversion.

As shown in Figure 3.4, Venezuelans or Singaporians are collective and authoritarian, so behavior tends to be for the good of society following authority of superiors, which is the diametric opposite of Americans or Australians, who are individualistic with small power distance, or more democratic. As we examine the risk and male/female dimensions in Figure 3.5, we notice that Americans, Australians, and Venezuelans are all masculine cultures, whereas the Singaporians are more feminine, or nurturing. Also the Singaporians are much more risk-tolerant than the Americans or Australians, and much more so than the Venezuelans. The Hofstede analysis provides an overview of cultural differences that helps illustrate national consumer and managerial differences.[63]

Businesspeople moving to another culture will experience stress and tension, often called culture shock. An individual who enters a different culture must learn to cope with a vast array of new cultural cues and expectations, as well as to identify which old ones no longer work. The authors of *Managing Cultural Differences* offer the following ten tips to deflate the stress and tension of cultural shock:

Be culturally prepared.
Learn local communication complexities.
Mix with the host and nationals.
Be creative and experimental.
Be culturally sensitive.
Recognize complexities in host cultures.
Perceive oneself as a culture bearer.
Be patient, understanding, and accepting of oneself and one's hosts.
Be most realistic in expectations.
Accept the challenge of intercultural experiences.[64]

63. Geert Hofstede, *Cultures and Organizations* (London: McGraw-Hill, 1991), pp. 23, 51, 83, 111.
64. Philip R. Harris and Robert T. Moran, *Managing Cultural Differences,* 2nd ed. (Houston: Gulf, 1987), pp. 212–215.

FIGURE 3.4

The Position of 50 Countries and 3 Regions on the Power Distance and Individualism—Collectivism Dimensions[a]

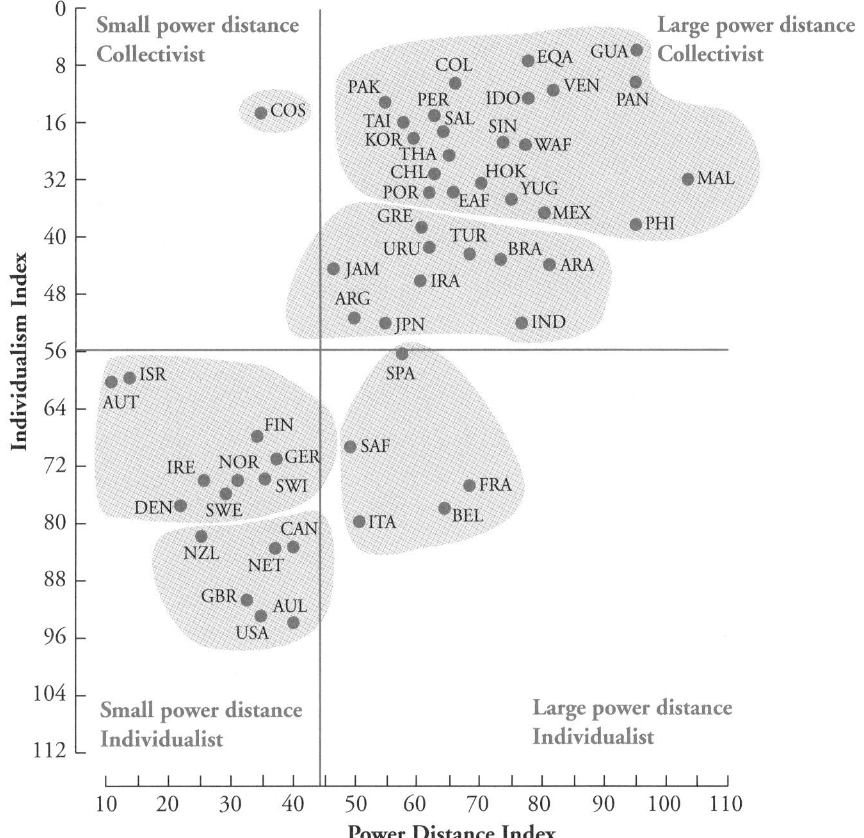

a. ARA, Arabic-speaking countries (Egypt, Iraq, Kuwait, Lebanon, Libya, Saudi Arabia, United Arab Emirates); ARG, Argentina; AUL, Australia; AUT, Austria; BEL, Belgium; BRA, Brazil; CAN, Canada; CHL, Chile; COL, Colombia; COS, Costa Rica; DEN, Denmark; EAF, East Africa (Ethiopia, Kenya, Tanzania, Zambia); EQA, Ecuador; FIN, Finland; FRA, France; GBR, Great Britain; GER, Germany F.R.; GRE, Greece; GUA, Guatemala; HOK, Hong Kong; IDO, Indonesia; IND, India; IRA, Iran; IRE, Ireland (Republic of); ISR, Israel; ITA, Italy; JAM, Jamaica; JPN, Japan; KOR, South Korea; MAL, Malaysia; MEX, Mexico; NET, Netherlands; NOR, Norway; NZL, New Zealand; PAK, Pakistan; PAN, Panama; PER, Peru; PHI, Philippines; POR, Portugal; SAF, South Africa; SAL, Salvador; SIN, Singapore; SPA, Spain; SWE, Sweden; SWI, Switzerland; TAI, Taiwan; THA, Thailand; TUR, Turkey; URU, Uruguay; USA, United States; VEN, Venezuela; WAF, West Africa (Ghana, Nigeria, Sierra Leone); YUG, Yugoslavia.

Source: Geert Hofstede, *Cultures and Organizations*, McGraw-Hill, 1991, pp. 23, 51, 83, and 111. Reprinted with permission of the McGraw-Hill Companies.

FIGURE 3.5

The Position of 50 Countries and 3 Regions on the Masculinity/Femininity and Uncertainty Avoidance Dimensions (for country name abbreviations see note to Figure 3.4).

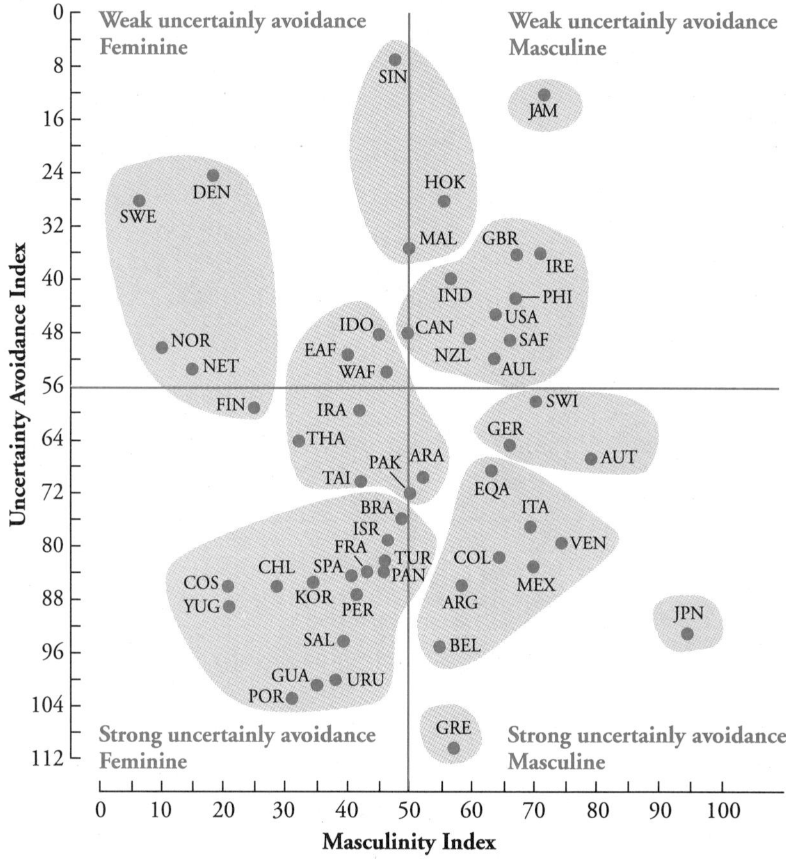

Source: Geert Hofstede, *Cultures and Organizations*, McGraw-Hill, 1991, pp. 23, 51, 83, and 111. Reproduced with permission of the McGraw-Hill Companies.

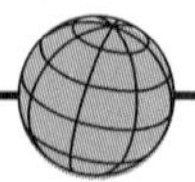

Conclusions

In this chapter, we introduced you to the wide variety of possible cultural and social influences present in global marketing operations. What we have presented here represents only the tip of the iceberg, a very small sample of all the potential factors.

It is essential for global marketers to avoid a cultural bias, or the self-reference criterion, when dealing with business operations in more than one culture. As the president of a large industrial company in Osaka, Japan, once explained, our cultures are 80 percent identical and 20 percent different. The successful businessperson is the one who can identify the differences and deal with them. Of course, this is a very difficult task, and few executives ever reach the stage where they can claim to be completely sensitive to cultural differences. The analytical concepts presented at the end of the chapter will help you to deal with cultural differences. These concepts will be refined further in Chapter 6.

QUESTIONS FOR DISCUSSION

1. Explain the difference between innate wants and needs and culturally derived wants and needs.
2. What process can a marketer use to ensure that an advertisement or brochure gives the desired message in an unfamiliar language?
3. How would marketing automobiles to a predominantly Islamic population differ from marketing to a predominantly Christian population?
4. How do the educational systems of the United States, Japan, England, and Germany affect the marketing of banking services to young adults aged sixteen to twenty-two?
5. What aspects of the culture influence the marketing of women's designer blue jeans in different countries? How do these cultural influences affect magazine advertising?
6. The country of origin of a product is said to influence consumer demand. Why do we prefer specific products from certain countries—for example, perfume from France, electronics from Japan, and beer from Germany?
7. What affect will the Internet have on cultural differences between France and India?
8. You have been asked to attend a meeting with Belgian, Turkish, and Japanese colleagues to develop a global plan for a new aftershave. Using Figures 3.4 and 3.5, what challenges would you face in the meeting? Assume your native culture.
9. When entering a new market, how can one "learn" the culture?

FOR FURTHER READING

Bradley, T. L. "Cultural Dimensions of Russia: Implications for International Companies in a Changing Economy." *Thunderbird International Business Review*, January/February 1999, vol. 41, no. 1, pp. 49–98.

Cavusgil, S. Tamer, and Pervez N. Ghauri. *Doing Business in Developing Countries.* Lincolnwood, Ill.: Routledge, 1990.

Chao, Paul. "Partitioning Country of Origin Effects: Consumer Evaluations of a Hybrid Product." *Journal of International Business Studies,* 2nd Quarter 1993, p. 291.

Cordell, Victor V. "Effects of Consumer Preferences for Foreign Sourced Products." *Journal of International Business Studies,* 2nd Quarter 1992, pp. 251–269.

De Mente, Boye. *Chinese Etiquette and Ethics in Business.* 2nd ed. Lincolnwood, Ill.: NTC Business Books, 1994.

———. *How to Do Business with the Japanese.* 2nd ed. Lincolnwood, Ill.: NTC Business Books, 1993.

Digh, Patricia. "Shades of Gray in the Global Marketplace." *HRMagazine,* April 1997, pp. 90–98.

Goodyear, Mary. "Divided by a Common Language: Diversity and Deception in the World of Global Marketing." *Journal of the Market Research Society,* April 1996, pp. 105–122.

Gulbro, Robert, and Paul Herbig. "Differences in Cross-Cultural Negotiations Behavior Between Manufacturing and Service Firms." *Journal of Professional Services Marketing,* November 1995, vol. 13, no. 1, pp. 23–28.

Harris, Lawrence E. *Who Prospers? How Cultural Values Shape Economic and Political Success.* New York: Basic Books, 1992.

Harris, Philip R., and Robert T. Moran. *Managing Cultural Differences.* 4th ed. Houston: Gulf, 1996.

Harris, R., and R. Davidson. "Anxiety and Involvement: Cultural Dimensions of Attitudes Towards Computers in Developing Societies." *Journal of Global Information Management,* January/March 1999, vol. 7, no. 1, pp. 26–39.

Hasan, H., and G. Ditas. "The Impact of Culture on the Adoption of IT: An Interpretive Study." *Journal of Global Information Management,* January/March 1999, vol. 7, no. 1, pp. 5–16.

Hitt, Michael A., M. Tina Dacin, Beverly B. Tyler, and Daewoo Park. "Understanding the Differences in Korean and U.S. Executives' Strategic Orientations." *Strategic Management Journal,* February 1997, pp. 159–167.

Hofstede, Geert. *Cultures and Organizations.* London: McGraw-Hill, 1991.

Holden, Nigel. *The Clash of Civilizations and the Remaking of World Order.* New York: Simon & Schuster, 1996.

———. "Viewpoint: International Marketing Studies—Time to Break the English Strangle-hold." *International Marketing Review,* 1998, vol. 15. no. 2, pp. 86–100.

Iyer, Gopalkrishnan. "Cultures and Societies in a Changing World." *Journal of Global Marketing,* 1996, vol. 9, no. 3, pp. 95–96.

Kaplan, Robert. *The Ends of the Earth.* New York: Random House, 1996.

Lipset, Seymour Martin. *American Exceptionalism.* New York: Norton, 1996.

Martenson, Rita. "Is Standardization of Marketing Feasible in Culture-Bound Industries? A European Case Study." *International Marketing Review,* Autumn 1987, pp. 7–17.

McCarthy, Dennis M. P. "International Economic Integration and Business Cultures: Comparative Historical Perspectives." *Business & Economic History,* Fall 1996, pp. 72–80.

Roth, Martin S., and Jean B. Romeo. "Matching Product Category and Country Image Perceptions: Framework for Managing Country-of-Origin Effects." *Journal of International Business Studies,* 3rd Quarter 1992, pp. 477–497.

Sowell, Thomas. *Race and Culture: A World View.* New York: Basic Books, 1994.

Terpstra, Vern, and Kenneth David. *The Cultural Environment of International Business.* 2nd ed. Cincinnati: South-Western, 1985.

Usunier, Jean Claude. *Marketing Across Cultures.* London: Prentice Hall, 1996.

Weiss, Stephen E. "Negotiating with 'Romans,'" Part 1. *Sloan Management Review,* Winter 1994, pp. 51–61.

———. "Negotiating with 'Romans,'" Part 2. *Sloan Management Review,* Spring 1994, pp. 85–99.

Williams, J. D., S. L. Han, and W. J. Qualls. "A Conceptual Model and Study of Cross-Cultural Business Relationships." *Journal of Business Research,* June 1998, vol. 42, no. 2, pp.135–144.

Zacharakis, Andrew. "The Double Whammy of Globalization: Differing Country and Foreign Partner Cultures." *Academy of Management Executive,* November 1996, pp. 109–110.

4

Political and Legal Forces

THE PURPOSE OF THIS CHAPTER IS TO IDENTIFY THE POLITICAL AND LEGAL forces that influence global marketing operations.

The first part of this chapter is concerned primarily with political factors; the second is devoted to the legal aspects of global marketing. The emphasis is on the regulations or laws that affect global marketing business transactions. Because many laws are actually politically inspired or motivated, it is difficult to separate political from legal forces. Nevertheless, some separation of the two areas is made to allow for a better organization of the subject matter. Figure 4.1 maps out the elements covered in the chapter and shows the relationships among them.

FIGURE 4.1

Relationship of Elements Covered in the Chapter

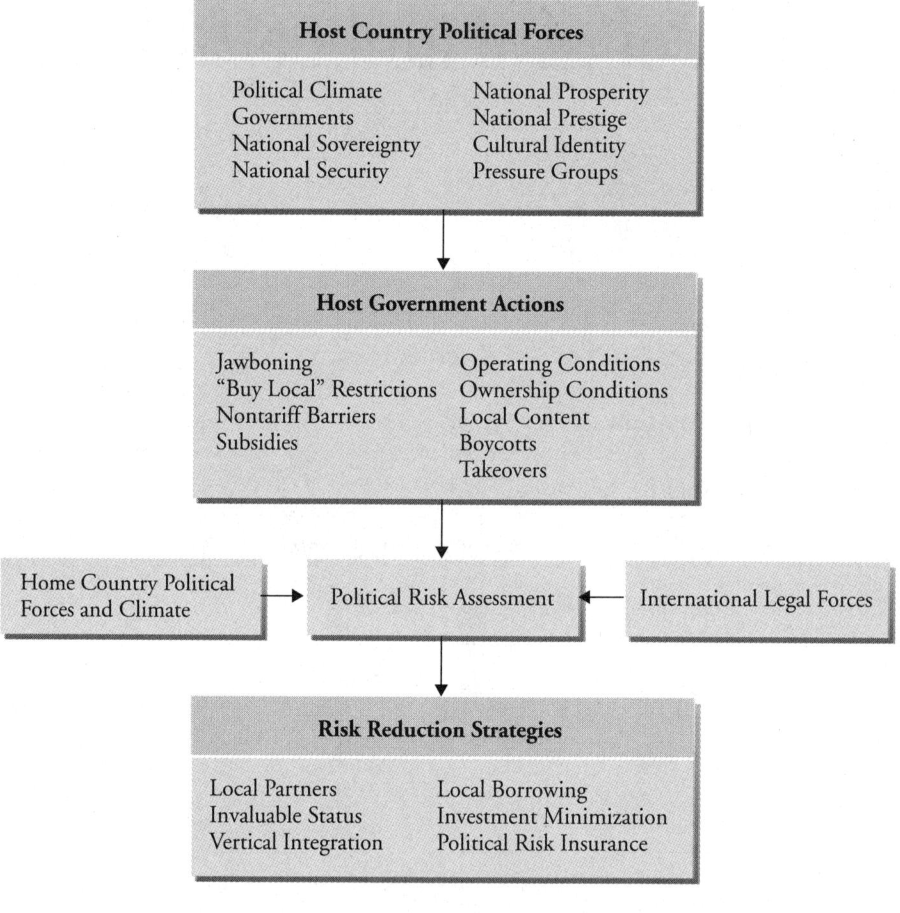

Dealing simultaneously with several political and legal systems makes the job of the global marketing executive a complex one. These factors often precipitate problems that increase the level of risk in the global marketplace. Global companies have learned to cope with such complexities by developing risk reduction strategies. These strategies are explained toward the end of the chapter.

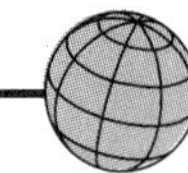

Host Country Political Forces

The rapidly changing nature of the global political scene is evident to anyone who regularly reads, listens to, or watches the various news media. Political upheavals, revolutions, and changes in government policy occur daily and can have an enormous impact on global business. As governments change, opportunities for new business may be lost or gained. For the executive, this means constant adjustments to maximize new opportunities and minimize losses.

Besides the global company, the principal players in the political arena are the host country governments, the home country governments, and the transnational bodies or agencies. Although we use the term *host country* extensively in the following sections, political actions take place increasingly in an environment of *regions*. One such example is the European Union (EU). Political actions of host countries can therefore apply to an entire region, or grouping of countries. Although we do not make an explicit distinction each time, we have decided to apply the term *host country* interchangeably, to both single countries or country groupings.

The respective interactions of these groups result in a given political climate that may positively or negatively affect the operations of a global business. The difficulty for the global company stems from the fact that the firm is simultaneously subject to all these forces, which often have conflicting influences, whereas a strictly domestic corporation has to deal with only one, namely the home country political climate. The situation is further complicated by the fact that companies maintain operations in scores of countries—meaning that companies must be able to simultaneously manage many sets of political relationships. In the following sections of this chapter, we discuss the host country political climate, the home country political climate, and transnational legal forces that regulate international trade. We also focus on political risk assessment and analyze the types of risk reduction strategies that may be employed to manage risk in such a complex world.

Political Climate

Any country that contains an operational unit (manufacturing, finance, sales, and so on) of a global company can be defined as a host country. By definition, global companies deal with many different host countries, each with its own political climate. In each country, the political climate is largely determined by the way the various participants interact with each other. It is influenced by the actions of the host country government and local special interest groups, as well as by the prevailing political philosophy.

Stable political climates are those in which existing relationships among the key players are not expected to change. Conversely, political climates are termed unstable when the nature of the interactions or their outcomes are unpredictable. Though the political climate of a country can be analyzed with respect to various segments of a society, for the purpose of this text we restrict ourselves to those aspects that relate to the business sectors.

Political instability can arise in any country. For example, in early 2000, the Freedom Party in Austria gained 27 percent of the electorate, enough to establish a coalition government with the People's Party. Jörg Haider, chairman of the Freedom Party, was a xenophobe who recommended that Austria close its borders to all immigrants. The rise of the Freedom Party led to mass demonstrations and contributed to foreign investors' fears. On February 29, 2000, Haider resigned as party chairman but will still be a political influence.[1]

There is a great deal of uncertainty about China's future, though it does not stem from the present direction of the economic course. Most China watchers agree that at some point China's politics will change greatly. Some think the Communist Party will evolve slowly and smoothly toward a more representative style of government. Others believe change will be accompanied by fireworks heard loudly outside of China. The difficulty will be China's ability to balance its inevitable economic growth with social stability.[2]

Governments

Businesses operate in a country at the discretion of its government, which can encourage or discourage foreign businesses through a variety of measures. The government plays the principal role in host countries in initiating and implementing policies regarding the operation, conduct, and ownership of businesses. In 2000, about 175 nations have been accepted as full members at the United Nations, giving some indication as to the large number of independent countries that exist at this time. Although each government may give the impression of acting as a single and homogeneous force, governments in most countries represent a collection of various, and at times conflicting, interests. Governments are sharply influenced by the prevailing political philosophy, existing local pressure groups or special interest groups, and the government's own self-interest. All of these factors lead to government actions that global companies must not only recognize but also actively incorporate into their marketing strategies. Of prime importance, then, is the marketer's ability to understand the rationale behind government actions.

To evaluate the political risk in a country and understand how decisions are made, examining the political structure is useful. Is it a democracy, dictatorship, monarchy, or socialist government? Knowing the political system aids under-

1. Eric Frey, "Haider Resigns as Chairman of Austria's Far-Right Party," *Financial Times*, February 29, 2000, p. 2.
2. "The Fight Over China's Future," *Economist*, January 11, 1997, pp. 75–76.

standing of the relationship between business and government. One way to classify governments is by the degree of representation of the population in government. Parliamentary governments hold regular elections so that government policies reflect the will of the people. All democracies are classified as parliamentary. Over the past decade, the world has seen a considerable shift toward democratic government. This was most apparent in eastern Europe, where communist governments were swept away in the 1989 political upheaval. However, changes in Latin America are equally significant. In the early 1980s, true democracies existed in only a few countries, Venezuela and Costa Rica among them. Now, most military dictatorships in that region have ceased, and democratic governments govern in virtually all Latin American countries.[3]

Trying to understand governmental behavior makes sense only if there is a rational basis for leaders' actions and decisions. As many political scientists have pointed out, these actions usually flow from the government's interpretation of its own self-interest. This self-interest, often called national interest, may be expected to differ from nation to nation, but it typically includes the following goals:

1. *Self-preservation*. This is the primary goal of any entity, including states and governments.
2. *Security*. To the extent possible, each entity seeks to maximize the opportunity for continued existence and to minimize threats from the outside.
3. *Prosperity*. Improved living conditions for a country's citizens are an important and constant concern.
4. *Prestige*. Most governments or countries seek prestige either as an end in itself or to help reach other objectives.
5. *Ideology*. Governments frequently protect or promote an ideology in combination with other goals
6. *Cultural identity*. Governments often intervene to protect their country's cultural identity.[4]

The interaction of governments with foreign business interests can be understood through a basic appreciation of their national interest. The goals cited above are frequently the source of governmental actions either encouraging or limiting the business activities of global companies. Many executives erroneously believe that such limiting actions will mostly occur in developing countries. On the contrary, there are many examples of restrictive government actions in the most developed countries, which indicates the universal nature of this type of

3. "Under Construction: Survey of Latin America," *Economist*, November 13, 1993, p. 5.
4. Vern Terpstra and Kenneth David, *The Cultural Environment of Global Business*, 3rd ed. (Cincinnati: South-Western, 1992), p. 203.

governmental behavior. Such restrictive behavior most often occurs when a government perceives the attainment of its own goals to be threatened by the activities or existence of a body beyond its total control, namely the foreign subsidiary of a company.

National Sovereignty and the Goal of Self-Preservation

A country's self-preservation is most threatened when its national sovereignty is at stake. Sovereignty gives a nation complete control within a given geographic area, including the ability to pass laws and regulations and the power to use necessary enforcement. Governments or countries frequently view the existence of sovereignty as a key to reaching the goal of self-preservation. Though sovereignty may, of course, be threatened by a number of factors, it is the relationship between a government's attempt to protect its sovereignty and a company's policies to achieve its own goals that are of primary interest to us.

Because subsidiaries, or branch offices, of global companies are substantially controlled or influenced by decisions made in headquarters, beyond the physical or legal control of the host government, such foreign companies are frequently viewed as a danger to the host country's national sovereignty. (It is important to recognize in this context that *perceptions* on the part of host countries are typically more important than actual facts.)

Many countries limit foreign ownership of newspapers, television, and radio stations for reasons of national sovereignty. Countries fear that if a foreign company controlled these media, it could influence public opinion and limit national sovereignty. The Australian-born Rupert Murdoch controls 70 percent of the major newspapers in Australia. He traded his Australian passport for an American passport to evade ownership restrictions in the United States. Kerry Packer, owner of Australia's largest magazine publishing company and television network, unsuccessfully tried to convince the Australian government that Murdoch was a foreigner and should reduce his holdings in Australia.[5] The U.K. Monopolies and Mergers Commission disallowed the sale of ICI's fertilizer business to the state-owned Finnish company Kemira Oy. Peter Lilley, the U.K. secretary of state for trade and industry at the time, felt that selling a U.K. business to a state-owned business was a "form of Nationalization through the back door."[6]

Over the past few years, globalization of the world economy has caused many interdependencies among countries. This has led to a decrease in the expression of national sovereignty issues. In fact, the tendency at this time is for a loosening of these restrictions. A worldwide trend toward liberalization and privatization that is sweeping most countries is opening up many opportunities previously

5. "Australian Media: Let Battle Commence," *Economist*, April 26, 1997, pp. 60–63.
6. "ICI Ready to Close Leith Plant After Government Veto of Finnish Takeover," *Sunday Times*, February 3, 1991, p. 35.

closed to global firms. We will therefore devote a special section later in this chapter to these issues.

Many attempts at restricting foreign firms have been curtailed by the worldwide General Agreement on Tariffs and Trade (GATT), which was superseded by the World Trade Organization (WTO). The WTO agreements still exclude a number of areas that governments, for their own interest, do not want to liberalize. One such area is the airline industry; governments remain heavily involved in setting policy, restricting access to airspace, and limiting landing rights. It is therefore not surprising that the takeoff and landing slots at European airports are dominated by the major domestic airlines. For example, Alitalia has 70 percent of the slots in Rome, Lufthansa 60 percent at Frankfurt, SAS 55 percent at Copenhagen, KLM 50 percent at Amsterdam, Swiss Air 50 percent at Zurich, Air France 45 percent at Paris, and British Airways 40 percent at London's Heathrow Airport.[7]

The Need for National Security

It is natural for a government to strive to protect its country's borders from outside forces. The military establishment typically becomes a country's principal tool to prevent outside interference. Consequently, many concerns about national security involve a country's armed forces or related agencies. Other areas sensitive to the national security are aspects of a country's infrastructure, its essential resources, utilities, and the supply of crucial raw materials, particularly oil. To ensure their security, host governments tend to strive for control of these sensitive areas and to resist any influence foreign firms may gain over such companies or agencies.

Examples of such government influence abound. The U.S. government, for one, does not typically purchase military material from foreign-controlled firms, even if they have subsidiaries in the United States. The U.S. government continues to control the sale of high-speed computers. In early 2000, President Clinton required a license on the sale of all computers capable of 12.3 billion or more operations per second. This executive order allows export of all but the extremely high-speed computers, which can be used for military purposes.[8]

The protection of national security interests such as defense and telecommunications through regulations requiring local sourcing is declining. This trend has been influenced by two factors. First, it is not economical for each country to have its own defense and telecommunications industry. The high cost of research and development means that in many cases the small local defense supplier will have inferior technologies. Second, the European Union has agreed to open up

7. "Let the Market Take Off," *Economist*, January 18, 1997, p. 74.
8. Nancy Dunne, "White House Cuts Computer Export Curbs," *Financial Times*, February 2, 2000, p. 5.

public spending to all EU companies. This opening of European public spending has caused many U.S. and Japanese firms to form alliances with European partners and to encourage the U.S. and Japanese governments to open up their public spending markets so their industries are not shut out of European markets. Mongolia has opened up all public projects to foreign suppliers and has eliminated all taxes on trade to stimulate foreign trade. Since Mongolia is now an independent country, trade and investment have become more important than defense. According to Prime Minister Narantsatsralt, this new policy, along with global support, helped Mongolia's gross national product (GNP) to grow by 3.4 percent from 1994 to 1998.[9]

Fostering National Prosperity

A key goal for government is to ensure the material prosperity of its citizens. Prosperity is usually expressed in national income or gross national product (GNP), and comparisons between countries are frequently made with respect to per capita income or GNP per capita figures. (Comparisons are also done on gross domestic product (GDP) and both GNP and GDP, adjusted by purchasing power parity to reflect comparable standard of living.) However prosperity is measured, most governments strive to provide full employment and an increasing standard of living. Part of this goal is to enact an economic policy that will stimulate the economic output of businesses active within the nation's borders. Global companies can assume an important role inasmuch as they add to a host country's GNP and thus enhance its income. However, any action that runs contrary to the host government's goals, though it may be in the best interest of the company, will likely cause a conflict between the foreign company and the host country government. Furthermore, a host country may take actions that unilaterally favor local industry over foreign competitors to protect its own standard of living and prosperity. Europe protects its agricultural industries with high tariffs. For example, in 1997, the average EU tariff on beef was 87.7 percent, cereals 67.8 percent, dairy products 57.7 percent, and sugar 61.8 percent.[10]

For many countries, a high level of imports represents a drain on their monetary resources and lost opportunities to expand their own industrial base. Under such circumstances, a host country may move toward a restriction of imports beyond the imposition of tariffs or customs duties. It puts up what are called nontariff barriers. Both the Italian and French governments have protected their local automobile industries from Japanese competition by using nontariff barriers. The Italian government has for many years restricted the import of Japanese automobiles to a total of 2,000 units annually. The French government, through selective

9. "Mongolian Premier Presents Paper on Country's Development Strategy," *Daily News Ulaanbaatar, BBC Worldwide Monitoring*, June 22, 1999, p. 1.
10. "Europe's Burden," *Economist*, May 22, 1999, p. 84.

use of import licenses, has limited Japanese producers to only 3 percent of the market.

For years the German government has supported local employment. However, rules of the EU open employment to any member of the EU. Given the high cost of German labor and the lack of flexibility of German trade unions, it is not surprising that 400,000 German construction workers are out of work, while over 190,000 other EU workers are employed on German construction sites.[11] In 1999, unemployment in Germany was at 11 percent, down from 12 percent in 1997. The high unemployment in Germany is often blamed on the social security cost of 42 percent of gross wages.[12]

Most host governments try to enhance a nation's prosperity by increasing its exports. To do this, some governments have sponsored export credit arrangements combined with some form of political risk insurance. (Some other methods of increasing exports are described in more detail in Chapter 18.) Particularly in Europe, heads of governments often engage in state visits to encourage major export transactions. Political observers often have pointed out that both the French president and the German chancellor spend a substantial amount of their state visits on business and trade affairs, more so than is typically the case for the president of the United States. Attracting global companies with a high export potential to open up operations in their countries is of critical interest to host governments. Frequently, such companies can expect special treatment or subsidies.

In many countries, regional or local governments can also influence decisions that affect global firms. For the U.S. location of new BMW and Daimler-Benz assembly plants, the relevant government was not a national one but state governments. Various local governments lobbied intensively for the plant. The winning state government for the Daimler-Benz plant, Alabama, had to offer a $253 million commitment in infrastructure improvements to attract the project. A year earlier, the government of South Carolina committed $150 million to attract a BMW plant.[13]

The host government's export and import policies are of interest to companies considering locating operations in a particular country. By collecting information on a government's policies or orientation, a company can make an optimal choice that may give it access to benefits not available in some other countries.

Enhancing Prestige

The pursuit of prestige has many faces; it does not always take the form of industrial achievement. Whereas the governments of some countries choose to sup-

11. "German Jobs: Odd Men In," *Economist*, June 14, 1997, p. 71.
12. John Grimond, "Survey: Germany: Wealth, but Not Work," *Economist*, February 6, 1999, p. G6.
13. Peter S. Canellos, "German Auto Plant Revs up in Alabama," *Boston Globe*, June 30, 1997, p. A1:4.

port team sports or individual athletes to enhance national prestige, other host governments choose to influence the business climate for the same reason. Having a national airline gives rise to national prestige. Other developed countries may prefer to see their industries achieve leadership in certain technologies such as telecommunications, electronics, robotics, or aerospace.

A host government trying to enhance its country's prestige will frequently encourage local or national companies at the expense of a foreign company. The French government suspended the sale of Thomson to the Lagardere Group because of the latter's plans to sell the multimedia division of Thomson to Daewoo Electronics, a South Korean firm. The French government was sensitive to the French workers' fear of working for Korean owners.[14] In another case, in 1991, the U.S. secretary of the interior raised a number of objections to Japanese ownership of the concessions in Yosemite National Park. Although the concessions are not a big business, the idea of part of Yosemite being in foreign hands challenged the nation's sense of prestige.[15] The U.S. sensitivity to foreign investors seemed to have diminished in 1999, with the Japanese owning many of Hollywood's entertainment companies; the Germans buying Chrysler, Bankers Trust, and Random House; and the British purchasing New England Electric and Amoco.[16]

In the future, companies will need to develop a keen sense for what constitutes national prestige as perceived by host governments. Businesspeople cannot expect host governments to have an explicit policy on such issues. Instead, companies will have to derive, from observing overt or covert government actions over time, some notions on national prestige. Once a company has a clear definition or idea of what constitutes prestige for a host government, it can avoid policies that are in direct conflict with government intentions or aspirations and can emphasize those actions that tend to enhance the host country's prestige.

Protecting Cultural Identity

With the global village becoming a reality, one of the major impacts felt by countries is in the area of culture. The breaking down of communications barriers has led to an increase in the activities of global, mostly U.S., media firms. These firms are most visible in entertainment, the production and distribution of movies, TV programs, videos, and music recordings. Even more important has been the role of TV companies through use of satellite transmission. Whereas most countries were able to determine broadcast policy on their own, the future is such that control over broadcasting, and therefore culture, is perceived to be in the hands of a few large, mostly U.S., firms.

14. "Keep It French," *Economist*, December 7, 1996, p. 5.
15. "That Tough New Line on Foreign Investment Is Only a Mirage," *Business Week*, January 21, 1991, p. 43.
16. "The British Are Coming: Foreign Investors Are Going on a Spending Spree in America, and That's Just Fine with Us," *Los Angeles Daily News*, December 16, 1998, p. N26.

MTV has over twenty international channels including MTV Latin America, MTV Nordic, MTV India, MTV Germany, MTV Italy, MTV Russia, MTV Southeast Asia, MTV UK, and others. MTV estimates it reaches 300 million households or about one-third of the world.[17] In Europe, where MTV reaches 85 million households, there are five local channels for the UK, Germany, Scandinavia, Italy, and the rest of Europe. In 2000 through 2001, MTV Europe will add four additional channels to serve local market tastes and at the same time will maintain the global MTV brand.[18] The European Parliament advocates curbs on foreign television to keep out U.S. sitcoms and game shows. France, Ireland, Portugal, and Belgium have quotas on their airwaves. Also, through lottery and cinema taxes, European films receive subsidies of $600 million per year.[19]

Increasing globalization—in business, in media, and in general—is likely to produce more of such moves by host governments. Global firms will therefore be well advised to understand the cultural content, or significance, of their products or services. Insensitivity to cultural ideals in any aspect of global marketing operations can lead to unwanted reactions.

Host Country Pressure Groups

Host country governments are not the only forces able to influence the political climate and, thus, to affect the operations of foreign companies. Other groups have a stake in the treatment of companies or in political and economic decisions that indirectly affect foreign businesses. In most instances, they cannot act unilaterally. Thus, they try to pressure either the host government or the foreign businesses to conform to their views. Such pressure groups exist in most countries and may be made up of ad hoc groups or permanently structured associations. Political parties are a common pressure group, though they frequently cannot exert much influence outside the government. Parties generally associated with a nationalist point of view frequently advocate policies restricting foreign companies. Environmental groups have had a major influence on consumers around the world, raising concerns about nuclear energy, oil transportation, waste disposal, rain forest destruction, fishing techniques, global warming, and so on. For example, scientists report that 1990 was the earth's warmest year on record since 1850, when people started recording the planet's temperature. The increased temperature is thought to be caused by human activities related to the escape of carbon dioxide, chlorofluorocarbons, and methane. There is a fear that this warming will have a drastic effect on climate, agriculture, and sea levels. In a French study, researchers reported that heat-trapping greenhouse gases are at their highest levels in 420,000 years, and U.S. researchers found that fifty-seven species of

17. Mimi Whitefield, "MTV Networks Global," *Miami Herald*, June 28, 1999, p. 9.
18. Katja Hoffman, "Youth TV's Old Hand Prepares for the Digital Challenge," *Financial Times*, February 18, 2000, p. 8.
19. Peter Cook, "Opposing the U.S. Culture," *Globe*, February 3, 1999. p. B2.

butterflies are altering their migratory patterns in response to heat changes.[20] DuPont, one of the world's largest producers of chlorofluorocarbons (CFCs), stopped making CFCs by 2000, investing $500 million in CFC alternatives.[21] Environmental groups also forced McDonald's to replace Styrofoam packing with cardboard. Although McDonald's internal market research showed that environmental issues have neither a positive nor a negative impact on sales, the company has agreed to work with the Environmental Defense Fund, an environmental pressure group, to reduce unnecessary and harmful waste.[22] In another case, the British-based Global Witness human rights group forced DeBeers, the world's largest gem supplier, to guarantee that none of its diamonds were from rebel groups in Angola, Guinea, and other war-torn nations.[23]

Some of the most potent pressure groups are found within the local business community itself. These include local industry associations and occasionally local unions. When local companies are threatened by foreign competition, they frequently petition the government to help by placing restrictions on the foreign competitors. In China, the state-owned newsprint factories were being hurt by cheap newsprint from the United States, Canada, and South Korea. The China Ministry of Foreign Trade and Economic Cooperation found that the foreign suppliers were dumping on the Chinese market. In 1999, the Chinese therefore assessed a tax of 55 to 78 percent on U.S., Canadian, and South Korean newsprint.[24]

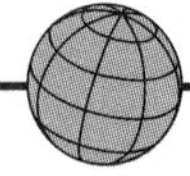

Host Government Actions

In the previous section, we focused on various governmental concerns and the underlying motivation for certain political actions. In this section, we analyze some of the typical policies host governments may choose to control foreign-based businesses. The relationships between the underlying motivations and the chosen policies are also discussed. The host governments' policies are presented in order of their severity, from the least to the most severe.

Jawboning

The intervention of governments in the business process in an informal way, often without a legal basis, is called *jawboning*. Governments use this form of in-

20. Dick Thompson, "What Global Warming?" *Time*, June 21, 1999, p. 62.
21. Natalie Noor-Drugan, "DuPont Hikes Prices: A Silver Lining for HFCs?" *Chemical Week*, May 13, 1998, p. 20.
22. Holman W. Jenkins Jr., "How to Save McDonalds," *Wall Street Journal Europe*, March 19, 1998, p. 12.
23. "DeBeers to Avoid Selling Dirty Diamonds," *Financial Times*, March 1, 2000, p. 22.
24. "China Starts New Antidumping Tax on Newsprint," *Dow Jones News Service*, June 3, 1999, p. 1.

tervention to prevent an act that, though legal, is perceived to be contrary to their own interests or goals. The effectiveness of jawboning lies in the possibility of stronger action at a later time should the "culprit" not fall into line.

Microsoft had difficulty gaining acceptance in China because the powerful Ministry of Electronics Industries (MEI) withheld endorsement of Microsoft Windows (specially adapted with Chinese characters). Microsoft had not cultivated this important local contact, so Compaq and AST, China's biggest PC suppliers, did not install Microsoft software in their PCs. However, Microsoft sales improved after Bill Gates visited China's president Jiang Zemin and signed an agreement with MEI to cooperate on software development.[25]

The leverage of host governments comes from the fact that foreign companies depend on permits and approvals issued by host governments. Such favored treatment may be at risk if a company proceeds against the expressed wishes of the host government, despite the fact that no laws were violated.

Such a jawboning action was also taken by the Japanese government. In a reaction to the fall in Japanese beef prices as a result of increased imports, the Japanese government issued "administrative guidance" to restrict imports to a certain level. Although this action was not legally binding, it reflects a step governments can undertake to interfere in the free marketplace. These actions are typical for many governments, and global firms will have to be aware of their impact.[26]

"Buy Local" Restrictions

Since governments are important customers of industry in virtually every country, they can use this purchasing power to favor certain suppliers. Frequently, local companies are favored over foreign imports. An industry, particularly subject to such local favoritism is the telecommunications industry, because telephone companies are state-run in most countries. For foreign companies, the case of Japan's Nippon Telegraph & Telephone Public Corporation (NTT) was particularly problematic. For years, NTT granted contracts exclusively to a few local suppliers, virtually shutting out foreign-based companies. Pressures from foreign governments led to global agreements under the umbrella of GATT, and other global organizations have established new rules that tend to prevent direct government intervention except for cases of national security and a few other exemptions. Opportunities for foreign firms to contract with NTT opended up with an accord signed with the U.S. in 1980 and renewed in 1997; this accord was continued even after NTT was broken up into smaller carriers in 1999.[27]

25. "Tony Walker, Chinese Lesson," *Financial Times*, February 23, 1995, p. 14.
26. "Japan's Request to Limit Purchases of Foreign Beef Is Likely to Anger U.S.," *Wall Street Journal*, August 9, 1993, p. A9.
27. "Japan, U.S. to Hold NTT, Computer Talks in Tokyo," *World News Connection*, May 25, 1999, p. 1.

Few areas have recently received as much attention as the local buying preference in public sector contracts. Different from import and export transactions, these contracts frequently deal with local construction. Access to such contracts has been opened up in the EU through the "Europe 1992" initiative, whereby all public sector contracts now require open bidding. The EU has instituted a requirement to report contracts above a threshold of 5 million European currency units (ECUs) (about U.S. $5 million). Supplies contracts have a lower limit of ECU 200,000; service contracts have the same limit. The 1992 Open Procurement rules were expected to generate annual public savings of 8 to 19 billion ECUs. Unfortunately, according to a study done for the European Commission, the public procurement policy failed because most countries have not incorporated it into their national laws and therefore it is not being enforced.[28]

U.S. construction companies are, with the help of the U.S. government, also trying to get access to the $278 billion Japanese public construction market. The 1988 Major Projects Agreement and the 1994 New Construction Market Access Pact between the Japanese and U.S. governments attempted to open the Japanese construction market.[29] However, the 560,000 construction companies in Japan exert significant influence in Japan through campaign contributions to politicians and through providing a large number of campaign workers.[30] A renewed effort to open the Japanese construction industry can be expected following Japan's bribery scandals involving public construction firms and politicians. A large number of construction firms were reported to follow *dango*, a system whereby contracts are shared among competing firms and a portion of the contract is regularly used as a payoff to politicians. According to a report by the Japanese Fair Trade Commission, 156 contractors were suspected of *dango* or bid rigging on 872 contracts on the new Kansai airport in 1996.[31] Although this scheme was not sanctioned by the Japanese government, its existence blocked global firms from gaining contracts on the basis of level competition.

Nontariff Barriers

Under the category of nontariff barriers we include any government action that is not an official custom tariff but that nevertheless inhibits the free flow of products between countries. These barriers may not necessarily add to landed costs but are more likely to result in a limitation on product flows. To a large extent, nontariff barriers are used by governments to keep imports from freely entering

28. Joe Sanderson, "The EU Green Paper on Public Procurement," *European Business Journal*, 1998, vol. 10, no. 2, pp. 64–66.
29. Jon Choy, "Japan's Construction Industry: The Economic Engine That Can't," *Japanese Economic Institute*, September 4, 1998, p. 6.
30. Sandra Sugawara, "Japanese Construction Trade Built on Cronyism," *Washington Post*, January 31, 1998, p. A1.
31. "KIX Highlights Construction Project Bidding Ills," *Mainichi Daily News*, June 24, 1998 p. 1.

the home market. Many types of measures may be taken. A common one is import restrictions or quotas.

Nontariff barriers are hard to detect and typically are not freely listed. International Game Technology (IGT), a U.S.-based maker of slot machines, began to target Japan as a major market in 1989. The company reacted to the fact that Japanese firms were suddenly its most important competitors in the United States, and it was not selling any machines in Japan, a market with 800,000 slot machines representing about two-thirds of the total worldwide installed base. When the company wanted to enter the Japanese market with its machines, it found out that the rules for regulators were hard to find. Only the eighteen members of a small industry group could get them. On trying to join the group, IGT learned that any potential member was required to have the support of three existing members, and the candidate firm needed three years of manufacturing experience in Japan before applying. Eventually, the company found its way through the myriad of regulations with the help of a local lawyer. Even then, IGT had to navigate many different regulatory hurdles before its products would be approved for sale in Japan.[32]

Nontariff barriers also affect the service industries. For example, limits on employing foreigners may prevent a consulting firm from using its critical human expertise, or restrictions on licensing professionals may hinder a supplier's ability to operate in a country.[33]

The use of nontariff barriers is growing. The World Bank estimates that nontariff barriers increased from 15 percent of industrial countries' imports in 1981 to 18 percent by 1986. The Institute for Global Economics estimates that if nontariff barriers were eliminated, world trade would increase by $330 billion.[34]

Subsidies

Government subsidies represent free gifts that host governments dispense with the intention that the overall benefits to the economy by far exceed such grants. They are a popular instrument used both to encourage exports and to attract global companies to a certain country.

Governments may also use direct or indirect subsidies to encourage industries that will be major exporters. Exporters bring multiple benefits, since they provide employment and bring increased revenue into the country through export sales. An example of a direct subsidy is when a government agrees to pay $1 for each pair of shoes to help a local producer compete more effectively in foreign mar-

32. "A Slot-Machine Maker Trying to Sell in Japan Hits Countless Barriers," *Wall Street Journal*, May 11, 1993, p. 1.
33. Douglas L. Fugate and Alan Zimmerman, "Global Services Marketing: A Review of Structural Barriers, Regulatory Limitations and Marketing Responses," *Journal of Professional Services Marketing*, 1996, vol. 13, no. 2, pp. 33–58.
34. "A Survey of World Trade," *Economist*, September 22, 1990, p. 8.

kets. Previously, GATT and now WTO agreements outlawed direct export subsidies but usually did not prohibit indirect subsidies. An indirect subsidy is the result of a subsidy on a component of the exported product. For example, a government may provide a subsidy on the canvas used to manufacture tents, which are then exported.

Subsidies are one way for government to support local industries. In most countries, subsidies amount to 2 to 3.5 percent of the value of industrial output. The rate of subsidy in the United States is estimated to be 0.5 percent, whereas it is 1.0 percent in Japan. In Europe, subsidies range from 0.9 percent of industrial output in Britain, to 3.1 percent in Germany, 5.3 in Italy, and a high of 5.6 percent in Greece.[35] The logic of the subsidies is that they improve global competitiveness and create or protect jobs. The European Union has tightened its policy on state aid to industry. However, European governments continue to support manufacturing industries, especially the automobile industry. There are 300 automobile assembly plants in Europe, with approximately 30 percent excess capacity.[36]

The treatment of local aircraft makers has been an issue between the U.S. and Europe for the past ten years. The French government points toward favorable treatment of Boeing by NASA and Pentagon contracts as another form of hidden subsidies. Boeing considered the 30 percent French ownership of Airbus to encourage local preference. An agreement in 1992 reduced tension between Airbus and Boeing, although in 1999, the U.S. Federal Trade Commission investigated both companies for price fixing. Also, the Airbus consortium was supposed to be converted into the European Aerospace and Defense Company in January 1999, but the conversion has been delayed by the French. Critics argue that Boeing has lost market share to Airbus not because of subsidies, but because of Boeing's low productivity—216 workers per plane at Boeing versus 143 for Airbus.[37]

Operating Conditions

Host governments have a direct influence on the operations of a foreign subsidiary by imposing specific conditions on the company's operations. The rules of conducting business may challenge the global company. For example, the requirement of *Mitbestimmung* (codetermination) in Germany necessitates the participation of labor on the management committee.[38] In Germany, there is a ban on bakers working between 10:00 P.M. and 4:00 A.M. The ban dates back to World War I, when supplies were short and authorities noticed that people ate less day-

35. "Subsidies to Industry," *Economist*, April 10, 1999, p. 105.
36. "A Handbrake on Subsidies: Governments Should Not Obstruct a Long Overdue Restructuring of the European Car Industry," *Economist*, February 13, 1999, p. 19.
37. Aerospace: Hubris at Airbus, Boeing Rebuilds," *Economist*, November 28, 1998, p. 64.
38. Janine Brewis, "Corporate Germany Starts to Listen to Its Shareholders," *Corporate Finance*, February 1, 1999, p. 18.

old bread than fresh bread. The law was repealed in November 1996, resulting in employment of 5,000 new bakery workers in six months.[39]

Operating conditions for global firms are of particular importance when they affect the freedom to run marketing programs. Host countries may restrict global firms in the area of pricing, advertising, promoting, selling, distributing, and many other elements. Some of those restrictions, and strategies to deal with them, are included in Chapters 10–15, which deal directly with marketing mix elements. Where such operating restrictions apply to all firms, domestic and global, the competitive threat is lessened; however, companies might still find such restrictions a problem when the way they have to operate varies from what they are accustomed to. Where operating restrictions apply to foreign firms only, the result will be a lessening of competitiveness, and companies should seriously consider these constraints before entering a market.

Kidnappings pose an extremely difficult operating condition. The number of kidnappings for ransom has risen in Latin America, especially in Colombia, where there were 4,000 in 1995; the same year, there were 800 in Brazil and Mexico and 200 in Ecuador. Senior business executives and political officials are the most common targets of these kidnappings.[40] Worldwide kidnapping for ransom increased 6% in 1999 to 1,786 cases. Ninety-two percent of the kidnappings took place in ten countries, with Latin America having 75% of the kidnappings for ransom.[41]

Local Content

Many host governments impose a local-content regulation that requires global firms to demonstrate that the value added derived from their products or services meets these limitations. For product-based companies, local-content laws mean that some part of the manufacturing must be done in the host country. Often, such restrictions are used to encourage local value-added activities. Occasionally, the regulations can also lead to the elimination of global competitors if the local market is not big enough to justify the manufacturing operation.

A constant point of discussion is the cars produced by Japanese transplant operations in the United States. Honda Motor Company, operating two U.S. assembly plants and assembling locally as much as two-thirds of its total U.S. sales volume, has been claiming a 50 percent local content. With less than that, Honda could not take advantage of a U.S.-Canadian free trade agreement, as it could have had with 100 percent local content. The company has had a dispute with the U.S. government on the classification of parts purchased from Japanese parts makers located in the United States. Some experts have not accepted Honda's characteri-

39. "German Jobs: Odd Men In," *Economist*, June 14, 1997, p. 72.
40. James Brook, "Kidnappings Soar in Latin America, Threatening Region's Stability," *New York Times*, April 7, 1995, p. A8.
41. Andrew Bolger, "Increase in Kidnapping for Ransom," *Financial Times*, April 24, 2000, p. 4.

zation of 75 percent local content.[42] In contrast, BMW has announced that its plant to be located in South Carolina will have a local content of 80 percent so that its cars can be treated as U.S.-made cars for purposes of trade, duties, and other regulations.[43]

Enforcing local content can also result in the elimination of global competitors. The European Commission required members of the EU to ensure 40 percent of their television programming to be of European source.[44] In the local application of this law, France interpreted it to mean that 60 percent of its programming should be from Europe and two-thirds of that portion from France alone. A similar law was applied to radio, where the French government mandated its eight national FM stations to raise the French language content of music to 40 percent, of which half must be originating from new French talent. This 1991 ruling had earlier been the source of a trade conflict between the EU and the United States, as it was also applied to movies.[45]

Regulations imposed by host governments dealing with local content are most often found for products that are purchased by local government institutions or that are in need of local government help, as through export financing. The recent trend in global trade negotiations has tended to reduce the restrictive character of some of these regulations. However, the local-content issue still remains an important aspect for global marketers, and they should be aware of it.

Ownership Conditions

Host governments sometimes pursue the policy of requiring that local nationals become part owners of the foreign company. These governments believe that this guarantees fair contributions to the local economy. The restrictions can range from an outright prohibition of full foreign ownership to selective policies aimed at key industries.

One country that has used ownership conditions extensively is India. India's Foreign Exchange Regulation Act of 1973 stipulated that foreign ownership may not exceed 40 percent unless the foreign firm or Indian company belongs to a key industry, manufacturing materials such as chemicals, turbines, machinery, tractors, or fertilizers.

International Business Machines Corporation (IBM) decided to leave rather than give up control. However, later changes in the government have brought a softening of India's stance, and the country is again courting firms that can contribute new technologies. Coca-Cola had also decided to leave rather than share its secret formula with the Indians. However, in 1988, Coke began negotiations to

42. "Honda: Is It an American Car?" *Business Week*, November 18, 1991, p. 81.
43. "BMW Expects U.S.-Made Cars to Have 80 Percent Level of North American Content," *Wall Street Journal*, August 5, 1993, p. A2.
44. "Cultural Wars," *Economist*, September 12, 1998, p. 97.
45. "Movies Eclipse Films," *Economist*, February 5, 1994, p. 89.

return to India without revealing the formula. The reintroduction of Coca-Cola in the Indian market took place in 1994.[46]

India's Bharatiya Janata Party (BJP) was elected in 1998 on a platform of protectionism, threatening to throw out foreign companies. However, once in power, the BJP opened up markets to outsiders and is expected to continue reforms mandated by the WTO.[47] The BJP's open-market policies did not, however, extend to Reader's Digest, which had left India in 1979, selling its business to Titan Industries and the Tata Group companies, with a license to publish. In 1998, the Indian Foreign Investment Board deferred a proposal for Reader's Digest to repurchase Reader's Digest India.[48] In fact, in some industries such as ports and toll roads, the Indian government is allowing 100 percent foreign ownership to boost infrastructure investments.[49] This demonstrates an important aspect in the control of foreign ownership. The 1960s and 1970s saw a tightening of the control over foreign ownership in many countries. During the late 1980s and particularly during the early 1990s, the trend has been toward trade liberalization, as countries recognized the catalytic nature of foreign investment. This new trend has brought the elimination of many restrictions. As a result, we will devote a special section later in this chapter to this new development, which is of crucial importance to global marketers.

Boycotts

The previously discussed policies are aimed at restricting or limiting the freedom of action of foreign firms. Boycotts, however, tend to completely shut out some companies from a given market. Typically, politically motivated boycotts tend to be directed at companies of certain origin or companies that have engaged in transactions with political enemies.

One of the most publicized boycott campaigns was the 1975 boycott waged by some Arab countries against firms that had engaged in business beyond simple export transactions with Israel. The boycott was administered by the Arab League. For example, one U.S. company on the Arab boycott list was Ford Motor Company, which supplied an Israeli car assembler with flat-packed cars for local assembly. Xerox was placed on the list after financing a documentary on Israel, and the Coca-Cola Company was added to the boycott list for having licensed an Israeli bottler. The boycott did not always include all Arab League member nations. The actual enforcement was, therefore, quite selective and differed by industry.

46. "Global Gallery," *Advertising Age*, January 17, 1994, pp. 1–18.
47. Mark Drajem, "India BJP Government Showed Reforms to Continue Despite Rhetoric," *Dow Jones International News*, May 7, 1999, pp. 1–2.
48. James Mathew and Anjan Mitra, "Readers Digest Re-entry Put on Ice," *Business Standard*, December 1, 1998, p. 9.
49. "India Opens Trade Doors," *International Business Asia*, January 18, 1999, p. 4.

The Arab League boycott became considerably less relevant with the changed political situation in the Middle East. By the end of the 1980s, many countries only selectively enforced it, and after the Iraq conflict, many more countries abandoned it.[50] For example, Coca-Cola only returned to the Gulf soft-drink market in 1994, because they traded with Israel. Coca-Cola sales have grown at a rate of 25 percent per year and now comprise 33 percent of the Gulf $1.2 billion market.[51]

It is expected that with the further improvement of the ties between the Palestinians and Israel, even direct economic linkages between Arab League member states and Israel will become possible.

Takeovers

No action a host government can take is more drastic than a takeover. Broadly defined, takeovers are any host government-initiated actions that result in a loss of ownership or a direct control by the foreign company. There are, of course, several types of takeovers.[52] *Expropriation* is a formal, or legal, taking over of an operation with or without the payment of compensation. Even when compensation is paid, there are often concerns about the adequacy of the amount, timeliness of the payment, and form of payment. *Confiscation* is expropriation without any compensation. The term *domestication* is used to describe the limiting of certain economic activities to local citizens; this means a takeover by either expropriation, confiscation, or forced sales. Governments may domesticate industry by imposing one of the following requirements: transfer of partial ownership to nationals, promotion of nationals to higher levels of management, or purchase of raw materials or components produced locally. If the company cannot meet these requirements, it may be forced to sell its operations in that country.

At one time, studies suggested that takeovers were becoming more frequent and were a major threat to companies operating abroad. Hawkins, Mintz, and Provissiero in 1975 found a total of 170 foreign takeovers of U.S. subsidiaries registered for the period 1946 to 1973. Comparing these findings with the total of 23,282 U.S. subsidiaries operating outside the United States yielded a takeover rate of about 0.7% percent.[53] These statistics were supported by a broader survey of all countries by the United Nations in which 875 takeovers were identified for the 1960–1974 period.[54] Ten countries had accounted for two-thirds of all takeovers, and fifty countries registered none at all. Nationalization of global

50. "Boycott of Israel Is Said to Relax," *New York Times*, June 9, 1993, p. A5.
51. "Coke Opens Saudi Bottling Plant in Cola War," *Agence France-Presse,* May 5, 1999, p. 1.
52. Richard D. Robinson, *International Business Management* (New York: Dryden, 1973), p. 374.
53. Robert G. Hawkins, Norman Mintz, and Michael Provissiero, "Government Takeovers of U.S. Foreign Affiliates," *Journal of International Business Studies*, Spring 1976, pp. 3–16.
54. Ibid.

firms peaked in the mid-1970s, when up to thirty countries were involved each year, affecting as many as eighty firms. By 1985, expropriations had declined, and almost no takeovers were recorded. Instead of nationalizations, countries engaged in the massive process of privatization.[55] In general, global marketers may have to fear nationalization, and the resulting total loss of an asset, far less in the future. The loss of operating control or freedom may prove to be a far greater political risk. Although takeovers seem less likely, in 1996 Hong Kong retailer Giordano had 11 stores in Shanghai closed and 25 other stores in China closed temporarily because of an investigation of possible tax violations. However, the Chinese government was at odds with Mr. Lai, Giordano's founder and publishing tycoon, for an article in his *Next* magazine criticizing then premier Li Peng. The Chinese stores were reopened in 1999 after Mr. Lai sold his interest in the Giordano company.[56]

This section has illustrated how host governments can act to impact the local operations of global companies. The previous section concentrated more on the motivations behind these governmental actions. Table 4.1 identifies and relates certain policy actions to the underlying goals discussed in this chapter. Though any combination of goal and action is possible, history tends to suggest that certain actions are more often associated with specific goals.

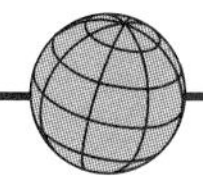

Home Country Political Forces

Managers of global companies need be concerned not only about political developments abroad. Many developments take place at home that can have a great impact on what a company can do globally. The political development in a company's home country tends to affect either the role of the company in general or, more often, some particular aspects of its operations. Consequently, restrictions can be placed on companies not only by host countries but by home countries as well. Therefore, an astute global manager must be able to monitor political developments both at home and abroad.

This section of the chapter explores home country policies and actions directed at global companies. Some of these actions are unique and have only recently come into existence to any large extent.

Home Country Actions

Home countries are essentially guided by the same six interests described earlier in this chapter: self-preservation, national security, prosperity, prestige, ideology,

55. "Multinationals," Survey, *Economist*, March 27, 1993, p. 19.
56. Kristi Hastings, "Giordano's Return to China Sends Shares Higher," *Asian Wall Street Journal*, June 10, 1999, p. 4.

TABLE 4.1

Host Government Goal and Policy Actions

Action	*Goal*					
	Self-Preservation	*Security*	*Prosperity*	*Prestige*	*Ideology*	*Cultural Identity*
Jawboning	X	X	X	X	X	X
"Buy local"	X	X	X			
Nontariff barriers	X		X			
Subsidies	X		X			
Operating restrictions	X	X	X			X
Local content			X			
Ownership conditions		X				X
Boycotts					X	
Takeovers	X	X	X		X	

X = Likelihood of using given action to accomplish that goal.

and cultural identity. In general, a home country government wishes to have its country's foreign companies accept its national priorities. As a result, home country governments at times look toward foreign companies to help them achieve political goals. They may engage in any or all the actions outlined earlier: jawboning, nontariff barriers, subsidies, operating restrictions, and so on.

How then do home country policies differ? In the past, home country governments have tried to prevent foreign companies from doing business on ideological, political, or national security grounds. In the extreme, this can result in an embargo on trade with a certain country. The U.S. government has taken unilateral actions in the past. Its embargo on trade with Cuba dates back to 1961, following the assumption of power of Fidel Castro. Since that time, U.S. businesses have been allowed neither to purchase from nor to sell to Cuba. Any U.S. company that wants to do business with Cuba must apply for a special license, but no such applications were granted until 1993. Discussions are under way to possibly change the trade embargo.[57] Another long-running trade embargo imposed by the U.S. government related to Vietnam. Imposed in 1975, this embargo was lifted in 1994.[58]

Unilateral embargoes, those imposed by one country only, expose businesses from that country to competitive disadvantage and thus are often fought by business interests. During the embargo against Vietnam, U.S. companies were kept out while firms from other nations were engaging in business with a nation of 70 million consumers. By mid-1993, global firms, excluding U.S. firms, had won on projects worth more than $6 billion.[59] In Cuba also, only the United States applied a trade embargo. After the visit by the Pope to Cuba in 1998, the Clinton administration resumed direct flights to Cuba, mail delivery, and cash contributions to independent charities and reduced restrictions on travel for academic, cultural, and athletic groups. Further opening of Cuba will be delayed until after the 2000 presidential elections as Vice President Gore does not want to jeopardize votes and financial contributions from anti-Castro Cuban Americans. [60]

Because there is a risk to the competitiveness of its business if a country takes unilateral actions restricting the business community, the emphasis has shifted toward taking multilateral actions together with many other countries. Such action may come from a group of nations or, increasingly, from the United Nations. The trade embargo by the global community against South Africa was one of the first such actions. Although, as a result of consumer group pressures, many companies had left South Africa to protest its apartheid regime, the embargo became applica-

57. Carla Anne Robbins, "Clinton Plans to Ease Some Restrictions on Humanitarian Aid, Travel to Cuba," *Wall Street Journal*, January 5, 1999, p. A4.
58. "Clinton Lifts Ban on Trade with Vietnam," *Wall Street Journal*, February 4, 1994, p. A12.
59. "Look East—But Don't Touch," *Financial Times*, September 16, 1993, p. 16.
60. Albert R. Hunt, "End the Anachronistic Embargo Against Cuba," *Wall Street Journal*, April 22, 1999, p. A23.

ble to a wider group of firms in the late 1980s when it was imposed by most countries. When the political situation in South Africa changed and apartheid was abolished, the United States, together with other nations, lifted the embargo in July 1991. Since 1994, the United States has been the largest foreign investor in South Africa, with some of the largest firms being Dow Chemical, Ford, General Motors, Coca-Cola, Hyatt, and Electronic Data Systems (EDS).[61]

Other multilateral actions by the global community are the trade sanctions enforced by the United Nations against Iraq as a result of the Gulf War in 1991; this embargo substantially restricts the type of trade companies can get involved with. The most recent embargo is against Serbia. Imposed in June 1992 and further tightened in April 1993 and again in May 1999, this embargo has virtually stopped orderly trade as NATO discusses reconstruction and the potential removal of President Slobodan Milošević.[62]

Home Country Pressure Groups

The kinds of pressures that international companies are subject to in their home countries are frequently different from the types of pressures brought to bear on them abroad. In many ways, international companies have had to deal with special interest groups abroad for a long time. But the type of special interest groups found domestically have only come into existence over the last ten to fifteen years. Such groups are usually well organized, tend to get extensive media coverage, and have succeeded in catching many companies unprepared. Although some of their actions have always been geared toward mobilizing support to get the home country government to sponsor specific regulations favorable to their point of view, special interest groups have also managed to place companies directly under pressure.

International companies can come under pressure for two major reasons: (1) for their choice of markets and (2) for their methods of business. A constant source of controversy involves global companies' business practices in three areas: product strategies, promotional practices, and pricing practices. Product strategies include the decision to cease marketing a certain product (such as pesticides or pharmaceuticals), usually for safety reasons. Promotional practices include the way the products are advertised or pushed through distribution channels. Pricing practices include the policy of charging higher or unfair prices.

61. Christopher Ogden, "Special Report South Africa, Less Aid More Trade," *Time*, May 24, 1999, p. 57.
62. Kelvin Galvin, "Clinton Imposes U.S. Trade Embargo on Serbia," *Associated Press Newswires*, May 1, 1999, pp. 1–2.

The infant formula controversy of the early 1980s involved participants from many countries and serves as a good example of the type of pressure sometimes placed on international companies. Infant formula was being sold all over the world as a substitute or supplement for breast-feeding. Though even the producers of infant formula agreed that breast-feeding was superior to bottle-feeding, changes had started to take place in western society decades ago that brought about the decline of infant breast-feeding. Following World War II, several companies expanded their infant formula productions in Third World countries, where birth rates were much higher than in developed countries. Companies that had intended their products to be helpful found themselves embroiled in controversy. Critics blasted the product as unsafe under Third World conditions. Because the formula had to be mixed with water, the critics charged that the sanitary conditions and contaminated water in developing countries led to many deaths. As a result, they urged an immediate stop to all promotional activities, such as nurses visiting new mothers and the distribution of free samples.

Nestlé Company, as one of the leading infant formula manufacturers, became the target of a boycott by consumer action groups in the United States and elsewhere. Under the leadership of INFACT, the Infant Formula Action Coalition, a consumer boycott of all Nestlé products was organized to force the company to change its marketing practices.[63] The constant public pressure resulted in the development of a code sponsored by the World Health Organization (WHO). This code, accepted by the Thirty-Fourth WHO General Assembly in 1981 (with the sole dissenting vote from the United States), primarily covered the methods used to market infant formula. Producers and distributors could not give away any free samples, had to avoid contact with consumers, and were not allowed to do any promotion geared toward the general public. The code was subject to voluntary participation by WHO member governments.[64] The effect of this controversy was that new regulations, or codes, eventually became part of the legal system.

Boycotts can have very visible effects. The 1990 boycott against tuna caught in nets that also trap and kill dolphins caused Heinz, owner of Star-Kist, to switch to dolphin-safe tuna. The other manufacturers quickly followed suit.[65] Surprisingly, local home country pressure groups can affect trade. A Massachusetts state law denies state contracts to companies that do business in Myanmar (formerly Burma), because of that country's brutal dictatorship; Massachusetts is considering a similar law for Indonesia (over the repression in East Timor). Apple, Motorola, and Hewlett-Packard all cited the Massachusetts law when pulling out of

63. "The Corporation Haters," *Fortune*, June 16, 1980, p. 126.
64. For a detailed background on the infant formula issue, see Christopher Gale, George Taucher, and Michael Pearce, "Nestlé and the Infant Food Controversy," (A) and (B) (Lausanne: IMD; London, Ontario: University of Western Ontario, 1979).
65. "P&G Can Get Mad, but Does It Have to Get Even?" *Business Week*, June 4, 1990, p. 27.

Myanmar. The law probably violates the WTO Procurement Agreement of 1995, which requires open, nondiscriminatory government contracts. In addition, a U.S. District Court judge ruled that the Massachusetts law interferes with the federal government's right to set foreign policy; however, it is expected the dispute will be appealed by Massachusetts to the U.S. Supreme Court.[66]

Global marketers must continue to be on the lookout for pressures from home country pressure groups or governments. Global trade sanctions imposed unilaterally are likely to occur again but typically affect only marginal markets. Pressure groups with specific interests, such as animal protection groups, environmentalists, or other such focus organizations, are likely to be of greater importance as global marketing develops.

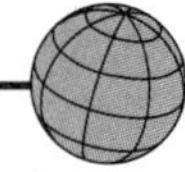

Sudden Changes in the Political Climate

The presence of political risk means that a foreign company can lose part or all of its investment in another country as a result of some political actions on the part of either the host country government or other pressure groups. The previous sections have detailed the various elements of political risk by describing the participants, their motivations, and their available options to participate and determine the political climate of a country. As we emphasized in the section on takeovers, the political climate of a country is hardly ever static. Instead, key decisions are often made during sudden and radical changes in the political climate of a host country. Sudden changes of power, especially when the new leadership is committed to a leftist economic and political philosophy, have frequently led to hostile political climates and takeovers. Such changes in government can happen as a result of open elections or unexpected coups d'état or revolutions.

The fall of the Iranian shah in 1980 is a typical example of a sudden change that caught many companies by surprise. The impact on U.S. business included a total of 3,848 claims of which 518 were for more than $250,000. The claims were being settled by The Hague Tribunal, which dispersed funds from $1 billion of Iranian assets, which were set aside after the release of the American diplomats who had been held hostage for fourteen months. The largest single settlement was $49.8 million, paid to R.J. Reynolds.[67] The damage was not only to U.S. companies. Many companies operating from Europe and Japan were forced to close either all or parts of their operations. The subsequent war between Iran and Iraq further limited the attractiveness of the area and caused additional losses to foreign investors.

66. "U.S. Court Hears Appeal of Massachusetts' Burma Law," *Dow Jones News Service*, May 4, 1999, p. 2.
67. "Slow Progress on Iran Claims," *New York Times*, November 14, 1984, pp. D1, D5.

For decades, sudden political change in a country meant sudden change in its economic policy, resulting in damage to global firms. As a result of the sweeping political change in eastern Europe since 1989, the splitting up of nations has actually been a dominant occurrence. The former Soviet Union has broken up into more than a dozen independent nations. Yugoslavia, as well, has disintegrated into several separate countries. More recently, Czechoslovakia ceased to exist as of January 1, 1993, resulting in two independent countries, the Czech Republic and Slovakia.[68] GTECH (based in the United States), the world's largest lottery company, negotiated with Czechoslovakia in 1991 following a successful negotiation for a computerized lottery contract with Poland. Talks with Czechoslovakia concluded in 1992, but implementation was delayed because of the daunting infrastructure problems with telecommunications. The sudden border cutting the country in half meant that even transporting simple personal computers across a city suddenly became an issue. GTECH had to renegotiate the contract and establish two systems with two different currencies. The backup center in Bratislava, the city that was the capital of Slovakia, also became the operations point for the new system for Slovakia. Both systems, now up and running, reached some 2,000 terminals in Czechia and 1,000 terminals in Slovakia.[69]

Faced with such a changing political climate, what can companies do? Globally active companies have reacted on two fronts. First, they have started to perfect their own intelligence systems to prevent being caught unaware when changes disrupt operations. Second, they have developed several risk-reducing business strategies that will help to limit the exposure, or losses, should a sudden change occur. The following sections will concentrate on these two solutions.

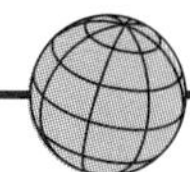

Political Risk Assessment

Because more than 60 percent of U.S.-based companies suffered some type of politically motivated damage between 1975 and 1980, many companies established systems to systematically analyze political risk.[70] To establish an effective political risk assessment (PRA) system, a company has to decide first on the objectives of the system. Another aspect concerns the internal organization, or the assignment of responsibility within the company. Finally, some agreement has to be reached on how the analysis is to be done.

68. Jean-Pierre Jeannet, "The Marketing Challenge in Eastern Europe," teaching note (European Case Clearing House), 1993.
69. "Two for One Split," *Providence Sunday Journal*, May 2, 1993, sec. F, p. 1.
70. "More Firms Are Hiring Own Political Analysts to Limit Risks Abroad," *Wall Street Journal*, March 30, 1981, p. 17.

Objectives of Political Risk Assessment

Potential risks have been described in detail in earlier sections of this chapter. Of course, companies everywhere would like to know about impending governmental instabilities so that no new investments will be placed in those countries. But even more important is the monitoring of existing operations and their political environment. Particularly with existing operations, not much is gained by knowing in advance of potential changes in the political climate unless such advanced knowledge can also be used for future action. As a result, political risk assessment is slowly moving from predicting events to developing strategies to help companies cope with changes. But first, political risk assessment has to deal with the potential political changes. Questions must be answered, such as, Should we enter a particular country? Should we stay in a particular country? What can we do with our operations in country X, given that development Y can occur?

Organization of Political Risk Assessment

In a study conducted in 1968 by the Conference Board, a U.S. research organization, more than half of the large U.S.-based global companies surveyed indicated that company internal groups were reviewing the political climate of both newly proposed and current operations. In companies that did not have any formalized systems for political risk assessment, top executives tended to obtain firsthand information through direct contact by traveling and talking with other businesspeople.[71]

This informal and unstructured approach once spelled trouble for a U.S. company. Eaton, a diversified U.S. manufacturer, built a plant in southern Normandy, France, that was notorious for its troublesome communist union.[72] If the company had known about the labor situation, it would never have built there, of course. As a result, Eaton established a group of full-time political analysts at its headquarters.

Since the 1980s, a number of organizations have developed risk assessment measurement systems. For example, *Institutional Investor* magazine surveys global financial advisors and rates every country on their creditworthiness on a scale of 0 to 100. These data are available to all subscribers.[73] The way Gulf Oil

71. Franklin Root, "U.S. Business Abroad and Political Risks," *MSU Business Topics*, Winter 1968, pp. 73–80; Stephen I. Kobrin et al., "The Assessment and Evaluation of Noneconomic Environments by American Firms: A Preliminary Report," *Journal of International Business Studies*, Spring–Summer 1980, pp. 32–47.
72. "The Multinationals Get Smarter About Political Risks," *Fortune*, March 24, 1980, p. 88.
73. Harvey D. Shapiro, "The World's a Dangerous Place," *Institutional Investor*, March 1999, vol. 33, no. 3, pp. 153–157.

was able to make use of its political risk assessment serves as an example of the power of correct information. Gulf's small team of analysts warned of the Iranian shah's probable fall several months before it was generally anticipated. The same group supported an exploration venture in Pakistan despite the Soviet invasion of Afghanistan that had just taken place. More risky was Gulf's decision to proceed with its operations in Angola. Prior to the civil war in Angola, Gulf's analyst foresaw that a Marxist group would emerge as the most powerful force among the three factions vying for control of the country. Gulf managers felt, however, that the Marxist government would provide both a stable and a reasonable government, so they decided to invest. Angola became one of Gulf's most important overseas production sources.[74]

Rather than rely on a centralized corporate staff, some companies prefer to delegate political risk assessment responsibility to executives or analysts located in the particular region. Exxon and Xerox both use their subsidiary and regional managers as a major source of information. The use of distinguished foreign policy advisers is practiced by others. Bechtel, the large California-based engineering company, made use of the services of Richard Helms, a former CIA director and U.S. ambassador to Iran. Henry Kissinger, a former U.S. secretary of state, has advised Merck, Goldman Sachs, and the Chase Manhattan Bank. General Motors and Caterpillar have also maintained outside advisory panels.[75]

Information Needs

Though expropriations and takeovers were a problem for companies in the past, companies now view other political actions as more dangerous. Some have seen delayed payments or restrictions on profit repatriation as the major problem.[76] Political stability, foreign investment climate, profit remittance, and taxation can all be more important than the fear of expropriation. In political risk assessment, it is suggested that international companies look for answers to six broad key questions:

1. How stable is the host country's political system?
2. How strong is the host government's commitment to specific rules of the game, such as ownership or contractual rights, given its ideology and power position?
3. How long is the government likely to remain in power?
4. If the present government is succeeded, how would the specific rules of the game change?

74. "Multinationals Get Smarter," p. 87.
75. Ibid.
76. "More Firms Are Hiring," p. 1.

5. What would be the effects of any expected changes in the specific rules of the game?

6. In light of those effects, what decisions and actions should be taken now?[77]

Another approach, used by an independent consultant on political risk, concentrated on viewing each country in terms of its political issues and the major political actors. The analysis was to determine which one of these actors would have the greatest influence with respect to important decisions.[78]

Several public or semipublic sources exist that regularly monitor political risk. The Economist Intelligence Unit (EIU), a sister company of the *Economist*, monitors some sixty countries on the basis of multiple factors. For 2000–2004, the top-ranked countries, in terms of business environment and low risk, are the Netherlands, the United Kingdom, the United States, and Canada. The bottom-ranked countries are Iraq, Iran, Nigeria, and the Ukraine.[79] The *International Country Risk Guide*, published monthly by Political Risk Services of East Syracuse, New York, includes financial, economic, and political risk forecasts and ratings for 130 countries.[80] The ratings vary from 100 (minimum risk) to 0 points for maximum risk. The indicators used include economic expectations versus reality, economic planning failures, political leadership, external-conflict risk, corruption in government, law-and-order tradition, political terrorism, and the quality of bureaucracy. The results of these rankings are shown in Table 4.2.

Different firms use different approaches and sources to assess political risk. Motorola often uses consultants to determine political risk. In 1987, for example, Motorola used consultants to evaluate the investment risk for a facility in a Southeast Asian country. A Far Eastern business information service reported on how other businesses were responding to the political climate. Another consultant analyzed financial risks. An academic analyzed factors relating to operating costs.[81]

What companies do with their assessments depends on the data they collect. Exxon, for one, integrated its political assessment with its financial plans; in cases where Exxon expects a higher political risk, the company may add 1 to 5 percent to its required return on investment.[82] Political risk assessment should also help the company stay out of a certain country when necessary. However, the collected data should be carefully differentiated so that the best decision can be made.

77. Bob Donath, "Handicapping and Hedging the Foreign Investment," *Industrial Marketing Management*, February 1981, p. 57.
78. "Multinationals Get Smarter," p. 98.
79. *Country Monitor*, Economic Intelligence Unit Limited, December 15, 1999, p. 12.
80. *International Country Risk Guide* (East Syracuse, New York: Political Risk Services, June 1997).
81. "How MNCs Are Aligning Country-Risk Assessment with Bottom-Line Concerns," *Business Global International Report to Managers of Worldwide Organizations*, June 1, 1987, pp. 169–170.
82. "Multinationals Get Smarter," p. 88.

TABLE 4.2

Country Risk, Ranked by Composite Risk Rating July 1999 Versus August 1998

Ranking 07/99	*Country*	*Composite Risk Rating 07/99*	*Composite Risk Rating 08/98*	*07/99 Versus 08/98**	*Rank in 08/98*
1	Luxembourg	88.9	92.0	−3.1	2
2	Singapore	88.0	88.8	−0.8	3
3	Finland	87.3	89.0	−1.7	3
3	Norway	87.2	92.5	−5.3	1
3	Switzerland	86.9	87.5	−0.6	5
3	Ireland	86.8	87.5	−0.7	5
7	Netherlands	86.0	87.8	−1.7	5
8	Denmark	84.7	87.8	−3.1	5
9	Taiwan	83.3	81.0	2.3	20
9	Austria	83.2	86.0	−2.8	9
9	United States	83.1	82.8	0.3	16
9	Germany	82.9	84.0	−1.1	10
9	Iceland	82.7	84.3	−1.6	10
14	Canada	82.4	83.5	−1.1	10
14	Sweden	81.8	83.8	−1.9	10
14	Brunei	81.8	83.0	−1.2	16
14	Botswana	81.7	79.3	2.5	26
14	Japan	81.5	81.0	0.5	20
19	Portugal	81.1	84.3	−3.2	10
20	United Kingdom	80.5	81.8	−1.3	18
20	Malta	80.4	80.8	−0.3	20
20	Australia	80.4	79.3	1.2	26
20	France	80.0	80.8	−0.7	20
24	Slovenia	79.1	NA	NA	NA
24	Namibia	78.6	77.3	1.4	38
26	Poland	78.0	81.3	−3.2	20
26	Belgium	77.5	82.0	−4.5	18
28	New Zealand	77.5	78.3	−0.8	32
28	El Salvador	77.4	76.0	1.4	41
28	Spain	76.5	79.3	−2.7	26
31	Costa Rica	76.5	76.5	0.0	38
31	Czech Republic	76.1	77.5	−1.4	32
31	Italy	76.0	83.8	−7.8	10
31	Kuwait	75.6	78.0	−2.4	32
31	United Arab Emirates	75.5	78.3	−2.7	32
36	Hungary	75.4	79.0	−3.6	26
36	Hong Kong	74.9	76.3	−1.3	41
36	Cyprus	74.6	79.0	−4.4	26
39	Lithuania	74.5	NA	NA	NA
39	Trinidad & Tobago	74.4	77.5	−3.1	32

TABLE 4.2

Country Risk, Ranked by Composite Risk Rating July 1999 Versus August 1998 (cont.)

Ranking 07/99	Country	Composite Risk Rating 07/99	Composite Risk Rating 08/98	07/99 Versus 08/98*	Rank in 08/98
39	Jordan	74.1	73.8	0.3	45
39	Greece	74.1	78.0	−3.9	32
39	Korea, Republic	73.8	68.0	5.8	67
44	China, Peoples' Republic	73.3	74.0	−0.7	45
44	Bahamas	72.7	79.5	−6.8	25
44	Argentina	72.7	74.3	−1.6	45
44	Dominican Republic	72.6	73.5	−0.9	45
48	Thailand	72.4	65.0	7.4	82
48	Slovak Republic	72.3	76.8	−4.5	38
48	Tunisia	72.2	73.3	−1.1	50
48	Bulgaria	72.1	66.0	6.1	77
48	Estonia	72.0	NA	NA	NA
48	Morocco	71.8	71.3	0.6	55
54	Oman	71.2	75.0	−3.8	43
54	Uruguay	71.2	73.0	−1.8	50
54	Bahrain	71.2	73.8	−2.5	45
54	Panama	71.0	73.3	−2.3	50
54	Latvia	70.9	NA	NA	NA
59	Malaysia	70.5	68.0	2.5	67
59	Syria	70.3	69.0	1.3	59
59	Jamaica	70.2	75.0	−4.8	43
59	Gabon	69.9	69.3	0.6	59
59	Philippines	69.8	68.5	1.3	59
64	Chile	69.1	79.0	−9.9	26
64	Croatia	68.8	NA	NA	NA
64	Guatemala	68.6	72.3	−3.6	53
64	Gambia	68.5	68.5	0.0	59
68	South Africa	68.4	69.8	−1.3	57
68	Mali	68.3	64.8	3.5	82
68	Saudi Arabia	68.3	72.3	−4.0	53
68	Mexico	67.8	67.5	0.3	67
68	Egypt	67.8	71.0	−3.2	55
68	Kazakstan	67.6	NA	NA	NA
68	Cote d'Ivoire	67.6	64.5	3.1	82
75	Peru	67.2	66.0	1.2	77
75	Iran	66.9	68.0	−1.1	67
77	Madagascar	66.3	64.5	1.8	82
77	Mongolia	66.0	67.0	−1.0	72
77	Suriname	66.0	66.8	−0.8	72

(continued)

TABLE 4.2

Country Risk, Ranked by Composite Risk Rating July 1999 Versus August 1998 (cont.)

Ranking 07/99	Country	Composite Risk Rating 07/99	Composite Risk Rating 08/98	07/99 Versus 08/98*	Rank in 08/98
77	Qatar	65.9	69.3	−3.3	59
77	Guyana	65.8	69.0	−3.2	59
82	Bolivia	65.1	70.0	−4.9	57
82	Paraguay	64.9	68.5	−3.6	59
84	Israel	64.4	69.0	−4.6	59
84	Papua New Guinea	64.1	67.3	−3.2	72
84	Burkina Faso	64.0	59.8	4.3	104
84	Uganda	63.8	64.3	−0.5	90
84	Bangladesh	63.8	66.0	−2.2	77
84	Sri Lanka	63.6	62.3	1.3	94
90	Senegal	63.3	64.5	−1.2	82
90	Ghana	63.0	62.3	0.8	94
90	Honduras	62.6	65.3	−2.7	82
93	Cameroon	62.3	61.8	0.5	94
93	Venezuela	61.8	66.0	−4.2	77
93	Zambia	61.8	61.0	0.8	103
93	Armenia	61.5	NA	NA	NA
93	Vietnam	61.5	63.0	−1.5	93
98	Guinea	61.3	61.5	−0.2	94
98	Yemen, Republic	61.3	66.0	−4.7	77
98	Kenya	61.3	61.8	−0.5	94
98	Libya	61.1	64.5	−3.4	82
98	Togo	61.0	60.3	0.8	104
98	India	60.8	63.5	−2.7	90
98	Malawi	60.8	64.8	−4.0	82
105	Cuba	60.1	62.0	−1.9	94
105	Niger	59.5	54.5	5.0	113
107	Albania	59.3	53.5	5.8	116
107	Belarus	58.6	61.5	−2.9	94
107	Mozambique	58.5	58.0	0.5	109
110	Brazil	57.8	67.8	−10.0	67
110	Nigeria	57.6	56.5	1.1	111
112	Ukraine	57.3	66.8	−9.5	72
112	Haiti	57.3	52.8	4.5	118
112	Tanzania	57.3	60.3	−3.0	104
112	Ethiopia	56.5	66.8	−10.2	72
116	Ecuador	56.4	62.0	−5.6	94
116	Myanmar	56.1	54.8	1.4	113
116	Azerbaijan	56.0	NA	NA	NA
119	Romania	54.6	62.3	−7.6	94

TABLE 4.2

Country Risk, Ranked by Composite Risk Rating July 1999 Versus August 1998 (cont.)

Ranking 07/99	Country	Composite Risk Rating 07/99	Composite Risk Rating 08/98	07/99 Versus 08/98*	Rank in 08/98
120	Turkey	53.7	51.3	2.4	119
121	Lebanon	52.8	55.8	−2.9	112
121	Colombia	52.7	60.0	−7.3	104
123	Algeria	52.1	58.5	−6.4	108
123	Zimbabwe	51.5	57.0	−5.5	110
123	Pakistan	51.5	54.8	−3.2	113
126	Nicaragua	51.3	53.8	−2.5	116
127	Russian Federation	50.0	63.8	−13.8	90
127	Moldova	49.5	NA	NA	NA
129	Congo, Republic	48.3	45.8	2.6	120
129	Guinea-Bissau	48.3	42.8	5.5	122
131	Indonesia	44.3	43.0	1.3	122
131	Liberia	43.5	41.0	2.5	124
133	Yugoslavia	42.1	38.8	3.4	126
134	Sudan	40.5	40.3	0.3	125
135	Iraq	39.9	38.8	1.2	126
136	Somalia	39.3	33.3	6.0	131
136	Angola	39.1	45.0	−5.9	121
136	Korea, D.P.R.	38.8	38.5	0.3	126
139	Congo, Dem. Republic	36.8	38.8	−2.0	126
140	Sierra Leone	36.0	33.5	2.5	130

Source: *International Country Risk Guide,* July 1999. Copyright © The PRS Group, L.L.C., East Syracuse, NY, USA.
NA: Data is not available for previous periods. Many of these countries have been reformed after the breakup of the U.S.S.R.
*The *International Country Risk Guide*, published monthly by Political Risk Services of East Syracuse, New York, includes financial, economic, and political risk forecasts and ratings for 130 countries. The ratings vary from 100 (minimum risk) to 0 points for maximum risk. The indicators used include economic expectations versus reality, economic planning failures, political leadership, external-conflict risk, corruption in government, law-and-order tradition, political terrorism, and the quality of bureaucracy.

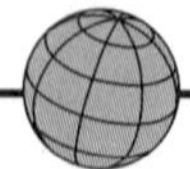

Risk Reduction Strategies

Determining or assessing political risk should not be a goal in itself. The value of political risk assessment is its integration of risk-reducing strategies that eventually enable companies to enter a market or remain in business. Many companies have experimented with different forms of ownership arrangements, production, and financing that were geared toward reducing political risks to an acceptable minimum. We will enlarge upon these alternatives with a discussion of the tools managers can use to deal with political risk rather than leave a market or refuse to enter one.[83]

Local Partners

Relying on local partners with excellent contacts among the host country governing elite is a strategy that many companies have used effectively. This could include from placing local nationals on the boards of foreign subsidiaries or accepting a substantial capital participation from local investors. For example, General Motors joined forces with Shanghai Automotive Industry Corporation (a state-owned firm) in a 50-50 joint venture to make Buicks, minivans, and compact cars. China's current tariffs on imported cars range from 80 to 100 percent, but they are expected to decline to 25 percent by 2005 as part of China's entry into the WTO. GM China has tailored the back seat, which is where the boss sits, with higher seats, more leg room, and its own radio and air conditioning controls.[84] Though many host countries require some form of local participation as a condition for entering their market, many foreign firms enlist local firms voluntarily. Diamond Shamrock, an U.S.-based company, built its chemical plant in South Korea with the help of a local partner to get more favorable operating conditions.[85]

Invaluable Status

Achieving a status of indispensability is an effective strategy for firms that have exclusive access to high technology or specific products. Such companies keep research and development out of the reach of their politically vulnerable subsidiaries and, at the same time, enhance their bargaining power with host governments by emphasizing their contributions to the economy. When Texas Instruments wanted to open an operation in Japan more than a decade ago,, the company was able, on the basis of its unique advanced technology, to resist pressures to take on a local partner. This occurred at a time when many other foreign companies were forced to accept local partners.[86] The appearance of being irreplaceable obviously helps reduce political risk.

Vertical Integration

Companies that maintain specialized plants, each dependent on the others in various countries, are expected to incur fewer political risks than firms with fully in-

83. The following sections are adapted from *Insurance Decisions*, published by the CIGNA companies, Philadelphia, 1996. Reprinted by permission.
84. "Investing in China Testing GM's Shock Absorbers Shanghai," *Economist*, May 1, 1999, p. 64.
85. "More Firms Are Hiring," p. 17.
86. Yves L. Doz and C. K. Prahalad, "How MNCs Cope with Host Government Intervention," *Harvard Business Review*, March–April 1980, p. 52.

tegrated and independent plants in each country. A firm practicing this form of distributed sourcing can offer economies of scale to a local operation. This can become crucial for success in many industries. If a host government were to take over such a plant, its output level would be spread over too many units, products, or components, thus rendering the local company uncompetitive because of a cost disadvantage. Further risk can be reduced by having at least two units engage in the same operation to prevent the company itself from becoming hostage to overspecialization. Unless multiple sourcing exists, a company could be virtually shut down if only one of its plants were affected negatively.

Local Borrowing

One of the reasons why Cabot Corporation prefers local partners is that it is then able to borrow locally instead of bringing foreign exchange to a host country.[87] Financing local operations from indigenous banks and maintaining a high level of local accounts payable maximize the negative effect on the local economy if adverse political actions were taken. Typically, host governments do not expropriate themselves, and they are reluctant to cause problems for their local financial institutions. Local borrowing, however, is not always possible, because of restrictions placed on foreign companies, which otherwise crowd local companies out of the credit markets.

Minimizing Fixed Investments

Political risk, of course, is always related to the amount of capital at risk. Given equal political risk, an alternative with comparably lower exposed capital amounts is preferable. A company can decide to lease facilities instead of buying them, or it can rely more on outside suppliers, provided they exist. In any case, companies should keep exposed assets to a minimum to limit damage due to political risk.

Political Risk Insurance

As a final recourse, global companies can purchase insurance to cover their political risk. With the political developments in Iran and Nicaragua in rapid succession and the assassinations of President Park of Korea and President Sadat of Egypt all taking place between 1979 and 1981, many companies began to change their attitudes on risk insurance. Political risk insurance can offset large potential losses. For example, as a result of the United Nations Security Council's worldwide embargo on Iraq until it withdrew from Kuwait, companies collected

87. "Multinationals Get Smarter," p. 98.

$100–$200 million from private insurers and billions from government-owned insurers.[88]

Companies based in the United States have two sources for such protection: government insurance and private insurance. The Overseas Private Investment Corporation (OPIC) was formed in 1969 by the U.S. government to facilitate the participation of private U.S. firms in the development of less developed countries. OPIC offers three kinds of political risk insurance in one hundred developing countries. The agency covers losses caused by currency inconvertibility, expropriation, and bellicose actions such as war and revolution.

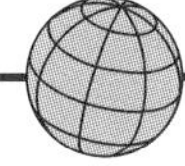

International and Global Legal Forces

In many ways, the legal framework of a nation reflects a particular political philosophy or ideology. Just as each country has its own political climate, so does the legal system change from country to country. The legal systems of the world are based on one of four sources—(1) common law derived from English law, found in the United Kingdom, the United States, Canada, and countries previously part of the English Commonwealth; (2) civil, or code, law based on the Roman law of written rules, found in non-Islamic and non-Marxist countries; (3) socialist law derived from the Marxist-socialist system, found in China and other socialist nations; and (4) Islamic law derived from the Koran, found in Iran, Iraq, Pakistan, and other Islamic nations. Thus, globally active companies find themselves in a situation in which they have to conform to more than one legal system. Although this is complicated enough, the difficulty in some cases of determining whose laws apply adds further to an already complex environment.

Here we discuss some of the current major legal challenges that require adjustment and consideration at the corporate level. In later chapters, we present the specific legal requirements covering certain aspects of the global marketing program. Such material appears in the chapters on pricing, advertising, and export mechanics, among others.

Of particular interest to us in this chapter are the laws pertaining to commercial behavior, such as laws against bribery and laws regulating competition and product liability. We also discuss the emergence of global courts.

Laws Against Bribery and Corrupt Practices

Though bribery in international business has been known to exist for years, the publicity surrounding some bribery scandals in the early 1970s caused a public furor in the United States about the practice. For example, in 1975 the U.S.-based company United Brands was accused of paying a bribe of $1.25 million in 1974 to

88. "Political Risk Insurers Fear Crisis Escalation," *Business Insurance*, 1990, vol. 24, no. 33a, p. 1.

a high government official in Honduras, later identified as that country's president,[89] to obtain a reduction of an export tax.

The Foreign Corrupt Practices Act (FCPA) of 1977 was intended to stop the payments of bribes. Though the act covers the whole range of record-keeping and control activities of a company both in the United States and abroad, its best-known section specifically prohibits U.S. companies, their subsidiaries, and representatives from making payments to high-ranking foreign government officials or political parties. The penalties for violation can be very stiff: an executive who violates the FCPA may be imprisoned for up to five years and fined up to $10,000. The company involved may be fined up to $1 million. Though the law prohibits outright bribery, small facilitating payments are not outlawed as long as they are made to government clerks without any policy-making responsibility.[90]

Bribery exists in both developed and less developed countries. In the United States, Salt Lake City officials used special funding to influence the Olympic site selection committee to pick their city for the 2002 Winter Olympics. The governments of Indonesia, Italy, Brazil, Pakistan, Zaire, and others have fallen partly because the people they governed no longer could stand having corrupt politicians.[91] The bribery scandals involving the construction industry in Japan and Italy are well known and have even led to enormous political change in those countries. In Italy, where bribing government officials by transferring large sums of money through their political parties was common, many leading politicians and business executives were jailed for the offense. One year later, bids for public works projects were reported to come in up to 40 percent below earlier cost estimates, and the Italian government is estimated to have saved up to $4.4 billion in 1994.[92] Other parts of the world in which bribery is common are China and Russia. In both countries, the changes toward more liberalization in trade have created opportunities for local officials to approve foreign investment. One source estimated that the "connection" payments in China amounted to 3 to 5 percent of operating costs of a project.[93]

IBM officials in Argentina allegedly paid $37 million in kickbacks for a $250 million contract with the state-owned Banco de la Nación. The officials involved have left IBM. This event followed charges in Mexico that IBM and city officials conducted an unlawful bidding process for the sale of a computer for the city's prosecutor's office. IBM settled the claim for $37 million, but the charges have

89. "Honduran Bribery," *Time*, April 21, 1975, p. 74.
90. Hurd Baruch, "The Foreign Corrupt Practices Act," *Harvard Business Review*, January-February 1979, p. 44.
91. "A Global War Against Bribery," *Economist*, January 1, 1999, p. 22.
92. "The Destructive Costs of Greasing Palms," *Business Week*, December 6, 1993, p. 133.
93. "Destructive Costs of Greasing Palms," p. 133.

not been dropped.[94] The two cases have cost IBM more than a loss of image. IBM lost the Banco de la Nación contract for $250 million as well as two contracts from the Argentina's tax authority worth $500 million. In July 1998, IBM said it would no longer bid on government contracts in Argentina or state contracts in other Latin American countries where it was the sole bidder. IBM headquarters has never admitted knowledge or responsibility for these events.[95]

Bribery is viewed differently by executives from various countries. In a 1993 survey in Asia, only 17 percent of Australian executives said they would offer a bribe (for business in Asia) if they risked losing a big sale. Japanese and U.S. executives had similar percentages at 27 and 22 percent. On the other hand, more than half of all Indonesian and Thai executives polled indicated they would bribe before losing an important client or deal. One expatriate executive noted that the Thai language does not have a word for bribe; they call it "commission."[96]

As a result of the difficulties in deciding which law applies, global companies have resorted to developing their own codes of ethics, particularly concerning bribes. When developing such a code, companies have to decide if they will apply one code worldwide or differentiate their standards by country or region. Experience over the past decade has shown that the level of ethical behavior is rising over time, and what was acceptable behavior at one time may suddenly be cause for prosecution under local laws. As a result, it makes sense for companies to adopt the highest available standard, even if it would not yet be the norm in a given country.

A number of studies have shown that corruption is closely linked to economic malpractice and that countries with high levels of corruption have lower economic investment and therefore lower economic growth rates. Higher corruption levels are also linked to lower investment in education, which pays big economic dividends. Shang-Jin Wei, a Harvard economist, argues that corruption acts as a tax on foreign investment. "An increase in the corruption level from that of Singapore to that of Mexico is equivalent to raising the tax rate by over 20 percentage points."[97]

A 1996 survey by the Hong Kong–based Political and Economic Risk Consultancy found that China, Vietnam, and Indonesia were the most corrupt. The lowest levels of corruption were reported for Switzerland, Australia, Singapore, the United States, and Britain. While most countries have laws aimed at fighting corruption, few apply them as strictly and consistently as does Singapore.[98]

94. "IBM's Last Tangle in Argentina," *Economist*, August 1, 1998, p. 31.
95. Ibid.
96. "Managing in Asia." Survey, *Far Eastern Economic Review*, September 16, 1993, p. 55.
97. "A Global War Against Bribery," *Economist*, January 1, 1999, p. 22.
98. "Singapore Remains a Graft-Free Haven," *Straits Times*, April 9, 1996, p. 3.

The thirty-four signatory nations of the Organization for Economic Cooperation and Development (OECD), which represent the world's largest economies, except China, agreed to adopt common rules to punish companies and individuals who bribe. Twelve countries have already changed their domestic laws to comply with the treaty, including Germany, Japan, the United States, the United Kingdom, and South Korea. It is too early to tell if the treaty and new laws will be effective, although the OECD will monitor the countries' antibribery laws and conduct audits to see it the laws are followed.[99]

Transparency International, an independent organization, tracks how public and global businesses view corruption in eighty-five countries. As of 1998, the ten least corrupt countries were Denmark, Finland, Sweden, New Zealand, Iceland, Canada, Singapore, the Netherlands, Norway, and Switzerland. At the bottom of the list were Cameroon, Paraguay, Honduras, Tanzania, Nigeria, Indonesia, Colombia, Venezuela, Ecuador, Russia, Vietnam, and Kenya. The United States was tied for seventeenth place from the top with Austria.[100]

Laws Regulating Competitive Behavior

Many countries have enacted laws that govern the competitive behavior of their firms. In some cases, as for the European Union, supranational bodies enforce their own laws. Unfortunately for global companies, these antitrust laws are frequently contradictory or differently enforced, adding great complexity to the job of the global executive. The United States, with its long-standing tradition of antitrust enforcement, has had considerable impact on the multinational operations of U.S. companies and is increasingly impacting those of foreign-based companies operating in the United States.

For example, Coca-Cola's proposed $1.75 billion takeover of Cadbury Schweppes PLC was reviewed by each of the European countries in which the company has operations, as well as by the European Commission.[101]

Competitors of Microsoft went to Mario Monti, the EU competition commission to protest that Microsoft's Windows 2000 was designed to extend its dominance in PC-operating systems, servers, and electronic commerce. If found guilty of breaking the EU competition laws, Microsoft can be forced to alter Windows 2000 or can be prohibited from selling in Europe, as well as fined up to 10 percent of their total worldwide revenue.[102] The EU has forced South Africa to phase

99. G. Pascal Zachary, "Industrial Countries to Adopt Rules to Curb Bribery," *Wall Street Journal*, February 16, 1999, p. A18.
100. Barbara Crossette, "Nations Rated by Corruption Level," *New York Times*, October 4, 1998, p. A4; the Corruption Perceptions Index can be found at www.transparency.de.
101. "Coke's Proposed Deal for Cadbury Brands Draws Probe by EC," *Wall Street Journal*, April 23, 1999, p. B10.
102. Michiyo Nakamoto, "Kodak Wins Deal to Sell Cut-Price Film in Japan," *Financial Times*, August 24, 1995, p. 5.

out the use of European regional names of alcoholic beverages, such as grappa, ouzo, port, and sherry by 2005.[103]

As of late, the European Union has its own merger task force to control mergers involving EU countries. During its first two years of existence, the task force dealt with 136 notifications. Of those, 103 dealt with short investigations of one month or less, and only a small percentage were fully investigated over four months.[104] In addition, the European Commission has proposed legislation to govern corporate mergers, acquisitions, and takeovers. DaimlerChrysler has been charged by the European Commission with violating antitrust rules by limiting dealers' ability to sell across borders from 1985 to 1996 in four European countries. If found guilty, DaimlerChrysler could be fined up to 10 percent of the worldwide sales in the year before the fine was levied. This could be as much as $142 billion, although the commission normally only fines 1 percent, which would still be a staggering $1.3 billion.[105]

Sometimes international firms can get caught between competing legal systems.[106] The recently proposed affiliation of British Airways and American Airlines has shown the potential need for a two-track approval process that would include both national and regional approval. Whereas the British authorities want the BA/AA alliance to sell 168 prime-time slots at Heathrow as a condition of approval, Karel Van Miert, the European competition commissioner, wants AA/BA to give up 230 Heathrow slots and reduce the number of flights to cities like New York. The U.S. Department of Transportation is expected to approve the deal if Britain and the United States agree on an open-skies air treaty that allows any carrier to fly between the two countries. The stumbling block had been the U.S. reluctance to allow foreign companies to offer domestic flights in the United States. Richard Branson, the owner of Virgin Atlantic Airways, is keen to offer a low-cost airline in the United States The AA/BA alliance may need to accommodate Mr. Branson.[107]

Product Liability

Though there are regulations or laws that directly affect all aspects of global marketing, regulations on product liability are included here because of their enormous impact on all firms. Specific regulatory acts, or laws, pertaining to other aspects of the marketing mix—namely pricing, distribution, and promotion—have been included in other chapters.

103. Nancy Dunne, "Exposed: Kodak's Path to the WTO," *Financial Times*, June 14, 1996, p. 5.
104. "Marriages Made in Brussels," *Financial Times*, January 19, 1993, p. 13.
105. Brandon Mitchener and Brian Coleman, "DaimlerChrysler May Face Stiff Fine Involving European Antitrust Rules," *Wall Street Journal*, April 15, 1999, p. A18.
106. "Mergers and Acquisitions: Blessed Are the Litigators," *Economist*, January 11, 1997, p. 68.
107. "Come Fly with Me: European and American Regulators Seem About to Approve Yet More Airline Alliances," *Economist*, June 20, 1998, p. 69.

Regulations on product liability are relatively recent in the United States. Other countries, as well, have laws on product liability; a major problem for global marketers is the differences in laws in different countries or regions. In the United States, product liability is viewed in the broadest sense, or along the lines of strict liability. For a product sold in defective condition that becomes unreasonably dangerous for the user, both producer and distributor can be held accountable.

Product liability laws have changed in Europe as well. In the mid-1970s, the European Commission (EC) proposed a set of regulations that was to supersede each member country's laws. Traditionally, the individual country laws had been rather lax by U.S. standards. In the United States, the plaintiff must prove that the product was defective at the time it left the producer's hand, whereas under the EC guidelines, manufacturers must prove that the product was not defective when it left their control. Nevertheless, there are differences due to the different legal and social systems. In the EU, trials are decided by judges and not common jurors. And the existing extensive welfare systems will automatically absorb many of the medical costs that are subject to litigation in the United States. Furthermore, it is typical for the loser in a court judgment in Europe to bear the legal costs. In the case of product liability cases, if a company is found to owe damages to a plaintiff, then it also will have to pay the plaintiff's legal costs according to typical fee standards. This differs substantially from the U.S. system, in which a winning plaintiff's lawyer typically is compensated through a predetermined percentage of the awarded damages, a practice that in the eyes of many experts has raised award damages and, as a result, liability insurance costs.

The rapid spread of product liability litigation, however, forces companies with global operations to review their potential liabilities carefully and to acquire appropriate insurance policies. Although an global marketing manager cannot be expected to know all the respective rules and regulations, executives must nevertheless anticipate potential exposure and, by asking themselves the appropriate questions, make sure that their firms consider all possible scenarios.

Bankruptcy Laws

Bankruptcy laws vary from country to country. In the United Kingdom, Canada, and France, the laws of bankruptcy favor the creditors. When a firm enters bankruptcy, an administrator is appointed. The administrator's job is to recover the creditors' money. In the United States, bankruptcy tends to protect the business from the creditors. Under Chapter 11 of the Federal Bankruptcy Code, the management prepares a reorganization plan, which is voted on by the creditors. In Germany and Japan, bankruptcies are often handled by the banks behind closed doors. The national bankruptcy systems have a wide variety of standards of openness to others. Also, creditor preference varies from country to country. For example, Swiss law gives preference to Swiss creditors. There is a need for a global bankruptcy law, but until establishment of world accountancy standards, there is little chance of a global bankruptcy code.[108]

Patents, Trademarks, and Copyrights

Patents and trademarks are used to protect products, processes, and symbols. Patents and trademarks are issued by each individual country, so marketers must register every product in every country they intend to trade in. The International Convention for the Protection of Industrial Property, honored by forty-five countries, gives all nationals the same privileges when applying for patents and trademarks. Also, the agreement gives patent coverage for one year after the trademark or patent is applied for in one country, thus limiting pirating of the product in other countries.

The United States has an extensive patent system open to anyone. The top ten companies receiving U.S. patents in 1997, in order of number received, were IBM, Canon, NEC, Motorola, Fujitsu, Hitachi, Mitsubishi, Toshiba, Sony, and Eastman Kodak. It is interesting to note that of the top ten patenting companies, only three were U.S. firms—the remainder were all Japanese.[109]

It does not seem, however, that all countries have open and accessible patent systems. It took AlliedSignal eleven years to get a patent on amorphous metal alloys approved in Japan. AlliedSignal alleges that the Japanese patent office dragged its feet while the Ministry for Trade and Industry (MITI) launched a catch-up program with thirty-four Japanese companies.[110] The patent system in Japan is slow and tends to pressure companies to reach agreements rather than assign penalties, so it is not surprising to see many of the Japanese firms using the United States to protect their intellectual knowledge. For example, Fujitsu is suing South Korea's Samsung over semiconductor patents before the U.S. International Trade Commission.[111] Smith Kline Beecham has gone to court in India to challenge the use of its zigzag toothbrush handle design by Hindustan Lever and three other Indian companies. Smith Kline Beecham has a very weak case as it did not register its design in India until 1993. Kewalraj of Mumbai, a local supplier, had already registered the design, which was subsequently purchased by Hindustan Lever.[112] Patent officials from Japan, U.S., Europe, and Canada met in Tokyo in May 1999 to discuss a global patent system whereby patents would be recognized

108. "Bankruptcy Laws," *Economist*, February 24, 1990, pp. 93–94.
109. "Intellectual Property: Big Business for Global Corporations," *Hindu*, December 9, 1998, p. 2.
110. "American-Japanese Trade—Low Tricks in High Tech," *Economist*, September 29, 1990, p. 90.
111. Jim Landers, "Many Japanese Firms Protect Patents in the United States," *Dallas Morning News*, September 23, 1998, p. 2.
112. "Patent Protection: India's Toothbrush War," *Economist*, November 23, 1996, p. 77.

in other countries. The global patent system was discussed at the 1999 WTO talks in Seattle.[113]

Pirating of products became a significant problem in the 1980s, affecting computers, watches, designer clothes, and industrial products. The sale of counterfeit goods ranging from Louis Vuitton bags and Rolex watches to car parts and medicines was estimated to be a hefty $150 billion a year. Patents, trademarks, and pirating will be discussed in more detail in Chapter 13.

Copyright laws and violations are also becoming an increasing concern for international executives. Disney entered China with its Chinese-speaking Mickey and Donald in 1987 but withdrew from the market in 1990 after rampant copyright violations. Following the passing of a new and stricter copyright law, Disney reentered the Chinese market in 1993. China's main draw is its 20 million births per year. Its one-baby policy also seems to have had a positive affect on Disney sales because families spend one-third to one-half of their disposable income on children, as each child enjoys the full attention of two parents and four grandparents.[114]

The worldwide cost of software piracy is estimated to be $11.4 billion, with 96 percent of Chinese software being pirated, compared with 77 percent in eastern Europe and 27 percent in the United States.[115] Microsoft won $100,000 in a lawsuit against two companies in China—a small amount compared with the $1.0 billion Microsoft estimates it has lost to pirated software in China. However, Microsoft believes that the Chinese government is serious about stopping piracy in China, having raided 70 to 80 factories in 1997 and confiscated their CD presses.[116]

U.S. businesses report they lose almost $2.5 billion to Chinese pirating of motion pictures, books, records, music, software, and video games. China's State Council on Intellectual Property reports it has destroyed 800,000 audio/video cassettes and 40,000 software programs and that it has levied fines of $3 million in 9,000 cases of trademark violation.[117] Although the information superhighway offers numerous opportunities for information exchange, the role of software patents, royalties, and encryption technology must be resolved. In 2000, China required that all Internet content providers have secure systems before they could receive licenses. The new rules were imposed to reduce leakage of state secrets but were expected to slow down the growth of the Internet in China.[118]

113. "Patents Officials See Need for Global Patent System," *Dow Jones International News*, May 20, 1999, p. 1.
114. Kathy Chen, "Chinese Babies Are Coveted Consumers," *Wall Street Journal*, May 15, 1998, p. B1.
115. "Software Piracy," *Economist*, June 27, 1998, p. 108.
116. "The Politics of Piracy," *Economist*, February 20, 1999, p. 64.
117. Tony Walker, "Chinese Lesson," *Financial Times*, February 23, 1995, p. 14.
118. James Kynge, "China Threatens Internet Operators with Secrecy Code, *Financial Times,* January 27, 2000, p. 1.

The importance of the copyright law for software also reached international trade discussion when the Japanese government began considering a change in the law that would allow Japanese companies to reengineer all software to make compatible products, even when the U.S. supplier would not authorize it.[119] Because of its importance to firms that depend on copyright protection, such as in the music, video, publishing, and software industries, international firms will have to pay increased attention to the enforcement of copyright law.

With counterfeiting and related infringements on the rise, companies must develop strategies to reduce their damaging effects. Possible responses are to (1) do nothing if the effect is minimal; (2) coopt the distributors through acquisition or licensing; (3) educate customers as to the value of "the real McCoy" through advertising; (4) investigate and bring legal action; (5) join coalitions like the International Anti-Counterfeiting Coalition, which brings pressure on governments and perpetrators; (6) use advanced technology such as special ink or raised letters that are difficult to copy; (7) continue to enhance the brand with new products, making it difficult for pirates to keep up.[120]

Regulatory Trends Affecting Global Marketing

In the past, international firms had to spend a large amount of energy to protect themselves from negative political decisions. Political risk consisted largely of losing operating freedom or, in the worst case, losing the asset in a country. The tremendous political change that has swept through the world over the past few years has actually brought an opening of trade and led to many more opportunities than in any five-year period since World War II. The key political events of total change in eastern Europe and the opening of countries such as China have significantly broadened the geographic boundaries within which international firms are allowed to participate.

Three major trends emerge, each present to different degrees in some parts of the world. The first such trend, *trade liberalization*, meaning the opening of many countries to international trade, has swept many formerly "locked" countries. Although this has clearly been the case in the formerly socialist countries of eastern Europe, trade liberalization and the corresponding opening of borders to imports and exports have also been of great importance in the emerging and developing economies. The second trend of importance is *deregulation*. This trend covers the various government actions aimed at allowing market forces more influence; it has resulted in a reduction of regulatory activities primarily in

119. "Decompilation: A Divisive Issue," *Nikkei Weekly*, December 20, 1993, p. 8.
120. Clifford J. Shultz and Bill Saporito, "Protecting Intellectual Property: Strategies and Recommendations to Deter Counterfeiting and Brand Piracy in Global Markets," *Columbia Journal of World Business*, Spring 1996, pp. 18–28.

the western economies but also elsewhere in the world. Finally, *privatization*, a third major trend, is today engulfing mostly the countries of eastern Europe. Governments in many countries are turning over ownership of companies, services, and agencies to private investors. We now look at each of these trends in greater detail in an effort to understand how they have affected the global marketing strategies.

Trade Liberalization In the early 1980s, international trade with large parts of the world was very restricted. The governments of eastern Europe, most of Latin America, and many Asian countries such as China and India tightly controlled what could be imported and thus severely restricted business opportunities for global firms. Chile, Mexico, and Argentina, however, began to open their borders to imports in the mid-1980s. Imports were expected to compete with high-priced local products; the resulting economic growth was then expected to lead to more export opportunities. In Mexico, this process started in 1986, when the country joined GATT. As a result, average tariffs were reduced from 22 to 9 percent, and import quotas and other trade limitations were eliminated.[121] This greatly expanded the market opportunities for foreign firms in Mexico from $12.5 billion to almost $40 billion in 1991.[122] The change required adjustments by global firms. Previously, any company that wanted to market its products in Mexico had to have a local production base. Now that imports are freely allowed, Cummins, a U.S.-based diesel engine manufacturer, reduced local production and is now exporting most products from its U.S. plants.[123]

India is another country that has turned to international trade liberalization in a major way. Following the initial trade liberalization in 1991, several steps were taken to make India a more attractive place for global firms to invest, including a much freer regulation of foreign exchange, permission to use foreign brand names where these were previously not permitted, and the right to raise equity stakes to 51 percent in many sectors.[124] As a result of the opening of India, many global firms have entered or reentered the Indian market, including Coca-Cola and Pepsi-Cola, the U.S. investment-banking firm of Morgan Stanley, Peugeot of France, Procter & Gamble, and General Electric.[125] Similar developments have led to trade liberalization between China and the rest of the world, including most of eastern Europe, as a result of the political changes that have swept through that area since 1989.[126]

121. "Across the Rio Grande," *Economist*, October 9, 1993, p. 67.
122. *World Competitiveness Report, 1993*, p. 223.
123. "No Such Thing as a Free Treaty," *Financial Times*, November 11, 1993, p. 13.
124. "Back in Charge," *Far Eastern Economic Review*, July 8, 1993, p. 8.
125. "India Clears Some Foreign Investments, Sending Bullish Signal on Reform Drive," *Wall Street Journal*, June 24, 1993.
126. "Cracking the China Market," Wall Street Journal Reports, *Wall Street Journal*, December 10, 1993; "China," Financial Times survey, *Financial Times*, November 18, 1993.

Deregulation A second trend affecting global marketing is the rapid deregulation of business everywhere. The United States is generally considered to have taken the lead with its deregulation of several industries, particularly transportation, airlines, banking, and telecommunications. The general ideas of deregulation were readily absorbed by some other governments, the United Kingdom among them. As part of the European integration drive, culminating in the "Europe 1992" initiative, deregulation also became an important issue in Europe. Typically, deregulation not only acts as a barrier to government intervention but also helps in opening doors to international competition.

The European Union is slowly opening its telecommunications market. The long-held monopolies of the national telephone companies in most European countries are to give way to more open competition along the U.S. and U.K. models. Although data communication has already been deregulated, the trend now is to include regular voice communications as well. Sprint and France Telecom are working together, and MCI WorldCom and Qwest International are setting up high-speed networks in Europe.[127] Deregulation will bring more competition, as the local phone companies can no longer count on their monopolies. It will also open up opportunities for other carriers, such as AT&T from the United States and the various regional operating companies. In mobile communications, these U.S. firms have already penetrated the market, usually linking up with local partners that were not previously active in telecommunications.

Similar efforts are under way in Asia, where telecommunications markets are growing rapidly. AT&T and British Telecom have taken a 30 percent ownership in Japan Telecom, the third-largest player in Japan.[128] Other efforts have taken place in financial markets, where substantial deregulation is under way in banking and insurance. The opening of Japanese financial markets, particularly with respect to financial derivatives, is of importance to international banks.[129] Deregulation is typically accompanied by liberalization and the opening of markets for foreign competitors. This trend, therefore, adds to the set of opportunities encountered by international firms.

Privatization The third trend affecting global marketing is the current rush toward privatization. Under privatization, countries sell government-owned agencies, organizations, and companies to private stockholders or other acquiring firms. Starting in the late 1970s and early 1980s, acts of privatization overtook nationalizations, and for the period 1990–1992, the United Nations counted more than 150 privatizations.[130] Some of the earliest examples of privatization came

127. "European Telecoms in a Tangle," *Economist*, April 24, 1999, p. 61.
128. "AT&T and BT Negotiate for 30% Joint Stake in Japan Telecom," *Wall Street Journal*, March 22, 1999, p. A4.
129. "Battle to Open Tokyo Markets Heats Up," *Wall Street Journal*, June 2, 1993, p. C1.
130. *World Investment Report 1993: TNCs and Integrated Production* (New York: United Nations Conference on Trade and Development, United Nations, 1993), p. 17.

from the United Kingdom, where the government privatized airlines (British Airways), telecommunications companies (British Telecom), and many utilities (British Airport Authority).

Privatization has swept through over one hundred countries, which have privatized 75,000 state-owned companies. The results have been good in central and eastern Europe as well as the Baltic States. The results have been poor in Russia, Armenia, Georgia, Kazakhstan, Moldova, Mongolia, and Ukraine. The International Monetary Fund (IMF) reports that much of the failures of privatization came from the turning over of mediocre assets to a large number of people who had neither the skills nor the financial resources to use them well. The urge to privatize gained steam as the formerly socialist countries of eastern Europe began to convert to a market economy.[131] The drive toward privatization was particularly strong in Poland, the Czech Republic, and Hungary. Philip Morris, the U.S.-based food and tobacco company, was able to acquire a stake in Czechia's Tabak, a company with a tobacco monopoly. The Czech government indicated that the monopoly would eventually end; however, Philip Morris expected to get a head start through the acquisition. Many privatizations in Poland and the Czech Republic occurred through the distribution of shares, or coupons, to the local population. Nevertheless, the effort to privatize state industry in many parts of Eastern Europe has resulted in significant opportunities for acquisitions for foreign firms. In Hungary, more than half of the revenue earned by the government through privatization came from foreign investors.[132]

Privatization has also become more common in other parts of the world. Argentina privatized almost its entire state holdings in a period of three years ending in 1993. This resulted in a net inflow of $19.1 billion for the sale of airlines, oil companies, gas companies, and other industrial firms.[133] Other privatization occurred in Brazil, where the government expects to raise $14 billion from the sale of Comgas, Cesp-São Paulo, three electric utilities, and Banespa S.A.[134]

Privatization is also coming in a big way to western governments, where some countries have held industrial stakes for a long time. France and Italy, with long traditions for industrial holdings, privatized some of their state-controlled industrial firms.[135] For example, the French sold 49 percent of France Telecom for FFR 150–200 billion![136] In Italy, privatization affected large banks and many state-run oil and chemical companies.[137]

The trend toward privatization is expected to continue, with some 1,300 separate deals anticipated worldwide, not including any activity in eastern Europe.

131. John Nellis, "Time to Rethink Privatization in Transition Economies," *Finance and Development*, June 1999, vol. 36, no. 2, pp. 16–18.
132. "Hungary's Privatization Falters After Flying Start," *Financial Times*, October 19, 1993, p. 4.
133. "Buying into Argentina Was the Easy Bit," *Financial Times*, December 7, 1993, p. 5.
134. Peter Fritsch, 'Brazil Resumes Its Drive to Privatize," *Wall Street Journal*, April 13, 1999, p. A10.
135. "State-Run Groups Get Used to New Identity," *Financial Times*, January 24, 1994, p. 13.
136. "Privatisation Takes French Leave," *Economist*, December 9, 1995, p. 59.
137. "After the Scandals, a Vast Sell-Off," *Business Week*, November 22, 1993, p. 56.

Whenever privatization occurs, it is typically related to a decreasing involvement of the local government in that particular industry or sector. This invariably leads to further trade liberalizations and deregulations. Both phenomena generate increased opportunities for global companies.

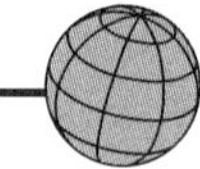

Conclusions

In this chapter we have outlined the major political and regulatory forces facing global companies. Our approach was not so much to identify and list all possible influences or actions that may have an impact on global marketing operations. Instead, we have provided only a sample of potential acts. It is up to executives with global responsibility to devise structures and systems that deal with these environmental influences. What is important to our discussion is to recognize that companies can adopt risk reduction strategies to compensate for some of these risks, but certainly not for all of them. For effective global marketing management, executives must be forward looking, anticipate potentially adversarial *or* positive changes in the environment, and not wait until changes occur. To accomplish these goals, systematic monitoring procedures that encompass both political and legal developments must be implemented.

The necessity of such monitoring for global firms has been demonstrated throughout this chapter. The past ten years have brought enormous political changes to this world, changes that are affecting the global marketing operations of global firms. Although these changes have resulted in the opening of many previously closed markets, numerous uncertainties remain. In many parts of the world, the existing trend toward open market economies is still questionable; substantial political and regulatory risks remain for many countries. Past experience has shown, however, that the traditional purpose of assessing political risk—to ensure that assets of firms would not be lost through takeovers or other arbitrary host government decisions—will have to give way to finding the true opportunities that might exist. As a result, the approaches and processes traditionally used by global firms to assess political risk will have to be redirected at political opportunity assessment.[138]

QUESTIONS FOR DISCUSSION

1. The construction industry in Japan has traditionally been dominated by domestic suppliers, with few foreign construction companies winning projects in Japan. What aspects of Japan's political forces may have influenced this control over the Japanese construction market? What political or legal forces may lead to the opening of this market for foreign firms?

138. Ideas expressed to authors by Clifton Clarke, retired vice president for global trade at Digital and now an independent consultant.

2. How successful has the opening of public procurement markets in Europe been? Why?
3. How could a country develop its own expertise in a product that is primarily imported—for example, automobiles in Egypt?
4. Develop a political risk analysis for a country of your choice. In which direction is the country going, and what effects would that have on global firms operating there?
5. What are the different methods a company can use to obtain and/or develop political risk assessment information?
6. John Deere has decided to enter the tractor market in Central America. What strategies could it use to reduce the possible effects of political risk?
7. While you are attempting to deliver a large computer system (selling price $1.4 million) to a foreign government, the minister of transportation advises you that a fee of $20,000 is required to ensure proper coordination of the customs clearance delivery process. What would you do?

FOR FURTHER READING

Akhter, Humayum, and Robert F. Lusch. "Political Risk and the Evolution of the Control of Foreign Business: Equity, Earnings, and the Marketing Mix." *Journal of Global Marketing*, Spring 1988, pp. 109–127.

Brouthers, K. D.; L. E. Brouthers; and G. Nakos. "Entering Central and Eastern Europe: Risk and Cultural Barriers." *Thunderbird International Business Review*, Sept-Oct 1998, Vol. 40, no 5. pp. 482–505.

Doz, Yves L., and C. K. Prahalad. "How Multinational Corporations Cope with Host Government Intervention." *Harvard Business Review*, March–April 1980, pp. 149–157.

Encarnation, Dennis J., and Sushil Vachani. "Foreign Ownership: When Hosts Change the Rules." *Harvard Business Review*, September-October 1985, pp. 152–160.

Erb, Claude B.; Campbell R. Harvey; and Tadas E. Viskanta. "Political Risk, Economic Risk, and Financial Risk." *Financial Analysts Journal*, November/December 1996, pp. 29–46.

Fukuyama, Francis. "Managing Global Chaos: Sources of and Responses to Global Conflict." *Foreign Affairs*, March/April 1997, pp. 175–185.

Harvey, Michael G., and Ilkka A. Ronkainen. "International Counterfeiters: Marketing Success Without the Cost and the Risk." *Columbia Journal of World Business*, Fall 1985, pp. 37–45.

Hauptman, Gunter. "Intellectual Property Rights." *International Marketing Review*, Spring 1987, pp. 61–64.

Huntington, Samuel P. "The Clash of Civilizations?" *Foreign Affairs*, 1993, Vol. 72, no. 3, pp. 22–49.

Huntington, Samuel P., and Myron Weiner. *Understanding Political Development*. Boston: Little, Brown, 1987.

Kim, Chan W. "Competition and the Management of Host Government Intervention." *Sloan Management Review*, Spring 1987, pp. 33–39.

Lodge, George C., and Erza F. Vogel. *Ideology and National Competitiveness*. Boston: Harvard Business School Press, 1987.

Marwick, Sandy. "The Outlook for Global Risk in 1997." *Risk Management*, November 1996, pp. 48–55.

O'Byrne, Shannon Kathleen. "Economic Justice and Global Trade: An Analysis of the Libertarian Foundations of the Free Trade Paradigm." *American Journal of Economics & Sociology*, January 1996, pp. 1–15.

Raddock, David M. *Assessing Corporate Political Risk*, Totowa, N.J.: Roowman & Littlefield, 1986.

Vogl, Frank. "Supply Side of Global Bribery." *IMF Publications Series*, June 1998, Vol. 35, no. 2, pp. 14–17.

Whitcomb, L. L.; C. B. Erdener; and C. Li. "Business Ethical Values in China and the U.S." *Journal of Business Ethics* (Netherlands), June 1998, Vol. 17, no. 8, pp. 839–853.

II Analyzing Global Marketing Opportunities

COMPETENCE LEVEL	GLOBAL ENVIRONMENT
ENVIRONMENTAL COMPETENCE	*Understanding the Global Marketing Environment* 2 3 4
ANALYTIC COMPETENCE	*Analyzing Global Marketing Opportunities* 5 6
STRATEGIC COMPETENCE	*Developing Global Marketing Strategies* 7 8 9
FUNCTIONAL COMPETENCE	*Designing Global Marketing Programs* 10 11 12 13 14 15
MANAGERIAL COMPETENCE	*Managing the Global Marketing Effort* 16 17 18

5 *Global Markets and Buyers*

6 *International and Global Marketing Research*

The Global Marketplace includes between 175 and 200 countries or territories. Global companies are constantly searching for the most appropriate markets and the best opportunities for their firms. Analyzing, classifying, and selecting opportunities for future business is an important aspect of global marketing management. In Part 2, we concentrate on the skills necessary to do this job well.

Chapter 5 provides concepts for analyzing opportunities within countries and groups of countries. We discuss the major market segments within each country's consumer, industrial, and government sectors and analyze the differences in these segments from market to market. The next chapter of this section, Chapter 6, covers the methods by which global companies collect market data and discusses ways to analyze this market research data for decision making.

We have given this section a largely analytic focus. Our aim in doing this has been to encourage analytic competence, which is necessary for success in global marketing.

5

Global Markets and Buyers

ASSESSMENT OF MARKET OPPORTUNITIES IS AN IMPORTANT ASPECT OF GLOBAL marketing. Every time a company decides to expand into foreign markets, it must systematically evaluate possible markets to identify the country or group of countries with the greatest opportunities. This process of evaluating worldwide opportunities is complicated for a number of reasons. First, there are between 175 and 210 countries and territories in the world; obviously, it is difficult to examine all these opportunities. Second, given the number of countries and resource limitations, the initial screening process is usually limited to the analysis of published data. Third, many possible markets are small, with little data available about specific consumer, business, or government needs.

Potential buyers often vary from country to country. The buyer can be a consumer, a business, or a government. The challenge for the global marketer is to recognize the differences while looking for the similarities that cut across markets. This chapter will identify the characteristics of different buyers.

In this chapter, outlined in Figure 5.1, we first discuss the process for selecting markets, both the selection techniques and the selection criteria. Then, to illustrate the screening process, we present a detailed case study of how this process can be used to select a market for dialysis equipment. In the final sections of the chapter, we discuss the rationale for grouping countries together and present the market groups in existence around the world today. Last, we discuss the variables influencing the different types of buyer: consumer, business, and government.

FIGURE 5.1

International Market Selection

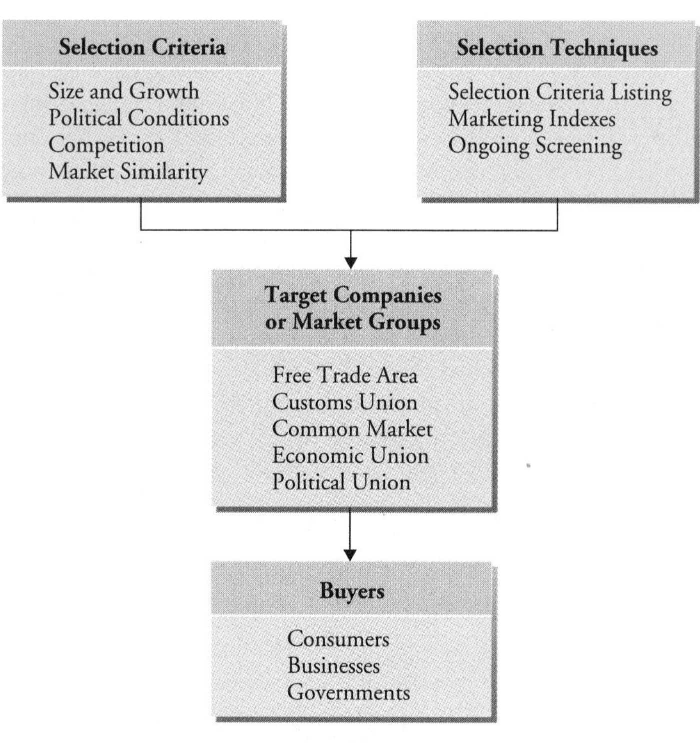

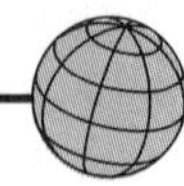

Screening Global Marketing Opportunities

Selection Stages

The assessment of global marketing opportunities usually begins with a screening process that involves gathering relevant information on each country and filtering out the less desirable countries. A model for selecting foreign markets is shown in Figure 5.2.

The model includes a series of four filters to screen out countries. The overwhelming number of market opportunities makes it necessary to break the process down into a series of steps. Although a firm does not want to miss a potential opportunity, it cannot conduct extensive market research studies in every country of the world. (The *World Bank Atlas* includes 206 countries and territories.)[1] The screening process is used to identify good prospects. Two common errors of country screening are (1) ignoring countries that offer good potential for the company's products and (2) spending too much time investigating countries that are poor prospects.[2] Thus, the screening process allows a global company to focus efforts quickly on a few of the most promising market opportunities by using published secondary sources available through online databases and websites.[3]

The first stage of the selection process uses macrovariables to discriminate between countries that represent basic opportunities and countries with little or no opportunity or with excessive risk. Macrovariables describe the total market in terms of economic, social, geographic, and political information. Often macroeconomic statistics indicate that the country is too small, as described by the gross national (or domestic) product. Possibly the gross national product seems large enough, but the personal disposable income per household may be too low. Political instability can also be used to remove a country from the set of possible opportunities.

In the second stage of the selection process, variables are used that indicate the potential market size and acceptance of the product or similar products. Often proxy variables are used in this screening process. A *proxy variable* is a similar or related product that indicates a demand for your product. For example, if you are attempting to measure the potential market size and receptivity for a palm-held communicator, possible proxy variables may be the number of telephone lines per person, personal computers per person, or cellular telephone usage. The number of telephone lines and cellular phones indicates communication needs, and the number of personal computers indicates a propensity to use advanced technologies. For example, the number of phone lines per 1,000 people is 661 in the United States, 570 in France, 554 in Finland, and 336 in Hungary.

1. *World Bank Atlas* 2000 (Washington, D.C.: World Bank, 2000).
2. Franklin R. Root, *Entry Strategies for Global Market* (New York: Jossey-Bass, 1998), p. 33.
3. See C. Samuel Craig and Susan P. Douglas, *International Marketing Research* (New York: John Wiley & Sons, 2000), pp. 66–67 and 100–102, for a detailed listing of secondary sources of information.

FIGURE 5.2

A Model for Selecting Foreign Markets

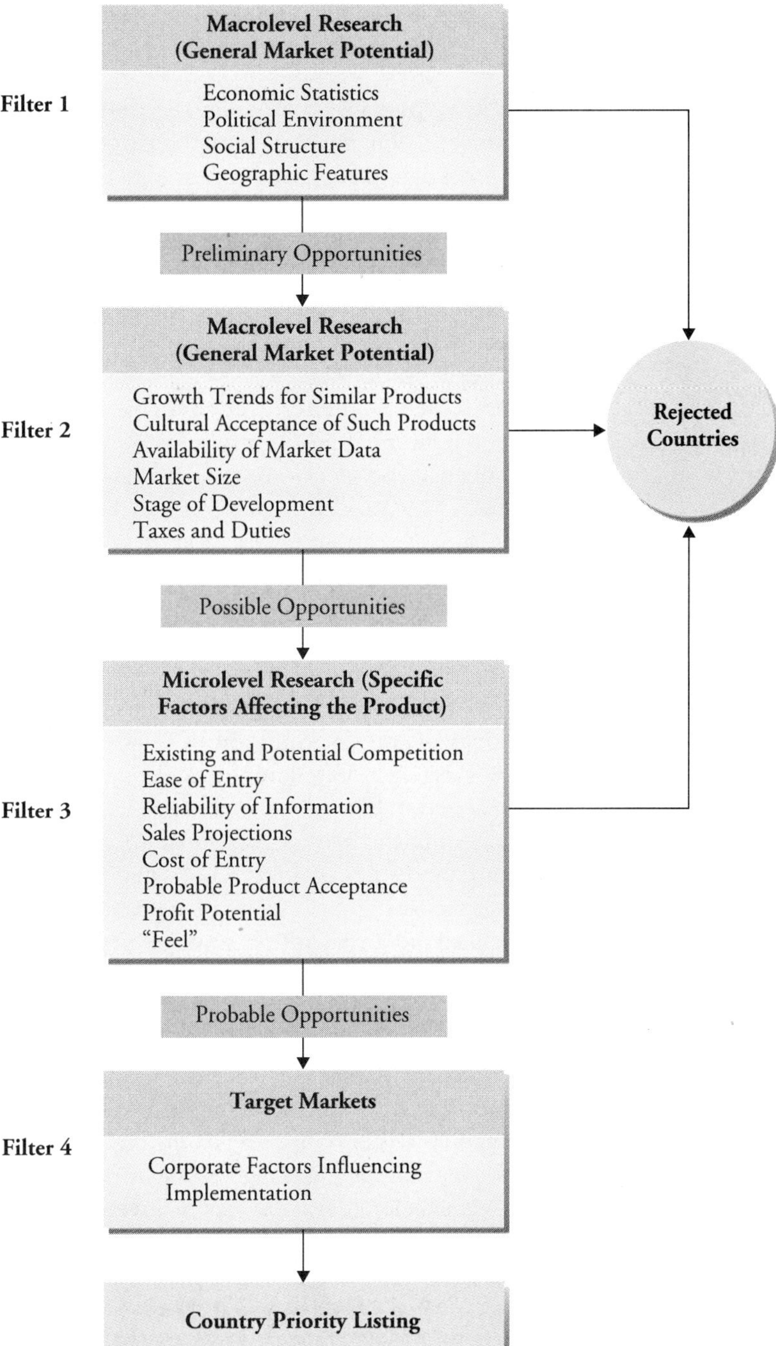

Source: R. Wayne Walvoord, "Export Market Research," *Global Trade Magazine*, May 1980, p. 83. Reprinted by permission.

The number of personal computers per 1,000 people is 459 in the United States, 208 in France, 349 in Finland, and 59 in Hungary. This indicates that Finland may be more receptive to advanced technology than France.[4] The year-to-year growth rates and the total sales of similar or proxy products are good predictors of market size and growth. Other factors in the second stage of the selection process can also be used to screen out countries, such as the stage of economic development, taxes, and duty requirements. If you do not plan to manufacture locally, a high import duty may eliminate a country from consideration in the second stage of the screening process.

The third stage of the screening process focuses on microlevel considerations such as competitors, ease of entry, cost of entry, and profit potential. Microlevel factors influence the success or failure of a specific product in a specific market. At this stage of the process, marketers may be considering only a small number of countries, so it is feasible to get more detailed, up-to-date information from the U.S. Department of Commerce, the U.S. State Department, and other companies currently operating in that country. The International Trade Administration of the Department of Commerce has an office in most major cities of the world and can provide information and contacts for many markets. Also, customs brokers and freight forwarders can help at this stage of the process.

The focus of the screening process switches from total market size to profitability. For example, based on the current and potential competitors, how much would you need to invest to gain a particular market share? Given the prices currently charged in the market, what margin can your company expect? Given the cost of entry and the expected sales, what is the expected profit? This stage of the analysis focuses on the quantitative profit expected, but many subjective judgments are made to arrive at the expected profit. For example, an Israeli manufacturer of pipe insulation found that the market price in the United Kingdom was \$10 per kilo versus \$6 per kilo in the United States, whereas its cost was \$5 per kilo. This indicated profit potential in the United Kingdom if the company could gain access to the market.

The fourth stage of the screening process is an evaluation and rank ordering of the potential target countries, based on corporate resources, objectives, and strategies. For example, although South Africa may have the same expected potential as Venezuela, Venezuela may be given a higher priority because successful entry into Venezuela can later be followed by entry into Colombia and Bolivia.

Criteria for Selecting Target Countries

The process of selecting target countries through the screening process requires that the companies identify the criteria to be used to differentiate desirable countries from less desirable countries. Research on global investment decisions has

4. World Bank Atlas 2000, pp. 50–51.

shown that the four critical factors affecting market selection are market size and growth, political conditions, competition, and market similarity.[5] In this section, we explain each of these factors and their uses in the market selection process.

Market Size and Growth It is obvious that potential market size and growth are an important factor in selecting markets. The larger the potential demand for a product in a country, the more attractive that market will be to a company.

Measures of market size and growth can be on both a macro and a micro basis. On a macro basis, it may be determined that the country needs a minimum set of potential resources to be worth further consideration. Table 5.1 summarizes the potential macroindicators of market size. A variety of readily available

TABLE 5.1

Macroindicators of Market Size

GEOGRAPHIC INDICATORS
Size of the country, in terms of geographic area
Climatic conditions
Topographical characteristics
DEMOGRAPHIC CHARACTERISTICS
Total population
Population growth rate
Age distribution of the population
Degree of population density
ECONOMIC CHARACTERISTICS
Total gross national product
Per capita gross national product
Per capita income (also income growth rate)
Personal or household disposable income
Income distribution

5. William H. Davidson, "Market Similarity and Market Selection: Implications for International Market Strategy," *Journal of Business Research*, December 1983, pp. 439–456.

statistics serve as macroindicators of market size. If you are screening countries for a firm that sells microwave ovens, you may decide not to consider any country with a personal disposable income per household of less than $10,000 per year. The logic of this criterion is that if the average household has less than $10,000, the potential market for a luxury item such as a microwave oven will not be great. However, a single statistic can sometimes be deceptive. For example, a country may have an average household income of $8,000, but there may be 1 million households with an income of over $10,000. These 1 million households will be potential buyers of microwaves. One commercially available report on the attractiveness of different countries for business is the *World Competitiveness Report*. Published annually, this report analyzes three hundred criteria to determine the overall competitiveness of the country and its strength by industry.[6] For a listing of population and gross national product macroindicators, see the table on the inside back cover of the book.

The macroindicators of market potential and growth are usually used in the first stage of the screening process, because the data are readily available and can be used to quickly eliminate countries with little or no potential demand. The macroindicators focus on the total potential demand (population) and ability to afford a product (per capita income). However, because the macroindicators of market size are general and crude, they do not necessarily indicate a perceived need for the product. For example, a country such as Iraq may have the population and income to indicate a large potential for razors, but the consumers, many of whom are Muslims, may not feel a perceived need for the product. In the third stage of the screening process, it is recommended that microindicators of market potential be used. Microindicators usually indicate actual consumption of a company's product or a similar product, therefore indicating a perceived need. Table 5.2 lists several examples of microindicators of market size.

These microindicators can be used to estimate market size. The number of households with televisions indicates the potential market size for televisions if every household purchased a new television. Depending on the life of the average television in use, one can estimate the annual demand. Although the actual consumption statistics may not be available for a certain product category, often the consumption of similar or substitute products is used as a proxy variable. For example, in determining the market size for surgical sutures, marketers may use the number of hospital beds or doctors as a proxy variable. The number of farms may indicate the potential demand for tractors, just as the number of cars is likely to indicate the number of tires needed.

The macro- and microindicators of market size allow the marketer to determine or infer the potential market size. Next, the marketer needs to evaluate the risk associated with each market opportunity.

6. *World Competitiveness Report 2000* (Lausanne: IMD, 2000).

TABLE 5.2

Microindicators of Market Size

Radios	Hotel beds
Televisions	Telephones
Cinema seats	Tourist arrivals
Scientists and engineers	Passenger cars
Hospitals	Civil airline passengers
Hospital beds	Steel production
Physicians	Rice production
Alcohol consumption	Number of farms
Coffee consumption	Land under cultivation
Gasoline consumption	Electricity consumption

Political Conditions The impact of a host country's political condition on market selection is described in studies by Stephan J. Kobrin and Franklin R. Root.[7] The influence of the host country's political environment was described in detail in Chapter 4. Though political risk tends to be more subjective than the quantitative indicators of market size, it is equally important. For example, the invasion of Kuwait in 1990 resulted in millions of dollars of U.S. assets being exposed to risk.

Any company can be hurt by political risk, from limitations on the number of foreign company officials and the amount of profits paid to the parent company, to refusal to issue a business license. Marketers can use a number of indicators to assess political risk.[8] Table 5.3 shows some indicators of political risk that may be used in country selection. Industrial disputes (strikes) can be a major disruption to business, and incidences vary greatly from country to country. The most strike-prone Organization for Economic Cooperation and Development (OECD) countries are Greece, Norway, and Canada.[9]

7. F. R. Root, "U.S. Business Abroad and Political Risks," *MSU Business Topics*, Winter 1968, pp. 73–80; S. J. Kobrin, "The Environmental Determinants of Foreign Direct Manufacturing Investment: An Ex-Post Empirical Analysis," *Journal of Business Studies*, Fall–Winter 1976, pp. 29–42.
8. R. Rummel and David Heenan, "How Multinationals Analyze Political Risk," *Harvard Business Review*, January–February 1978, pp. 67–76.
9. "Greece is OECD's Most Strike Prone Nation," *Financial Times*, April 9, 1998, p. 7.

TABLE 5.3

Indicators of Political Risk

Probability of nationalization	Percentage of the voters who are communist
Bureaucratic delays	Restrictions on capital movement
Number of expropriations	Government intervention
Number of riots or assassinations	Limits on foreign ownership
Political executions	Soldier/civilian ratio
Number of socialist seats in the legislature	

Historically, extractive industries such as oil and mining have been susceptible to the political risk of expropriation. More recently, the financial, insurance, communication, and transportation industries have been targets of expropriation. As shown in Table 5.3, many aspects of political risk assessment can be analyzed based on historical data. Unfortunately, historical indicators are not always that accurate because political conditions can change radically with a new government. Some of the syndicated services that rate political risk are the World Political Risk Forecast by Frost & Sullivan; the Business International Rating of 57 Countries; the Business Environment Risk Index; the Political Risk Index of the Economist Intelligence Unit. For example, if you are considering opportunities in South America, it is noteworthy that the Economist Intelligence Unit Country Risk Service estimates the country risk to be 75 in Venezuela, 70 in Mexico, 65 in Argentina, and 50 in Brazil, whereas Colombia is 40 and Chile 20. Other things being equal, Chile and Colombia would be less risky.[10] In addition to these major sources of information, global companies often consult banks, accounting firms, and domestic government agencies for political risk information.[11] The risk assessment services provided by Business International, Frost & Sullivan, Political Risk Services, and others are all useful long-term measures of risk. These do not preclude the need to keep attuned to the current events of the day, be they the collapse of the Berlin Wall, the invasion of Kuwait, the crushed student uprising in Tiananmen Square, or the invasion of Kosovo by the Serbs. These critical events may not have been predicted by the risk assessment services, yet each had a profound effect on business in that area.

10. "Country-Risk Ratings," *Economist*, June 22, 1996, p. 100.

11. F. T. Haner with John S. Ewing, *Country Risk Assessment* (New York: Praeger, 1985), p. 171.

Competition The number, size, and quality of the competition in a particular country affect a firm's ability to enter and compete profitably. In general, it is more difficult to determine the competitive structure of foreign countries than to determine the market size or political risk. Because of the difficulty of obtaining information, competitive analysis is usually done in the last stages of the screening process, when a small number of countries are being considered.

Some secondary sources are available that describe the competitive nature of a marketplace. The International Market Reseach Mall (ecnext.imrmall.com) publishes an online listing of available research reports. These reports tend to concentrate on North America and Europe, but some reports can be obtained on Japan, the Middle East, and South America. Such research reports usually cost between $500 and $5,000, with the average fee being about $1,200. In some cases, there may be no research report covering a specific country or product category, or it may be too expensive. Another reliable source of information is the U.S. government. The U.S. Department of Commerce and the State Department (or the equivalent in other countries) may be able to provide information on the competitive situation. Also, in almost every country, embassies employ commercial attachés whose main function is to assist home companies entering that foreign marketplace. Embassies of the foreign country being investigated may also be able to help marketers in their analysis. For example, in investigating the competition for farm implements in Spain, you can call or write the Spanish embassy in Washington, D.C., and secure a list of manufacturers of farm implements in Spain. In developing countries, the United States Agency for International Development (U.S. AID) is a very good source of information.

The World Wide Web has opened up a number of sources of global market information, such as:

Stat-USA	*www.stat-usa.gov* National Trade Data Bank Global Business Procurement Opportunities
I-Trade	*www.i-trade.com* Index of Free Services Market Your Company Index of Fee-Based Services
International Trade Administration	*www.ita.doc.gov* International Trade Administration Assistance Centers Information Directory

Other sources of competitive information vary widely, depending on the size of the country and the product. Many of the larger countries have chambers of commerce or other in-country organizations that may be able to assist potential investors. For example, if you were investigating the Japanese market for electronic measuring devices, the following groups could assist you in determining the competitive structure of the market in Japan:

- U.S. Chamber of Commerce in Japan
- Japan External Trade Organization (JETRO)
- American Electronics Association in Japan
- Japan Electronic Industry Development Association
- Electronic Industries Association of Japan
- Japan Electronic Measuring Instrument Manufacturers Association

The final and usually most expensive way to assess the market is to go to the country and interview potential customers and competitors to determine the size and strength of the competition. As a trip to a potential market is always required before a final decision is made, it should not be overlooked as an important part of the screening process. If you are well prepared in advance, two to three days in a country talking to distributors, large buyers, and trade officials can be extremely valuable in assessing the competitiveness of the market and the potential profitability.

Market Similarity Strong evidence exists that market similarity can be used for country selection. A study of 954 product introductions by fifty-seven U.S. firms found a significant correlation between market selection and market similarity.[12]

The concept of market similarity is simple. A firm tends to select countries based on their similarity to the home market. Therefore, when a company decides to enter foreign markets, it will first enter the markets that are most similar. For example, a U.S. firm will enter Canada, Australia, and the United Kingdom before entering less similar markets such as Spain, South Korea, or India. Measures of similarity are (1) aggregate production and transportation, (2) personal consumption, (3) trade, and (4) health and education.[13]

As shown in Table 5.4, the selection of foreign markets tends to follow similarity very closely. Although language similarities were not measured in the study, it is worth noting that the top three markets all use the same language. Using market similarity as a selection variable is relatively simple. One can use the similarity ranking shown in Table 5.4, update it with the most recent economic data, or develop other criteria for determining similarity.

The premise behind the selection of similar markets is the desire of a company to minimize risk in the face of uncertainty. Entering a market that has the

12. Davidson, "Market Similarity and Market Selection."
13. Ibid.

TABLE 5.4

Correlation of Similarity and Position in the Entry Sequence

	Similarity to the United States	***Position in Investment Sequence***
Canada	1	2
Australia	2	3
United Kingdom	3	1
West Germany	4	6
France	5	4
Belgium	6	10
Italy	7	9
Japan	8	5
Netherlands	9	12
Argentina	10	15
Mexico	11	8
Spain	12	13
India	13	16
Brazil	14	7
South Africa	15	14
Philippines	16	17
South Korea	17	18
Colombia	18	11

Source: Reprinted by permission of the publisher from "Market Similarity and Market Selection: Implications for International Market Strategy," by William H. Davidson, *Journal of Business Research*, vol. 11, no. 4, p. 446. Copyright 1983 by Elsevier Science Publishing Co., Inc.

same language, a similar distribution system, and similar customers is less difficult than entering a market in which all these variables are different. The benefits of similarity need to be balanced against the available market size, however. For example, Australia may be similar but may have relatively little demand compared with China or Indonesia, which are dissimilar.

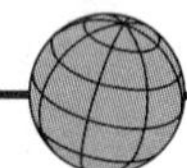

Techniques of Making Market Selection Decisions

The framework for making market selection decisions usually follows the systematic screening process shown in Figure 5.2. Different techniques can be used to accomplish the screening processes. These techniques vary from simple listings of selection criteria to complex combinations of different criteria into an index. These techniques will be discussed individually.

Listing of Selection Criteria

The simplest way to screen countries is to develop a set of criteria that are required as a minimum for a country to move through the stages of the screening process. To illustrate the screening methodology, we have outlined the screening process that could be used by a manufacturer of kidney dialysis equipment as an example (see Table 5.5).

The minimum cutoff number for each criterion will be established by management. As we move through the screening process, the criteria become more specific. The following text gives the rationale for each of the screening criteria and cutoff points.

Macrolevel Gross National Product Introduction of dialysis equipment in a new market requires a significant support function, including salespeople, service people, replacement parts inventory, and an ensured continuous supply of dialysate fluid, needles, tubing, and so on. Some countries lack the technical infrastructure to support such high-level technology. Therefore, management may decide to consider only countries having a minimum size of $15 billion gross domestic product (GDP) or gross national product (GNP), thus excluding many of the developing economies of the world from consideration. (Note that the dialysis screening was done with 1985 data.) Also, dialysis requires substantial government support. A tradeoff then develops between acceptable expenditures for dialysis and acceptable kidney-related death rates. GDP per capita is an indicator of the level at which this tradeoff will occur. The lower the GDP per capita, the lower the expected government expenditure for dialysis equipment, given other pressing societal needs such as food and shelter. Therefore, the GDP per capita over $1,500 would have been set as a minimum. These economic factors would

TABLE 5.5

Screening Process Example: Targeting Countries for Kidney Dialysis Equipment

Filter Number	Type of Screening	Specific Criteria
1	Macrolevel research	GDP over $15 billion GDP per capita over $1,500
2	General market factors relating to the product	Less than 200 people per hospital bed Less than 1,000 people per doctor Government expenditures over $100 million for health care Government expenditures over $20 per capita for health care
3	Microlevel factors specific to the product	Kidney-related deaths over 1,000 Patient use of dialysis equipment—over 40 percent annual growth in treated population
4	Final screening of target markets	Numbers of competitors Political stability

have limited the market to the following twenty-eight countries in the world, excluding North America:

All of Europe except Hungary	Venezuela
Iceland	Australia
the former U.S.S.R.	Iran
New Zealand	Argentina
South Africa	Iraq
Brazil	

General Market Factors Related to the Product: Medical Concentration Hemodialysis is a sophisticated procedure that requires medical personnel with advanced training. In order for a country to support advanced medical equipment, it requires a high level of medical specialization. Higher levels of medical concentration allow doctors the luxury of specialization in a field such as nephrology (the study of kidneys).

Management may determine that a population of less than 1,000 per doctor and a population of less than 200 per hospital bed indicate that medical personnel will be able to achieve the level of specialization needed to support a hemodialysis program. This second step of the screening process would have eliminated Iran, Iraq, Brazil, and Venezuela. As can be expected, the majority of countries with high GNP and GDP per capita have a high level of medical concentration.

Public health expenditures show the government's contribution to the medical care of its citizens—a factor of obvious importance in hemodialysis. Management may believe that countries that do not invest substantially in the health care of their population generally are not interested in making an even more substantial investment in a hemodialysis program. Thus, countries that do not have a minimum of $20 expenditure per capita or $100 million in total expenditures for health care would have been eliminated from consideration. This would have screened out Austria, Portugal, Yugoslavia, the former U.S.S.R., and South Africa. Thus, eighteen countries have the ability to purchase and satisfactorily support dialysis equipment. Dialysis programs were already under way in most of these countries.

The third stage of the screening process will identify which countries will provide the best opportunities for the sale of kidney dialysis machines.

Microlevel Factors Specific to the Product Management may decide that there are two microlevel factors to consider: (1) the number of kidney-related deaths and (2) the growth rate of the treated patient population.

1. *Kidney-related deaths*. The number of deaths due to kidney failure is a good indicator of the number of people in each country who could have used dialysis equipment. The company will be interested only in countries with a minimum of 1,000 deaths per year due to kidney-related causes. A lower death rate indicates that the country has little need for dialysis equipment or that the market is currently being well served by competitive equipment. The Netherlands, Argentina, Norway, Switzerland, and Sweden would have been eliminated from analysis on these grounds.
2. *Growth rate of the treated patient population*. Analysis of the growth rate of the kidney treatment population demonstrates a growth in potential demand. Newly opened markets with the greatest growth potential are the best targets for a new supplier of dialysis equipment. These are the countries in which the treated patient population continues to grow at a minimum of 40 percent per year. This criterion would have excluded all but the following: Italy, with 75.1 percent; Greece, with 63.4 percent; and Spain, with 60.1 percent. Competition in all three of these markets is substantially less than in the United States, Japan, and the remainder of western Europe.

Final Screening of Target Markets The screening process identified three target countries. To select one of these countries, an analysis of the competition and political stability is conducted. Discussions with the five major suppliers of dialysis equipment may indicate that Italy already has two local suppliers. Greece is being served by the four major European suppliers. Spain has a strong preference for U.S. equipment and is served by only one supplier. An evaluation of the political environment in each country would have indicated that Greece has a stable government; Italy's government is stable but is not increasing its medical expenditures; Spain is making a transition to a stable democracy.

After evaluating the data, management would most likely have selected Spain for the initial market entry. The final decision would have been based on the following review of each market. Greece would have been discounted as a potential market for the following reasons:

1. There is significant competition from other companies.
2. The corporate income tax is higher than that of Spain.
3. Products are subject to a "turnover" tax.
4. The inflation rate is high.

Similarly, Italy would have been discounted for these reasons:

1. There is extensive foreign as well as local competition.
2. The projected growth for dialysis equipment is slower than in Spain.
3. Products are subject to a 14 percent value-added tax.
4. The inflation rate is extremely high.

Spain would have been chosen for the following reasons:

1. The political outlook is stable; it appears that the transition to democracy will continue.
2. There is aggressive government support for health care.
3. A very high growth rate is predicted for kidney equipment (23 percent).
4. Competition at this time is minimal.
5. Spain imposes no value-added tax.
6. Government subsidies for home use of dialysis equipment will stimulate demand.
7. The inflation rate is lower than in Italy or Greece.
8. U.S. products and firms have a favorable reputation in the country.

The screening of markets for dialysis equipment is an example of how to analyze the world market and select a few countries for entry. The screening process must be tailored to the specific product or service.

Market Indexes for Country Selection

Another technique for analyzing country selection criteria is to develop indexes that combine statistical data and allow the marketer to look at a large number of variables quickly. For example, for the past thirty-four years Business International, now the Economic Intelligence Unit (EIU), has published market indicators that allow managers to quickly compare country opportunities. The EIU publishes three indexes: market size, market growth, and market intensity.

Market size is the measure of total potential based on the total population (double-weighted), urban population, private consumption expenditure, steel consumption, cement and electricity production, and ownership of telephones, cars, and televisions. *Market growth* is an indicator of the rate of increase in the size of the market. The growth is determined based on an average of several indicators over five years: population; steel consumption; cement and electricity production; and ownership of passenger cars, trucks, buses, televisions, and telephones. The *market intensity* index measures the richness of a market or the concentration of purchasing power. The average world intensity is designated as 1.0, and each country is calculated in proportion to the average world intensity. Intensity is calculated for each market by averaging the per capita consumption of steel, ownership of telephones and televisions, production of cement and electricity levels, private consumption expenditure (double-weighted), ownership of passenger cars (double-weighted), and proportion of urban population (double-weighted). Figure 5.3 shows the twelve largest countries and their percentages of the world market. The size of the circle represents the relative market size.

The EIU market indexes allow a quick visual review of the world's major markets. The United States, much of Europe, and Japan are big markets with low growth and high intensity. China, Germany, and Indonesia offer higher growth rates and lower levels of market intensity.[14]

Ongoing Market Screening

The market screening process requires a significant amount of effort. After the target country is selected, there is a tendency to focus on the selected markets and ignore the rejected countries. However, the world market is continually changing, and countries that were rejected last year may provide significant opportunities just one year later. For example, Finland has long favored domestic banks, making it very difficult for foreign banks to operate. The move toward a single European market has caused Finland to become concerned about the limited access it provides to its banking market. So Finland's financial markets are suddenly much more accessible. The events in eastern Europe have also made countries such as Poland more attractive.

14. "EIU Market Indexes," *Crossborder Monitor*, August 28, 1996, p. 12.

FIGURE 5.3

EIU Market Indexes: Size, Growth, and Intensity of the Twelve Largest Markets

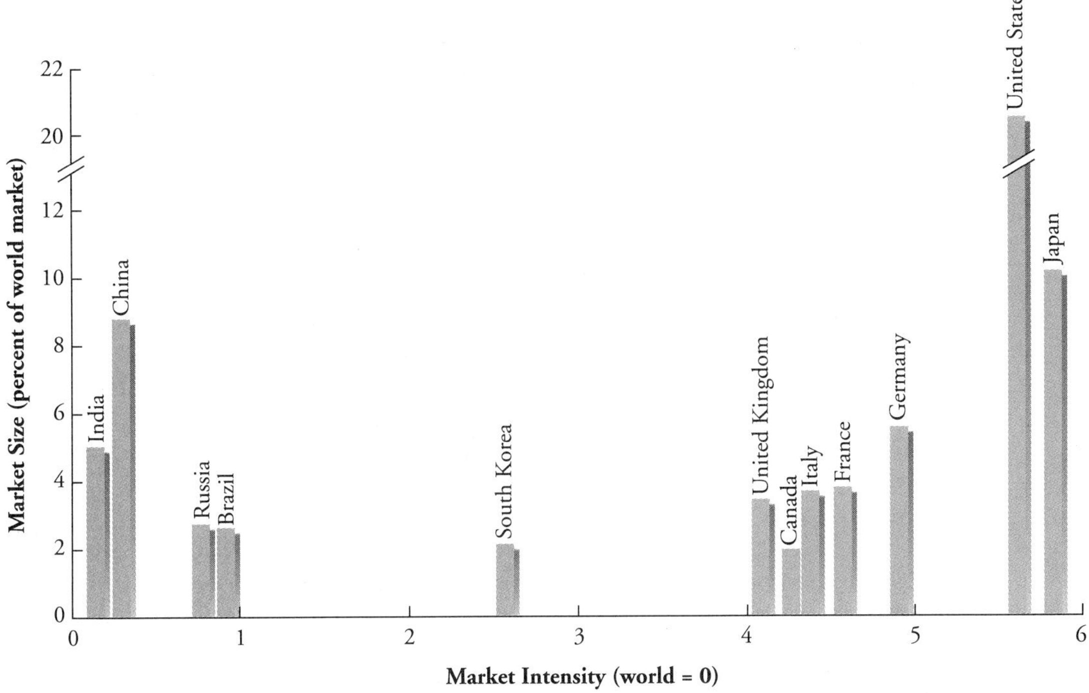

Source: © Cross Border Monitor, 1998. Reproduced by permission of the Economist Intelligence Unit, NA, Inc.

For example, Makro Cash & Carry, a Dutch retailer, has a network of 15 stores in Poland and added 3 more in 1999. The Warsaw store posted the best results of Makro's 130 stores worldwide, and by 2000, Makro expects to reach sales of 7 billion zlotys.[15]

Political and economic events can also make an attractive market suddenly undesirable. Iraq and Jordan became less attractive after the invasion of Kuwait, as did Serbia after the invasion of Kosovo and the resulting North Atlantic Treaty Organization. (NATO) bombings.[16] For most companies, it is necessary to have an ongoing monitoring and screening of world markets to spot new emerging opportunities, as well as to identify new potential risks.

15. "Growth in Turnover," *Rzecpospolita*, April 28, 1999, p. 10.
16. John Reed, "Combat Fatigue Hits Yugoslav Economy," *Wall Street Journal*, October 12, 1988, p. A16.

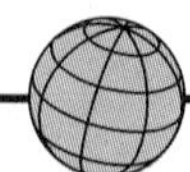

Grouping Global Markets

There are many ways to group international markets. The chapters on political, economic, and cultural environments demonstrated that the interaction between these variables causes each country to be unique, therefore making it difficult to group countries together. Despite these difficulties, it is often necessary to group countries together so they can be considered as a single market or as a group of similar markets. In this segment of the chapter, we explore the rationale for grouping markets and the various ways that marketers can group countries together.

Rationale for Grouping Markets

The two principles that often drive the need for larger market groupings are critical mass and economies of scale. *Critical mass*, a term used in physics and military strategy, indicates that a minimum amount of effort is necessary before any impact will be achieved. *Economies of scale* is a term used in production situations; it means that greater levels of production result in lower costs per unit, which obviously increases profitability.

The costs of marketing products within a group of countries are lower for three reasons. First, the potential volume to be sold in a group of countries is sufficient to support a full marketing effort. Second, geographic proximity makes it easy to travel from one country to another, often in two hours or less. Third, the barriers to entry are often the same in countries within an economic grouping—for example, the European Union. Finally, in pursuing countries with similar markets, a company gains leverage with marketing programs. There is some debate over the long-term role of market groupings. Although the European Union has become a strong grouping with a single currency, many economic groupings may become subordinate to the role of the World Trade Organization (WTO). Also, given the broad membership of the WTO and strong enforcement powers, the regional market groupings will generally need to conform to the rules and practices of the WTO when dealing with all other WTO countries.

Marketing Activities Influenced by Country Groupings

The major activities used to enter a new market are market research, product development or modification, distribution, and promotion. Each of these activities can be influenced by economies of scale and critical mass. In this section, we show how each of these four activities relates to country groupings.[17]

17. Vern Terpstra, "Critical Mass and International Marketing Strategy," *Journal of Academy of Marketing Sciences*, Summer 1983.

Market Research In the screening process, marketers use many readily available secondary sources of market information. As stated previously, these secondary sources are acceptable for selecting target countries, but they are not sufficient to develop a marketing strategy to penetrate a specific market. Before entering a new market, the company will need to invest in the acquisition of knowledge about the specific aspects of marketing the product in each country. Normally, the following questions must be answered:

1. Who makes the purchase decisions?
2. What decision criteria do consumers use to select the product?
3. How must the product be modified?
4. What are the channels of distribution?
5. What are the competitive price levels?

These and many other questions must be answered before the first product can be shipped. The cost of acquiring this knowledge will often be higher than domestic market research, because of the travel distances, cultural differences, and language differences. Given the sizable investment required to obtain this firsthand market knowledge, there are economies of scale if two or more countries can be included in the same market research study.

Product Development/Modification Development of new products and modifications of current products require a large investment. Given the cost, there are obvious economies of scale when these costs are spread over a number of markets. This is particularly true if the markets are similar, so that the same modified product can be sold in a number of markets. For example, Procter & Gamble's Head & Shoulders dandruff shampoo is manufactured in a single European plant; however, the company takes advantage of European Union regulations by selling the product throughout Europe with a "Eurobottle" label in eight languages.[18]

Distribution The distribution aspect of marketing is particularly important in serving international markets. In the case of exporting, the marketer is faced with all the mechanics of getting the product from the domestic market to the foreign market, which includes documentation, insurance, and financial arrangements. Also, the shipping rates will vary, depending on the size of the shipment. Less than carload- or container-sized orders will be calculated at a higher price per pound than full carloads or containers. The mechanics and shipping aspects of exporting are influenced by economies of scale and critical mass. If one plans to

18. "Unilever Aims to Bolster Lines in U.S." *Wall Street Journal*, June 19, 1987, p. 6.

ship only a small amount each month to a South American country, it may not be worth the effort. Without a critical mass of business, it does not pay to learn the mechanics and process the paperwork. Also, if you do not have sufficient volumes to ship, transportation costs will escalate.

The distribution systems within foreign markets also are influenced by the number of markets served. Many distributors and dealers in foreign markets handle numerous markets. For example, Caps Gemini, a large software development and distribution firm, has operations in every European country. Given the multicountry nature of many distributors, it can be beneficial to enter a group of similar markets through the same distribution channels.

Promotion A major task of the global company is promotion, which includes advertising and personal selling. Advertising is used as a communication device to give customers a message about a product via television, radio, or print media. In many parts of the world, these three forms of communication cross country boundaries. For example, a message on German television will be seen in Switzerland. Also, it's much cheaper to shoot one commercial for all of Europe and to have one Euromarket manager with junior product managers for each country rather than full marketing managers at country levels.[19] So, there may be economies of scale in grouping two or more markets together when entering a new area.

Selling is a very important part of the promotional process, which usually requires a local sales force. Establishing and managing a sales force is a large fixed expense that lends itself to economies of scale. Spreading the cost of a sales office, rent, secretarial staff, sales support, sales managers, and sometimes the salesperson over two or three countries can be very cost-effective.

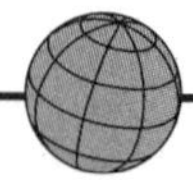

Growth of Formal Market Groups

Countries have used the concept of market groupings for centuries. The British Commonwealth preference system linked the markets of the United Kingdom, Canada, Australia, New Zealand, India, and former colonies in Africa, Asia, and the Middle East. The growth of market groups since World War II was encouraged by the success of the European Economic Community, now called the European Union (EU). The EU expanded in 1994/95 to include former European Free Trade Association (EFTA) members Sweden, Austria, and Finland.

As discussed in Chapter 2, a market group is created when two or more countries agree to reduce trade and tariff barriers between themselves, therefore creating a trade unit. Successful trade units or market groups are based on favorable

19. "A Universal Message, Pan-European Ads Are Increasingly Common," *Financial Times*, May 27, 1993, p. 18.

economic, political, or geographic factors. A country will agree to join a trade unit based on one or more of these factors, *if* the expected benefits of becoming part of the trade unit exceed the disadvantages and loss of sovereignty caused by joining the group.

Economic Factors

The major benefit of every market group is usually economic. Member countries of the group experience reduced or eliminated tariffs and duties that stimulate trade between member countries. They also have common tariff barriers against firms from nonmember countries. Joining together with other countries gives members a greater economic security, reducing the impact of competition from member countries and increasing the group's strength against foreign competitors. For example, in 1999 the United States planned to impose tariffs valued at $500 million on Louis Vuitton handbags from France, pecorino cheese from Italy, and cashmere sweaters from Britian after a six-year battle over Europe's banana policy favoring former colonies in Africa and the Caribbean. The EU ambassadors were able to confer with the WTO as a unit of fifteen countries and propose similar retaliatory action against the United States.[20]

Consumers benefit from the reduced trade barriers through lower prices. Economies that are complementary rather than directly competitive tend to make better members of a market group. Most of the problems within the European Union have revolved around agricultural products; member countries are threatened by products such as eggs, milk, meat, and chicken from other member countries.

Political Factors

In most countries, the political system and its ideology are dominant forces. The political system usually reflects the aspirations of the nation. It's easy to see, then, why market groups are made up of countries with similar political aspirations. A major impetus for the original formation of the European Community was the need for a unified entity to protect against the political threat of the former U.S.S.R.

Geographic Factors

Countries that share common borders tend to function better in a market group for the simple fact that it is easier to move goods back and forth across the truck

20. Helene Cooper, "U.S. Starts Its Threatened Banana Fight with Europe," *Wall Street Journal*, March 4, 1999, p. A2.

and railroad systems. Also, countries that share boundaries have experienced each other's cultures and are likely to have a history of trade.

Types of Market Groups

There are five different types of market groups: free trade area, customs union, common market, economic union, and political union. When a country enters an agreement with another country or group of countries, the resulting association falls into one of these five categories. The level of integration and cooperation between countries depends on the type of group they form. Figure 5.4 shows which aspects of global integration are included in each type of agreement.

Major Market Groups

Market agreements that formed the major market groups are shown in Table 5.6. The next sections describe most of these market groups and the agreements that brought them together. The sections are divided according to geographic area.

FIGURE 5.4

Forms of International Integration

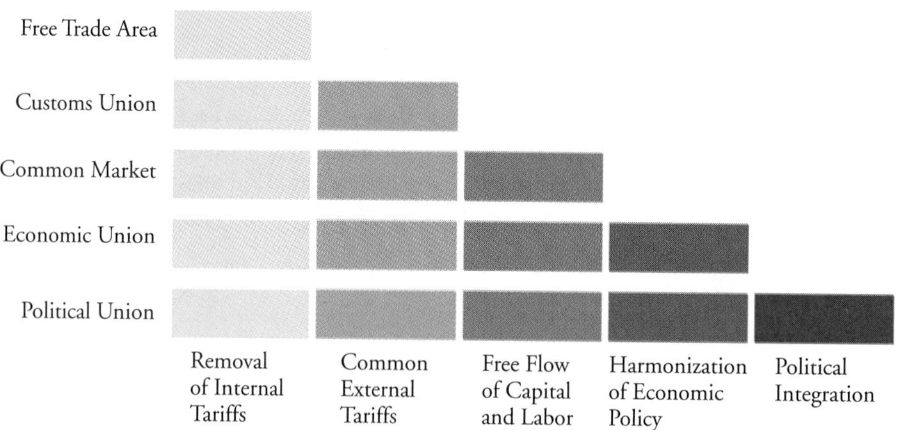

Source: Ruel K. Kahler and Roland L. Kramer, *International Marketing*, 5th ed., 1983, p. 343. Reprinted by permission of Southwestern Publishing Company.

TABLE 5.6

Summary of Market Agreements

European Agreements

EUROPEAN ECONOMIC AREA (EEA)

Austria
Belgium
Denmark
Finland
France
Germany
Greece
Iceland
Ireland
Italy
Liechtenstein
Luxembourg
Netherlands
Norway
Portugal
Spain
Sweden
United Kingdom

EUROPEAN UNION (EU) (Customs union)

Austria
Belgium
Denmark
Finland
France
Germany
Greece
Ireland
Italy
Luxembourg
Netherlands
Portugal
Spain
Sweden
United Kingdom

EUROPEAN FREE TRADE ASSOCIATION (EFTA) (Free trade area)

Austria
Finland
Iceland
Liechtenstein
Norway
Sweden
Switzerland

EUROPEAN MONETARY UNION (EMU)

Austria
Belgium
Finland
Ireland
The Netherlands
France
Germany
Italy
Luxembourg
Portugal
Spain (Economic Union)

COMMONWEALTH OF INDEPENDENT STATES (CIS) (Ad hoc group)

Azerbaijan
Armenia
Belarus
Estonia
Georgia
Kazakhstan
Kyrgyzstan
Latvia
Lithuania
Moldova
Russia
Tajikistan
Turkmenistan
Ukraine
Uzbekistan

African Agreements

EAST AFRICA COOPERATION (Customs union)

Ethiopia
Kenya
Sudan
Tanzania
Uganda
Zambia

FRENCH AFRICAN COMMUNITY

Benin
Burkina Faso
Cameroon
Central African Republic
Chad
Congo
Ivory Coast
Equatorial Guinea
Gabon
Guinea Bissau
Mali
Niger
Senegal
Togo

ARAB MAGHREB UNION (Common market)

Algeria
Libya
Mauritania
Morocco
Tunisia

ECONOMIC COMMUNITY OF WEST AFRICAN STATES (ECOWAS) (Customs union)

Benin
Burkina Faso
Cape Verde
Gambia
Ghana
Guinea
Guinea-Bissau
Ivory Coast
Liberia
Mali
Mauritania
Niger
Nigeria
Senegal
Sierra Leone
Togo

(continued)

TABLE 5.6

Summary of Market Agreements (cont.)

American Agreements

MERCOSUR (SOUTHERN COMMON MARKET) (Common market)

Argentina	Paraguay
Brazil	Uruguay

ANDEAN COMMON MARKET (ANCOM) (Common market)

Bolivia	Peru
Colombia	Venezuela
Ecuador	

CENTRAL AMERICAN INTEGRATION SYSTEM (Common market)

Costa Rica	Honduras
El Salvador	Nicaragua
Guatemala	Panama

CARIBBEAN COMMUNITY AND COMMON MARKET (CARICOM) (Common market)

Antigua and Barbuda	Jamaica
Bahamas	Montserrat
Barbados	Saint Kitts-Nevis
Belize	Saint Lucia
Dominica	Saint Vincent and the Grenadines
Grenada	Suriname
Guyana	Trinidad and Tobago
Haiti	

U.S.-CANADA FREE TRADE AGREEMENT (Free trade area)

Canada	United States

NORTH AMERICAN FREE TRADE AGREEMENT (NAFTA) (Free trade area)

Canada	United States
Mexico	

Asian Agreements

ARAB COMMON MARKET (ACM) (Common market)

Egypt	Syria
Iraq	Kuwait
Jordan	

ECONOMIC COOPERATION ORGANIZATION (ECO) (Ad hoc arrangement)

Afghanistan	Pakistan
Azerbaijan	Tajikistan
Iran	Turkey
Kazakhstan	Turkmenistan
Kyrgyzstan	Uzbekistan

ASSOCIATION OF SOUTH EAST ASIAN NATIONS (ASEAN) (Free trade area)

Brunei	Myanmar
Cambodia	Singapore
Indonesia	Philippines
Laos	Thailand
Malaysia	Vietnam

ASIA PACIFIC ECONOMIC COOPERATIVE (APEC)

Australia	New Zealand
Brunei	Papua New Guinea
Canada	Philippines
Chile	Singapore
China	South Korean
Hong Kong	Taiwan
Indonesia	Thailand
Japan	United States
Malaysia	Vietnam
Mexico	

Source: Data from *1997 World Bank Atlas.* Adapted with permission from The World Bank.

Europe Europe has four major market groups: the European Economic Area (EEA), the European Union (EU), the European Free Trade Area (EFTA), and the Commonwealth of Independent States (CIS).

The European Economic Area. The European Economic Area was officially begun on January 1, 1994, and includes the fifteen member countries of the European Union (to be discussed later) plus Norway, Liechtenstein, and Iceland. The EEA grew out of a 1984 agreement between the EU (which was called the European Community at the time) and EFTA to join together to form the European Economic Space (EES). As members of the EEA, Norway and Iceland enjoy all the trading rights and obligations of the EU except in farming and fishing.[21] It took ten years to form the EEA because of the difficulty of getting EFTA countries to agree to the rules and policies established by the EU, especially the legal strictures against monopolies and state aid to businesses.[22] The EEA will in time be replaced by the EU as the latter expands and Norway and Iceland decide to join the EU.

The European Union. The European Union was established in 1993 as a result of the drive toward a single market by the twelve members of the European Community (EC) in 1992. With the removal of all internal tariffs and common external tariffs and the free flow of goods, capital, and people, the EU is a true common market. The members of the EU have agreed to the Maastricht Treaty, which established the European Monetary Union (EMU) in 1999, although the United Kingdom, Greece, Denmark, and Sweden did not join the EMU. The EMU united the currencies of the EMU members, with the European Central Bank dictating economic policy to the member country banks. The outlook for EMU is still mixed. Although Greece has been approved for admission in 2001, no date has been set for the UK, Denmark, or Sweden to join the EMU. There are also twelve additional countries who have applied to become part of the EU, with Hungary and Poland hoping to become members in 2004. All EU members can apply for EMU membership.[23]

The EU, referred to as the European Community until 1993, was called the European Common Market when it was established in 1958. The EU has grown from the original six countries to fifteen countries, increasing its role over time through the establishment of the European Parliament, the Court of Justice, and the European Currency Unit (ECU).

The relaunch of the EU and the creation of the single European market, often referred to as "1992," were initiated by Lord Cockfield, the British commissioner

21. "The Five Nordic Countries Remain Defiantly Different from the Rest of Europe," *Economist*, January 23, 1999, p. 3.
22. "European Economic Area," *Economist*, January 8, 1994, pp. 49–50.
23. Michael Smith and Stefan Wagstyl, "Late Starters Strain to Catch Favourites for EU," *Financial Times*, February 15, 2000, p. 2.

to the EU and author of the internal market white paper published on June 14, 1985.[24] The white paper explained the logic for a single market and summarized the impediments into three areas: physical barriers at frontiers, technical barriers within different countries, and barriers designed to protect fiscal regimes. It took two years for the white paper to be approved by EU members and become the Single European Act. There was a compelling logic for the single market. Europe, although bigger than the United States and Japan in population, was underperforming its two largest competitors on almost every economic measure.

The EU commissioned a number of studies to measure the potential impact of a single market. Paolo Cecchini, a senior official of the EU, coordinated thirty different studies and expected economic outcome of the 1992 initiative.[25] This report, known as the Cecchini report, documented the costs of continuing in a divided market and the benefits of building an integrated one.[26] The report summarized the economic gains if the EU implemented the single market as follows:

- A rejuvenation of the EU economy, adding 4.5 percent to GDP
- A reduction in inflation, with a fall in consumer prices of 6.1 percent
- A reduction in the cost of public programs through open bidding
- The creation of 1.8 million new jobs in the EU, reducing unemployment[27]

To illustrate the potential impact of The Europe 1992 Initiative, consider the pharmaceutical industry. The drug industry has a separate regulatory body, applying its own criteria for approving medicines, and mutual approval of licenses is nonexistent. Each country has a different system for pricing and paying for drugs. Also, rules regarding drug advertising vary from country to country. Within the spirit of the single market, the European Union is moving on several fronts to harmonize the EU drug industry. The European Medicines Agency opened its offices in 1996 and began reviewing drugs for use throughout the EU, therefore eliminating the need for pharmaceutical manufacturers to get drugs approved individually in all fifteen EU countries.

The European Free Trade Association. The European Free Trade Association was created in 1959 by countries that did not join the EU. The EFTA consisted of Austria, Finland, Iceland, Liechtenstein, Norway, Sweden, and Switzerland and operated as a free trade area. As the EU single market became a reality in 1992, the EFTA countries of Sweden, Austria, and Finland applied and were ad-

24. Lord Cockfield, "Completing the Internal Market," white paper to the European Council (Luxembourg: Office of Publications of the European Communities, 1985).
25. Nicholas Colchester and David Buchan, *Europe Relaunched* (London: Economist Books, 1990), pp. 32–33.
26. Paolo Cecchini, *The European Challenge 1992: The Benefits of a Single Market* (London: Wildwood House, 1988).
27. James W. Dudley, *1992 Strategies for the Single Market* (London: Kogan Page, 1989), pp. 34–35.

mitted as EU members. Switzerland voted not to be part of the EEA. Eventually, the EFTA will disappear as an independent market group.

The Commonwealth of Independent States. The collapse of the Berlin Wall in 1989, the breakup of the fifteen republics of the Soviet Union (e.g., Estonia, Latvia, Lithuania), and the opening of eastern Europe to free elections in 1990 resulted in the creation of the Commonwealth of Independent States. The CIS is really a very loose collection of nations that replaces the Council for Mutual Economic Assistance (COMECON). COMECON was formed in 1949 as a political union of eight eastern European communist countries, later joined by Cuba and Vietnam. Until 1990, these ten countries were tightly controlled by the Soviet Union, and COMECON operated as an enforced political group. COMECON countries depended on the Soviet Union as a major customer. In exchange, the Soviet Union provided oil and defenses against NATO forces.

The future of CIS as a single market group is doubtful. The eastern European countries of Poland, Hungary, and the Czech Republic have agreed to cooperate with the EU on trade, economic, industrial, and scientific issues; tourism; transport; communications; and environmental pollution. Given the economic and political difficulties in Russia, the former republics are more likely to cooperate with the western European groups than with Russia.

Russia, with 150 million citizens hungry for consumer goods, is the largest single market in the CIS. Although the risks are high, the potential is great. The financial crisis and devaluation of the ruble in 1998 caused the price of imports to quadruple. Nestlé, a Swiss food company and one of the top foreign investors in Russia, opened a new production line in its factory in Rossiya. Andreas Schlaepfer, head of Nestlé in Russia, said, "Unlike [its] competitors, who build sweet factories from scratch, Nestlé took over an existing plant making existing Russian brands. Cost cutting is easier as we use less expensive Russian sugar and less expensive cocoa." Nestlé was expected to make $500 million in Russia in 1999.[28] The collapse of Russian currency has given local producers like Svoboda, a Moscow-based shampoo company, a big boost. Svoboda has taken share from Procter & Gamble, Unilever, and Colgate.[29]

The North Atlantic Treaty Organization. Although primarily a political organization, the North Atlantic Treaty Organization (NATO) has taken on more of an economic role with the demise of the Soviet military power. NATO was originally established to protect western Europe from the Soviet Union. Now NATO has moved eastward, admitting Poland, Hungary, and the Czech Republic in1998.[30] The Russian government opposes expansion of NATO but accepted the creation of the NATO-Russian Consultative Council.[31] This allowed Russia to

28. "Russia: Sweet Flows the Volga," *Economist*, June 5, 1999.

29. "Russian Consumer Googs: The Joys of Devaluation," *Economist*, November 28, 1998, p. 66.

30. Carla Anne Robbins, "Senate Ratifies Treaty to Add 3 Nations from Former Warsaw Pact to NATO," *Wall Street Journal*, May 1, 1998, p. B2.

31. Ibid.

participate in discussions of NATO issues such as terrorism, crime, nuclear proliferation, and regional defense but without voting or veto power. China is also concerned about the growth of NATO. China had not opposed NATO in the past because it helped enforce the U.S.-Japanese Security Agreement, which limits Japanese military investments. China now fears the strengthening of NATO, as shown by the bombing in Serbia and the May 7, 1999, bombing of the Chinese Embassy in Belgrade, as a western plan to contain China's growth as a global power. It was not surprising in June 1999 that China agreed to buy fifty Su-30 fighter aircraft from the Russians.[32]

Africa The continent of Africa has seven major market agreements in force: the Afro-Malagasy Economic Union, the East Africa Customs Union, the Maghreb Economic Community, the Casablanca Group, the Economic Community of West African States, the West African Economic Community, and the French African Community. The success of the EU has prompted African countries to get together to form these groups. Unfortunately, however, the groups have had little success in promoting trade and economic progress, because most African nations are small and have limited economic infrastructure to produce goods.

The French African Community (CFA) was established in 1985 as a monetary union. The member countries have fixed their currencies to the French franc. Since 1985, the combination of declining prices; tax, fiscal, and monetary policies; and the appreciation of the French franc against the U.S. dollar have resulted in a 30 percent currency appreciation, which has reduced the competitiveness of exports from these countries.[33]

The European disengagement from Africa is complete, with only France continuing to provide significant military and financial aid. The United States has no serious military or geostrategic interest in Africa. There has been a trend toward democratic elections throughout Africa. Democracy, along with the rebirth of South Africa, should halt the decline of living standards throughout Africa.[34] South Africa reached a free trade agreement with the EU in March 1999. This agreement will allow approximately $20 billion of free trade between South Africa and the EU members.[35]

Latin America There are five major market agreements in Latin America: MERCOSUR; the Andean Common Market, the Central American Common Market, the Caribbean Community and Common Market, and the Latin American Integration

32. "China's Foreign Policy: Dangerous Limbo," *Economist*, July 10, 1999, pp. 36–37.
33. "Devaluation Is Overdue," Special section: "Africa: A Continent at Stake," *Financial Times*, September 1, 1993, p. vii.
34. "Africa for the Africans," *Economist*, September 7, 1996, Sub-Saharan African section, pp. 3–18.
35. Clive Sawyer, "EU Leaders Approve Trade Deal with South Africa," *Cape Argus*, March 25, 1999, p. 1.

Association. Latin America faced a number of problems that made it difficult to achieve significant economic integration and cooperation between countries before the mid-1990s. Political turmoil, the low level of economic activity, and extreme differences in economic development from country to country were stumbling blocks to the success of regional market agreements.

MERCOSUR, the Southern Common Market, was formed in 1991 and includes Argentina, Brazil, Paraguay, and Uruguay. Both Chile and Bolivia have signed free trade agreements with the group. Although it is one of the newer regional trading groups, MERCOSUR's intergroup trade has grown from $4 billion in 1990 to $18 billion in 1997 as members cut tariffs sharply on most goods except sugar and cars.[36] MERCOSUR expects to reach free-trade-area status by 2000 with 100 percent of all goods. MERCOSUR has also begun the process of becoming a customs union, establishing common external tariffs for imports from countries outside MERCOSUR. MERCOSUR is expected to develop relationships with the Andean group countries like Colombia, Ecuador, Peru, and Venezuela. January 1999 was set as a target date for MERCOSUR and the Andean Common Market to establish a free trade zone.[37] Latin American and EU leaders held a two-day summit in June 1999 to explore the possibility of a Latin America–Europe free trade zone.[38]

The Andean Common Market, which includes Colombia, Ecuador, Peru, Venezuela, and Bolivia, has sped up its reduction of tariffs with the free trade zone through the elimination of all tariffs between member countries. Economic realities have sidelined many ideological struggles in Latin America. As Ecuador's minister of industries and commerce said, "We decided to take a risk. Rather than seeing the dangers of trading with a more developed country such as Colombia, we began seeing the opportunities. If Mexico was seeking free trade with the United States, then it was because they saw opportunities of growth."[39]

The Caribbean Community and Common Market (CARICOM) group of fourteen Caribbean island nations represents only 15 million people and is working closely with the North American Free Trade Agreement (NAFTA) to develop a trading relationship or possibly receive preferential treatment for textiles, apparel, footwear and other leather goods, and petroleum. CARICOM, which accounts for $6 billion in trade with the United States, is working with the United States to improve trade and transportation.[40]

36. "The Americas Mercosur's Malaise," *Economist*, April 24, 1999, p. 31.
37. Estrella Gutierrez, "Andean Community Setting Out on a New Stage of Integration, *International Press Service*, April 1, 1998.
38. Robert Wielaard, "EU, Latin America Use Regional Changes to Chart a New Course," Associated Press Newswires, June 30, 1999.
39. "Andes Nations Regain a Taste for Free Trade," *Financial Times*, December 8, 1992, p. 6.
40. Drew Robb, "Central America and the Caribbean," *World Trade*, September 1998, vol. 11, no. 9, pp. 30–33.

President Clinton held a conference of the leaders of the thirty-four Western Hemisphere countries (all except Cuba) in 1994, at which the group agreed to negotiate a Free Trade Area of the Americas (FTAA) by 2005. The future of regional agreements will depend upon the economies of trading partners. If Brazilian inflation is kept in check and Chile's growth continues, some further integration of NAFTA, MERCOSUR, and the Andean group is likely.[41]

North America The U.S.-Canada Free Trade Agreement, which became effective in 1989, removes barriers to trade and investment for most agricultural, industrial, and service businesses. The agreement eliminates tariffs for products manufactured in either country and then exported to the other. If less than 50 percent of the manufacturing cost takes place in the United States or Canada, then the goods are subject to the normal tariff. As two-thirds of Canada's imports from the United States were already duty-free, the agreement has not had much economic significance. The main impact of the agreement is a psychological "kick in the backside," according to an economist of the Canadian Manufacturing Association.[42]

The North American Free Trade Agreement (NAFTA) was signed by the heads of state of Canada, Mexico, and the United States in October 1992 and passed by the governments in late 1993. NAFTA provides for the gradual ending of tariffs and trade barriers, over ten years for most goods and services and over fifteen years for some agricultural products.[43] NAFTA, with a free trade area of 390 million people and an $8.8 trillion output, has attracted considerable investment, especially in Mexico. Sony, Matsushita, and Sanyo, all Japanese electronic firms, have built factories in Mexico, with most of the output going to the U.S. market duty-free.[44]

Middle East There are two market agreements in the Middle East: the Arab Common Market and the Economic Cooperation Organization. The Arab Common Market was formed in 1964 by Egypt, Iraq, Kuwait, Jordan, and Syria. Progress has been achieved toward the development of free trade and eliminations of tariffs between member countries. Equalization of external tariff is expected in the future. The Economic Cooperation Organization (ECO) was originally established by Pakistan, Iran, and Turkey to expand mutual trade and business ventures. In late 1992, the countries of Afghanistan, Azerbaijan, Kyrgyzs-

41. "Now the Hemisphere," *Economist*, October 12, 1996, p. 27, MERCOSUR survey.
42. Bernard Simon, "Trade Pact Brings Canada New Hopes and Fears," *Financial Times*, February 12, 1991, p. 3.
43. "North American Free Trade," special section, *Financial Times*, May 12, 1993, p. 27.
44. "Mexico's Northern Border Is Modern Manufacturing on the Move: The Tijuana Triangle," *Economist*, June 20, 1998, p. 13.

tan, Turkmenistan, Uzbekistan, Kazakhstan, and Tajikistan joined ECO. Linking primarily Islamic countries, ECO is sizable enough, with 300 million people, to support economic initiatives. At meetings held in 1999, the ECO members agreed to cooperate on custom documentation, reducing narcotics and arms trade, and improving trade in the region.[45]

Asia The Association of South East Asian Nations (ASEAN) includes Brunei-Cambodia, Indonesia, Laos, Malaysia, Myanmar (formerly Burma), Singapore, the Philippines, Thailand, and Vietnam. All ASEAN countries, except Singapore, have an abundance of labor and developing economies. Seeking closer economic integration and cooperation between the member countries, ASEAN members began cutting intra-ASEAN tariffs in 1993, working toward an ASEAN free trade area by the year 2008.[46] The aim is to reduce most tariffs with ASEAN to a maximum of 5 percent in a series of cuts over fifteen years.[47] In a U.S.-ASEAN Business Council meeting held in June 1999, United Parcel Service announced a commitment of $500 million in Asia, with a major logistics center in Singapore to support the ASEAN markets and the rest of Asia.[48] ASEAN is expected to grant membership to Cambodia in the future after more evidence of this country's political stability.[49] With its present nine countries, ASEAN is not wealthy but has a population of 500 million, more than Europe or North America. Japan has suggested a summit with its ASEAN neighbors, but because of either Southeast Asians' long-standing suspicions of Japan or ASEAN's fear of antagonizing China, ASEAN's relationship with Japan has remained neutral.[50]

The Asia Pacific Economic Cooperation (APEC) initiative includes eighteen members: the seven nations of ASEAN and the United States, Australia, Canada, New Zealand, Japan, Papua New Guinea, Taiwan, Brunei, Indonesia, Malaysia, Singapore, Philippines, Thailand, South Korea, Chile, Mexico, and China, Hong Kong. APEC was started by the United States and Australia to promote the multilateral interests of the member countries. The APEC trade group has been supported by U.S. president Bill Clinton as his vision of the "new Pacific community."

The future of country groupings in Asia is unclear. ASEAN is a large group in terms of population, but it is not an economic power. APEC is a weak collection of countries to promote trade, but it is not a formal union; no agreements

45. "Economic Cooperation Organization Ends Session in Uzbek Capital," *Narodnoye Slovo*, June 15, 1999, p. 1.
46. "Progress Toward a Free Trade Area," *Financial Times*, December 2, 1992, p. 12.
47. "Fortress Asia?" *Economist*, October 24, 1992, p. 35.
48. Matthew C. Quinn, "International Business: UPS Betting on Southeast Asia," *Atlantic Constitution*, June 17, 1999, p. E2.
49. "ASEAN Looks to a New Year," *Economist*, December 19, 1998, p. 47.
50. "Japan and Asia: Not So Fast," *Economist*, January 18, 1997, p. 37.

have been formatted. APEC depends on the mutual dependence between East Asia and the United States. As the Japanese economy recovers, as China absorbs Hong Kong and Macau, as the China-Taiwan issue is resolved, and as the Korean tension is settled, Asia will face uncertainty. No matter what happens, China will undoubtedly be the focal point of the economic development of Asia.[51]

In an increasingly global trade environment, with 135 members in the WTO, there is considerable discussion of the role of the eighty regional trade groups that grant preferential access to each other's markets. With all of the WTO members except Japan and South Korea belonging to one or more regional trade groups, there is concern about the real value of trade groups. Trade groups' preferential treatment of their members creates trade diversion and ignores the principle of comparative advantage discussed in Chapter 2. Jagdish Bhagwati, an economics professor at Columbia University, argues that the regional trade groups act as stumbling blocks rather than as building blocks to freeing world trade.[52]

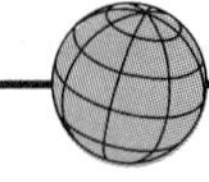

Global Buyers

All buyers go through a similar process to select a product or service for purchase. Although the process will be similar from country to country, the final purchase decisions will vary because of the differences in the social, economic, and cultural systems. International buyers differ by who actually makes the decision to buy, what they buy, why they buy, how they buy, when they buy, and where they buy. To assume that buyers in different countries use the same buying processes and the same selection criteria can be disastrous. When launching disposable diapers worldwide, Procter & Gamble established a global marketing team in Cincinnati, believing babies' diaper needs should be the same around the globe. They later found out that although mothers in most countries are concerned about keeping their babies' bottoms dry, Japanese mothers had different needs. In Japan, babies are changed so frequently that thick absorbent diapers were not necessary and could be replaced by thin diapers that take up less space in the small Japanese home.[53]

In every marketing situation, it is important to understand potential buyers and the process they use to select one product over another. Most elements of a marketing program are designed to influence the buyer to choose one product

51. Barry Wain, "Two Takes on Asians' Future," *Asian Wall Street Journal*, April 12–13, 1996, p. 8.
52. "A Question of Preference: Do Regional Trade Agreements Encourage Free Trade?" *Economist*, August 22, 1998, p. 62.
53. Brian Dumaine, "P&G Rewrites the Rules of Marketing," *Fortune*, November 6, 1989, p. 48.

FIGURE 5.5

Global Buyer Analysis Process

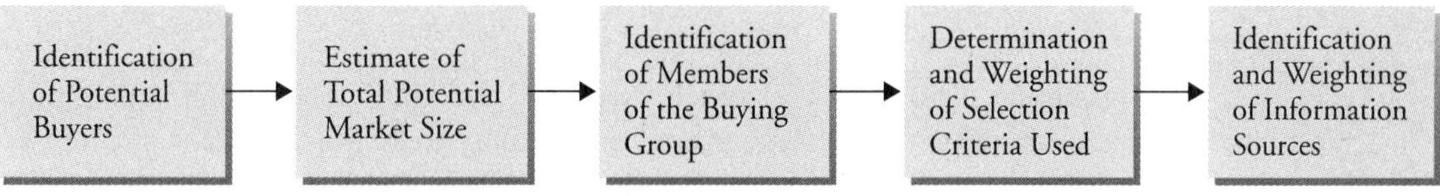

over competitors' products. Figure 5.5 summarizes a process that can be used to analyze the global buyer.

In the case of each type of buyer—consumer, business, and government—the marketer must be able to identify who the buyers are, the size of the potential market, and how they make a purchase decision. For example, in automobile purchases in Italy, who usually makes the decision, the husband or wife? When a Japanese company purchases a computer system, what type of people are involved? Is price more important than the reputation of the computer manufacturer? When a young man in Germany decides to open a savings account, what information sources does he use to select a bank?

Having set a framework for understanding global buyers, we now examine each type of buyer—consumers, businesses, and governments—in the final sections of this chapter.

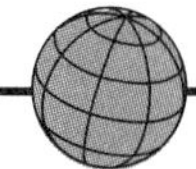

The Consumer Market

Consumers around the world have many similar needs. All people must eat, drink, and be sheltered from the elements. Once these basic needs are met, consumers will seek to improve their standard of living with a more comfortable environment, more leisure time, and an increased social status. Although basic needs and the desire for an improved standard of living are universal throughout the world, people's ability to achieve these objectives is not universal. The economic, political, and social structure of countries affects the ability of consumers to fulfill their needs and the method they use to do so. To understand a consumer market, we must examine the following four aspects of consumer behavior:

1. The ability of people to buy
2. Consumer needs

3. Buying motives
4. The buying process

Ability to Buy

To purchase a product, a consumer must have the ability to buy. The medium of exchange in most societies is currency. The ability to buy a product is affected by the amount of wealth a country possesses and the distribution of its wealth. A country accumulates wealth by the sale of goods to other countries (exports) and the sale of goods within the country. These inflows of money are offset by the outflows of money to pay for necessary imports.

A very important indicator of total consumer potential is gross national product (GNP) because it indicates the value of production in a country, which is an indicator of market size. The GNP per capita shows the value of production per consumer, which is a crude indicator of potential per consumer. The per capita national income is better than the GNP as a measure of gross consumer purchasing power, because it eliminates capital consumption and business taxes, which are not part of personal income. GNP and GNP per capita can vary significantly from country to country.

The total wealth in a country is an important indicator of market potential. With a GNP per capita of $32,350 in Japan and $25,580 in Sweden, it is expected the demand for automobiles will be greater in those countries than in Niger with GNP per capita of 200 or India with $440.[54]

The accumulated income (GNP) is divided among the members of a society. The government has a major influence on the distribution of wealth. A large government will take a large share of the wealth through taxes or ownership of industries. The government also sets policies and laws to regulate the distribution of wealth. For example, a graduated income tax, with a 60 to 90 percent tax on high levels of income and no taxes on low levels of income, will help to distribute income evenly. The revenue that remains in the private sector will be distributed among workers, managers, and owners of industries. Low wages and unemployment will tend to increase the size of the lower-income class. Concentration of business ownership in a few families will decrease the size of the upper class. Income distribution across the population of a country can distort the market potential in a country. For example, if a few people have all the wealth and the remainder are poor, there may be few people in the middle. Countries such as Sierra Leone, Guatemala, Guinea-Bissau, Paraguay, and Panama have the largest disparity between the income held by the top 20 percent and the bottom 20 percent of the population. The countries of Slovakia, the Czech Republic, Austria,

54. *World Bank Atlas 1999* (Washington, D.C.: World Bank, 1999).

Norway, and Finland have the lowest inequity between the top and bottom 20 percent of the population.[55]

Consumer Needs

Money is spent to fulfill basic human needs. One framework of consumer needs was developed by Abraham Maslow. Maslow's hierarchy-of-needs model explains that humans will tend to satisfy lower-level needs, such as the physiological needs for food, clothing, and shelter, before attempting to satisfy higher-level needs, such as safety, belongingness, or esteem. In Figure 5.6, the consumption patterns within different countries illustrate Maslow's theory. The figure shows that the structure of consumption for each country varies depending on the income per capita. A developing country, such as China, spends over 50 percent on food, whereas developed countries, such as France or the United States, spend less than 20 percent on food. Although it is possible to generalize about the order of consumer purchases based on Maslow's hierarchy of needs, the patterns may vary by country.

Buyer Motivation

The ability to buy is influenced by a variety of economic elements that are much easier to identify and qualify than elements in the motivation to buy. As mentioned earlier, all consumers have some similarities as members of the human race. Unfortunately, however, buyer behavior is not uniform among all humans. Buyer behavior is learned, primarily from the culture. As a marketer moves from culture to culture (within and between countries), buyer behavior will differ.

As we discussed in Chapter 3, culture refers to widely shared norms or patterns of behavior within a large group of people.[56] These norms can directly affect product usage. For example, mothers in Brazil feel that only they can properly prepare foods for their babies, and therefore they are reluctant to buy processed foods. This cultural norm in Brazil caused difficulty for Gerber despite the fact that its products were selling well in other Latin American countries.[57]

Social class is a grouping of consumers based on income, education, and occupation. Consumers in the same social class tend to have similar purchase patterns. The perceived class structure and the distribution of income will affect purchase behavior. Culture not only influences the consumer behavior, it also affects the conduct of businesses. Harris and Moran suggest that cross-cultural training is

55. "High Inequality Countries," *Economist*, June 12, 1999, p. 98.
56. Henry Assael, *Consumer Behavior and Marketing Action*, 3rd ed. (Boston: Kent, 1987), p. 15.
57. Ann Helmings, "Culture Shocks," *Advertising Age*, May 17, 1982, p. M-9.

FIGURE 5.6

Consumer Expenditure Patterns of Selected Countries (Percentage of Total Spending)

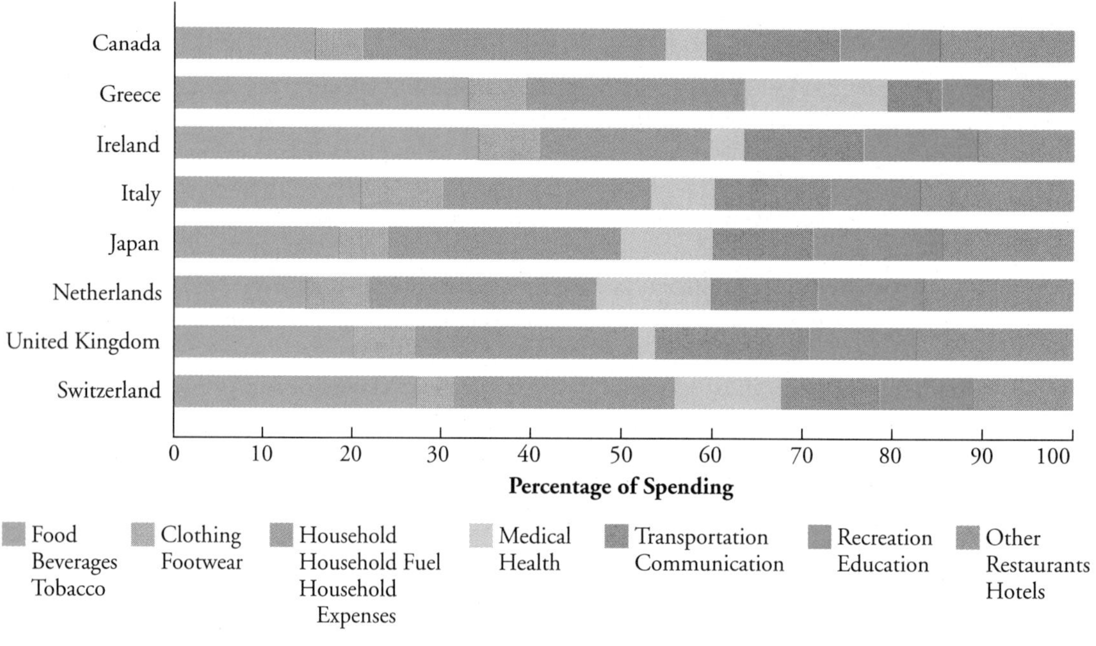

very important for managers to be successful in dealing with business people of different cultures.[58]

Consumers belong to a variety of different groups that also influence purchase behavior. For example, it is difficult to sell insurance in Muslim countries because religious leaders claim it is a form of usury and gambling, both of which are explicitly prohibited in the Koran.[59]

Family Structure The structure of the family and the roles assigned to each member play an important part in determining who makes a decision and who does the influencing. Table 5.7 shows the results of a study that examined and

58. Philip R. Harris and Robert T. Moran, *Managing Cultural Differences*, 2nd ed. (Houston: Gulf, 1987), pp. 3–24.
59. D.E. Allen, "Anthropological Insights into Consumer Behavior," *European Journal of Marketing*, vol. 5 (Summer 1971), p. 54.

TABLE 5.7

Mean Number of Purchase Decisions by Product Type

Product	United States	Venezuela	Product	United States	Venezuela
Groceries			Vacations		
Husband	.23	.23	Husband	1.00	1.51
Joint	.60	.69	Joint	3.68	3.18
Wife	3.20	3.08	Wife	.40	.41
Furniture			Savings		
Husband	.41	1.16	Husband	1.00	1.07
Joint	3.41	2.71	Joint	1.61	1.60
Wife	2.23	2.16	Wife	.44	.34
Major appliances			Housing		
Husband	.98	1.97	Husband	.34	.87
Joint	3.21	2.10	Joint	2.47	1.82
Wife	.85	.93	Wife	.34	.39
Life insurance			Doctor		
Husband	2.65	3.38	Husband	.03	.10
Joint	1.23	.55	Joint	.35	.42
Wife	.15	.05	Wife	.62	.49
Automobiles					
Husband	2.59	4.16			
Joint	3.06	1.42			
Wife	.41	.40			

Source: Robert T. Green and Isabella Cunningham, "Family Purchasing Roles in Two Countries," *Journal of International Business Studies*, Spring–Summer 1980, p. 95. Reprinted by permission.

compared decision-making roles in families from the United States and Venezuela. Nine products/services were picked, and each family surveyed was asked to identify which member made the decision to purchase the product. The overriding contrast between the two samples involved the role of the husband. More joint decisions regarding major purchases were made in the United States than in Venezuela. In all purchase decisions, except groceries and savings, the Venezuelan husband made more decisions than the U.S. husband. Families in the United States make more joint decisions than Venezuelan families.

Global marketers must be aware that variations in family purchasing roles may exist in foreign markets because of the social and cultural differences. Marketing strategy may change based on the respective role of family members. For example, a U.S. manufacturer of appliances or furniture may find it advisable to incorporate the husband into a Venezuelan marketing strategy to a larger extent than in the United States.

Family structure, particularly the number of two-parent families (versus single-parent families), will affect the level of household income. Also, families with two working parents will have a higher level of pooled income than single-parent or one-working-parent families. The pooling of incomes will positively influence the demand for consumer durables and luxury goods.

Religion As we noted in Chapter 3, religion affects behavior patterns by establishing moral codes and taboos. What, when, and how consumers buy is a function of their religion. Traditional Catholics do not eat meat on Fridays during Lent, and Orthodox Jews are forbidden ever to eat pork. The Christian Sabbath is on Sunday, the Jewish Sabbath on Saturday, and the Muslim Sabbath on Friday. Religion influences the attitudes and beliefs of people with regard to interests, work, leisure, family size, family relationships, and so on. Many of these affect the type of products people purchase, why they buy them, and even which newspapers they read. For example, in some countries, if too much attention is given to the body in advertisements, the product may be rejected as immoral.

Educational Systems Formal education involves public or private institutions where learning takes place in a structured environment. The literacy rate is the standard measurement used to assess the extent and success of educational systems, and it normally varies directly with economic development.

In Europe and Japan the literacy rate exceeds 90 percent (see Table 3.2), whereas in some developing countries it is below 50 percent. A low level of literacy affects marketers in two ways: first, it reduces the market for products that require reading, such as books and magazines; second, it reduces the effectiveness of advertising.

Education includes the process of transmitting skills, ideas, attitudes, and knowledge. In effect, the educational process transmits the existing culture and traditions to the next generation. Often the goals of an educational system will include broader political goals, such as India's programs to improve agriculture and reduce the birthrate.

Buying Process

It is difficult to generalize about consumer behavior in each country of the world and for every product category because consumption patterns vary considerably. The differences are caused by consumers' ability and motivation to buy. For example, consumption patterns for beer vary tremendously from country to country. In France, as shown in Figure 5.7, the average consumption is 28 liters per person, versus 140 liters in Ireland or 8 liters in the United States.

FIGURE 5.7

Beer Consumption for Selected Countries (in Liters per Person, 1997)

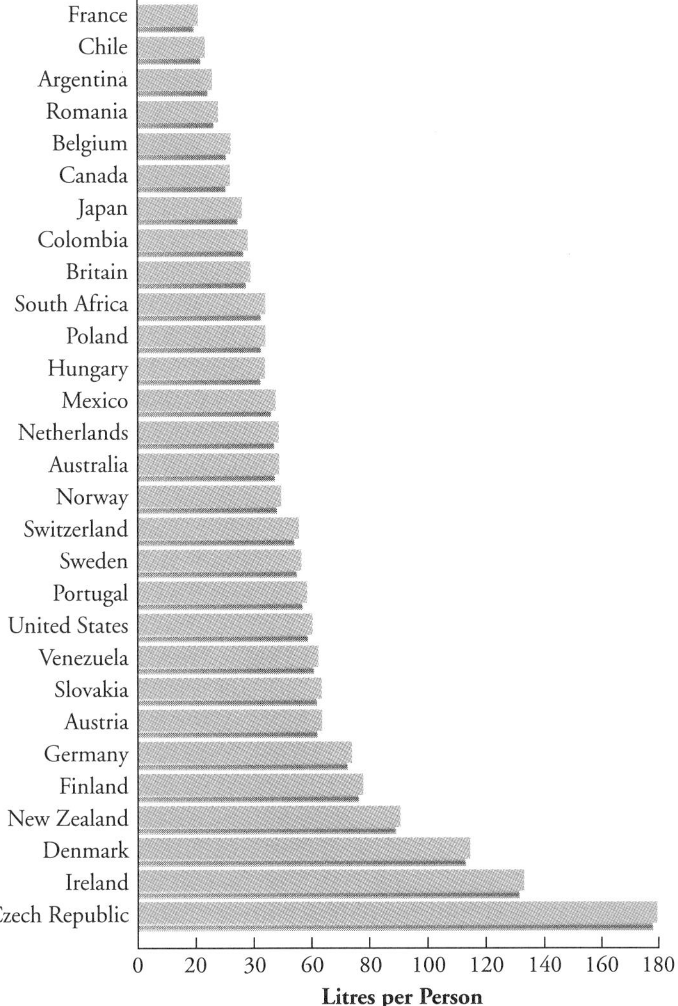

Source: Economist, November 28, 1998, p. 108.

The high consumption of wine in Europe versus the United States is offset by the high U.S. consumption of soft drinks. The average American drinks five times as many soft drinks as a French consumer, three times as many as an Italian, and two and one-half times as many as a German.[60]

Patterns of consumption also vary with services. For example, about 15 percent of the world's countries have 95 percent of all telephones. Studies by the Brookings Institution, the University of Texas, Stanford University, the University of Cairo, and the Massachusetts Institute of Technology indicate that telephones have significant economic benefits to the consumer in excess of the cost and contribute to a rise in per capita income. For example, the World Bank reported that when Sri Lankan farmers received telephones, prices of produce increased from 55 percent of Colombian prices to 85 percent, as a result of buyers having access to better information.[61] The United Nations has established a fund to speed up the adoption of telephones around the world.

Business Markets

Business buyers around the world are much more predictable than consumers because they are more influenced by the economic considerations of cost and less by social or cultural factors. For example, a purchasing agent in Japan who is buying specialty steel for his company will attempt to get the best possible product at the lowest cost, which is similar to how a purchasing agent in the United States or Germany would act. The criteria that business buyers use will be much the same around the world. However, the buying process used by business buyers and the negotiation process are influenced by local culture and vary from country to country. The terms *business buyer* and *industrial buyer* are used interchangeably in this chapter, although business buyers normally include all types of businesses, whereas industrial buyers are limited to manufacturing businesses.

Buying Motives

Industrial buying is less affected by such cultural factors as social roles, religion, and language than is consumer buying. Purchasing agents, regardless of background, will be primarily influenced by the use of the product, its cost, and the terms of delivery.

Industrial products, such as raw materials or machinery, are sold to businesses for use in a manufacturing process to produce other goods. Given that the objective of the manufacturer is to maximize profit, the critical buying criterion will

60. *Beverage Industry Annual Manual* (Cleveland: Harcourt, Brace, Jovanovich, 1987), p. 16.
61. "Third World Telephones," *Economist*, December 17, 1983, pp. 82–85.

focus on the performance of the product purchased versus its cost. This is called the *cost-performance criterion*, and it is used along with other buying criteria such as service, dependability, and knowledge of the selling company.

Because the cost-performance criterion is critical, the economic situation in the purchasing country will affect the decision process. Cost-performance is a function of the local cost of labor and the scale of operation. As can be seen in Figure 5.8, which lists manufacturing labor cost averages in selected countries, wage levels vary from country to country. Thus, selling an industrial robot that replaces three workers in the manufacturing of a certain product will be more easily justified in Japan or Germany, where average labor costs are 40 percent more than in the United States, than it will be in Spain, where labor cost is 20 percent less than in the U.S.

Labor costs play a key role in the level and type of manufacturing. Countries with a surplus of labor normally have lower labor costs, as supply exceeds demand. These lower pay rates result in a certain type of manufacturing that is labor-intensive. Therefore, these countries will be less apt to purchase sophisticated automatic machinery because the same job can be done with cheaper labor. China's main objective, for example, is to import technology that optimizes its vast population. Companies wishing to export to labor-intensive countries must be aware that labor-saving measures may not be appreciated or readily applied. On the other hand, highly developed countries with a high labor rate are prime targets for automated manufacturing equipment. Countries with high labor rates have begun to see an emergence of service industries, which require human labor instead of machines. Labor in these areas is expensive, for a great deal of expertise is needed. Thus, a country normally moves from labor-intensive to capital-intensive and then to technology-intensive industry.

Factors Influencing Global Purchasing

In many situations, a buyer will have the choice of purchasing a domestic product/service or a foreign product/service. The buyer's perceptions of product quality may be influenced by feelings of nationalism, the product's country of origin, and the firm's competence with global transactions. Although it is assumed that industrial buyers will be completely rational and purchase products based on concrete decision criteria such as price, quality, and performance, research has shown that professional purchases are influenced by the country of origin, even when all other variables are held constant.[62]

The global company must recognize the country-of-origin stereotypes and use this information when developing a marketing strategy. Highly nationalistic countries tend to encourage economic self-sufficiency even at the expense of eco-

62. Phillip D. White and Edward W. Cundiff, "Assessing the Quality of Industrial Products," *Journal of Marketing*, January 1978, pp. 80–86.

FIGURE 5.8

Labor Costs per Worker-Hour for Selected Countries

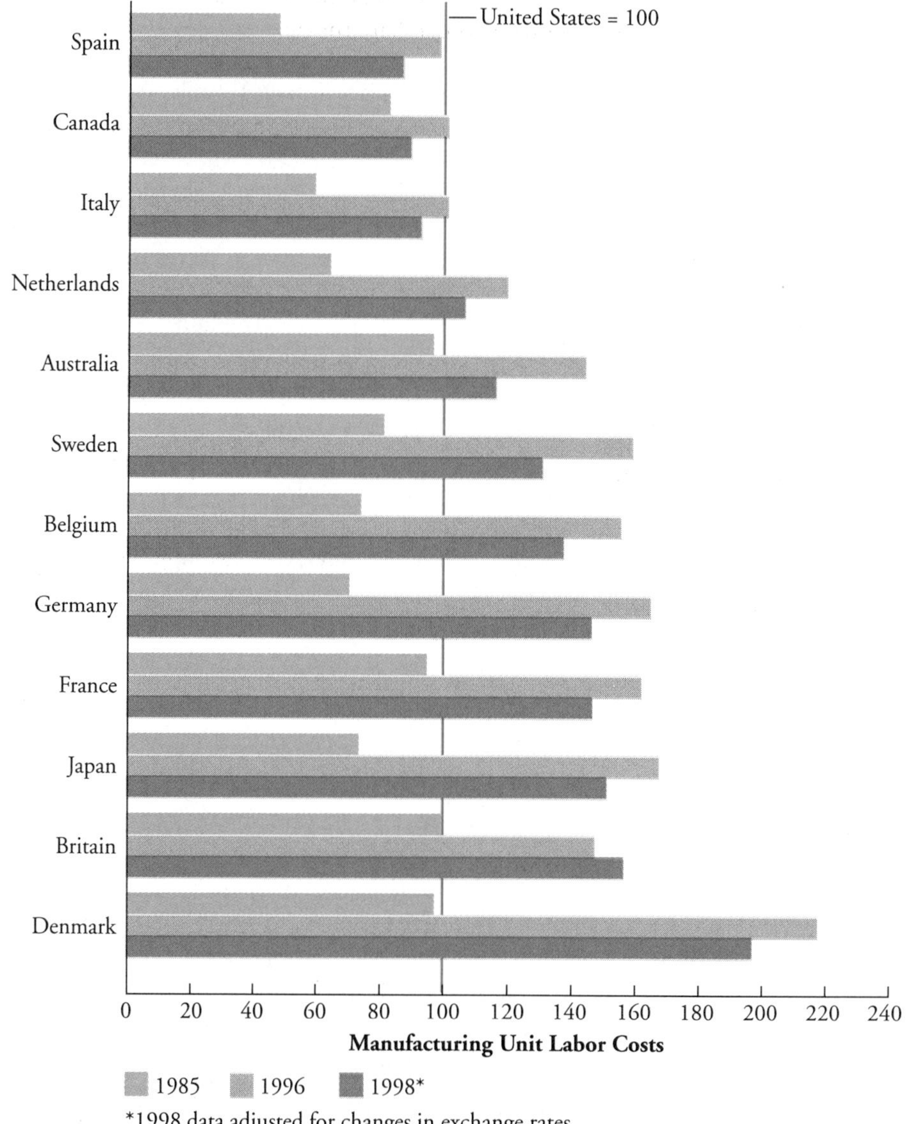

Note: United States = 100.

Source: Economist, December 19, 1998, p. 148. Copyright © 1998 The Economist Newspaper Group, Inc. Reprinted by permission. Further reproduction prohibited.

nomic efficiency, which will have a negative effect on the global company. A study of purchasing behavior by Swedish companies found that buyers preferred to deal with domestic suppliers but would use foreign suppliers when necessary.[63] The study also found that the purchasing firm's competence for global business is positively related to the use of global suppliers. International purchasers generally have broad market knowledge, an ability to handle foreign cultural patterns, and a knowledge of international trade techniques.[64] Given the results of this analysis, the global company should pay close attention to the level of nationalism in a country, the country-of-origin stereotypes, and the competence level of the purchasing function to deal with global suppliers.

Government Markets

A large number of international business transactions involve governments. For example, 80 percent of all international trade of agricultural products is handled by governments. The U.S. government buys more goods and services than any other government, business, industry, or organization in the world.[65] Selling to governments can be both time consuming and frustrating. However, governments are large purchasers, and selling to them can provide enormous returns.

The size of government purchases depends on the economic or political orientation of the country. In highly developed, free-market countries, the government has less of a role than in state-controlled markets, where most buying is under direct control of the state. Less developed countries lack the economic infrastructure to facilitate private companies; thus, governments play a major role in overseeing the purchase of foreign products. The amount of government purchases is also a function of state-owned operations. For example, in the United States the only government-owned operation is the postal system, whereas in India the government owns not only the postal system, but also the telecommunications, electric, gas, oil, coal, railway, airline, and shipbuilding industries.

The Buying Process

Governmental buying processes tend to be highly bureaucratic. In order to sell to the U.S. Department of Defense, a firm has to get on a bidding list for each branch of the armed forces. These bidding lists are issued on an annual basis; thus, a firm not able to get on the list must wait a full year to try again.

63. Lars Hallen, "International Purchasing in a Small Country: An Exploratory Study of Five Swedish Firms," *Journal of International Business Studies*, Winter 1982, pp. 99–111.
64. Ibid.
65. *Selling to the Government Markets: Local, State, Federal* (Cleveland: Government Product News, 1975), p. 2.

Governments make it harder for a foreign firm to sell to them; many place their own domestic firms ahead of foreign operations. Also, negotiating with foreign governments can be a very formal process. Understanding cultural differences is essential in order not to overstep boundaries.

Government procurement processes vary from country to country. The following sections describe purchasing processes in Belgium and in the European Union.

Marketing to the Belgian Government[66] In Belgium, 90 percent of all public contracts are awarded to the lowest bidder. The remaining 10 percent are granted through "invitation to tender," with factors other than price coming into play. These other factors may include the company's financial viability, technical competence, and postsale service. Central government supplies, excluding data processing and telecommunications, must be bought through the Central Supplies Office. Regional, local, and quasi-governmental bodies, such as Sabena Airlines, purchase supplies independently. Here are several recommendations to companies that wish to sell to the Belgian government:

- Manufacture in Belgium. Preference is given to a local supplier if other things are equal.
- Develop a European image. A strong EU image has favored companies such as Siemens and Philips.
- Use the appropriate language. Although both Flemish and French are officially accepted, ask which is preferred in the department that is accepting the bid.
- Emphasize the recruitment of labor following the winning of a contract. Companies are favored if they will employ Belgian people.
- When new technology is involved, get in at the beginning. It is often difficult and expensive for the government to change to a different technology at a later date.
- Whenever possible, use local contractors. The Belgian government likes a bidder to use as many local contractors as possible.

Obviously, bidding for Belgian government work is particularly difficult for suppliers with no local participation of subcontractors or manufacturing in Belgium or the EU. However, every government market has some limitations.

Economic and Political Needs of Governments

Firms involved in selling to foreign governments not only must have an understanding of the political and economic structures, they must also be able to evalu-

66. The information in this section has been drawn from Business Global, "How to Sell to Belgium's Public Sector," *Business Europe*, October 2, 1981, pp. 314–315.

ate a country's industrial trends vis-à-vis the national system. Factors to be considered are the government's responsibility to industry, government priorities, national defense, high-tech industrial efficiency, and financial self-sufficiency. The level of economic development involves not only the GNP but the state of production. China, for example, is pushing for modernization but does not want production techniques at the expense of its large labor pool. The desire to reduce unemployment is a major interest to most countries. Governments are also confronted with balance of payments problems. Trade deficits—importing more than exporting—will affect the position of a country's currency with respect to foreign currencies. The more the government imports, the more expensive the products become because the government must use more foreign exchange.

Governments tend to protect their domestic industry to shrink high unemployment and GNP deficits. Whether products are for consumer, industrial, or government use, protection in the form of tariffs, subsidiaries, and quotas is levied if domestic industries are threatened. Because governments look out for their domestic companies, they will stay clear of those products and services on which restrictions are imposed.

Protection of domestic products and services extends beyond that imposed by foreign governments. The threat of reducing national security has prompted governments to institute restrictions on various domestic products. The transfer of technology such as nuclear plants, computers, telecommunications, and military weapons is usually restricted so that these critical technologies do not get into the wrong hands.

Conclusions

The world marketplace is large and complex. The global company needs to systematically evaluate the entire world market on a regular basis to be sure that company assets are directed toward the countries with the best opportunities. The basis for an evaluation of countries should be a comparative analysis of different countries. Certain ones may be unsuitable because of their unstable political situation, and others may have little potential because their population is small or the per capita income is low. The screening process gives the firm information about market size, competition, trade regulations, and distribution systems that will form the basis for the development of a market strategy. As global firms evaluate different consumer, business, and government market opportunities, they must be aware of the nature of the differences between countries.

The nature of the world marketplace has changed as a result of the development of major regional market groups. The economic integration of a number of countries offers great opportunities to companies. Many national markets, such as those in Europe, that are small individually become significant when combined with other countries. By locating production facilities in one country of a market group, the global company has access to the other countries with little or no trade restrictions. The market groups also increase competition. Local producers that for years completely dominated their national markets thanks to tariff protection now face competition from many other member countries.

The development of these market groups can also have negative effects on global companies. If a company is unable or unwilling to build a manufacturing plant in a certain market group, it may be unprofitable to export to that market. There are often more regulations between market groups, making it more complicated and expensive to move goods from one group to another. Also, the market group does not necessarily reduce the complexity of the consumer and cultural differences. For example, although Germany and Spain are both in the EU, the marketing programs, products, and strategies for success in each market will differ.

The success of market groups formed after World War II, particularly the EU, indicates that such groups will continue to grow. The potential entry of some eastern European countries into the EU, as well as the expansion of NAFTA to include other Central or South American countries, supports the growth of market groups and the growing interdependence of trading partners. Global companies need to monitor the development of new groups and any changes in the structure of current groups, because changes within market groups will result in changes in market size and competition.

The largest business markets for U.S. goods are in countries that have a sophisticated industrial infrastructure, such as Canada, Japan, Germany, and England. These countries have a large industrial base, a financial basis, and a transportation network. These countries are also large importers and exporters of goods and services.

Developing countries offer a different type of market opportunity. They have specific economic needs that must be met with limited financial resources. In these situations, the government is likely to get involved in the purchase process, offering concessions to get the correct product or agreement. In many cases, the government will be the decision maker.

QUESTIONS FOR DISCUSSION

1. Searching for the best global opportunity often requires an analysis of all the countries of the world. How will the initial screening differ from the final screening of possible countries to enter?
2. If you were evaluating opportunities for caviar but found that no countries had data on caviar consumption, what other indicators would you use to evaluate the size of each country's market?
3. Using Figure 5.3, compare the potential for caviar consumption in Germany, India, and South Korea.
4. In the sale of hair shampoo, what are the advantages of grouping countries together rather than marketing to each country individually?

5. What are the differences between a free trade area, a customs union, and a common market? If you were marketing to a grouping of countries but only had a manufacturing plant in one of the countries, which of the three types of agreements would you prefer? Why?
6. What are the reasons for the growth in the establishment of country groupings?
7. What critical factors influence a consumer's ability to purchase a product such as a stereo system?
8. Given the data on family decision making in the United States and Venezuela in Table 5.7, how will the marketing of automobiles be different in the two countries?
9. Will the buying process be more similar from country to country for deodorant or delivery vans? Why?
10. If you are selling a product such as nuclear power plants, which are purchased mostly by governments, how would you prepare to sell to Belgium, Egypt, and Mexico? What process should be used to understand the government buying process in each of these countries?

FOR FURTHER READING

Graig, C. Samuel, and Susan P. Douglas. *International Marketing Research*. John Wiley & Sons, 2000.

Craig, C. Samuel, and Susan P. Douglas. "Responding to the Challenges of Global Markets: Change, Complexity, Completion and Conscience." *Columbia Journal of World Business*,Winter 1996, pp. 6–18.

Fishburn, Dudley, ed. *World in 1991*. London: The Economist Publications, 1991.

Ganesh, Jaishankar. "Converging Trends Within the European Union: Insights from an Analysis of Diffusion Patterns. *Journal of Global Marketing*, November 1998, vol. 6, no. 4.

Hilton, Andrew. "Mythology, Markets, and the Emerging Europe." *Harvard Business Review*, November-December 1992, pp. 50–54.

Lal, Deepak. "Trade Blocs and Multilateral Free Trade." *Journal of Common Market Studies*, September 1993, pp. 349–358.

Levy, Brian. "Korean and Taiwanese Firms as International Competitors: The Challenges Ahead." *Columbia Journal of World Business*, Spring 1998, pp. 43–52.

Longhammer, Rolf J. "The Developing Countries and Regionalism." *Journal of Common Market Studies*, June 1992, pp. 211–231.

Malhotra, Naresh K., James Agarwal, and Imad Baalbaki. "Heterogeneity of Regional Trading Blocs and Global Marketing Strategies: A Multicultural Perspective." *International Marketing Review*, 1998, vol. 15, no. 6, pp. 476–506.

Mitchell, Vincent W., and Michael Grentorex. "Consumer Purchasing in Foreign Countries: A Perceived Risk Perspective." *International Journal of Advertising*, 1990, vol. 9, no. 4, pp. 295–307.

Papadopoulos, Nicolas, Louise A. Heslop, and Jozsef Beracs. "National Stereotypes and Product Evaluation in a Socialist Country." *International Marketing Review*, 1990, vol. 7, no. 1, pp. 32–47.

Pinkerton, Richard L. "The European Community—'EC '92': Implications for Purchasing Managers." *International Journal of Purchasing and Materials Management*, Spring 1993, pp. 19–26.

Quelch, John, Erich Joachimsthalen, and Jose Luis Nueno. "After the Wall: Marketing Guidelines for Eastern Europe." *Sloan Management Review*, 1991, vol. 32, no. 2, pp. 82–93.

Russow, Lloyd C., and Andrew Solocha. "A Review of the Screening Process Within the Context of the Global Assessment Process." *Journal of Global Marketing*, 1993, vol. 7, no. 1, pp. 65–85.

Tam, Jackie L. M., and Susan H. C. Tai. "The Psychographic Segmentation of the Female Market in Greater China." *International Marketing Review*, 1998, vol. 15, no. 1, pp. 61–77.

van Rij, Jeanne Binstock. "Trends, Symbols and Brand Power in Global Markets: The Business Anthropology Approach." *Strategy & Leadership*, November/December 1996, pp. 18–24.

6

Global Marketing Research

PREVIOUSLY, WE INTRODUCED YOU TO A VARIETY OF CONSUMERS, MARKETS, and environments. Our main purpose in Chapter 6 is to provide you with a method for collecting the appropriate data and a framework in which to analyze the environment, the market, and the consumers for your product. Figure 6.1 presents an overview of global market research and analysis.

Although this chapter is written around the research issues in an international environment, our emphasis is managerial rather than technical. Throughout the chapter, we focus on how companies can obtain useful and accurate information that will help them to make more informed strategic and marketing decisions described in later chapters.

FIGURE 6.1

International Marketing Research and Analysis

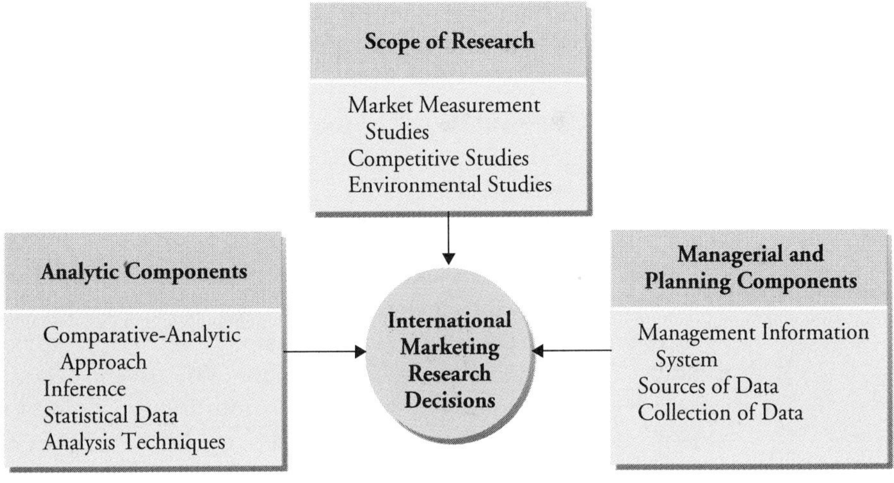

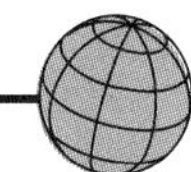

The Scope of Global Marketing Research

Global marketing research is meant to provide adequate data and cogent analysis for effective decision making on a global scale. In contrast to marketing research that has a domestic focus, global research covers a multitude of environments, and there is a scarcity of comparable, relevant data. Because of this limitation, flexibility, resourcefulness, and ingenuity on the part of the researcher are often required to overcome the numerous obstacles encountered in carrying out the research task.

The analytical research techniques practiced by domestic businesses also apply to global marketing projects. The key difference is in the complexity of assignments because of the additional variables that must be dealt with. Global marketers have to judge the comparability of their data across a number of markets; they frequently are faced with making decisions based on limited data. Traditionally, marketing research has been charged with the following three broad areas of responsibility:

1. *Market studies*. One of the most frequent tasks of researchers is to determine the size of a market and the needs of potential customers. From this data, it is possible to estimate expected sales for a product in a country or set of coun-

tries, which is an important input into the development of a global marketing program.

2. *Competitive studies*. To provide insights about competitors, both domestic and foreign, is an important assignment for the global marketing researcher. The researcher must study the general competitive behavior of industries in the various markets within which the firm will compete.

3. *Environmental studies*. Given the added environmental complexity of global marketing, managers need factual and timely input on the international environment—particularly relating to the economic, political, and legal elements of the potential markets.

Global marketing research is used to make both strategic and tactical decisions. Strategic decisions include the selection of what markets to enter, how to enter them (exporting licensing, joint venture), and where to locate production facilities. Tactical decisions are decisions about the specific marketing mix to be used in a country. Table 6.1 shows the various types of tactical marketing decisions needed and the kinds of research used to collect the necessary data.

New-product development or product adaptation will require product benefit research and product testing to meet environmental conditions, customer tastes, and competitive constraints. For example, CPC International did consumer research on Skippy peanut butter in Hungary. There was no question with the taste, look, and packaging, but Hungarian consumers were critical about the texture. Chunky style was favored over creamy style. This research helped determine product texture as well as focus the advertising and direct in-store displays and sampling.[1]

Advertising, sales promotion, and sales force decisions all require data from the local market in the form of testing. The type of information required is often the same as that required in domestic marketing research, but the process is made more complex by the variety of cultures and environments.

The Importance of Global Marketing Research

The complexity of the global marketplace, the extreme differences that exist from country to country, and the frequent lack of familiarity with foreign markets accentuate the importance of global marketing research. Before making market entry, product position, or market mix decisions, a marketer must have accurate information about the market size, customer needs, competition, and so on. Marketing research provides the necessary information to avoid the costly mistakes of poor strategies or lost opportunities.

1. "Hungary for Skippy, CPC Spreads Peanut Butter Brand in New Market," *Advertising Age*, September 2, 1991, p. 36.

TABLE 6.1

Global Marketing Decisions Requiring Marketing Research

Marketing Mix Decision	Type of Research
Product policy	Focus groups and qualitative research to generate ideas for new products
	Survey research to evaluate new product ideas
	Concept testing, test marketing
	Product benefit and attitude research
	Product formulation and feature testing
Pricing	Price sensitivity studies
Distribution	Survey of shopping patterns and behavior
	Consumer attitudes toward different store types
	Survey of distributor attitudes and policies
Advertising	Advertising pretesting
	Advertising posttesting, recall scores
	Surveys of media habits
Sales promotion	Surveys of response to alternative types of promotion
Sales force	Tests of alternative sales presentations

Source: C. Samuel Craig and Susan P. Douglas, *International Marketing Research,* © 1983, p. 32. Reprinted by permission of Prentice-Hall, Inc. Englewood Cliffs, NJ.

Marketing research can guide product development for a foreign market. Based on a research study conducted in the United States, one U.S. firm introduced a new cake mix in England. Believing that homemakers wanted to feel that they participated in the preparation of the cake, the U.S. marketers devised a mix that required homemakers to add an egg. Given the success in the U.S. market, the marketers confidently introduced the product in England. The product failed, however, because the British did not like the fancy American cakes. They preferred cakes that were tough and spongy and could accompany afternoon tea.

The technique of having homemakers add an egg to the mix did not eliminate basic taste and stylistic differences.[2]

Companies are spending more on in-company research to keep up with volatile market segments. There are over 100 million young, affluent, media-literate, music-loving Europeans whose needs are changing. PepsiCo's research found that the youth market was ready for a new cola that did not contain sugar. However, Pepsi also found the youth market, especially males, was adverse to a diet soda; therefore, the soft drink giant launched Pepsi Max as a trendy, cool, sugar-free cola. The TV campaign showed Pepsi Max drinkers "Living Life to the Max," performing death-defying stunts.[3]

Whirlpool found that market research could help speed up market entry. Although fewer than one-third of European households owned microwave ovens, research suggested that European consumers would buy a microwave that performed like a conventional oven. Whirlpool therefore introduced a model that incorporated a broiler coil for top browning and a unique dish that sizzles the underside of the food. This new product, the Crisp, became one of Europe's best-selling microwaves.[4]

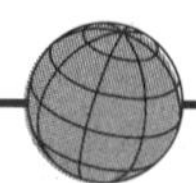

Challenges in Planning Global Research

Global marketing researchers face five principal challenges:

1. Complexity of research design
2. Lack of secondary data
3. Costs of collecting primary data
4. Coordination of research and data collection across countries
5. Establishing comparability and equivalence[5]

Whereas domestic research is limited to one country, global research includes many countries. The research design is made more complex because the researcher defining the possible target market must choose which countries or segments should be researched. This initial step in the research process is further complicated by limited secondary information. Even if the appropriate secondary information exists, it may be difficult to locate and acquire. Thus, researchers are

2. David A. Ricks, *Blunders in International Business*, Third Edition (New York: Blackwell, 1999), pp. 130–136.
3. Juliana Koranteng, "Tracking What's Trendy, Hot Before It's Old News," *Advertising Age International*, May 1996, p. 130.
4. "How to Listen to Consumers," *Fortune*, January 11, 1993, p. 77.
5. C. Samuel Craig and Susan P. Douglas, *International Marketing Research:* (New York: Wiley, 2000), pp. 16–19.

forced either to spend considerable resources finding such data or to accept the limited secondary data that are available. In many countries, the cost of collecting primary data is substantially higher than in the domestic market. This is particularly the case for developing countries. Consequently, researchers have to accept tradeoffs between the need for more accurate data and the limited resources available to accomplish the tasks.

Even gathering demographics from country to country is no easy task. There are a wide variety of problems with using national census data. For example, the U.S. census is taken every ten years. Canada and Japan do one every five years. Germany did one in 1987, twenty-seven years after its previous census in 1960. Although the United States, Canada, Australia, New Zealand, Mexico, Sweden, and Finland collect income data, many countries do not. Educational levels can be used to determine socioeconomic status, but educational systems vary widely from country to country, making comparisons very crude. Switzerland and Germany publish data on noncitizens. Canada collects data on religion. Both these topics are excluded from the U.S. census. Marital status and head of household information varies from country to country. Ireland only recognizes single, married, or widowed. Latin America often combines cohabiting with marital categories. These major differences from country to country make even the simplest demographic analysis challenging.[6]

Because companies can ill afford for each subsidiary to obtain its own expensive primary data, coordination of research and data collection across countries becomes necessary. The borrowing of research results from one country to another is hindered by the general difficulty of establishing comparability and equivalence among various research data. Definitions of housewives, socioeconomic status, incomes, and customers vary widely in Europe, even where the research is measuring the same thing.[7] Full comparability can only be achieved when identical procedures are used. One study found that, even with the same scales measuring the same attributes of products, different cultures exhibit different degrees of reliability because of different levels of awareness, knowledge, and familiarity.[8] With research capabilities differing from country to country, global marketing research administration becomes a real challenge. Companies that can successfully manage this task will be in a situation to avoid costly duplication of research.

Along with all the problems of data collection and comparability, balancing between the needs of national subsidiaries and headquarters can pose a challenge. Market research agencies report that treading the diplomatic path between head office staff and national subsidiaries of global firms is probably the biggest

6. Donald B. Pittenger, "Gathering Foreign Demographics Is No Easy Task," *Marketing News*, January 8, 1991, p. 23.
7. Tom Lester, "Common Markets," *Marketing*, November 9, 1989, p. 41.
8. Ravi Parameswaran and Attila Yaprak, "A Cross-National Comparison of Consumer Research Measures," *Journal of International Business Studies*, Spring 1987, p. 45.

problem they face on global research projects. This obstacle is increasingly recognized as companies make the conceptual switch to treating Europe as a single market.[9]

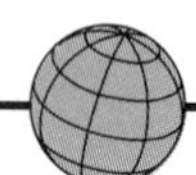

Conceptual Framework: The Comparative Analytic Approach

We have discussed the scope of marketing research situations and the difficulties encountered in conducting research. Although an understanding of the difficulties of collecting information for foreign markets helps to increase the quality of information obtained, an overall conceptual framework is necessary to provide the analyst with the relevant questions to ask. Consequently, this section of the chapter focuses on building a framework that can guide global marketing managers in the formulation of market research studies.

Pioneered by T. A. Hagler in the late 1950s, comparative research actually led to the establishment of global marketing as a discipline.[10] Comparative marketing focuses on the entire marketing system, but this macro approach becomes less important as specific problems at the company level need to be analyzed. However, the comparative approach can be adapted to specific micromarketing problems.

Marketing as a Function of the Environment

Comparative marketing analysis emphasizes the study of the marketing process in its relationship to the environment. The marketing process is viewed as a direct function of environment. Under changed environmental conditions, the existing marketing processes are also expected to change. In a dual-country analysis employing the comparative approach, the marketing environment in one country is investigated with respect to its effect on the marketing process. The resulting functional relationship is transferred to a second country, whose environment may be known but whose marketing process will be assessed based on the earlier analysis of the relationship between the marketing process and the environment in another country.

This situation is illustrated in Figure 6.2.[11] The comparative marketing analysis allows the researcher to understand the relationship between the environment and the marketing process in one country and then to transfer that knowledge to another country, *adjusting* for differences in the environment.

9. Robin Cobb, "Client Diplomacy," *Marketing*, May 17, 1990, p. 31.
10. Jean Boddeyn, "A Framework for Comparative Marketing Research," *Journal of Marketing Research*, May 1966, pp. 149–153; *Comparative Management and Marketing* (Glenview, Ill.: Scott, Foresman, 1969).
11. Jean-Pierre Jeannet, "International Marketing Analysis: A Comparative-Analytic Approach," working paper, 1981.

FIGURE 6.2

Managerial Approach to Comparative Analysis

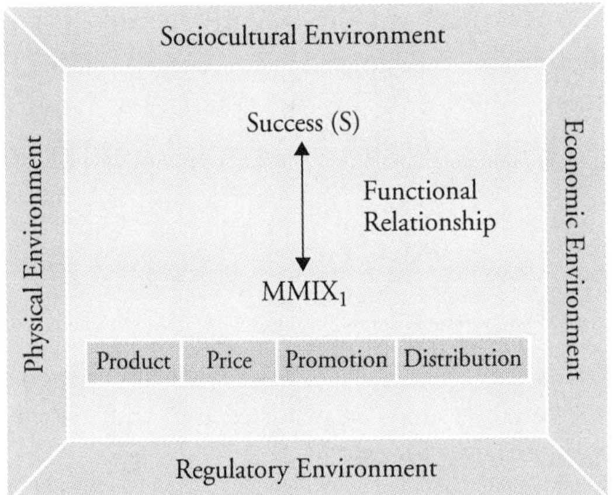

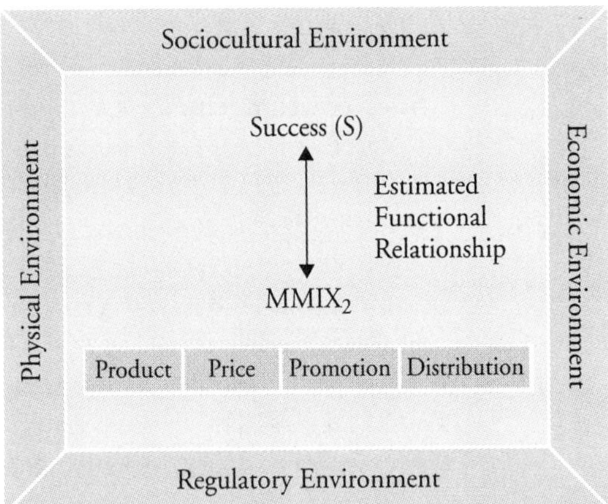

Example: McDonald's In the United States (the home country), McDonald's achieved its success through an aggressive, well-structured marketing mix. The elements may be described as follows:

- *Product/service design:* A standardized product of high and consistent quality emphasizing speed of service and long opening hours
- *Price:* A low-price policy
- *Distribution:* Placing restaurants primarily in areas where customers live—suburban and urban locations
- *Promotion:* A strong advertising campaign that focuses on the consumer, particularly young people, via heavy use of television promotion

In the early 1970s, several other countries were targeted for possible expansion, and an assessment had to be made as to the best approach for McDonald's to pursue. The traditional approach views success in the United States as a function of McDonald's effective marketing strategy, or as a direct result of the company's own efforts. The comparative analytic approach advanced here, however, views McDonald's success as a function of a given set of marketing mix variables that are effective because of the country's environment. The main emphasis falls on the domestic environmental variables that allowed McDonald's marketing mix to be successful.

The difference between the two approaches is important. The comparative analytic view sees McDonald's primarily as having been able to take advantage of an existing opportunity, whereas the traditional approach views McDonald's success primarily as a direct result of its own efforts.

Viewing the Marketing Mix as a Function of the Environment Viewing a successful marketing mix as a function of the existing environment emphasizes an environmental view of the marketing process.[12] This view is of great importance. Success is no longer defined as unilateral or solely a function of the marketing mix. Thus, the company is viewed as taking advantage of a given opportunity rather than creating one by its own actions.

Understanding the Marketing Environment

The first step in the comparative analytic approach is to look at the environmental factors. The critical environmental variables may be grouped into four major categories: physical, social/cultural, economic, and regulatory.

Physical Variables Included in physical variables are constraints with respect to the conditions of the product's use or the physical properties of the particular market. These are population, population density, geographic area, climate, and the physical conditions of the product's use (surroundings, space and size requirements, and so on). Variables such as population have an effect on the absolute size of any target market and, similar to climate, tend to be subject to little change over time. The physical-use conditions relate to a product's function in any given environment. As a result, we view the consumption of the product or service as a *physical event* directly influenced by physical environmental variables that have to be recognized to determine a marketing mix.

Turning again to the McDonald's example, several variables from the physical environment have contributed toward McDonald's success in the United States. An important influence on McDonald's distribution or location policies was the concentration of the U.S. population in suburbia. Opening 11,368 units in the United States was possible because of the absolute size of the population, which is about 270 million people.[13] It is important to recognize that the market size is often finite and that any country with a different population would, of course, not offer the same opportunities, all other things being equal. The physical-use conditions of McDonald's are less restrictive because they are directly shaped by the firm's policies and the building of outlets. The situation is different in cases in

12. Robert Bartels, "Are Domestic and International Marketing Dissimilar?" *Journal of Marketing*, July 1968, pp. 56–61.
13. Robert F. Hartley, "McDonald's: Could There Be Storms on the Horizon?" *Marketing Mistakes and Successes* (New York: Wiley, 1998), p. 273.

which consumers take products home for consumption and are restricted by their own physical environments, such as apartment or kitchen size, electrical systems, and so on.

Social/Cultural Variables Social/cultural variables include all relevant factors from the social and cultural background of any given marketing environment, including local cultural background (race, religion, customs, habits, and languages), educational system, and social structure (individual roles, family structure, social classes, and reference groups).

As we have mentioned before, the social/cultural environment is a primary influence on the role expectations of buyers and sellers, regardless of the differences in the physical environment. Since the social/cultural environment does not change rapidly over time, many domestic marketers can lose sight of the fact that they've subconsciously chosen a marketing mix that incorporates many social/cultural values. Defining the social forces that impact on a marketing mix is the first step in shedding the cultural bias that affects so many managers unknowingly.

In the case of McDonald's, several social and cultural forces greatly affected its success. For one, the value that U.S. society placed on time favored the consumption of meals with minimum time effort. Saving time, in fact, created the desire for meals purchased outside the home on an unplanned or impulse basis. The result was a burgeoning demand for low-priced food that was available any time and that could be purchased with minimum shopping effort. Another important factor was the prevailing family structure in the United States and the trend toward a youth-oriented culture. Beginning with the 1970s, the decision-making role in families changed to such an extent that children often made the selection of a place to eat. McDonald's special emphasis on children and teenagers as advertising targets was successful largely because the strategy capitalized on these existing social trends.

The changing role of the wife in the typical U.S. household resulted in an ever-increasing number of women accepting employment outside the home. Whether this trend resulted in a lower valuation of the home-cooked meal in a social sense is debatable; nevertheless, it greatly increased the acceptability of eating meals outside the home.

Not to be underestimated is the habit or heritage of the hamburger itself. Truly, the hamburger represents a long-standing tradition of the U.S. food and restaurant scene, and hamburger made up the daily meal of many Americans before McDonald's arrived on the scene. It is fair to state, then, that the company's success stemmed to a considerable degree from the selection of an already existing and widely popular product. Aside from the type of service, the product did not represent an innovation. Of course, there are other reasons for dining out, and U.S. customers often make other choices, but the social and cultural influences to a large extent prepared the ground for the success of an operation such as McDonald's.

Adjusting a marketing mix to consumer needs and tastes is very important, as McDonald's discovered in the Philippines. Whereas McDonald's used its standard menu in the Philippines, Jollibee, a local family-owned hamburger chain, tailored its menu to Philippine tastes. Jollibee offered a slice of pineapple on its Aloha Burger, as well as thin noodles, tofu, fish, and squid, along with rice instead of French fries. Consequently, Jollibee enjoys 57 percent of the Philippine hamburger market, while McDonald's has only captured 36 percent.[14] Jollibee has 325 stores in the Philippines compared with McDonald's less than 200 stores.[15] McDonald's also found it needed to adapt its menu in India, where the Maharaja Mac is made from lamb, not beef or pork, in respect for the Hindus' reverence of cows and the Muslims' abstinence from pork.[16]

What is important then is to isolate the salient social and cultural variables that have an impact on the success of a company's products or services. The combined sociocultural variables create the *sociocultural event* that becomes an essential part of the consumption and use of any product or service. Understanding the nature of the sociocultural event in one country as the starting point for analyzing the respective variables in another country is the basis of the comparative analytic model.

Economic Variables Under the economic category, we include all aspects of the economic environment, on both a macro and micro level, such as gross national product (GNP), GNP per capita, price levels, income distribution, and prices of competitive products and services.

Economic considerations affect most consumption or buying decisions. To the extent that income levels of consumers differ from country to country, the tradeoffs consumers make in order to maximize economic satisfaction are different. Different price levels for products also cause changes in buying behavior even under a constant income level. The global marketer must isolate the specific income and price variables to arrive at a given combination, termed the *economic event*, that affects the success of a given product or service. The comparative analytic model suggests that the elements and nature of the economic event with regard to another market can largely be found by first investigating the relevant factors in a company's home market.

For McDonald's, a significant variable of the economic environment was the income level of the U.S. population and the resulting disposable income available for frequent visits to fast-food restaurants. It is still more expensive to frequent a fast-food outlet than to prepare an equivalent meal at home; consequently, the success of fast-food outlets does not so much stem from their price advantage

14. Farland Chang, "Western Ideas, Asian Empire," CNNfn: Entrepreneurs Only, June 7, 1999.
15. Al Labita, "Jollibee to Open More Fast Food Outlets in U.S.," *Business Times* (Singapore), March 22, 1999, p. 20.
16. Robert F. Hartley, *Marketing Mistakes and Successes* (New York: Wiley, 1998), p. 237.

over food purchased in stores. Instead, it was the *relative price advantage* of fast-food restaurants over the more traditional, simple diner-type restaurants that ensured the tremendous success of fast-food outlets. Consuming a meal at a place such as McDonald's becomes an economic event to the extent that economic variables are introduced into the consumer's decision-making process affecting the particular product or service choice.

Regulatory Variables The regulatory environment includes all actions of governments or agencies influencing business transactions, such as commercial law or codes, consumer protection laws, product liability laws, regulatory agencies (for example, the U.S. Food and Drug Administration, the U.S. Department of Commerce, and the International Chamber of Commerce), local regulations, and zoning laws.

Regulations do not tend to stimulate needs or demands for services and products. Instead, they act in an *enabling manner* (or disabling manner, depending on the point of view) by restricting choices for the international corporation or by prescribing the nature of its marketing effort. Companies have to be aware of the particular regulations that make an existing marketing program effective because such an approach may not be duplicated in other countries even if it were desirable from a business point of view.

The possible effect of the regulatory environment can be illustrated by returning to our example. Certainly, the use of television advertising to reach children was one of the reasons for McDonald's success in the United States. But in many other countries, particularly those in Europe, such advertising is banned outright. On an operational level, it may be difficult to get teenage help in some countries or impossible to keep operating during hours customary in the United States. Since the United States has in many ways a more liberal regulatory environment, companies often face situations in which operations cannot be carried out in the accustomed fashion. This is true even when the target customers in other countries would respond positively to U.S. methods or practices and even when the relevant physical, economic, and social events indicate that their use would be beneficial.

Analyzing Environmental Variables

The importance of environmental variables to international marketing has been emphasized by previous writers. Robert Bartels highlighted physical, social, and economic variables in his environmental marketing concept.[17] Robert Buzzell included a similar set of variables in his analysis of elements that may prevent a standardization of marketing programs across several countries.[18] Furthermore, War-

17. Bartels, "Are Domestic and International Marketing Dissimilar?"
18. Robert D. Buzzell, "Can You Standardize Multinational Marketing?" *Harvard Business Review*, November–December 1968, pp. 102–113.

ren Keegan concentrated on the same variables as influencing extension versus adaptation decisions for product design or communications strategy.[19] The comparative analytic approach is different in that it focuses on the situational variables and selects the salient environmental variables that may affect the product's or service's success in any country. Since the selected environmental variables are the ones most clearly related to the success of a product or service in the home country, they can be referred to as *success factors*.

Traditionally, marketers have viewed success factors as variables under marketing management's control. With the comparative analytic approach, success factors are treated as a function of the environment, which means that success is recognized as a function of a given scenario of outside factors not always subject to management's control. Typically, marketing programs succeed because managements take advantage of opportunities or positive constellations of success factors. Therefore, we are "allowed" to be successful provided we spot the opportunity. This view results in a greater appreciation of the role that environmental variables play in marketing and also tends to avoid traditional tendencies to overestimate the impact of management's own actions in the marketplace.

The comparative analytical approach provides a methodology for marketers to analyze their success in current markets as a function of the marketing mix and the environment. It also provides an approach for isolating the critical environmental variables. These variables become the focus of the international market research process. In the McDonald's example, the variables we analyzed were population size, population density, family structure, role of the mother, income levels, and availability of advertising media to reach children. As we look at other countries, we must examine these environmental variables and adjust the McDonald's marketing mix appropriately.

The Research Process

Although conducting marketing research globally usually adds to the complexity of the research task, the basic approach remains the same for domestic and international assignments. Either type of research is a four-step process:

1. Problem definition and development of research objectives
2. Determination of the sources of information
3. Collection of the data from primary and secondary sources
4. Analysis of the data and presentation of the results

19. Warren J. Keegan, *Global Marketing Management*, 6th ed. (Upper Saddle River: Prentice Hall, 1999), pp. 398–402.

Although these four steps may be the same for both global and domestic research, problems in implementation may occur because of cultural and economic differences from country to country.

Problem Definition and Development of Research Objectives

In any market research project, the most important task is to define what information you are after. This process, which can take weeks or months, determines the choice of methodologies, the types of people you survey, and the appropriate time frame in which to conduct your research.[20]

Problems may not be the same in different countries or cultures. This may reflect differences in socioeconomic conditions, levels of economic development, cultural forces, or the competitive market structure.[21] For example, bicycles in a developed country may be competing with other recreational goods such as skis, baseball gloves, or exercise equipment, whereas in a developing country, they may be a form of basic transportation competing with small cars, mopeds, and scooters.

The comparative analytic approach can be used to isolate the critical environmental variables in the home market. These variables should be included in the problem definition and research objectives.

Determination of Data Sources

For each assignment, researchers may choose to base their analyses on primary data (data collected specifically for this assignment) or to use secondary data (already collected and available data). Since costs tend to be higher for research based on primary data, researchers usually exhaust secondary data first. Often called desk research or library research, this approach depends on the availability of material and its reliability. Secondary sources may include government publications, trade journals, and data from international agencies or service establishments such as banks or advertisement agencies.

The quality of government statistics is definitely variable. For example, Germany reported that industrial production was up by 0.5 percent in July 1993 but later revised this figure, reporting that production had actually declined by 0.5 percent, an error of 100 percent in the opposite direction. An *Economist* survey of twenty international statisticians rated the quality of statistics from thirteen developed countries based on objectively, reliability, methodology, and timeliness. The leading countries were Canada, Australia, Holland, and France, while the worst

20. Michael Brizz, "How to Learn What Japanese Buyers Really Want," *Business Marketing*, January 1987, p. 72.
21. Craig and Douglas, *International Marketing Research*, pp. 16–19.

were Belgium, Spain, and Italy.[22] According to a report by the U.S. and Foreign Commercial Service in Beijing, Chinese government statistics are often collected by individual ministries or reported by state-owned enterprises and are riddled with *shuifen* ("water content"). China has begun to crack down on fraudulent statistics, using new laws to discipline local officials who exaggerate their success.[23]

Although a substantial body of data exists from the most advanced industrial nations, secondary data are less available for developing countries. Not every country publishes a census, and some published data are not considered reliable. In Nigeria, for example, the population total is of such political importance that published census data are generally believed to be highly suspect. For reasons such as this, companies sometimes have to proceed with the collection of primary data in developing countries at a much earlier stage than in the most industrialized nations.

Data Collection

Collecting Secondary Data For any marketing research problem, the analysis of secondary data should be a first step. Although not available for all variables, often data are available from public and private sources at a fraction of the cost of obtaining primary data.

Collection of data includes the task of calling, writing, or visiting the potential secondary sources. Often, one source will lead to another source until you find the desired information or determine that it does not exist. A good approach to locating secondary sources is to ask yourself who would know about most sources of information on a specific market. For example, if you wanted to locate secondary information on fibers used for tires in Europe, you may consider asking the editor of a trade magazine on the tire industry or the executive director of the tire manufacturing association or the company librarian for Akzo, a Dutch company that manufacturers fibers. Web-based databases, microfilm, and compact disks are excellent sources of information available in most business libraries. Searches on these systems can quickly identify articles, books, and financial information on most business topics, marketing, and companies. Some of these Web-based and commercial sources are

Web Sites
www.country.data.com
www.eiu.com
www.esomar.nl
www.euromonitor.com
www.europa.eu.int
www.ffas.usda.gov

22. "The Good Statistics Guide," *Economist*, September 11, 1993, p. 65.
23. "China: What's in a Number? Worries About Reliability Plague All Who Use Chinese Statistics," *East Asian Executive Reports*, September 15, 1997, pp. 8, 14.

www.greenbook.org
www.oecd.org
www.ita.doc.gov
www.prsgroup.com
www.stat-usa.gov
www.un.org
www.worldbank.org

Commercial Organizations

Advertising Age international issues (www.adage.com)

Coplin, W. D. and O'Leary, K. eds. (1999) Country Forecasts. Political Risk Yearbook, Vol. 4. Political Risk Group, East Syracuse, NY.

Dun and Bradstreet (annual) *Exporters Encyclopedia*. Dun and Bradstreet, New York.

Economist Intelligence Unit (www.eiu.com), London.

Euromonitor (www.euromonitor.com), London.

Europa Publications *World Yearbook* (www.europe.eu.int).

Gale Country and World Rankings Reporter.

IMD (annual) *The World Competitiveness Yearbook*. IMD, Lausanne, Switzerland.

JETRO (annual) *Economic Yearbook*. Jetro, Tokyo.

Media Guide International. Directories International, New York.

Political Risk Group. *Political Risk Yearbook* (www.prsgroup.com).

Pricewaterhouse Coopers Information Guides—*Doing Business in* . . . Pricewaterhouse Coopers, New York.

The Nikkei Weekly, *Japan Economic Almanac* (1997) Nikon Keizai Shimbun, Tokyo.

UN (1997) *Human Development Report 1997*. United Nations Development Programme, New York: Oxford University Press.

It would be impractical to list all the secondary data sources available on international markets, but some secondary data sources would be banks, consulates, embassies, foreign chambers of commerce, libraries with foreign information sections, foreign magazines, public accounting firms, security brokers, and state development offices in foreign countries. A good business library and the local U.S. Department of Commerce are always helpful places to start a search for secondary data. Table 6.2 lists some of the major sources of published secondary data.

There are problems associated with the use of secondary data, namely (1) lack of necessary data, (2) level of accuracy of the data, (3) lack of comparability of the data, and (4) timeliness of the data. In some cases, no data have been collected. For example, many countries have little data on the number of retailers, wholesalers, and distributors.

TABLE 6.2

Major Sources of Secondary Data

U.S. DEPARTMENT OF COMMERCE
- *Foreign Trade Report:* U.S. exports by commodity and by country
- *Global Market Surveys:* Global market research on targeted industries
- *Country Market Surveys:* Detailed reports on promising countries covering fifteen industries
- *Business America:* Magazine presenting domestic and international business news
- *Overseas Marketing Report:* Trade forecasts, regulations, and market profiles prepared for all countries

INTERNATIONAL MONETARY FUND
- *International Financial Statistics:* Monthly report on exchange rates, inflation, deflation, country liquidity, etc.

NATIONAL TECHNICAL INFORMATION SERVICES
- *Market Share Reports:* Reports the size of 88 markets and identifies export opportunities

UNITED NATIONS
- *Yearbook of Industrial Statistics:* Statistics of minerals, manufactured goods, electricity, and gas
- *Statistical Yearbook:* Population, production, education, trade, wages
- *Demographic Yearbook:* Population, income, marriages, deaths, literacy

WORLD BANK
- *Country Economic Reports:* Macroeconomic and industry trends
- *World Development Report:* Population, investment, balance of reports, defense expenditures

EUROMONITOR PUBLICATIONS
- *European Marketing Data and Statistics:* Population, employment, production, trade, standard of living, consumption, housing, communication

PREDICASTS
- *Worldcasts:* Economics, production, utilities

THE ECONOMIST
- *E.I.U. World Outlook:* Forecasts of trends for 160 countries
- *Marketing in Europe:* Product markets in Europe—food, clothing, furniture, household goods, appliances
- *Business International Data Base:* Economic indicators, GNP, wages, foreign trade, production, and consumption

The accuracy of data varies from country to country, with data from highly industrialized nations likely to be more accurate than data from developing countries.[24] This variability is a result of the mechanism for collecting data. In industrialized nations, relatively reliable procedures are used for national accounting and for collecting population and industry statistics. In developing countries, where a major portion of the population is illiterate, the data may be based on estimates or rudimentary procedures. Also, statistics could be manipulated for political reasons. For example, a study by the International Labor Organization found the actual unemployment in Russia to be over 14.2 percent, or 10.4 million people, compared with the official figure of 1.7 million people.[25] The growth of global market opportunities is causing companies to demand cross-border standards for audience measurement. Currently there are differences in critical variables like household size that cause country-to-country differences. Even within a market, these differences can be a problem. For example, in Argentina, the three ratings companies—IPSA Nielsen, IBOPE of Brazil, and Mercados y Tendencias—have conflicting results for video viewing, which was approximately 50 percent of the market.[26]

Data may not be directly comparable from country to country. The population statistics in the United States are collected every ten years, whereas population statistics in Bolivia are collected every twenty-five years. Also, countries may calculate the same statistic but in different ways. For example, there are a number of indicators of national wealth. Gross national product (GNP) is the gross value of production in a country. Gross domestic product (GDP) is the value of all goods and services produced and is often used in place of GNP. GDP per capita is one of the most common measures of market size, suggesting the economic wealth of a country per person. Recently, the International Monetary Fund (IMF) decided that the normal practice of converting the local currency of GDP into dollars at market exchange rates understates the true size of developing economies relative to rich ones. Therefore, IMF has decided to use purchasing power parities, which take into account the differences in international prices. As shown in Table 6.3, GDP per head is much higher based on purchasing power. For example, the 1998 GDP per head in China jumped from $860 to $3,070, an increase of 280 percent.[27]

Another problem with GDP statistics is the hidden, or underground, economy not shown in government statistics. For example in Greece, Spain, and Italy, the hidden economy is 20 to 30 percent of GDP, while in Japan and Switzerland it is less than 4 percent of GDP.[28] When using official GDP statistics, it is important to remember that they do not reflect the true size of the economy.

24. "The Good Statistics Guide," *Economist*, September 11, 1993, p. 65.
25. "Russia's Unemployment Rate Rises Year-On-Year," *Interfax News Agency*, June 21, 1999, p. 1.
26. Jeffery D. Zbar, "Need Seen for Standard in TV Audience Data," *Advertising Age International*, p. 131.
27. World Bank Atlas (Washington, D.C.: World Bank, 1999), pp. 42–43.
28. "Working in the Shadows," *Economist*, February 12, 1994, p. 81.

TABLE 6.3

Market Exchange Rates and Purchasing Power Parity in Developing Countries, 1998

	GNP Per Capita $	
Country	**Market Exchange Rates**	**Purchasing Power Parity**
China	$ 750	$ 3,051
India	440	2,060
Brazil	4,630	6,460
Mexico	3,840	7,450
Indonesia	640	2,407
South Korea	8,600	13,286
Thailand	2,160	5,524
Pakistan	470	1,652
Argentina	8,030	11,728
Nigeria	300	740
Egypt	1,290	3,146
Philippines	1,050	3,725
Malaysia	3,670	7,699
Turkey	3,160	6,594

Source: 2000 World Bank Atlas, Washington, D.C., 2000, pp. 42–43.

Government statistics vary in reliability from country to country. In the United Kingdom, inaccurate GDP growth data, which was sharply revised upward in the early 1980s, is blamed for inflationary economic policies. Mr. Tim Holt, who now runs the Central Statistics Office in the United Kingdom, advises that changes to GDP figures have been less than 0.1 percent since 1995.[29] Even government statistics are faulty; a recent U.S. study showed the Consumer Price Index is overstated by 1 to 2 percent per year. The traditional methods of measuring are based on units of physical goods like cotton, steel, corn, and gloves, which were accu-

29. "Few Damned Lies," *Economist*, March 30, 1996, p. 54.

rate indicators in the 1940s when farming, mining, and manufacturing made up over 50 percent of the country's output. Now these sectors account for less than 30 percent. The bulk of U.S. output consists of services that benefit consumers and create value difficult to measure, like electronic banking. Leonard Nakamura, an economist at the Federal Reserve, argues that GDP in the United States is understated by 2 to 3 percent per year because the full value of new services, new goods, and product improvements is not taken into account.[30]

Finally, age of the data is a constant problem. Population statistics are usually two to five years old. Industrial production statistics can be one to two years old. With different growth rates, it is difficult to use older data to make decisions.

To test the quality of secondary data, marketers should investigate the following:

1. When were the data collected?
2. How were the data collected?
3. What is the expected level of accuracy?
4. Who collected the data, and for what purpose?

Collecting Primary Data If secondary data are not available or usable, the marketer will need to collect primary data. Experienced global researchers indicate that although secondary data may be available, going directly to potential consumers, distributors, and retailers may sometimes be less expensive in the long run than spending considerable time in libraries, embassies, and trade associations.

Once secondary sources of information have been exhausted, the next step is to collect primary data that will meet the specific information requirements for making a specific management decision. Often primary sources will reveal data not available from secondary sources. For example, Siar Research International found that over 50 percent of Kazakhstan men shave every day, while most Azerbaijan men shave only once a week.[31]

Sources of primary data are those in the target country who will purchase or influence the purchase of products. They are consumers, businesses, or governments. Collecting the appropriate data requires the development of a process for doing so. The primary data collection process involves developing a research instrument, selecting a sample, collecting the data, and analyzing the results. These steps are the same in domestic and international environments. The process of collecting data in different cultures creates a number of challenges for the global marketer. These challenges include comparability of data, willingness of the potential respondent to participate, and ability of the respondent to understand and communicate.

30. "The Unmeasurable Lightness of Being," *Economist*, November 23, 1996, pp. 85–86.
31. "Sharp as a Razor in Central Asia," *Economist*, June 5, 1993, p. 36.

Comparability of data is important irrespective of whether research is conducted in a single-country or multicountry context. Research conducted in a single country may be used at a later date to compare with the results of research in another country.[32] For example, if a product is tested in France and is successful, the company may decide to test the Italian market. The test used for the Italian market must be comparable with the test in the French market to assess the possible outcome in Italy. Significant differences exist from country to country. For example, a survey of Europeans found the French twice as likely as the European average (22 percent versus 11 percent) to try a product endorsed by a celebrity.[33] Obviously, that research would have a big impact on how a new product is marketed in France.

A second challenge in research is the willingness of the potential respondent. For example, in many cultures a man will consider it inappropriate to discuss his shaving habits with anyone, especially with a female interviewer. Respondents in the Netherlands or Germany are notoriously reluctant to divulge information on their personal financial habits; the Dutch are more willing to discuss sex than money. Through careful planning, researchers can design instruments and techniques to overcome or avoid cultural limitations.[34] For example, in some cultures, it may be necessary to enlist the aid of a local person to obtain cooperation.

Another challenge in survey research involves translation from one language to another. Translation equivalence is important, first to ensure that the respondents understand the question and second to ensure that the researcher understands the response. Idiomatic expressions and colloquialisms are often translated incorrectly. For example, the French translation of a *full* airplane became a *pregnant* airplane; in German, *"Body by Fisher"* became a *corpse by Fisher.*[35] In a recent case, Braniff found its translation of *to be seated in leather* became *to be seated naked* in Spanish.[36] To avoid these translation errors, experts suggest the technique of back-translation in the local dialect, so that *ji xuan ji*, which means "computers" to Chinese and Taiwanese does not become "calculators" to Singaporians or Malaysians through mistranslation.[37] First, the questionnaire is translated from the home language into the language of the country where it will be used, by a bilingual who is a native speaker of the foreign country. Then this version is translated back to the home language by a bilingual who is a native speaker of the home language. Another translation technique is parallel translation, in which two or more translators translate the questionnaire. The results are compared, and differences are discussed and resolved.

32. Craig and Douglas, *International Marketing Research*, p. 132.
33. "Hunting the Euro-Consumer," *Financial Times*, June 28, 1993, p. 4.
34. Robin Cobb, "Marketing Shares," *Marketing*, February 22, 1990, p. 44.
35. Ricks, *Blunders in International Business*, 3rd ed. (Blackwell, UK, 1999), p. 39.
36. "Braniff, Inc.'s Spanish Ad Bears Cause for Laughter," *Wall Street Journal*, February 9, 1987, p. 5.
37. Kevin Reagan, "In Asia, Think Globally, Communicate Locally," *Marketing News*, July 19, 1999, pp. 12–14.

TABLE 6.4

Comparison of European Data Collection Methods

	France	The Netherlands	Sweden	Switzerland	U.K.
Mail	4%	33%	23%	8%	9%
Telephone	15	18	44	21	16
Central location/ streets	–	52	37	–	–
Home/work	–	–	8	44	54
Groups	13	–	5	6	11
Depth interviews	12	12	2	8	–
Secondary	4	–	4	8	–

Source: Emanual H. Demby, "ESOMAR Urges Changes in Reporting Demographics, Issues Worldwide Report," *Marketing News*, January 8, 1990, p. 24. Reprinted by permission of the American Marketing Association.

Data can be collected by mail, by telephone, or face to face. The technique will vary by country. The European Society for Opinion and Market Research (ESOMAR) recently reported on interviewing techniques used in Europe. As shown in Table 6.4, face-to-face interviews at home or work are very popular in Switzerland and the United Kingdom, whereas interviews in shopping areas are popular in France and the Netherlands. Telephone interviewing dominates Swedish data collection.[38]

Data collection and privacy concerns being raised in the European Union (EU) may affect market research globally. The EU Data Privacy Directive passed in 1995 requires unambiguous consent from a person for each use of his or her personal data.[39] This regulation could seriously limit the use of telephone interviews that ask questions related to health problems, political beliefs, sex habits, and so on. All fifteen EU nations have data privacy legislation and a government privacy commission to enforce the EU policy. This legislation stipulates that data cannot be sent to a non-EU member country unless that country has an adequate level of privacy protection. The U.S. Department of Commerce is working with EU offi-

38. Emanual H. Demby, "ESOMAR Urges Changes in Reporting Demographics, Issues Worldwide Report," *Marketing News*, January 8, 1990, p. 24.
39. James Heckman, "Marketers Waiting, Will See on EU Privacy," *Marketing News*, June 7, 1999, p. 4.

cials to develop the International Safe Harbor Privacy Principles for non-EU countries.[40]

In Japan, consumers will generally not respond to telephone interviews. Only 5 percent of interviews are done by telephone; 30 percent are conducted in business offices, 20 percent by mail, 19 percent in the surveyor's office, 14 percent in focus groups, and the rest in other ways.[41] Although personal interviews are expensive and time consuming, the Japanese preference for face-to-face contact suggests that personal interviews yield better information than data collected by mail or telephone. In fact, Japanese managers are skeptical about western-style marketing research. Senior and middle managers will often go into the field and speak directly with consumers and distributors. This technique of collecting information, called "soft data," though less rigorous than large-scale consumer studies, gives the manager a real feel for the market and the consumers.[42]

Japanese firms have begun to do more market research. For example, Matsushita (Panasonic) visited 10 million households in 1992 to determine consumer needs for electronic products.[43]

Another technique for collecting marketing research data is focus groups. The researcher assembles a set of six to twelve carefully selected respondents to discuss a product. The focus group is often used at the early stage of a new product concept to gain valuable insights from potential consumers. The research company assembles the participants and leads the discussion, avoiding the potential bias from a company representative. Of course, the discussion leader must speak in the mother tongue of the participants. Representatives of the company can observe the focus group via video- or audiotaping, through a one-way mirror, or sitting in the room. In some countries, such as Japan, it may be difficult to get participants to criticize a potential product. Experienced focus group companies are resourceful at using questioning techniques and interpreting body language to get the full value from this research technique.[44]

Sample Selection After developing the instrument and converting it to the appropriate language, the researcher will determine the appropriate sample design. Due to its advantage of predicting the margin of error, researchers generally prefer to use probability sampling. The great power of a probability sample lies in the possibility of predicting the corresponding errors: (1) sampling errors, or the chance of not receiving a true sample of the group investigated; (2) response

40. "EU Denies Breakdown in Data Privacy Talks with The U.S.," *Dow Jones International*, May 31, 1999, p. 1.
41. H. Lee Murphy, "Japanese Keeping Fewer Secrets from U.S. Firms, *Marketing News*, June 21, 1999, p. 4.
42. Johny K. Johansson and Ikujiro Nonaka, "Market Research the Japanese Way," *Harvard Business Review*, May–June 1987, pp. 16–22.
43. "Marketing in Japan, Taking Aim," *Economist*, April 24, 1993, p. 74.
44. Catherine Bond, "Market Research—Spy in a Corner," *Marketing*, August 17, 1989, p. 35.

errors, or the deviation of responses from the facts due to either incorrect recall or unwillingness to tell the truth; and (3) nonresponse errors, or uncertainty of the views held by members of the sample that were never reached.[45] For these reasons, probability samples are generally preferred by researchers.

In many foreign countries, however, the existing market infrastructure and the lack of available data or information substantially interfere with attempts to use probability samples. Sampling of larger populations requires the availability of detailed census data, called *census tracks*, and maps from which probability samples can be drawn. Where such data are available, they are often out of date. Thus, stratification is prevented.[46] Further difficulties arise from inadequate transportation that may prevent fieldworkers from actually reaching selected census tracks in some areas of the country. Sampling is particularly difficult in countries having several spoken languages because carrying out a nationwide survey is impractical.

Research Techniques

A variety of analytic techniques can be used in international marketing research. Although these techniques may be used in domestic marketing research, they are often modified to deal with the complexities of international markets.

Demand Analysis

Demand for products or services can be measured at two levels: aggregate demand, for an entire market or country, and company demand, as represented by actual sales. The former is generally termed *market potential*, whereas the latter is referred to as *sales potential*. A very useful concept developed by Richard D. Robinson views both market and sales potential as a filtering process (see Figure 6.3). According to Robinson, demand or potential demand can be measured at six successive levels, the last and final level representing actual sales by the firm.[47] The six levels of demand are explained as follows.

Potential Need Of course, the country's consumers will not purchase the product if there is no need. Therefore, the researcher has to pose the question: Is there a potential need, either now or in the future? Potential need for a product

45. Paul E. Green and Donald S. Tull, *Research for Marketing Decisions*, 4th ed. (Englewood Cliffs, N.J.: Prentice Hall, 1978), pp. 111–112.
46. W. Boyd Harper, Jr., Ronald E. Frank, William F. Massy, and Mostafa Zoheir, "On the Use of Marketing Research in the Emerging Economies," *Journal of Marketing Research*, vol. 1 (November 1964), pp. 20–23.
47. Richard D. Robinson, *Internationalization of Business*, 2nd ed. (Chicago: Dryden Press, 1984), p. 36.

FIGURE 6.3

Market Potential and Sales Potential Filter

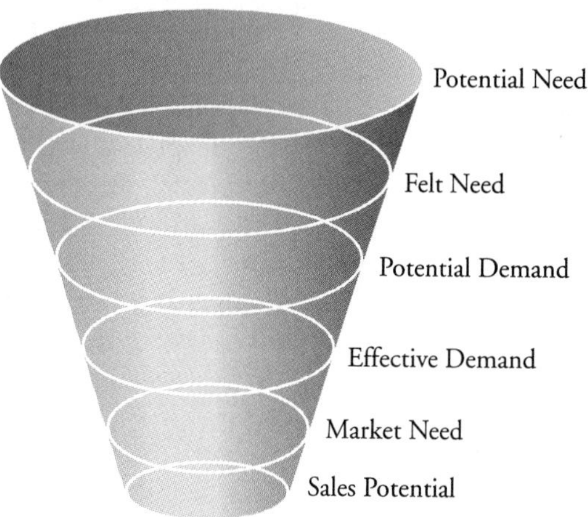

Source: Reprinted from *Internationalization of Business*, 2nd ed., by Richard D. Robinson, p. 36. Copyright © 1984 with permission of the author.

or service is primarily determined by the demographic and physical characteristics of a country. The determinants are a country's population, climate, geography, natural resources, land use, life expectancy, and other factors termed part of the physical environment. The potential need could only be realized if all consumers in a country used a product to the fullest extent regardless of social, cultural, or economic barriers. This represents the ideal case that actually may never be reached.

Felt Need Though a potential need as defined above may exist to the uninvolved observer, one should not assume that everyone in a market actually feels a need for the product or service under investigation. Because of different life styles, some consumers may not feel a need for a product. For instance, though a farmer in a developing country who drives his produce to a local market in an animal-drawn cart potentially has a use for a pickup truck, he actually may not feel the need for one. Thus, felt need is substantially influenced by the cultural and social environment, including the amount of exposure consumers or buyers have to modern communications. The key task for the researcher is to evaluate the extent to which the potential need is culturally and socially appropriate among the target customers.

Potential Demand The felt need represents the aggregate desire of a target population to purchase a product. However, lack of sufficient income may prevent some customers from actually purchasing the product or service. The result is the potential demand, or the total amount the market would be ready to absorb. Economic variables preventing the realization of sales are generally beyond the control of any individual company. For example, the average income per household may seem to indicate a large demand for washing machines, but the distribution of income is skewed so that 10 percent of the population has 90 percent of the wealth. To identify if potential demand is blocked, a firm must look at income distribution data.

Effective Demand Though potential demand might exist, regulatory factors might prevent prospective customers from being able to satisfy their demand. Included are regulations on imports, tariffs, and foreign exchange; specific regulations on product standards with respect to safety, health, and pollution; legal aspects such as patents, copyrights, and trademarks; fiscal controls such as taxes, subsidies, or rationing and allocations; economic regulations, including price controls and wage controls; and political regulations, including restrictions on buying foreign goods, the role of the government in the economy, and the power of the government to impose controls.

The presence of any of the above-cited factors can cause the potential demand to be reduced to a lower level—in other words, to effective demand. Therefore, marketing research needs to uncover the extent to which regulatory factors are present and to determine the possible actions a firm may take to avoid some of the impact on demand.

Market Demand The extent to which the effective demand can be realized depends substantially on the marketing infrastructure available to competing firms in a country. The degree to which a country's transportation system has been developed is important, as well as its efficiency in terms of cost to users. Additional services that marketers use regularly are storage facilities, banking facilities (particularly for consumer credit), available wholesale and retail structure, and advertising infrastructure. The absence of a fully developed marketing infrastructure will cause market demand to be substantially below effective demand. Marketing research will determine the effectiveness of the present marketing system and locate the presence of any inhibiting factors.

Sales Potential The actual sales volume that a company will realize in any country is essentially determined by its competitive offering vis-à-vis other firms who also compete for a share of the same market. The resulting market share is determined by the relative effectiveness of the company's marketing mix. In determining sales potential, the researcher will have to assess whether the company can meet the competition in terms of product quality and features, price, distribution, and promotion. The assessment should yield an estimate of the company's market share, given the assumptions about the company's mode of entry (see Chapter 9) and marketing strategy (see Chapter 8).[48]

The difficulty, of course, lies in determining the various demand levels and collecting the facts that can be used to determine actual potential and sales forecasts. Consider a situation in which a company is investigating a market that already has had experience with the product to be introduced. In such a case, the research effort is aimed at uncovering the data on present sales, usage, or production to arrive at the market demand (see Figure 6.3). Consequently, this is primarily an effort in collecting data from secondary information sources or commissioning professional marketing research through independent agencies when necessary.

Analysis by Inference

Available data from secondary sources are frequently of an aggregate nature and do not satisfy the specific needs of a firm focusing on just one product and a given time frame. A company must usually assess market size based on very limited data on foreign markets. In such cases, market *assessment by inference* becomes a necessity. This technique uses available facts about related products or other foreign markets as a basis for inferring the necessary information for the market under analysis. Market assessment by inference, a low-cost method that is analysis based, should take place before a company engages in any primary data collection at a substantial cost. Inferences can be made based on related products, related markets' sales, and related environmental factors.

Related Products Few products are consumed or used alone without any ties to other prior purchases or products in use. Relationships exist, for example, between replacement tires and automobiles on the road and between electricity consumption and the use of appliances. In some situations, it may be possible to obtain data on related products and their uses as a basis for inferred usage of the particular product to be marketed. From experience in other, similar markets, the analyst is able to apply usage ratios that can provide for low-cost estimates. For example, the analyst can determine the number of replacement tires needed per *X* automobiles on the road. A clear understanding of usage patterns can be gained from performing a comparative analysis as described earlier.

Related Markets' Size Quite frequently, if market size data are available for other countries, this information can be used to derive estimates for the particular country under investigation. For example, consider that market size is known for

48. Franklin R. Root, *Entry Strategies for International Markets* (New York: Jossey-Bass, 1999), p. 41.

the United States and estimates are required for Canada, a country with a comparable economic system and comparable consumption patterns. Statistics for the United States can be scaled down by the relative size of either GNP, population, or other factors to about one-tenth of U.S. figures. Similar relationships exist in Europe, where the known market size of one country can provide a basis for an inference about a related country. Of course, the results are not exact, but they provide a basis for further analysis. The cost and time lag for collecting primary market data often force the analyst to use the inference approach.

Related Environmental Factors A more comprehensive analysis can be provided after a full comparative analysis as outlined previously. After data are collected on the relevant environmental variables for a given product, an inference may be made on the market potential. The estimate's reliability would depend on the type of data available on the success factors. Actual data on success factors are of course preferable to inferences based on the demand structure in a related market. Reed Moyer described a series of additional methods suited for forecasting purposes that often involve the use of historic data.[49] Some of these methods are described in abbreviated form.

Analysis of Demand Patterns By analyzing industrial growth patterns for various countries, researchers can gain insights into the relationship of consumption patterns to industrial growth. Relationships can be plotted between GDP per capita and the percentage of total manufacturing production accounted for by major industries. During earlier growth stages with corresponding low per capita incomes, manufacturing tends to center on necessities such as food, beverages, textiles, and light manufacturing. With growing incomes, the role of these industries tends to decline, and heavy industry assumes a greater importance. By analysis of such manufacturing patterns, forecasts for various product groups can be made for countries at lower income levels, since they often repeat the growth patterns of more developed economies.

Similar trends can be observed for a country's import composition. With increasing industrialization, countries develop similar patterns modified only by each country's natural resources. Energy-poor countries must import increasing quantities of energy as industrialization proceeds, whereas energy-rich countries can embark on an industrialization path without significant energy imports. Industrialized countries import relatively more food products and industrial materials than manufactured goods, which are more important for the less industrialized countries. Understandably, these relationships can help the analyst determine future trends for a country's economy and may help determine future market potential and sales prospects.

49. Reed Moyer, "International Market Analysis," *Journal of Marketing Research*, vol. 5 (November 1968), pp. 353–360.

Multiple-Factor Indexes

This technique has already been successfully used by domestic marketers. It entails the use of proxies to estimate demand if the situation should prevent the direct computation of a product's market potential. A multiple factor measures potential indirectly, using proxy variables that intuition or statistical analysis reveals to be closely correlated to the potential for the product under review.

A good example for such an approach is Ford Motor's analysis for its overseas tractor business.[50] To evaluate the attractiveness of its various overseas markets, the company developed a scale and rated each country on attractiveness and competitive strength. These two dimensions were measured based on the following criteria:

Country attractiveness
- Market size
- Market growth rate
- Government regulations
  - Price controls
  - Nontariff barriers
  - Local content
- Economic and political stability
  - Inflation
  - Trade balance
  - Political stability

Competitive strength
- Market share
- Product fit
- Contribution margin
  - Profit per unit
  - Profit percentage, net of dealer cost
- Market support
- Quality of distribution system
- Advertising versus competition

These items were evaluated by Ford's executives and rated on a ten-point scale for each item. The items were combined based on the relative weight of each item to determine the coordinates of the X and Y axes. Figure 6.4 illustrates Ford's use of the market evaluation system for Ford's key countries. The weights are indicative of the firm's effort to rank markets via multiple-factor indexes.

Competitive Studies

As every marketer knows, results in the marketplace do not depend only on researching buyer characteristics and meeting buyer needs. To a considerable extent, success in the marketplace is influenced by a firm's competition. Companies competing on an international level have to be particularly careful with monitoring competition, because some of the competing firms will most likely be located abroad, thus creating additional difficulties in keeping abreast of the latest developments.

50. Gilbert D. Harrell and Richard O. Kiefer, "Multinational Strategic Market Portfolios," *MSU Business Topics*, Winter 1981, pp. 5–15.

FIGURE 6.4

Key-Country Matrix

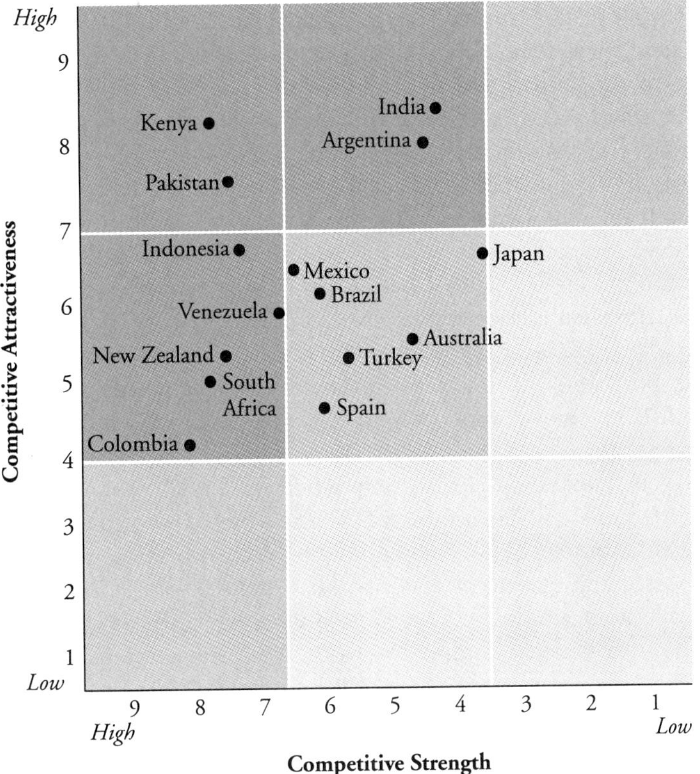

Source: Gilbert D. Harrell and Richard O. Kiefer, "Multinational Strategic Market Portfolios," *MSU Business Topics*, Winter 1981, p. 13. Reprinted by permission.

When Honda first entered the U.S. motorcycle industry in 1959, the British and U.S motorcycle firms that dominated the industry did not pay much attention. Honda's entry with a 50 cc bike posed little threat to the macho bikes of Harley Davidson and Triumph. But thirty years later, 80 percent of the bikes are Japanese, competing from 50 cc to 1,400 cc. Many companies fail to spot competitors until it is too late. Swiss watchmakers were blind-sided by competitors not even in the same business. While the Swiss were making increasingly more complex mechanized watches, Casio launched basic digital watches that sold at half the price of cheap mechanical watches. Only with the launch of the fashionable electronic Swatch watch in 1985 were the Swiss able to regain some of their lost market. The $2.8 billion Swatch Group plans to expand in India with an assembly operation targeting the middle and low-end price range with the Swatch and Tissot brands.[51]

First, a company must determine who its competitors are. The domestic market will certainly provide some input here. However, it is of great importance to include any foreign company that either presently is a competitor or may become one in the future. For many firms, the constellation of competitors will most likely change over time. The U.S. company Caterpillar once considered other domestic competitors its major competitors both domestically and abroad. However, the Japanese firm Komatsu has now established itself as the second-largest firm for earthmoving equipment, forcing Caterpillar to concentrate more resources on tracking this new competitor. Although only 15 percent of Komatsu's revenue is in the United States and Europe, given the economic slowdown in Asia, Komatsu is focusing on the United States with its backhoe loader.[52] Therefore, included in a company's monitoring system should be *all* major competitors, both domestic and foreign. The monitoring should not be restricted to activity in the competitors' domestic market only but must include competitors' moves anywhere in the world. Many foreign firms first innovate in their home markets, expanding abroad only when the initial debugging of the product has been completed. Therefore, a U.S. firm would lose valuable time if, say, a Japanese competitor's action would only be picked up on entry into the U.S. market. Any monitoring system needs to be structured in such a way as to ensure that competitors' actions will be spotted wherever they tend to occur first. Komatsu, Caterpillar's major competitor worldwide, subscribed to the *Journal Star*, the major daily newspaper in Caterpillar's hometown, Peoria, Illinois. Also important are the actions taken by subsidiaries; they may signal future moves elsewhere in a company's global network of subsidiaries.

Table 6.5 contains a list of the type of information a company may wish to collect on its competitors. Aside from the general business statistics, a competitor's profitability may shed some light on its capacity to pursue new business in the future. Learning about others' marketing operations will allow the investigating company to assess, among other things, the market share to be gained in any given market. Whenever major actions are planned, it is extremely helpful to know what the likely reaction of competitive firms will be and to include them in a company's contingency planning. And, of course, monitoring a competitor's new products or expansion programs may give early hints on future competitive threats.

Analysis that focuses on studying the products of key competitors can often miss the real strength of the competitor. To understand an industry and where

51. Iqbal Singh Ahmedabad, "Swatch May Launch Low-End Watches," *Business Standard*, April 6, 1999, p. 8.
52. Peter Marsh, 'Japan's Komatsu to Enter U.S. Heavy-Equipment Market," *Financial Times*, December 7, 1998, p. 19.

TABLE 6.5

Monitoring Competition: Facts to Be Collected

OVERALL COMPANY STATISTICS
Sales and market share profits
Balance sheet
Capital expenditures
Number of employees
Production capacity
Research and development capability
MARKETING OPERATIONS
Types of products (quality, performance, features)
Service and/or warranty granted
Prices and pricing strategy
Advertising strategy and budgets
Size and type of sales force
Distribution system (includes entry strategy)
Delivery schedules (also spare parts)
Sales territory (geographic)
FUTURE INTENTIONS
New product developments
Current test markets
Scheduled plant capacity expansions
Planned capital expenditures
Planned entry into new markets/countries
COMPETITIVE BEHAVIOR
Pricing behavior
Reaction to competitive moves, past and expected

it is headed over the next five years, studying the core competencies in an industry is important. For example, Chaparral Steel, a profitable U.S. steelmaker, sends its managers and engineers to visit competitors, customers, and suppliers' factories to identify the trends and skills that will lead steelmaking in the future. Chaparral also attends trade shows and visits university research departments to spot new competencies that may offer an opportunity or pose a threat.[53]

There are numerous ways to monitor competitors' activities. Thorough study of trade or industry journals is an obvious starting point. Also, frequent visits can be made to major trade fairs where competitors exhibit their products. At one such fair in Texas, Caterpillar engineers were seen measuring Komatsu equipment.[54] Other important information can be gathered from foreign subsidiaries located in the home markets of major competitors. The Italian office equipment manufacturer, Olivetti, assigned a major intelligence function to its U.S. subsidiary because of that unit's direct access to competitive products in the U.S. marketplace. A different approach was adopted by the Japanese pharmaceutical company Esei, which opened a liaison office in Switzerland, home base to several of the world's leading pharmaceutical companies.

There is a widespread impression that U.S. and European firms are much less vigilant than their Asian competitors. For example, Mitsubishi has between 650 and 800 employees in New York to gather intelligence information about their U.S. competitors. The South Koreans are not far behind; the intelligence systems of their three largest trading companies were developed by an ex-colonel of the South Korean military intelligence. The systems require real-time reporting to a central processing unit by every branch manager around the world.[55] The examples from Japan and Korea suggest that a business intelligence system requires a coordinated effort that draws on the knowledge of the entire organization. To keep track of a firm's competitors is an important international research function. Kodak learned through competitive intelligence that Fuji was planning a new camera for the U.S. market. Kodak launched a competing model just one day before Fuji. Motorola discovered through one of its intelligence staff (fluent in Japanese) that the Japanese electronics firms planned to build new semiconductor plants in Europe. Motorola changed its strategy to build market share in Europe before the new capacity was built. This type of intelligence can be critical to a firm.[56]

53. C. K. Prahalad and Gary Hamel, "The Core Competence of the Corporation," *Harvard Business Review*, May-June 1990, pp. 79–91.
54. Ibid.
55. Benjamin Gilad, "The Role of Organized Competitive Intelligence in Corporate Strategy," *Columbia Journal of World Business*, Winter 1989, p. 32.
56. "High Price of Industrial Espionage," *Times of London*, June 5, 1999, p. 31.

Environmental Studies

Frequently it becomes necessary to study the international environment beyond the customary monitoring function that most global executives perform. Of particular interest are the economic, physical, sociocultural, and political environments.

In any focus on the economic environment, the primary interest will be on the economic activity in target countries. Major economic indicators are GNP growth, interest levels, industrial output, employment levels, and the monetary policy of the country under investigation. Studies focusing on a country are frequently undertaken when a major decision regarding that country has to be made. This could include a move to enter the country or to significantly increase the firm's presence in that market through large new investments.

Also frequently studied are the international economy and the role of the various supranational organizations as these affect the business climate for global companies. For example, it is important for companies active in Europe to learn about the possible impact or likelihood of new regulations or decisions of the European Union. Frequently, reviews of such agencies or groups are ordered when a major move is imminent and information is needed on the potential impact of these decisions.

Since the physical environment tends to be the most stable aspect of the foreign marketing environment, such studies are frequently made for major market entry decisions or when the introduction of a new product requires a special analysis of that particular aspect of the environment. Included within the physical environment are population and related statistics on growth, age composition, birthrates, and life expectancy, as well as data on the climate and geography of a country.

Of particular interest is the sociocultural environment, already described in some detail in Chapter 3. The salient factors include social classes, family life, lifestyles, role expectations of the sexes, reference groups, religion, education, language, customs, and traditions. Market researchers have classified these statistics as *psychographics*. The primary interest to the global company is the potential effect of these variables on the sale of its products. Since the sociocultural environment is also unlikely to change over the short run and changes that do occur tend to be of a more gradual nature, such studies are most likely ordered when a major marketing decision in the local market is contemplated. As a company gains experience in any given country, its staff and local organization accumulate considerable data on the social and cultural situation that can be tapped whenever needed. Therefore, a full study of these environmental variables is most useful when the company does not already have a base in that country and past experience is limited.

Frequently management will investigate the regulatory environment of a given country because those influences can substantially affect marketing operations anywhere. Today, regulatory influences can originate with both national and supranational organizations. National bodies tend to influence the marketing scene within the borders of one country only, whereas supranational agencies have a reach beyond any individual country. National regulations may include particular rulings affecting all businesses, such as product liability laws, or may be targeted at individual industries only. In the United States, the latter type would include regulatory agencies such as the U.S. Food and Drug Administration (FDA) and the U.S. Department of Commerce. Examples of supranational regulations are those issued by the European Union with respect to business within the member nations, and the United Nations' Center for Transnational Corporations' nonbinding code of conduct for international companies.

Regulatory trends can be of great importance to global companies and may even lead to new opportunities. It is generally accepted by most observers that U.S. safety and emission control regulations for passenger automobiles are the world's most stringent. Recognizing this fact, the French company Peugeot has maintained a small beachhead in the U.S. market, even with a small and insignificant sales volume, primarily to gain the experience of engineering cars under these stringent conditions. The company feels that this experience can be usefully applied elsewhere as other countries adopt similar regulations. Consequently, a company will not monitor the regulatory environment to adopt products and marketing operations to meet with only local success. In addition, firms may find it useful to keep informed about the latest regulations regarding their business in countries that have preceded other countries with pertinent legislation even if they may not conduct any business there.

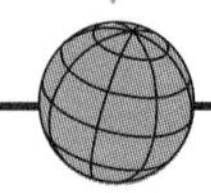

Developing a Global Information System

Companies that already are or plan to become global marketers must look at the world marketplace to identify global opportunities. To evaluate the full range of opportunities requires a global perspective for market research. Although many global players started in the triad of North America, Japan, and Europe, this only represents 15 percent of the planet's population. Eastern Europe offers interesting opportunities, with a combined GNP from the former East Germany, Hungary, and Czechoslovakia. This region has relatively well-trained and low-paid workers. Indonesia, the fifth-most populated country in the world, has cut government paperwork by 67 percent in an effort to stimulate growth and attract foreign investors. China, with the second-largest economy and the largest population, offers significant opportunities. India, the second-largest country, with 800 million people, has been eliminating regulations to open its markets. For example, in 1988, Indians bought 6 million television sets, up from only

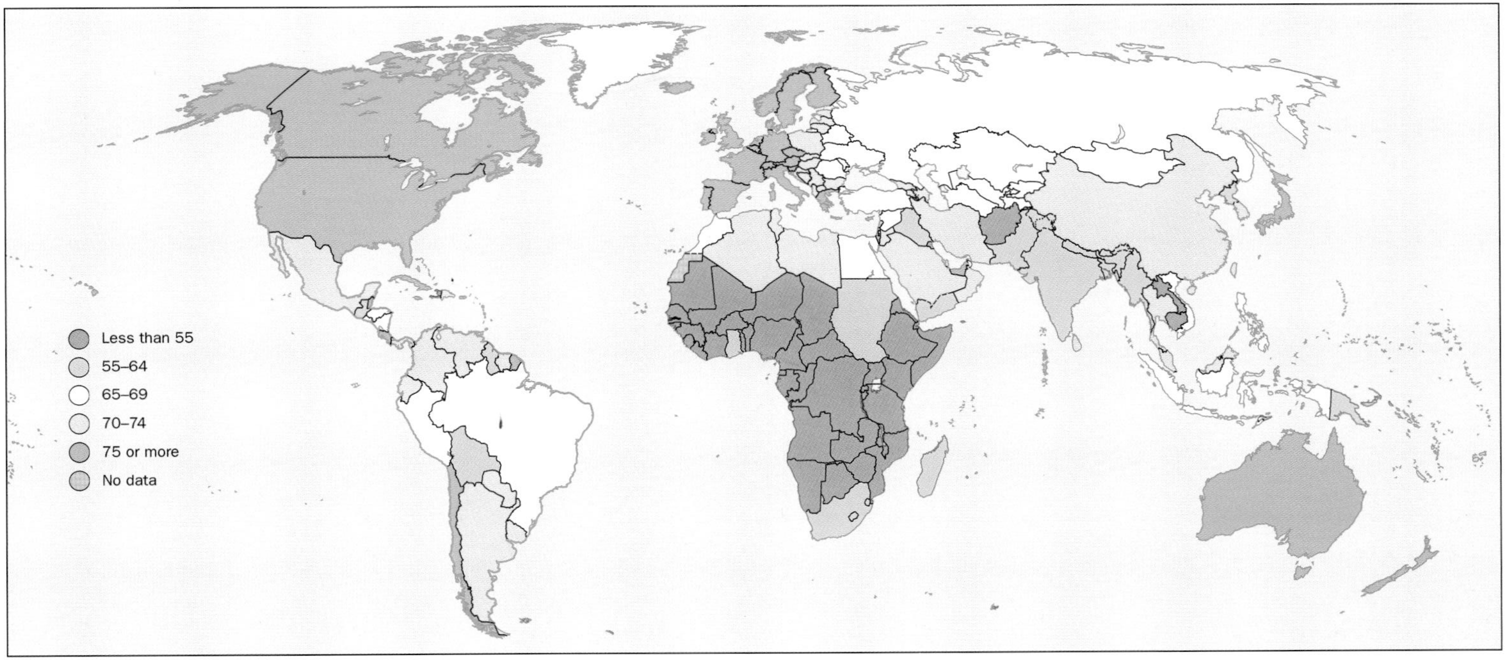

Less than 55
55–64
65–69
70–74
75 or more
No data

Life expectancy

Life expectancy at birth, 1998

The average number of years a newborn baby would live if patterns of mortality prevailing for all people at the time of its birth were to stay the same throughout its life.

Distribution of world population among economies grouped by life expectancy at birth

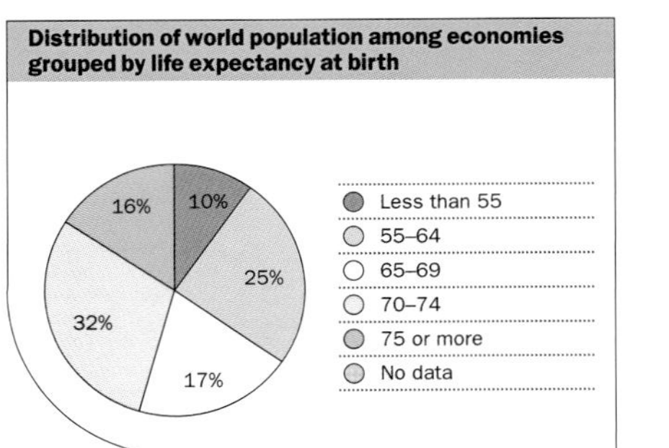

16%
10%
25%
32%
17%
Less than 55
55–64
65–69
70–74
75 or more
No data

Life expectancy at birth, 1998, years

East Asia & Pacific
69
Europe & Central Asia
69
Latin America & Caribbean
70
Middle East & North Africa
68
South Asia
62
Sub-Saharan Africa
50
High income
78
0
20
40
60
80
100

Life expectancy at birth, 1998, years

	Economies	GNP $ millions 1998	Population millions 1998	GNP per capita $ 1998
Less than 55	41	171,948	569	300
55–64	22	803,150	1,498	540
65–69	29	1,900,669	1,024	1,860
70–74	54	3,195,695	1,874	1,710
75 or more	48	22,750,913	931	24,430
No data	12	12,293	1	16,110

Source: Adapted from the *2000 World Bank Atlas*.

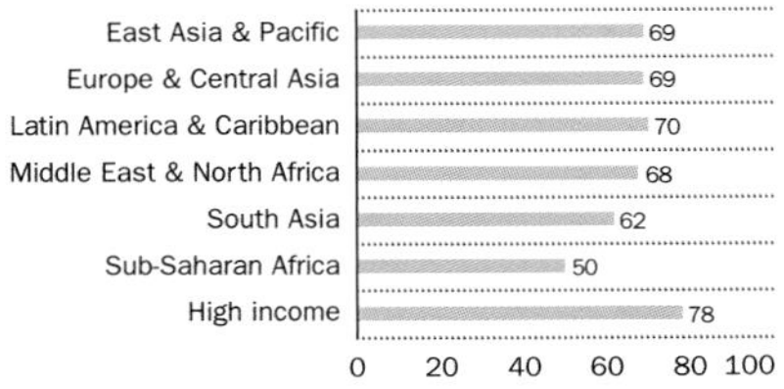

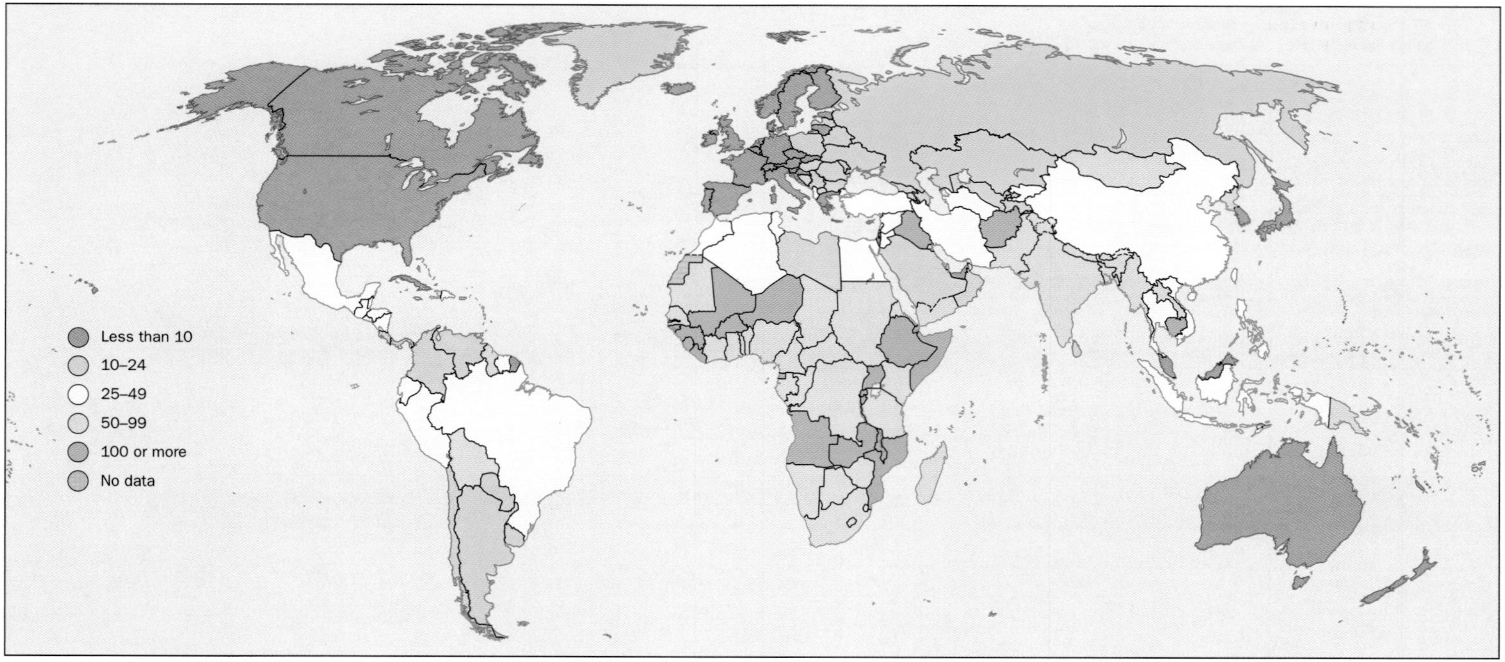

Less than 10
10–24
25–49
50–99
100 or more
No data

Infant deaths

Infant mortality rate, 1998

The number of deaths of children under one year of age per thousand live births.

Infant mortality rate, 1998, per 1,000 live births

	Economies	GNP $ millions 1998	Population millions 1998	GNP per capita $ 1998
Less than 10	45	23,133,794	988	23,410
10–24	53	1,646,354	567	2,900
25–49	33	3,083,432	2,282	1,350
50–99	42	851,913	1,796	470
100 or more	21	106,882	263	410
No data	12	12,293	1	16,110

Infant mortality rate, 1998, per 1,000 live births

East Asia & Pacific
35
Europe & Central Asia
22
Latin America & Caribbean
31
Middle East & North Africa
45
South Asia
75
Sub-Saharan Africa
92
High income
6
0
20
40
60
80
100

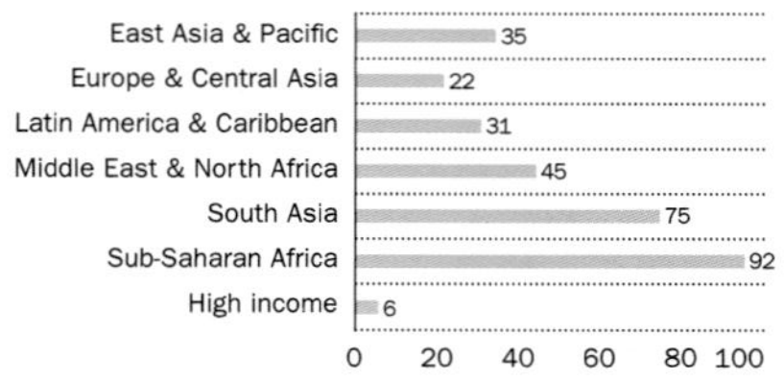

Distribution of world population among economies grouped by infant mortality rate

Less than 10
10–24
25–49
50–99
100 or more
No data
4%
17%
10%
39%
30%

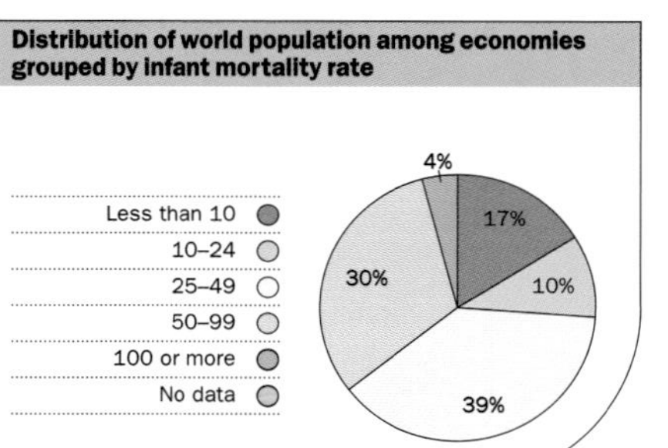

Source: Adapted from the *2000 World Bank Atlas.* Reprinted by permission of The World Bank.

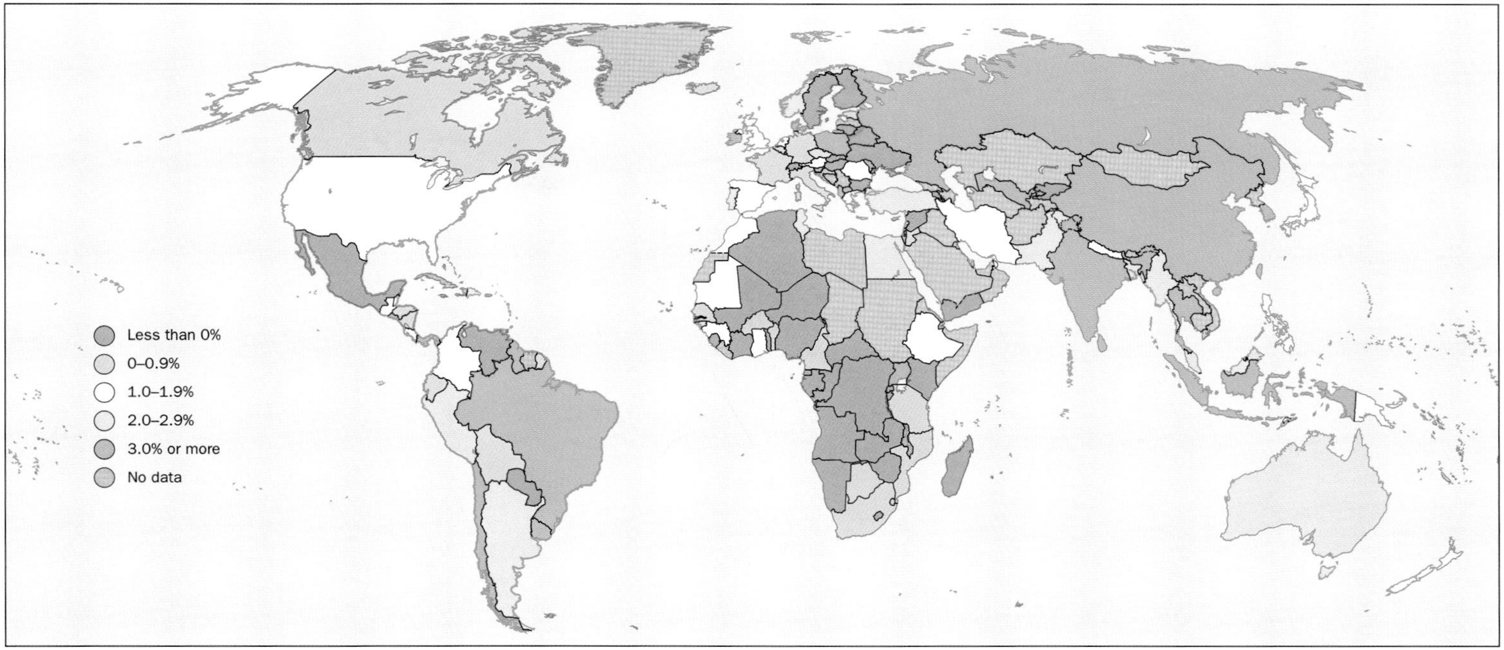

Less than 0%
0–0.9%
1.0–1.9%
2.0–2.9%
3.0% or more
No data

Change in personal spending

Private consumption per capita growth rate, 1990–98

The average annual percentage change in a country's private consumption per capita.

Distribution of world population among economies grouped by private consumption growth rate

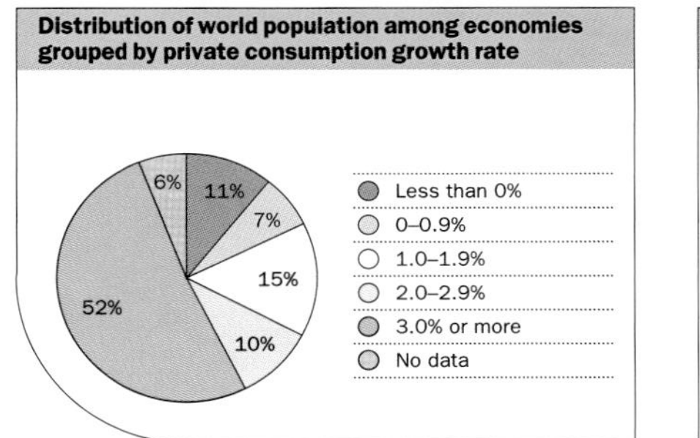

Private consumption per capita growth rate, 1990–98, percent per year

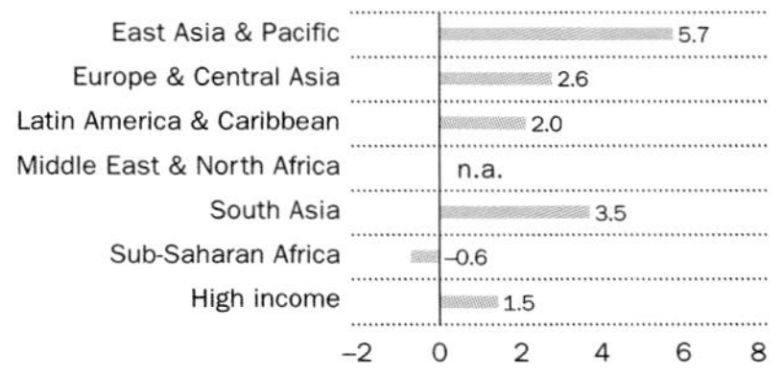

East Asia & Pacific 5.7
Europe & Central Asia 2.6
Latin America & Caribbean 2.0
Middle East & North Africa n.a.
South Asia 3.5
Sub-Saharan Africa –0.6
High income 1.5

–2 0 2 4 6 8

Private consumption per capita growth rate, 1990–98, percent per year

	Economies	GNP $ millions 1998	Population millions 1998	GNP per capita $ 1998
Less than 0%	42	1,435,916	627	2,290
0–0.9%	25	5,885,741	411	14,310
1.0–1.9%	22	14,998,393	893	16,800
2.0–2.9%	19	1,729,719	579	2,990
3.0% or more	30	4,186,967	3,040	1,380
No data	68	597,930	347	1,720

Source: Adapted from the *2000 World Bank Atlas.*
Reprinted by permission of The World Bank.

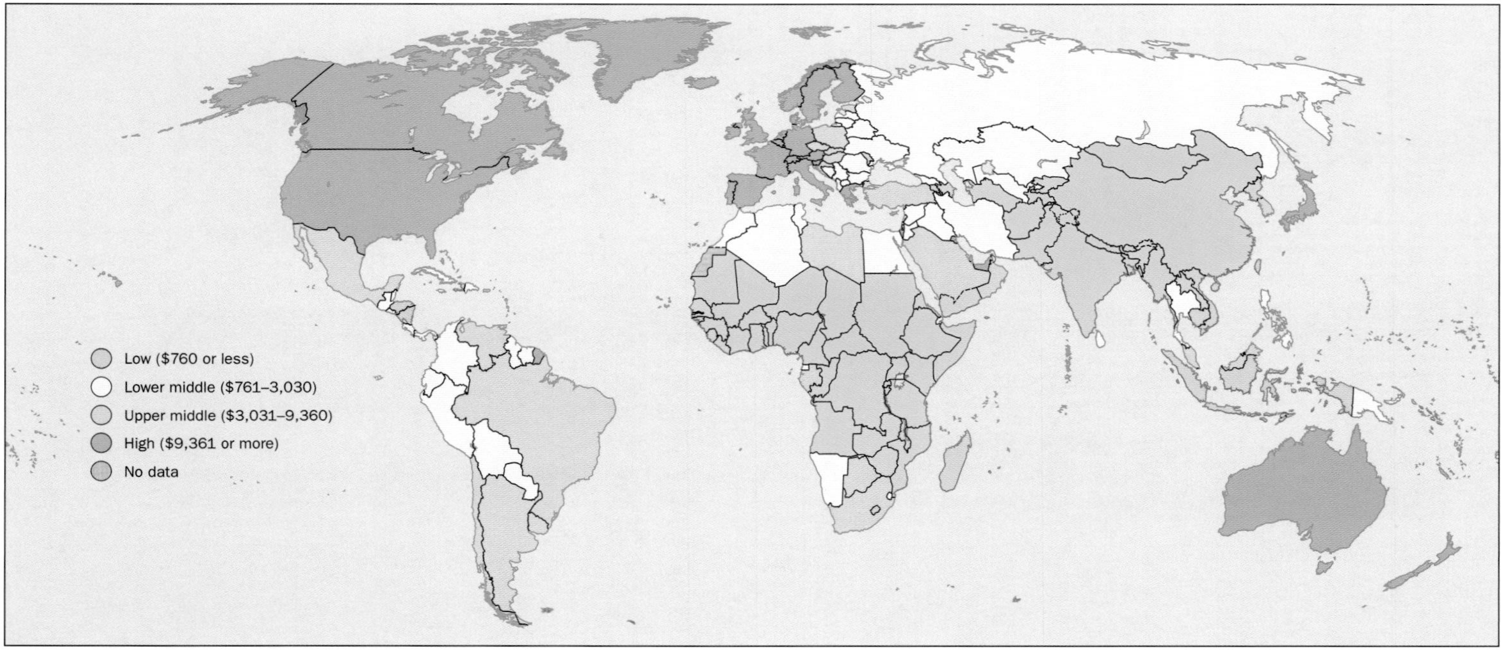

Low ($760 or less)
Lower middle ($761–3,030)
Upper middle ($3,031–9,360)
High ($9,361 or more)
No data

Income per person

GNP per capita, 1998

Gross national product—the sum of gross value added by resident producers (plus taxes less subsidies) and net primary income from nonresident sources—divided by midyear population.

Distribution of world population among economies grouped by GNP per capita

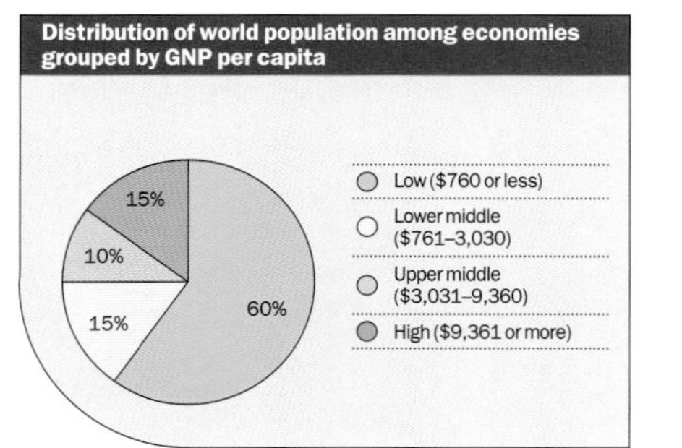

15%
10%
15%
60%
Low ($760 or less)
Lower middle ($761–3,030)
Upper middle ($3,031–9,360)
High ($9,361 or more)

GNP per capita, 1998, $

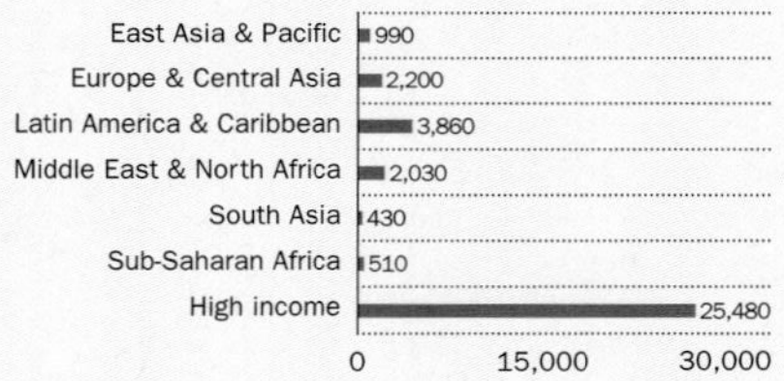

East Asia & Pacific
990
Europe & Central Asia
2,200
Latin America & Caribbean
3,860
Middle East & North Africa
2,030
South Asia
430
Sub-Saharan Africa
510
High income
25,480
0
15,000
30,000

GNP per capita, 1998, $

	Economies	GNP $ millions 1998	Population millions 1998	GNP per capita $ 1998
Low ($760 or less)	63	1,841,645	3,536	520
Lower middle ($761–3,030)	57	1,541,422	886	1,740
Upper middle ($3,031–9,360)	35	2,859,822	588	4,870
High ($9,361 or more)	51	22,591,778	886	25,480
World	206	28,834,667	5,897	4,890

Source: Adapted from the *2000 World Bank Atlas*. Reprinted by permission of The World Bank.

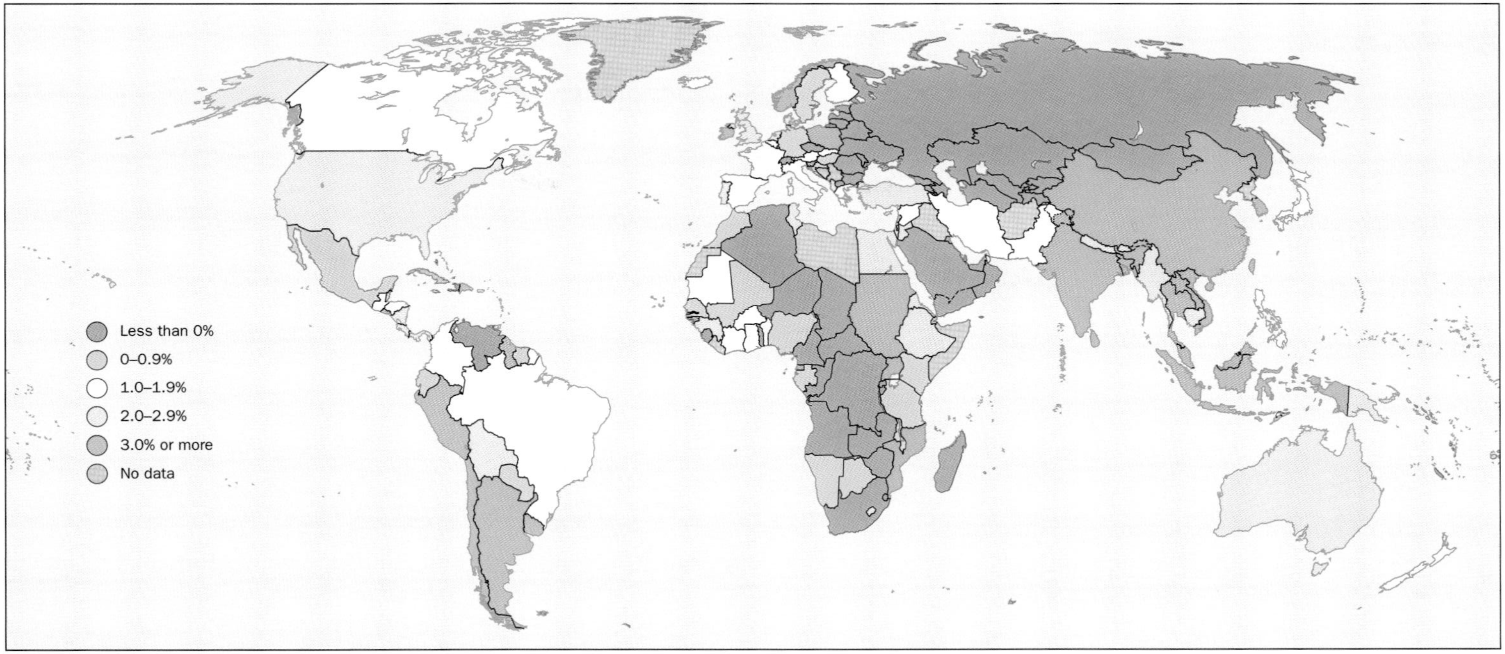

Income growth

GNP per capita growth, 1990–98

The average annual percentage change in a country's real GNP per capita. To exclude the effects of inflation, constant price GNP is used in calculating the growth rate.

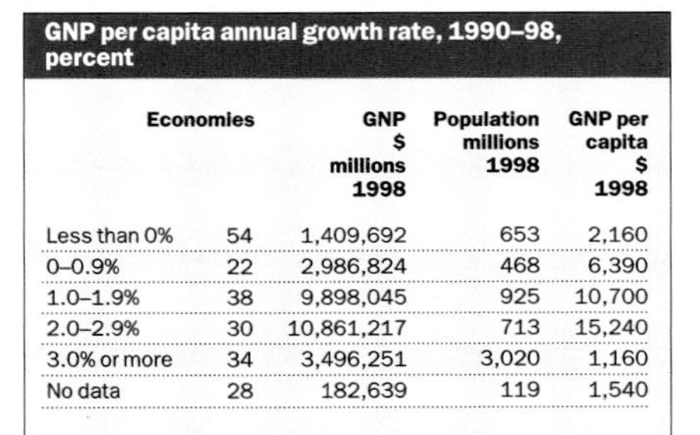

GNP per capita annual growth rate, 1990–98, percent

	Economies	GNP $ millions 1998	Population millions 1998	GNP per capita $ 1998
Less than 0%	54	1,409,692	653	2,160
0–0.9%	22	2,986,824	468	6,390
1.0–1.9%	38	9,898,045	925	10,700
2.0–2.9%	30	10,861,217	713	15,240
3.0% or more	34	3,496,251	3,020	1,160
No data	28	182,639	119	1,540

Index of GNP per capita, 1980–98, 1980 = 100

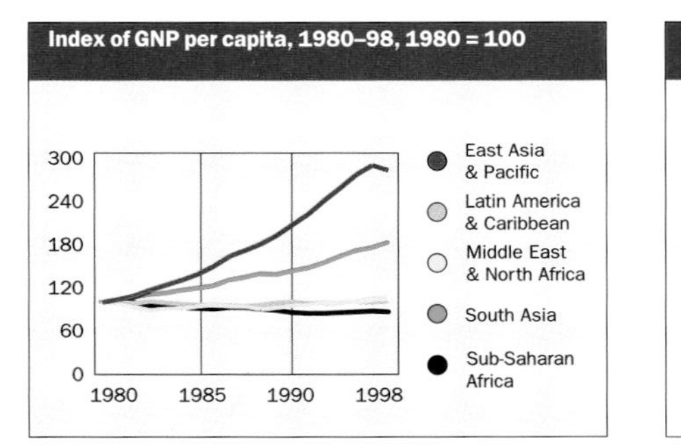

Distribution of world population among economies grouped by GNP per capita growth rate

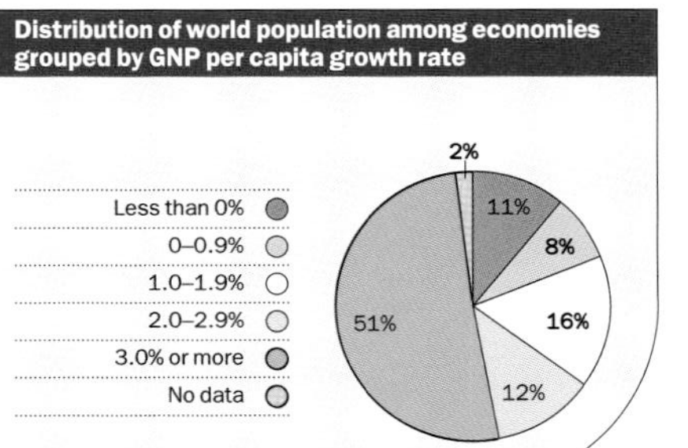

Source: Adapted from the *2000 World Bank Atlas*. Reprinted by permission of The World Bank.

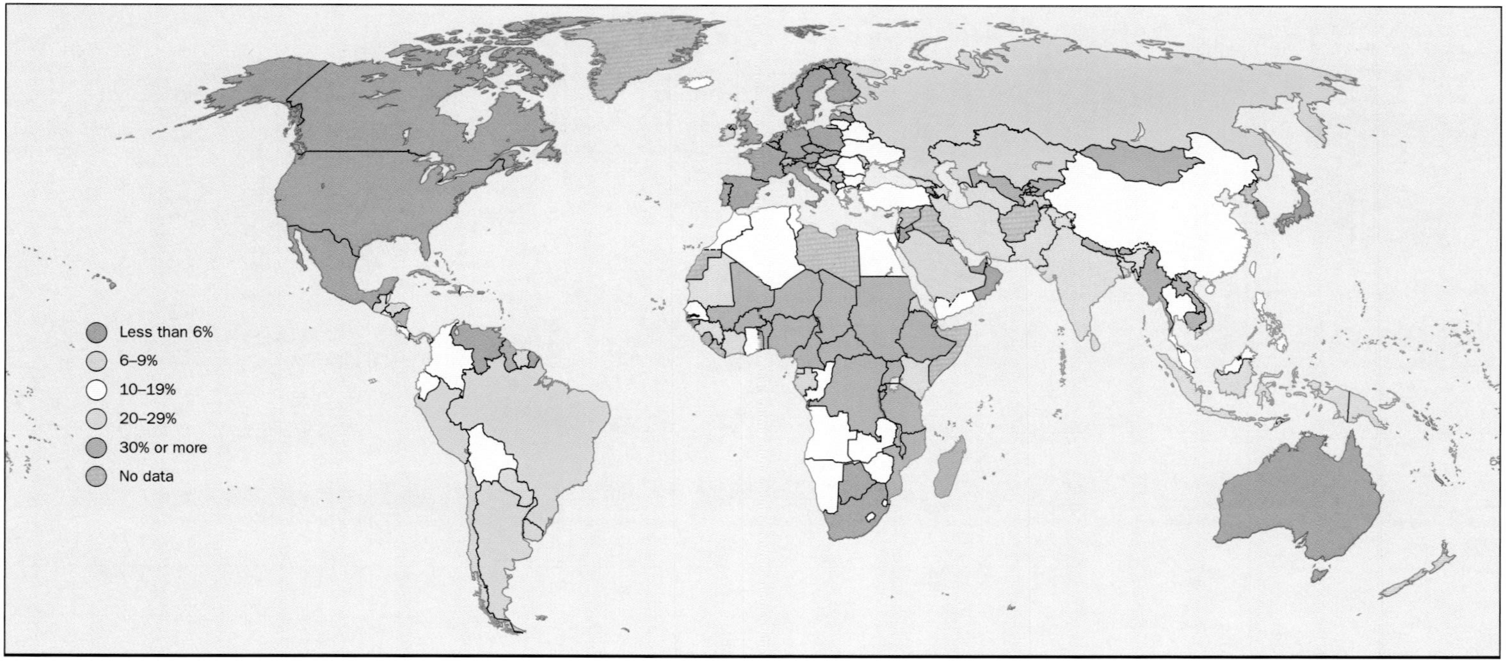

Less than 6%
6–9%
10–19%
20–29%
30% or more
No data

Agriculture

Agriculture share in GDP, 1998

The value added in a country's agricultural sector as a percentage of gross domestic product.

Distribution of world population among economies grouped by agriculture share in GDP

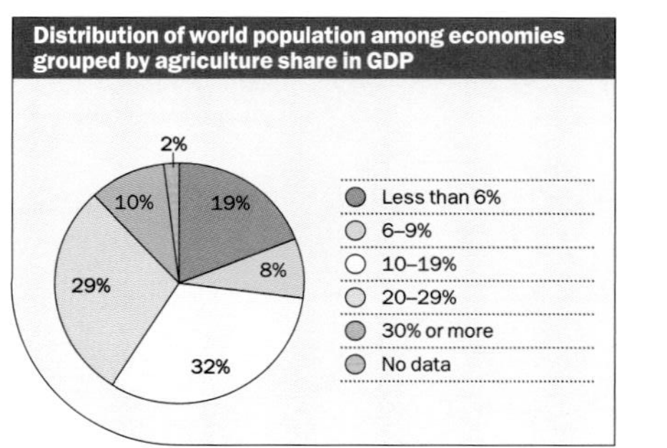

2%
10%
19%
29%
8%
32%
Less than 6%
6–9%
10–19%
20–29%
30% or more
No data

Agriculture share in GDP, 1998, percent

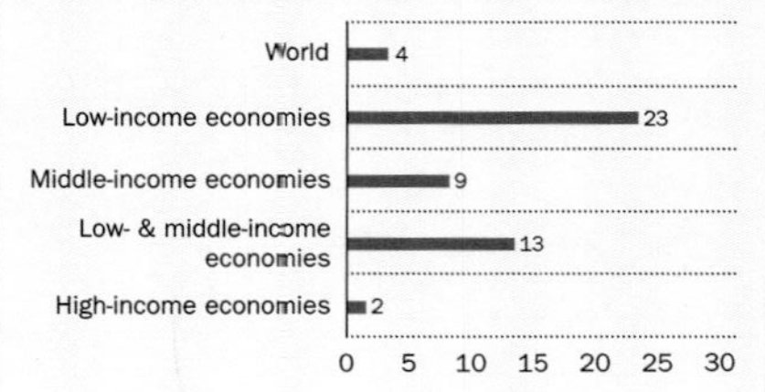

World
4
Low-income economies
23
Middle-income economies
9
Low- & middle-income economies
13
High-income economies
2
0 5 10 15 20 25 30

Agriculture share in GDP, 1998, percent

	Economies	GNP $ millions 1998	Population millions 1998	GNP per capita $ 1998
Less than 6%	46	23,191,029	1,131	20,500
6–9%	23	1,936,482	473	4,100
10–19%	40	2,071,226	1,867	1,110
20–29%	26	884,291	1,703	520
30% or more	37	260,571	584	450
No data	34	491,068	140	3,520

Source: Adapted from the *2000 World Bank Atlas*. Reprinted by permission of The World Bank.

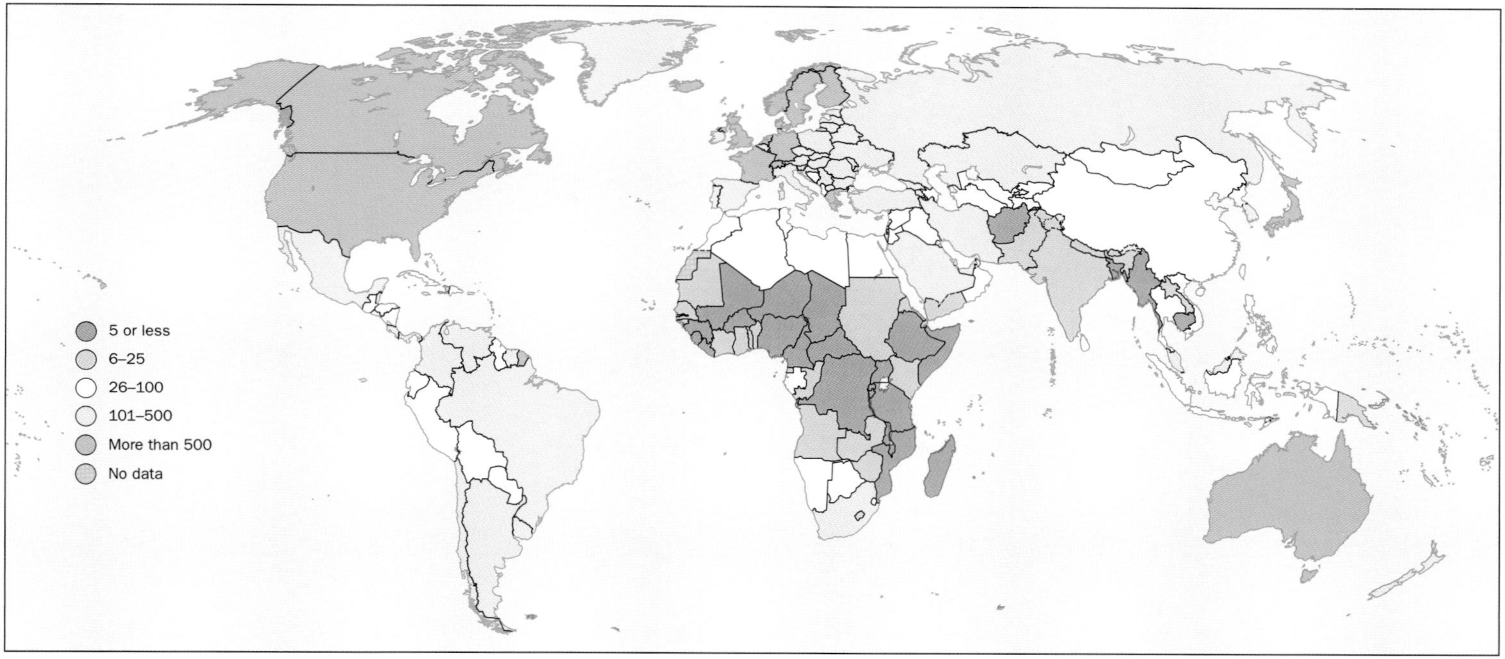

5 or less
6–25
26–100
101–500
More than 500
No data

Telephone lines

Telephone mainlines per 1,000 people, 1998

Telephone lines connecting a customer's equipment to the public switched telephone network, per 1,000 people.

Distribution of world population among economies grouped by telephone mainlines per 1,000 people

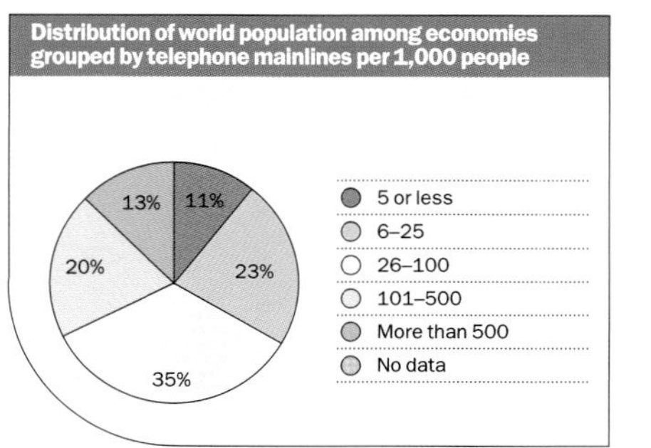

11%
23%
35%
20%
13%
5 or less
6–25
26–100
101–500
More than 500
No data

Telephone mainlines per 1,000 people, 1998

East Asia & Pacific
70
Europe & Central Asia
200
Latin America & Caribbean
123
Middle East & North Africa
81
South Asia
19
Sub-Saharan Africa
14
High income
567
0
150
300
450
600

Telephone mainlines per 1,000 people, 1998

	Economies	GNP $ millions 1998	Population millions 1998	GNP per capita $ 1998
5 or less	24	166,045	627	260
6–25	29	573,875	1,328	430
26–100	48	1,837,693	2,038	900
101–500	75	6,324,651	1,163	5,440
More than 500	25	19,922,148	738	27,000
No data	5	10,256	3	3,200

Source: Adapted from the *2000 World Bank Atlas.* Reprinted by permission of The World Bank.

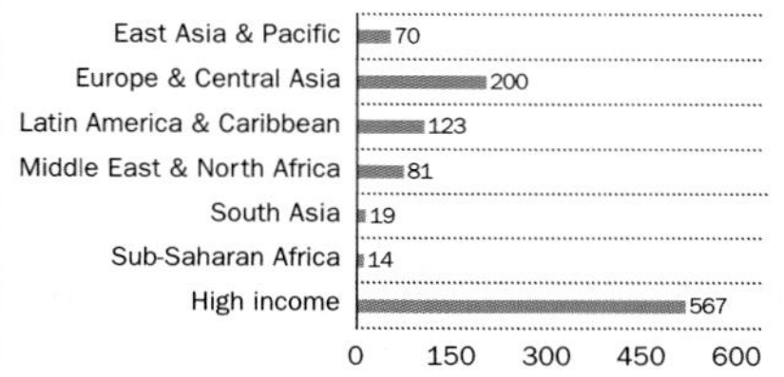

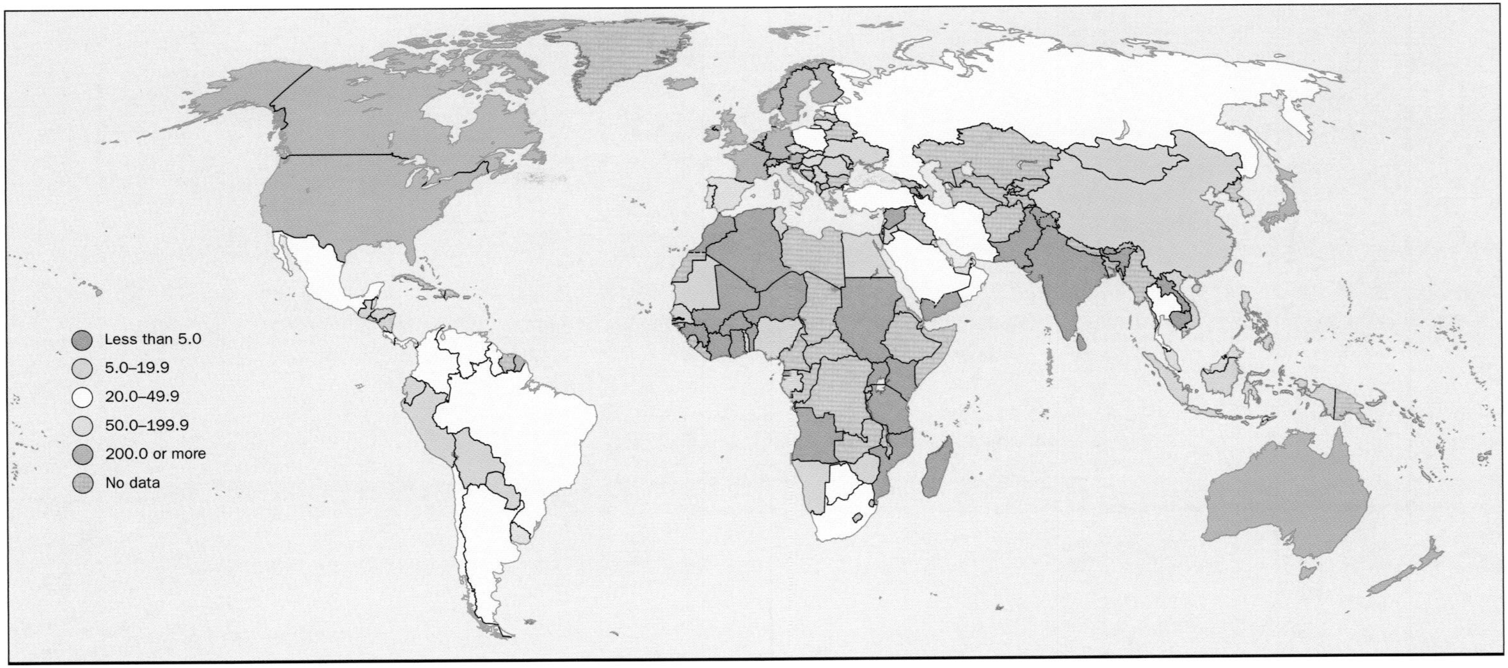

Less than 5.0
5.0–19.9
20.0–49.9
50.0–199.9
200.0 or more
No data

Personal computers

Personal computers per 1,000 people, 1998

The estimated number of self-contained computers designed to be used by a single individual, per 1,000 people.

Personal computers per 1,000 people, 1998

Economies		GNP $ millions 1998	Population millions 1998	GNP per capita $ 1998
Less than 5.0	28	687,278	1,474	470
5.0–19.9	28	1,541,443	1,983	780
20.0–49.9	22	2,945,534	832	3,540
50.0–199.9	24	2,977,309	253	11,760
200.0 or more	24	20,221,961	739	27,380
No data	80	461,142	617	750

Personal computers per 1,000 people, 1998

East Asia & Pacific
14.1
Europe & Central Asia
34.6
Latin America & Caribbean
34.0
Middle East & North Africa
9.9
South Asia
2.9
Sub-Saharan Africa
7.5
High income
311.2
0
125
250
375

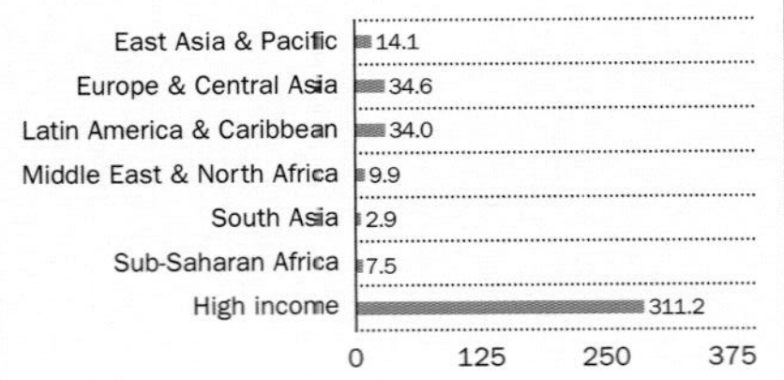

Distribution of world population among economies grouped by personal computers per 1,000 people

Less than 5.0
5.0–19.9
20.0–49.9
50.0–199.9
200.0 or more
No data
25%
10%
13%
4%
14%
34%

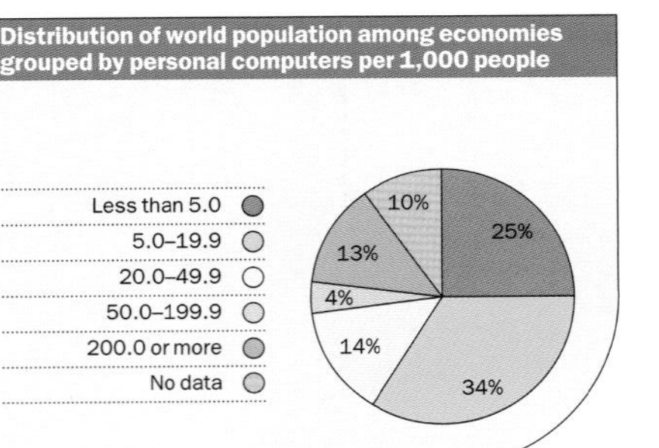

Source: Adapted from the *2000 World Bank Atlas*. Reprinted by permission of The World Bank.

150,000 sets a decade earlier.[57] In approaching the marketplace from a global perspective, companies need to look not only at countries but also at industries and segments.

The forces that affect industry should be analyzed to determine the competitiveness of the industry and the role of the major forces, such as buyers, suppliers, new entrants, substitutes, and competitors.[58] In addition, companies need to look for global industry shifts and position themselves to take advantage of them. For example, a retailer examining the do-it-yourself market may notice that the car servicing industry is shifting because of changes in automotive technology. Given the mechanical reliability of today's cars, the maintenance needs of second-hand car owners beyond the warranty are limited to a few options that do not require skilled labor on complex equipment. These repairs can be done in specialty workshops at a lower cost and more conveniently than by the authorized dealer.[59] Predicting this type of industry shift opens opportunities for the vigilant company.

Globalization also means that companies are looking for new ways to segment markets, especially where demographics fail. There is a trend toward classifying consumers based on lifestyles, attitudes, and preferences rather than nationalities. If you plan to build a global brand, you need segments that are similar regardless of nationality.[60] The arrival of personal computers in the 1980s moved information technology from the mainframe to the desktop. Now with local and wide area networks, along with high-speed networking, technology allows managers to tap large volumes of mixed data, voice, graphics, and video. Furthermore, the Internet has removed the walls between corporations and organizations, offering access to unbelievable amounts of data. According to IBM chairman Louis Gerstner, the implications of network computing "will transform every business and institution in the world."[61]

The demand for quality multicountry research has spurred the market research industry to expand beyond traditional national boundaries. Mintel, primarily a U.K.-based market research company, changed its name to Mintel International to reflect its concentration on the world market. Industry experts expect a rapid increase in the demand for multicountry research.[62]

57. Thomas A. Stewart, "How to Manage in a New Era," *Fortune*, January 15, 1990, p. 29.
58. Michael E. Porter, *Competitive Strategy: Techniques for Analyzing Industries and Competitors* (New York: Free Press, 1980).
59. Xavier Gilbert and Paul Stebel, "Taking Advantage of Industry Shifts," *European Management Journal*, 1990, vol. 7, no. 4, p. 399.
60. Mary Goodyear, "Bold Approaches to Brave New Worlds," *Marketing Week*, March 23, 1990, pp. 52–55.
61. Paul Taylor, "The Threshold of a Significant Change," *Financial Times*, February 7, 1996, Information Technology section, p. xvi.
62. Donna Dawson, "Booming Reports," *Marketing*, December 14, 1989, p. 37.

In 1999, Nielsen introduced its first pan-European research service, called Quartz, which provides simulated market tests based upon consumer reactions in five European countries. Twenty-five multinationals, including Nestlé, Procter & Gamble, and Danone Group, have already signed up for the service. Europanel, a consortium of Europe's leading consumer panel companies, has developed a pan-European service called the European Market Measurement Database. It tracks the movement of consumer goods throughout western Europe, based on information from 55,000 households. ACNielsen, the leading global market research firm, offers services in over one hundred countries and had 1998 revenues of $1.4 billion.[63] The global research companies have purchased a number of national market research companies.

Global market research companies have experienced rapid growth in recent years as a result of expanding research services, new research measuring devices, and innovative techniques. The largest industrial market research companies are shown in Table 6.6. Electronic scanner data are now available in many markets, offering very fast retail consumer data for marketers.[64] As a revolutionary communication tool, the Internet is also pushing research horizons, and revenues, as companies measure consumer response.

The top twenty-five global research firms made up 52 percent of the total market in 1995; this figure is expected to climb to 60 percent by 2000. The larger firms have been acquiring smaller firms to expand their global abilities. For example, ACNielsen has operations in ninety-four countries, versus twenty-five in 1990, and acquired the Surveys Research Group in Asia for $150 million in 1995.[65]

To assist decision making about marketing on a global scale, researchers must provide more than data on strictly local factors within each country. All firms that market their products in overseas markets require information that allows analysis across several countries or markets. However, leaving each local subsidiary or market to develop its own database does not usually result in an integrated marketing information system (MIS). Instead, authority to develop a centrally managed MIS must be assigned to a central location, with reports given directly to the firm's chief international marketing officer. Jagdish Sheth made a very effective case for a centralized marketing research staff that would monitor buyer needs on a worldwide basis.[66] Sheth favors the establishment of a longitudinal panel in selected geographical areas encompassing all major markets, present and potential. By assessing client needs on a worldwide basis, the company ensures that products and services are designed with all buyers in mind. This avoids the traditional

63. "ACNielsen and Catalina Marketing Develop Powerful New Loyalty Marketing Approach," *P. R. Newswire*, June 4, 1999.
64. Kenneth Wylie, "100 Leading Research Companies," *Advertising Age*, May 20, 1996, p. 39.
65. "Market Research Data Wars," *Economist*, July 22, 1995, pp. 60–61.
66. Jagdish N. Sheth, "A Conceptual Model of Long-Range Multinational Marketing Planning," *Management International Review*, 1971, no. 4–5, pp. 3–10.

TABLE 6.6

Top 25 Global Research Organizations

Rank 1998	Rank 1997	Organization	Headquarters	Country	No. of countries with subsidiaries/branch offices[1]	Full-time employees	Total research revenues[2] (millions)	Percent change from 1997[3]	Revenues from outside home country US$ (millions)	Percent of total
1	1	ACNielsen Corp.	Stamford, Conn.	U.S.	80	20,700	1,425.4	0.8%	$1,035.0	72.6%
2	–	IMS Health Inc.	Westport, N.Y.	U.S.	74	8,000	1,084.0	7.6	672.5	62.0
3	3	The Kantar Group Ltd.	London	U.K.	1	4,347	674.9	13.6	406.1	60.2
		Research International	*London*	*U.K.*	*24*	*1,770*	*328.0*	*13.5*	*211.2*	*64.4*
		Millward Brown	*Naperville, Ill.*	*U.S.*	*15*	*1,377*	*226.4*	*17.9*	*134.6*	*59.5*
		Other Kantar	*London*	*U.K.*	*14*	*1,200*	*120.4*	*7.8*	*0.2*	*50.0*
4	4	Taylor Nelson Sofres plc.	London	U.K.	35	4,500	548.8	10.7	386.9	70.5
5	5	Information Resources Inc.	Chicago	U.S.	17	4,600	511.3	2.1	114.3	22.4
6	9	NFO Worldwide Inc.	Greenwich, Conn.	U.S.	32	3,100	424.3	8.3	58.2	37.7
		NFO Worldwide Inc.	*Greenwich, Conn.*	*U.S.*	*21*	*2,180*	*250.4*	*6.4*	*80.3*	*32.1*
		Infratest Burke AG	*Munich*	*Germany*	*12*	*920*	*173.9*	*10.9*	*77.9*	*44.8*
7	–	Nielsen Media Research	New York	U.S.	2	2,486	401.9	12.1	10.4	2.6
8	6	GfK Group AG	Nuremberg	Germany	33	3,111	353.0	6.5	174.0	49.3
9	12	IPSOS Group S.A.	Paris	France	20	1,538	226.3	12.8	160.2	0.8
10	7	Westat Inc.	Rockville, Md.	U.S.	1	1,203	205.4	12.9	—	—
11	10	The Arbitron Co.	New York	U.S.	2	609	194.5	10.0	7.6	3.9
12	11	United Information Group Ltd.	London	U.K.	5	1,058	181.6	6.9	61.3	33.8
13	13	Maritz Marketing Research Inc.	St Louis, Mo.	U.S.	3	720	169.1	18.3	42.3	25.0
14	15	The NPD Group Inc.	Port Washington, N.Y.	U.S.	13	970	138.5	24.7	22.2	16.0
15	14	Video Research Ltd.	Tokyo	Japan	2	343[4]	137.5[4]	3.7[4]	—	—
16	16	Market Facts Inc.	Arlington Heights, Ill.	U.S.	2	915	136.5	21.4	20.3	14.9
17	18	Marketing Intelligence Corp.	Tokyo	Japan	2	366	80.2	4.4	0.4	0.5
18	25	IBOPE Group	Rio de Janeiro	Brazil	7	1,400	72.5	28.1	15.0	20.7
19	25	J.D. Power and Associates	Agoura Hills, Calif.	U.S.	5	475	64.8	25.8	6.8	10.5
20	19	Audits & Surveys Worldwide Inc.	New York	U.S.	4	241	58.3	−15.4	19.4	33.3
21	24	Opinion Research Corp. International	Princeton, N.J.	U.S.	5	422	58.2	7.2	18.0	31.0
22	23	Dentsu Research Inc.	Tokyo	Japan	1	118	55.2	10.0	3.1	5.2
23	–	Burke Inc.	Cincinnati, Ohio	U.S.	3	239	52.4	19.6	10.6	20.2
24	–	Sample Institut GmbH & Co. KG	Molln	Germany	6	346	51.9	3.9	27.0	52.1
25	–	Roper Starch Worldwide Inc.	Harrison, N.Y.	U.S.	3	344	51.3	13.6	10.6	20.7
		Total				62,151	$7,357.8	8.6%	$3,482.2	47.3%

[1]Includes countries which have subsidiaries with an equity interest or branch offices or both. [2]Total revenues that include nonresearch activities for some companies are significantly higher. This information is given in the individual company profiles.
[3]Rate of growth from year-to-year has been adjusted so as not to include revenue gains or losses from acquisitions or divestitures; see company profiles for explanation. Rate of growth is based on home-country currency. [4]For fiscal year ending March 31.
Source: Reprinted from *Advertising Age*, May 24,1999. Reprinted with permission from Advertising Age International. Copyright, Crain Communications Inc. 1999.

pattern of initially designing products for the company's home market and looking at export or foreign opportunities only once a product has been designed.

A principal requirement for a worldwide MIS is a standardized set of data to be collected from each market or country. Though the actual data collection can be left to a firm's local units, they will do so according to central and uniform specifications.

Companies are only analyzing a small percentage of the data currently available, and in the case of retail, data available are doubling every year. A new technique of data mining has been developed to extract previously unknown, yet comprehensive and actionable, information from large databases and to use this information to make critical business decisions. Coca-Cola is linking up with its bottlers partners around the world to share information and best practice. In a planned seven-year rollout, Coca-Cola anticipates boosting revenue by sharing sales information and communicating more effectively with its partners. The new system will upgrade and expand data warehouses, decision support systems, and a worldwide Intranet to improve communications.[67]

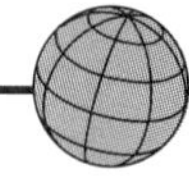

Conclusions

In this chapter, we discussed the major challenges and difficulties in securing necessary data for global marketing. We have shown that effective marketing research is based on a conceptual framework combined with a thorough but flexible use of conventional marketing research practices. The major difficulties are the lack of basic data on many markets and the likelihood that research methods will have to be adapted to local environments. The final challenge of global marketing research is to provide managers with a uniform database covering all the firm's present and potential markets. Such a database will allow for cross-country comparisons and analysis as well as the incorporation of worldwide consumer needs into the initial product design process. Given the difficulties in data collection, to achieve this global comparability of data is indeed a challenge for even the most experienced professionals.

The value of market research cannot be understated, especially in new developing markets. The use of properly conducted market research can reduce or eliminate most global marketing mistakes. Market research can uncover local adaptation needs, potential name problems, promotion requirements, and appropriate market strategies.[68] Sound global marketing research techniques uncover potentially costly and often embarrassing situations.

67. Bob Violino, "Extended Enterprise—Coca-Cola Is Linking Its IT System with Those of Worldwide Bottling Partners as It Strives to Stay One Step Ahead of the Competition," *Information Week*, March 22, 1999, pp. 46–54.

68. David A. Ricks, *Blunders in International Business,* Third Edition, Blackwell: Oxford, 1999, p. 159.

The world has changed greatly since the first edition of this text in 1987. At that time, market information around the world was sparse and unreliable, especially in developing and undeveloped countries. Now through the efforts of the United Nations, global market research companies, and on-line data sources, information is available for every market in the world, from Canada and Mexico to Uzbekistan and Mongolia. Global marketers can use the widely available information to make better market decisions and marketing strategies.

QUESTIONS FOR DISCUSSION

1. Why is it so difficult to do marketing research in multicountry settings?
2. What role does the Internet play in global market research?
3. Comparative marketing analysis is a powerful technique that provides the basis for the study of global marketing. What is the comparative approach, and how is it applied to multicountry environments?
4. What are the advantages and disadvantages of secondary and primary data in global marketing?
5. What are the challenges of using a market research questionnaire developed in one country and used in several other countries?
6. If you were estimating the demand for vacuum cleaners, what type of inference analysis would you use? Give a specific example.
7. If you headed Kodak, how would you monitor reactions around the world to a major competitor such as Fuji Film?

FOR FURTHER READING

Asay, Sylvia, and Charles B. Hennon. "The Challenge of Conducting Qualitative Family Research in International Settings." *Family and Consumer Sciences Research Journal*, June 1, 1999, pp. 409–420.

Craig, C. Samuel, and Susan P. Douglas. *International Marketing Research: Concepts and Methods*. New York: Wiley, 1999.

Davis, Harry L., Susan P. Douglas, and Alvin J. Silk. "Measure Unreliability: Hidden Threat to Cross-National Marketing Research," *Journal of Marketing*, Spring 1981, pp. 98–109.

Green, Robert, and Philip D. White. "Methodological Considerations in Cross-National Consumer Research." *Journal of International Business Studies*, Fall–Winter 1976, pp. 81–88.

Greenbaum, Thomas L. "Understanding Focus Group Research Abroad." *Marketing News*, June 3, 1996, pp. H14, H36.

Helgeson, Neil. "Research Isn't Linear When Done Globally." *Marketing News*, July 19, 1999, p. 13.

Keillor, Bruce D., and G. T. M. Hult. "A Five-Country Study of National Identity Implications for International Marketing Research and Practice." *International Marketing Review*, 1999, vol. 16, no. 1, pp. 65–84.

Medina, Jose F., Sharon E. Beatty, and Joel Saegert. "Consumer Acquisition Patterns in an Industrializing Country: A Study of Global Convergence of Demand." *Journal of Global Marketing*, 1996, vol. 10, no. 2, pp. 5–25.

Mundorf, Norbert, Rudy Roy Dholakia, Nikhilesh Dholakia, and Stuart Westin. "German and American Consumer Orientations to Information Technologies: Implications for Marketing and Public Policy." *Journal of International Consumer Marketing*, 1996, vol. 8, no. 3, 4, pp. 125–143.

Murphy, H. Lee. "Japanese Keeping Fewer Secrets from U.S. Firms." *Marketing News*, June 21, 1999, pp. 4–6.

Netemeyer, Richard G., Srinivas Durvasula, and Donald R. Lichtenstein. "A Cross-National Assessment of the Reliability and Validity of the CETSCALE." *Journal of Market Research*, August 1991, pp. 320–327.

Peterson, Robin T. "Screening Is First Step in Evaluating Foreign Market." *Marketing News*, November 9, 1990, p. 13.

"Research Companies Push Global Expansion." *Advertising Age*, March 8, 1993, p. 31.

Winters, Lewis C. "International Psychographics." *Marketing Research: A Magazine of Management and Application*, September 1992, pp. 48–49.

III Developing Global Marketing Strategies

COMPETENCE LEVEL	GLOBAL ENVIRONMENT	
ENVIRONMENTAL COMPETENCE	*Understanding the Global Marketing Environment*	2 3 4
ANALYTIC COMPETENCE	*Analyzing Global Marketing Opportunities*	5 6
STRATEGIC COMPETENCE	*Developing Global Marketing Strategies*	7 8 9
FUNCTIONAL COMPETENCE	*Designing Global Marketing Programs*	10 11 12 13 14 15
MANAGERIAL COMPETENCE	*Managing the Global Marketing Effort*	16 17 18

Increasingly, companies are being asked to design their marketing strategies from a global point of view. Globalized marketing strategies require an ability to look at business and competitive developments all over the world and to digest often conflicting information into a workable plan. Global marketing strategies require skills and conceptual understanding that are different from those required for developing domestic strategies.

In this section, we concentrate on the global marketing strategies firms must be able to develop to be successful. No company can be all things to all people, and global marketing managers have to learn to focus and build on their company's strengths. Future global marketing managers need to have the strategic competence necessary to develop global marketing programs that will ensure the success of their firms.

Chapter 7 deals with the global mindset required of future global marketing managers. Chapter 8 concentrates on the major strategic decisions faced by firms active in global marketing. The chapter introduces the most recent concepts on globalization of marketing strategies. The various alternative entry strategies will be the subject of Chapter 9.

7

Developing a Global Mindset

Different Types of Marketing Mindsets

Knowledge Components for the Global Mindset

Analytical Global Marketing Skills

Customer-Based Global Logics

Industry-Based Global Logics

Global Market and Opportunity Assessment

Individual Skills for a Global Mindset

THE SLOGAN "THINK GLOBALLY, ACT LOCALLY" IS FREQUENTLY USED TO describe the managerial challenge faced by global marketers.[1] It captures the need to think in global terms about a business or a market while at the same time doing appropriate local tailoring to meet the particular requirements of the local customers. In this chapter, we give some background on what is meant by thinking globally. If this is a truly different type of thinking, requiring a new mindset (namely, a global one), one should be able to differentiate it from a more traditional mindset. We have therefore decided to offer detailed ideas

1. Gurcharan Das, "Local Memoirs of a Global Manager," *Harvard Business Review*, March–April 1993, pp. 38–47.

about what this new global marketer with a global perspective ought to be able to do, how he or she should be able to think, and what kind of skills could be expected from such a person. This chapter is different from others, as it does not focus primarily on existing business practice. Instead, we concentrate on developing new analytic tools that will make the adoption of a global perspective more likely.

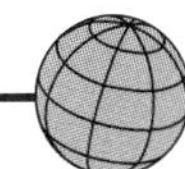

Categorizing Global Marketing Mindsets[2]

The mindset is the outlook or frame of mind that the marketer carries around the world. The global perspective, or mindset, is characterized by a different view of the opportunities and the facts of the world market. The global marketing perspective is more encompassing than the domestic, international, multinational, or even panregional perspective. It is a new, truly different dimension in managerial thinking that transcends traditional labels and shapes the outlook of global marketers. (See Figure 7.1 for a more detailed account of the concepts discussed in this chapter.)

Domestic Mindset

The *domestic perspective* is characterized by the fact that all basic anchor points of a marketer are based on a single-country experience, his or her domestic market. A marketing executive growing up in the United States and professionally active in the U.S. market has only a single-country, domestic mindset. The same is true for a German manager growing up and living in Germany only. Thus, the domestic mindset is always single-country in nature. As we all know, marketers must constantly refer to their own experience as they go about making marketing decisions. Facts are not always spelled out completely, and executives typically fill in the blanks from their own cultural experience. The domestic mind tends to fill in those blanks from its own domestic market or cultural perspective.

Falling back on one's own cultural or domestic experience base comes very naturally to executives. As we showed in Chapter 3, violating cultural norms in another country is commonplace because executives, or companies, go to a different country and automatically transfer some of their underlying assumptions to the new locale. The reverse, however, is also true. When data from a different country are available, executives with a domestic perspective often find that set of data meaningless, or discomfiting, preferring instead business data from their own country.

The concept of the domestic perspective is not new to global marketing. For some time, executives have referred to such a perspective as ethnocentric, or bound in only one culture.[3] This reaction of spurning data, facts, or readings from

2. Jean-Pierre Jeannet, "The Age of the Global Mind," *Unternehmung*, 1991, vol. 45, no. 2, pp. 132–142.
3. Howard V. Perlmutter, "The Tortuous Evolution of the Multinational Corporation," *Columbia Journal of World Business*, January–February 1969, p. 12.

FIGURE 7.1

Elements of the Global Mindset

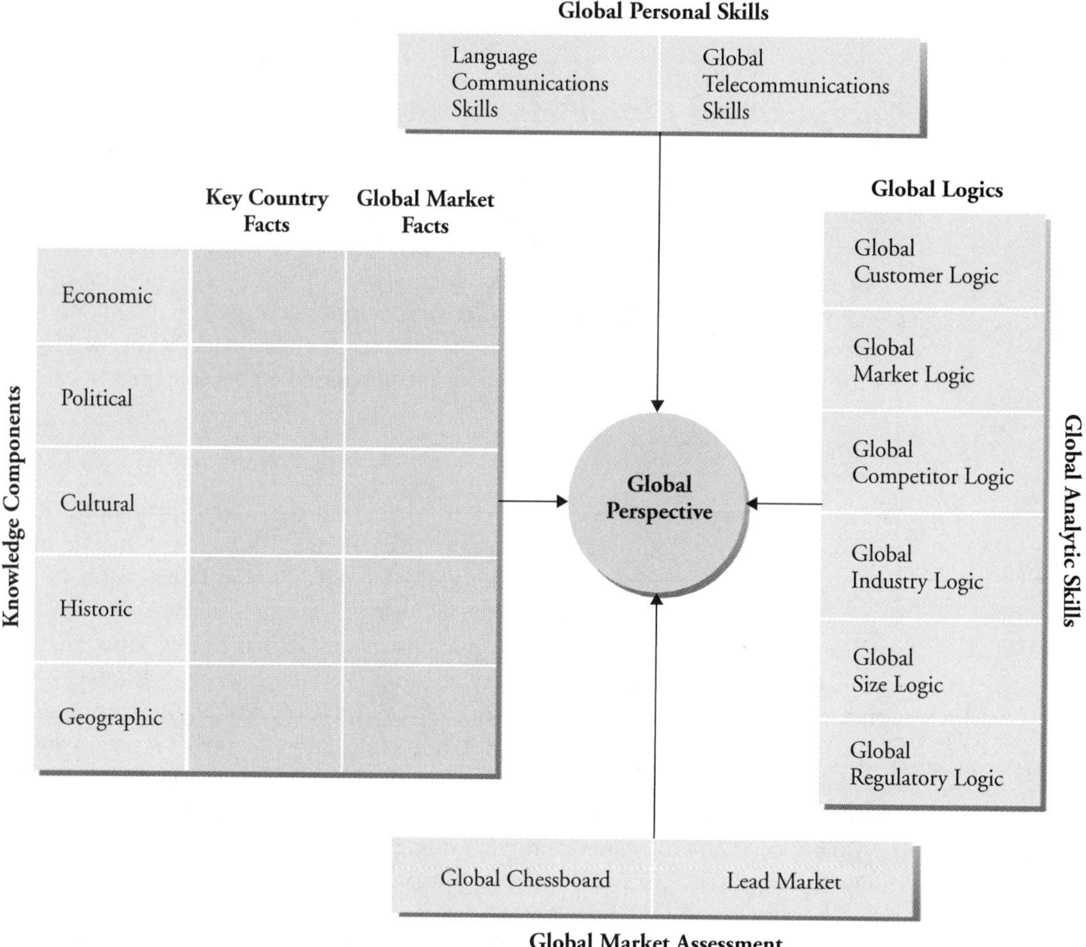

elsewhere is sometimes referred to as the not-invented-here (NIH) syndrome, a concept well known in engineering and scientific circles. It generally results in the rejection of new ideas that are not homegrown and stands in the way of adopting best practice in marketing, particularly when the idea originated in some distant market. Clearly, for marketing professionals to become effective in our new global economy, they must be able to step out of a domestic mindset and adapt a different, more open type of thinking.

International Mindset

Marketing executives with an international mindset have broadened their reference points to other markets, typically through some longer international or overseas stay. A Japanese executive who has spent four years with the U.S. subsidiary can be expected to have broadened his or her perspective to an international one, allowing for incorporation of Japanese and U.S. reference points in that person's mind.

In many firms, executives are sent on international assignments for the single purpose of enhancing their perspective. The number of Americans working for U.S. firms overseas is estimated at about 250,000.[4] There are many expatriate employees from other countries as well. Although working overseas provides a new perspective for the manager, substantial barriers exist that limit opportunities. For one, sending a manager overseas is typically three times more costly than hiring locals.[5] The experience of Tetra Laval, a global Swedish-based firm, indicates that moving a French manager to the United States cost 50 percent more than hiring a local (U.S.) manager. Conversely, moving a U.S. manager into France and providing the required overseas package drove up costs to 150 percent above hiring a local (French) manager.[6] The extra costs include cost-of-living allowances, different taxation schemes, and the expense of sending an entire family to a different country.

An international experience can take several different forms. Many students spend some time abroad in overseas university programs. To the extent that they have contact with the local environment, international experience is gained. Likewise, the large number of international students in U.S. business schools gain international experience through their stay in the United States. At Babson College in Massachusetts, all full-time M.B.A. students are required to participate in an international component, taking them overseas to a certain country.

Sometimes, the impetus for international experience can be an unforeseen event. John Aliberti, an engineer with Union Switch and based in Pittsburgh, had little international experience when his company needed someone to visit China in search of contracts. An expert in the type of railroad engineering systems desired by Chinese railroad executives, Aliberti was sent to China having no prior experience with the culture. He quickly immersed himself in the culture, history, and politics of the country and after many trips to China became highly effective in conducting business there although he speaks or writes little Chinese. According to his firm, the Chinese value Aliberti's professional expertise.[7]

4. "Thriving in a Foreign Environment," *New York Times*, December 5, 1993, p. F17.
5. Ibid.
6. "Tethered to Pittsburgh for Years, an Engineer Thrives on Trips to Asia," *Wall Street Journal*, November 19, 1996, p. 1.
7. Kenichi Ohmae, *The Borderless World* (London: Collins, 1990), ch. 2, pp. 17–31.

All such experiences provide an international perspective as the student or executive gains in-depth knowledge of a foreign country. Although it is international experience in just one country, many experts believe that such a manager would be less subject to the NIH syndrome. By broadening the domestic, single-country perspective to an international (dual-country) view, the individual would in all likelihood respond more openly to an initiative in a new country than would the domestic-minded executive, for whom any international contact would be a first-time affair.

Multinational Mindset

A still smaller set of executives, having gone through several overseas experiences or assignments, has reached a multinational perspective. These executives know more than one overseas country well. Often their assignments span a region, or even more than one region. In many large international firms, such as Citibank, Nestlé, Unilever, and BP, executives undertake a series of assignments, each of which may extend three to four years, in different locations. These executives not only become knowledgeable about one market or culture but have also learned how to master new ones, not yet experienced.

The cadre of executives with a multinational mindset are, however, still largely bound by their cultural and foreign experiences. Their skill derives from the detailed knowledge of those markets they have experienced personally. While characterizing the multinational perspective as incorporating a greater quantity of in-depth international experience is fair, it still is not to be confused with a global perspective, the unique mindset we describe in more detail in a following section.

Some executives believe that a multinational mindset is developed as a result of a series of single-country assignments. However, even when executives move around the world assuming ever greater responsibility, they frequently receive these assignments in the context of a single-country market. It would not be unusual for an executive to be "promoted" from smaller to larger countries but still tend to have assignments that limit responsibility to the assigned country. Therefore, the development of a truly global outlook, encompassing many different countries or markets at the same time, is stifled. A global mindset is not merely the accumulation of a series of single-country experiences; instead, it goes far beyond this approach and reflects an altogether different type of thinking.

Panregional Mindset

The panregional mindset is a variant of both the multinational and the global mindset. It incorporates the ability to think across a region, such as Europe, and incorporate the realities of a large number of countries at once. A marketing manager with extensive experience across a number of European markets would be called a Pan-European manager. Panregional managers gain their experience from exercising marketing responsibility across a number of markets. In the case of Europe, this might consist of more than twenty different countries.[8] Other panregional experiences might be gained in Asia and Latin America.

Panregional managers, because of the very nature of their responsibility, are much closer to the thinking of marketing managers with a global mindset since the need to think across many markets simultaneously is a precursor to the global mindset. We shall therefore move on right away to our fifth and final mindset.

Global Mindset

With the global mindset we are stepping into a type of perspective fundamentally different from the four previously described.[9] The global perspective encompasses *all* cultures or nationalities; it might be described as a mind hovering like a satellite over the earth.[10] The global mindset calls for a manager with a capability to maintain equal "mental" distance from all regions of the world. However, such a manager should not be construed as a person without any cultural anchor. Rather, the executive with the global perspective maintains that point of view with respect to his or her business or profession. A personal cultural anchor point is still required for personal balance.

Marketing managers with a global mindset are able to keep the entire global opportunity for a business in mind and are able to think across multiple markets rather than compartmentalize issues on one market at a time. They are able to see the "big picture" and are sensitive to the linkages between markets and trends across the world.

International, panregional, and multinational mindsets depend on experience gained from direct contact with one or several other countries and cultures. The marketing executive with a global mindset achieves that view throughout the world, even for areas where no direct prior experience exists. This ability is essential because managers who act with global responsibility for a product, a segment, a category, or some other project could not possibly have been personally exposed to all those countries before.

Although we have not yet said so explicitly, the global mindset is also an attitude. Executives with a global mind display an innate curiosity about the developments of this world. They recognize a need for continued, permanent, lifelong

8. The authors are indebted to Clifton Clarke, formerly with Digital Equipment Corp. and now an independent consultant, for his observations on the attitudinal dimensions of the global mindset.
9. Vern Terpstra and Kenneth David, *The Cultural Environment of International Business*, 2nd ed. (Cincinnati: Southwestern, 1985).
10. Ferdinand Schevill, *A History of the Balkans* (New York: Dorset, 1991).

learning because much of what they know becomes obsolete over time. Executives who aspire to a global mindset need to recognize the integration of industries into a global economy. In this new global economy, they must see their industry as an interconnected whole and appreciate that events generated in this dynamic drive the shape of their industry and their customers' needs over time. This global mindset, then, is both an attitude as well as a cognitive capability to exercise a certain set of new analytic skills.

A marketing executive who wants to achieve a global mindset will have to think differently about the worldwide opportunity. The following sections of this chapter establish more clearly what those differences are. We will concentrate on the particular knowledge required for a global mindset, the new global analytic skills to be applied, the strategic concepts to be understood, the personal skills to be mastered, and the managerial capabilities to be acquired.

Knowledge Components for the Global Mindset

In the previous section, we described the kind of outlook, or mindset, a marketing manager with a global perspective would bring to an assignment. Although such an outlook is important, it cannot suffice alone. The marketing manager with a global mindset will need knowledge about the world markets. The knowledge components described in this section represent core knowledge but are not necessarily complete. However, the ones we discuss would most likely account for a vast majority of the necessary factual knowledge; they might serve as a guide to aspiring global marketing managers who are just in the process of acquainting themselves with the world. Again, with the world constantly changing, such knowledge can never be viewed as final or static. It is in constant need of updating.

Key Market Knowledge

With the world consisting of more than two hundred countries and territories, it would be impossible for anyone to have a firsthand and factual knowledge of all of these markets. Instead, a knowledge of *key markets* would have to suffice. We understand key markets as the top twenty markets in a given industry, recognizing that the list of top twenty might vary depending on the line of business. Since in most countries, 80 percent or more of the economic activity can be expected to come from the top twenty markets, we have structured the knowledge components around such a list. For the purpose of this book, we use the listing of the top twenty countries by gross domestic product (GDP) as a measure (Table 7.1). Since these markets are of strategic value, marketing managers need to understand the parameters that shape the market dynamics.

TABLE 7.1

Top 20 Countries Ranked by Gross Domestic Product (1999)

Ranking	Country	(US$ billions)
1	USA	$8,508.9
2	Japan	3,786.2
3	Germany	2,118.3
4	France	1,418.7
5	United Kingdom	1,377.8
6	Italy	1,160.7
7	China	960.9
8	Brazil	776.8
9	Canada	595.3
10	Spain	545.0
11	Mexico	415.0
12	Netherlands	374.4
13	Australia	359.8
14	India	345.8
15	Argentina	336.9
16	Korea	301.6
17	Russia	272.9
18	Switzerland	262.6
19	Taiwan	261.4
20	Belgium	248.4

Source: The World Competitiveness Yearbook 1999, Lausanne: IMD Institute, 1999, p. 350.

TABLE 7.2

Key Areas of Market Economic Knowledge

GNP	Export volume
GNP growth	Import volume
GNP per capita	Foreign trade position
Major industrial sectors	Monetary policies
Inflation rate	Foreign reserve position
Interest level	Employment level

Economic Knowledge

Although statistical knowledge has some value, marketing managers need even more to have an understanding of the economic dynamics in a key market. It would be important to know the present stage of the economic cycle. Another part of required knowledge would be the type of economic system and the structure of the economy. Understanding a country's monetary system and foreign exchange regime is part of the course, as is an up-to-date knowledge of foreign exchange trends. The marketer with a global perspective ought to know economic developments in the key markets, so that a clear tapestry of the economic activity emerges. Key areas of market economic knowledge are listed in Table 7.2. Real understanding comes from combining these facts into a composite understanding of the present and future economic situation of any key market.

Political Knowledge

The global marketing manager needs to know the current and future political trends for each key market. This knowledge will certainly include knowledge of the important political institutions and a sense as to how the country is governed. Among other things, managers need to know the importance of the various political parties, their political programs, something about their leaders, and a sense of the electoral chances for success. Country analysis, as it has been practiced traditionally, will not be sufficient to understand the dynamics in key markets. Companies have to learn to understand the key drivers in the industrial policies of countries. Increasingly, governments strive for added competitiveness, often in the form of generating more exports. The resulting economic policies affect players in that country and, given today's global economy, often radiate across other countries.

Executives used to be concerned about political risk as it related to expropriations, or loss of assets; today's globally thinking manager worries more about opportunities lost or missed. The future development of the political system in China is of great interest to companies with major plants there, not because they are anxious about losing them, but because political policy affects their future growth or profitability. The same can be said for Russia or any other part of the world where major changes might occur. The executive with a global mindset is always alert to relevant developments in the leading markets of the company's industry.

Cultural Knowledge

Each key market has its own cultural heritage.[11] A manager with a global mindset is expected to understand those major cultural traits and how they may shape customers or business executives in the market. Such cultural knowledge would certainly include an understanding of the type of language, or languages, spoken—for example, knowing in the case of Brazil that Portuguese is the official language, whereas for Belgium it is French and Flemish (Dutch). Additional knowledge of particular literature, arts, or music might be important. (In the case of Japan, for example, it would imply some understanding of such traditional arts as kabuki and No.) Each country values its own leading artists, writers, and composers, and familiarity with them is integral to key country understanding. Included in cultural knowledge would be an understanding of the religious background of the key country. As we explained in detail in Chapter 3, the business environment is significantly affected if the country has a Christian, Muslim, or other religious tradition. For many countries, some understanding of the more popular local sports may be part of knowing the local culture.

Historic Knowledge

Executives often underestimate the value of appreciating a country's history. Many developments that appear to be of a short-term political nature are driven by the longer-term historical experiences of a country. How groups of executives relate to each other is also influenced by that heritage. Although global marketers typically know the historical background of their own country, few know the key historical developments or defining moments that shaped the present in their relevant key markets. Marketers need not know history for history's sake but should learn the relevant historical facts that still shape, or influence, the political and economic life of a country in the present time. Looking over the list of top twenty economies (Table 7.1) would quickly indicate where

11. Jutikkala Eino and Pirinen Kauko, *A History of Finland*, 4th ed. (Espoo: Eino & Kauko, 1984).

gaps exist. As the tragic developments in a country such as the former Yugoslavia demonstrate, the actions we witness today are rooted in history, dating back as many as six hundred years.[12] Commenting on the defining historic moments of Finland, some executives believe that knowledge of Finland's history—and especially its 1939 war with the then Soviet Union—is important in understanding the determination that some Finnish companies apply to the conquering of world markets.[13]

Geographic Knowledge

Part of a thorough understanding of a key market is knowledge of its main geographic features. This may include knowing the locations of key cities and the logistics of getting in and out of the country. Knowing the size of a country, its key dimensions, and its topography is also essential.[14] Another critical component of the geographic knowledge of key markets is an understanding of its transportation infrastructure, which might include seaports and airports for freight shipments, rail and highway systems, and telecommunications infrastructure.

Understanding Global Market Facts

Up to now, we have discussed knowledge about a company's key markets. Those facts are about individual countries only. A much larger body of knowledge about the global economy, politics, history, culture, and geography embraces all countries and plays an increasingly important role in today's business environment. A marketing manager with a global mindset would appreciate this overarching global structure just as much as each individual key market.

Understanding *global economic forces*, rather than individual-country economic forces, requires knowledge about world trade, international economic structures, and the various international institutions that play a role in the creation of the global economy. Many of those—including the International Monetary Fund (IMF), the World Trade Organization (WTO), the Group of Seven (G7, consisting of the leaders of the largest seven economies of the world), and regional bodies such as the European Union (EU), the North American Free Trade Agreement (NAFTA), and the Association of South East Asian Nations (ASEAN)—have been described in earlier chapters in greater detail. In this category, we include understanding the current global economic trends that will shape the structure of the world economy over the next decades.[15]

12. Philip R. Cateora, *International Marketing*, 7th ed. (Homewood, Ill.: Irwin, 1990), ch. 7, p. 209.
13. Robert B. Reich, *The Works of Nations* (New York: Knopf, 1991).
14. Henry Kissinger, *Diplomacy* (New York: Simon & Schuster, 1994).
15. Paul Kennedy, *The Rise and Fall of the Great Powers* (New York: Random House, 1987). See also Paul Kennedy, *Preparing for the Twenty-First Century* (New York: Random House, 1993).

The equivalent body of knowledge in the political realm consists of understanding how *global political forces* affect the global marketing environment. This knowledge goes beyond the political structures of any individual country but includes the role played by bodies such as the United Nations and an appreciation of the geopolitical realities of the day. The disappearance of communist regimes in eastern Europe could not be treated as a single-country event alone but would need to be understood in the context of world political forces.[16]

Country-specific history has also its equivalent in a new body of knowledge that we could describe as world history. The understanding required is not the knowledge of just one country but the historical trends and development over time, including a group of countries, a region, or even the entire world. Paul Kennedy's *Rise and Fall of the Great Powers* is but one example of such a new body of historical knowledge that aims at a global perspective in history.[17] In the same vein would be Denis de Rougemont's comprehensive work on the history and development of Europe, which incorporates the philosophical and historical development of an entire continent or region.[18] Equivalent knowledge exists on *world culture*, where the current media trends might be included; *world geography*, where a clear understanding of world trade patterns and trade routes could be included; and the history of *world trade*.[19]

The Importance of Acquiring Global Key Market Knowledge

To some extent, the knowledge we are describing in this section may be viewed as strictly factual, the kind contained in a library. However, executives do not always consult their library when making decisions about the importance of key markets. Rather, any decisions can be made based upon erroneous, unverified knowledge and thus can result in less than optimal global marketing strategies. Significantly "underestimating" a country's population without checking might lead to the elimination of a market that otherwise should be part of a global marketing strategy. Many recent studies have shown that knowledge about key markets or world affairs varies considerably between countries and that U.S. managers particularly may be approaching global marketing battles with less factual knowledge than managers from other countries.[20] A realistic strategy of acquiring knowledge of key markets and the global marketplace thus can be an important ingredient in the success of individual executives and companies.

16. Denis de Rougemont, *The 28 Centuries of Europe* (Paris: Payot, 1996).
17. Kennedy, *The Rise and Fall of the Great Powers*. See also Kennedy, *Preparing for the Twenty-First Century*.
18. "What's Going On?" *Wall Street Journal*, March 30, 1994, p. A16.
19. Ohmae, *Borderless World*, p. 114.
20. "The World Automotive Suppliers," *Financial Times*, June 28, 1993, Survey, sec. IV.

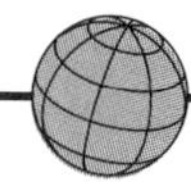

Analytical Global Marketing Skills

Acquiring a global marketing perspective is much more than mastering global marketing facts. Marketing managers who want to plot strategy with a global mindset will be challenged to process the vast amount of data they acquire in different ways. In this section, we examine the thinking and analytic routines the minds of executives have to go through as they chart global marketing strategies from a large set of data.

For space reasons, we do not give a complete summary of the analytic competence required by global marketers. Basic marketing analysis, used for both single-country and multicountry situations, are not covered here. We concentrate on some of the unique marketing analytic skills, concepts, and tools that are relevant primarily in global marketing. These topics are grouped around the concept of the *global logic*, with special emphasis on how it applies to global marketing.[21]

The Global Logic Concept

Writers have used the term *global logic* in the past to connote a given relationship in global markets.[22] Here we use *global logic* as a *condition in the marketplace that requires a company to adopt a global strategy*. When the global logic is very strong, there is almost a mandate to pursue its marketing operations on a global scale, leading to a global imperative. Furthermore, if the global logic were disregarded, the firm presumably would suffer negative competitive consequences. Wherever present, the company facing a global logic in its business must accommodate that logic or suffer competitively.

Whereas the global logic applies to the entire business strategy of a firm, the more specific *global marketing logic* describes the forces that demand the adoption of a global marketing strategy. The global marketer must understand the source of the global marketing logic, as the strategic response might differ. The sources of a global marketing logic might rest with the customer base, thus creating a global *customer* logic or a *global information* logic. They may also come from the purchasing approaches, resulting in a global *purchasing* logic. The industry environment may generate its own global logic sources. The strategies pursued by competitors are at the source of the global *competitor* logic. The industry and the relevant key success factors can combine to create a global *industry* logic. The presence of a strong critical mass requirement can lead to the global *size* logic. And finally, we can identify a global *regulatory* logic relating to the regulatory environment. We will now explore each of these sources of global marketing logic in more detail.

21. Jean-Pierre Jeannet, *Siemens AT: Brazil Strategy* (Lausanne: IMD Institute, 1993).
22. "Capturing the Global Consumer," *Fortune*, December 13, 1993, p. 166.

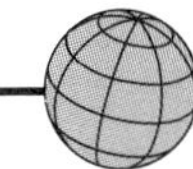

Customer-Based Global Logics

Customer-based global logics were at the beginning of marketing globalization. Many firms in the early 1980s began to review their globalizing customers and determine the need for globalization from their customer base. As a result, it does make sense to begin our review of globalization drivers from the customer angle. Different from the approaches taken initially, we have divided the customer-based global logic into several different specific logics that may not all apply equally for each industry. In fact, it is important to recognize that the pressure for globalization not only stems from what customers want to buy, but equally how they buy it, and where they get their information from.

Global Customer Logic

A company faces a global customer logic when its customers demand the same product in most countries and, in particular, when the same customer purchases a given product or service in many different locations, or countries. However, in few cases is the nature of demand so homogeneous that there are virtually no differences among countries. More likely, levels of similarities and dissimilarities exist. How does the marketer answer the question, "Do we have a global customer?" (See Figure 7.2.)

Analyzing the nature of the demand across countries is a starting point. Traditionally, companies have segmented their business or markets along product/market

FIGURE 7.2

Global Customer Logic

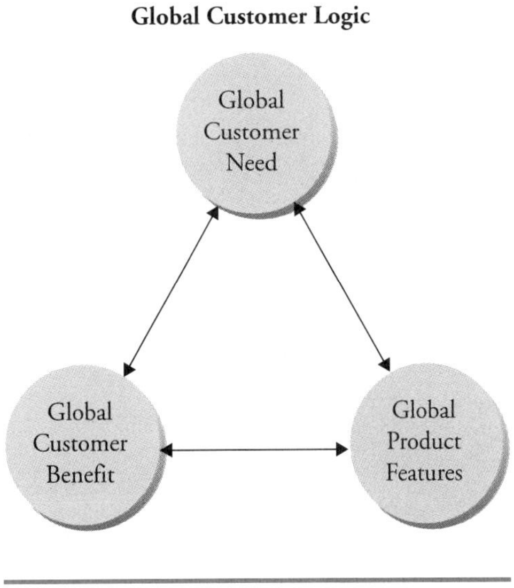

and country/geographic territories. This traditional matrix, depicted in Figure 7.3, captures the view that, as a company moves from one country to the next, significant changes occur in its marketing environment. The traditional view, emphasizing the country or geographic differences, is characterized through the presence of thick vertical lines, each one of these lines representing significant country differences. A company viewing its business this way would constantly emphasize the difference in its global marketing strategies. However, due to the differences,

FIGURE 7.3

Global Market Segmentation Matrix

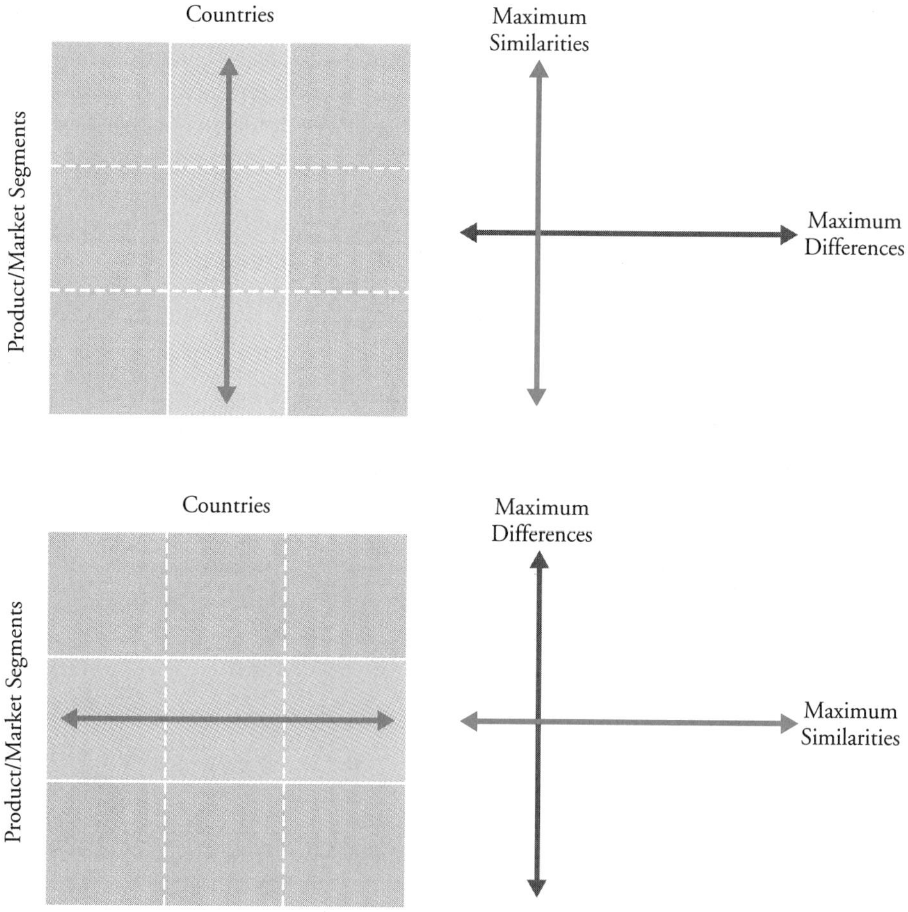

Countries

Product/Market Segments

Maximum Similarities

Maximum Differences

Countries

Product/Market Segments

Maximum Differences

Maximum Similarities

once a company is in a given country, experience can be leveraged through to other product lines. This we call leveraging on the vertical axis.

The opposite view may be taken by a company that finds that while country differences exist, still larger and more significant differences exist across segments, product lines, or industry sectors. In that situation, the horizontal lines between the segments are thick and solid, with the vertical lines separating countries fine and broken. In such a situation, the emphasis on the analysis is on the horizontal axis, where leverage occurs across a segment, product line, or sector. Similarities across countries are significant and can be exploited. We describe this as the horizontal view.

The marketer with a global mindset will discern the differences between geographic differences and segment-specific similarities. For products more rooted in customs, such as food, differences along geographic lines may be greater than those across segment lines. As one moves more toward new technological products and into industrial products and services, the geographic differences are often smaller than the segment or industry differences. The particular matrix faced by a company, with its specific grid of "lines" on either the geographic or segment level, depends on the type of industry. We therefore cannot speak of a generalizable matrix; instead, the global marketer must be able to determine the relevant type of matrix that confronts his or her company.

Although such an analysis might show to what extent a market may differ across many countries, a company has other ways to test for global customer logic.

More likely, a partial global customer logic may exist. Few products, particularly consumer products, are demanded by consumers in exactly the same form because the comparison across countries is lacking. The ultimate form of global product, which entails essential similarity in features and form, is rarely achieved. This is a function of the differences in requirements among countries.

If a given underlying need for a product or service exists across many countries, this is a *global need*. A product or service subject to global need would show its presence worldwide, with consumers in most countries indicating such a need. Many generic needs such as the need for communications, food, and so on are global needs. Marketing products that fit a global need could be undertaken with multidomestic approaches, offering each country its own version of that product bundle. Whether or not a product or service would be subject to a still more powerful global logic would depend on other things.

The second phase of customer globalization occurs at the benefit level. Companies whose customers derive the same benefit from a product or service will face a much more far-reaching form of global logic. Benefits touch on the content of marketing communications. When a company needs to accommodate a *global benefit*, it will sooner or later move toward some form of global communication.

When customers desire similar features in products, a company is said to face a *global product logic*. Similarity in features allows companies to standardize products and to market more homogeneous products across world markets.

Not all companies face identical customer logic. A company may face a global product logic, requiring homogeneous products, but encounter significant differences in benefits sought among customers. For other firms, the opposite may be true; a customer base seeks similar benefits around the world but requires different product features. Companies have to be ready to accommodate different levels and intensity of global logic, with corresponding differences in their strategic response.

Global Information Logic

Recently, we have come across another type of logic that is different from the first but also relates to the customer base, namely, the *information acquisition strategy* of a company's customers.[23] By information acquisition we mean the way customers scan the environment, the type of media they read or are exposed to, and to what extent they go to obtain information about products and services a long distance from home.

Traditional coverage of information acquisition is well documented in standard marketing textbooks.[24] Typically, consumers or business customers would scan the local media before making a particular purchasing decision. There was very little, if any, global information logic in the customer base that influenced international firms.

More recent developments, however, have made such influences more pervasive and thus affect the presence of a global information logic. Many business-to-business customers in technology-driven sectors tend to read specific magazines or publications from mostly the United States, thus making that information available to buyers in other countries. A Japanese buyer, reviewing a U.S.-based industry publication, thus acts to acquire information on a global scale, not just locally. This is particularly true for such sectors as information technology, communications, computers, electronic commerce, and medical instruments, where the U.S. market is viewed as the lead market and developments in the United States are quickly spotted elsewhere.

As a next step, buyers might go to specific trade shows with a global attendance. Such shows exist in both the United States and Europe, and for some industries they are the most important events. Telecom is a major trade show taking place every four years in Geneva, Switzerland. Visitors come from all over the world, thus creating a global information acquisition opportunity. Other important trade shows can be identified for many specific industries.

23. Stephen Allen, Case Series: "Note on the Construction Machinery Industry" (ECCH no. 393-068-5, 1993); "Caterpillar and Komatsu in 1988" (ECCH no. 393-069-1, 1993); "Caterpillar and Komatsu in 1993" (ECCH no. 393-070-1).

24. "PepsiCo Critics Fear Glass Is Half Empty," *Wall Street Journal*, September 30, 1996, p. B4.

The ever more frequent travel by business executives exposes many buyers to information outside their home country. To the extent they follow up and actively pursue such information, a global information logic exists.

In consumer industries, this development has been even more pronounced. Information sources have geographically spread through cable TV channels and satellite TV, making it possible for consumers to sit in their living room in Germany and watch a program transmitted from the United Kingdom. To reach such consumers, companies in Germany may have to advertise via a foreign channel, although the customer is in many ways viewed as a domestic customer. Sports events, such as the Olympics or world championships, create other strong global information logics. The commitment of advertisers to the Olympics in Nagano, Japan, was not primarily driven by the potential exposure to event visitors, or even the Japanese market. Instead, these companies were pursuing customers looking in via television from many countries. The actual event site is immaterial. The companies are primarily interested in the audience generated by the event.

Possibly the most important change in our information acquisition is the development of the Internet and the World Wide Web (WWW). This new electronic network, which is taking the world by storm, is rapidly becoming a new mode for looking for product or service information. Consumers anywhere can enter the WWW and locate product information in a different country, thus creating strong global information logic.

Any company seeking to understand thoroughly the forces that shape the global marketplace must recognize the changing way by which customers acquire information. Neglecting global information logic in a business would put the company's entire communications strategy at risk, and any global strategy designed will need to be based upon a thorough understanding of this logic.

Global Purchasing Logic

Across the world, customers show different types of purchasing behavior and processes. A company is subject to a global purchasing logic to the extent that its customers search the world for best products as opposed to purchasing within a given local market only. In many industries, the time has passed when a customer buys within the confines of one country only. Although this is less the case in consumer goods markets, industrial buyers are becoming accustomed to look for the best bargain on an international, regional, even worldwide basis.

Automobile companies' purchasing behavior for parts used in assembling cars provides an example.[25] Total parts costs have traditionally accounted for 50 percent of total product costs for car makers. Typically, parts purchases are sent out for bid each year, splitting supply contracts among several companies to "bid

25. Christopher Lorenz, "The Birth of a Transnational," *McKinsey Quarterly*, Autumn 1989, p. 72.

down" prices. In recent years, these companies have begun to pay more attention to parts cost as a way to increase efficiency. In some of the high-technology sectors of parts (for example, automotive electronics, which includes automatic breaking systems or engine management systems), research costs have amounted to about 10 percent of parts costs for parts suppliers. With each part supplier paying for its own research to fit components into specific car models, car companies have in fact paid for the same set of research costs several times. This has led some companies—GM was first among them—to concentrate parts purchases on just fewer suppliers, at times even a single supplier, per car model and to give them a contract over the entire model life cycle.

Parallel to this development, car companies have begun to insist on best prices and now engage in worldwide sourcing. Rather than purchasing from a number of nearby plants, a car company will source a greater distance away for lower costs. In some cases, parts are flown in by cargo aircraft from long distances away on a regularly determined schedule, "just in time." This has changed the way companies purchase parts and locate plants, making the entire world the shopping plaza for firms that no longer source in the same country or nearby. Thus, the automotive parts and components industry has become subject to a strong global purchasing logic wherein buyers, car companies in this case, search the world for the best bargain. Many car components suppliers have had to adjust to this demand, often turning local firms into global suppliers if they wanted to survive.[26] The presence of global sourcing or global purchasing practices in an industry is therefore one of the strongest indications of the presence of a significant global purchasing logic.

The presence of a gray market is another indicator. Gray markets exist where prices for a given product or service between two countries are widely different. Customers aware of that price difference begin to purchase in the low-price area and move the products into the high-price area. These gray-market activities are not illegal, and in Chapter 10 we explore this phenomenon in greater detail. However, we need to understand that industries in which such activities persist are subject to a global purchasing logic. Many international firms experience this phenomenon constantly. One U.S. pharmaceutical company reported that a significant portion of its products sold through Dutch drugstores were in fact purchased in France through unofficial channels. The price differences between France and the Netherlands were significant and were caused largely by different pricing mechanisms applied by the two governments. Behavior such as that of the buyers in the Netherlands demonstrates a transparent market, with buyers well informed as to where better prices exist. Again, when companies face such purchasing behavior, they need to accommodate the global purchasing logic through specific global marketing strategies.

26. "On the Verge of a World War in White Goods," *Business Week*, November 2, 1987, p. 41.

This test of global purchasing logic is therefore often present in industry or business-to-business markets. It happens far less in consumer marketing, because individual consumers usually buy a given product or service in one location only. Citicorp, the leading U.S.-based international bank, has encountered similar requirements among its wealthy customers looking for private banking services. The company began to offer a Citigold service to upwardly mobile Asian private customers with access to banking services wherever Citicorp has a branch—worldwide.[27] For some leisure or travel-related products, such as films, hotels, or even telephone services, a global purchasing logic exists because travelers demand these products to be present wherever they are.

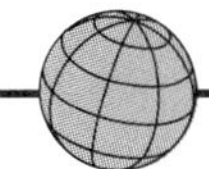

Industry-Based Global Logics

When the debate on the merits of globalization began in the early 1980s, the predominant assumption among proponents of globalization was the belief that consumers, or customers, were becoming more similar, thus driving the trend toward globalization. This section was largely devoted to these trends and explained in detail sources of the various pressures that might compel firms to adopt some form of a global marketing strategy. However, there are still many firms for which pressure from the customer base itself is not sufficiently strong to warrant all-out global marketing strategies. Instead, as the experience of countless other firms has shown, different forces, often related to an industry's competitive behavior, or inherent industry economics, may outshine customer-based forces as a source for globalization. These industry-based global logics in the form of global competitive logic, global industry logic, global size slogic, and global regulatory logic will be our focus for this next section.

Global Competitor Logic

When the need to develop a global marketing strategy stems from the behavior of a company's major competitors, we are speaking of a *global competitor logic*. Global pressures rooted in competitive actions can be observed from specific competitive patterns. First and foremost, a firm might face global competitor logic when the company encounters the same competitors consistently wherever it markets. In some industries, particularly those of industrial equipment, a small set of internationally active companies pursue major orders, such as for aircraft, power plants, turbines, and similar large installations. Whenever a large public tender is opened up, the same sales teams pursue the contract, independent of

27. Stephen Allen, Case Series: "Note on the European Major Home Appliance Industry—1990" (ECCH no. 393-091-5); "Whirlpool Corporation" (ECCH no. 393-095-1, 1993); "Electrolux" (ECCH no. 393-094-1, 1993); "General Electric: Major Appliances" (ECCH no. 393-093-1, 1993).

the country in question. This is a clear sign of global competitor logic. The presence of other globally active players who can reach into most markets requires all players to adopt a global marketing strategy to remain competitive themselves.

In extreme situations, leading companies engage in what we call a ***global chess game***. Picturing the world market as a chessboard, the global chess game implies a consistent, direct, and competitor-oriented move that is highly cognizant of the various market positions of each player. The competitive situations of Kodak versus Fuji Film have continued over many years and have taken place both in the U.S. market and in Japan, Kodak wanting to protect its business in the United States and Fuji aiming to maintain its lead in Japan.[28] The battle of Caterpillar versus Komatsu is another typical example of such competitive games, in which two players face off worldwide and pursue competitive advantages in many territories.[29] Over the years, Caterpillar had been able to navigate the turbulances in the international environment to its advantage while keeping its rival in check.[30] One of the most intense global competitive battles being waged presently pits Coca-Cola Co. against PepsiCo, armed with their leading brands of Coke and Pepsi, respectively. Pepsi found itself outmaneuvered when its bottler in Venezuela was acquired overnight by Coke, resulting in a complete loss of local distribution for Pepsi.[31] As in a chess game, the competitors' moves are very open and visible, and each company continually takes into account the next move of the opponent.

The presence of significant global competitor logic is derived from the number of relevant competitive theaters. Companies must understand when they are competing in a single, global competitive theater, or arena, in which the eventual outcome or ranking denotes their competitive position on a worldwide basis. In one global competitive arena, it will make sense to consider market share on a global, not national, basis. Indicating the presence of a single competitive arena is the fact that the outcome in the world market race is more important than the ranking in any single national market. For a company such as Boeing, the global market share for wide-bodied passenger jets is more important than the market share in any given country.

A company might find, rather than one global theater, many individual-country theaters, thus calling for country-by-country competition. In such a case, looking at market share and competitive position on a country-by-country basis would be more relevant. Intermediate strategies are called for by regional competitive

28. Kenichi Ohmae, *The Mind of the Strategist* (New York: McGraw-Hill, 1992), ch. 3.
29. "White Goods Empire: 400 Villages Crown Electrolux Market King," *Business International*, August 11, 1986, p. 250.
30. "Job of Wiring China Sets Off Wild Scramble by Telecom Giants," *Wall Street Journal*, April 5, 1994, p. 1.
31. "Successful But Cautious," *Financial Times*, July 23, 1991, p. 1, Sec. III, Survey on Pharmaceuticals.

theaters, where the relevant unit of analysis then becomes the region, such as Europe, North America, or Asia. Global competitive logic is strongest where the company faces one single relevant global theater and weakest when the relevant competitive theater is one country only. (See Figure 7.4.)

Recent developments in some industries have shown, however, that care must be exercised in the analysis of global competitive theaters. An analysis in the white goods industry in 1980 might not have found much presence of any global competitor logic, as main players were confined to regions (e.g., U.S. firms to the United States and European firms to parts of Europe). The aggressive competitive behavior of one single player, in this case Electrolux of Sweden, led to the acquisition of Zanussi, a major Italian producer, and White Westinghouse, a major U.S.

FIGURE 7.4

Global Competitive Theaters

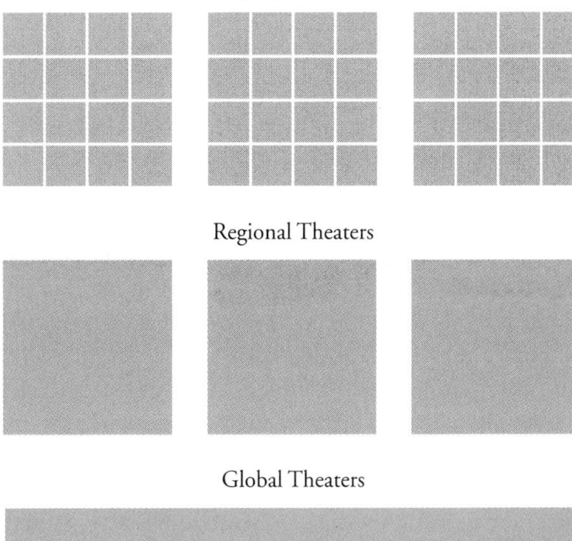

company, in the 1980s transforming an entire industry. Major U.S. firms reacted. Maytag purchased Hoover of the UK, Whirlpool acquired the appliance business of Philips of the Netherlands, and GE entered into a close agreement with GEC of the United Kingdom.[32] These moves were triggered by a perceived threat to their position by Electrolux. As a result, an entire industry with little global competitor logic was transformed into an industry with an overwhelming global competitive logic.[33] For Maytag and GE Appliances, the globalization strategies did not create permanent positive results and Maytag later disinvested itself of its European acquisitions. On the other hand, Bosch Siemens, originally only active in Europe, has now announced several acquisitions in the U.S. market and made it clear that any major player needed to be among the top firms both in Europe and the United States.[34] Clearly, firms without any accommodation of that global competitive logic risk competitive disadvantage over the longer term. In many other industries as well, a sudden shock move by one major player has brought about a complete competitive reorganization and a sudden emergence of a global competitive logic.

Global Industry Logic

Conceptually, every industry requires some basic dos and don'ts of its participants. A company that violated these competitive rules would invariably suffer competitive disadvantage and, in the long run, go out of business. These basic rules of competition, required from any player that wants to be a member of this industry, have traditionally been called *key success factors* (KSFs).[35] When an industry is characterized by similar KSFs across the world, a global industry logic exists that would make transferring this experience from one country to another important.

Each company, successful in its home market, has learned how to deliver on the KSFs in its industry. An important indicator of global industry logic is the transferability of these KSFs across the world. If the lessons of competition and the basic competitive requirements for a company to sustain itself in an industry are essentially the same, the first and most important condition for a global industry logic exists. When a company competes in a global industry, leveraging any experience across many countries becomes of great importance. Firms that do this effectively gain a competitive advantage.

The presence of a significant global industry logic will often draw competitors into leveraging their experience into other countries, therefore also creating a secondary effect in the global competitor logic. The experience in the white-

32. "A Drug Giant's Allergic Reaction," *Business Week*, February 3, 1997, pp. 122–125.
33. "Novartis Throws Up Clash of Strategies," *Financial Times*, December 18, 1996, p. 25.
34. "Dogfight Over London—and Paris, Rome, Madrid . . . " *Business Week*, August 12, 1996, p. 48.
35. "The Last Frontier," *Business Week*, September 18, 1995, pp. 58–65.

goods industry serves as an example. As mentioned above, Electrolux was the first player to pursue a global strategy, prompting many competitors into following suit for fear of competitive disadvantage. The cause of Electrolux's original intent to change its strategy from essentially a country-by-country or even regional one centering on Scandinavia to pursuing a broader global strategy rested with some new assumptions. The Electrolux managers were not tempted by a sudden emergence of customers who all wanted the same appliances. Instead, they realized that while appliances were different on the outside from country to country, the important components hidden from view were essentially the same. As costs for appliances became an important element, the costs for key components could only be driven down if the company gained economies of scale on compressors, pumps, and other elements present in millions of appliances.[36]

Electrolux believed that a competitive cost position for large component volume was dependent on gaining market share by acquiring other appliance makers in foreign countries. Electrolux was able to combine its component manufacturing with that of the acquired firms, reducing costs and investing in new models otherwise not affordable. This fundamental economic logic in the appliance business was not just restricted to Electrolux's local market but applied to the world market as a whole. It was on this global industry logic that the company acted, causing a competitive effect that changed the entire industry worldwide. Leveraging this type of component system may play a role in one industry, but in other industries, companies may be able to leverage some other parts of the value chain. Whether a strong global industry logic exists in a given industry will depend on the presence of such leverage points.

Global Size Logic

A very particular logic is the one driven by *critical mass*. For many firms, a *minimal size* of a key activity needs to be sustained before they can safely compete in a given industry. The presence of some form of critical mass in the economics of an industry therefore easily relates to a global logic if that necessary critical mass cannot be achieved anymore in a single market. When companies need to pursue global markets to get over the critical mass hurdle, a global size logic exists.

Such critical mass issues exist in many industries. In the commercial airplane building business, the development of a new passenger jet requires huge sums of money. Airbus, together with Boeing the leading builder of commercial airliners, estimates its new A3XX design, intended to transport anywhere from 555 to 750 passengers, to require an investment of anywhere from $11 to $15 billion.[37] No single domestic market is large enough to provide sufficient volume to justify

36. "Europe's Sell-Off to End All Sell-Offs," *Business Week*, October 21, 1996, p. 54.
37. "Giant Bows to Colossal Pressure," *Financial Times*, September 22, 1995, p. 13.

such an investment, thus creating a size logic that drives for maximum market coverage to recoup investment costs. In the pharmaceuticals industry, the development of a new drug, ranging from compound development through to toxicology and testing, tends to cost about $230 million.[38] In both instances, the amount of money a company may pay for research and development is limited. In few industries does this limit exceed 10 percent of sales/revenue, and in the pharmaceuticals industry it was estimated to have reached 20 percent of sales.[39] Whatever the acceptable percentage in a given industry, the relationship determines the volume the company needs to sell to pay off the entire development of a system or new product. In many industries, the minimal sales level to be achieved over the product life cycle exceeds the volume a company can expect to obtain in even as large a market as the United States. The desire to achieve relevant size on a global basis has fueled a number of recent mergers in the pharmaceutical industry. The merger between Zeneca of the United Kingdom and Astra of Sweden was driven by the need to obtain critical mass.[40] At the time of its announcement, the world's largest merger in terms of stock value was between two Swiss pharmaceutical companies, Sandoz and Ciba-Geigy. Both firms, now trading under the new company name of Novartis, were believed to be ranked too low in the pharmaceutical industry tables, but combining their forces could vault them into the number two spot behind Glaxo of the United Kingdom.[41]

The pursuit of new markets to pay off initial large investments for development is at the heart of the global size logic. What many of these companies have found is that the development or adjustment of an initial product to new markets is minor once the first step has been taken. Although we have cited mostly high-technology companies or industries so far, the same development can be seen in the motion picture industry, where true profitability often can only be achieved from foreign sales. Critical mass may be encountered in many ways. It may consist of a reservations or computer system in one industry or the logistics system for another. Each industry must be analyzed separately and may show different patterns.

Global Regulatory Logic

More recently, it has become apparent that governments, through their regulatory influence, can significantly affect the rationale for pursuing global strategies.

38. "World Phone Inc.?" *Business Week*, November 18, 1996, pp. 54–55.
39. Ibid.
40. Kenichi Ohmae, *Triad Power: The Coming Shape of Global Competition* (New York: Free Press, 1985), pp. 122–124.
41. "Can the Queen of Cosmetics Keep Her Crown?" *Business Week*, January 17, 1994, p. 90.

Although in the past, government regulations have always had an impact on business, they tended to be country-specific in scope and, in general, did not push a company to pursue global marketing strategies. In several industries, recent trends toward deregulation, which implies a lowering of the regulatory threshold, have opened up markets to foreign competitors and thus provided an impetus to globalization. Furthermore, some countries are treading the path of trade liberalization, allowing for more international entries into previously prohibited markets; this too has stimulated the growth of global logic.

Such deregulation has had major repercussions in the international airlines industry. New types of accords, so-called open-sky agreements, have been signed between the United States and other governments, giving more access to international airlines in both the U.S. and the U.K. markets. Such trends are causing some airlines to seek links with former competitors. The Star Alliance, an alliance between Lufthansa of Germany, United Airlines of the United States, Air Canada, Thai International, and Scandinavian Airlines resulted in additional annual revenue of $225 million alone for Lufthansa, and allowed the German carrier to boost is trans-Atlantic traffic by more than 20 percent, twice the industry growth rate.[42]

One of the industries most affected by recent regulatory activity is the telecommunications industry. With deregulation sweeping the world and resulting in most governments selling off their stakes in state monopolies, telecommunications companies suddenly have access to many more markets than before. The deregulatory fever, often taking the form of privatizations of government-owned phone companies, is rapidly expanding the telecommunications market in many countries. Increasingly, it is being followed by a market opening that allows for multiple carriers in a given country.[43]

Nippon Telegraph and Telephone (NTT) of Japan is expanding its international operations, taking on companies such as AT&T of the United States, by taking stakes in companies that provide services related to the Internet and telecommunications.[44] The U.K.-based firm Cable & Wireless expanded its network into Japan by acquiring a small independent local operator, thus creating new competition for NTT.[45] Deutsche Telecom, already having lost considerable market share to newly licensed local competitors such as Mannesmann, tried unsuccessfully to acquire Tecom Italia to expand its business.[46] Deutsche

42. "Job of Wiring China Sets Off Wild Scramble by the Telecom Giants," *Wall Street Journal*, April 5, 1994, p. 1.
43. Jean-Pierre Jeannet, "Lead Markets: A Concept for Designing Global Business Strategies," working paper, IMEDE International Management Institute, May 1986.
44. "The Managed Care Remedy," *Financial Times*, September 9, 1996, p. 17.
45. "International Communications," Financial Times Survey, pts. 1 and 2, *Financial Times*, September 19, 1996.
46. "Welcome to the Revolution," *Fortune*, December 13, 1993, p. 76.

Telecom also owns part of a venture, Global One, that includes Sprint of the United States and France Telecom to provide telecommunications services to international companies. That market segment was estimated at some $23 billion worldwide and is growing rapidly.[47] This major upheaval in the telecommunications industry, induced by regulatory changes, has also affected the equipment industry. Increasingly, switches carrying voice traffic are losing their luster, and companies who used to depend on that business, such as Lucent of the United States (formerly part of AT&T), Siemens of Germany, and Alcatel of Europe, now must concentrate on equipment that focuses on carrying data or mobile phone traffic.[48]

As these examples demonstrate, governments or other regulatory bodies can become major drivers forcing companies to take a global view of their markets. A company may thus have to review its situations carefully and monitor the regulatory pressure for indications of impending changes in the world market.

Integrating Global Logics into a Composite View

In this section we have focused on major global logics and how they might influence companies in designing global marketing strategies. We have described seven prototype, or generic, global logic forces, ones that we have found extremely useful for explaining the globalization pressures in a large number of industries. Conceivably, there could be others that might be more or less appropriate for a given industry.

Although we have discussed these global logics one at a time, a company will of course be exposed simultaneously to a number of them, and some will be more important than others. By plotting them on a single graph (see Figure 7.5), an analyst can get an impression of the nature of the pressures. Some firms might find the customer or purchasing logics stronger; other firms might find industry-based logics exerting greater pressure. Most likely, the graphs (spiderwebs) created would be different from industry to industry. Judging from the graphs, a firm facing a large footprint, exhibited by a larger area covered by the connected points, is said to face greater global logic than one facing a smaller footprint.

Any firm would have to have a clear understanding of the particular set of forces it faces. Global logic patterns are rarely symmetrical, and it is important to understand the dominating global logic in a given industry. In Chapter 8, we make a direct connection between the particular set of global logic forces faced by a firm and the suggested generic global marketing strategy best suited to that situation.

47. "Telecommunications in Business," Financial Times Survey, *Financial Times*, June 10, 1996.
48. "Ready to Cruise the Internet," *Business Week*, March 28, 1994, p. 180.

FIGURE 7.5

Global Logics

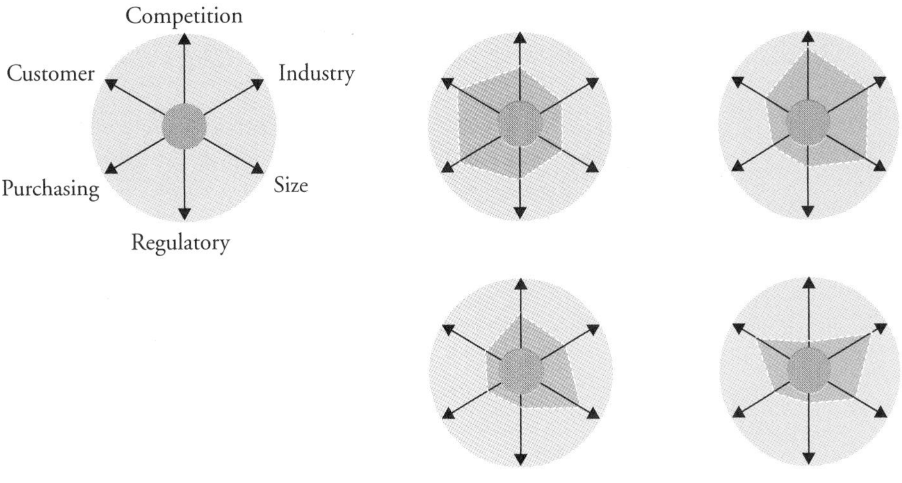

Global logic forces, furthermore, are not static. A company might well be able to describe the present constellation of global logics it faces. Equally important, however, are the trends and the expected forces that will enter the picture in the future. A company would thus be advised not only to analyze the present situation but also to understand the nature of the constellation as it will evolve in a particular industry. Effective global marketing strategies need to take into account the expected constellation as the dominant factor.

The fundamental importance of the concept of global logic is its general validity. Once global logic exists in a given industry, all firms in the world market become subject to its dictates. A company facing considerable global logic pressures simply cannot avoid taking relevant action because global logic must be accommodated. Eventually and inevitably, firms that disregard global logic face substantial competitive penalties over time.

Global Market and Opportunity Assessment

To bring a global perspective to the analysis of marketing opportunities requires a new approach to the analysis of data. Traditionally, international marketers did a large amount of their analysis on a country-by-country basis. By contrast, marketing with a global mindset requires that additional analytic market assessment skills be acquired. This section introduces the global chessboard and lead markets as two new skills and concepts. They are to be viewed as additional skills beyond those already described in Chapter 6.

The World Market as a Global Chessboard

In the earlier passage on global competitor logic, we spoke of competition as a form of global chess. Rather than describing the rules of this game, we will concentrate on drawing analogies between the world market and the chessboard (see Figure 7.6). The global chessboard is not a square board consisting of sixty-four equal squares. Rather, it consists of many squares, one for each of the approximately two hundred countries that presently exist. Also contrary to regular chess, in which each space is of equal size, the spaces on the global chessboard vary in size. In this game, square size represents market size, or typically gross national product (GNP): countries with large GNPs are presented by large squares, countries with small GNPs by correspondingly smaller ones. The United States, as the country with the largest GNP, representing about 20 percent of world GNP, would make up 20 percent of this global chessboard. Other countries would follow, each in proportion to its GNP.

The rules of the game in global chess require the capture of the most important strategic spaces on the board. However, contrary to regular chess, the global chessboard is a moving board, with the various squares subject to constant change driven by the particular dynamics of changing economic circumstances of

FIGURE 7.6

The Traditional Versus the Global Chessboard

The Global Chessboard Differs

Has One Square for Each Country (200 plus)

The Squares are not all equal in Size (Driven by GNP or Related Metric)

The Board Changes During Play (Political and Economic Developments)

FIGURE 7.6

The Traditional Versus the Global Chessboard (*Continued*)

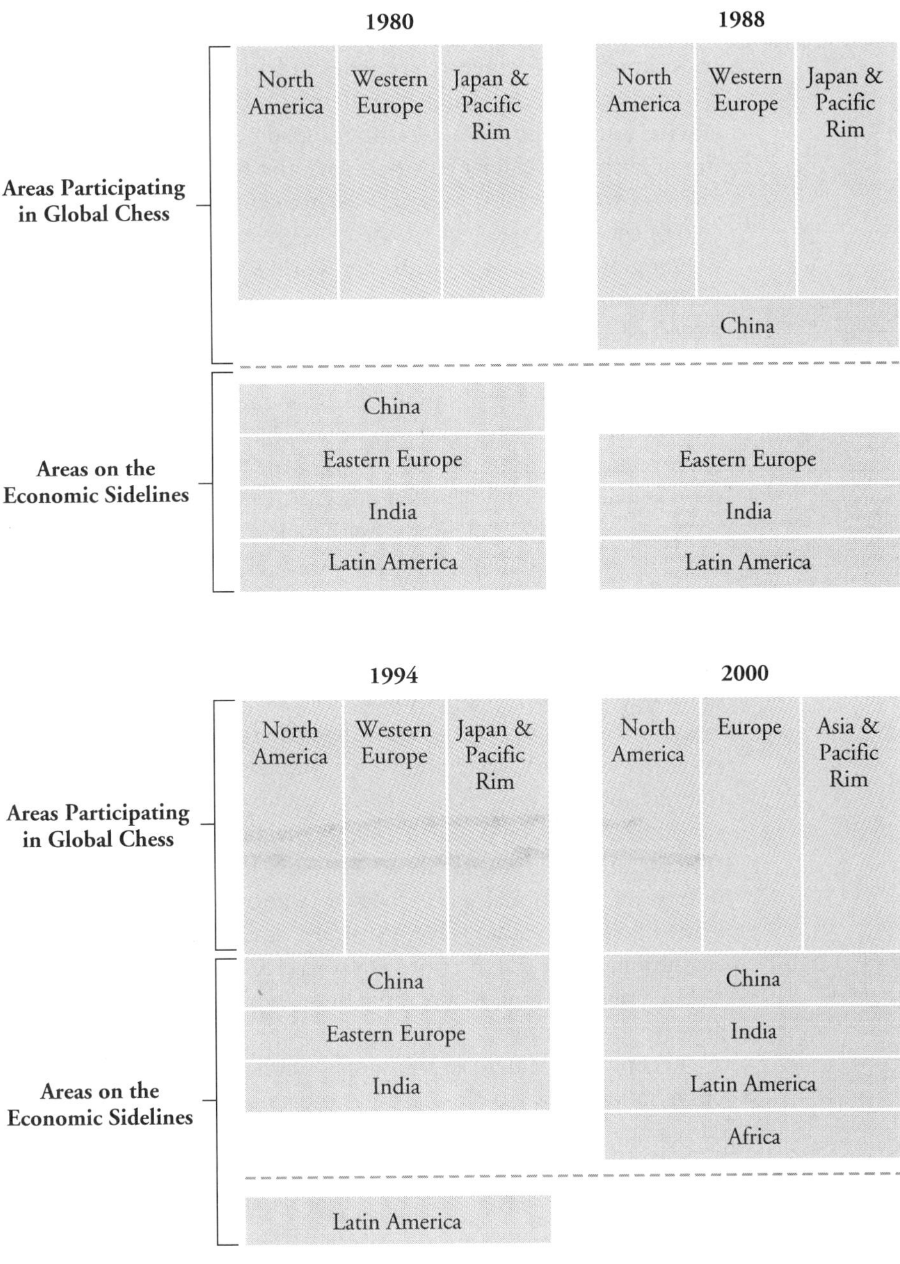

the countries involved. Despite the large number of global chess squares, the ones that really count are those squares companies can move products, services, people, capital, and profits freely across borders. Countries that are behind insurmountable trade barriers or that do not allow free transfer of imports or exports are excluded from the global chess board, as any market position in those countries cannot be leveraged to other countries.

Traditionally, the major members of the global chessboard were markets considered part of the triad, contributing some 75 percent of world GNP.[49] Consisting of Europe (western Europe then), the United States, and Japan, the triad market area was crucial for any global marketer. Having a strong position in at least two of the three areas and a credible presence in the third was viewed as essential for global success. L'Oréal, the world's largest cosmetics company, had a market share of 22 percent in Europe, compared with only 7.5 percent in the United States. Leadership in cosmetics was hotly contested with Procter & Gamble of the United States and Unilever, another European firm. With the U.S. representing the largest single market in the global cosmetics industry, eventual global leadership will be decided on the outcome of the U.S. market battle. The U.S. market has become, therefore, a "must win" market for L'Oréal, causing it to invest disproportionately more in the United States versus other countries.[50]

The triad concept, in the eyes of Kenichi Ohmae, was helpful to create a sense of priorities among the many existing countries. In some ways, it consisted of selecting a few key markets from the global chessboard. That global chessboard, however, has undergone substantial changes in the past few years. Not only has it gained many additional markets, pushing the total up toward two hundred, but the world marketplace has also seen different countries rise in importance and others decline. If we define the relevant part of the chessboard as those countries open to free trading, we have seen a boom in the emergence of new relevant markets.

The tremendous political changes leading to liberalization, privatization, and deregulation have led to many countries joining the global chessboard. In addition to the traditional industrialized countries consisting of western Europe, the United States, Canada, Japan, Australia, and New Zealand, other major countries are surging into prominence. These include the group of Asian countries (South Korea, Taiwan, Hong Kong, Singapore) typically dubbed the "Tigers" for their aggressive export drive.

Recent newcomers to the global chessboard include China (where relatively open trade is now possible), India, and a number of Latin American countries (notably Brazil, Mexico, Argentina, and Chile). As all of these countries begin to abandon their old restrictive trade practices, they become important pieces in the

49. Harley Hahn and Rick Stout, *The Internet Complete Reference* (Berkeley, Calif.: Osborne McGraw-Hill, 1994).

50. "The Internet and Your Business," *Fortune*, March 7, 1994, p. 88.

global chess game for market dominance. The same is the case for the former eastern European countries. Over the last five years, the major expansion in the global chessboard has forced a rethinking of the triad concept. The relevant free market is now distributed into three major trading regions: North America, consisting of the United States, Canada, and Mexico, bound together in NAFTA; Europe, consisting of the EU countries and the associate countries; and finally Asia, consisting of Japan, China, India, and the many Asian Pacific Rim countries that are growing rapidly.

The dynamics of the global chessboard are not limited to new countries joining the game through trade liberalization. Some of these countries, China and India notably, are experiencing remarkable growth, as we explained in earlier chapters. That growth is represented with an ever larger square on the global chessboard represented by China, thus enhancing its importance in the competitive calculations of global firms. A market such as China, if shut off from the rest of the world economy, not accessible for international firms via imports or exports, would be a far less important piece on the global chessboard.

Although we can imagine the world as a global chessboard with each country represented by its size of GNP, individual firms competing in their own specific industry will be required to see the chessboard as it is shaped by that industry's perspective: each country, or local market, is represented with respect to the market size, or relevant industry "metric," for that industry. The chessboard for Ford will be determined by the size of the automotive markets in the various countries. The chessboard of IBM or Apple will be represented by the size of the computer markets. Global marketers, therefore, face chessboards that differ by industry and on which each industry will have its own key markets as determined by size.

The telecommunications market provides an excellent example of the shifting importance of individual countries on the overall global chessboard. Having become the fastest-growing market for telecommunications installations, China's annual spending was expected to reach $18 billion. This contrasts with only $2 billion per year in 1990.[51] The reason for this enormous growth is the need to bring more phone lines into China, where the density of telephones was less than two phones per one hundred inhabitants in 1994, amounting to no more than 40 million lines. By the year 2000, the Chinese government intended to increase phone density to ten lines per one hundred inhabitants—still behind the United States, where the density was fifty lines per one hundred inhabitants. However, the investment necessary to reach the goal by the year 2000 amounted to building the equivalent of one regional U.S. operating company (referred to as a "Baby Bell") every single year. Telecommunications firms that must invest large sums of money to develop the next generation of digital systems will find it critical to

51. "Suppliers Surf the Internet Wave," Financial Times Review, Information Technology, *Financial Times*, December 4, 1996, p. I.

participate in the Chinese market for future competitiveness. Some experts have indicated that China might well become the largest single market for telecommunications networking and infrastructure equipment. Should this come to pass, the Chinese market would become the cornerstone of any global marketing strategy of telecommunications firms, raising it to the status of a "must win" market where future global leadership would be determined.

Global marketers aspiring to a global mindset will need to constantly evaluate the state of the global chessboard. This evaluation, gauging the importance of key markets, not only will have to be made on present data but needs to consider growth rates and the state of the chessboard many years into the future. Moreover, this survey must occur at both the macroeconomic level and the particular industry level relevant to the company.

Marketers will not only have to develop a new sense of understanding and assessing countries one at a time but must also be able to judge the importance of one piece of the global chessboard versus the rest of the pieces.

Understanding Lead Markets

Once the global chessboard relevant to a particular industry and a particular company has been determined, the marketer with a global mindset will need to understand the interrelationships of those markets. To do so, the first step is to identify the lead market, or markets, relevant to a particular part of the business. The *lead market* is the particular geographic market, or country, that is ahead in its development of the rest of the world and where initial new developments tend to set a trend for other markets to follow. The lead market thus serves the function of a bellwether.[52]

The identification of a lead market has strategic importance for companies. Those who can identify their own lead markets relevant to their industry will be able to leverage learning out of those markets for the rest of their international or global operations. The knowledge about lead markets gives the global marketer a window on future opportunities. It also helps identify those countries as strategic in importance.

One can distinguish several types of lead market categories. First, there are customer-driven lead markets based upon the location of the country with the most advanced customers. A company would have to look at its industry and try to evaluate where the most advanced customers tend to be. If those customers are concentrated in one particular country or region, we have the presence of a lead market with respect to customer demand. Charting the demand coming from that lead market might tell where the rest of the customers in other parts of the world are headed.

52. "Here Comes the Payoff from PCs," *Fortune*, March 23, 1992, p. 51.

One can distinguish among other types of lead markets as well. Operations-based lead markets are those that contain the most efficient participants in an industry, particularly with respect to producing the products or services in question. A third category consists of the product lead market, which contains the country where the most advanced products in that industry emerge. Again the emphasis is on industry participant, not on customer. And finally, one may distinguish the lead market based upon management systems and the companies that consistently apply the most advanced management systems in that industry. More recently, we have applied the term *benchmarking* for measuring a company's performance against others that are best in its category. The lead market, by definition, would contain the firms against whom others would benchmark their own operations. What is different in global terms is the requirement that these benchmark operations must in fact be leading in the world, or of a world-class stature.

When the U.S. government undertook a major effort to reform the U.S. health care system in 1993, the impact of some of those discussions was felt around the world. Already, many companies involved in health care, such as insurance companies, hospitals, pharmaceutical firms, and medical equipment manufacturers, had long been under pressure to become more cost-effective. In the United States, the health maintenance organization (HMO) was founded as a way to begin to replace fee-for-service care with managed care. By 1990, less than 10 percent of Americans were covered by managed care contracts. By 1996, this number had grown to 75 percent under managed-care of some form. This trend, coming as a result of the cost pressures of ever-increasing medical expenses, was also present in European and other overseas markets. Now that governments elsewhere are trying to rein in health expenditures, they are looking for answers to the United States and its new types of care options. In this way, the U.S. health industry is becoming the lead market for other countries, and firms who successfully adapt to its demands are likely to find that they can do the same elsewhere.[53]

As with many of the concepts described earlier in this chapter, lead market identification is not a one-time exercise. Marketers who aspire to a global perspective have to monitor the performance of their lead markets continuously. Furthermore, lead markets, most of which at one time were concentrated in the United States, have become dispersed, with many countries sharing in some of them over time. A company must therefore understand the migration pattern of lead markets and adjust its understanding of the global chessboard accordingly. The search for lead markets is an attempt to identify the driving wheel of a complicated machine in which each country, or market, is characterized by a single cog wheel in a complex structure (see Figure 7.7). Marketers who understand the process and can clearly identify the "driving" market have an advantage. Chapters

53. "Videoconferencing: Industry Expects Sales to Soar," *Financial Times*, June 10, 1996, p. ix.

FIGURE 7.7

Lead-Market Relationships

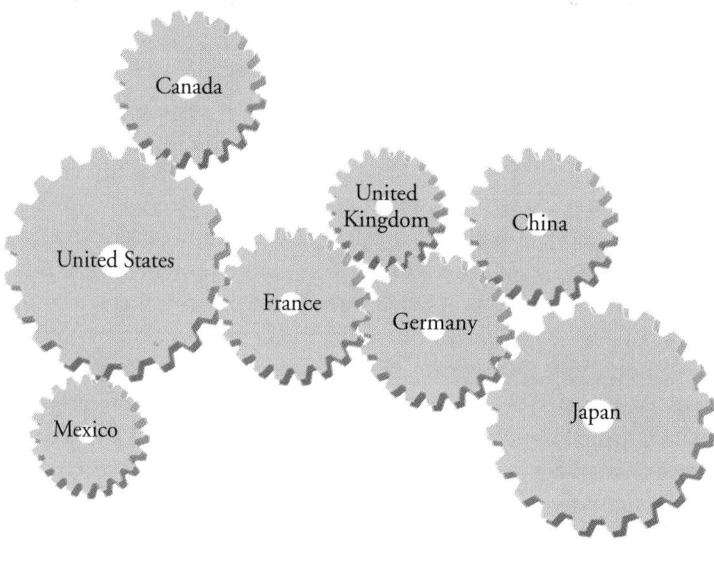

8 and 9 include special sections dealing with strategic actions by which global firms can take advantage of their presence in lead markets.

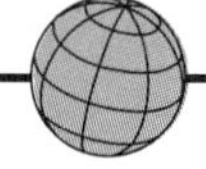

Individual Skills for a Global Mindset

Most of the previous section described analytic and conceptual requirements for a marketer with a global mindset. We believe that certain individual requirements are also indispensable. These skills have been identified over the years through the authors' own interactions with many international executives. Some of them come from the authors' experience with sending many students on overseas assignments. In themselves, these skills do not alone add up to a global mindset. However, without them, even the conceptual understanding of a global perspective on marketing could be diminished.

Global Language Communications Skills

A first category of skills can be grouped under global language communications skills. Here we want to emphasize the language aspects, treating them separately from technological aspects of communications. Presumably, the global manager must be a multilingual manager. Although this is typically the case with managers from many countries, English has reached the point of becoming the global business language. The use of English as the global business language has been further reinforced through the development of the Internet. In our new global world, what, then, is the value of learning and speaking a foreign language?

Typically, a major benefit of learning a foreign language comes from also learning about the foreign culture. However, in this global world with many major markets speaking many different languages, which one should a manager learn? This choice has baffled many students of global management. Will the language acquired also be the language that is desired sometime in the future? Companies hiring young executives for future overseas assignments often emphasize that having learned one language is an indication of the young executive's promise to learn another one for the next international appointment.

This pattern is illustrated by the career patterns of two former students, both of whom were hired by international firms. The first student, a U.S. national, joined a U.S. company in Latin America. The student won this assignment because of his proven Spanish language skills. After a few years, the student found himself transferred to Italy, for which he had no prior knowledge. His proven language skills in Spanish were used as an indication that he would quickly acquire another language. Our second student, also a U.S. national, had acquired some French during his undergraduate years. He was hired into the head office of a Swiss international firm in which the business language was English. The company hired him because his learning of French indicated to them that the student had promise of being able to function in different environments. After an initial training period of two years, this student found himself in the newly formed subsidiary in Moscow, where again a very different language applied. These two situations illustrate the advantage of learning one foreign language, while cautioning those who do so that their particular choice of language may have little bearing on their first real overseas assignment.

While learning a foreign language is still needed for longer stays in a country, most marketing executives who act in the global marketplace tend to spend little time in any one market. Moving about, making many brief trips, invariably causes them to use English as the key language in international business. Although executives in many parts of the world are increasingly familiar with English, this does not mean that their understanding is perfect. Those who work within the network of a U.S.-based international company can expect to find most written documents produced everywhere to be in English. Executives working for an international firm's operation in the United States, however, may find themselves limited if they cannot speak some of the language of the head-office country. This is especially true for French, Italian, and German firms; the firms located in smaller countries, such as the Netherlands, Sweden, and Switzerland, tend to use English as their corporate language. When meeting local customers abroad, particularly those who are not engaged in international business per se, knowing the local language can still be important. Of course, that capability would be present in a company's local subsidiary or with a distributor or agent who can speak English.

Native English speakers use many idiomatic expressions that are not clear to those for whom English is a second language, however perfectly they may speak it. Misunderstandings thus can arise. A proven strategy is to eliminate such local, idiomatic expressions from the English spoken to arrive at something we call "global English." This capability will become ever more important, as we shall show in later chapters, such as in dealing with new forms of global organizations and global teams. Even more important is the use of nonidiomatic English when using email or similar forms of communication. Although it is important to recognize that foreign-language skills will help managers gain cultural empathy with a different culture, it is at the same time necessary to realize that a marketing executive with a global mindset will still need to know the key markets for that industry. Knowledge described in the first part of our chapter will be required and can be acquired even without foreign-language skills for that particular market.

Global Telecommunications Skills

A second set of important communications skills is of a more technical nature. The communications revolution has brought about new forms of international telecommunications possibilities that substantially change the nature of how international marketing gets transacted. For marketers who aspire to a global perspective, such knowledge would be critical. We cannot describe these new forms of technology here in great detail, and it is not the purpose of this text to equip all readers with that knowledge. However, we can give some background and will point out the application of these techniques to the way global marketing is conducted.

Communications with customers and business partners overseas have changed considerably over the past decades. Exchanges that once took weeks in regular mail have now been condensed into reaction times that approach immediate response. The real challenge is to bridge the gap between what is technologically possible and what has actually been used. To the detriment of their global marketing positions, many firms do not yet use the full technological capabilities.

Much international communication traffic travels over telephone lines. In global marketing, making international phone connections is now an everyday occurrence. With direct-access dialing to most countries, the phone has become an easy way to overcome communication gaps. Between 1981 and 1991, international calls into and out of the United States grew from 500 million to 2.5 billion per year.[54] The telephone, however, can only bridge the distance gap, giving the

54. "Welcome to the Revolution," *Fortune*, December 13, 1993, p. 76.

ability to overcome distances. It still requires that both initiator and recipient of the call be there at the same time. When calls have to be made from New York to Japan (Tokyo is fourteen hours ahead of New York), it becomes difficult to make calls at a time when both parties are in their offices. Even with Europe, where the time difference is only six hours (from the East Coast of the United States), common office-time overlaps amount only to two to three hours each day.

With much of global marketing taking place in different time zones, companies have had to use other means of communicating. In the past, they used telex machines. Today, much of this communications is carried by fax machines, which are now in wide use in every type of international marketing operation. Similarly, use of international courier services such as Federal Express, UPS, or DHL can speed documents across continents overnight, whereas transmittal used to take weeks through regular mail.

More recently, data communication over both fixed and mobile networks is placing telephones into the hands of business executives in even remote areas. Combining telephones with mobile data transmission capabilities has extended fixed telephone networks to many parts of the world.[55] What we have come to expect in terms of on-the-desk transmission (for example, credit card purchases) is now available through mobile networks. The effect of this new technology is to extend the reach of many firms beyond their own natural borders, bridging distance and time gaps in such a way that round-the-clock processing of orders is becoming a possibility. E-commerce, or e-business, is the latest form, bringing two business partners closer together and bridging both the distance and the time gap in dramatic ways.

Electronic mail, once used only to communicate within the premises of a single firm, is now available, via regular phone lines and the Internet, for communicating with clients and companies worldwide. By many accounts, email has taken over from phones as the preferred way of communications in business, greatly affecting how global firms reach into other markets. For the U.S. market, it was estimated that some 3.4 trillion email messages were delivered in 1998, and more than 70 percent of those were business-related messages.[56]

As more and more companies avail themselves of an Internet gateway for their in-company electronic mail systems, executives have instant access to the Internet's thousands of computer networks. The popularity of the World Wide Web (WWW) has spawned a huge number of company web sites on the Internet. Although many of these sites only disseminate information, more and more firms have begun actually to transact business online. The Internet is better able to provide place and time independence than phone or fax and is more immediate in

55. "Telecommunications in Business," Financial Times Survey, *Financial Times*, June 10, 1996.
56. "Is E-Mail Marketing for You," *Direct*, April 1, 1999.

response. The Internet is also more cost-effective and offers smaller firms worldwide access without any established distribution system. Even smaller companies can take advantage of e-commerce capabilities with costs of as little as $100 per month for up to fifty items, or $1,000 per month for up to one thousand items.[57] In many business-to-business marketing areas, the access to the World Wide Web is used to build stronger supply partnerships and to integrate supply chains across international borders. These developments are likely to revolutionize the ease of doing business globally, and to make global marketing and purchasing much more common than in the past.[58]

The development of new "groupware" software, such as Lotus Notes, allows many users within a single company to share information simultaneously, with immediate updates as if everyone were connected to the same computer or workstation. Groupware—or software for teams not all located in the same place or frequently out of the office at one time or another—has allowed firms to create virtual teams whose members may in fact be located in different offices in different countries. This has affected the way these firms operate globally.

Another recent development in telecommunications is videoconferencing. Through connections over special telephone lines, companies have installed video systems that allow teams of managers to see each other as they talk although they are separated by thousands of miles. With participants sitting in front of cameras and with a separate projector for documents, such conferences are becoming the norm to avoid costly and time-consuming travel. Teleconferencing also allows firms to project scarce technical specialists into the offices of their clients to support products or services and thus gain a competitive advantage. Although very powerful (it does bridge the distance gap), the videoconference still requires executives at both ends to be present at the same time.[59]

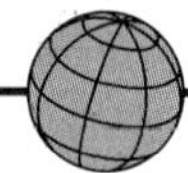

Conclusions

As we pointed out in Chapter 1, a growing need for global mindsets exists in today's global business environment. In this chapter, we explained in more detail what such a global mindset, or global perspective, consists of. It is nevertheless important to indicate here that the need for marketers with a global mindset is not just limited to companies operating in the major industrialized nations. The need for a global perspective extends to marketers from all parts of the world, from both developed and emerging countries.

57. "E-Commerce for Small Firms: Help or Hindrance," *National Post*, July 12, 1999, p. E4.
58. "e-Business: Global Links—Companies are turning to the internet for tighter integration with suppliers overseas," *Information Week*, March 23, 1998, p. 18.
59. "Videoconferencing: Industry Expects Sales to Soar," *Financial Times*, June 10, 1996, p. ix.

The need for a global perspective results from the pervasiveness of the global logic. Any company that is part of the global economy and operating in an industry with some form of global logic will require marketing managers with a global mindset. Since the global logic works on companies large and small and is independent of the company's location, the need for the type of skills, knowledge, and concepts explained in this chapter is considered universal.

In this chapter, we have described the global mindset in greater detail. Acquiring a global mindset is aided by gaining knowledge about key markets and an understanding of the wider framework of the global economy and politics. Understanding the concepts of global logics and having the ability to analyze for their presence in a company's industry are a second prerequisite. Marketers with a global perspective will also have to adopt new ways to understand and prioritize the world market, such as through the analogy of the global chess game. And finally, the global mindset is gained through the acquisition of special communications skills that help overcome time and place differences and allow companies to project their skills beyond their own borders.

What separates the global mindset from other approaches to international and global marketing is the ability to think about the entire global opportunity at once, and to view each individual market in relationship to the whole world economy. This perspective, with a sense for the strategic necessity, will allow global marketers to set the right priorities and to guide their firms through a mass of potential or theoretical possibilities, not all of which can realistically be pursued. This is a sharp departure from the long-standing tradition of analyzing individual markets one at a time. Although the single-market analysis competency will still be part of the necessary tool kit of the global marketer, that alone will no longer suffice as a guide through the multitude of possibilities.

As many more firms find themselves drawn into the global economy and forced to pursue global marketing strategies, the need for marketing managers with a capability to adopt the global perspective can be expected to rise dramatically over the next decade. A global mindset can be acquired; it is not an innate skill. Managers from all countries face the same challenges, or the same hurdles, in acquiring it. Those who do better at it are likely to gain a competitive advantage over their peers who lack it. And finally, firms with a larger cadre of marketing executives who have cultivated a global mindset can be expected to outperform those who lack this key human resource.

QUESTIONS FOR DISCUSSION

1. How does a global perspective differ from an international or multinational perspective?
2. Explain the concept of a global logic.
3. In the automobile manufacturing industry, where do you find a global logic? Which of the sources of the global logic predominates?
4. What is the managerial meaning of the concept of the global chessboard?

5. Select a country and do a factual analysis that satisfies the section on global key markets.
6. What differentiates single-market assessment from global market assessment?
7. Select an industry and perform a global chessboard analysis on it, determining relevant metrics and identifying lead markets.
8. Select an industry and perform a global logic analysis on it along the lines of Figure 7.5. What implications can you draw from your "spiderweb"?

FOR FURTHER READING

Bartlett, Christopher A., and Sumantra Ghoshal. "What Is a Global Manager?" *Harvard Business Review*, September–October 1992, pp. 124–132.

Dyer, Jeffrey H. Dong Sung Cho, and Wujin Chu. "Strategic Supplier Segmentation," *California Management Review*, January 1, 1988, vol. 40, p. 57.

Jeannet, Jean-Pierre. *Managing with a Global Mindset*. London: Financial Times/Prentice Hall, 2000.

Ohmae, Kenichi. *Triad Power: The Coming Shape of Global Competition*. New York: Free Press, 1985.

Porter, Michael E., ed. *Competition in Global Industries*. Boston: Harvard Business School Press, 1986.

Pucik, Vladimir. "Creating Leaders That Are World-Class," *Australian Financial Review*, October 28, 1998, p. 10.

Taylor, William. "The Logic of Global Business: An Interview of ABB's Percy Barnevik," *Harvard Business Review*, March–April 1991, pp. 91–105.

Tung, Rosalie L. "American Expatriates Abroad," *Journal of World Business*, June 22, 1998, vol. 33, no. 2, p. 125.

8

Global Marketing Strategies

IN THIS CHAPTER WE INTRODUCE THE READER TO THE COMPLEX CHOICES FACED by companies as they develop global marketing strategies. Companies need not just make a decision on whether or not to adopt a global marketing strategy, but more important, they need to select from a variety of generic global marketing strategies. First, companies have to review and consider their internationalization patterns, ranging from opportunistic, or unplanned patterns, to fully planned patterns of globalization, which involve subjecting a pattern to global logics. Second, firms have to select an appropriate expansion strategy, which might result either in global market reach through market coverage or in globalizing their asset base through building companies in many markets. Third, companies must determine the

FIGURE 8.1

Global Marketing Decision Elements

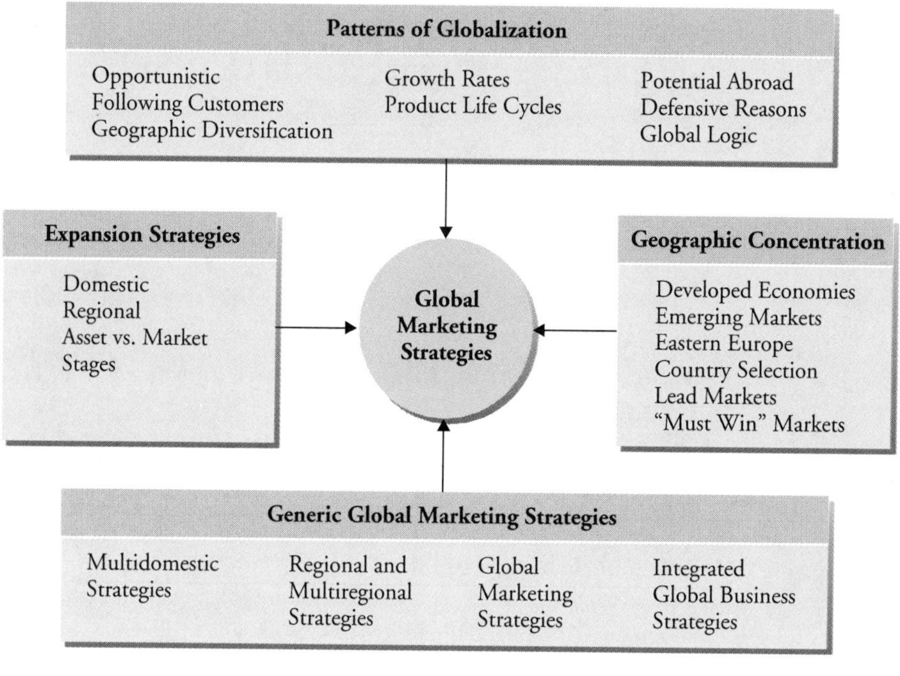

desired geographic concentration strategy, which includes a selection of the markets the company intends to cover. The chapter ends with an review of the various generic global marketing strategies and their selection criteria. Figure 8.1 summarizes the topics discussed in the chapter.

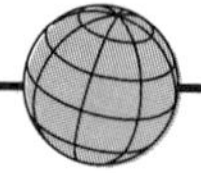

Patterns of Globalizing Marketing Operations

Whether to compete globally is a strategic decision that will fundamentally affect the firm, including its operations and its management. For many companies, the decision to globalize remains an important and difficult one. Typically, there are many issues behind a company's decision to begin to compete in foreign markets. For some firms, going abroad is the result of a deliberate policy decision; for others, it is a reaction to a specific business opportunity or a competitive challenge.

Opportunistic Global Market Development

Probably the most common reason for global expansion is the recognition that opportunities exist in foreign markets. Many companies, particularly those in the United States, promote their products in trade journals or through other media to their U.S. customers. These publications are also read by foreign business executives, who place orders that are initially unsolicited. Because these transactions are usually more complicated and more involved than a routine shipment to domestic customers, the firm has to make the decision whether to respond at that time. The company can also adopt a more aggressive policy and actively pursue foreign customers, moving beyond filling unsolicited orders. Thus, some firms have built sizable foreign businesses by first responding to orders and then taking a more proactive approach later. Most large, internationally active companies were built initially around an opportunistic strategy, although today these firms have moved to a more orchestrated and deliberate strategy in their approach to global marketing. Furthermore, smaller growing firms and start-up companies are increasingly taking a planned approach to their internationalization since the strategic value of expanding globally is becoming more important for them.

Following Customers Abroad

For a company whose business is concentrated on a few large customers, the decision to globalize is usually made when one of its key customers moves abroad to pursue international opportunities. Many of the major U.S. automobile component suppliers are operating plants abroad to supply their customers in foreign locations. PPG Industries, a major U.S.-based supplier of car body paints to the U.S. automobile industry, did little overseas business other than licensing its technology to other foreign paint makers until the early 1980s, when it followed its major customers abroad and began to directly service them in Europe and elsewhere. The company began to sell to non-U.S. car companies as well and achieved the leading position in supplying paints to car manufacturers worldwide.[1] Similar trends can be observed as Japanese and European automobile manufacturers set up their own operations in the United States. These moves tend to be followed by a series of component suppliers who do not want to lose out on a new business opportunity.[2]

R. R. Donnelley & Sons Co., the largest U.S.-based printer of magazines, catalogs, and directories, was a largely domestic company until 1978, when it made its first foreign acquisitions. Fifteen years later, international revenue was still only 8 percent of its more than $4 billion in sales. However, the company

1. Jean-Pierre Jeannet, "The World Paint Industry," case (Lausanne: IMD International, 1993).
2. Jean-Pierre Jeannet and Kurt Schaer, "Siemens Automotive Technology: Brazil Strategy," case (Lausanne: IMD Institute, 1993).

believed that within a decade this percentage might rise to 40 or 50 percent. Its international business has developed primarily on the strength of its customers' requests. Some of Donnelley's main client groups (for example, computer firms, software houses, and telecommunications firms) are rapidly expanding overseas and want Donnelley to go with them, supplying documents and manuals overseas. The company entered into a joint venture (JV) with Bell Atlantic, a regional U.S. phone operator. The JV company itself entered into a venture with the Shanghai Telephone Directory Company with the purpose of transforming the traditional yellow page directory format into a comprehensive guidebook on communication, commerce, investment, and hopping. The Shanghai telephone directory accounts for almost half of the yellow pages advertising revenue in China.[3]

The service sector has seen similar expansions triggered by client moves overseas. The establishment of international networks of major U.S. professional services firms, such as Deloitte Touche Tohmatsu, was motivated by a desire to service key domestic clients overseas. Deloitte has 28,000 employees and professionals in its U.S. operation, and another 54,000 spread over some 130 country operations. Many of the firm's service lines have adopted a globalized structure, such as the secure e-business practice.[4]

Pursuing Geographic Diversification

A need to diversify beyond a single country can also be behind moves to internationalize a company. Although diversification is a lesser factor for U.S.-based companies, firms in other parts of the world often do not want their operations to be dominated or to become overly dependent on the economy of a single country. Saint-Gobain, a large French company founded by King Louis XIV some 330 years ago, and with a long-standing tradition in glass and building materials, for years followed a strategy to break out of its France-only position. Acquiring large companies in the same field in Germany and the United Kingdom, the company was able to reduce French sales to 25 percent of corporate sales. The acquisition of Norton Company, a U.S.-based maker of abrasives and ceramics, and Carborundum of Canada, significantly strengthened Saint-Gobain's position in the United States. With sales of almost $21 billion, about two-thirds of its 120,000 employees work outside France, its domestic market. The company now ranks as the number one worldwide producer for several business lines, including flat glass, insulation, ductile iron pipes, major industrial ceramics, and abrasives, and it ranks as the number two worldwide in containers, reinforcements, and building materials for roofing and cladding products.[5]

3. "China Gets the Message," *Journal of Commerce* (Special), September 23, 1998, p. 1C.
4. "Deloitte & Touche Secure E-Business Practice to Globalize," *PR Newswire*, July 2, 1999.
5. "Compagnie de St.-Gobain," *Industry Week,* June 7, 1999, p. 38.

Exploiting Different Economic Growth Rates

Economic growth rates are subject to wide variations among countries. A company based in a low-growth country may suffer a competitive disadvantage and may want to expand into faster-growing countries to take advantage of growth opportunities. The area of the Pacific Rim (which includes Japan, South Korea, Taiwan, China, Hong Kong, Thailand, Singapore, Malaysia, and Indonesia) experienced above-average growth rates in the second half of the 1980s, which in turn prompted many international firms to invest heavily in expanding in that region. Although the region suffered from a substantial economic recession in 1998, many of the region's economics have rebounded and are rapidly making up for lost ground.[6]

The chemicals industry in Asia has experienced above-average annual growth rates, ranging between 12 percent for China and 7 to 9 percent for several other Asian Pacific Rim countries. This enormous growth, expected to make the Asian chemicals market the largest in the world in the year 2000, has attracted investment by many chemicals companies from the United States and Europe. Bayer, a large German-based chemicals company, plans to invest some $5 billion in Asia by the year 2010, when Asia's share of the world chemicals market is expected to reach 32 percent, up from its present 29 percent. Specifically, Bayer expects its Asian sales to reach about 25 percent of corporate sales. Major investments are planned in Thailand and China, where the company has already invested in a dozen specialized joint ventures.[7]

Exploiting Product Life Cycle Differences

When the market for a firm's product becomes saturated, a company can open new opportunities by entering foreign markets where the product may not be very well known. Thus, adding new markets extends the product's life cycle. Among U.S. firms following this strategy are many consumer goods marketers, such as Philip Morris, Coca-Cola, and PepsiCo. They often target markets where the per capita consumption of their products is still relatively low. With economic expansion and the resulting improvement in personal incomes in the new market, these companies expect to experience substantial growth over time—though operations in the United States are showing little growth. One 1990 report showed that Coca-Cola sold 189 twelve-ounce servings per person annually in the United States. Its international average was only 37 servings, although this

6. "Buoyant Tiger Returns to High Growth and Reform," *Financial Times*, November 4, 1999, Special Survey on Taiwan, P. I.
7. "Bayer Plans Investments in Asia Through 2010," *Chemical Market Reporter*, February 22, 1999, p. 28.

varied between 215 in Iceland, 173 in Mexico, 111 in West Germany, 61 in the United Kingdom, 35 in Japan, and 26 in France. China trailed with 0.3 servings per capita. The company believes that if the per capita consumption in China ever reaches the levels of other Asian countries, such as Australia, Coca-Cola of China would become as large as the entire existing Coca-Cola company.[8]

Industrial products and service companies experience product life cycle differences as well. Electronic Data Systems (EDS), the largest computing services company in the United States, is exploiting its skill at outsourcing in Europe. In the United States, many companies have for many years contracted for computing services rather than having their own computer centers. EDS believed that Europe was some five years behind the U.S. trend, and Asia Pacific was still several years behind Europe.[9]

Pursuing Potential Abroad

Some firms maximize their domestic market and then reach out for more potential abroad. With a 1998 market share of 45 percent in the United States, Anheuser-Busch dominates the U.S. beer market. However, with opportunities for growth outside the United States more attractive, Anheuser-Busch has also been entering a number of major international markets and is trying to build a global brand for Budweiser, something no other brewery has ever been able to pull off. A latecomer to international expansion, the company did not even establish an international department until 1982. Since then, the company has built up major stakes in key international markets although international volume is still only about 7 percent of total corporate volume. Anheuser-Busch introduced several of its brands in Japan. In China, where Budweiser is priced of two to three times higher than locally brewed premium brands, the company is building both brewing capacity and local distribution capabilities. China has become Anheuser's fifth-largest overseas market. The company's largest international market is Canada, where the Budweiser brand is brewed under license by Labatt. The company also owns a substantial stake in Grupo Modelo, the brewer of Corona, now the top-selling import in the United States.[10]

China is attracting many international brewing companies because of its sheer size. Although per capita consumption is still considerably behind major markets of Europe and the United States, in volume terms the Chinese market has already surpassed Germany and is expected to even surpass the United States within the next five years. Among the leading international brewers, Anheuser-Busch is competing

8. Richard Seet and David Yoffie, "Internationalizing the Cola Wars (A): The Battle for China and Asian Markets," Harvard Business School, Case 9-795-186, 1995.
9. "Hungry American Eyes European Sales," *Financial Times*, March 23, 1993, p. 19.
10. "This Bud's for Them: Anheuser-Busch Takes Closer Aim at Foreign Markets," *New York Times*, June 23, 1999, p. C1.

against Fosters from Australia, and Heineken, Beck, and Carlsberg from Europe. China's share of world beer consumption has risen from 6 percent in 1990 to 14 percent in 1998. Excess capacity among foreign brewers, however, and the need to charge steep premium prices, has caused substantial losses among the international brewers present in the Chinese market.[11] Pursuing even such substantial potential abroad can still require long-term investments, with payback years away.

Globalizing for Defensive Reasons

Sometimes companies are not particularly interested in pursuing new growth or potential abroad but decide to enter the international business arena for purely defensive reasons. When a domestic company sees its markets invaded by foreign firms, that company may react by entering the foreign competitor's home market in return. As a result, the company can learn valuable information about the competitor that will help in its operations at home. A company may want to slow down a competitor by denying it the cash flow from its profitable domestic operation that could otherwise be invested into expansion abroad. For these reasons, companies who had not needed to compete internationally find themselves suddenly forced to expand abroad.

Many U.S. companies opened operations in Japan to get closer to their most important competitors. For example, major companies such as Xerox and IBM use their local subsidiaries in Japan to learn new ways to compete with the major Japanese firms in their field. Likewise, many European firms want to be represented in the U.S. market because they can learn about new opportunities more directly than if they waited in their home markets for U.S. firms to arrive with new products or technologies.

Pursuing a Global Logic or Imperative

In Chapter 7, we covered the concept of a global logic. The strong presence of a global logic in a company's business or industry can be a major force propelling a firm to establish international and global operations. If a global logic is ignored, the firm is likely to suffer negative competitive implications, such as lower long-term profitability.

Many of the reasons for internationalization cited earlier in this section represent choices companies can make, but they do not represent compelling rationales that would lead to competitive disadvantages in case of nonaction. The situation is different, however, for companies facing strong global logics. The stronger a global logic in a given area or along a given dimension, the stronger the necessity to accommodate and comply.

11. "Over a Barrel," *Forbes*, December 14, 1998, p. 156.

A strong global logic thus creates an imperative for a firm to globalize its marketing operation. When this occurs, the steps to globalize are no longer voluntary, opportunistic, or based on what a company might like to do. Global marketing under the pressures of the global logic becomes a must. The global imperative, or global logic, demands accommodation, and steps to globalize the marketing operations have become necessary for competitive survival. This type of pressure is becoming more and more typical for many firms, thus driving globalization of marketing operations.

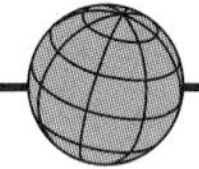

Pathways to Global Expansion

To succeed in global marketing, companies need to look carefully at their geographic expansion. To some extent, a firm makes a conscious decision about its extent of globalization by choosing a posture that may range from entirely domestic without any international involvement to a global reach where the company devotes its entire marketing strategy to global competition. Each level of globalization will profoundly change the way a company competes and will require different strategies with respect to marketing programs, planning, organization, and control of the international marketing effort.

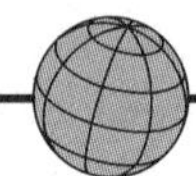

Domestic Marketing Strategies

A company with a strictly domestic marketing strategy has decided not to actively involve itself in any global marketing. Clearly, such companies are not the main interest for our text, but there nevertheless are situations in which a company should not or cannot become an active participant in global marketing.

When a company has a very limited product range that appeals only to its own local market, global marketing will not be advisable unless the company is prepared to expand its product line. In many service-oriented businesses, customer relations are such that business is only done within a narrow or limited geographic trading range. To expand to new business centers, other affiliates will have to be built, again requiring considerable capital assets. Also, some industries are substantially domestic, with individual companies not directly competing beyond their own local markets. And newly started companies may not be in a position to expand abroad before their domestic market is satisfied.

Over the past twenty-five years, an ever-increasing number of domestic industries have become subject to a increasing global logic, as described in Chapter 7. These developments may have been triggered by a foreign company's arriving on the scene and changing the competitive situation.

The major appliance industry serves as an excellent example of an industry that has turned from purely domestic to international in scope. By many industry observers, the foray of Sweden-based Electrolux into the United States through the acquisition of the WCI Group (1998) is credited with the true transition from primarily domestic to an international and global industry.[12] Electrolux's transition triggered a reaction among the leading U.S.-based firms of GE Appliances, Whirlpool, and Maytag. Whirlpool joined the fight for global leadership and began to rapidly expand its business in Europe, acquiring major business from Philips of the Netherlands in 1989. Maytag also invaded Europe and acquired the operations of Hoover. However, these investments did not meet expectations, and Maytag later divested its Hoover assets in Europe and Australia. GE Appliances followed a more tentative strategy, engaging in a series of alliances and joint ventures in Europe but not entering the battle for control of that market. Ten years later, the strategies of most major players in the appliance industry have changed. Whirpool and Electrolux continue to battle for global leadership. Whirpool is leading in the U.S. market, number three in Europe, and well positioned in the other areas of the world. The company had to pull back from some markets, such as Brazil, where profitability was not in line with expectations. Electrolux consolidated its position in the United States through the creation of Frigidaire Home Products. Both firms, however, are still some distance from achieving their target returns, indicating that a transition from domestic to global is not always followed by immediate improvements in returns.[13]

Many well-known firms with large domestic shares have eventually had to align themselves with other firms to make up for lack of international coverage. Gerber Foods, a well-established U.S.-based producer of baby foods, was acquired by Sandoz of Switzerland (now a unit of Novartis Nutrition), which had an extensive overseas marketing network to sell Gerber products. Gillette acquired Duracell, a leading U.S.-based batteries manufacturer, reasoning that it could introduce Duracell batteries in the many overseas markets where Gillette had experience, such as Brazil, India, China, and Indonesia. Duracell did not have the necessary resources to grow overseas on its own.[14] Kao of Japan, a leading maker of detergents, soaps, and toiletries, also has had a largely domestic history (with barely 20 percent of its revenue from international markets), to the extent that neither Procter & Gamble nor Unilever, its two big international rivals, see Kao as a threat outside Japan.[15] The risk of this domestic market position became apparent when the Japanese market for household goods shrank by 2 to 3 percent in 1996, forcing Kao to look for international markets to maintain its overall competitiveness against Procter & Gamble and Unilever, which were active in its home market.[16]

12. "Globalization: The Second Decade." *Appliance Manufacturer*, May 1, 1999, p. 34.
13. Ibid.
14. "Gillette to Buy Duracell for $7 Billion," *New York Times*, September 13, 1996, p. D1.
15. "Should We Kow-Tow to Kao?" *Economist*, March 30, 1996, p. 68.
16. "Kao Wants to Clean-Up in Markets Overseas," *Nikkei Weekly*, February 10, 1997, p. 17.

With more and more industries subject to the global logic, fewer companies can safely select purely domestic marketing strategies. Increasingly, firms will have to accommodate the global logic by pursuing various levels of globalization. The following sections describe different globalization pathways companies may adopt.

Regional and Multiregional Marketing Strategies

Mapping out a regional marketing strategy implies that a company will concentrate its resources and marketing efforts on one or possibly two of the world's regions. Emphasizing North America or Europe can be the result of a regional strategy. Other regions a company may want to concentrate on are Latin America, the Pacific Basin, and Asia. In such a situation, the company has expanded beyond a domestic environment but, as we will show later, has not yet reached a multinational or global state.

Companies pursue a pathway toward a regional marketing strategy for a number of reasons. Such firms are competing in the region of which their home market is a part; neighboring markets within the same region are invaded because of market or product similarity requiring few adaptations. Regional strategies are also encouraged when customer requirements in one region are substantially different from those in others. Under those circumstances, different sets of competitors and market structures may exist, and industry participants may not invade each other's regions or market territories. When such a fragmentation exists, a firm can compete on the basis of knowing its own region best by being closer to its customers. As we have already observed in some of the industries moving from domestic to global, the global logic often does not stop at the regional level. Although an improved strategy for some firms, regional marketing strategies may only be a stop on the way toward a more completely global direction. Some firms, and the appliance industry serves again as our example, compete for market share globally but operate their businesses in distinct regional groupings. Electrolux, operating a European appliance group and a North American one, is a case in point.[17]

Asset Globalization Versus Market Globalization

International and global pathways can be classified along two dimensions. Along the *geographic dimension*, describing a company's geographic reach of a marketing operation or market coverage expressed through number of countries, we can identify pathways ranging from domestic to international, regional, or global.

17. "Globalization: The Second Decade." *Appliance Manufacturer*, May 1, 1999, p. 34.

FIGURE 8.2

Market Coverage Versus Asset Distribution

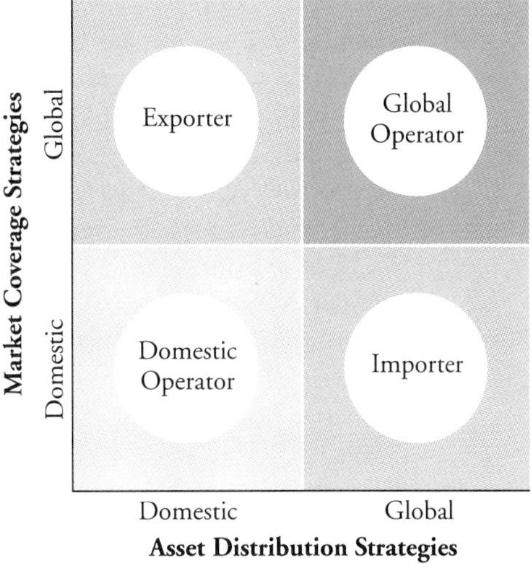

Companies may adopt various patterns of geographic strategies. Along a second axis, the *asset distribution*, companies' pathways may be described in terms of their asset distribution strategies. The asset strategy describes a company's investment patterns in terms of plants, logistics operations, and other physical assets. Asset strategies may range from domestic, single-country, to regional and eventually global, reflecting the way a company's assets are distributed geographically around the world.

Companies' strategies may therefore fall into several categories.[18] (See Figure 8.2 for a matrix of the patterns.) Global market strategies are pursued by those firms who serve the entire world market and whose marketing operations stretch across the world. Global asset strategies are pursued by firms who dot their plants, support operations, and other fixed assets across the world. Clearly, there are combinations as well. The company with a local market and asset strategy is the typical domestic company, both producing and marketing in only one market. The company with a global market strategy but local asset strategy would be the typical exporter, marketing all over the world but producing in a single market. Boeing, the passenger aircraft manufacturer, exemplifies such a strategy. When a company markets globally and its assets are also distributed globally, we

18. Vijay Jolly, "Global Competitive Strategies," in *Strategy, Organizational Design, and Human Resource Management*, ed. Charles C. Snow (Greenwich, Conn.: JAI Press, 1989), pp. 55–110.

may speak of a truly global company. And finally, some firms whose markets are largely domestic pursue a global asset strategy by sourcing products overseas. Such firms may be classified as classic importers. Schwinn Bicycles of the United States would typify such a strategy.[19]

In addition to market coverage and asset distribution, we identify a third dimension, which we call *idea sourcing*. By that, we refer to the sources of new business ideas for the creation of new enterprises. Traditionally, business ideas have come from nearby, typically the home or domestic market of the company founder. While concentrating on home-grown ideas would be appropriate if an entrepreneur lived in the lead market for a given industry, executives and entrepreneurs elsewhere in the world benefit from importing ideas, or new business concepts, and realizing them locally. In retailing, the entertainment industry, e-commerce, and many service businesses, local entrepreneurs all over the world pick up new ideas from lead market countries, frequently the United States, and implement them locally.

A relatively new firm demonstrating idea sourcing abroad is Submarino, a Brazil-based Internet bookseller. The company, originally started as Booknet in São Paulo, was emulating Amazon.com's U.S. strategy by acting as an Internet-based distributor for Spanish and Portuguese books. With financing from some U.S.-based venture capital firms, the company embarked on an aggressive growth strategy and has already opened offices in Spain, Argentina, and Mexico. Submarino's long-term strategy is to become the leading online shopping destination in the Spanish- and Portuguese-speaking world.[20]

A domestic idea sourcing strategy is limiting, whereas a global idea sourcing strategy entails scouring the entire world for the best new ideas. Again, the market exploitation and asset distribution of the resulting business might be either domestic or global. It is important to remember that pursuing a global marketing strategy does not require a physical presence in every country. We need to accept that different types of geographic strategies exist but that they all have a global context and they all require marketing managers with the global mindset described in the previous chapter.

Stages of Global Market Development Pathways

Tracking the development of the large global corporations today reveals a recurring, sequential pattern of expansion. Typically, these companies began their business development phase by entrenching themselves first in their domestic markets. Often, international development did not occur until maturity

19. Jean-Pierre Jeannet and Robert Howard, "Schwinn Bicycle Company," case (European Case Clearinghouse, 1993).
20. "Where the Risk Is Riskier Yet," *New York Times*, December 16, 1999, p. C1.

was reached domestically. After that phase, these firms began to turn into companies with some international business, usually on an export basis. As the international side of their sales grew, the companies increasingly distributed their assets into many markets and achieved what was once termed the status of a multinational corporation (MNC). Pursuing multidomestic strategies on a market-by-market basis, companies began to enlarge and build considerable local presence. Only during their latest phase have these firms begun to transform themselves into global marketing behemoths whose marketing operations are closely coordinated across the world market rather than developed and executed locally.

This traditional sequencing of the growth from domestic to international, to multidomestic or multinational to global, seems to be followed by most firms, and also by many newly formed companies. However, some newer firms are jumping right into the latest, or global, category, and not necessarily going through the various stages of development (see Figure 8.3). This leap reflects two trends. First, the time companies have to get their global market positions in key markets is getting ever shorter, forcing many newly formed companies to attempt to conquer domestic and global markets at the same time. Second, newer firms realize that they do not have to "learn" in the same sequence older ones did; they can take advantage of the most recent forms of market development—global forms. One example, Logitech, the Swiss computer-input device maker, serves to illustrate the point. Logitech's market coverage and its marketing strategy were global virtually from its inception, skipping many of the earlier, intermediate forms of international market development. The company not only opened sales offices rapidly throughout the world but also added factories

FIGURE 8.3

Sequencing Internationalization Strategies

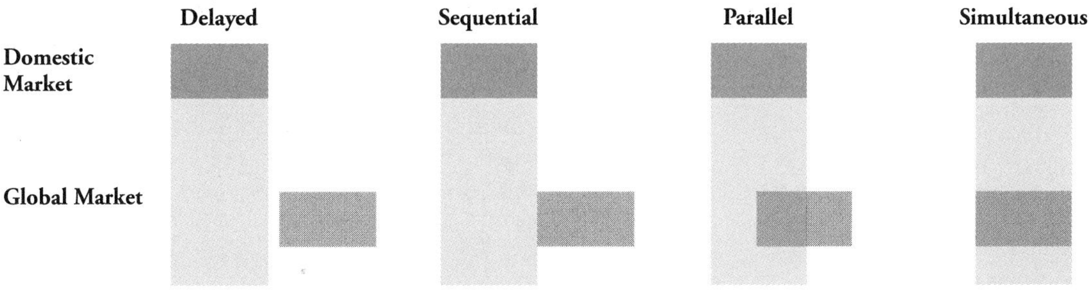

in Taiwan, the United States, Switzerland, and Ireland.[21] Logitech built is business to become the world's leading PC mouse maker, with an annual output of 73 million mice made from plants in Taiwan and China and attaining a global market share of 50 percent.[22]

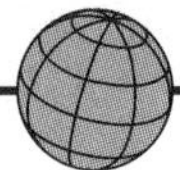

Geographic Market Choices

Once a company commits to extending its business internationally, management is confronted with the task of setting a geographic or regional emphasis. A company may decide to emphasize developed nations, such as Japan or those of Europe and North America. Alternatively, some companies may prefer to pursue primarily developing countries in Latin America, Africa, or Asia. Management must make a strategic decision to direct business development in such a way that the company's overall objectives are congruent with the particular geographic mix of its activities.

Emphasizing Developed Economies

Developed economies account for a disproportionately large share of world gross national product (GNP) and thus tend to attract many companies. In particular, firms with technology-intensive products have concentrated their activities in the developed world. Although competition from both other international firms and local companies is usually more intense in those markets, doing business in developed countries is generally preferred over doing business in developing nations. This is primarily because the business environment is more predictable and the investment climate is more favorable.

Developed countries are located in North America (the United States and Canada), western Europe, and Asia (Japan, Australia, New Zealand). Although some global firms such as IBM operate in all of these countries, many others may be represented in only one or two areas. Very early in their development, U.S. international companies established strong business bases in Europe, then, more recently, in Japan. Japanese firms tend to start their overseas operations in the United States and Canada and then move into Europe.

The importance of developing a competitive position in the major developed markets was first articulated by Kenichi Ohmae. Ohmae maintained that for most industries it was important to compete effectively in the three parts of the *triad* of the United States, Europe, and Japan. Companies were said to need to be strong in at least two areas and have a representation in the third; real global competitors were advised to have strong positions in all three areas. The three areas

21. Vijay Jolly, "Logitech International (A)," case (Lausanne: IMD International, 1991).
22. "PC Mouse Maker Logitech Still No. 1," *Taiwan Economic News*, June 8, 1999.

of the strategic triad account for about 80 percent of most industries, thus determining the outcome of the competitive battle.[23] Even more so, ten of the most international-trade-minded developed countries (the United States, Canada, the United Kingdom, Germany, France, the Netherlands, Sweden, Switzerland, Japan, and Australia) account for 50 percent of the world's international trade, 70 percent of its inward investment, and 90 percent of its foreign direct investment. As a result, companies that see themselves as world-class marketers cannot afford to neglect these pivotal markets.[24]

Because of the importance of the triad countries in international trade, global companies expend great efforts to balance their presence such that their sales begin to mirror the relative size of the three regions. A company underrepresented in one area or another will undertake considerable investment, often in the form of acquisitions, to balance the geographic portfolio. Alcatel, a leading European manufacturer of telecommunications equipment, had staked out the enterprise market for communications equipment as an area of expansion. With 50 percent of the global opportunity for this market located in the United States, the company began a major investment drive into the LAN (local area network) switching business and acquired Xylan Corp. and Assured Access Technology, two California-based firms.[25]

Europe, the third leg of the triad, has been the focus of investment from the United States and from Japanese companies. The attraction of Europe for Japanese firms was enhanced through the adoption of the common currency (euro) on January 1, 1999, covering 11 of the 15 EU countries. (see Chapter 4). Investments surpassed $1 billion in 1997, triggered by an understanding that the resulting "Euroland" covering the eleven countries who adopted the common currency would experience higher returns.[26]

Although the triad concept was first understood as referring to the United States, western Europe, and Japan, more recent use of the concept tends to emphasize three regions rather than countries. With the advent of the North American Free Trade Agreement (NAFTA) in 1992, North America has become a more relevant concept than just the United States. In Europe, the relevant concept is the European Union (EU), which has been expanded to fifteen western European countries. And finally, many firms refer to the third leg of the triad as the Asia Pacific region rather than just Japan. Including other rapidly growing Asian countries in the triad has brought about a considerably increased focus. Most

23. Kenichi Ohmae, *Triad Power: The Coming Shape of Global Competition* (New York: Free Press, 1985).
24. "Subramanian Rangan: Seven Myths to Ponder Before Going Global," *Financial Times*, Mastering Strategy, Part 10, November 29, 1999, p. 2.
25. "Alcatel Open to More Acquisitions," *Business World*, March 25, 1999.
26. "Japanese Investors Likely to Look to Europe for Better Returns," *Asian Wall Street Journal*, October 1, 1998, p. 22.

European and U.S. global firms, traditionally weak in that part of the world, have undertaken considerable efforts to balance their market positions. In a recent survey among managers of international firms, investment in the Asia Pacific region was rated as highest in importance, ranking equal to investment in their home countries and ahead of any other region. Whirlpool of the United States, the world's largest white goods company, set up a regional headquarters for Asia in Singapore. The company indicated that with its past investments in Europe and Latin America, the remaining missing piece was the Asia Pacific region, where unit sales are expected to outpace both Europe and North America. Whirlpool has entered into several joint ventures in Asia and has acquired several controlling interests in four appliance companies in China and two in India.[27]

Emphasizing Emerging Markets

Emerging markets differ substantially from developed economies by geographic region and by the level of economic development. Markets in Latin America, Africa, the Middle East, and Asia are also characterized by a higher degree of risk than markets in developed countries. Because of the less stable economic climates in those areas, a company's operation can be expected to be subject to greater uncertainty and fluctuation. Furthermore, the frequently changing political situations in developing countries often affect operating results negatively. As a result, some markets that may have experienced high growth for some years may suddenly experience drastic reductions in growth. In many situations, however, the higher risks are compensated for by higher returns, largely because competition is often less intense in those markets. Consequently, companies need to balance the opportunity for future growth in the developing nations with the existence of higher risk.

Unilever, the large Dutch-British consumer goods company, met intensive competition in its traditional markets in Europe and the United States, where it has about two-thirds of its volume. Faced with lower growth in those markets, the company moved aggressively into emerging markets, where annual growth has averaged 5 percent or more in most of its core business categories. The company declared five geographic areas as top targets: central and eastern Europe, Latin America, India, and Southeast Asia. In China, Unilever has invested some $800 million over the past years. Although still accounting for only a small portion of Unilever's sales, the potential in China is viewed as huge. The company planned to obtain half of its global sales from emerging countries over the next ten years.[28]

27. "Asia Challenges Whirlpool Technology," *Research Technology Management*, September 1, 1998, p. 4.

28. "China: Unilever Seeks Market in China," *China Daily*, June 21, 1999, p. 5.

Banco Santander, the leading Spanish commercial and investment bank, decided to pursue emerging markets on the basis that traditional markets in Europe and North America were overbanked. As a result, the company launched a major drive to develop its competitive position in Latin America. In 1996, the bank made major acquisitions in Chile, entered pension fund management in Argentina, and acquired large banks in Mexico and Colombia, as well as Venezuela's second-largest bank.[29] Following its merger with BCH SA, another Spanish bank, Santander commanded some 1,400 retail branches throughout the region and was expected to reach for a market share of about 10 percent in each market.[30]

Hyundai, the largest of Korea's three major car manufacturers with sales of 1.2 million units in 1995, has also aggressively pursued emerging markets. Hyundai acquired old car plants in recently liberalizing countries, especially in eastern Europe and the former Soviet Union. The company further expanded with plants into Turkey, India, Egypt, and Botswana. These are all markets with still small car markets, and with few competitors in place.[31]

The past experience of international firms doing business in developing countries has not been especially positive. Trade restrictions forced companies to build local factories, exposing themselves to substantial risk. However, with the present trend toward global trade liberalization and privatization, many formerly closed countries have opened their borders.

Many firms were seriously affected by the economic crisis in Mexico in the early 1990s. Whirlpool, the U.S.-based household goods company, saw its results severely affected by the economic situation in Brazil. Currency devaluation in that country resulted in a substantial net charge against income. Furthermore, annual sales in Brazil, measured in hard currency, declined by $200 million as a result of the devaluation. Actual shipments were expected to fall 10 to 15 percent in Brazil.[32] Although the potential is usually superior in emerging markets, global companies have to expect annual fluctuations that far exceed those experienced in developed markets of North America or Europe.

Expanding in Eastern Europe

The economic liberalization of the countries in eastern Europe opened a large new market for many international firms. The market typically represents about 15 percent of the worldwide demand in a given industry, about two-thirds of that

29. "A Banking Dynasty on the Move," *New York Times*, January 1, 1997, p. 61.
30. "Santander-BCH Bank Merger Creates Overlap in Latin America Market," *Dow Jones Business News*, April 16, 1999.
31. "Fast Drive Out of the Shadows," *Financial Times*, June 17, 1996, p. 17.
32. "Whirlpool Says Net Fell By 65 Percent on Impact of Brazil Devaluation," *Wall Street Journal*, April 16, 1999, p. B2.

accounted for by Russia and other countries of the former Soviet Union. Although many companies consider this market as long-term potential with little profit opportunity in the near term, a number of firms have moved to take advantage of opportunities in areas where they once were prohibited from doing business.

The first wave of investments into eastern Europe was led by companies marketing industrial equipment, such as U.S.-based Otis. In Poland, where Otis has been operating since 1975, the company had reached a market share of 30 percent. Otis was attracted to the Polish market because its 60,000 operating elevators were mostly old and the replacement and service markets were promising.[33]

Companies marketing consumer goods tended to enter the region later. One of the leaders was Procter & Gamble, the U.S.-based consumer products company. P&G set up regional centers for each product line, making the Czech Republic its center for detergents and Hungary its center for personal care products.[34] Procter & Gamble began its Russian operations in August 1991 in St. Petersburg. The company slowly introduced a line of products while expanding its geographic reach. According to company surveys, only 10 to 15 percent of the Russian population could afford western consumer goods.[35]

The behavior of international car manufacturers demonstrates an aggressive approach to eastern Europe. Low labor costs, at rates only a fraction of what they are in western Europe, attracted international firms to build cars in eastern Europe (see Table 8.1). Initial low sales levels promised substantial future growth as the markets of eastern Europe improved the income levels of their populations. In Poland, automobile sales jumped 40 percent from 1995 to 1996, and in Hungary about 20 percent over the same one-year period. To capitalize on this potential, many firms moved to set up assembly plants and car component factories, or acquired local firms.[36]

Setting up car plants in eastern Europe serves several purposes. First, as the example of Hungary shows, those companies that manufacture locally have a clear marketing advantage. Japan's Suzuki and GM/Opel are tied for first place, with about 20 percent of the market each. Although the market in Hungary is still small (about 75,000 units in 1997) and below the peak of 90,000 units achieved in 1995, the demand is expected to grow in the future. Suzuki not only makes its small hatchback Swift model for local distribution but also exports it to other European destinations, thus taking advantage of lower labor costs. GM, Ford, and Daewoo have all started their own finance activities in Hungary to support local marketing operations.[37] Other firms have started to develop the Russian market.

33. "Otis Signs $5 Million Contract with TPSA," *Polish Press Agency*, June 9, 1999.
34. "P&G Sets Up E. Europe Units," *Advertising Age*, June 24, 1991, p. 6.
35. "Crash Russian Course for Procter & Gamble," *New York Times*, December 19, 1993, p. 5.
36. "Into the East at Full Throttle," *Financial Times*, February 13, 1997, p. 11.
37. "Target for Investment," Hungary Survey, *Financial Times*, December 16, 1996, p. III.

TABLE 8.1

Operations of Automobile Firms in Eastern Europe

Company Name	*Country*	*Type of Operation*	*Investment*[a]
GM/Opel	Poland	Car assembly New car plant	DM 30 mio DM 500 mio
	Hungary	New engine & car plant	DM 1.0 bio
	East Germany	New car plant	DM 1.0 bio
Ford Motor	Poland	Car & van assembly	DM 54 mio
Volkswagen	Poland	Car & van assembly	DM 54 mio
	Hungary	New Audi engine & car plant	DM 1.0 bio
	Slovakia	Assembly & gearbox plant	DM 215 mio
	Czech	Skoda acquisition (70% stake), new car plant & models	DM 3.7 bio
	Eastern Germany	2 plants, new engine & cars	DM 3.2 bio
Fiat	Poland	FSM (78% stake) new plant & models	DM 1.8 bio
Suzuki	Hungary	New car plant (80% stake)	na
Daewoo	Poland	Acquisitions of FS Lublin & FSO, new plants & models	DM 1.34 bio

[a]Some investments staged over several years into 2000–2002 period.
Source: Financial Times, February 13, 1997, p. 11. Reprinted by permission.

GM began with the production of Chevrolet Blazers in 1997 and reached an output of 50,000 units per year in 1998. But bureaucratic impediments and uncertainties have made most global automotive companies cautious on the Russian market, although they are fully aware of its long-term potential.[38]

Few companies can match Germany's Volkswagen in its expansion into eastern Europe. Aside from setting up assembly plants, new car plants, and engine plants, the company also invested in a new model range through its stake in Skoda, the leading Czech company with a long tradition in the automotive industry. In 1996, VW unveiled a new model, Octavia, as part of the company's strategy to make Skoda its low-budget brand throughout Europe and to become VW's answer to cheaper imports from Asia. On the coattails of the introduction of Octavia, VW hoped to raise Skoda's output from about 200,000 units to 400,000 units in 1998.[39] Skoda's latest model, Felicia, was engineered largely in Czechia and is doing very well in many European markets.[40]

Like Volkswagen, Daewoo has launched an aggressive strategy in eastern Europe. The company began by acquiring a range of old-line automakers in Poland (FS Lublin and FSO), the Czech Republic (Avia), and Romania (Oltcit). Its promised investment amounts to $1.43 billion for its two Polish plants and $900 million for its Romania operation, with the eventual goal of producing a full line of cars and core components and attaining a volume of 500,000 units.[41] In the area of the former Soviet Union, Daewoo invested in a car plant in Uzbekistan. Making the only such major investment in that central Asian republic, the company hoped to produce 160,000 vehicles by the year 2000.[42] In Poland, the company has invested more than $1 billion becoming number two (behind Fiat) and selling 170,000 vehicles annually.[43] Daewoo has declared its intention to make Poland its main base in Europe and to locate its research center there. In 1999, the company expected to use Poland also as an export base with some 40,000 vehicles built there sold in many other European markets.[44] This and other Daewoo investments in eastern Europe are part of a strategy to invest in "overlooked markets." By the end of 1999, Daewoo's parent company in Korea was undergoing drastic restructuring because of a heavy debt load taken on in building its overseas business.[45]

38. "Russia's Vast Potential Drawing U.S. Auto Makers," *Tribune Business News* (Detroit Free Press), August 18, 1998.
39. "Octavia Becomes VW's Spearhead in Budget Car Battle," *Financial Times*, October 1, 1996, p. 21.
40. "The Frugal Felicia Proves to Be a Firm Favourite," *Western Morning News* (Devon, U.K.), July 7, 1999.
41. "A Drive into the Fast Lane," *Financial Times*, February 28, 1996, p. 11.
42. "Passport for Uzbeks to Daewooistan," *Financial Times*, September 27, 1996, p. 7.
43. "Daewoo Rules Out Drastic Reduction in Overseas Business," *Agence France-Press*, July 21, 1999.
44. "Japan Eager for Investments in Poland," *Polish News Bulletin*, July 2, 1999.
45. "Battle of Wills," *Far Eastern Economic Review*, August 26, 1999, p. 10.

Country Selection

At some point, the development of any global marketing strategy will come down to selecting individual countries in which a company intends to compete. There are more than two hundred countries and territories from which companies have to select, but very few firms end up competing in all of these markets. The decision on where to compete, the country selection decision, is one of the components of developing a global marketing strategy.

Why is country selection a strategic concern for global marketing management? Adding another country to a company's portfolio always requires additional investment in management time and effort and in capital. Although opportunities for additional profits are usually the driving force, each additional country also represents a new business risk. It takes time to build up business in a country where the firm has not previously been represented, and profits may not show until much later on. Consequently, companies need to go through a careful analysis before they decide to move ahead.

Analyzing the Investment Climate A complete understanding of the investment climate of a target country will help in the country selection decision. The investment climate of a country is made up of its political situation, its legal structure, its foreign trade position, and its attitude toward foreign investment or the presence of foreign companies. In general, companies will try to avoid countries with uncertain political situations. The impact that political and legal forces can have on the operations of a foreign company abroad was described in detail in Chapter 4.

A country's foreign trade position can also determine the environment for foreign firms operating there. Countries with a strong balance of payments surplus or strong currencies that are fully convertible are favored as good places to invest. Countries with chronic balance of payments difficulties and those where there are great uncertainties about the transferability of funds are viewed as risky and, as such, are less favored by foreign investors. These aspects were described in greater detail in Chapter 2. Consequently, assessing a country's investment climate will require a thorough and skillful analysis. However, investment climate is not the only determinant for a country being selected for entry.

Determining Market Attractiveness Before a country can be selected for addition to a firm's portfolio of countries, management needs to assess the overall attractiveness of that country with respect to the firm's products or services. Initially, this requires a clear indication of the country's market size. It may consist of analyzing existing patterns of demand. Also needed are data on growth—both past and future—that will allow a firm to determine market size not only as it relates to the present situation but also with respect to potential.

Analyzing demand patterns allows a company to plot where on the product life cycle a given product or service can be located. Also, a firm may want to analyze potential competitors in that country to achieve an understanding of how it can compete. Finally, companies should get to know a new country's market enough to be able to determine if their way of competing and marketing is allowed in that country. Some markets may be very attractive, but if the firm's key strength cannot be employed, success is questionable.

The analytic approach required for an in-depth assessment of a country's market attractiveness was covered in great detail in Chapters 5, 6, and 7. Analyzing international markets and the company's prospective international buyers—the ability to perform marketing research and analysis on an international scale—is a prerequisite to sound country selection decisions.

Targeting Lead Markets

In Chapter 7, we introduced the concept of a lead market and its importance to global marketing strategists. In the context of selecting markets for special emphasis, the lead market concept can help in identifying those countries where a company should place extra emphasis.

By 1984, the United States is no longer the only lead market in many key industries (see Figures 8.4 and 8.5). In electronics or semiconductor manufacturing, Japan has captured the lead in a number of segments. This loss of leadership to Japan and other countries has become pronounced in a number of areas of the electronics industry. The worldwide share of U.S. semiconductor manufacturers had slipped to less than 40 percent by 1990.[46] The lack of capital investment in the semiconductor industry has also caused difficulties for U.S. manufacturers of semiconductor testing equipment. When Japanese firms became the world leaders in semiconductors, their position was also exploited by Japanese test equipment manufacturers.[47]

In a demonstration of the dynamic nature of lead markets, U.S. semiconductor makers were able to reverse this trend. In 1988 the U.S. market share amounted to 43 percent, compared with 48 percent for Japanese firms; by 1994 the relative strength was 48 percent for the United States versus 36 percent for Japanese suppliers. Much of this success was credited to the formation of Sematech, a consortium founded in 1987 linking eleven of the largest U.S.-based chip manufacturers. Matching the U.S. government's investment of $690 million by 1994, the consortium was also able to improve the position of semiconductor equipment makers, whose share had rebounded to just above 50 percent from a low of 45 percent in 1990. Clearly, as the United States became the lead market again in chip manufacturing, U.S. equipment suppliers could improve as they benefited from being exposed to pressures from new developments and better practices.[48]

46. "U.S. Semiconductor Industry Slips Further in World Markets, " *Financial Times*, February 22, 1991, p. 14.
47. "Pillar of Chip Industry Eroding," *New York Times*, March 3, 1989, p. D1.
48. "A Declaration of Chip Independence," *New York Times*, October 6, 1994, p. D1.

FIGURE 8.4

U.S.-Based Firms Lead in Most World Markets . . . But Trail in a Few

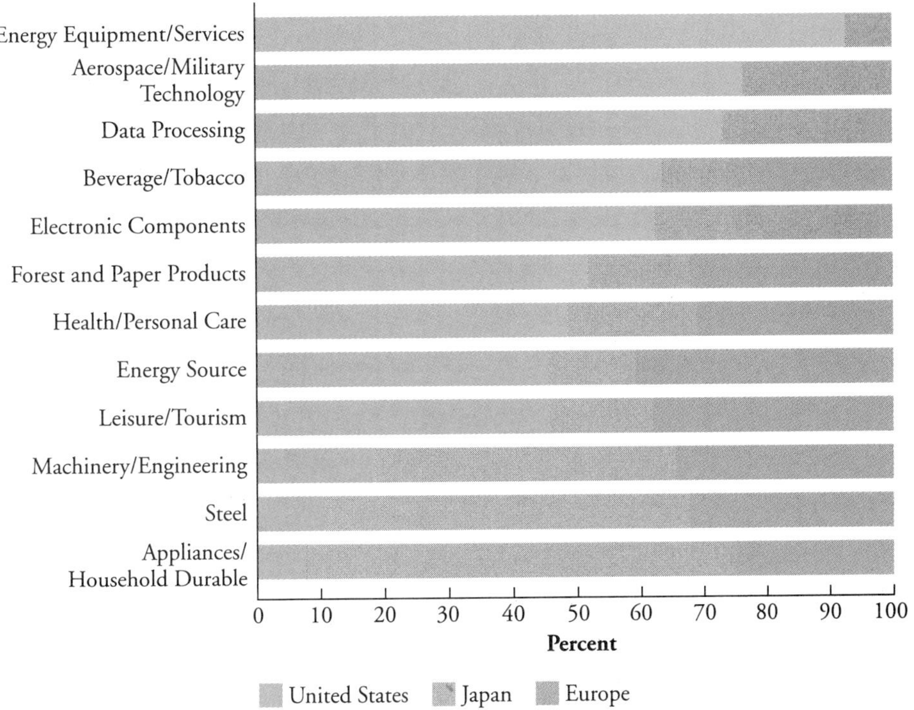

Source: Wall Street Journal, September 9, 1994, p. A10 (data from Alexis de Tocqueville Institution, Arlington, Va.). Reprinted by permission of the Wall Street Journal via Copyright Clearance Center.

Taiwan provides a good example of how newly industrializing countries can become lead markets by wresting competitive positions away from developed nations. For many years behind the innovations elsewhere, Taiwanese electronics companies have now become world leaders in several important product categories. Elitegroup and First International are the world's largest independent manufacturers of printed circuit boards. GVC, another Taiwanese company, has risen to the leading position as modem producer, surpassing Hayes of the United States. For such important components as pointing devices (the computer mouse), scanners, and motherboards, Taiwan accounted for some 70 percent of the world market share in 1992. As a result of the rising importance of these firms, leading U.S. companies such as Digital, Apple, and

FIGURE 8.5

Leading Research Nations

Field	Rank 1	2	3	4	5
Astrophysics	USA	SWI	NET	CHL	GBR
Biochemistry	USA	SWI	SWE	GBR	DEN
Chemistry	USA	SWI	ISR	NET	SWE
Earth Sciences	USA	AUS	GBR	SWI	FRA
Immunology	SWI	USA	BEL	GBR	SWE
Computer Science	ISR	USA	SWI	CAN	DEN
Engineering	DEN	SWE	USA	SWI	AUS
Multidisciplinary	USA	SWI	DEN	SWE	CAN
Agriculture	SWE	GBR	DEN	CAN	NET
Materials Science	USA	DEN	NET	ISR	SWI
Mathematics	DEN	NOR	GBR	USA	NET
Clinical Medicine	USA	CAN	GBR	SWE	DEN
Microbiology	USA	SWI	GBR	NET	ISR
Molecular Biology	SWI	USA	DEN	GBR	ISR
Neuroscience	SWE	USA	SWI	GBR	DEN
Ecology	SWE	NOR	USA	SWI	AUS
Plant and Animal Science	GBR	SWE	DEN	USA	AUS
Pharmacology	SWI	NZL	GBR	USA	SWE
Physics	SWI	DEN	USA	NET	ISR
Psychology	USA	SWE	DEN	GBR	CAN

AUS = Australia
BEL = Belgium
CAN = Canada
CHL = Chile
DEN = Denmark
FRA = France
GER = Germany
GBR = Great Britain
ISR = Israel
NET = Netherlands
NZL = New Zealand
NOR = Norway
SWE = Sweden
SWI = Switzerland
USA = United States

Source: Table from *Tages Anzeiger* (Zurich, Switzerland), February 11, 1997, p. 6. Reprinted by permission.

Motorola are engaging local firms in joint design projects for microprocessors.[49] Taiwan, through agreements with many western chip makers, has reached the number four rank worldwide in semiconductor industry, and its computer industry has risen to the number three position worldwide.[50] Taiwan, with its efficient business culture and propensity for speed in product development, has become the site of choice for manufacturing operations. In certain industries, international firms must be present in Taiwan if they intend to keep abreast of the changes.

It is essential for globally competing firms to monitor lead markets in their industries, or better yet, to build up some relevant market presence in those markets. Toray Industries, a leading Japanese company in a number of plastic and textile industries, runs its artificial leather affiliate, Alcantara, from Italy. Although Japanese firms have tended to stay away from Italy as a market for investment, Alcantara is highly successful, primarily because it depends on design for its leather products, and Toray management considers Italy as number one in the world in design. The result is excellent styling for new Toray products, which are strong enough to attract customers on looks alone. Thus, locating in lead markets gives companies lessons to learn for other markets and at the same time makes them more competitive on a worldwide basis.[51]

Targeting "Must Win" Markets

As global marketers eye the array of countries available for selection, they soon become aware that not all countries are of equal importance on the path to global leadership. Markets that are defined as crucial to global market leadership, markets that can determine the global winners among all competitors, markets that companies can ill afford to avoid or neglect—such markets are "must win" markets.

The starting point for analyzing which markets are "must" markets is the relevant global chessboard that best depicts the industry in question. Not all industries show the same countries as "must win" markets, and typically, absolute size is an important criterion for their selection. In the past, the United States has been the largest single market for many industries, thus becoming the decisive piece in global competitive struggles. With the rapid rise of China and its ongoing industrialization, that giant is increasingly assuming a key role thanks to the sheer size of this 1.2-billion-people market. With China pulled into the global chessboard as a result of its market opening, sales in many consumer goods areas are growing rapidly. Procter & Gamble of the United States had just a few products and $50 million in sales in China, By 1999, volume had grown to $1 billion.

49. "Power Switch," *Far Eastern Economic Review*, December 16, 1993, p. 44.
50. "Acer's Semiconductor Unit Weighs Market Listing as Picture Brightens," *Dow Jones Business News*, January 20, 1999.
51. "Manager's Hands-Off Tactics Right Touch for Italian Unit," *Nikkei Weekly*, February 3, 1997, p. 17.

Among its fifteen products in China, P&G's best-selling brand is Head & Shoulders shampoo.[52]

Currently the second-largest beer market in the world, China has attracted as many as sixty foreign brewers, who have entered into some fifty joint ventures and have invested some $500 million. However, size alone is no assurance of profits. Fosters of Australia plunged in and quickly ran up a loss, eventually pulling back. San Miguel of the Philippines invested $300 million into breweries in China and lost $20 million on Chinese operations in the first half of 1998 alone but was able to run things around and substantially reduce that loss in 1999.[53] Carlsberg of Denmark, a brewer with a large international business, predicts that China will be the world's largest beer market in the near future, taking that distinction from the United States.[54] Carlsbad entered into a major joint venture in Shanghai, eventually investing as much as $1 billion in the country, even at a time when other foreign brewers were pulling back because of lack of profits.[55]

Similarly, McDonald's views China as one of its biggest single opportunities. Building twenty-seven restaurants in China between 1990 and 1995, the fast-food company expects to double its size every year until reaching 600 restaurants in early 2003.[56] In Beijing alone, McDonald's ran some thirty-four outlets and expected to have as many as one hundred in a short period of time.[57]

China's automotive industry is also growing rapidly. In 1991, 50,000 cars were sold in China. By 1998, the number had grown to 510,000.[58] Volkswagen of Germany had been one of the first companies to set up in China, starting with a joint venture as early as in 1984. In the first five months of 1999, it boasted a 60 percent market share in China and achieved sales of 122,000 unites. Success of both its Volkswagen and Audi lines prompted the company to announce plans to invest another $1.6 billion in China over the next few years.[59] Passenger car ownership in China will likely increase from 2 million in 1994 to 22 million by 2010. This would mean producing about 3.5 million units annually, a feat that would make China the fourth-largest producer behind the United States, Japan, and Germany. Car manufacturers not investing in China are rightfully anxious that they may miss out on the chance of a lifetime. Any producer entrenched there would

52. "Procter & Gamble Warns on Soft Sales in China," *Asian Wall Street Journal*, October 1, 1999, p. 4.
53. "Power Play," *Far Eastern Economic Review*, August 26, 1999, p. 38.
54. "Carlsberg Sees China as Top Market," Survey on Danish Food Industry, *Financial Times*, June 7, 1994, p. III-12.
55. "Carlsberg A/S," *Food and Drink Weekly*, October 26, 1998.
56. "Chinese Market Offers Big Expansion for Big Mac," *Financial Times*, February 20, 1995, p. 4.
57. "Fast Food, Western Colas Highlight China Growth," *National Catholic Reporter*, January 29, 1999, p. 15.
58. "China Makes World-Class Cars," *China Business Information Network*, June 16, 1999.
59. "Volkswagen to Invest Another $1.63 Billion in China," *China Online*, June 21, 1999.

be able to capitalize on the large volume advantage in the export business as well, beating competitors all over the world on the basis of cost.

The massive scale of China as a "must" market has also lured many Japanese companies to the scene. Matsushita, a leading maker of consumer electronics, with brands such as Panasonic, had created some thirty-four joint ventures by 1996, thirty-one of them in just 1994–1996. These JVs employ some 20,000 local residents and are dotted all over the country. Matsushita's massive presence is viewed as one of the main reasons why the company has become a leader in VCRs and color televisions.[60] By 1999, China had about 320 million television sets and 40 million CVDS installed.[61]

Competing for a "must" market such as China has its risks, too. Compaq, the U.S. PC maker, experienced considerable growth in sales in China but had great difficulty collecting from its independent dealers and distributors. Microsoft also was fighting pirated software by adjusting its local price and initiating legal action.[62] With an installed base of 11 million PCs and 2.1 million Internet users, China is an attractive market for any information technology-related company.[63] Annual PC sales in 1997 amounted to 3 million units, growing at more than 40 percent. Industry experts estimated that the Chinese market will grow at a high rate through 2002, when annual PC sales might reach 11 million. At that point, China would be tied with Japan as number two worldwide in PC sales, moving up from the sixth spot in 1997.[64] If a market is in the "must win" or decisive category, however, companies will have to find solutions to overcome such difficulties. Contrary to other markets, "must win" markets cannot be avoided if global market leadership is at stake.

Identifying Generic Global Marketing Strategies[65]

Generic strategies are general classifications of prototype strategies that help us understand different approaches to globalization. The concept has been widely used by writers on business and corporate strategies, including Michael E. Porter.[66] Generic strategies, such as differentiation, cost leadership, and the like,

60. "Matsushita Manages Growth Despite Slower Economy," *Nikkei Weekly*, February 10, 1997, p. 20.
61. "China: Gates Launches Venus Project as Cheap Alternative to PCs," *China Daily*, March 14, 1999.
62. "PC Producers Find China to be a Chaotic Market," *Asian Wall Street Journal*, April 9, 1996, p. 1.
63. "China: Gates Launches Venus Project as Cheap Alternative to PCs," *China Daily*, March 14, 1999.
64. "Mr. Grove Goes to China," *Fortune*, August 17, 1998, p. 154.
65. For more details see Jean-Pierre Jeannet, *Managing with Global Mindset* (London: Financial Times Pitman, 2000).
66. First published in Michael E. Porter, *Competitive Strategy: Techniques for Analyzing Industries and Competitors* (New York: Free Press, 1980); more recently in Michael E. Porter, *The Competitive Advantage of Nations* (New York: Free Press, 1990), pp. 39–40.

are archetypes that describe fundamentally different ways to compete. Believing that firms can select from among a great many different fundamental types of global strategies, we would like to offer a way to conceptualize the different types (see Figure 8.6) and a framework for understanding the choices today's companies face.

To many readers, the term *global marketing strategy* probably suggests a company represented everywhere and pursuing more or less the same marketing strategy. However, global marketing strategies are not to be equated with global standardization, although they may be the same in some situations. *A global marketing strategy represents the application of a common set of strategic marketing principles across most world markets*. It may include, but does not require, similarity in products or in marketing processes. A company that pursues a global marketing strategy looks at the world market as a whole rather than

FIGURE 8.6

Level of Geographic Marketing Strategy Integration

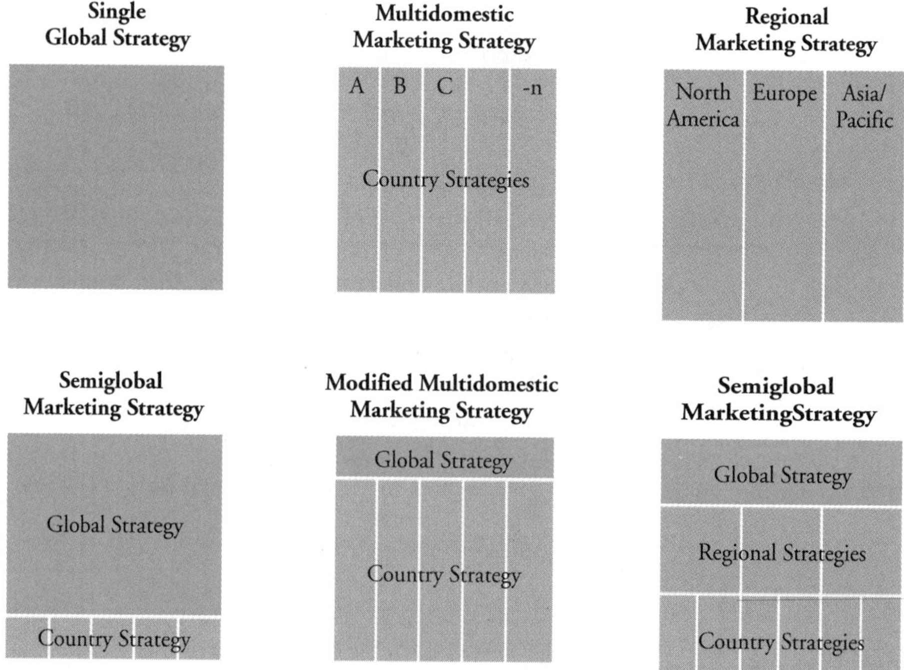

at markets on a country-by-country basis, which is more typical for multinational firms.

Standardization deals with the amount of similarity companies want to achieve across many markets with respect to their marketing strategies and marketing mix. Standardization may also apply to general business policies or the modes of operation a company may want to pursue. *Globalization*, on the other hand, deals with the integration of the many country strategies and the subordination of these country strategies to one global framework. As a result, it is conceivable that one company may have a globalized approach to its marketing strategy but leave the details for many parts of the marketing plan to local subsidiaries.

Few companies will want to globalize all of their marketing operations. The difficulty then is to determine which marketing operations elements will gain from globalization. Such a modular approach to globalization is likely to yield greater returns than a total globalization of a company's marketing strategy.[67]

Globalization of a firm's marketing operations may take several forms. Major drivers are the differences in the environment and the different sources of global logic, as described in Chapter 7. The major sources of global logic can be grouped into two distinctive sets. Customer-based global logics, consisting of global customer, information, and purchasing logics, tend to affect the marketing variables such as product design, branding, and communications. Such globalization patterns frequently are taking place "in public," as globalization of products, communications, and brands is visible to all concerned. Industry-based global logics, such as competitive, industry, and size (critical mass) logics, mostly affect the integration aspects of global operations, ranging from manufacturing to research and development, logistics, and distribution. Because this type of globalization path takes place within the organization, these aspects are often hidden from view.

The two forces—customer-based and industry-based logics—combine into various paths of globalization, explaining differences in global marketing practices among international firms. When the global logic is low for both customer- and industry-based factors, companies tend to opt for multidomestic marketing strategies. Faced with strong customer-based global logic but weak industry-based global logic as a result of differences in the competitive and industry structures across many markets, companies are able to pursue global marketing mix strategies. Confronted with different customer pressures across the world but high industry-based global logic, companies may adopt a global leverage strategy by concentrating on synergy in operations. Finally, when both sets of global logics,

67. John Quelch, "Customizing Global Marketing," *Harvard Business Review*, May-June 1986, pp. 59–68.

FIGURE 8.7

Generic Global Marketing Strategies

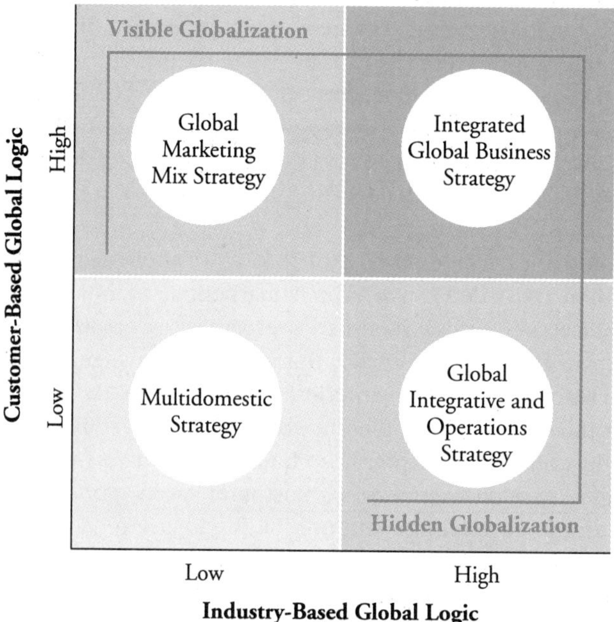

industry- and customer-based ones, are strong, a firm may find an integrated global business strategy most appropriate. Figure 8.7 depicts those different globalization patterns.

Multidomestic Marketing Strategies

Although we explore organization issues in more detail in Chapter 16, some general principles of how multidomestic firms are organized should be introduced at this point. To a large extent, international firms operating as multidomestic firms have organized their businesses around countries or geographic regions. Although some key strategic decisions with respect to products and technology are made at the central or head office, the initiative of implementing marketing strategies is left largely to local-country subsidiaries. As a result, profit and loss responsibility tends to reside in each individual country. At the extreme, this leads to an organization that runs many different businesses in a number of countries—

therefore the term *multidomestic*. Each subsidiary represents a separate business that must be run profitably.

As we discussed in Chapter 1, multinational corporations tend to be represented in a large number of countries and the world's principal trading regions. Many of today's large internationally active firms may be classified as pursuing multidomestic strategies.

A large number of U.S. firms listed by *Fortune* magazine in its *Fortune* 500 list have traditionally operated multidomestically. This includes such well-known firms as General Motors, Ford, IBM, Gillette, General Electric, and Kodak, as well as major service businesses, including Citibank and Chase, two of the largest U.S.-based financial services organizations. Common to most of these firms is their very large percentage of sales and profits generated from overseas business. For IBM and Gillette, more than half of their volume is generated overseas. Overseas firms such as Unilever, Royal Dutch–Shell, and Nestlé are foreign-based firms with only a small portion of their sales coming from their domestic or home market. The ranks of international firms have also been joined by many Japanese firms, as well as firms from newly industrialized countries such as South Korea, Taiwan, and some developing countries.

Nestlé, the world's largest food company, though represented in most markets of the world, is a typical practitioner of the multidomestic strategy.[68] Including its operating companies, such as Carnation, Rowntree, and Buitoni, among others, it has traditionally practiced a decentralized approach to management. Local operating managers, thought to be much more in tune with local markets, are given the freedom to develop marketing strategies tailored to local needs. In the foods business, where considerable differences exist among countries' cultures and consumer habits, competitive environments, market structures, and practices, decentralization was judged by management to be imperative.[69] Like many other companies pursuing a multidomestic strategy Nestlé has begun a move toward a more centralized management structure, which has resulted in a reorganization around major business lines. In order to reap the benefits of global leverage, companies realize that the multidomestic business model leaves too many initiatives to local levels, thus resulting in missed opportunities.

Regional and Multiregional Strategies

Regional marketing strategies focusing on Europe, Asia, or Latin America represent a halfway point between multidomestic and truly global strategy types. Con-

68. "Nestlé Shows How to Gobble Markets," *Fortune*, January 16, 1989, p. 74.
69. Helmut Maucher, "Global Strategies of Nestlé," *European Management Journal*, 1989, vol. 7, no. 1, pp. 92–96.

ceptually, they are not global because the coordination takes place across one single region only, with pan-European strategies standing out as the first real regional marketing strategies created, because of the run up to the European Union integration.

On the other side, regional strategies are marketing strategies across a number of countries, although in close proximity. For Europe, this might include some fifteen different main markets. The fact that several countries are involved with a closely coordinated strategy means that regional marketing strategies are no longer multidomestic either. The thought process that companies go through to determine their appropriate regional strategy across, say, ten Asian markets is identical to the analysis a company would apply to determine the best global marketing strategy across its top twenty global markets. The global mindset is thus closely related to a pan-European mindset, at least on a conceptual level, with the major difference stemming from the type of markets included in the analysis, but not from the type of conceptual approach. The many different regional marketing strategies (see Figure 8.8) typically center around any one of the three large trading blocs of North America (United States, Canada, and Mexico), Europe, and the Asia Pacific area (Japan, and the Pacific Rim countries). A global strategy, by comparison, would include all the major triad regions. Regional strategies may be structured around penetrating just one regional market or several markets.

We speak of a North American strategy if a company has integrated its marketing strategy for the United States, Canada, and Mexico. Passage of NAFTA caused many firms to adopt an integrated North American strategy by merging the operations of the three signature countries. A pan-European strategy occurs when a firm integrates its strategy across Europe. And finally, a firm adopting a pan-Asian strategy integrates its marketing strategy across the Asia Pacific region. Companies may also integrate two regions into a trans-Pacific strategy or a trans-Atlantic strategy.

Pan-European Strategies Pan-European marketing strategies have received considerable attention due to the European integration to create a single European market. As a result, many companies have begun to integrate their marketing strategies across Europe, striving for such things as pan-European brands, pan-European products, and pan-European advertising strategies.

In a 1992 study, some 80 percent of consumer goods companies indicated an interest in a pan-European strategy, but only a fourth admitted to having begun the process of integration, and less than 20 percent of that fourth believed their process of pan-European marketing integration had been completed.[70] Since

70. "Who Favors Branding with Euro Approach?" *Advertising Age International*, May 25, 1992, pp. 1–16.

FIGURE 8.8

Regional Marketing Strategies

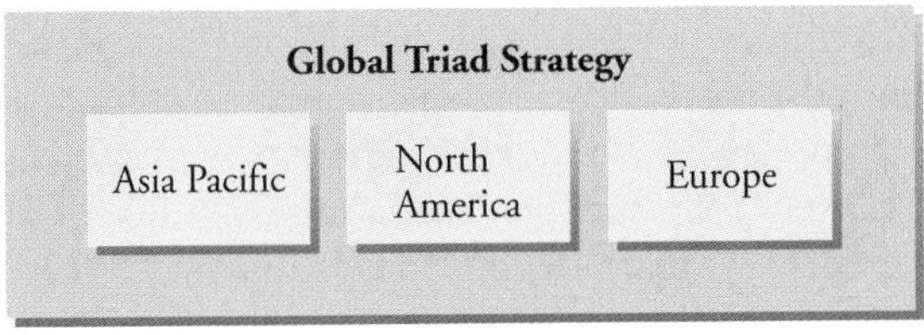

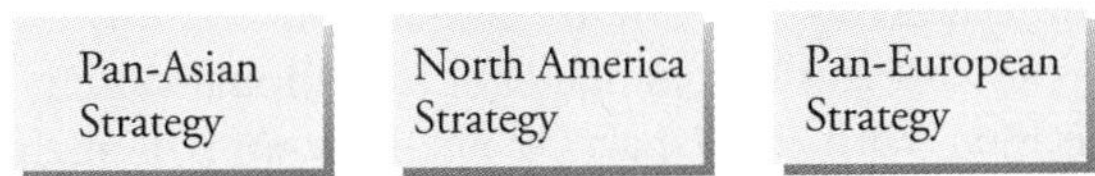

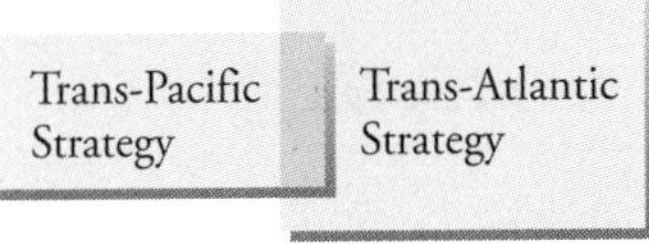

that time, many more firms have begun to integrate their European marketing operations as the European Union moved towards a single currency starting in 1999.

Lever, a European company active in the detergent field, began to switch its strategy in the mid-1980s, after Procter & Gamble from the United States adopted pan-European strategies. Lever appointed European brand managers and started coordinating many of its policies. To avoid alienating consumers who may still require local differences, Lever has implemented this process step by step. Most brands still retain some local variations, but the company continues to strive for more uniform and standardized products across most of its European markets.[71]

Pan-Asian Strategies Much has been written about pan-European strategies, which deal with countries that are relatively similar; the opposite is true of

71. "In Pursuit of the Elusive Euroconsumer," *Wall Street Journal*, April 23, 1992, p. B1.

pan-Asian strategies. Differences in Asia across the various markets are much greater, and thus much less is known about such pan-Asian, pan-ASEAN (Association of South East Asian Nations), or even pan-Pacific strategies.

Among the major companies building such pan-Asian strategies are the large automotive manufacturers. Toyota, with its strong position in Japan, has been building its market position in other Asian countries by tying together a string of operations. The company is aggressively enhancing plant capacity in various Asian countries, closely followed by Honda Motor.[72] Both companies are also building distinct models for that market. Honda launched its City model as its first low-priced "Asia car"; the City catapulted Honda into market leadership in Thailand, the largest single car market in Southeast Asia. Close behind is Toyota with its Soluna model. Toyota expects this car to be the basis for its market penetration in many Asian countries. Exports from Thailand are now developed for both firms.[73] Both Toyota and Honda changed the traditional design practices for the industry by beginning with local parts availability and then designing a model from there. This resulted in models that could take advantage of the low-cost labor pool in Asia and did not require costly components imported from other parts of the world.[74]

Global Marketing Strategies

In the early phases of development, global marketing strategies were assumed to be of one type only. Typically, these first types of global strategies were associated with offering the same marketing strategy across the globe. The debate centered on whether a company could gain anything from this strategy and what its preconditions would be. As marketers gained more experience, many other types of global marketing strategies became apparent. Some of those were much less complicated and exposed a smaller aspect of a marketing strategy to globalization. In this section, we explore the various generic types of global marketing strategies and indicate the conditions under which they may best succeed (see Figure 8.9).

Integrated Global Marketing Strategy When a company pursues an integrated global marketing strategy, most elements of the marketing strategy have been globalized. Globalization includes not only the product but also the communications strategy, pricing, and distribution, as well as such strategic elements as segmentation and positioning. Such a strategy may be advisable for

72. "Japan Moves into Higher Gear," *Financial Times*, March 27, 1996, p. 13.
73. "Thailand Becoming Major Exporter of Cars," *Dow Jones International News*, July 2, 1999.
74. "New Entries in Asian Car Race," *Financial Times*, February 11, 1997, p. 24.

FIGURE 8.9

Level of Global Marketing Strategy Integration

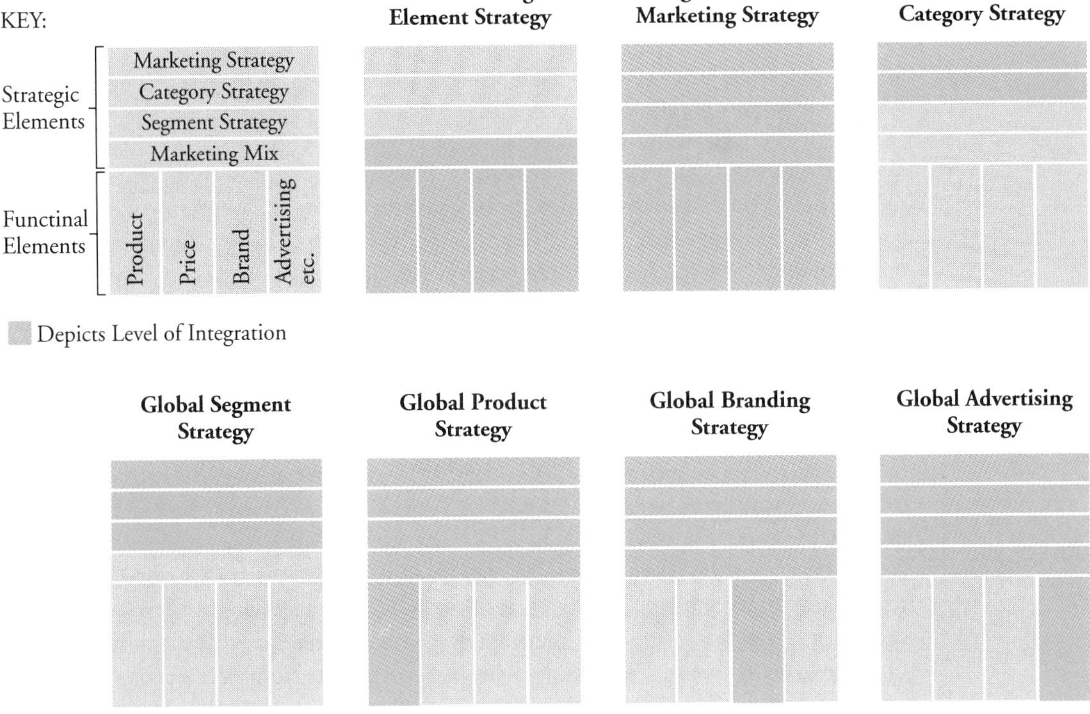

companies that face completely globalized customers along the lines defined earlier. It also assumes that the way a given industry works is highly similar everywhere, thus allowing a company to unfold its strategy along similar paths in country by country.

One company that fits the description of an integrated global marketing strategy to a large degree is Coca-Cola. That company has achieved a coherent, consistent, and integrated global marketing strategy that covers almost all elements of its marketing program, from segmentation to positioning, branding, distribution, bottling, and more.[75] This globally integrated marketing strategy is also aided by a

75. David Yoffie and Richard Seet, "Internationalizing the Cola Wars (A): The Battle for China and Asian Markets," Harvard Business School, Case 9-795-186, 1995.

constant and intensive global logic faced by Coca-Cola from both its customers and the industry, as evidenced by the relentless competitive struggle with its archrival PepsiCo. We cover this classic global battle in more detail later in this chapter.

Reality tells us that completely integrated global marketing strategies will continue to be the exception. However, there are many other types of partially globalized marketing strategies; each may be tailored to specific industry and competitive circumstances.

Global Product Category Strategy Possibly the least integrated type of global marketing strategy is the global product category strategy. Leverage is gained from competing in the same category country after country and may come in the form of product technology or development costs. Selecting the form of global product category implies that the company, while staying within that category, will consider targeting different segments in each category, or varying the product, advertising, and branding according to local market requirements. Companies competing in the multidomestic mode are frequently applying the global category strategy and leveraging knowledge across markets without pursuing standardization. That strategy works best if there are significant differences across markets and when few segments are present in market after market.

Several traditional multinational players who had for decades pursued a multidomestic marketing approach—tailoring marketing strategies to local market conditions and assigning management to local management teams—have been moving toward the global category strategy. Among them are Nestlé, Unilever, and Procter & Gamble, three large international consumer goods companies doing business in food and household goods.

Nestlé, for decades relying on regional executives who supervised many local companies, has adopted a series of strategic business units (SBUs) along product categories, such as for beverage, confectionery, or milk products. Senior executives at the head office took on responsibility for those categories. Previously, the same categories existed, but without profit and loss responsibility.[76] A similar move has been made by Procter & Gamble, the U.S.-based producer of consumer goods. For several of its categories, such as disposable baby diapers, senior head-office executives now carry out the function of coordinating and sharing information across one category on a global basis. Most recently, Procter & Gamble decided to structure its entire organization around seven product categories with global responsbility.[77] Unilever, the Dutch-British company in similar businesses

76. Ray A. Goldberg and Elizabeth Ashcroft, "Nestlé and the Twenty-First Century," Harvard Business School, Case No. 9-596-074, 1995.

77. P&G Moves Forward with Reorganization," *Chemical Market Reporter*, February 1, 1999, p. 12.

as Nestlé and Procter & Gamble, is focusing its business on some fourteen main categories.[78]

Global Segment Strategy A company that decides to target the same segment in many countries is following a global segment strategy. The company may develop an understanding of its customer base and leverage that experience around the world. In both consumer and industrial industries, significant knowledge is accumulated when a company gains in-depth understanding of a niche or segment. A pure global segment strategy will even allow for different products, brands, or advertising, although some standardization is expected. The choices may consist of competing always in the upper or middle segment of a given consumer market or for a particular technical application in an industrial segment.

Segment strategies are relatively new to global marketing. Industrial firms in particular have begun to adopt them. ICI Nobel Explosives, a world leader in explosives for use in various types of mining, has adopted a global segmentation strategy according to key mining segments, such as deep mining, surface, and so on. Since the mining companies are increasingly pursuing global strategies themselves, it has begun to make sense for ICI to coordinate its strategies by segments and to leverage products, experience, and sales activities around the world. Among financial services firms, several companies have adopted global segment strategies. Citibank, a unit of recently formed CitiGroup, runs several segment strategies for different categories of private banking clients. Deloitte Touche Tohmatsu, a leading professional services firm, has adopted global strategies for several key client segments, such as for the financial services industry and telecommunications.

Global Marketing Mix Element Strategies These strategies pursue globalization along individual marketing mix elements such as pricing, distribution, communications, or product. They are partially globalized strategies that allow a company to customize other aspects of its marketing strategy. Although various types of strategies may apply, the most important ones are global product strategies, global advertising strategies, and global branding strategies. Typically, companies globalize those marketing mix elements that are subject to particularly strong global logic forces. A company facing strong global purchasing logic may globalize its account management practices or its pricing strategy. Another firm facing strong global information logic will find it important to globalize its communications strategy. DSM, a Dutch chemical company, faced strong purchasing logic in its engineering plastics sector. The requirements of more and more cus-

78. "Giant Breaks Free from the Shackles," *Financial Times*, February 12, 1997, p. 20.

tomers to expecting a coordinated global approach led to the formation of a new global account management structure with responsibilities that cut across geographic lines.

Global Product Strategy Pursuing a global product strategy implies that a company has largely globalized its product offering. Although the product may not need to be completely standardized worldwide, key aspects or modules may in fact be globalized. The company may elect to add a global product strategy if the product or services offered fit the description of global products discussed earlier. Global product strategies require that product use conditions, expected features, and required product functions be largely identical so that few variations or changes are needed. Companies pursuing a global product strategy are interested in leveraging the fact that all investments for producing and developing a given product have already been made. Global strategies will yield more volume, which will make the original investment easier to justify.

Ford Motor Company adopted a global product strategy. Previously organized as regional profit centers, the company reorganized around global models, or products. At the same time, Ford was working on a new "world car" program to develop a replacement for the older Escort models. Escorts, although marketed in both the United States and Europe, were developed separately for each market. Code-named CW170, Ford's new model is to be developed and launched by the European competency center for small and medium-sized cars, one of five such centers within Ford.[79]

Other companies with relatively homogeneous products have already achieved global product status. For example, in the mobile phone handset industry, the products are largely standardized phones with the exception of fitting to different local telecommunications standards. Although features may differ from country to country, substantial modules, or elements, of the products are identical.

Global Branding Strategies Global branding strategies consist of using the same brand name or logo worldwide. Companies want to leverage the creation of such brand names across many markets, because the launching of new brands requires a considerable marketing investment. Global branding strategies tend to be advisable if the target customers travel across country borders and will be exposed to products elsewhere.

Spending some $140 million on its brand name, U.S.-based athletic shoe manufacturer Reebok embarked on a global branding strategy, consolidating all of its advertising under the Leo Burnett advertising agency. The company wants to become a leading sports and fitness brand in the athletic shoe market,

79. "Ford Maps Out a Global Ambition," *Financial Times*, April 3, 1995, p. 9.

estimated at $12 billion, and in the process achieve a 30 percent world market share.[80]

Global branding strategies also become important if target customers are exposed to advertising worldwide. This is often the case for industrial marketing customers, who may read industry and trade journals from other countries. Increasingly, global branding has become important also for consumer products, where cross-border advertising through international TV channels has become common. Even in some markets such as eastern Europe, many consumers had become aware of brands offered in western Europe before the liberalization of the economies in the early 1990s. Global branding allows a company to take advantage of such existing goodwill. Companies pursuing global branding strategies may include luxury product marketers, who typically face a large fixed investment for the worldwide promotion of a product. In Chapter 12, we look at the various alternatives to global branding in more detail.

Global Advertising Strategy Globalized advertising is generally associated with the use of the same brand name across the world. However, a company may want to use different brand names, partly for historic purposes. Many global firms have made acquisitions in other countries, resulting in a number of local brands. These local brands have their own distinctive market, and a company may find it counterproductive to change those names. Instead, the company may want to leverage a certain theme or advertising approach that may have been developed as a result of some global customer research. Global advertising themes are most advisable when a firm may market to customers seeking similar benefits across the world. Once the purchasing reason has been determined as similar, a common theme may be created to address it. The difficulties encountered with selecting common themes are discussed at length in Chapter 12.

Composite Global Marketing Strategy The above descriptions of the various global marketing models give the distinct impression that companies might be using one or the other generic strategy exclusively. Reality shows, however, that few companies consistently adhere to only one single strategy. More often, companies adopt several generic global strategies and run them in parallel. A company might for one part of its business follow a global brand strategy while at the same time running local brands in other parts. The earlier descriptions were deliberately offered in pure form to allow the reader a clearer understanding. This simplification was not intended to disguise the fact that many firms are a mixture of different approaches, thus the term *composite*.

80. "Why Reebok Fired Chiat, Once and for All," *Advertising Age*, September 20, 1993, p. 3.

Integrated Global Business Strategies

A company that faces a high degree of both customer-based and industry-based global logics is in a position to consider an integrated global business strategy. In this case, not only the marketing strategy, as discussed in the previous section, is globalized, but also other aspects of the business strategy. Typically, globalization also involves research and development (R&D), production, logistics, information technology, finance, accounting, and many other key functions relevant to the business.

In the context of global marketing as we perceive it here, the issues of globalizing nonmarketing functions are beyond the scope and purpose of this text.[81] However, global marketers need to understand the challenge of fitting into a global business strategy. This challenge stems from relating marketing to other core functions, particularly product development, research and development, and manufacturing. Integration means that those functions, like the marketing function, do not exist on a single-country basis only, but that several or all regions share in common manufacturing, research, or development.

In the early phases of a firm's international development, the marketing responsibility is frequently the first to globalize. Manufacturing, research, and other core functions tend to remain attached to the domestic, or original, home market. In a true international business strategy, this umbilical cord would be cut and the functions would serve all markets on an equidistant basis, without bias to home markets. Such resource sharing, or integration, makes sense if the firm faces a strong industry, competitive, or size logic as described in the previous chapter.

Looking at global business strategies, companies have several choices to make. We explain two main forms in the next section: first, the global focus strategy and, second, the global business unit.

Formulating Global Focus Strategies As outlined earlier in this chapter, geographic extension is one of two key dimensions in the strategy of an international company. The second dimension is concerned with the range of a firm's product and service offerings. To what extent should a company become a supplier of a wide range of products aimed at several or many market segments? Should a company become the global specialist in a certain area by satisfying one or a small number of target segments, doing this in most major markets around the world?

Even some of the largest companies cannot pursue all available initiatives. Resources for most companies are limited, often requiring a tradeoff between product expansion and geographic expansion strategies. Resolving this question is necessary to achieve a concentration of resources and efforts in areas where they

81. See Jeannet, Jean-Pierre, *Managing with a Global Mindset*, for more details.

will bring the most return. We can distinguish between two models: on the one hand, we have the broad-based firm marketing a wide range of products to many different customer groups, both domestic and overseas; on the other hand, we have the narrowly based firm marketing a limited range of products to a homogeneous customer group around the world. Both types of companies can be successful in their respective markets.

Companies such as Procter & Gamble, Unilever, and Nestlé are all examples of consumer goods firms practicing a broad-based product strategy. In most markets, these firms offer many brands and product lines. Among industrial marketers, General Electric follows a similar strategy. Some of these firms, however, are broken down into a large number of strategic business units, or divisions with a limited product range aimed at a limited market segment, and within each business unit the chosen strategy may be much more focused.

Firms with a narrow product range include Hertz and Avis, the U.S. car rental companies, and Rolex, the Swiss watch manufacturer. These firms have a common strategy of a narrow and clearly focused product line with the intent of dominating the chosen market segment across many countries. Many specialty equipment manufacturers in the fields of machine tools, electronic testing equipment, and other production process equipment tend to fit this pattern of niche, or focus, marketing.

The trend today is for companies to expect their businesses to develop a worldwide position and for some (such as GE) to become number one or two worldwide. This requires a business to develop its competitive position across all major markets, in particular across the major regions of North America, Asia Pacific, and Europe. The preference is for businesses (or strategic business units in large corporations) to focus on a particular line or segment by extending that offering around the globe. This has also led companies to pursue global marketing strategies per business line rather than corporatewide. Rather than having a single global strategy for one corporation, companies will let each operating division set the appropriate type of global strategy best suited to its markets and industry environment.

A company such as GE may pursue many different global marketing strategies, not just one. Each business is to develop its own, and there may well be different global marketing strategies for different businesses. In this sense, each business is given a global mandate, which means that it is required to develop its business on a worldwide basis. As a result, each operating division such as GE Appliances, GE Capital, GE Plastics, and GE Medical Systems has its own form of global strategy.[82] GE Capital, which concentrates on financial services, is one of the largest units of its kind and consists of twenty-eight operating units specializing in different segments of the financial services market. GE Capital has invested heavily in Europe, where it got involved with GPA, the large Irish aircraft leasing firm, and the card

82. "GE's Brave New World," *Business Week*, November 8, 1993, pp. 64–69.

finance companies of a number of European retailers. The company also invested in financing companies in Asia and in Japan specifically, where it acquired loans from several banks, including Japan's Long-Term Credit Bank.[83] Needless to say, the global marketing strategy of GE Capital will have to be quite different from the global marketing strategy of other units, such as GE Plastics.

Creating Global Business Units Many firms have come to realize that a strong global presence in one given product was becoming a strategic requirement. Since traditional multinational firms, often competing through a multidomestic strategy, have realized the weakness of their unfocused patterns of global coverage, they have begun to assemble business units that have a better global focus. Many are striving to change their business to reflect more a coherent market position whereby a business consists of strong units in major markets. Avoiding globally unfocused strategies, international firms have either retrenched to become regional specialists or changed their business focus to adopt global niche strategies, selective globalization, or complete globalization (see Figure 8.10).

A strategy of *complete globalization* is selected by firms that essentially globalize all of their business units. This pattern is typical of companies such as General Electric of the United States (as discussed earlier) and Siemens of Germany. Such firms end up with some dozen or more globally positioned businesses, each charting its own global marketing strategy. *Selective globalization* is adopted by firms that globalize several, or many businesses but also exit from others because financial resources may be limited. Examples of selective globalization include ICI of the United Kingdom, where some units, such as man-made fibers, polyurethane, and acryclics, were sold off or spun off to strengthen the market positions of others. *Global niche strategies* are selected by firms that focus on one or very few businesses worldwide and exit from others to make up for a lack of resources. Nokia, the Finnish telecommunications company, employs such niche strategies. The company exited from computers, paper, and other sectors to concentrate on cellular phones and telecommunications infrastructure.[84] Nokia eventually became a global leader in both sectors, beating both Motorola and Ericsson which had traditionally been strong in those businesses.[85] An equally focused strategy is pursued by Newbridge, a Canadian-based networking solutions company for Internet service providers, and telecommunications providers, with customers located in more than 100 countries and employing some 6,000 people.[86] In general, companies with a narrow product or business focus but globally

83. "GE Profit Jumped 15 Percent to $2.82 Billion," *Wall Street Journal*, July 9, 1999, p. A3.
84. "How Nokia Wins in Cellular Phones," *Fortune*, March 21, 1994, pp. 38–40.
85. "Land of Midnight Mobiles," *Financial Times*, October 30, 1998.
86. "SAP Chosen by Newbridge Networks for Its Business Transformation Project," *Canada Newswire*, July 20, 1999.

FIGURE 8.10

Global Business Strategies

marketed perform better than firms with a broad product line. Since the establishment of strong global marketing positions requires substantial resources, many firms have begun to adopt the narrow focus model by spinning off business no longer viewed as part of the company's core operations.

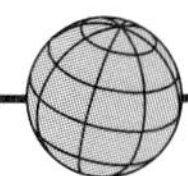

Competitive Global Marketing Strategies

As firms compete globally for markets, the competitive game changes and different elements are considered than those that characterize the traditional single-market competition. The purpose of this section is to give some background on the shifting and varied competitive game by highlighting some well-known battles in the global marketplace.

Two types of games emerge as of particular interest to us. First, there are a number of heated global marketing duels in which two firms compete with each other across the entire global chessboard. The second game pits a global company versus a local company—a situation frequently faced in many markets. Both are discussed in depth here for illustrative purposes.

Global Firm Versus Global Firm

One of the longest-running battles in global competition is the fight for market dominance between Coca-Cola and PepsiCo, the world's largest soft-drink companies.[87] Traditionally, the two have been relatively close in the U.S. market, but Coca-Cola has long been the leader in international markets. With international markets growing much more rapidly than the domestic market, the advantage continues to shift in favor of Coca-Cola. Coca-Cola, with its Coke brand, outsells Pepsi in nine of the world's ten largest markets. Pepsi leads only in the Middle East and is within striking distance only in Canada. In terms of worldwide market share, Coke leads Pepsi by 46 percent to 21 percent, better than a two-to-one margin. Coke derives 71 percent of its revenue from international sales, Pepsi is 71 percent U.S. based. Coke generates 80 percent of its earnings abroad, and Pepsi, 80 percent from the United States.[88]

The battle for global market share is an ongoing one that erupts simultaneously on several fronts. One of the most dramatic actions took place in Latin America. Venezuela was the only market in Latin America where Pepsi led Coke by a substantial margin (76 percent share versus 13 percent), thanks to its long-standing ties with the local bottler. In a dramatic play for share, Coke negotiated with Pepsi's Venezuelan bottler to acquire a controlling interest in that company. The day after the deal was announced, on August 16, 1996, the Venezuelan bottler was switched to bottling Coke, and Pepsi lost its distribution literally overnight.[89] It took Pepsi thirty months and a combined investment of more than $500 million to reestablish itself in the country.[90] Pepsi's other large Latin American bottler, Argentina-based Baesa, with operations in several Latin American markets, also suffered as it found itself unable to dislodge Coke in Brazil, one of the world's largest markets, where Coke leads Pepsi with a five-to-one advantage.[91]

87. "Pepsi Gets Back in the Game," *Time Magazine*, April 26, 1999, p. 44.
88. "How Coke Is Kicking Pepsi's Can," *Fortune*, October 28, 1996, pp. 70–84.
89. Ibid.
90. "PepsiCo's Venezuelan Joint Venture Inaugurates $32 Million Plant," *Financial Times*, May 27, 1999, p. 19.
91. "Debt-Laden Baesa's Loss Narrows, but Outlook Still Raises Doubts," *Wall Street Journal*, February 12, 1997, p. B4.

Coke and Pepsi are fighting it out in other competitive arenas as well. In Europe, Coke consolidated its bottling with a few major anchor bottlers with regional and international reach. Coke was able to concentrate its own activities on brand building and franchise creation while its bottling partners were running distribution and local operations. In eastern Europe, where Pepsi traditionally was ahead of Coke, Coca-Cola was able to change its strategy following the extensive liberalization that came in the wake of the demise of the communist regimes.[92]

A final major arena, and potentially the largest prize, is Asia. While its U.S. market was growing slowly, Coke believed that in the major markets of China, India, and Indonesia, which together are home to almost half the world's population, Coke would be able to double its business every three years for the indefinite future.[93] Although Coke and Pepsi were relatively evenly matched at the outset, Coke was able to pull ahead of Pepsi in China by a 44 percent to 12 percent margin in major cities.[94] Similar to its strategy elsewhere, Coca-Cola relied on anchor bottlers who knew both the business and the region well. For China, it was relying on Swire Pacific, a Hong Kong–based firm, and Kuok, from Malaysia. Both firms had been bottlers for Coke in their respective markets.[95]

Finally, Coke had left India many years ago when forced to give up control of its business. Upon return in 1993, Coke found Pepsi already established. In the race for local dominance, Coke acquired a leading local soft-drink firm, Parle, with some fifty-four bottling plants. Coke is rapidly building up its Indian operation and has already overtaken Pepsi in this large market. It is expected to invite another anchor bottler into India from among its established Asian bottlers.

The Coke versus Pepsi fight has even affected sports sponsorships. Coke, which had landed a deal to sponsor the Argentine national football (soccer) team, used that affiliation to its advantage. Pepsi, in a move to retaliate, signed a deal to sponsor the annual football championship series on an exclusive basis—calling it "Torneo de Pepsi"—and secured exclusive promotional opportunities throughout the season on key games. The sponsorship cost Pepsi $8 million over two years.[96]

One local market where Pepsi was able to move ahead of Coca-Cola was India. Coke had been present for many years but under new licensing regulations was forced to leave in 1977. When the laws were liberalized, Pepsi beat Coke into

92. "A New Red Flag Flies over Eastern Europe," *Financial Times*, June 2, 1992, p. 19.
93. "Coke Pours into Asia," *Business Week*, October 28, 1996, p. 72.
94. "Coke Knows How to Make Things Go Better in China," *Financial Post* (Harbin, China), March 28, 1998, p. 20.
95. "Coke Pours into Asia," *Business Week*, October 28, 1996, p. 72.
96. "PepsiCo Secures $8 Million Argentine Soccer Deal," *Financial Times*, March 4, 1997, p. 19.

India by 3 years. During their period of absence, Parle, a local bottler, developed an alternative cola, Thums Up, and Limca, a lemon drink. When Coca-Cola returned to India, the company believed it would be easy to acquire Parle's brands and then substitute it with Coke and catch up with Pepsi. However, the Indian market had become accustomed to life without colas. Although Pepsi outsells Coke in India, Coca-Cola beats PepsiCo on a corporate level due to its local brands. Coke even began to export the local brands and target them at Indian expatriate communities in other Asian countries.[97]

As can be expected in true global competition, Coke and Pepsi square off in all important markets. There is true global competitive logic in this business requiring both firms to coordinate their strategies across markets, leverage their knowledge and resources, and go beyond the local resources.

Many other well-known match-ups mirror the soft-drink global marketing wars. Unilever, a Europe-based firm, and Procter & Gamble of the United States clash in many markets, particularly in laundry products. The two firms compete with each other in most world markets, and action in one market easily spills over into others, causing observers to describe the competitive action as "The Great Soap Wars."[98]

An equally bruising battle is under way between Kodak of the United States and Fuji of Japan.[99] Whereas Fuji has successfully entered the U.S. market and gained some 25 percent share to put pressure on Kodak at home, the U.S. firm has had great difficulty expanding in Japan.[100] Despite efforts by the U.S. government, the World Trade Organization has not found any evidence of unfair practices in the Japanese market on the import of foreign film.[101]

Local Company Versus Global Firm

As we have shown, global firms are able to leverage their experience and market position in one market for the benefit of another. Consequently, the global firm is often a more potent competitor for a local company. The example of how Procter & Gamble dealt with two local competitors in the Swiss disposable diaper market illustrates such a competitive dynamic.

In the mid-1970s, the Swiss market for baby diaper products consisted of cloth diapers, still the largest segment, and some disposable products such as inserts for traditional diapers.[102] Having observed the success of disposable diapers

97. "For Coke in India, Thumbs Up Is the Real Thing," *Wall Street Journal*, April 29, 1998, p. B1.
98. "Unilever: Bureaucracy Buster," *Forbes*, January 25, 1999, p. 40.
99. "Kodak Losing U.S. Market Share to Fuji," *Wall Street Journal*, May 28, 1999, p. A3.
100. "Fuji: Beyond Film," *Business Week*, November 22, 1999, p. 132.
101. "U.S. Urges Japan to Further Open Up the Film Market," *Wall Street Journal*, August 8, 1998, p. A4.
102. For more details, see Jean-Pierre Jeannet, *Competitive Marketing Strategies in a European Context* (Lausanne: IMEDE, International Management Development Institute, 1987).

in the United States and in other larger markets, the Swiss company Moltex introduced its own version of the disposable diaper. Although a considerable habit change was needed, the company supported its product with little advertising and relied primarily on Switzerland's largest supermarket chain, Coop, for support. Moltex quickly gained a 35 percent market share.

When Procter & Gamble wanted to introduce its Pampers brand one year later, the large U.S. company found the channels blocked; Coop, its largest potential retail customer, was unwilling to stock another brand. Moltex had strengthened its hand with the trade by offering larger discounts and higher margins. In an effort to outflank the blocked channel, Pampers were introduced through drugstores, department stores, and in hospitals through heavy sampling. Once initial distribution was attained, the Pampers brand was supported with considerable advertising aimed at the consumer. Despite its distribution handicap, Pampers became the brand leader.

When Coop realized the profitability of the disposable diaper market, the chain introduced its own store brand. Moltex, up to that time the only brand carried by this chain, lost its most important distribution overnight. However, Procter & Gamble was able to continue to expand its market share and maintain dominance despite a substantial premium price, because the company had continued to build its brand image with consumers by supporting it with advertising. In the end, the supermarket chain began to carry Pampers. Moltex, having lost distribution, was relegated to minor brand status.

Why was Procter & Gamble able to overcome substantial local competition despite a late entry into the Swiss market for disposable diapers? Moltex had learned of the considerable market potential in disposable diapers by observing market trends abroad. However, the company had adopted a marketing strategy that did not consider the marketing strength of its principal and most likely competitor, Procter & Gamble, though P&G was already on the Swiss market with other products and could be expected to follow suit soon. Local market connections to the retail trade were not sufficient to overcome the marketing expertise of a global firm.

Our second example should make clear that local firms can in fact compete effectively against much larger international companies if they compete wisely.

Ramlösa, the leading Swedish bottler of mineral water, is a local firm that was able to compete effectively against Perrier of France, probably the most successful marketer of mineral water worldwide. Ramlösa sold its mineral water primarily in Sweden, with some minor export business to neighboring Norway and Finland. Ramlösa executives had watched Perrier invade market after market in Europe and finally dominate the premium segment for mineral water worldwide.[103]

103. Ibid.

In the early 1980s, when Perrier was repeating its attack on the premium segment of Denmark, Ramlösa executives realized that it would not be long before Perrier would invade their market also. In Sweden, Ramlösa enjoyed a market share of close to 100 percent, and it was feared an aggressive new entrant like Perrier might lower Ramlösa's share considerably. Having studied Perrier's strategy in other European markets, Ramlösa searched for a response and in 1981 finally decided to launch its own premium brand of mineral water. The company invested in expensive packaging and bottles, advertised to obtain a premium image, and increased the price by almost 50 percent although the mineral water of the premium brand was identical to that sold under its regular label. The sales volume of the premium brand did end up decreasing the sales of the regular brand, but Ramlösa was not unhappy, because the profitability of the premium brand per unit was substantially higher than its regular brand.

When Perrier finally entered the Swedish market in 1983, it followed its proven strategy of aiming at the premium spot. However, with Ramlösa already owning the premium spot with its top brand, Perrier was forced to enter on a premium versus premium strategy. This resulted in such a high price that Perrier gained very little market share over Ramlösa. By correctly spotting and predicting the Perrier strategy in advance, Ramlösa was able to design a response that prevented Perrier from unfolding the approach that had been so successful elsewhere.

Although global firms have superior resources, they often become inflexible after several successful market entries and tend to stay with standard approaches when flexibility is called for. In general, the global firms' strongest local competitors are those who watch global firms carefully and learn from their moves in other countries. With some global firms requiring several years before a product is introduced in all markets, local competitors in some markets can take advantage of such advance notice by building defenses or launching a preemptive attack on the same segment.

Global Strategies for Companies Originating in Emerging Economies

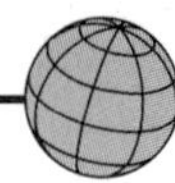

Much of our discussion so far has concerned itself with major international firms based in the developed economies of the United States, Europe, and Japan. One important trend, however, has been the creation of international enterprises based in countries that typically have attracted foreign investment but where businesses traditionally saw themselves as local only. In the early 1980s, international strategies by major firms in South Korea and Taiwan began to emerge. More recently, firms from Latin America and many other emerging economies have joined the select group of multinational firms. Some of those new players we have described in Chapter 1.

The Thailand-based group Charoen Pokphand is a typical example of a developing global company based in an emerging country. Set up in the early 1920s by Chinese emigrants as a vegetable seed store in Bangkok, the company has expanded to become the largest animal feed supplier in Asia and the fourth-largest worldwide. It has pursued a policy of vertical integration in its feed business and has expanded into many other businesses ranging from chemicals and gasoline service stations to telecommunications. With sales of $5 billion in 1992, the company was widely expected to become one of the leading agribusinesses, if not *the* leading agribusiness, worldwide by the year 2000. Investments in China are playing a big role in its growth.[104]

Latin America has also been a place where local companies have increasingly pursued international and global strategies. Vitro, Mexico's largest glass manufacturer, with $3.3 billion in sales its largest industrial company, has tended to pursue joint ventures with foreign investors for the Mexican market. In 1993, the company acquired Anchor Glass, the second-largest U.S. glass manufacturer. This move was prompted by the expectation of trade liberalization with the United States.[105] Cemex, another Mexican company, is the largest cement producer in the Western Hemisphere and the third-largest worldwide. The company began its drive to internationalize with the acquisition of Mexican plants of some foreign cement companies, eventually expanding across its border into the United States. In 1992, Cemex acquired two large cement plants in Spain, taking the company into Europe.[106] The expansion by Cemex into international markets was partly triggered as a response to the invasion of its market by Holderbank, a Swiss-based company and the world's largest cement producer. Cemex has now grown its international operations into some twenty countries and generates half of its income abroad. Its expansion into Asia just recently began with an investment in the Philippines.[107]

In the future, we can expect to see global marketing strategies adopted by firms from all parts of the world. As markets become increasingly accessible to all firms, the trend toward globalization will continue. Firms in developing and emerging economies, which are as affected by the global logic as those based in the developed world, will begin to concentrate on their own strengths and develop global marketing strategies for a particular sector. This is a key reason why

104. "Overseas Chinese Investments in China—Patterns of Growth, Diversification, and Finance: The Case of Charoen Pokdhand," *China Quarterly*, September 1, 1998, p. 610.
105. "Bottling Up Competitors," *Financial Times*, November 10, 1993, sec. IV, p. 4, Survey on Mexico.
106. "Cemex Embarks on a $1.85 Billion Gamble," *Financial Times*, July 22, 1992, p. 14.
107. "Mexico's Cemex Wins Bet on Acquisitions," *Wall Street Journal*, April 30, 1998, p. A14.

managers in emerging markets will need a global mindset as much as their peers in developed countries.

Conclusions

Any company engaging in global marketing operations is faced with a number of very important strategic decisions. At the outset, a decision in principle needs to be made committing the company to some level of internationalization. Increasingly, firms will find that the presence of a strong global logic demands that global marketing must be pursued for competitive reasons and that it is often not an optional strategy. Once committed, the company needs to decide where to go, both in terms of geographic regions and specific countries.

During the 1990's, a changing competitive environment has considerably affected these choices. In the past, companies have moved from largely domestic or regional firms to become global. As multidomestic companies, these firms competed in many local markets and attempted to meet the local market requirements as best they could. Although many firms still approach their international marketing effort this way, an increasing number are taking a global view of their marketplace.

The global firm operates differently from the multidomestic or regional company. Pursuing a global marketing strategy does not necessarily mean that the company is attempting to standardize all of its marketing programs on a global scale. Furthermore, a global marketing strategy also does not imply that the company is represented in all markets of the world. Rather, a global marketing strategy requires a new way of thinking about global marketing operations. Global companies are fully aware of their strengths across as many markets as possible. Consequently, the global company will build its marketing strategy on the basis of a thorough understanding of global logic pressures and will enter any markets dictated by the overall global logic it faces in any given industry.

A global company is also keenly aware of the value of global size and market share. As a result, a number of strategic decisions, such as which markets to enter, will become subject to the overall global strategy. Rather than making each market pay its way separately, a global firm may aim to break even in some markets if this will help its overall position by holding back a key competitor. As strategy begins to resemble that of a global chess game, companies have to develop new skills and learn about new concepts to survive. Understanding and exploiting the lead market principle will become more important.

Globalization of many industries today is a fact. Some companies have no choice but to become globalized; once key competitors in their industries are globalized, other firms must follow. This leads to a rethinking of the strategic choices and inevitably will lead to new priorities. Globalization is not simply a new term for something that has existed all along; it is a new competitive game requiring companies to adjust to and learn new ways of doing business. For many companies, survival depends on how well they learn this new game.

As we have seen in this chapter, *globalization* has become a multifaceted term requiring companies to carefully monitor their markets. Globalization may occur in several parts of a firm's business and may require different responses whether it occurs at the customer, market, industry, or competitor level. As a result, there are many types of generic global marketing strategies a firm may choose from, moving the fundamental choice away from *whether* a global marketing strategy should be pursued toward *which* global marketing strategy should be adopted.

Global marketing strategies are also becoming an issue for firms not typically associated with globalization. Smaller firms, although *focused*, will increasingly find benefits from a global marketing strategy. To make the best of their limited resources, these firms will likely select niche strategies but pursue global reach in many key markets. Furthermore, many of the new venture start-ups will join the global game from the outset as they compete for key markets globally. Such venture firms will implement global marketing strategies early and by design, in contrast with their earlier international brethren such as Nestlé, Unilever, and others, who more often became global *accidentally* rather than as the result of an explicit and intentional strategy.

QUESTIONS FOR DISCUSSION

1. What reasons are there for small firms to pursue a global strategy? Should they do this at all?
2. Investigate the geographic portfolio of three large *Fortune* 500 companies. What differences do you see, and what do you think accounts for these differences?
3. Contrast global with other types of geographic expansion strategies. In particular, how does a global expansion strategy differ from a multinational strategy?
4. How can a local company best compete against global firms?
5. What are the major advantages of a global niche strategy?
6. Why should firms in emerging countries pursue global marketing strategies?
7. Contrast global integration strategies with global marketing strategies.
8. Contrast regional with global marketing strategies.

FOR FURTHER READING

Abegglen, James C. *Sea Change*. New York: Free Press, 1994.

Alahutta, Matti. "Growth Strategies for High Technology Challengers." *Acta Polytechnica Scandinavica*, Electrical Engineering Series No. 66, Helsinki University of Technology, Helsinki, 1990.

Bartlett, Christopher A., and Sumantra Ghoshal. *Managing Across Borders*. Boston: Harvard Business School Press, 1989.

Ghoshal, Sumantra. "Global Strategy: An Organizing Framework." *Strategic Management Journal*, 1987, vol. 8, pp. 425–440.

Jeannet, Jean-Pierre, *Managing with a Global Mindset*, London: Financial Times/Pitman, 2000.

Ohmae, Kenichi. *Triad Power: The Coming Shape of Global Competition*. New York: Free Press, 1985.

Pavlinek, Petr, and Adrian Smith. "Internationalization and Embeddedness in East-Central European Transition," *Regional Studies*, October 1, 1998, p. 619.

Porter, Michael E. *The Competitive Advantage of Nations*. New York: Free Press, 1990.

Porter, Michael E., ed. *Competition in Global Industries*. Boston: Harvard Business School Press, 1986.

Reich, Robert B. "Who Is Them?" *Harvard Business Review*, March–April 1991, pp. 77–88.

Thomsen, Stephen, and Malko Miyake. "Recent Trends in Foreign Direct Investments," *Financial Market Trends*, June 1, 1998, p. 95.

9

Global Market Entry Strategies

COMPANIES PURSUING A GLOBAL MARKETING STRATEGY MUST DETERMINE THE type of presence they expect to maintain in every market where they compete. One major choice concerns the method of entering any selected market. A company may want to export to the new market, or it may prefer to produce locally. A second major choice involves the amount of direct ownership desired. Should the company strive for full ownership of its local operation, or is a joint venture preferable? These initial decisions on market entry tend to be of medium- to long-term importance, leaving little room for change once a commitment has been made. Therefore, it is important to treat these decisions with the utmost care. Not only is the financial return to the company at stake, but the extent to which the

FIGURE 9.1

Market Entry Strategies

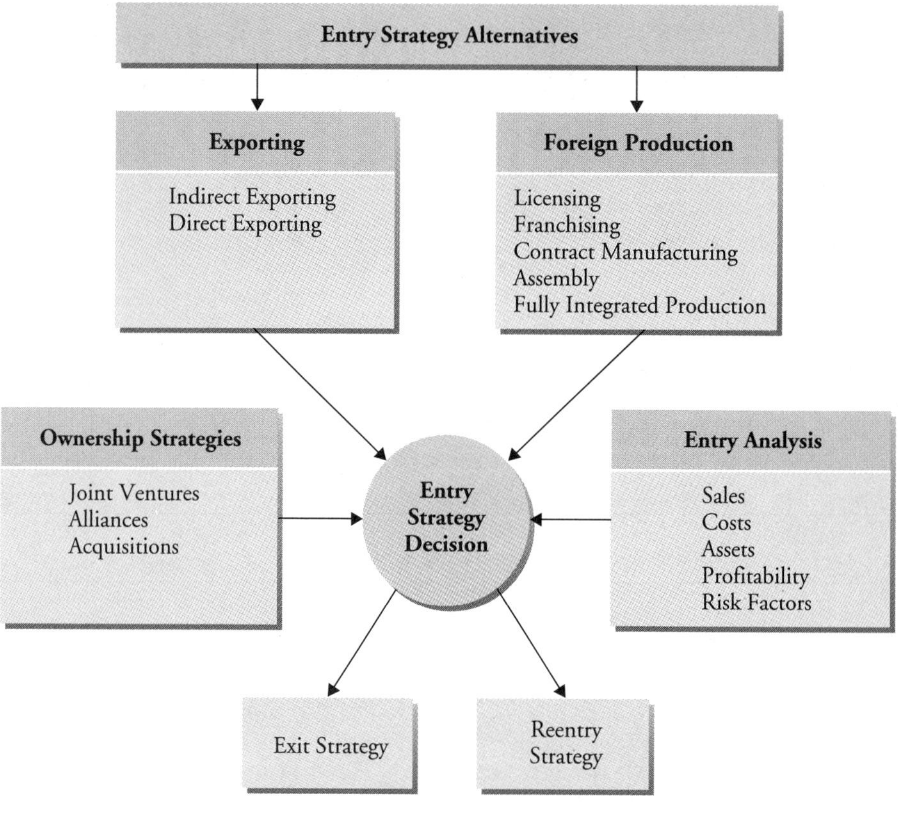

company's marketing strategy can be employed in the new market also depends on these decisions.

In this chapter, we concentrate on the major entry strategy alternatives by explaining each one in detail and citing relevant company experiences. We also treat the entry strategy from an integrative point of view and offer guidance as to how a specific strategy may be selected to suit a company's needs. For an overview of all chapter topics, see Figure 9.1.

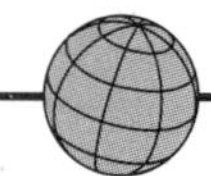

Exporting as an Entry Strategy

Exporting to a foreign market is a strategy many companies follow for at least some of their markets. Since many countries do not offer a large enough opportunity to justify local production, exporting allows a company to centrally manufacture its products for several markets and, therefore, to obtain economies of scale. Furthermore, since exports add volume to an already existing production operation located elsewhere, the marginal profitability of such exports tends to be high.

Few companies are as committed to exporting as Filofax, the U.K.-based marketer of personal organizing systems. Filofax relies for almost two-thirds of its revenues on international sales, all exports from the United Kingdom. In some of its largest markets in Europe, Filofax has been achieving substantial growth. It has also begun to acquire distributors located in its various markets and is turning them into fully owned subsidiaries. This arrangement, however, is the exception, not the rule: in most foreign markets, the company exports through independent local distributors.[1]

A firm has two basic options for carrying out its export operations. It can contact foreign markets through a domestically located (in the exporter's country of operation) intermediary—an approach called *indirect exporting*. Alternatively, it can use an intermediary located in the foreign market—an approach termed *direct exporting*. The use of various types of export intermediaries is described in detail in Chapter 15.

Indirect Exporting

Several types of intermediaries located in the domestic market are ready to assist a manufacturer in contacting international markets or buyers. The major advantage for using a domestic intermediary lies in that individual's knowledge of foreign market conditions. Particularly for companies with little or no experience in exporting, the use of a domestic intermediary provides the exporter with readily available expertise. The most common types of intermediaries are brokers, combination export managers, and manufacturers' export agents. Group selling activities can also help individual manufacturers in their export operations.

Even large companies may avail themselves of indirect exporting opportunities. Jaguar, the British luxury car maker, used indirect exporting to enter the Chinese market. The company appointed Inchcape, a U.K.-based services and international marketing group, as its importer/distributor for China. The same firm was also Jaguar's importer into Hong Kong. Inchcape was to set up Jaguar China through its Inchcape Pacific distribution arm and expected to create dealerships as joint ventures.[2]

1. "Personal Organizers Make It to Siberia," Financial Times Exporter, *Financial Times*, 1995, p. 9.
2. "Jaguar to Enter Chinese Car Market," *Financial Times*, October 4, 1993, p. 6.

Direct Exporting

A company engages in direct exporting when it exports through intermediaries located in the foreign markets. Under direct exporting, an exporter must deal with a large number of foreign contacts, possibly one or more for each country the company plans to enter. Although a direct exporting operation requires a larger degree of expertise, this method of market entry does provide the company with a greater degree of control over its distribution channels than would indirect exporting. The exporter may select from two major types of intermediaries: agents and merchants. Also, the exporting company may establish its own sales subsidiary as an alternative to independent intermediaries. Of the about 300,000 manufacturing companies in the United States, only about 10 percent are actively exporting. Almost 85 percent of the U.S. exports, however, are accounted for by the top 250 U.S. companies, which means that a substantial amount of exporting is performed by many small to medium-sized manufacturers. Most of these companies get started by using distributors overseas. However, most foreign distributors represent other competing brands as well; they frequently push whatever brand offers the best margin.

Successful direct exporting depends on the viability of the relationship built up between the exporting firm and the local distributor or importer. By building the relationship well, the exporter saves considerable investment costs. However, success is not always ensured. Freeman Corp., a privately held U.S. maker of hardwood products with sales of $10 million, already had some 30 percent of its volume in exports to the Middle East and Europe. Through a Japanese trading company, Freeman contacted a Japanese firm that wanted to buy its wood products in the form of extra-thick veneer. The Japanese firm wanted to import Freeman's product, use a new slicing technology, and sell the products locally. However, when the Japanese firm ran into difficulty with the process, it stopped ordering the product. Having granted exclusive distribution rights to the Japanese trading company, Freeman was unable to change the distribution activity of the Japanese importer. To recover its investment in new machines to produce the special hardwood floor veneer, the company ended up suing the Japanese firm.[3]

Independent Distributor Versus Sales Subsidiary The independent distributor earns a margin on the selling price of the products. Although the independent distributor does not represent a direct cost to the exporter, the margin the distributor earns represents an opportunity that is lost to the exporter. By switching to a sales subsidiary to carry out the distributor's tasks, the exporter can earn the same margin. For example, a manufacturer of electronic equipment exports products priced at $7,500 each (at the factory in Boston). With airfreight,

3. "For Japan Inc., a Kentucky Whipping," *Business Week*, November 8, 1993, p. 56.

tariffs, and taxes added, the product's landed costs amount to \$9,000 each. An independent distributor will have to price the products at \$13,500 to earn a desired gross margin of $33\frac{1}{3}$ percent. Instead, the exporter can set up a wholly owned sales subsidiary, in this case to consist of a manager, a sales manager, several sales agents, clerical staff, a warehousing operation, and the rental of an office and a warehouse location. If the total estimated cost amounts to \$450,000 annually, then the point at which the manufacturer can switch from an independent distributor to a company-owned sales subsidiary is calculated as follows:

With increasing volume, the incentive to start a sales subsidiary grows. On the other hand, if the anticipated sales volume is small, the independent distributor will be more efficient since sales are channeled through a distributor who is maintaining the necessary staff for several product lines. Sega, the Japanese video game company, experienced cost pressures from exports in its European operation. Following rapid growth, European sales declined, and the slump immediately affected Sega's cost structure. As a result, Sega had to restructure its European operation, and its sales subsidiaries in Austria, Belgium, and the Netherlands were closed. In those countries, as in many other European markets, Sega continued to market through independent agents, serving only the United Kingdom, France, Germany, and Spain through sales subsidiaries. The total cost of this restructuring amounted to \$245 million.[4] Research has shown that firms marketing products that require the development of special skills or special working relationships tend to have their own sales subsidiaries.[5]

The lack of control frequently causes exporters to shift from an independent distributor to wholly owned sales subsidiaries. Volkswagen, the leading importer into Japan, with a volume of 53,000 VW/Audi cars, had used Yanase as its exclusive importer to Japan for almost forty years. In 1992, Volkswagen wanted to expand to a level of 100,000 units and replaced Yanase with the creation of its own sales subsidiary, Volkswagen Audi Nippon. VW also entered into a cooperation with Toyota to open additional channels. Upset by this approach, Yanase signed up as the importer of Opel, GM's German subsidiary, abandoning its long-standing relationship with VW. As a result, Opel had to switch its previous relationship with Isuzu, a GM affiliate located in Japan that had performed below expectations.[6] Following the switch, Volkswagen sales took a 40 percent plunge. The company reasoned that its \$300 million predelivery inspection center, opened in Japan in 1992, was scaled for 100,000 imported cars a year. Since the existing dealer arrangement did not promise to reach that volume, the company had to go it alone and create its own sales

4. "Sega to Scale Down European Sales Operations," *Financial Times*, February 28, 1996, p. 1.
5. Erin Anderson and Anne T. Coughlan, "International Market Entry and Expansion in Independent or Integrated Channels of Distribution," *Journal of Marketing*, January 1987, pp. 71–82.
6. "Yanase Set to Unveil Opel Distribution Deal," *Financial Times*, April 29, 1992, p. 26.

subsidiary and network.[7] Although sales continue to improve, 1997 volume amounted to still only 49,340 units.[8] In the meantime, GM has been able to expand its linkages with Yanase, adding Cadillac and Saab to its Opel brand in Japan, and planning for a volume of 80,000 Opels in 2000.[9] Although the strategic rationale for the shift was clear, this example shows that such distribution changes are difficult to accomplish.

The Company-Owned Sales Office (Foreign Sales Subsidiary) Many companies export directly to their own sales subsidiaries abroad, sidestepping independent intermediaries. The sales subsidiary assumes the role of the independent distributor by stocking the manufacturer's products, selling to buyers, and assuming the credit risk. The sales subsidiary offers the manufacturer full control of selling operations in a foreign market. Such control may be important if the company's products require the use of special marketing skills, such as advertising or selling. The exporter finds it possible to transfer or export not only the product but also the entire marketing program that often makes the product a success.

The operation of a subsidiary adds a new dimension to a company's international marketing operation. It requires the commitment of capital in a foreign country, primarily for the financing of accounts receivables and inventory. Also, the operation of a sales subsidiary entails a number of general administrative expenses that are essentially fixed in nature. As a result, a commitment to a sales subsidiary should not be made without careful evaluation of all the costs involved.

When Chrysler began to export its Jeep Cherokee to Japan, the U.S. company became dissatisfied as it saw the sticker price driven some 50 percent higher than at home by a range of importing expenses. Major costs were incurred by a series of tests required by its local importer. Eventually, Chrysler came to the conclusion that a lower and more competitive price in Japan could not be achieved by using independent importers.[10] With an investment of $100 million, Chrysler was able to buy a majority stake in the local importer.[11]

When General Motors began to plan for the export of its Saturn car to Japan, the GM division opted to open its own sales subsidiary. With the eventual goal of selling some 30,000 vehicles annually, the company sidestepped Yanase, its Japanese importer.[12] Having to recruit its own dealerships for the

7. "Volkswagen's Looser Rein Unfetters Sales," *Nikkei Weekly*, October 10, 1994, p. 9.
8. "Sato to Retire from VW's Japan Unit," *Automotive News*, June 29, 1998, p. 43.
9. "GM to Strengthen Marketing Ties in Japan," *Nikkei/Dow Jones International News*, March 9, 1999; "GM Japan, Yanase Team Up to Promote GM's Opel Cars in Japan," *Dow Jones International News*, June 10, 1998.
10. "Costly Ride to Showroom in Japan," *Herald Tribune*, May 17, 1995, p. 13.
11. "Chrysler in $100 Million Japanese Deal," *Financial Times*, June 28, 1995, p. 16.
12. "GM Revving Up for Big Push into Japan," *Nikkei Weekly*, August 21, 1995, p. 1.

launch, Saturn could only find about 10 dealers and ended up with a volume of only 1,400 units in its first sixteen months of operations in Japan.[13] Clearly, going on its own in a difficult market turned out to be much harder than Saturn had anticipated.

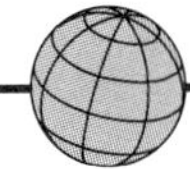

Foreign Production as an Entry Strategy

Many companies realize that to open a new market and serve local customers better, exporting into that market is not a sufficiently strong commitment to realize strong local presence. As a result, these companies look for ways to strengthen their base by entering into one of several ways to manufacture. The following section is devoted to explore the various types of local manufacturing that can be entered—ranging from licensing all the way to fully integrated production facilities. The purpose of this section is to relate manufacturing to market entry and not to treat international or offshore production in a disconnected way. Out interest lies only in establishing production for the purpose of securing a local market. Many companies engage today into offshore production that is simply a way of maximizing product supply or minimizing costs. A company building a new factory in China to have access to lower cost production and then exporting its products to the United States is not truly entering the Chinese market for enhanced presence, and thus would not be of interest to us as global marketing executives. However, a firm building a new factory in Japan with the expressed strategy of improving the Japanese market position is of interest to us. It is for the latter companies that the foreign production section is intended.

Licensing

Under licensing, a company assigns the right to a *patent* (which protects a product, technology, or process) or a *trademark* (which protects a product name) to another company for a fee or royalty. Using licensing as a method of market entry, a company can gain market presence without an equity investment. The foreign company, or licensee, gains the right to commercially exploit the patent or trademark on either an exclusive (the exclusive right to a certain geographic region) or an unrestricted basis.[14]

Licenses are signed for a variety of time periods. Depending on the investment needed to enter the market, the foreign licensee may insist on a longer licensing

13. "How Does GM's Saturn Sell Cars in Japan? Very Slowly," *Wall Street Journal*, August 25, 1998, p. B1.
14. For a thorough analysis of licensing among MNCs, see Piero Telesio, *Technology Licensing and Multinational Enterprises* (New York: Praeger, 1979).

period to pay off the initial investment. Typically, the licensee will make all necessary capital investments (machinery, inventory, and so forth) and market the products in the assigned sales territories, which may consist of one or several countries. Licensing agreements are subject to negotiation and tend to vary considerably from company to company and from industry to industry.

Reasons for Licensing Companies use licensing for a number of reasons. For one, a company may not have the knowledge or the time to engage more actively in international marketing. The market potential of the target country may also be too small to support a manufacturing operation. A licensee has the advantage of adding the licensed product's volume to an ongoing operation, thereby reducing the need for a large investment in new fixed assets. A company with limited resources can gain advantage by having a foreign partner market its products by signing a licensing contract. Licensing not only saves capital because no additional investment is necessary but also allows scarce managerial resources to be concentrated on more lucrative markets. Also, some smaller companies with a product in high demand may not be able to satisfy demand unless licenses are granted to other companies with sufficient manufacturing capacity.[15]

In some countries where the political or economic situation appears uncertain, a licensing agreement will avoid the potential risk associated with investments in fixed facilities. Both commercial and political risks are absorbed by the licensee. In other countries, governments favor the granting of licenses to independent local manufacturers as a means of building up an independent local industry. In such cases, a foreign manufacturer may prefer to team up with a capable licensee despite a large market size, because other forms of entry may not be possible.

International paint firms, with operations in both Europe and North America, have had difficulties penetrating the Japanese market. As a result, many have signed licensing agreements with Japanese firms. PPG of the United States and Courtaulds of the United Kingdom both licensed Nippon Paint for automotive and marine paints, respectively. DuPont licensed Kansai, the other leading Japanese paint company, for its automotive paints. It was expected that these agreements, although not providing any penetration of the Japanese market, would keep the Japanese out of western markets. In other markets, however, PPG decided to stay away from licensing.[16]

The French pharmaceutical company Sanofi has become a major user of licensing. Volume under license, but attributable to its licensees, accounts for as

15. "Licensing May Be the Quickest Route to Foreign Markets," *Wall Street Journal*, September 14, 1990, p. B2.

16. "The Pace of Change Slows," *Financial Times*, March 27, 1991, Sec. III, p. 1, Survey, World Paints and Coatings.

much as 60 percent of Sanofi's own trading volume of about $2 billion. A new entrant into the drug business, the company soon realized that it could do only a limited number of research projects if it had to bring them from the lab to trial and eventual market entry. Sanofi therefore decided to engage in active licensing, letting other pharmaceutical companies market its newly discovered drugs. In the case of Plavix, a drug that reduces blood-clot risk in heart patients, Sanofi licensed Bristol-Myers Squibb to market the drug in the United States. As a result of this licensing and sharing, Sanofi was able to maintain some thirty research and development projects that, on their own, might cost as much as $400 million to bring to market. With this strategy Sanofi advanced to twenty-fifth place in the pharmaceutical industry and achieved sales of $3.5 billion.[17]

Disadvantages of Licensing A major disadvantage of licensing is the company's substantial dependence on the local licensee to produce revenues and, thus, royalties, usually paid as a percentage on sales volume only. Once a license is granted, royalties are paid only if the licensee is capable of performing an effective marketing job. Since the local company's marketing skills may be less developed, revenues from licensing may suffer accordingly. PepsiCo experienced the limitations of relying on a licensing partner in France. Pepsi was licensed through Perrier, the French mineral water company. However, the retail structure in France changed, and supermarkets emerged as important channels. Other French brands, such as Badoit and Evian, did better in those channels. The resulting decline for Perrier also had a negative impact for Pepsi, which lost almost half its market share.[18] This led to the breakup of the relationship, PepsiCo choosing to develop the French market on its own in the future.

Another disadvantage is the resulting uncertainty of product quality. A foreign company's image may suffer if a local licensee markets a product of substandard quality. Ensuring a uniform quality requires additional resources from the licenser that may reduce the profitability of the licensing activity.

The possibility of nurturing a potential competitor is viewed by many companies as a disadvantage of licensing. With licenses usually limited to a specific time period, a company has to guard against the situation in which the licensee will use the same technology independently after the license has expired and, therefore, turn into a competitor. Although there is a great variation according to industry, licensing fees in general are substantially lower than the profits that can be made by exporting or local manufacturing. Depending on the product, licensing fees may range anywhere between 1 percent and 20 percent of sales, with 3 to 5 percent being more typical for industrial products.

17. "French Drug Maker Reaps Profits with Offbeat Strategy," *Wall Street Journal*, November 14, 1996, p. B4.
18. "C'est là for Coke and Pepsi," *Financial Times*, February 18, 1991, p. 15.

Conceptually, licensing should be pursued as an entry strategy if the amount of the licensing fees exceeds the incremental revenues of any other entry strategy, such as exporting or local manufacturing. A thorough investigation of the market potential is required to estimate potential revenues from any one of the entry strategies under consideration.

Franchising

Franchising is a special form of licensing in which the franchiser makes a total marketing program available, including the brand name, logo, products, and method of operation. Usually, the franchise agreement is more comprehensive than a regular licensing agreement inasmuch as the total operation of the franchisee is prescribed.

Numerous companies that successfully exploited franchising as a distribution form in their home market are exploiting opportunities abroad through foreign entrepreneurs. Among these companies are McDonald's, Kentucky Fried Chicken, Burger King, and other U.S. fast-food chains with operations in Latin America, Asia, and Europe. Service companies such as Holiday Inn, Hertz, and Manpower have also successfully used franchising to enter foreign markets. About 80 percent of all McDonald's restaurants are franchised, and as of 1999 the firm operated about 24,500 stores in 116 countries.[19]

Local Manufacturing

A common and widely practiced form of market entry is the local manufacturing of a company's products. Many companies find it to their advantage to manufacture locally instead of supplying the particular market with products made elsewhere. Numerous factors such as local costs, market size, tariffs, laws, and political considerations may affect a choice to manufacture locally. The actual type of local production depends on the arrangements made; it may be contract manufacturing, assembly, or fully integrated production. Since local production represents a greater commitment to a market than other entry strategies, it deserves considerable attention before a final decision is made.

International firms with plants in Taiwan, Malaysia, Thailand, and other foreign countries have little intention of penetrating these markets with the help of their new factories. Instead, they locate abroad to take advantage of favorable conditions that reduce manufacturing costs, and the products are slated for markets elsewhere. This cost savings strategy has been employed by many U.S. companies in the electronics industry and has more recently been adopted by Japan-

19. www.mcdonalds.com.

ese and European firms as well. The motivation behind the location of plants in foreign countries may, therefore, be related at times to cost cutting rather than to entering new markets. Such decisions, of a sourcing or production nature, are not necessarily tied to a company's international marketing entry strategy and therefore are not of concern to us here.

Morinaga, Japan's leading dairy company, built a new powdered milk plant in China not so much to enter the Chinese market, but instead to establish a low-cost base from which to capture share in other Asian markets. Its own home base, Japan, had become less competitive as a result of cost increases and the high value of the Japanese currency. Main target markets were Vietnam, Thailand, Indonesia, and the Middle East. For sales of its tofu, however, Morinaga was considering eventual production in the United States since that market is gaining increasing importance for that product.[20]

Contract Manufacturing Under contract manufacturing, a company arranges to have its products manufactured by an independent local company on a contractual basis. The manufacturer's responsibility is restricted to production. Afterward, products are turned over to the international company, which usually assumes the marketing responsibilities for sales, promotion, and distribution. In a way, the international company "rents" the production capacity of the local firm to avoid establishing its own plant or to circumvent barriers set up to prevent the import of its products. Contract manufacturing differs from licensing with respect to the legal relationship of the firms involved. The local producer manufactures based on orders from the international firm, but the international firm gives virtually no commitment beyond the placement of orders.

Chrysler, which had to abandon the European market as part of a retrenching effort during its difficult 1970s, returned to Europe in 1988 on an export basis. The company needed a manufacturing base as its European sales grew substantially to 84,000 units in 1995 and were expected to pass 100,000 in 1996.[21] Chrysler now has a contract manufacturing agreement with Daimler-Puch, an Austrian group, to build its Jeep Cherokee model under contract at a yearly volume of 47,000 units. The Austrian partner, however, is supplied with stamped metal parts from Chrysler's U.S. facilities. The agreement extends to the year 2004.[22]

Typically, contract manufacturing is chosen for countries with a low-volume market potential combined with high tariff protection. In such situations, local production appears advantageous to avoid the high tariffs, but the local market

20. "Morinaga Bases Global Strategy on Chinese Production Arm," *Nikkei Weekly*, May 29, 1996, p. 25.
21. "Chrysler Aims to Crack Europe," *Herald Tribune*, May 31, 1996, p. 15.
22. "Chrysler Committed to Production in Europe," *Financial Times*, January 7, 1997, p. 17.

does not support the volume necessary to justify the building of a single plant. These conditions tend to exist in the smaller countries in Central America, Africa, and Asia. Of course, whether an international company avails itself of this method of entry also depends on its products. Usually, contract manufacturing is employed where the production technology involved is widely available and where the marketing effort is of crucial importance in the success of the product.

Assembly By moving to an assembly operation, the international firm locates a portion of the manufacturing process in the foreign country. Typically, assembly consists only of the last stages of manufacturing and depends on the ready supply of components or manufactured parts to be shipped in from another country. Assembly usually involves heavy use of labor rather than extensive investment in capital outlays or equipment.

Motor vehicle manufacturers have made extensive use of assembly operations in numerous countries. General Motors has maintained major integrated production units only in the United States, Germany, the United Kingdom, Brazil, and Australia. In many other countries, disassembled vehicles arrive at assembly operations that produce the final product on the spot.

The opening of the Vietnam market in 1991 led to a series of car assembly operations. The Vietnamese government controlled the number of parts to be imported very tightly and prohibited the construction of large-scale plants. In 1996, only 6,000 passenger cars were allowed to be built. To protect their interests in this low-volume but high-potential market, car makers have signed twelve assembly operations, most of them on a joint venture basis. Many of the world's leading auto manufacturers are represented, such as Daewoo of Korea; Mitsubishi, Daihatsu, Toyota, and Isuzu of Japan; and Ford and Chrysler of the United States.[23] As of 1999, fourteen different car ventures were operating in Vietnam, with a combined total output of 140,000 units. With annual demand estimated at only 35,000 new units per year, it will take some time until the market is large enough to support full-scale manufacturing operations for most car companies.[24]

Often, companies want to take advantage of lower wage costs by shifting the labor-intensive operation to the foreign market; this results in a lower final price of the products. In many cases, however, the local government forces the setting up of assembly operations either by banning the import of fully assembled products or by charging excessive tariffs on imports. As a defensive move, foreign companies begin assembly operations to protect their markets. However, successful assembly operations require dependable access to imported parts. This is

23. "Vietnam's Ardor for Carmakers Jams Market," *Nikkei Weekly*, September 23, 1996, p. 28.
24. "Ford Vietnam Targets Bigger Automobile Market Slide," *Saigon Time Daily*, July 2, 1999.

often not guaranteed, and in countries with chronic foreign exchange problems, supply interruptions can occur.

Full-Scale Integrated Production To establish a fully integrated local production unit represents the greatest commitment a company can make for a foreign market. Since building a plant involves a substantial outlay in capital, companies only do so where demand appears assured. International companies may have any number of reasons for establishing factories in foreign countries. Often, the primary reason is to take advantage of lower costs in a country, thus providing a better basis for competing with local firms or other foreign companies already present. Also, high transportation costs and tariffs may make imported goods uncompetitive.

Establishing Local Operations to Gain New Business. Some companies want to build a plant to gain new business and customers. Such an aggressive strategy is based on the fact that local production represents a strong commitment and is often the only way to convince clients to switch suppliers. Local production is of particular importance in industrial markets where service and reliability of supply are main factors in the choice of product or supplier.

When Polaroid Corp. opened an assembly plant for instant cameras in the former Soviet Union in 1991, the company knew that in-country assembly was the only way to have its products sold in that country. Short of foreign exchange, Polaroid would not have been able to get access to sufficient hard currency to keep up an importing operation. Building a local assembly plant reduced the hard-currency drain. The strategy was to earn the foreign exchange needed to purchase components needed for local assembly. Without this strategy, Polaroid would not have been able to cover the market.[25] Polaroid used its local base to develop the market. In 1995, Russian sales had grown to about $200 million, or almost 10 percent of corporate sales. This development was helped by the fact that local regular film processing was notoriously of bad quality, making instant film the choice over regular film. With the market established and free trade possible, Polaroid closed its Russian factory in 1997. However, it was still enjoying substantial sales from instant films generated from its installed based of more than 6 million instant cameras.[26]

When the Indian government began to liberalize its car market by allowing importation of parts and participation of foreign firms, many international car companies began to review their position in the Indian market. With duties on imported parts still at 50 percent, the economic benefit from setting up local plants was great. Many companies announced major investments. Hyundai of Korea committed to a major investment and in 1999 was producing at a rate of 6,500

25. "Polaroid's Russian Success Story," *New York Times*, November 24, 1991, Sec. 3, p. 1.
26. "Polaroid Adjusts Its Focus in Russian Market," *Moscow Times*, February 17, 1998, p. v.

units monthly, a level close to breakeven, and had captureed some 10 percent market share. Some products were also exported.[27] Daewoo, another Korean company, was readying its plant to roll out the Matiz, a car developed for the Indian market, in 1999.[28] Toyota entered the market with plans to launch a purposely built car for India in early 2000 and a target volume of 20,000 units annually.[29] Finally, Honda, another foreign car company to set up in India, was planning to begin exporting locally assembled units to Sri Lanka and steering wheel subassemblies to Thailand.[30]

Establishing Foreign Production to Defend Existing Business. Many times, companies establish production abroad not to enter new markets but to protect what they have already gained through exporting. Changing economic or political factors may make such a move necessary. The Japanese car manufacturers, who had been subject to an import limitation of assembled cars imported from Japan, began to build factories in the United States in the 1980s to protect their market share.

In 1982, Honda became the first Japanese car manufacturer to set up production in the United States. In 1993, Japanese car manufacturers produced, for the first time, more cars in the United States than they exported to that country from Japan. (In 1992, Japanese exports had still outnumbered U.S. local production by some 100,000 vehicles.)[31] U.S. production was expected to increase from 2.5 million to about 2.7 million units by 1997. Major producers are Toyota, Honda, Nissan, Mitsubishi, Mazda, and Suzuki. Japanese automobile manufacturers have also built up capacities in Europe and in Asia.

As mentioned above, Japanese manufacturers' reasons for the local production were partly political, as the United States imposed import targets for several years. Also, with the value of the yen increasing to one hundred yen per U.S. dollar, exports from Japan became uneconomical compared with local production. Thus, to defend market positions, Japanese car companies instituted a longer-term strategy of making cars in the region where they are sold.

Moving with an Established Customer. Moving with an established customer can also be a reason for setting up plants abroad. In many industries, important suppliers want to keep a relationship by establishing plants near customer locations; when customers build new plants elsewhere, suppliers move too. The automobile industry, with its intricate network of hundreds of component suppliers feeding into the assembly plants, is a good example of how compa-

27. "Hyundai to Step Up Production of Euro-II Santro," *The Hindu*, July 3, 1999.
28. "Daewoo to Cut Stake in Local Outfit to 51 Percent," *Financial Express*, July 26, 1999.
29. "India Launch of Toyota Model in January 2000," *Business Standard*, February 13, 1999, p. 16.
30. "Honda Increasing Transactions Between Asian Units," *Dow Jones News Service*, July 5, 1999.
31. "Local Auto Output in U.S. Set to Exceed Exports from Japan," *Nikkei Weekly*, December 6, 1993, p. 9.

nies follow customers. As Japanese car manufacturers have built plants in the United States and in Canada, Japanese parts suppliers have become concerned that U.S. production will partially replace car shipments from Japan and that a reduction in parts volume will result. To counter this possibility, Japanese suppliers have built some four hundred component plants in the United States and in Canada in the early 1990s.[32]

In similar fashion, Detroit's major automotive parts and component suppliers, such as tire companies and battery manufacturers, long ago opened manufacturing facilities abroad to supply General Motors' and Ford's various foreign facilities.

Shifting Production Abroad to Save Costs. When Mercedes-Benz was looking at new opportunities in the automotive market, the company targeted the luxury sports vehicle segment. In the United States, its major market, the company was suffering a 30 percent cost disadvantage against major Japanese and U.S. competitors. Mercedes-Benz decided to locate a new factory for such sports vehicles outside of Germany, despite the fact that the company had never before produced cars outside Germany. Mercedes-Benz chose the United States because it expected total labor, components, and shipping costs to be among the lowest in the world.[33] By 1999, the plant had already reached a volume of 80,000 units annually and was employing some 1,500 workers.[34] However, since we are primarily concerned with creating markets globally, for the purposes of this text, the cost savings issue is less our concern.

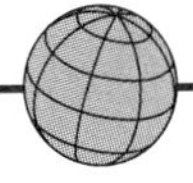

Ownership Strategies

Companies entering foreign markets have to decide on more than the most suitable entry strategy. They also need to arrange ownership, either as a wholly owned subsidiary (discussed above), in a joint venture, or—more recently—in a strategic alliance.

Joint Ventures

Under a joint venture (JV) arrangement, the foreign company invites an outside partner to share stock ownership in the new unit. The particular participation of the partners may vary, with some companies accepting either a minority or majority position. In most cases, international firms prefer wholly owned subsidiaries for reasons of control; once a joint venture partner secures part of the operation,

32. "Successful Transplants," *Financial Times*, March 27, 1991, p. 2, Survey, Automotive Components.
33. "Why Mercedes Is Alabama Bound," *Business Week*, October 11, 1993, p. 138.
34. "Picking Up an ML320 at Factory Adds to Fun," *Washington Times*, April 23, 1999, p. E13.

the international firm can no longer function independently, which sometimes leads to inefficiencies and disputes over responsibility for the venture. If an international firm has strictly defined operating procedures, such as for budgeting, planning, and marketing, getting the JV company to accept the same methods of operation may be difficult. Problems may also arise when the JV partner wants to maximize dividend payout instead of reinvestment, or when the capital of the JV has to be increased and one side is unable to raise the required funds. Experience has shown that JVs can be successful if the partners share the same goals, with one partner accepting primary responsibility for operations matters.

Reasons for Entering into Joint Ventures Despite the potential for problems, joint ventures are common because they offer important advantages to the foreign firm. By bringing in a partner, the company can share the risk for a new venture. Furthermore, the JV partner may have important skills or contacts of value to the international firm. Sometimes, the partner may be an important customer who is willing to contract for a portion of the new unit's output in return for an equity participation. In other cases, the partner may represent important local business interests with excellent contacts to the government. A firm with advanced product technology may also gain market access through the JV route by teaming up with companies that are prepared to distribute its products.

Many international firms have entered Japan with JVs. During the 1960s and 1970s, the Japanese market was viewed as a difficult environment, much different from other industrialized markets, and government regulations tightly controlled equity participation in ventures. When McDonald's entered Japan in 1971, it did so in a joint venture with Fujita & Company, a trading company owned by a private Japanese businessman. Den Fujita insisted on some practices that differed from the typical U.S. approach of McDonald's, such as opening the first store in the fashionable Ginza shopping district rather than going to a suburban location, and owning most of the stores rather than franchising.[35] The chain grew enormously, with some 2,400 restaurants operating in Japan by 1998 and annual sales of more than $3 billion. Each year, the chain adds 400 to 500 new restaurants.[36]

With Fujita's skill at locating real estate and obtaining government permits for new outlets, the McDonald's Japan operation in itself was approached as a JV partner by Toys "R" Us. The toy manufacturer assumed McDonald's Japan's 20 percent interest in the new venture would help land good retail sites. A more recent Fujita deal involved Blockbuster Video, which also helped open up retail outlets. Development of the video rental chain has been slow, however, and the venture has been folded into a new Japanese entity, Geo.[37]

35. "Den Fujita, Japan's Mr. Joint-Venture," *New York Times*, March 22, 1992, Sec. 3, p. 1.
36. "McDonald's Co. Japan Ltd.," *Nation's Restaurant News*, January 1, 1998, p. 112.
37. "Blockbuster Sells Japan Video Business to Fujita," *Nikkei/Dow Jones International News*, July 13, 1999.

JVs were at one time the only way an international firm could hope to establish a base in Japan. Many of the existing ventures, therefore, were formed in the 1960s and 1970s. Today, international firms do find it possible to have full ownership. Despite this change, however, new joint ventures continue to be signed when companies enter markets unknown to them. America Online entered Japan in 1996 with a JV with Mitsui & Co., a large trading company, and Nihon Keizai Shimbun, a large publisher, with America Online holding 50 percent of the equity.[38] Growth has been substantial, with 200,000 subscribers reached in early 1999.[39]

Joint Ventures to Enter China. Given the country's large economic potential, many foreign firms have been attracted to China. Within two years of the adoption of China's law on joint ventures in 1979, more than four hundred joint venture contracts had been signed between Chinese and foreign firms. By 1991, some ten thousand joint ventures involving foreign investors had been formed in China. At least one hundred of them had been closed, not including a number of dormant ventures.[40]

Swiss-based Schindler, a leading elevator manufacturer, was the first foreign firm taking advantage of China's law on joint ventures, in 1979.[41] The company took a 25 percent equity position with the goal of both becoming a major supplier of elevators in China and using the venture as a production base for its growing business in the Far East.[42] Selling a total of thirty thousand lifts over the first eighteen years of operation, the JV has become one of China's leading lift suppliers. Other leading firms, such as Otis, Thyssen, Mitsubishi, and Hitachi, all maintain JVs in China.[43] Schindler did get to use its Chinese JV as an export base, exporting some four hundred lifts and elevators to other countries and as a result maintaining its number 1 position in China.[44]

Gillette, the U.S. razor blade manufacturer, has also gone through extensive JV experience in China. In the early 1980s, the company formed a first, small JV called Shenmei Daily Use Products with Chinese authorities in a province northeast of Beijing. That plant had produced older-technology blades under a local brand name for several years. However, annual production was only 60 million units in a market of 1 billion units, and the northern location was too far away from the booming provinces in the south. Gillette therefore formed a second JV with the Shanghai Razor Blade Factory, obtaining 70 percent ownership and

38. "America Online Breaks into Japan's Booming Market," *International Herald Tribune*, Asia/Pacific Edition, May 9, 1996, p. 15.
39. "AOL Japan Subscribers Top 2000,000," *Asia Pulse*, January 22, 1999.
40. "Foreigners Find China Ventures Difficult to Quit," *Wall Street Journal*, March 12, 1991, p. A15.
41. "Schindler Gives Chinese Business a Lift," *Financial Times*, August 29, 1986, p. 6.
42. "Swiss Lift Maker Expands in China," *Financial Times*, December 14, 1988, p. 6.
43. "China Elevator Maker Lifts Performance Expectations," *China Daily*, June 1, 1998.
44. "Toppest Export Recorded in Schinler Elevator of Suzhou," *AsiaPort Daily News/China Market News*, July 27, 1998, p. 5.

management control.[45] Having had the foresight to acquire local plants and engage them into joint ventures early reaped huge profits for Gillette. The Shanghai plant evolved into Asia's largest blade plant, and in 1998 Gillette controlled 80 percent of China's $51 million razor blade market.[46] The Gillette pattern of market entry into China follows the experience of other firms, suggesting a regional entry strategy aimed at the major regions or provinces. The entire operation might be controlled from one Chinese city, with Shanghai, Beijing, or Hong Kong as the most frequently cited names.

Few companies can match the experience of Thailand's Charoen Pokphand Group (CP) in JVs in China (see Chapter 8). Most observers consider the Thai company with its 110 joint ventures the largest foreign investor in China. With Heineken, CP started to produce beer in Shanghai in 1989. With another Chinese partner, Shanghai Motor Corp., CP set up one of the world's largest motorcycle plants with a planned capacity of 2 million units, accounting for up to 20 percent of China's market. Other ventures are in the areas of banking, retailing, and agrobusiness. The company's top management credits its success to its ethnic Chinese contacts as well as its ability to make decisions quickly and not to bottle up and bog down business discussions in voluminous details, something western firms typically do before they sign on.[47] Although the company went through some restructuring in China in 1999, selling some non-agro industry businesses, CP remains the largest foreign investor, employing about 60,000 workers, with assets exceeding $4 billion and revenues of $3.6 billion.[48] When China first opened its market to international firms, JVs were the only alternative.

Today, with ownership laws more liberalized, international firms can own either all or a majority of a venture. As those firms become more experienced at operating in China, the value and the need of relying on a JV partner might decrease over time. However, JVs remain the primary ownership model for China.

Joint Ventures in Eastern Europe. With the liberalization of industry and trade in eastern Europe over the past few years, many international firms have pursued joint ventures in those countries. Originally, western firms were not allowed to own any stock, capital, or real estate, and joint ventures were thus the norm. Then, although the political and economic situations were still in flux, restrictions on foreign investments were lifted in many countries, and foreign firms were allowed to start new companies with full ownership. However, because of the difficulties of operating in unknown environments, many foreign firms nevertheless continue to prefer JVs with local partners.

Since 1987, when the first JVs with western firms were allowed, more than 10,000 ventures have been registered. However, only about 20 percent of those

45. "Many Chinese Make Light Work of Razor Sales Targets," *Financial Times*, June 14, 1993.
46. "The Next CEO's Key Asset: A Worn Passport," *Business Week*, January 19, 1998, p. 76.
47. "Thai Group Spreads Throughout China," *Nikkei Weekly*, October 28, 1996, p. 30.
48. "CP Committed to Businesses in China," *Bangkok Post*, July 1, 1999, p. 2.

actually began business operations. Because many Russian JVs fail during the first year of operation, the average survival rate of Russian JVs is only about 2.5 years.[49] The difficulties of running a JV are enormous since Russia does not yet have a market economy as we have come to know it in the West. Because of the often unreliable nature of supplies, lack of modern machinery, and lack of technological know-how, ventures that intend to exploit cheap Russian labor or raw material often fail. Ventures aimed largely at satisfying domestic demand, with exports a secondary goal, have much greater chances for success.[50]

The structure of the McDonald's venture in Russia is a classic way of operating as an island within the country and as much as possible independent of local suppliers. With its partner, the city of Moscow, McDonald's built a $45 million processing plant to make its own beef patties, pasteurize its own milk, and bake its own buns. Raw materials for this plant, however, are obtained from Russian sources, and the company has a number of specialists working with suppliers on quality. Transportation is arranged with its own trucks.[51] The initial restaurant is the world's busiest McDonald's, in 1999 serving 20,000 customers a day. The company has expanded to forty-seven outlets and 7,000 employees.[52] McDonald's has invested $130 million in Russia and purchases 75 percent of its supplies locally.[53]

Not all companies have been so successful. U.S. firms make up the largest share of foreign investment in Russia, with more than five hundred U.S. firms operating directly in the country. Following economic difficulties in 1997, some fifty firms left or closed operations. Among those were Dunkin' Donuts, Pizza Hut, and Ben and Jerry's Ice Cream.[54]

A very successful JV is operated in St. Petersburg between Gillette of the United States and Leninets, a Russian consumer products company. Gillette built a $60 million plant and got a 65 percent stake in the operation.[55] Designed for an output of 860 million blades a year, the operation employs 500 people and has annual revenues of $200 million. Gillette began to develop the Russian market with small-scale imports in 1989 and grew its Russian business to become one of the company's top ten markets. Russia, with its 2 billion blade volume, was the third-largest blade market in the world and thus of critical importance to Gillette. With the older double-edged blades still accounting for 80 percent of volume, there was still substantial growth for Gillette's twin-blade systems. A new expansion was announced in 1998 that would employ another 350 workers.[56]

49. "Successful Joint Ventures in Russia," *World Trade*, August 1, 1998, p. 42.
50. Jeffrey M. Hertzfeld, "Joint Ventures: Saving the Soviets from Perestroika," *Harvard Business Review*, January–February 1991, pp. 80–91.
51. "Big Macs Rake in the Roubles," *Financial Times*, June 2, 1993, p. 2.
52. "Russian McWorkers Have Beef with McDonald's," *Wall Street Journal*, June 25, 1999.
53. "Many U.S. Firms Leaving Russia," *Times Union* (Albany, NY), April 6, 1999, p. E4.
54. Ibid.
55. "Gillette Forms Soviet Link to Make Shavers," *Financial Times*, March 5, 1991, p. 26.
56. "Gillette Expands in Russia with New Blade Plant," *Business Wire*, March 30, 1998.

Joint Venture Divorce: A Constant Danger Not all joint ventures are successful and fulfill their partners' expectations. One study found that between 1972 and 1976 some ninety major ventures failed in Japan alone. Many of these ventures involved large U.S.-based firms such as General Mills, TRW, and Avis. Another study showed the failure of 30 percent of investigated joint ventures formed before 1967 between U.S. companies and partners in other industrialized countries. In most cases, the ventures were either liquidated or taken over by one of the original partners.[57]

Glaxo, the large U.K.-based pharmaceutical company, entered Japan with a joint venture in 1994. Traditionally, a local partner in Japan was considered necessary for an international company in the medical field since Japan's health culture is unique. Among other distinctions, Japanese doctors both prescribe and sell drugs. However, Glaxo was not satisfied with its performance in Japan, the world's second-largest pharmaceuticals market, where its market share amounted to only 2 percent, compared with 5 percent worldwide. Buying back the other half of the JV business for almost $600 million, Glaxo assumed full control.[58]

Not all joint ventures in Japan end as failures. One of the most successful is the collaboration between Caterpillar of the United States and Mitsubishi Heavy Industries. For years, Caterpillar had a JV with Mitsubishi for the production of bulldozers and other heavy construction equipment. However, the market in Japan, where building operations must take place under very tight space situations, became increasingly attractive for excavators. These machines were never at the center for Caterpillar; so when the market took off in Japan, the company decided to form a second JV, Shin Caterpillar-Mitsubishi. But the new JV was not only for Japan. It was also made responsible for hydraulic excavator design worldwide for both Caterpillar and Mitsubishi and included the Mitsubishi manufacturing in Japan. Outside Japan, Caterpillar was to remain independent for manufacturing and distribution, while all excavator products were to carry the name Caterpillar. Excavator sales of the combined company grew 75 percent worldwide in four years; in Japan, Mitsubishi recovered its declining market share.[59] Based upon this success, Caterpillar assigned additional responsibility to the JV and now sources key components from Japan for its operations elsewhere.[60]

Corning executives, who have extensive joint venture experience, have learned a number of lessons to make joint ventures successful. Because a partner is involved in all dealings, time must be taken to explain any unilateral decisions.

57. J. Peter Killing, "How to Make a Global Joint Venture Work," *Harvard Business Review*, May–June 1982, p. 121.
58. "Glaxo to Buy Out Partner in Japan for $594 Million," *Financial Times*, November 22, 1996, p. 15.
59. "Digging a Mutual Trench," *Financial Times*, March 11, 1991, p. 10.
60. "American Companies in Japan," *Japan-U.S. Business Report*, vol. 1999, no. 352, January 1, 30, 1999.

A senior executive at Corning advises the following cautions for firms considering a joint venture:[61]

1. Do not enter into JVs with partners that are initially overconcerned with control or how to split up if the venture should fail.
2. The venture must be able to get the resources to grow and should not be restricted technologically or geographically.
3. The venture must develop its own culture.
4. Venture managers need good access to top management at the parent companies.
5. Stay away from partners who are overly centralized and have no experience in sharing responsibility.

Despite the difficulties involved, it is apparent that the future will bring many more joint ventures. Successful international and global firms will have to develop the skills and experience to manage JVs successfully, often in different and difficult environmental circumstances. And in many markets, the only viable access to be gained will be through JVs.

Strategic Alliances

A more recent phenomenon is the development of a range of strategic alliances. Alliances are different from traditional joint ventures, in which two partners contribute a fixed amount of resources and the venture develops on its own. In an alliance, two entire firms pool their resources directly in a collaboration that goes beyond the limits of a joint venture. Although a new entity may be formed, it is not a requirement. Sometimes, the alliance is supported by some equity acquisition of one or both of the partners. In an alliance, each partner brings a particular skill or resource—usually, they are complementary—and by joining forces, each expects to profit from the other's experience. Typically, alliances involve either distribution access, technology transfers, or production technology, with each partner contributing a different element to the venture.

Technology-Based Alliances A survey conducted by the Maastricht Economic Research Institute reviewed 4,182 alliances. Most of these technological alliances were in the biotechnology and information technology industries. The most commonly cited reasons for entering an alliance were access to markets, exploitation of complementary technology, and a need to reduce the time taken for an innovation.[62]

61. "Hard Work on Joint Ventures," *Financial Times*, January 22, 1990, p. 30.
62. "Holding Hands," *Economist*, March 27, 1993, Survey of Multinationals, p. 14.

One of the companies most experienced with technological alliances is Toshiba, a major Japanese electronics company. The company's first technological tie-ups go back to the beginning of this century, when it contracted to make light bulb filaments for U.S.-based General Electric. The company has since engaged in alliances with many leading international companies, among them United Technologies, Apple Computer, Sun Microsystems, Motorola, and National Semiconductor, all of the United States, and such European firms as Olivetti, Siemens, Rhône-Poulenc, Ericsson, and SGS-Thomson.[63] More recently, Toshiba entered a wide-ranging alliance with the U.S.-based Carrier Company, a leader in air conditioning equipment. Both Toshiba and Carrier placed their respective Japanese units into the alliance, forming a new company owned to 60 percent by Toshiba. The Japanese company's $1.1 billion air conditioning equipment unit was merged with Carrier's Japanese unit. As part of this wide-ranging alliance, the two firms also formed manufacturing JVs in the United Kingdom and Thailand. Toshiba sales organizations in several Asian and European countries will also be merged with Carrier units. Carrier will get access to Toshiba's leading technology in lighter and commercial air conditioning equipment, whereas the U.S. firm has been traditionally strong in the large systems.[64]

Production-Based Alliances Particularly in the automobile industry, a large number of alliances have been formed over the past years. These linkages fall into two groups. First, there is the search for efficiency through component linkages, which may include engines or other key components of a car. Second, companies have begun to share entire car models, either by producing jointly or by developing them together. U.S. automobile manufacturers have been very active in creating global alliances with partners, primarily in Japan. Many of these alliances are production based. With the development of a new car model generation now surpassing $2 billion, companies such as Ford have created tight alliances with partners. For Ford, the major Japanese partner is Mazda, of which Ford owns 25 percent of the equity. The two firms have collaborated intensively with the creation of more than ten projects over the years. Despite the ownership tie between Ford and Mazda, the two companies have had their differences over how to cooperate. In 1997, Ford was actually pulling out of a sales alliance with Mazda for Ford-produced recreational vehicles in the United States. Moreover, the companies are phasing out a production agreement under which Mazda was building 100,000 cars for Ford on one of its U.S. lines. Mazda would still like to use Ford as a production base for Europe, and the two automakers are discussing a deal for assembling pickup trucks in Southeast Asia.[65] (For several examples of other U.S. firms engaged in production alliances, see Figure 9.2.)

63. "How Toshiba Makes Alliances Work," *Fortune*, October 4, 1993, p. 116.
64. "Carrier and Toshiba Make It Official, Form Global Strategic Alliance," *Business Wire*, April 1, 1999.
65. "Mazda Ends Ford Sales Agreement," *Financial Times*, September 28, 1994, p. 9.

FIGURE 9.2

International Alliances of U.S. and Japanese Automobile Manufacturers (as of March 1993)

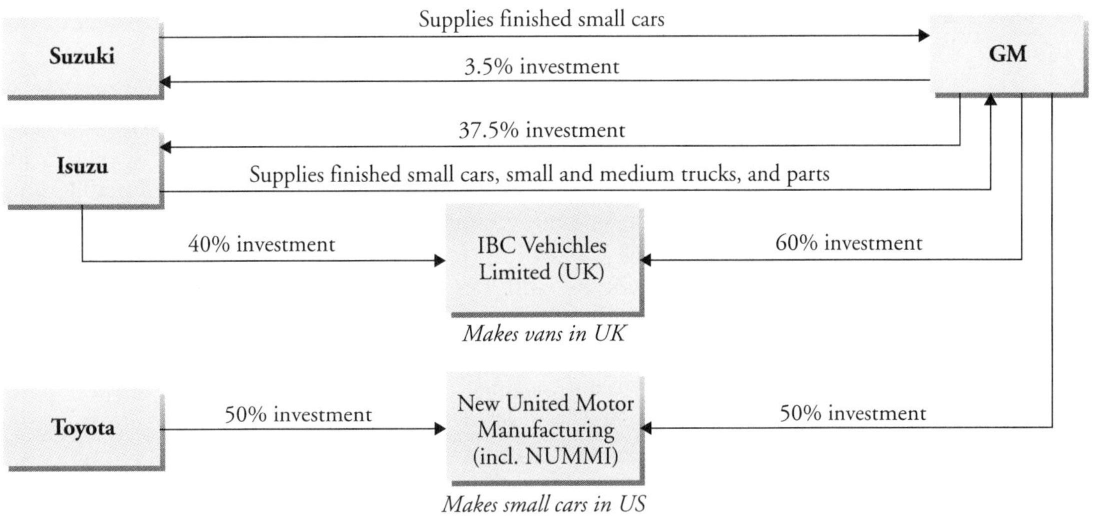

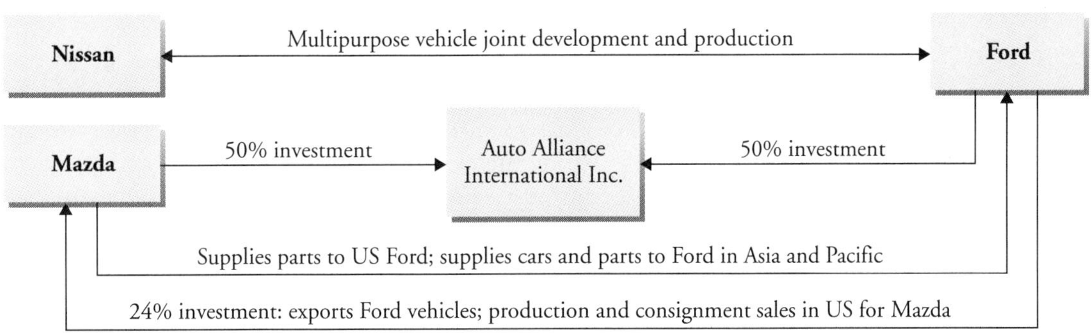

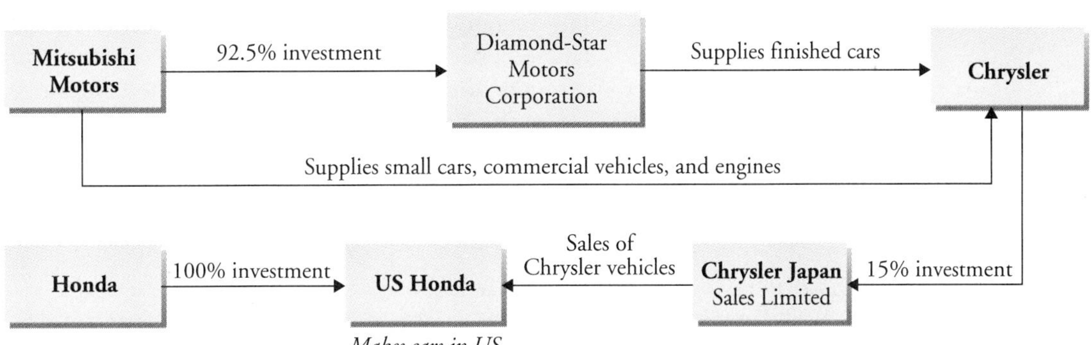

Source: Japan Automobile Manufacturers' Association. From "Japan Braces Itself for the U.S. Roadshow," *Financial Times*, August 19, 1993. Reprinted by permission.

Alliances have also been known to run into trouble when their respective partners changed strategic direction. Volvo of Sweden and Renault of France entered a far-reaching production alliance in 1990. The two companies agreed to a series of interlocking deals linking each other's truck and bus divisions. Separately, Renault bought 25 percent of Volvo's car operation and another 10 percent of Volvo Corporation. In return, Volvo acquired 20 percent of Renault, with an option for another 5 percent later on. In 1993, both Volvo and Renault came to the conclusion that a full-scale merger was necessary. What had begun as a venture of equals (50:50) was to turn into a 65:35 deal, with Renault of France holding the majority. Since Renault was a state-controlled company, this caused difficulties. Furthermore, Volvo was rapidly improving its profitability, whereas Renault was sliding into a period of poor financial results. In the end, the deal did not go through, because of resistance by Volvo shareholders and senior managers.[66] Following the abandonment of the full merger, the two companies decided to unravel their existing cross-shareholdings, and many of the anticipated joint projects were shelved. This shows that even two originally willing partners can have difficulties moving into a full alliance.

Volvo had better success with a more limited production alliance involving Mitsubishi of Japan. In 1995, the two firms entered a car manufacturing JV in the Netherlands, NedCar, that provided for the plant's vehicle capacity of 180,000 units to be shared equally by the partners. What differentiated this agreement from most others was its arrangement for the two firms to build two different models in the same plant. Sharing the facility gave both car makers economies of scale neither would have enjoyed when going alone, and neither company had enough volume to utilize an entire car plant full-time.[67] Things got even more complicated, however, after Ford Motor acquired Volvo's car operation in 1999. Mitsubishi Motor has long ties to Chrysler, now part of DaimlerChrysler and a global competitor of Ford. The production agreement expires in 2004.[68]

Distribution-Based Alliances Alliances with a special emphasis on distribution are becoming increasingly common. General Mills, a U.S.-based company marketing breakfast cereals, had long been number two in the United States, with some 27 percent market share compared to Kellogg's 40 to 45 percent share. With no effective position outside the United States, the company entered into a global alliance with Nestlé of Switzerland. Forming Cereal Partners Worldwide, owned equally by both companies, General Mills used the local distribution and

66. "Driven by the Need to Survive," *Financial Times*, September 3, 1993, p. 17; "Hard Slog to Make the Marriage Work," *Financial Times*, September 7, 1993, p. 19; "Why Volvo Kissed Renault Goodbye," *Business Week*, December 20, 1993, p. 54.
67. "NedCar Gets into Its Stride," *Financial Times*, December 28, 1995, p. 16.
68. "Mitsubishi Motors May Start Dutch Joint Venture Independently," *Dow Jones Business News*, June 30, 1999.

marketing skills of Nestlé in Europe, the Far East, and Latin America. In return, General Mills provided the technology and the experience of how to compete against Kellogg's. Cereal Partners Worldwide (CPW) was formed as a full business unit with responsibility for the entire world except the United States. General Mills initially invested $103 million but has since invested more than $300 million annually to expand the business. CPW passed $800 million in sales in 1998 and was close to reaching an operating profit. Its market share outside the United States had reached almost 20 percent.[69]

While Nestlé was getting access to a new product line, breakfast cereals, from General Mills by making its distribution network available, the company engaged in a different alliance with Coca-Cola. Forming Coca-Cola Nestlé Refreshments, the two partner companies intended to market Nestlé's new ready-to-drink coffees and teas through the Coca-Cola distribution system worldwide.[70] Nestlé had developed the products and already held a leading position in instant coffee. But ready-to-drink products are sold mainly through vending machines. This latter distribution was well known to Coca-Cola, whose Georgia brand canned coffee is its leading product in Japan. It was also in Japan that Nestlé had become aware of the opportunity in ready-to-drink coffees and had already signed a JV with Otsuka Pharmaceutical.[71]

In Japan, the ready-to-drink market was growing rapidly. This fact inspired both Nestlé and Coca-Cola to work together to bring these products to other markets. Both invested $100 million into the venture, which excludes the Japanese market (where both already had their own arrangements). Success elsewhere depended very much on the development and distribution of vending machines. Japan's thirsty consumers can tap some 5.4 million vending machines, some 2.2 million just for canned drinks. However, vending machines in Japan can be displayed in the streets with little fear of vandalism. Elsewhere in the world, such a strategy is not possible. This was believed to impact on the growth of such drinks outside Japan.[72]

The Future of Alliances Although many older alliances were spawned by technology exchange and were contracted among manufacturing companies, some of the most innovative arrangements are signed by service firms. Many of these, however, have proved to be short-lived in a never-ending rearrangement among the world's leading players.

In telecommunications, the global logic of both the operating business and client needs has driven companies to create a series of new organizations. Large telecommunications carriers compete in groupings of constantly shifting alliances.

69. "Is the Cereal Bowl Half Full or Half Empty," *Star-Tribune* (Mpls-St. Paul), August 16, 1998, p. 1D.
70. "Coca-Cola Names Teasley as Chief of Joint Venture," *Wall Street Journal*, March 14, 1991, p. B6.
71. "War of the Sales Robots," *Forbes*, January 7, 1991, p. 294.
72. "Getting the Coffee Market in the Can," *Financial Times*, December 10, 1990, p. 17.

One is WorldPartner, which includes AT&T, the Japanese KDD, Singapore Telecom, and Unisource of Europe, itself a combination of several European firms. The alliance serves about seven hundred international clients, including MasterCard and Whirlpool, in thirty-five countries. The competing alliances are GlobalOne with Sprint, Deutsche Telekom, France Telecom, and Concert (BT and MCI).[73]

No less active in forming international alliances are airlines. Delta had joined Sabena, Austrian Airlines, and Swissair in an alliance termed Atlantic Excellence. When Delta saw more opportunity to anchor its European business in Paris with Air France, it abandoned the other partners. Swissair quickly signed a code share agreement with American Airlines and sold its stake in Delta. Austrian Airlines saw its future with Lufthansa and left the alliance as well.[74] Other competing alliances were Star Alliance (United Airlines and Lufthansa), Wings (Northwest, KLM, and Alitalia), and Oneworld (British Airways and American Airlines). A recent study found that some two hundred international airlines were members of at least one alliance. These alliances allow airlines to offer fuller services and more extensive routes, as well as cost savings. Lufthansa estimates that its membership in Star Alliance saved it more than $270 million in 1998.[75]

Although many alliances have been forged in a large number of industries, the evidence is not yet in as to whether these alliances will actually become successful business ventures. Experience suggests that alliances with two equal partners are more difficult to manage than those with a dominant partner. Furthermore, many observers question the value of entering alliances with technological competitors, such as between western and Japanese firms. The challenge in making an alliance work lies in the creation of multiple layers of connections, or webs, that reach across the partner organizations. Eventually such connections will result in the creation of new organizations out of the cooperating parts of the partners. In that sense, alliances may very well be just an intermediate stage until a new company can be formed or until the dominant partner assumes control.[76]

Entering Markets Through Mergers and Acquisitions

Although international firms have always made acquisitions, the need to enter markets more quickly than through building a base from scratch or entering some type of collaboration has made the acquisition route extremely attractive. This trend has probably been aided by the opening of many financial markets, making the acquisition of publicly traded companies much easier. Most recently even unfriendly takeovers in foreign markets are now possible.

73. "Telstra to Join Global Club," *Sydney Morning Herald*, May 18, 1998, p. 37.
74. "Delta, Air France Play Global Partnership Catch Up," *Airline Financial News*, June 28, 1999.
75. "Aviation Alliances—Who Do They Benefit the Most," *Deutsche Presse-Agentur*, July 1, 1999.
76. George Taucher, "Beyond Alliances," *IMEDE Perspective for Managers*, no. 1 (Lausanne: IMEDE, 1988).

The advantage of the acquisition strategy was already demonstrated in the case of Rover in the United Kingdom. Originally tied to Honda in an alliance, BMW was able to purchase Rover and thus undo the alliance with Honda. Along with the acquisition cost of $848 million for Rover came further investments of about $700 million over the first three years. This funding would have to be compared to the expense of building the same business from scratch.[77] Reckitt & Coleman of the United Kingdom had always had a business in household cleaners in the United States. However, competing with Procter & Gamble, the British rival was always a distanced player. The company therefore jumped at the chance to buy L&F Household from Eastman Kodak. The acquisition included the U.S. brand Lysol, accounting for $360 million in sales. Bringing in several other brands, and adding some $775 million in new volume, Reckitt & Coleman considered the acquisition both faster and cheaper than building the same business on its own.[78]

Mergers are also transacted among leading international firms. In the packaging industry, the most important recent merger was the combination of Crown Cork & Seal of the United States with the European group Carnaud/Metalbox (CMB), itself the result of an earlier merger of a French and a U.K. firm. Involving 152 Crown factories and 190 CMB plants, the two companies complement each other's business lines and geographies. Together, they wield much more power in purchasing raw materials.[79] Even more complex are mergers of two firms with a wide range of geographic interests. Coca-Cola acquired the worldwide beverage interests of Cadbury Schweppes and all related brands in some 155 countries. However, because of specific regulatory difficulties, not all country operations could be acquired by Coca-Cola. Those in the United States, Norway, Switzerland, and some European Union member states were excluded.[80] In general, global mergers with overlapping interests frequently force the acquiring company to divest other units to satisfy regulators, thereby reducing the overall value of the merger.

Nevertheless, international mergers and acquisitions are difficult to make work. In the first nine months of 1995, KPMG Peat Marwick identified 2,216 cross-border mergers, 427 involving U.S. target firms. A separate study indicated that of 89 American firms acquired over the 1977–1990 period, most failed to achieve their targets for their foreign buyers. U.S. companies fared equally poorly, with Ford's acquisition of Jaguar of the United Kingdom cited as an example of a company hopelessly far from recouping its original investment of $2.5 billion.[81]

77. "The World Is Not Always Your Oyster," *Business Week*, October 20, 1995, p. 132.
78. "Cleaning Up Its Act to Fight the Giants," *Financial Times*, September 27, 1994, p. 17.
79. "A Strong Magnetic Attraction," *Financial Times*, May 24, 1995, p. 12.
80. "Coca-Cola Completes Acquisition of Schweppes Brands in 155 Countries," *Dow Jones Business News*, July 30, 1999.
81. "The World Is Not Always Your Oyster."

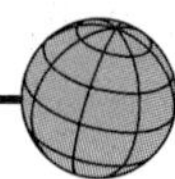

Preparing an Entry Strategy Analysis

Of course, assembling accurate data is the cornerstone of any entry strategy analysis. The necessary sales projections have to be supplemented with detailed cost data and financial need projections on assets. The data need to be assembled for all entry strategies under consideration (see Figure 9.3). Financial data are collected not only on the proposed venture but also on its anticipated impact on the existing operations of the international firm. The combination of the two sets of financial data results in incremental financial data incorporating the net overall benefit of the proposed move for the total company structure.

For best results, the analyst must take a long-term view of the situation. Asset requirements, costs, and sales have to be evaluated over the planning horizon of the proposed venture, typically three to five years for an average company. Furthermore, a thorough sensitivity analysis must be incorporated. Such an analysis may consist of assuming several scenarios of international risk factors that may adversely affect the success of the proposed venture. The financial data can be adjusted to reflect each "new" set of circumstances. One scenario may include a 20 percent devaluation in the host country, combined with currency control and difficulty of receiving new supplies from foreign plants. Another situation may assume a change in political leadership, to a group less friendly to foreign investments. With the help of a sensitivity analysis approach, a company can quickly spot the key variables in the environment that will determine the outcome of the proposed market entry. The international company then has the opportunity to further add to its information on such key variables or at least to closely monitor their development.

In this section, we provide a general methodology for the analysis of entry decisions. It is assumed that any company approaching a new market is looking for profitability and growth. Consequently, the entry strategy must support these goals. Each project has to be analyzed for the expected sales level, costs, and asset levels that will eventually determine profitability (see Table 9.1).

Estimating Sales

An accurate estimate of the market share or sales volume is crucial to the entry strategy decision. Sales results will largely depend on the company's market share and the total size or potential of the market. The market share to be gained is primarily competitively determined. The foreign company can influence the market share through a strong marketing mix, which in turn is dependent on the level of financial commitment for marketing expenditures. The various types of entry strategies also allow a foreign firm to aim for varying degrees of market share. Typically, direct or indirect exporting results in a lower market share than do local sales subsidiaries or local production, owing to a weaker market presence.

FIGURE 9.3

Considerations for Market Entry Decisions

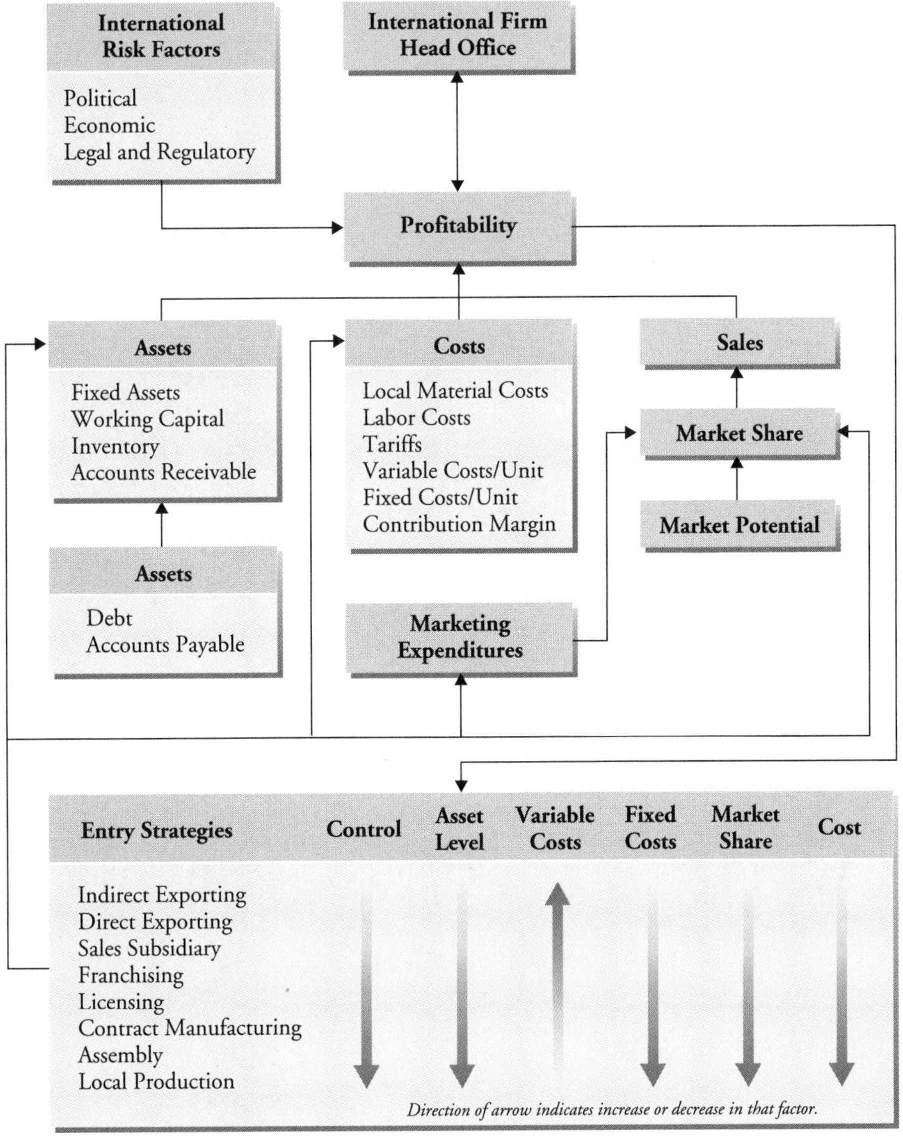

TABLE 9.1

Financial Analysis for Entry Strategies

Financial Variables	*Local Values*	*Decreases Elsewhere (Due to New Operation)*	*Incremental Value*
ASSETS Cash Accounts receivable Inventory Equipment Buildings Land TOTAL	New amount of assets needed to sustain chosen entry strategy in local market	Assets liquidated or no longer needed due to shift of operation	Net new assets required
LIABILITIES Accounts payable Debt TOTAL	New amount of liabilities incurred due to entry strategy	Reduction or change in liabilities due to shift in operation	Net liabilities incurred
NET ASSETS			Net asset requirement
COSTS Unit variable costs (VC) Material costs Labor costs Purchases TOTAL	Amount of VC in newly selected operations	Diseconomies of scale due to volume loss by shifting production to new subsidiary	Net variable costs across all subsidiaries resulting from new entry mode
Fixed and semifixed costs Supervision Marketing General administrative expenses TOTAL	Local fixed costs due to selected entry mode	Lost contribution if production shifted elsewhere	Net fixed burden of new entry mode Incremental total costs
TOTAL UNIT COSTS			
SALES	Local sales of chosen entry mode	Lost sales in other units of the MNC subsidiary network	Net additional sales of entry strategy
TOTAL SALES			

This weaker presence causes a loss of control over local intermediaries; also, to some extent, the exporter must depend on independent firms to carry out its marketing functions.

Of course, market potential is not subject to the influence of the international firm seeking entry. The size of a local market combined with the expected market share often determines the outcome of an entry strategy analysis. Local assembly or production with correspondingly high levels of assets and fixed costs needs large volumes to offset these costs, whereas exporting operations can usually be rendered profitable at much lower sales volumes than can other entry strategies.

Particularly in markets with considerable growth potential, it becomes essential to forecast sales over a longer period of time. A low expected volume right now may indicate little success for a new subsidiary, but data on volume expected in, say, three to five years may suggest a change in the future entry strategy. Since it is often impossible to shift quickly into another entry mode once a firm is established, special attention has to be focused on the need to ensure that the chosen entry strategy offers a long-term opportunity to maximize profits.

Estimating Costs

The international firm will have to determine the expected costs of its operation in a foreign country with respect to both manufacturing and general administrative costs. Unit variable costs may vary depending on the chosen strategy: local production, assembly, or exporting. To establish such costs, analysts must take local material costs, local wage levels, and tariffs on imports into consideration. Again, unit variable costs should be expected to vary according to the entry strategy alternatives considered.

Necessary fixed costs represent another important element in the analysis. Administrative costs tend to be much smaller for a sales subsidiary than for a local manufacturing unit. Through use of a contribution margin analysis, breakeven for several levels of entry strategies can be considered. Government regulations and laws may also affect local costs and substantially change costs over time.

Cost levels may differ substantially from country to country. The task of estimating and forecasting costs in the international environment requires the added awareness that environmental factors of a political, economic, or legal nature can render a careful analysis invalid. Such possibilities always need to be considered from the outset.

Estimating Asset Levels

The level of assets deployed greatly affects the profitability of any entry strategy. The assets may consist of any investments made in conjunction with the entrance into (or exit from, for that matter) the new market. Such investments may include working capital in the form of cash, accounts receivable, and/or inventory, or fixed assets such as land, buildings, machinery, and equipment. The amount of assets required depends to a great extent on the particular entry strategy chosen. Exporting and sales subsidiaries require an investment in working capital only, with little additional funds for fixed facilities. Local assembly and production, however, demand substantial investments. Often, local financing can reduce the net investment amount of the international firm. For an adequate comparison of the various entry strategies, an asset budget should be computed for each alternative considered.

Forecasting Profitability

Conceptually, a company should maximize the future stream of earnings, discounted at its cost of capital. Other companies may prefer to concentrate on return on investment (ROI) as a more appropriate measurement of profitability. In either case, profitability is dependent on the level of assets, costs, and sales. Several exogenous international risk factors influence profitability and therefore must be included in the analysis. The outcome of such an analysis determines the selection of the entry strategy. In the following sections, each of these factors will be described and their possible impact on profitability will be indicated.

Assessing International Risk Factors Aside from the normal business risk factors that every company also confronts in its home market, the existence of more than one economy or country involves additional risks. Each country hosting a foreign subsidiary may take actions of a political, economic, or regulatory nature that can completely obliterate any carefully drawn-up business plan. As discussed in Chapter 4, political turmoil in many parts of the world greatly affects business and investment conditions. For example, following the departure of the shah of Iran in 1979, the country's political stability deteriorated to such an extent that business could not be conducted as usual. Many foreign operations were taken over by the government or ceased to exist. Similar effects on businesses were witnessed in other countries, particularly Nicaragua (in 1979) and Turkey (1978 to 1980).

As covered in Chapter 2, different economic systems add to uncertainties, which are reflected in currency changes or diverging economic trends. Manufacturing costs are particularly sensitive to various changes. Many times, a company has shifted production from one country to another on the basis of the latest cost data only to find out a few years later that costs have changed because of fluctuations of macroeconomic variables beyond company control. Local labor costs, for example, are very sensitive to local inflation and foreign currency changes; they have fluctuated considerably over the years.

Maintaining Flexibility The ability to switch from one mode of entry into another may be an important requirement of the initial arrangement. Data General of the United States was able to shift its entry strategy following the changes in the investment laws in Japan in 1978.[82] Data General had, in 1971, signed a licensing agreement with a consortium of seven Japanese companies, called Nippon Minicomputer. A few years later, Data General realized that most of its customers in Japan were other multinationals who wanted to buy Data General minicomputers through direct purchase agreements with its head office in the United States. Since the company could not make a licensee obey such agreements, Data General negotiated to buy a 50 percent stake in Nippon Minicomputer in 1979, which was later raised to 85 percent in 1982. The local organization was changed to Nippon Data General (NDG), but Japanese management was left in place. This step approach to an integrated production and sales organization was very successful for Data General, and the company was able to obtain a leadership position in the Japanese market.

Assessing Total Company Impact Once profitability on a local level has been established and the relevant international risk factors included, analysis must turn to the company as a whole. The expected profits of the new market entry have to be analyzed along with the overall impact on the total organization. Replacing imports with local production may cause a loss of sales or output at the existing facility, which may counterbalance the new profits gained from the plant opening. Such an impact may also exist with respect to assets, costs, and sales, depending on the entry strategy. As a result, the global firm aims at maximizing incremental profits achieved on incremental assets and sales. A promising opportunity abroad may suddenly appear less attractive when allowances are made for displacement in other parts of a global company.

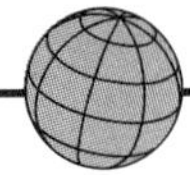

Entry Strategy Configuration

This chapter has been dedicated to explaining the various entry strategy modes available to international and global firms. In reality, however, most entry strategies consist of a combination of different formats. We refer to the process of deciding on the best possible entry strategy mix as *entry strategy configuration.*

Rarely do companies employ a single entry mode per country. A company may open up a subsidiary that produces some products locally and imports others to round out its product line. The same foreign subsidiary may even export to other foreign subsidiaries, combining exporting, importing, and local manufacturing into one unit. Furthermore, many international firms grant licenses for patents and trademarks to foreign operations, even when they are fully owned. This is done for additional protection or to make the transfer of profits easier. In many

82. "Data General Shows Friendly Takeovers Are Possible in Japan," *Business International*, August 6, 1982, p. 249.

cases, companies have bundled such entry forms into a single legal unit, in effect *layering* several entry strategy options on top of each other.

Bundling of entry strategies is the process of providing just one legal unit in a given country or market. In other words, the foreign company sets up a single company in one country and uses that company as a legal umbrella for all its entry activities. However, such strategies have become less typical—particularly in larger markets, many firms have begun to unbundle their operations.

When a company *unbundles*, it essentially divides its operations in a country into different companies. The local manufacturing plant may be incorporated separately from the sales subsidiary. When this occurs, companies may select different ownership strategies, for instance, allowing a JV in one operation while keeping full ownership in another part. Such unbundling becomes possible in the larger markets, such as the United States, Germany, and Japan. It also allows the company to run several companies or product lines in parallel. ICI, the large U.K. chemicals company, operates several subsidiaries in the United States that report to different product line companies back in the United Kingdom and are independently operated. Global firms granting global mandates to their product divisions will find that each division will need to develop its own entry strategy for key markets.

Portal or E-Business Entry Strategies

The technological revolution of the Internet with its wide range of connected and networked computers has given rise to the virtual entry strategy. Using electronic means, primarily web pages, email, file transfer, and related communications tools, firms have begun to enter markets without ever touching down. A company that establishes a server on the Internet and opens up a web page can be contacted from anywhere in the world. Consumers and industrial buyers who use modern Internet browsers, such as Netscape, can search for products, services, or companies and in many instances even make purchases online.

Of 5 million Internet hosts in 1995, about 3.372 million were in North America, compared to 1 million in western Europe, 151,000 in Asia, and 192,000 in the Pacific Area. About 27 percent of these hosts served commercial purposes. About 80,000 companies were connected to the Internet in 1995, with sales still relatively small.[83] By 1999, the number of global Internet users had passed 145 million by some counts. Business-to-consumer volume in e-commerce was expected to grow from $10 billion to $400 billion by 2002, and business-to-business trade from $43 billion to $1.3 trillion by 2003. Cisco, a U.S.-based Internet equipment supplier, believes that by 2010 some 25 percent of all retail transactions would be Internet-based.[84]

83. "The Internet," Survey, *Economist*, July 1, 1995.
84. "E-Commerce to Take Retailing to Another Realm," *South China Morning Post*, July 10, 1999, p. 2.

Whatever the forecasts, most experts agree that the opportunity for Internet-based commerce will be huge. Although the cost of creating a web presence is small, global marketing alone is beyond a mere web page. Once a business has a web address, interested buyers from anywhere in the world can contact the address. Consequently, the Internet will eliminate some of the hurdles that plagued smaller firms from competing beyond their borders.[85] Although it is difficult to guess the actual trading done from international customers at all Internet sites, the trend is clear if one follows some major Internet companies.

Amazon.com, the leading Internet retailer, early on established a presence overseas. Following its web presence in the United States, it opened a second one in the United Kingdom (Amazon.Co.uk) by acquiring Bookpages, an existing U.K. Internet book retailer. In Germany (Amazon.de), the company purchased Telebuch. Both international web sites are patterned after the U.S. one. The German site is entirely in German, and the merchandise inventory is specific to the different markets.[86] Although first in the United States, Amazon is typically encountering established foreign competitors in overseas markets. Each of its own operations has its own fulfillment operation that packages and ships from local stocks. A customer, however, can always order from the United States but will have to pay the extra charges for shipment and delivery.

U.S. portal sites, such as America Online (AOL), are also engaged in expanding internationally. Different from Amazon, AOL has tended to engage in joint ventures in overseas markets. In Europe, AOL established a venture in 1995 with Bertelsmann, a leading German media company. Its Japan operation was established in 1997 with Mitsui & Co., a Japanese trading house, and Nihon Keizai Shimbun, a publisher. Although clearly dominant in the United States, AOL is facing stiff local competition. In the United Kingdom, the company has to overcome the aggressive marketing of Freeserve, a U.K.-based Internet service provider that dropped monthly charges.[87] In Brazil, with its 6.8 million Internet users one of the world's most important markets, AOL ran into trouble with its recent start as it had to battle established local providers, some supported by foreign venture capital. AOL is cooperating in Latin America with the Venezuela-based Cisneros group.[88] AOL wants to expand its international membership. As of 1999, in the United States, it had 19 million members, and 3.2 million internationally.[89]

E-commerce is big business in most foreign markets. It is expanding rapidly through Asia, where China, Australia, South Korea, Taiwan, and Hong Kong are

85. "The Internet Age," *Business Week*, 70th Anniversary Issue, October 4, 1999, p. 70.
86. "Internet Retailing: A New Leaf," *Economist*, October 23, 1999, p. 72.
87. "AOL Searching for New President of Foreign Unit," *Wall Street Journal*, October 28, 1999, p. B21.
88. "SOL Waltzes into Brazil, Unprepared for the Samba," *Wall Street Journal*, December 11, 1999, p. B2.
89. "AOL Searching for New President of Foreign Unit."

the main user markets. Forecasts vary widely, but one source estimated the number of Chinese Internet users at about 500,000 in 1999, expected to grow to 80 million in a few years as access to personal computers and the Net expand.[90] In India, where the creation of commercial software has become a major export industry, the leading portal service, Satyam Infoway, has acquired a smaller company with a search engine that provides access to Indian sports, culture, and food recipes, something of great value to the many Indians living overseas. All main players in this market are local and provide local content. Currently, India, with its small population of 500,000 Internet subscribers, is yet too small for a large number of players.[91]

A third group of major Internet players with global ambitions are service providers, such as Schwab or Merrill Lynch. Although the first wave of Merrill's online trading is targeted for U.S. brokerage clients, the future points toward using this service abroad.[92] Financial services firms, however, battle with legal restrictions and the need to obtain regulatory approval for offering certain services to a given country. On the other hand, it is virtually impossible for governments to police the access. Most likely, financial services firms will have to provide special access, or qualifying service, to local customers before they can sign on. Given the low cost of the Internet, it is very likely that many more established firms will use the Internet as the first point of contact for countries where they do not yet have a major base.

There are many challenges to would-be Internet-based global marketers. One of the biggest is language. One research company estimated that by 2002, 60 percent of the world's Internet users and 40 percent of the e-commerce revenue will be from outside the United States, mostly from non-English-speaking areas. Although many people are able to surf the Net in English, they still prefer to do transactions in their local language. The second big challenge is the fulfillment side of the e-business. Here we are dealing with completing a sale, shipping, collecting funds, and providing after-sales service to customers all over the world.[93]

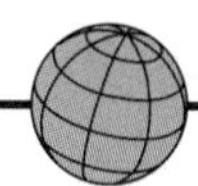

Exit Strategies

Circumstances may make companies want to leave a country or market. Other than the failure to achieve marketing objectives, there may be political, economic, or legal reasons for a company to want to dissolve or sell an operation. International companies have to be aware of the high costs attached to the liquida-

90. "China's Online Date with Destiny," *Financial Times*, December 18, 1999, p. 8.
91. "Portals in a Storm as Contest in India Heats Up," *Financial Times*, December 10, 1999, p. 22.
92. "Joining Crowd, Merrill to Offer On-Line Trades," *Herald Tribune International*, June 3, 1999, p. 13.
93. "Idiom App Speaks Your Language," *Computer World*, May 31, 1999, p. 66.

tion of foreign operations; substantial amounts of severance pay may have to be paid to employees, and any loss of credibility in other markets can hurt future prospects.

Consolidation

Sometimes, an international firm may need to withdraw from a market to consolidate its operations. This may mean a consolidation of factories from many to fewer such plants. Production consolidation, when not combined with an actual market withdrawal, is not really what we are concerned with here. Rather, our concern is a company's actual abandoning its plan to serve a certain market or country.

In the 1970s, several U.S.-based multinational firms had to retrench their international operations and shrink back onto a U.S. base. Chrysler sold its European operations in the United Kingdom and France to European car manufacturers, mostly Peugeot, and concentrated on the U.S. market. In the late 1980s, Avon Products sold 60 percent of its successful Japanese company for some $400 million. This came after it offered 40 percent of its Japanese company to the public in 1987. The money was needed to reduce Avon's debt in the United States. Avon had started its Japanese subsidiary twenty years before and had reached sales of $285 million.[94]

Nissan, the Japanese car manufacturer, had been assembling cars in Australia since 1976. The smallest of the five assemblers, Nissan lost money after 1989. Its 10 percent market share was not sufficient to support a local assembly operation.[95] Nissan's exit from Australia in 1992 related to production only and not to its selling and dealership operations. However, the company suffered for many years as the Japanese yen went through a strong period and artificially raised prices on cars imported from Japan. The company did not reach breakeven again until 1997.[96]

Political Reasons

Changing political situations have at times forced companies to leave markets. Procter & Gamble, the giant U.S.-based consumer goods manufacturer, sold its Cuban subsidiary in 1958, one year before Castro won Cuba's civil war. P&G also disposed of its Chilean subsidiary shortly before the election victory of a leftist regime in Chile in 1970. Had the company stayed in those markets, the subsidiaries would most likely have been expropriated.

94. "Saying Sayonara Is Such Sweet Sorrow," *Business Week*, March 12, 1990, p. 52; "Avon Agrees to Sell Rest of Japanese Unit," *New York Times*, February 22, 1991, p. D5.
95. "Auto Industry Seen Paring Operations," *Nikkei Weekly*, February 15, 1992, p. 8.
96. "Nissan Gets Back on Track," *The Age*, April 20, 1999, p. 2.

Changing government regulations can at times pose problems, prompting some companies to leave a country. India is a case in point. There, the government adopted its Foreign Exchange Regulation Act in 1973 to require most foreign companies to divest themselves of 60 percent of their subsidiaries by the end of 1977. Companies that manufactured substantially for export or whose operations used advanced technology were exempted. Since IBM's Indian operation did little exporting and sold mostly older computer models, the computer manufacturer was asked to sell 60 percent of its equity to Indian citizens. Coca-Cola decided to leave the market rather than sell a controlling ownership to local investors.

Exit strategies can also be the result of negative reactions in a firm's home market. When the political situation in South Africa was open to challenge on moral grounds, many multinational corporations exited that country by abandoning or selling their local subsidiaries. In 1984, some 325 U.S. companies were maintaining operations in South Africa. Two years later, this number had decreased to 265; the total amount of U.S. direct foreign investment was estimated at U.S. $1.3 billion. One of the U.S. firms that left was Coca-Cola; others included General Motors, IBM, Motorola, and General Electric. Some European firms also withdrew from that country, Alfa-Romeo of Italy, Barclays Bank of the United Kingdom, and Renault of France among them.[97]

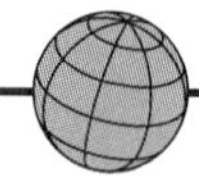

Reentry Strategies

Several of the markets left by international firms over the past decades have changed in attractiveness, making companies reverse their exit decisions and enter those markets a second time. In India, for example, the government relaxed its restrictive ownership legislation in view of its overall policy of economic liberalization. When the restrictive Foreign Exchange Regulation Act was introduced in India in 1973, some two hundred of five hundred companies with large investments exited, selling their stakes to local companies. Following liberalization in August 1991, approximately one hundred firms raised their equity stakes to the allowable 51 percent. Typical of this strategy is Gillette, which had entered India with a minority stake in the mid-1980s.[98] Coca-Cola, after having left the market completely in 1977, reentered again in 1993 to counter the earlier first-time entry of rival PepsiCo. Coca-Cola accomplished its return to the Indian market by acquiring Parle, India's leading local cola company.[99] General Motors returned to India after a much longer absence. After producing cars in India from 1928 to

97. "South Africa: Time to Stay—or Go?" *Fortune*, August 4, 1986, p. 45; "If Coke Has Its Way, Blacks Will Soon Own 'The Real Thing,'" *Business Week*, March 27, 1987, p. 56; "High Risks and Low Returns," *Financial Times*, November 25, 1986, p. 10.
98. "Back in Charge," *Far Eastern Economic Review*, July 8, 1993.
99. "Coca-Cola Invasion Starts to Worry Businessmen," *Financial Times*, November 9, 1993, p. 6.

1953, GM left because of poor economic prospects. It later developed licensing agreements with Hindustan Motors. This developed into the announcement of a full-scale 50–50 venture to jointly produce GM models in India again.[100]

The changing situation in South Africa is largely a function of the political evolution in that country. International sanctions, as well as sanctions imposed by the U.S. government and some 150 cities, states, and counties, resulted in 214 U.S. firms exiting between 1984 and 1991.[101] Since July 1991, when the ban on investing in South Africa was lifted, some of those firms have returned. Among them is Honeywell, a manufacturer of industrial controls equipment. The company returned by repurchasing the industrial distributor it had sold to local interests in 1985.[102]

The majority of the companies now entering South Africa are firms that purposely did not deal directly with that country when it remained under white minority rule. Digital Equipment (since acquired by Compaq) waited for the formal lifting of sanctions by the African National Congress, the leading black political party, and entered on July 1, 1993. Digital was attracted by the fact that many of its key customers, such as some of the leading international oil companies, had always maintained operations there and its products had found their way to South Africa through non-Digital channels.[103] Today, U.S. companies have again taken a substantial lead with investment in South Africa, accounting for almost 86,000 directly related jobs.[104]

Conclusions

The world contains more than two hundred individual countries or markets. Thus, entry decisions are the strategy decisions international companies must make most frequently. Since the type of entry strategy can clearly affect later market success, these decisions need to be based on careful analysis. Companies often find it difficult to break out of initial arrangements, another reason why special attention must be given to this type of decision. In some of the more difficult markets, such as Japan, making the correct entry decision can become a key competitive advantage for a firm and can unlock markets otherwise inaccessible to a foreign company.

To survive in the coming global battles for market dominance, companies have to become increasingly bolder and more creative in their entry strategy choices. Long gone are the days when entry was restricted to exporting, licensing, foreign manufacturing, and joint ventures. New concepts such as global

100. "Indian Venture for 20,000 Cars a Year," *Financial Times*, May 12, 1994, p. 15.
101. "As U.S. Firms Return to Land of Apartheid, Lotus Feels Its Way," *Wall Street Journal*, Wednesday, May 26, 1993.
102. "Honeywell's Route Back to South Africa Market," *New York Times*, January 31, 1994, p. D1.
103. "Digital Sets Up Shop in South Africa," *Boston Sunday Globe*, July 11, 1993, p. 65.
104. "US Still SA's Biggest Investor," *Business Day* (South Africa), February 15, 1999, p. 2.

alliances have become common, and international firms will have to include acquisitions, venture capital financing, and complex government partnerships as integral elements in entry strategy configurations. The myriad of new entry alternatives has raised the level of complexity in international marketing and will remain an important challenge for managers.

This added complexity will make detailed analysis and comparisons of entry strategy alternatives more difficult. For adequate analysis, companies have to take into consideration not only present cost structures but also the ever-changing economic and political environment. Rapidly fluctuating foreign exchange rates have changed the cost of various entry alternatives and have forced companies to shift their approach. Economic changes are likely to continue, and companies will be forced to reevaluate their entry strategy decisions on an ongoing basis. Entry strategies will rarely be permanent but will have to be adapted to the most recent situation.

Although most companies have preferences as to which entry strategy they would pursue given no objections or obstacles, firms increasingly will be adopting a flexible approach. Establishing a sales subsidiary may be the best alternative for entering some countries, whereas joint ventures may be necessary to enter other countries. Managers will be forced to learn to manage with a variety of entry strategies, and they will be less able to repeat the same entry patterns all over the world. A high degree of managerial flexibility will thus be required of international companies and their executives. We can also expect that the future will bring other types of entry strategies that will challenge international managers anew.

QUESTIONS FOR DISCUSSION

1. Contrast the entry strategies practiced by Boeing and IBM. What differences do you find, and what explains these differences?
2. Would entry strategies differ for companies considering Germany, Japan, and China? If so, in what way and for what reasons?
3. How will the entry strategy of a new start-up firm differ from that of a mature multinational company?
4. What difficulties and special problems can be expected from a firm practicing only franchising as an entry strategy?
5. Perform a literature search on alliances and try to determine the reasons particular alliances were made.
6. It has been speculated that alliances between Japanese and western firms work primarily to the benefit of Japanese companies. Comment.
7. Explain the concept of entry strategy configuration and the strategies of layering, bundling, or unbundling entry strategies.

FOR FURTHER READING

Bleeke, Joel, and David Ernst. "The Way to Win in Cross-Border Alliances." *Harvard Business Review*, November–December 1991, pp. 127–135.

Erramilli, Krishna M., and C. P. Rao. "Service Firms' International Entry-Mode Choice: A Modified Transaction–Cost Analysis Approach." *Journal of Marketing*, 57 (July 1993), pp. 19–38.

Harrigan, Kathryn R. *Strategies for Joint Ventures*. Boston: D. C. Heath, 1985.

Kanter, Rosabeth Moss. *When Giants Learn to Dance*. New York: Simon & Schuster, 1989.

Killing, J. Peter. *Strategies for Joint Venture Success*. New York: Praeger, 1983.

Kogut, Bruce, and Harbir Singh. "The Effect of National Culture on the Choice of Entry Mode." *Journal of International Business Studies*, Fall 1988, pp. 411-432.

Lawrence, Paul, and Charalambos Vlachoutsicos. "Joint Ventures in Russia: Put the Locals in Charge." *Harvard Business Review*, January-February 1993, pp. 44-54.

Parkhe, Arvind. "Interfirm Diversity, Organizational Learning, and Longevity in Global Strategic Alliances." *Journal of International Business Studies*, 4th Quarter 1991, pp. 579-601.

Root, Franklin R. *Entry Strategies for International Markets*. Revised and expanded ed. Lexington, Mass.: D. C. Heath, 1994.

Shan, Weijan. "Environmental Risks and Joint Venture Sharing Arrangements." *Journal of International Business Studies*, 4th Quarter 1991, pp. 555-578.

Yoshino, Michael Y., and U. Srinivasu Rangan. *Strategic Alliances*. Cambridge: Harvard Business School Press, 1995.

IV Designing Global Marketing Programs

COMPETENCE LEVEL	GLOBAL ENVIRONMENT
ENVIRONMENTAL COMPETENCE	*Understanding the Global Marketing Environment* 2 3 4
ANALYTIC COMPETENCE	*Analyzing Global Marketing Opportunities* 5 6
STRATEGIC COMPETENCE	*Developing Global Marketing Strategies* 7 8 9
FUNCTIONAL COMPETENCE	*Designing Global Marketing Programs* 10 11 12 13 14 15
MANAGERIAL COMPETENCE	*Managing the Global Marketing Effort* 16 17 18

Assembling a global marketing program requires an analysis of how the environment will affect the four marketing mix elements: product, distribution, pricing, and communications. In Part 4, we focus on how companies adapt to different marketing environments by adjusting certain elements of their marketing programs to ensure market acceptance. In concentrating on these issues, our aim is to help you increase functional competence. Marketing managers not only must be knowledgeable about the global environment, but they also must posses the solid, functional skills necessary to compete successfully in the global marketplace, adapting to local conditions where necessary and providing a global solution where possible.

Chapter 10 outlines the differences between domestic global pricing and how companies can deal with problems arising from different prices in different markets. In Chapter 11, we give an overview of communications strategies, sales force management, and promotional policies for global companies. Chapter 12 looks at global advertising and the challenges faced by companies running advertising programs simultaneously in many countries. In Chapter 13, we concentrate on product and service strategy issues for global markets. In Chapter 14, we discuss how to manage the new-product development process in a global environment. Important distribution and channel decisions are discussed in Chapter 15.

10

Pricing for Global Markets

THIS CHAPTER PROVIDES AN OVERVIEW OF THE KEY FACTORS THAT AFFECT pricing policies in a global environment. We assume that you understand the basic pricing decisions that companies must make in a single-country or domestic environment. In this chapter, we focus on the unique aspects of global pricing. (See Figure 10.1 for a chapter overview.)

The material is organized around six major issues. First we look at internal factors and company policies as they affect global pricing policies. Costs and how they affect price determination are major concerns. The second section is devoted to the market factors companies must consider in setting prices, such as competi-

FIGURE 10.1

Global Pricing Strategies

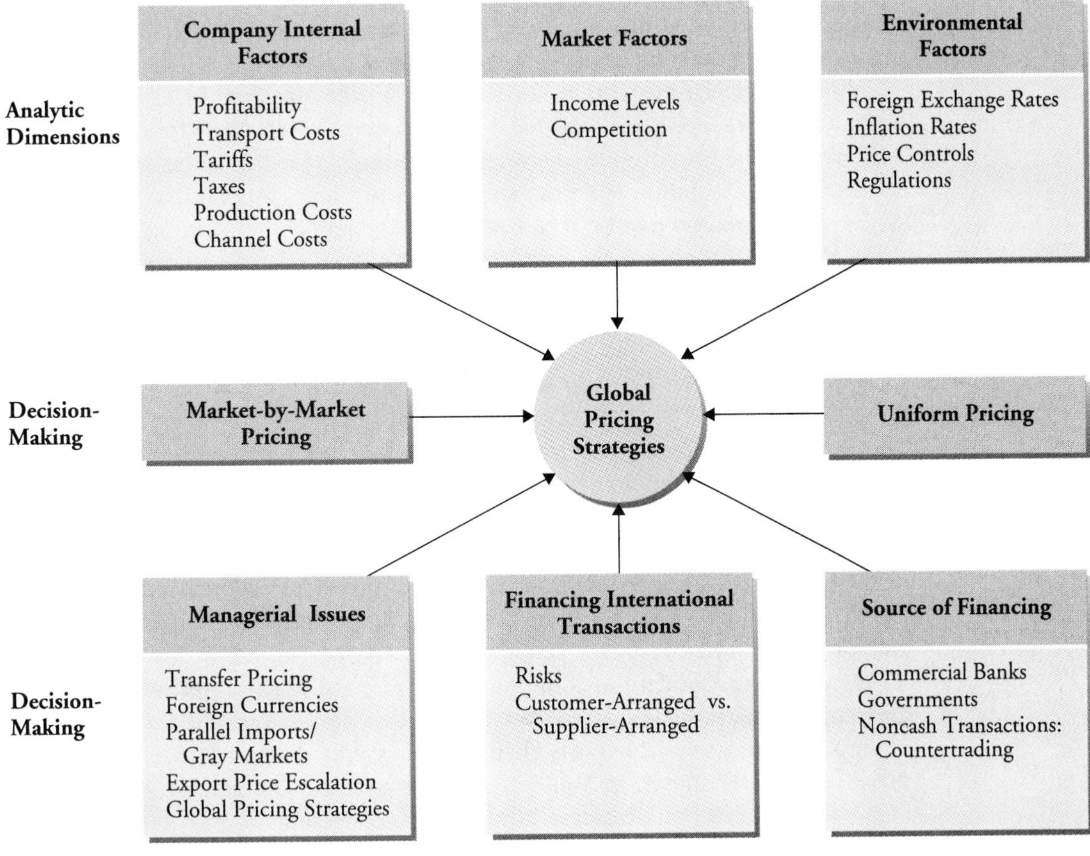

tion and the income levels of various countries. The third segment focuses on the environmental variables, such as foreign exchange rates, inflation, and legal constraints, that are not controlled by individual firms but that play an important role in shaping pricing policies. The fourth section covers managerial pricing issues, such as transfer pricing—price arbitrage and countertrade—issues of great concern to companies active globally. The chapter ends with sections on two financing issues: risks and financial sources, critical areas that have received increased attention from global firms.

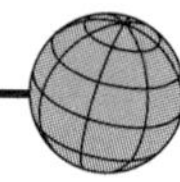

Company Internal Factors

Most companies begin pricing deliberations based on their own internal cost structure. Therefore, it makes sense to look at internal costs before considering other issues. Included under internal factors are profits and the requirement for profits as they impact internal pricing procedures.

Also of concern are country-to-country transfer costs, such as tariffs, transportation, insurance, taxes, and local channel costs. Such costs frequently make exported products more expensive than domestic ones, and this fact must be taken into consideration if a company wants to compete effectively. However, such costs do not have to be taken as given. Companies can, through various actions, affect the level of these costs. It is the purpose of this section to point out the options available to companies in managing their global costs.

Profit and Cost Factors

The basis for any effective pricing policy is a clear understanding of the cost and profit variables involved. Experience shows that clear definitions of relevant costs and of profits are often difficult to achieve. On the other hand, the field of global marketing offers many examples of firms that have achieved substantial profits through flexible or nonconventional costing approaches. Therefore, understanding the various cost elements can be considered a prerequisite for a successful global pricing strategy.

According to standard accounting practice, costs are divided into two categories: fixed costs and variable costs. Fixed costs do not vary over a given range of output, whereas variable costs change directly with output. The relationship of these variables is shown in Table 10.1 using a fictitious example, Western Machine Tool, Inc., a manufacturer of machine tools selling at $60,000 per unit in the U.S. market.

The total cost of a machine tool is $54,000. Selling it at $60,000, the company will achieve a profit of $6,000 before taxes from the sale of each unit. However, if one additional unit is sold (or not sold), the marginal impact amounts to more than an additional profit of $6,000 (or loss of the same amount), because the extra cost of an additional unit will be limited to its variable costs only, or $26,000, as shown in Table 10.2. For any additional units sold, the marginal profit is $34,000, or the amount in excess of the variable costs. This amount may also be referred to as the *contribution margin*.

Another example is used to illustrate the relationships between variable costs, fixed costs, and contribution margin. Western Machine Tool has a chance to export a unit to a foreign country, but the maximum price the foreign buyer is willing to pay is $50,000. Machine Tool, using the full cost pricing method, argues that the company will incur a loss of $4,000 if the deal is accepted. However, since

TABLE 10.1

Profit and Cost Calculation for Western Machine Tool, Inc.

Selling price (per unit)			$60,000
Direct manufacturing costs			
Labor	$10,000		
Material	15,000		
Energy	1,000	$26,000	
Indirect manufacturing costs			
Supervision	5,000		
Research and development contribution	3,000		
Factory overhead	5,000	13,000	
General administrative cost			
Sales and administrative overhead	10,000		
Marketing	5,000	15,000	
Full costs			54,000
Net profit before tax			$ 6,000

only $26,000 of additional variable cost will be incurred for a new machine because all fixed costs are incurred anyway and are covered by all prior units sold, the company can go ahead with the sale and claim a marginal profit of $24,000, using a contribution margin approach. In such a situation, a profitable sale may easily be turned down unless a company is fully informed about its cost composition.

Cost components are subject to change. For example, if growing export volume adds new output to a plant, a company may achieve economies of scale that allow operations at lower costs, both domestically and abroad. Furthermore, as the experience curve indicates, companies with rapidly rising cumulative production may reap overall unit cost reductions at an increasing rate because of the higher output caused by exporting.[1]

1. For a detailed discussion of the experience curve concept, see Derek F. Abell, *Managing with Dual Strategies* (New York: Free Press, 1993), Chapter 9.

TABLE 10.2

Marginal Profit Calculation for Western Machine Tool, Inc.

Selling price (per unit)			$60,000
Variable costs			
Direct manufacturing costs			
Labor	$10,000		
Material	15,000		
Energy	1,000	26,000	
Total variable costs			26,000
Contribution margin (selling price minus variable costs)			$34,000

Transportation Costs

Global marketing often requires the shipment of products over long distances. Since all modes of transportation, including rail, truck, air, and ocean, depend on a considerable amount of energy, the total cost of transportation has become an issue of growing concern to global companies. High-technology products are less sensitive to transportation costs than standardized consumer products or commodities. In the latter case, the seller with the lowest transportation costs often has the advantage.

For commodities, low transportation costs can decide who gets an order. For expensive products, such as computers or sophisticated electronic instruments, transportation costs usually represent only a small fraction of total costs and rarely influence pricing decisions. For products between the two extremes, companies can substantially affect unit transportation costs by selecting appropriate transportation methods. The introduction of container ocean vessels has made large-scale shipment of many products possible. Roll-on, roll-off ships (ro-ro carriers) have reduced ocean freight costs for cars and trucks to very low levels, making exporters more competitive vis-à-vis local manufacturers. World seaborne trade increased 2.7 percent in 1988 to 5.21 billion tons, dominated by oil, grain, iron ore, coal, and other bulk commodities. Containerized cargo increased 3.9 percent in 1998 to a total of 160 million-twenty ton units.[2] The international firm

2. Felix Chan, "World Container Cargo Volumes Forecast to Rise," *Business Times* (Singapore), July 7, 1998, p. SHIP 1.

must continuously search for new transportation technologies to reduce unit transportation costs and, thus, enhance competitiveness.

Tariffs

When products are transported across national borders, tariffs have to be paid unless a special arrangement exists between the countries involved. Tariffs are usually levied on the landed costs of a product, which include shipping to the importing country. Tariffs are normally assessed as a percentage of the value.

Tariff costs can have a rippling effect and increase prices considerably for the end user. Intermediaries, whether they are sales subsidiaries or independent distributors, tend to include any tariff costs in their costs of goods sold and add any operating margin on this amount. As a result, the impact on the final end-user price can be substantial whenever tariff rates are high.

The intricacies of managing through duty and regulations are illustrated by Land Rover, the British producer of the Range Rover four-wheel-drive (4WD) sports utility vehicle, marketed in the United States since 1987. When the U.S. tariffs for light trucks were increased from 2.5 percent to 25 percent to stem the imports, 4WD vehicles were classified as multipurpose vehicles subject to a higher tariff. But Land Rover complained that its $40,000 vehicle was classified as a heavy-duty truck, pointing out that it has four doors and not just two as the typical light truck. Thus, the higher duty was avoided. In 1991, however, the United States began to charge a 10 percent surtax on luxury vehicles above $30,000, thus potentially affecting the sales of the Range Rover. The U.S. tax authorities classified four-wheel-drive vehicles as trucks, and the Range Rover again avoided the tax. To ensure compliance, however, the Range Rovers are shipped to the United States as cars to avoid the truck surcharge but have an increased weight of 6,019 pounds, from 5,997 pounds, because the tax authorities' truck definition starts at vehicles of 6,000 pounds.[3] Tariffs always penalize someone. In 1999, the U.S. imposed a 100 percent tariff on printed bed linens from Europe in retaliation against the European Union tariffs on Latin America bananas. The linen producers in Italy, France, and Portugal lost sales, as well as the retailers in the United States who specialized in this product.[4] BMW faced a similar situation in Egypt, with duties of 135 percent of the value of the car, plus a 45 percent sales tax. BMW set up an assembly plant in a duty-free zone near Cairo, and monthly sales increased from thirty-five to one hundred cars.[5] Although tariffs

3. "What's in a Name?" *Economist*, February 2, 1991, p. 60.
4. Brent Felgner, "Bed Imports Look to Peel Away Tariff," *Home Textiles Today*, April 26, 1999, pp. 1, 46.
5. "BMW Invests to Avoid Tariffs," *Corporate Location*, Sept/Oct 1997, p. 57.

have declined over recent years, they still influence pricing decisions in some countries. To avoid paying high duties, as we have seen in Chapter 9, companies have shipped components only and established local assembly operations because tariffs on components are frequently lower than on finished products. The automobile industry is a good example of how companies can reduce overall tariff costs by shifting the place of production and shipping knocked-down cars to be assembled on the spot. Such a move may be called for when tariffs are especially high.

Taxes

Local taxes imposed on imported products also affect the land cost of the products. A variety of taxes may be imposed. One of the most common is the tax on value added (VAT) used by member countries of the European Union (EU).

Each EU country sets its own value-added tax structure (see Figure 10.2). However, common to all is a zero tax rate (or exemption) on exported goods. A company exporting from the Netherlands to Belgium does not have to pay any tax on the value added in the Netherlands. However, Belgian authorities do collect a tax on products shipped from the Netherlands at the Belgium rate. Merchandise shipped to any EU member country from a nonmember country, such as from the United States or Japan, is assessed the VAT rate on landed costs, in addition to any tariffs that may apply to those products.

Local Production Costs

Up to this point, we have assumed that a company has only one producing location, from which it exports to all other markets. However, most global firms manufacture products in several countries. In such cases, operating costs for raw materials, wages, energy, or financing may vary widely from country to country, allowing a firm to ship from a particularly advantageous location to reduce prices or costs. Increasingly, companies produce in locations that give them advantages in freight, tariffs, or other transfer costs. Consequently, judicious management of sourcing points may reduce product costs and thus result in added pricing flexibility.

Channel Costs

Channel costs are a function of channel length, gross margin, and logistics. Many countries operate with long distribution channels, causing higher total costs and end-user prices because of the additional number of intermediaries. Also, gross margins at the retail level tend to vary from country to country because of the dif-

FIGURE 10.2

European VAT Rates, February 1997 (in percentages)

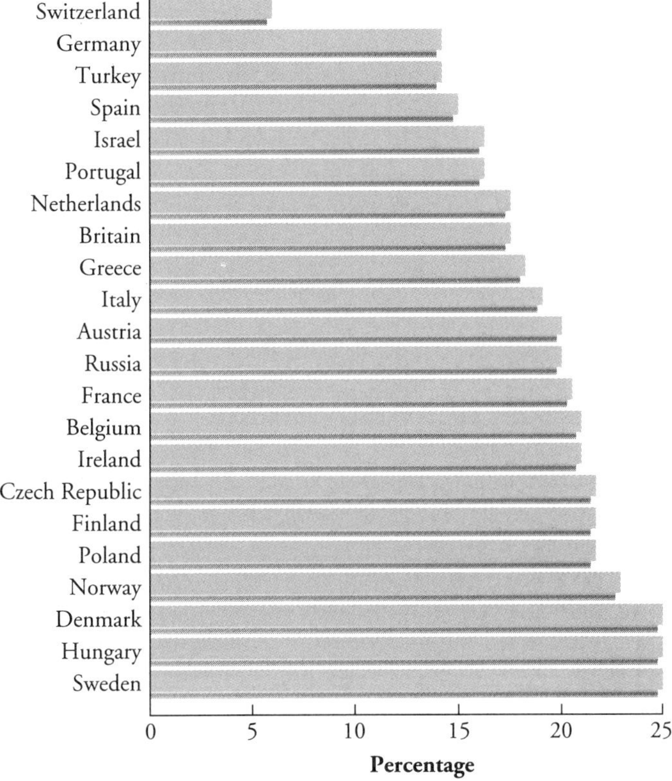

Source: The Economist, March 1, 1997, p. 106. From "Economic Indicators," © 1997 The Economist Newspaper Group, Inc. Reprinted with permission. Further reproduction prohibited.

ferent logistics systems. All of these factors can add extra costs to a product that is marketed globally.

Campbell Soup Company, a U.S.-based firm, found that its retailers in the United Kingdom purchased soup in small quantities of twenty-four cans per case of assorted soups, requiring each can to be hand-picked for shipment. In the United States, the company sold one variety to retailers in cases of forty-eight cans per case, which were purchased in large quantities. To handle small purchases in England, the company had to add another level of distribution and new facilities.

As a result, distribution costs are 30 percent higher in England than in the United States.[6]

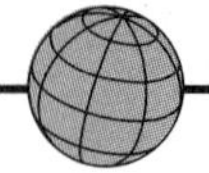

Market Factors Affecting Pricing

Companies cannot establish pricing policies in a vacuum. Although cost information is essential, prices also have to reflect the realities of the marketplace. The challenge in pricing for global markets is the large number of local economic situations to be considered. Two factors stand out and must be analyzed in greater detail: income levels and competition.

Income Levels

The income level of a country's population determines the amount and type of goods and services bought. When detailed income data are not available, incomes are expressed by gross national product (GNP) or gross domestic product (GDP) divided by the total population. This measure, *GNP per capita* or *GDP per capita,* is a surrogate measure for personal income and is used to compare income levels among countries. To do so, all GNPs/GDPs have to be converted to the same currency. If you look at the table on the inside back cover of the book, you'll see that GNP per capita figures for key countries were expressed in U.S. dollars.

As mentioned in Chapter 6, GNP/GDP per capita converted to dollars based on market exchange rates tends to understate the true purchasing power of a country's consumers. It is more accurate to look at developing countries' GNP or GDP per capita converted to dollars based on purchasing power parity. The World Bank's latest estimate of China's GNP/GDP per capita based on purchasing power parity is $3.8 trillion, which is ahead of Japan and approximately one-half of that of the United States.[7] To respond to the purchasing power of different countries, Coca-Cola prices its product as a proportion of disposable income.[8]

As a result of widely differing income and price levels, elasticity of demand for any given product can be expected to vary greatly. Countries with high income levels often display lower price elasticities for necessities such as food, shelter, and medical care. These lower elasticities in part reflect a lack of alternatives, such as "doing it yourself," which forces buyers in these countries to purchase such goods even at higher prices. For example, in many countries with low income levels, a

6. Philip R. Cateora and John L. Graham, *International Marketing*, 10th ed. (New York: Irwin McGraw Hill, 1999), p. 562.
7. "Global Giants," *Economist*, May 8, 1999, p. 109.
8. "The Ascent of Everest: Coca-Cola's Plans for a New Global Sales Assault," *Financial Times*, January 16, 1992, p. 10.

considerable part of the population has the additional alternatives of providing their own food or building their own shelters should they not have sufficient money to purchase products or services on a cash basis. Availability of such options increases price elasticity, as these consumers can more easily opt out of the cash economy than can consumers in developed economies. Global companies theoretically set product price by considering the price elasticity in each country. However, there are forces at work that do not always allow this practice because prices may vary widely across several countries. The danger of disparate price levels is examined later, in the managerial issues in global pricing segment of this chapter.

Competition

The nature and size of competition can significantly affect price levels in any given market. A firm acting as the sole supplier of a product in a given market enjoys greater pricing flexibility. The opposite is true if that same company has to compete against several other local or global firms. Therefore, the number and type of competitors greatly influence pricing strategy in any market. The public postal, telephone, and telegraph (PTT) services of some countries are a public monopoly, allowing them to charge high rates with no threat of competition. As the Japanese telecommunications market has opened up, U.S. and other suppliers have been quick to respond. AT&T World Access offered international calling opportunities at approximately half the standard rate offered by Japanese providers.[9] The opening of telecom markets is destroying the fortresses previously held by the PTTs. For example, after the German telecom market was opened in 1998, fifty-one new companies entered the field, taking one-third of the market from Deutsche Telekom and dropping long-distance rates by 90 percent.[10]

Also important is the nature of the competition. Local competitors may have different cost structures from those of foreign companies, resulting in different prices. Market prices for the same product may vary from country to country, based on the competitive situation. Heinz, the U.S.-based food company and the world leader in ketchup, with 50 percent world market share, began to expand on its 1 percent market share in Japan after a liberalization of the policy regarding some food imports. The company faced major price competition by the leading Japanese ketchup producer. However, Heinz decided not to follow suit but to keep prices at the higher level to indicate quality and to protect its profitability.[11]

But foreign companies do not always have to be at a disadvantage when competing with local companies. In the wake of the substantial strengthening of the

9. Joshua Ogawa, "AT&T Adds Corporate Call Back Service," *Nikkei Weekly*, November 4, 1996, p. 9.
10. Gautam Naik and William Boston, "Deregulation Dismays Deutsche Telekom," *Wall Street Journal*, January 14, 1999, p. 1.
11. "Ketchup War Will Be Fought to the Last Drop," *Financial Times*, February 21, 1990, p. 18.

Japanese yen in 1998, the Japanese car manufacturers did not cut prices in the United States. They enjoyed strong sales in the U.S. market. The profits will be repatriated back to Japan and will help the weak markets in Asia.[12]

Occasionally, price levels are manipulated by cartels or other agreements among local competitors. Cartels are forbidden by law in the United States, but some governments allow cartels provided they do not injure the consumer. Following a five-year-long investigation, the European Union fined twenty-three western European chemical companies $80 million for the price fixing of two plastic products. The companies were found guilty of forming secret pricing cartels to keep up the price of polyvinyl chloride (PVC) and low-density polyethylene.[13] The U.S. Justice Department found four graphite electrode manufacturers guilty of conspiring to suppress and eliminate competition between 1992 and 1997. The two Japanese, one German, and one U.S. companies paid fines totaling $284 million.[14] Cartels may be officially recognized by a local government or may consist of competitors following similar pricing practices. In general, new market entrants must decide whether to accept current price levels or to set price levels different from those of the established competition.

The U.S. government has a very strict approach to cartels, and any cartel such as described above clearly would be against existing U.S. laws. Furthermore, U.S. companies may find themselves in violation of U.S. laws if they actively participate in any foreign cartel.

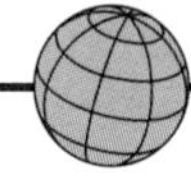

Environmental Factors Affecting Price

We have thus far treated pricing as a matter of cost and market factors. A number of environmental factors also influence pricing on the global level. These external variables, uncontrolled by any individual company, include the general economic environment, foreign exchange, inflation, government price controls, and government regulations. These factors restrict company decision-making authority and can become dominant concerns for country managers.

Exchange Rate Fluctuations

One of the most unpredictable factors affecting prices is foreign exchange rate movement. As the exchange rate moves up and down, it affects all producers.

12. William Dawkins, "A Yen for Appreciation," *Financial Times*, November 12, 1996, p. 15; Lisa Shuchman and Gregory L. White, "Japan Car Makers to Hold U.S. Prices," *Wall Street Journal*, June 18, 1999, p. A15.
13. "Don't Save the Yen," *Economist*, February 8, 1997, p. 18.
14. "Bruce Ingersoll, "Germany's SGL to Pay $135 Fine," *Wall Street Journal*, May 5, 1999, p. B12.

Since a company's costs are often in its domestic currency, as this currency weakens, it means that the company's goods are cheaper in another currency. For example, when the euro was launched in January 1999, each euro was valued at $1.20. By July 1999, the euro had dropped to $1.00. Therefore, Cotherm, a French producer of thermostats and sensors that exports to China and Brazil, was able to reduce prices and maintain profits and market share.[15] In Chapter 2, we explained the reasons behind these foreign currency fluctuations.

Though foreign exchange fluctuations can present new opportunities, they may also make operations more difficult, particularly for companies operating in countries with appreciating currencies. As the dollar and the pound became stronger against the euro, it meant that items manufactured in the United States or the United Kingdom would be more expensive in the eleven euro countries and that therefore export demand would drop. The Confederation of British Industry estimated that 15,000 to 20,000 jobs would be lost in the United Kingdom by August 1999 because of the strong pound sterling.[16] In 1999, Korean shipbuilders were able to offer prices well below that of Japanese shipbuilders because of the fast appreciation of the yen versus the Korean won. Korean shipbuilding volume increased 37 percent in 1999 over 1998 even though world orders declined 15 percent.[17]

Inflation Rates

The rate of inflation can affect product cost and may force a company to take specific action. Inflation rates have traditionally fluctuated over time and, more important, have differed from country to country. In some cases, inflation rates have risen to several hundred percent. When this happens, payment for products may be delayed for months, harming the economy because of the local currency's rapid loss of purchasing power. A company would have to use a last-in, first-out (LIFO) method of costing or, in the extreme, a first-in, first-out (FIFO) approach to protect itself from eroding purchasing power. A company can usually protect itself from rapid inflation if it maintains constant operating margins (gross margin, gross profit, net margin) and makes constant price adjustments, sometimes on a monthly basis.

Historically, inflation has been a problem in countries like Brazil. The United States and Europe have successfully managed inflation by raising interest rates whenever the economy starts to heat up, keeping inflation at 0 to 2 percent. One

15. David Woodruff, "Weakened Euro May Enliven Economies," *Wall Street Journal*, April 15, 1999, p. A17.
16. Helene Cooper, "British Exports Suffer as Euro Goes Forward," *Wall Street Journal*, September 14, 1998, p. A1.
17. Lee Jong-Seung, "Competitive Prize Edge Sinks Rivals," *Business Korea*, January 2000, pp. 24–25.

FIGURE 10.3

Currencies Against the Dollar, Percentage Change, December 31, 1998 to March 24, 1999

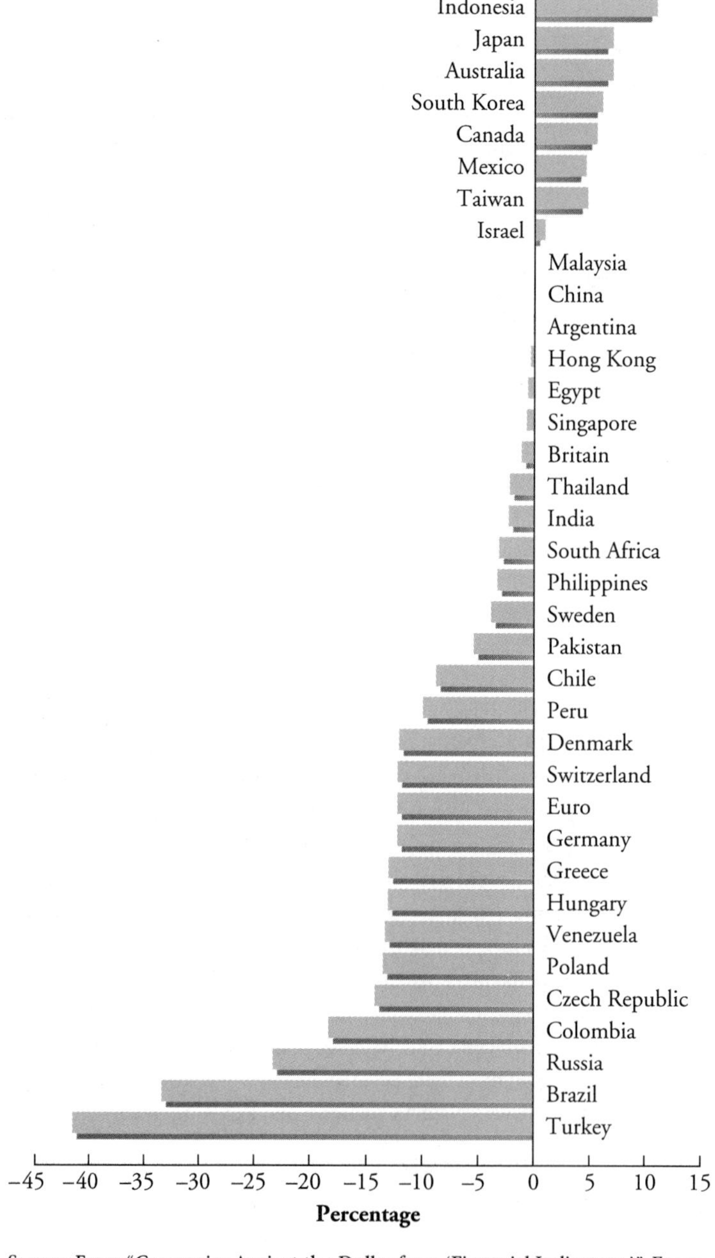

Source: From "Currencies Against the Dollar from 'Financial Indicators,'" *Economist*, March 27, 1999, 110. © 1999 The Economist Newspaper Group, Inc. Reprinted with permission. Further reproduction prohibited.

exception is Greece, where consumer prices rose 5 percent in 1998 and were estimated to rise only 3 percent in 1999, the country's lowest inflation rate since 1972.[18]

In countries with extremely high inflation, companies may price in a stable currency, such as the U.S. dollar, euro, or yen, and translate prices into local currencies on a daily basis. Vision Express, which has been very successful in Russia, charges customers in dollars to avoid the inflation that lifts prices rapidly. Most of the customers, entrepreneurs and businesspeople, seem to be able to get dollars. In fact, a 1998 study by the Russian central bank found that 20 percent of transactions in their economy were in dollars.[19] The U.S. dollar was reasonably strong in 1999, appreciating against most currencies except some Asian currencies such as the Indonesian rupiah, the Japanese yen, the Australian dollar, the South Korean won, as shown in Figure 10.3. One of the big losers against the dollar in the beginning of 1999 was the Brazilian real, which dropped 34 percent versus the dollar since the end of 1998.

Price Controls

In some countries, government regulatory agencies influence the prices of products and services. Controls may be applied to an entire economy to combat inflation; regulations may be applied only to specific industries, such as the pharmaceutical industry. In the European Union, where many aspects of the countries' economies are coordinated, methods of controlling prices for drugs may vary considerably. In the United Kingdom, drug prices are established through the Pharmaceutical Price Regulation Scheme (PPRS). Though companies are allowed to set prices for individual drugs, the government limits their overall profitability. (However, company profit targets are established through confidential negotiations and are set differently for each company.) Furthermore, the British National Health Service recently introduced price limits for drugs that qualify for customer reimbursement. Aventis Pharmaceuticals, the Franco-American pharmaceutical group, cut its U.K. price on a sleeping pill called Zimovane from 98 to 16 pence to avoid being blacklisted (taken off government reimbursement).[20] Italy uses a similar restrictive list combined with price controls and varying levels of reimbursements. France uses a method of strict price controls to contain overall health costs, and Germany also maintains a restrictive list for some drugs but otherwise lets the companies set their own prices. In the United States, by contrast, prices for some drugs are established through negotiations between the drug company, the federal Medicare program, and several private insurance companies

18. "Greece," *Economist*, February 13, 1999, p. 106.
19. George Melloan, "Another Russian Crisis," *Wall Street Journal*, June 2, 1998, p. A23.
20. "Britain to Cut Price It Pays for Drugs by 2.5%," *Financial Times*, August 10, 1993, p. 14.

that reimburse their customers for drug costs. Because of the strong government policy limiting prices of drugs in many countries, consumers pay less than in the United States. The same $100 of drugs in the United States would cost $76 in Canada, $67 in the United Kingdom, $47 in Sweden, and $32 in Australia.[21]

The European Union is attempting to harmonize EU car prices without resorting to price controls. Twice a year, car manufacturers must publish comparative EU price lists for selected new cars. In each EU country, car prices are expected to be within 12 percent over the long term and within 18 percent over periods of a year.[22] If car manufacturers do not stay within these differentials, they may lose the right to use selective dealer distribution. BMW, the owner of the U.K.-based Rover, announced in 1999 that it would cut price differentials on all its new cars to less than 10 percent.[23] A report by the EU found cars sold in the U.K. were priced 35 percent higher than those in the Euro-zone countries in 2000. EU competition commissioner, Mario Monti, said he will prosecute violations of EU competition rules when the car-sales exception from EU law expires in 2002.[24]

Regulatory Factors: Dumping Regulations

The practice of selling a product at a price below actual costs is referred to as *dumping*. Because of potential injuries to domestic manufacturers, most governments have adopted regulations against dumping. Antidumping actions are allowed under provisions of the World Trade Organization (WTO) as long as two criteria are met: "sales at less than fair value" and "material injury" to a domestic industry.[25] The first criterion is usually interpreted to mean selling abroad at prices below those in the country of origin. However, the WTO rules originally adopted by the General Agreement on Tariffs and Trades (GATT) in 1968 prohibit assessment of retroactive punitive duties and require all procedures to be open. The United States differs from the WTO in its dumping regulations, determining "fair market value" and "material injury" sequentially rather than simultaneously. Also, the U.S. government will assess any duty retroactively and has on numerous occasions acted to prevent antidumping practices from injuring domestic manufacturers.

The U.S. government has taken dumping actions on numerous occasions over the past decade. In one recent case, the U.S. government charged Asian sweater makers with dumping on a volume of $1.25 billion. In another case, dumping

21. Carol Gentry, "Bay State May Negotiate Price of Pharmaceuticals," *Wall Street Journal*, December 9, 1998, p. NE1.
22. "Long Term Benefits from Japan's Bitter Pill," *Financial Times*, June 15, 1990, p. 21.
23. Tim Burt, "BMW to Smooth Price Variations," *Financial Times*, July 1, 1999, p. 7.
24. Brandon Mitchener, "European Commission Raids Offices of Renault in Antitrust Probe," *Dow Jones Business News*, April 19, 1999.
25. Franklin R. Root, *International Trade and Investment*, 3rd ed. (Cincinnati: Southwestern, 1973), p. 296.

charges were leveled against ball-bearing imports on the basis of a suit filed by a U.S. producer.[26]

The United States is not alone in taking antidumping actions. There were 225 WTO antidumping cases opened in 1998 by twenty-six countries. In the 1980s and early 1990s, 80 percent of antidumping charges were brought by the United States, Canada, the European Union, and Australia, often against Asian countries. Many of the new antidumping cases have been brought to the WTO by developing countries such as South Africa, India, Brazil, Indonesia, and Mexico, with the United States, the EU, Canada, and Australia bringing less than one-third of the cases. Forty-three of the cases were brought against the EU and its members.[27] Global marketers have to be aware of antidumping legislation that sets a floor under export prices, limiting pricing flexibility even in the event of overcapacity or industry slowdown. On the other hand, antidumping legislation can work to a company's advantage, protecting it from unfair competition.

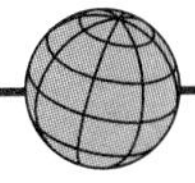

Managerial Issues in Global Pricing

Now that we have given you a general overview of the context of global pricing, we direct your attention toward managerial issues. These recurring issues require constant management attention; they are never really considered solved. The issues are transfer pricing, quoting in foreign currencies, gray-market pricing, and export price escalation.

Determining Transfer Prices

A substantial amount of global business takes place between subsidiaries of the same company. It is estimated that in-house trading between subsidiaries accounts for one-third of the volume among the world's eight hundred largest multinationals. The cost to the importing or buying subsidiary depends on the negotiated transfer price agreed on by the two involved units of the international firm. How these prices are set is a major issue for global companies and governments. Because negotiations on transfer prices do not represent arm's-length negotiations between independent participants, the resulting prices frequently differ from free-market prices.[28]

Companies may deviate from arm's-length prices for two reasons. They may want to (1) maximize profits and/or (2) minimize risk and uncertainty.[29] To

26. "When One Man's Dumping Is Another Man's Good Price," *Financial Times*, May 9, 1990, p. 10.
27. "World Trade: Poorer Nations Starting More Dumping Cases," *Financial Times*, May 6, 1999, p. 21.
28. For a conceptual treatment, see *Transfer Pricing* (Washington, D.C.: Tax Management, Inc., 1995).
29. Sanjaya Lall, "Transfer-Pricing by Multinational Manufacturing Firms," *Oxford Bulletin of Economics and Statistics*, August 1973, pp. 173–175.

pursue a strategy of profit maximization, a company may lower transfer prices for products shipped from some subsidiaries while increasing prices for products shipped to others. The company will then try to accumulate profits in subsidiaries where it is advantageous and keep profits low in other subsidiaries.

Impact of Tax Structure Different tax, tariff, or subsidy structures by country frequently invite such practices. By accumulating more profits in a low-tax country, a company lowers its overall tax bill and thus increases profit. Likewise, tariff duties can be reduced by quoting low transfer prices to countries with high tariffs. When countries use different exchange rates for the transfer of goods as opposed to the transfer of capital or profits, advantages can be gained by increasing transfer prices rather than transferring profits at less advantageous rates. The same is true for countries with restrictions on profit repatriation. Furthermore, a company may want to accumulate profits in a wholly owned subsidiary rather than in one that is minority owned; by using the transfer price mechanism, it can avoid sharing profits with local partners.

Companies may also use the transfer price mechanism to minimize risk or uncertainty by moving profits or assets out of a country with chronic balance-of-payment problems and frequent devaluations. Since regular profit remittances are strictly controlled in such countries, many firms see high transfer prices as the only way to repatriate funds and thereby to reduce the amount of assets at risk. The same practice may be employed if a company anticipates political or social disturbances or a direct threat to profits through government intervention.

In actual practice, companies choose a number of approaches to transfer pricing. Market-based prices are equal to those negotiated by independent companies or at arm's length. Of thirty U.S.-based firms, 46 percent were reported to use market-based systems. Another 35 percent used cost-based systems to determine the transfer price. Costs were based on a predetermined formula, which may include a standard markup for profits.[30]

Internal Considerations Rigorous use of the transfer pricing mechanism to reduce a company's income taxes and duties and to maximize profits in strong currency areas can create difficulties for subsidiary managers whose profits are artificially reduced. In such cases, managers may be subject to motivational problems when the direct-profit incentive is removed. Furthermore, company resource allocation may become inefficient since funds are appropriated to units whose profits are artificially increased; conversely, resources may be denied to subsidiaries whose income statements were subject to transfer price–induced reductions. It is generally agreed that a transfer price mechanism should not seri-

30. Scott S. Cowen, Lawrence C. Phillips, and Linda Stillabower, "Multinational Transfer Pricing," *Management Accounting*, January 1979, pp. 7–22.

ously impair either morale or resource allocations, since gains incurred through tax savings may easily be lost through other inefficiencies.

External Problems Governments do not look favorably on transfer pricing mechanisms aimed at reducing their tax revenues. U.S. government policy on transfer pricing is governed by tax law, particularly Section 482 of the Revenue Act of 1962.[31] The act is designed to provide an accurate allocation of costs, income, and capital among related enterprises to protect U.S. tax revenue. The U.S. Internal Revenue Service (IRS) accepts the following transfer price methods:

> Market prices are generally preferred by the IRS, either based on a comparable uncontrolled price method or a resale price method. As far as cost-plus pricing is concerned, the IRS will accept cost-plus markup if market prices are not available, and economic circumstances warrant such use. Not acceptable, however, are actual cost methods. Other methods, such as negotiated prices, are acceptable as long as the transfer price is comparable to a price charged to an unrelated party.[32]

U.S. transfer pricing regulations have continued to evolve. If a comparable arms-length transaction cannot be located, the IRS can use the comparable profits method to gauge the appropriate tax burden. In addition, the IRS requires all companies to maintain detailed explanations of the rationale and analysis supporting the transfer pricing policy. As a result of the U.S. IRS tax regulations, the countries of the Organization for Economic Cooperation and Development (OECD) have agreed to a new set of transfer pricing guidelines close to the U.S. rules.[33] According to a study by the General Accounting Office, 67 percent of all the foreign-controlled companies doing business in the United States, or 40,195 companies, do not pay any U.S. taxes. In the same report, the large* 15,363 U.S. companies pay an average of $8.1 million per year in taxes, whereas the large 2,767 foreign companies pay only $4.2 million per year. Senator Byron L. Dorgan (Democrat, North Dakota) estimates that foreign-controlled companies doing business in the United States are failing to pay $45 billion owed in U.S. taxes. Transfer pricing is the primary method used to avoid taxes.[34]

Given the strengthening of government regulations all around the world, it is necessary for global businesses to document the arms-length principle. According to a study of 280 multinational companies operating in Europe, eighty-five percent had been audited in the past three years on transfer pricing.[35] In 1992, the U.S. IRS

* Note: Large firms had either $250 million in assets or $50 million in sales.

31. Ibid., p. 18.
32. Ibid., p. 19.
33. Michael C. Durst, "United States: Transfer Pricing," *International Tax Review* (London), February 1999, pp. 56–60.
34. William Glanz, "Foreign Firms Skirt U.S. Tax Laws," *Washington Times*, April 15, 1999, p. 14.
35. Foo Eu Jin, "Transfer Pricing Poses Threat to Firms," *Business Times* (Malaysia), March 10, 1999, p. 3.

developed the Advanced Pricing Agreement Program (APA), which became effective on December 31, 1993. Under this program a company can obtain approval from the IRS for its transfer pricing procedures. This new process reduces the expense and uncertainty around transfer pricing, which is done in an open nonadversarial process.[36] Asia, Australia, Japan, and Korea all have formal advanced pricing arrangements, and China, India, and New Zealand have informal programs. [37]

Quoting Price in a Foreign Currency

For many global marketing transactions, it is not always feasible to quote in a company's domestic currency when selling or purchasing merchandise. Although the majority of U.S. exporters quote prices in dollars, there are situations in which customers may prefer quotes in their own national currency. For most import transactions, sellers usually quote the currency of their own country. When two currencies are involved, there is the risk that a change in exchange rates may occur between the invoicing date and the settlement date for the transaction. This risk, the foreign exchange risk, is an inherent factor in global marketing and clearly separates domestic from international business. Astro-Med Inc., a small manufacturer of high-quality printers based in Warwick, Rhode Island, experienced firsthand the reaction of a customer when the export price list was quoted in U.S. dollars. During the negotiations for a printer quoted at $200,000, its German customer balked at being presented with a price list, sales manual, and brochures, all for the U.S. market.[38] A research study of 671 companies in the United States, Finland, and Sweden found that companies that respond to customer's currency requests benefit from a larger volume of export business.[39] In such circumstances, special techniques are available to protect the seller from the foreign exchange risk.

The tools used to cover a company's foreign exchange risk are either (a) hedging in the forward market or (b) covering through money markets. These alternatives are given because of the nature of foreign exchange. As we discussed in Chapter 2, for most major currencies, international foreign exchange dealers located at major banks quote a spot price and a forward price. The *spot price* determines the number of dollars to be paid for a particular foreign currency purchased or sold today. The *forward price* quotes the number of dollars to be paid for a foreign currency bought or sold 30, 90, or 180 days from today. The forward price, however, is not necessarily the market's speculation as to what the spot price will be in the future. Instead, the forward price reflects interest rate differen-

36. Steven Harris, "U.S. Programme Sets the Standard," *International Tax Review* (London), April 1999, vol. 10, no. 4, pp. 35–38.
37. Michael Happell, "Asia: An Overview," *International Tax Review*, February 1999, pp. 7–9.
38. "Learning the Language of EC Trade," *Providence Journal-Bulletin*, March 1, 1989, p. C1.
39. Saeed Samiee, Patrick Anckar, and Abo Akademi, "Currency Choice in Industrial Pricing: A Cross-National Evaluation," *Journal of Marketing*, vol. 62, no. 3. (July 1998), pp. 25–27.

tials between two currencies for maturities of 30, 90, or 180 days. Consequently, there are no firm indications as to what the spot price will be for any given currency in the future. For a review of foreign exchange markets, see Chapter 2.

A company quoting in foreign currency for purchase or sale can simply leave settlement until the due date and pay whatever spot price prevails at the time. Such an uncovered position may be chosen when exchange rates are not expected to shift or when any shift in the near future will result in a gain for the company. With exchange rates fluctuating widely on a daily basis, even among major trading markets such as the United States, Japan, Brazil, and the United Kingdom, a company will expose itself to substantial foreign exchange risks. Since global firms are in business to make a profit from the sale of goods rather than from speculation in the foreign exchange markets, management generally protects itself from unexpected currency fluctuations.

One such protection lies in the forward market. Instead of accepting whatever spot market rate exists on the settlement in thirty or ninety days, the corporation can opt to contract for future delivery of foreign currency at a firm price, regardless of the spot price actually paid at that time. This allows the seller to incorporate a firm exchange rate into the price determination. Of course, if a company wishes to predict the spot price in ninety days and is reasonably certain about the accuracy of its prediction, a choice may be made between the more advantageous of the two: the expected spot or the present forward rate. However, such predictions should only be made under the guidance of experts familiar with foreign exchange rates.

An alternative strategy, covering through the money market, involves borrowing funds to be converted into the currency at risk for the time until settlement. In this case, a company owes and holds the same amount of foreign currency, resulting in a corresponding loss or gain when settling at the time of payment. As an example, an exporter holding accounts receivable in Japanese yen and unwilling to absorb the related currency risk until payment is received may borrow yen for working capital purposes. When the customer pays in the foreign currency, the loan, also denominated in that same currency, is paid off. Any fluctuations will be canceled, resulting in neither loss nor gain.

How to Incorporate a Foreign Exchange Rate into a Selling Price Quote

To illustrate the incorporation of a foreign exchange rate into a price quote for export, assume that a U.S. company needs to determine a price quote for its plastic extrusion machinery being sold to a Canadian customer. The customer requested billing in Canadian dollars. The exporter, with a list price of U.S. $12,000, does not want to absorb any exchange risk. The daily foreign exchange rates on July 16, 1999, are U.S. $.6749 spot price for one Canadian dollar and $.6769 in the sixty days forward market.[40] The exporter can directly figure the Canadian

40. "Currency Trading," *Wall Street Journal*, July 16, 1999, p. C15.

dollar price by using the forward rate, resulting in an export price of $17,780.41 in Canadian currency. Upon shipping, the exporter would sell at $17,727.88 (in Canadian money) forward with sixty days delivery and, with the rate of $.6769 per Canadian dollar, receive U.S. $12,000. Consequently, wherever possible, quotes in foreign currencies should be made based on forward rates, with respective foreign currency amounts sold in the forward market.

Selection of a Hedging Procedure To illustrate the selection of a hedging procedure, assume that a U.S. exporter of computer workstations sells two machines valued at $24,000 to a client in the United Kingdom. The client will pay in British pounds quoted at the current (spot) rate (July 16, 1999) of $1.5650, or £15,335.46. This amount will be paid in two months (sixty days). As a result, the U.S. exporter will have to determine how to protect such an incoming amount against foreign exchange risk. Although uncertain about the outcome, the exporter's bank indicates that there is an equal chance for the British pound spot rate to remain at $1.5650 (Scenario A), to devalue to $1.45 (Scenario B), or to appreciate to $1.65 (Scenario C). As a result, the exporter has the option of selling the amount forward in the sixty days forward market, at $1.5684.

	A	B	C
Spot rate as of July 16, 1999	$1.5650	$1.5650	$1.5650
Spot rate as of September 16, 1999 (estimate)	1.45	1.65	$1.5650
U.S. dollar equivalent of £15,335.46 at spot rates on July 16, 1999	24,000.00	22,236.42	25,303.51
Exchange gain (loss) with hedging	0	(1,763.58)	1,303.51

Source: "Foreign Exchange," *Wall Street Journal*, July 16, 1999, p. C15.

The alternative available to the exporter is to sell forward the invoice amount of £15,335.46 at $1.5684 to obtain a sure $23,947.98, a cost of $52.02 on the transaction. In anticipation of a devaluation of the pound, such a hedging strategy would be advisable. Consequently, the $52.02 represents a premium to ensure against any larger loss. However, a company would also forgo any gain as indicated under Scenario C. Acceptance for hedging through the forward market depends on the expected spot rate at the time the foreign payment is due. Again, keep in mind that the forward rate is not an estimate of the spot rate in the future.

Dealing with Parallel Imports or Gray Markets

One of the most perplexing problems global companies face is the phenomenon of different prices between countries. When such price differentials become large, individual buyers or independent entrepreneurs step in and buy products in low-price countries to reexport to high-price countries, profiting from the price differential. This arbitrage behavior creates what experts call the "gray market," or "parallel imports," because these imports take place outside of the regular trade channels controlled by distributors or company-owned sales subsidiaries. Such price differences can occur as a result of company price strategy, margin differences, or currency fluctuations. Levi Strauss sells its 501 Jeans in Paris at twice the price paid in the U.S.; therefore, it is not surprising that EU retailers are buying much of their Levi's inventory from unofficial sources outside the EU. The current EU legislation allows for parallel trading between countries within the EU but does not allow parallel imports of unofficial branded products from outside of the EU. Levi is suing twenty-four European retailers, including Tesco, the U.K. supermarket giant, for parallel importing from outside the EU. The brand owners argue that parallel imports hurt the consumer because the goods are old, damaged, different specifications, or even fakes. Consumer groups and retailers argue that parallel imports increase competition, give the consumer more choice, and lead to lower prices. EU commissioners are considering elimination of the law banning parallel trading from outside the EU.[41]

Parallel importing has become a big problem in the European pharmaceutical industry, where wholesalers buy truckloads of branded ulcer and cancer drugs at bargain-basement prices in Spain and Portugal and resell them in Britain and Germany, where prices are higher. The northern European countries have paid the higher prices to support the higher costs of research and development. One study estimated that the parallel trade from Spain to Britain, France, Germany, and the Netherlands cost the seven leading drug companies $300 million in 1996. Drug companies sought protection from the European Court of Justice, but the court ruled that wholesalers have the right to trade goods freely throughout Europe regardless of different fixed prices among the various states.[42]

As the European Union transitions to a common currency, two things happened. First, pricing has become more transparent, and customers expect lower prices. For example, a pack of twenty aspirin cost 11 cents in Spain and 19 cents in Germany in 1997. Retailers in Germany expect a price close to the Spanish price, or they will buy from a Spanish distributor.[43] Second, there will be no foreign exchange cost. Heinz-Walter Kohl, head of corporate finance at Bayer,

41. "Parallel Imports: Hardly the Full," *Economist*, February 27, 1999, p. 72.
42. "Pharmaceuticals Drug Trafficking," *Economist*, December 17, 1996, p. 65.
43. "When the Walls Come Down," *Economist*, July 5, 1997, p. 61.

estimated the common European currency will save Bayer up to DM 50 million ($28.5 million) in exchange costs each year.[44]

Fluctuating currency values can also create opportunities for parallel imports, as observed earlier in this chapter. The fluctuating currency value in Indonesia has led to a flourishing parallel import trade. With the value of the dollar fluctuating between Rp 14,000 and Rp 17,000, customers can buy Epson inkjet printers and Toshiba notebooks on the gray market for $5 to $50 less than from an authorized dealer.[45]

Chinese National Tobacco reports that 90 percent of the foreign cigarettes sold in China are smuggled in, costing the Chinese government over $1 billion in lost tax revenue. The volume of smuggled cigarettes is high because of the equally high Chinese tariff. Local distributors pay only $500 per case (10,000 cigarettes) for smuggled products versus $700 per case for legally imported cigarettes. Philip Morris and BAT, the two largest suppliers, do not condone the practice; nevertheless, they spend about $120 million on advertising and sports sponsorship in China and the government estimates that over $100 million of Philip Morris cigarettes enter China illegally per year.[46]

For the United States alone, parallel, or gray-market, annual volume was estimated to be $130 billion. A typical example of gray markets is Lanza Research Company, which sold shampoo at a 40 percent discount to Libya and Malta. However, when Quality King International purchased the shampoo in Malta and reimported it into the United States, Lanza sued Quality King in federal court based on copyright law but lost the suit in the U.S. Supreme Court.[47]

Corporate users of international telecommunications services have begun to enjoy the benefits of parallel trading of long-distance telephone services. Although long-distance service in Japan is available through Kokusai Denshin Denwa (KDD) at a cost of $4.36 per minute to the United States, companies can use call-back service for a rate of $1.77 per minute or less. The caller simply dials a number in the United States, which recognizes the call without answering it, then calls back and allows the user to take advantage of inexpensive phone rates.[48]

Global companies can deal with parallel, or gray, markets at two levels. Once such practices occur, a firm may use a number of strategies in a reactive way. These range from confronting the culprit to price cutting, supply interference, and emphasis of product limitations all the way to acquisition of the diverter in-

44. "EMU Boost for Bosch," *Financial Times*, July 8, 1997, p. 2.
45. "Parallel Imports Takes a Chunk Out of Distributor Profits," *Asia Computer Weekly*, December 21, 1998, p. 3.
46. Craig Smith, "Smugglers Stoke BAT's Cigarette Sales in China," *Wall Street Journal*, December 18, 1996, p. A16; Craig S. Smith and Wayne Arnold, "China's Antismuggling Drive to Hurt U.S. Exporters," *Wall Street Journal*, August 5, 1998, p. A12.
47. "Gray Goods Cleared by Court," *Chain Store Age* (New York), April 1998, p. 34.
48. Joshua Ogawa, "Call Back Market Ringing Up a Storm," *Nikkei Weekly*, October 21, 1996, pp. 1, 19.

volved. A number of proactive strategies may be implemented to prevent the practice from occurring at all. A company may provide product differentiation solely to prevent gray markets from developing. Strategic pricing may be used to keep prices within limits. Cooperation may be achieved with dealers willing to cooperate. And, finally, companies may use strict legal enforcement of contracts and even resort to lobbying governments with the aim of adding regulations that may prevent the practice. For example, international drug companies argued in hearings before the Israeli Knesset (parliament), that parallel imports endanger public health because of fake and fraud medicines.[49]

The pricing situation in the EU is especially interesting since the introduction of the euro, which allows easy price comparisons from country to country. A recent study by the French *L'Express* found prices within Europe could vary by up to 500 percent. For example, a 1.5 liter of Coca-Cola cost .7 euro in Portugal and 1.9 euro in Finland; a Sony premium 180-minute videocassette cost 1.98 euro in Portugal and 10.52 euro in France. A proactive strategy to develop a European pricing corridor is recommended by some experts. The price corridor would take into account the price elasticities of different markets and maximize the potential European profit margin rather than gravitating to the lowest price availability in Europe, if the parallel trading is successful.[50]

Product arbitrage will always occur when price differentials get too large and when transport costs are low in relation to product value. Global companies will have to monitor price differentials more closely for standardized products in particular. Products that are highly differentiated from country to country are less likely to become parallel traded.

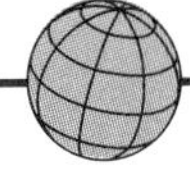

Managing Export Price Escalation

The additional costs described earlier may raise the end-user price of an exported product substantially above its domestic price. This phenomenon, called export price escalation, may force a company to adopt either of two strategic patterns. First, a company may realize its price disadvantage and adjust the marketing mix to account for its "luxury" status. By adopting such a strategy, a company sacrifices volume to keep a high unit price. For example, in Guangzhou, China, Pizza Hut found that the typical price per person per meal was 40 to 50 renminbi (RMB), whereas a value meal at McDonald's was 16 to 25 RMB. Pizza Hut determined it was necessary to position itself as a casual dining restaurant with table service, rather than counter service, to differentiate its offerings from the

49. "Israel Adopts Dutch Drug Import Pricing System," *Marketletter* (London), February 23, 1998, p. 1.
50. Stephan A. Butscher, "Maximizing Profits in Euro-Land," *Journal of Commerce*, May 5, 1999, p. A5.

fast-food restaurants.[51] Alternatively, a company may grant a "discount" on the standard domestic price to bring the end-user price more in line with prices paid by domestic customers. Such discounts may be justified under marginal-contribution pricing methods. Because of reduced marketing costs at the manufacturer's level, particularly when a foreign distributor is used, an export price equal to a domestic price is often not justified. Legal limits such as antidumping regulations prevent price reductions below a certain point. Customary margins, both wholesale and retail, may differ considerably among countries, with independent importers frequently requiring higher margins than domestic intermediaries do.

Global Pricing Strategies

As global companies deal with market and environmental factors, they face two major strategic pricing alternatives. Essentially, the choice is between the global single-price strategy and the individualized country strategy.

To maximize a company's revenues, it would appear to be logical to set prices on a market-by-market basis, looking in each market for the best combination of revenue versus volume yielding maximum profit. This strategy was common for many firms in the early part of their international development. For many products, however, noticeable price differences between markets are taken advantage of by independent companies or channel members who see a profit from buying in lower-price markets and exporting products to high-price markets. For products that are relatively similar in many markets and for which transportation costs are not significant, substantial price differences will quickly result in the emergence of the gray market. As a result, fewer companies have the option of pricing on a market-by-market basis. As the markets become more transparent, the information flows more efficiently; and as products become more similar, the trend away from market-by-market pricing is likely to continue.

McDonald's, the leading U.S. fast-food chain, has taken the route of pricing its products according to local market conditions. Its key product, the Big Mac, priced at $2.43 in the United States, ranged from $1.19 in Malaysia to $3.97 in Switzerland. The third column in Table 10.3 shows the cost of a Big Mac in each country divided by its cost in the home market, giving the implied purchasing power of the local currency. Comparing these figures to the actual exchange rate, you can see which currencies are overvalued or undervalued based on the Big Mac; for example, the Swiss franc is overvalued by 64 percent, whereas the Chinese yuan and the Malaysian ringgit are undervalued by 51 percent.[52] The so-called Big Mac index has been studied by many economists. Annaert and De-

51. Author's interview on June 16, 1999, Guangzhou, China, with Henry Yip, General Manager of Pizza Hut Southern China.

52. "Big MacCurrencies: The Economist Offers Some Hot Tips on Exchange Rates," *Economist*, April 3, 1999, p. 66.

TABLE 10.3

The Hamburger Standard

	Big Mac prices in local currency	in dollars	Implied PPP* of the dollar	Actual $ exchange rate 30/03/99	Under (−)/ over (+) valuation against the dollar, %
United States†	$2.43	2.43	—	—	—
Argentina	Peso2.50	2.50	1.03	1.00	+3
Australia	A$2.65	1.66	1.09	1.59	−32
Brazil	Real2.95	1.71	1.21	1.73	−30
Britain	£1.90	3.07	1.28‡	1.61‡	+26
Canada	C$2.99	1.98	1.23	1.51	−19
Chile	Peso1.25	2.60	518	484	+7
China	Yuan9.90	1.20	4.07	8.28	−51
Denmark	DKr24.75	3.58	10.19	6.91	+47
Euro area	Euro2.52	2.71	0.97§	1.08§	+11
France	FFr8.50	2.87	7.20	6.10	+18
Germany	DM4.95	2.72	2.04	1.82	+12
Italy	Lire4,500	2.50	1,852	1,799	+3
Netherlands	Fl5.45	2.66	2.24	2.05	+10
Spain	Pta375	2.43	154	155	0
Hong Kong	HK$10.2	1.32	4.20	7.75	−46
Hungary	Forint299	1.26	123	237	−48
Indonesia	Rupiah14,500	1.66	5,967	8,725	−32
Israel	Shekel13.9	3.44	5.72	4.04	+42
Japan	¥294	2.44	121	120	0
Malaysia	M$4.52	1.19	1.86	3.80	−51

TABLE 10.3

The Hamburger Standard (cont.)

	Big Mac prices in local currency	in dollars	Implied PPP* of the dollar	Actual $ exchange rate 30/03/99	Under (−)/ over (+) valuation against the dollar, %
Mexico	Peso19.9	2.09	8.19	9.54	−14
New Zealand	NZ$3.40	1.82	1.40	1.87	−25
Poland	Zloty5.50	1.38	2.26	3.98	−43
Russia	Rouble33.5	1.35	13.79	24.7	−44
Singapore	S$3.20	1.85	1.32	1.73	−24
South Africa	Rand8.60	1.38	3.54	6.22	−43
South Korea	Won3,000	2.46	1,235	1,218	+1
Sweden	SKr24.0	2.88	9.88	8.32	+19
Switzerland	SFr5.90	3.97	2.43	1.48	+64
Taiwan	NT$70.0	2.11	28.8	33.2	−13
Thailand	Baht52.0	1.38	21.4	37.6	−43

*Purchasing-power parity: local price divided by price in United States.
†Average of New York, Chicago, San Francisco and Atlanta. ‡Dollars per pound. §Dollars per euro.
Source: "The Hamburger Standard," *Economist*, April 3, 1999, p. 66.

Ceuster found that since 1986, when the Big Mac index began, the three most undervalued currencies outperformed the three most overvalued currencies by 2.6 percent per year.[53] (See Table 10.3 for more comparisons.) Certainly, McDonald's can maximize its pricing according to the competitive forces of each individual country without much fear of parallel imports.

For many consumer products, there are still substantial price differences across many countries. For a price comparison of the cost of a movie ticket in major European cities, see Figure 10.4. Many theorize that large differences in

53. "Something for Investors to Chew Over," *Economist*, December 7, 1996, p. 68.

FIGURE 10.4

Price of a Movie Ticket in Major European Cities

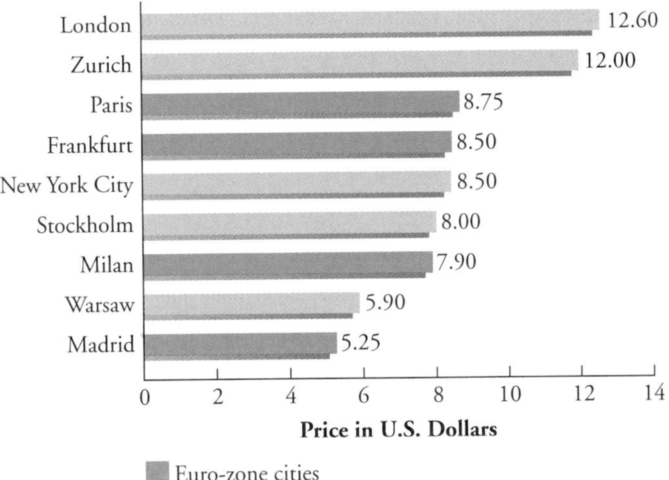

Source: "Price of a Movie Ticket in Major Metropolitan Areas' from "Prices at the Europlex" *The Economist*, March 27, 1999, p110. Copyright © 1999 The Economist Newspaper Group, Inc. Reprinted with permission. Further reproduction prohibited.

prices will cause consumers to cross the border for a lower price. Thus, given that a Swatch costs 39.2 euros in Belgium and 25.7 euros in Italy, or that a bottle of Chanel No. 5 perfume is 42.2 euros in the Netherlands and 34.8 euros in Belgium, many theorize consumers will cross the border to spend less. However, the price differences often reflect the VAT (value-added sales tax), labor rates, regulatory burdens, transportation, or real estate cost differences. Mr. Jan Haars, group treasurer of Unilever, predicts about a 10 percent price difference across Europe.[54]

Employing a uniform pricing strategy on a global scale requires that a company, which can determine its prices in local currency, will always charge the same price everywhere when the price is translated into a base currency. In reality, this becomes very difficult to achieve whenever different taxes, trade margins, and customs duties are involved. As a result, there are likely to be price differences due to those factors not under control of the company. Keeping prices identical aside from those noncontrollable factors is a challenge. Firms may start

54. G. Pascal Zachary, "Euro Is Unlikely to End Differences in Prices Soon," *Wall Street Journal*, January 1, 1999, p. A 16.

out with identical prices in various countries but soon find that prices have to change to stay in line with often substantial currency fluctuations.

Although it is becoming increasingly clear for many companies that market-by-market pricing strategies will cause difficulties, many firms have found that changing to a uniform pricing policy is rather like pursuing a moving target. Even when a global pricing policy is adopted, a company must carefully monitor price levels in each country and avoid large gaps that can then cause problems when independent or gray-market forces move in and take advantage of large price differentials.

Financing Global Marketing Transactions

As many global marketers have observed, the ability to make financing available at a low cost can become the deciding factor that beats competitors. In the context of global marketing, financing should be understood in its broadest sense (see Figure 10.5). Not only does it consist of direct credits to the buyer, it also includes a range of activities that enable the customer to afford the purchase. In this section we examine financing provided by the selling company, as well as financing through the financial community and government-sponsored agencies.

Risks

Financing global marketing transactions involves a host of risks over and above those encountered by strictly domestic operations. Global companies have to be aware of these risks and understand the methods available for reducing risk to an acceptable level. The four major risks are commercial risk, foreign currency risk, transfer risk, and political risk.

Commercial risk refers to buyer ability to pay for the products or services ordered. This risk is also typical for a domestic operation. As a result, companies are accustomed to checking the financial stability of their customers and may even have internally approved credit limits. Although checking credit references in a domestic environment poses no great difficulty, such information is not always readily available in every market. Companies can rely on their banks or on credit reporting agencies where such organizations exist. Past experience with a commercial customer abroad may frequently be the only indicator of a firm's financial stability.

Foreign currency risk exists whenever a company bills in a currency other than its own.[55] For U.S. companies billing in Japanese yen, a currency risk exists because the value of the yen versus the dollar is subject to market fluctuations

55. Chuck C.Y. Kwok, "Hedging Foreign Exchange Exposures: Independent Versus Integrative Approaches," *Journal of International Business Studies*, Summer 1987, p. 33.

FIGURE 10.5

Financing Global Marketing Transactions

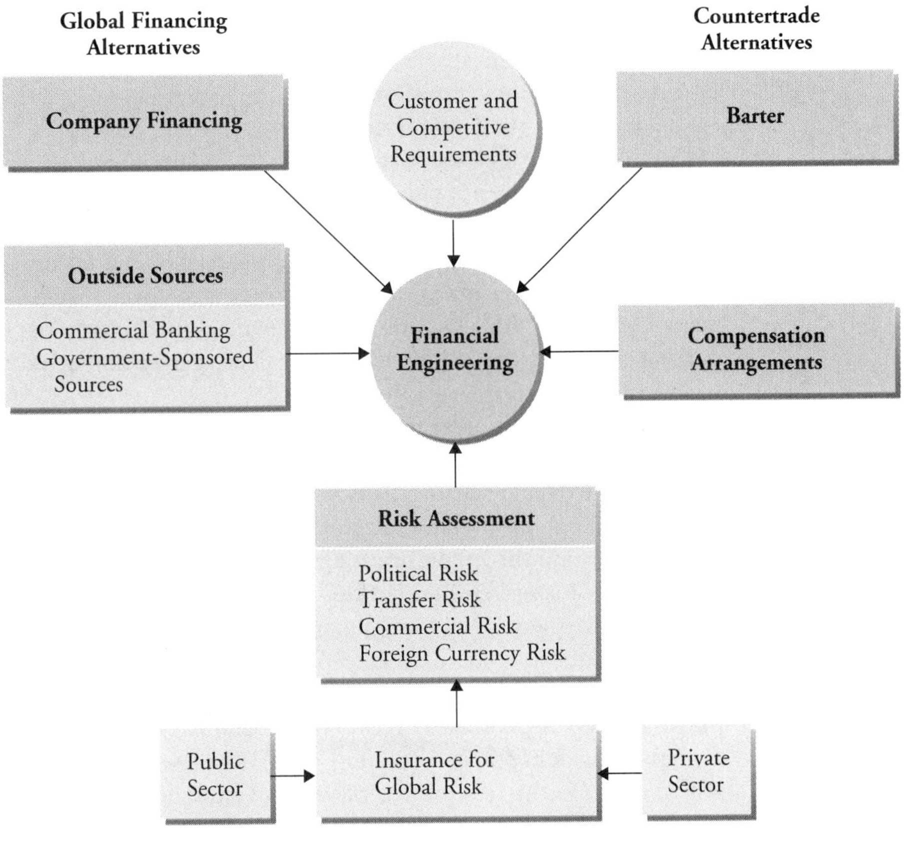

and, therefore, cannot be determined at the outset. Foreign currency risk grows with the length of credit terms and with the instability of a foreign currency. For example, in June 1998, the dollar was worth 142 yen, a drop of 40 percent from the 1995 high of 102 yen to the dollar. This weakening of the yen meant that all countries exporting to Japan found their product more expensive when converted to yen. Also, South Korea and Taiwan, whose products compete with the Japanese exports, found lower prices as the weak yen was converted to dollars, sterling, or Swiss francs.[56] For example, in 1997, Andrew Carol Jr.,

56. "The Yen: Asian Nightmares," *Economist*, June 13, 1998, p. 68.

president and CEO of the American Automobile Association, stated, "The free fall of the yen is becoming a serious problem that is disrupting business planning and threatening many U.S. exports opportunities. Having depreciated more than 50 percent from its peak in 1995, it has become a run-away train that is threatening serious market disruptions."[57] On the other hand, when the yen started to recover in 1999, this appreciation made Japanese exports more expensive. Sony reported that the 5 percent appreciation in the yen cost the firm 54 billion yen in the last quarter of 1998. Nissan predicted a 60-billion-yen loss for its fiscal year ending March 31, 1999.[58] Suppliers can ensure themselves against foreign currency fluctuations, as was described in more detail earlier in this chapter.

Invoicing in their own currency, suppliers shift the currency risk to the customer. The customer may not be in a position to cover that risk, as is the case in many countries with unsophisticated financial markets. In such a case, the exporting company frequently must choose between selling in a foreign currency or having no deal at all.

Although the customer may be able to pay, payments often get delayed by bureaucracies, creating a *transfer risk*. Transfer delays prevail in countries where the foreign exchange market is controlled and where the customer has to apply for the purchase of foreign currency before payment takes place. Delays of up to 180 days beyond the credit terms agreed on are not unusual and add to the costs of exporter or supplier. In countries where a foreign exchange shortage prevents immediate payment of all foreign currency–denominated debts, complex debt restructuring negotiations may take place, causing additional delays. Many countries have had to negotiate such extensions at one time or another, including Brazil, Mexico, Argentina, Turkey, Poland, and Zaire.

Financing for global marketing operations is also subject to *political risk*, which includes the occurrence of war, revolutions, insurgencies, or civil unrest, any of which may result in nonpayment of accounts receivable. In some instances, civil unrest may demand rescheduling of foreign trade debt, as in Poland in the early 1980s. In other situations, political unrest may bring about a new government that cancels foreign debt, as happened in Iran following the downfall of the shah in 1979.

The global marketer needs to understand the risks of providing financing to customers. In cases in which the supplier shoulders all global risks, companies may want to build extra costs into their prices. Smaller price adjustments may be required when only a portion of the global credit risk is carried.

57. "Worth Repeating," *Fortune*, March 3, 1997, p. 27.

58. Robert L. Simison, "Japan's Nissan Reports Wider Loss," *Wall Street Journal*, May 21, 1999, p. 1; Bill Spindle, "Weak Sales Prove Drag on Results for Sony," *Wall Street Journal*, January 1, 1999, p. A13.

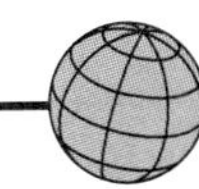

Customer-Arranged Versus Supplier-Arranged Financing

As discussed in this section, financing arranged by suppliers goes beyond the open-account practices that will be described in Chapter 18. In this context, supplier financing is viewed as any term beyond the usual thirty to ninety days customary for open-account shipment.

Because credit risks are higher for clients abroad, companies have a preference for shorter payment terms with foreign clients. However, many customers may not be able to purchase under shortened credit terms. Consequently, companies may charge an interest rate on the outstanding amount. When companies cannot get at least market interest rates, they may try to capture the additional cash through higher prices. However, most clients today are adept at comparing total costs to themselves, and opportunities for hiding interest costs behind higher list prices are limited.

Since most companies do not consider themselves to be in the business of financing their customers, they prefer to assist clients in finding suitable financing opportunities. One such exception is financing without recourse, a relatively new method (explained below) for financing shipments abroad.

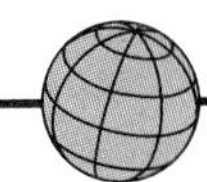

Sources of Financing

Companies can choose from a wide selection of alternatives to finance global marketing transactions: traditional financing through commercial banks, government-sponsored loans, or countertrade. The global marketer is increasingly expected to be knowledgeable about complicated financial arrangements. As buyers compare acquisition costs, including any necessary financing, providing such financing becomes a matter for marketing management to handle. The following sections offer you a general background on the most common financing alternatives practiced by many global companies today.

Commercial Banks

Commercial banks, whether domestic or foreign, are usually willing to finance transactions only to first-rate credit risks. This fact makes financing unavailable to any but the largest companies. Furthermore, commercial banks avoid long-term financing and prefer short maturities. When selecting a commercial bank, inquire about the following: size of the global department, number and locations of foreign branches or correspondent banks, charges for letters of credit, and experience with government financing programs.

Commercial banks that have loaned heavily to developing countries have recently experienced difficulties with repayment and interest payments on outstanding loan portfolios. Therefore, banks located in developed countries have hesitated to lend further to developing countries, forcing exporters to look elsewhere to finance their clients.

Clients outside the developed countries of Europe and Asia have also found local financing difficult. Especially for purchases in currencies other than their own, foreign buyers in developing countries are increasingly dependent on financing from abroad. For larger industrial projects, this is now almost the rule. With commercial banks only partially able to close the gap, both buyers and suppliers are availing themselves of other financing sources.

Forfaiting: Financing Without Recourse[59] *Forfaiting*, or financing without recourse, means that the seller of merchandise can transfer a claim, resulting from a transaction in the form of a bill of exchange, to a forfaiting house by including the term *without recourse* as part of the endorsement. The collection risk is thus transferred to the forfaiting house, and the seller receives on presentation of documents the full amount minus a discount for the entire credit period. Generally, the forfaiting houses prefer working with invoices guaranteed by foreign banks or governments.[60] The discount varies with the country risk and the currency chosen for financing. Typical maturities range from six months to several years.

Nonrecourse financing offers the advantage of selling products over medium terms at market rates. Such transactions are not possible through commercial banks. An exporter may obtain a firm quote on a given business deal ahead of time, allowing inclusion of the discount rate into the price calculation. This ensures that the net payout meets normal profitability standards. Forfaiting has become very popular for companies in developed countries selling to developing markets in eastern Europe and Latin America. The export forfaiting market is estimated to be \$30 to \$50 billion, or 5 percent of world trade.[61] For example, when Sortex, a California manufacturer of agricultural processing equipment, sold \$100,000 of equipment to a company in Argentina, it turned to London Forfaiting. The forfaiting loan was guaranteed by the buyer's bank, and the equipment was shipped. After Sortex received the paperwork from the customer and its local bank that the equipment had arrived in Argentina, London Forfaiting paid Sortex.[62]

59. This section is based on Carol Lustig, "Forfaiting: A European Customer Finance Technique Comes to the U.S.," *Business Credit*, Nov/Dec 1998, pp. 26–29.
60. "Congratulations, Exporter, Now About Getting Paid," *Business Week*, January 17, 1994, p. 98.
61. Rupert Wright, "Forfaiting for Fun and Profit," *Euromoney*, December 1997, pp. 140–141.
62. Daniel S. Levine, "Forfaiting," World Trade, December 1998, pp. 55–56.

Government-Sponsored Financing: The Export-Import Bank

With the ability to assemble the best financing package often determining the sale of capital equipment or other large-volume transactions, governments all over the world have realized that government-sponsored banks can foster exports and, therefore, employment.[63] Government-subsidized financing now exceeds that which commercial banks and exporters formerly provided. For this purpose, the United States created its Export-Import Bank (Eximbank for short) in 1934. Other countries, particularly members of the Organization for Economic Cooperation and Development (OECD), have established their own export banks, also aimed at assisting their respective exporters with the financing of large transactions. Japan committed funds to provide 15 trillion yen of insurance coverage per year for developing countries and political risk insurance for Japanese companies investing overseas. The export insurance plan was to cover up to 97.5 percent of the value for prepaid contracts.[64]

The Export-Import Bank and its affiliated institutions, the Foreign Credit Insurance Association (FCIA) and the Private Export Funding Corporation (PEFCO), make a number of services available to U.S. exporters. Eximbank has special services for short-, medium-, and long-term financing requirements.

Short-Term Financing Financing requirements of 180 days or less are considered short-term. For such commitments, Eximbank does not make direct financing available. Instead, through the Foreign Credit Insurance Association, Eximbank offers export credit insurance to the U.S. exporter. This insurance covers the exporter for commercial risk, such as nonpayment by the foreign buyer; political risk, such as war, revolution, insurrection, and expropriation; and currency inconvertibility. The cost of such insurance averages less than half of 1 percent per $100 of gross invoice value. With such insurance in force, the exporter has the choice of carrying accounts receivable on the company records or refinancing with a commercial bank at domestic interest rates, provided the transaction is insured. In general, commercial risks are insured up to 90 percent of the invoiced value. Political risks are covered for up to 100 percent of the merchandise value, depending on the type of policy selected.

In 1983, about $7.5 billion, or 3.8 percent, of U.S. exports were insured by the FCIA.[65] Total premium costs were about 0.2 percent of the insured volume. In

63. This segment draws heavily from official publications of the Export-Import Bank of the United States, Washington, D.C., 1979.
64. "Japan to Make Trade Insurance Operations Into Independent Agency," *Dow Jones International News*, January 6, 1999.
65. *Der Monat* (Swiss Bank Corporation), April 1985.

the same year, FCIA paid out $193 million to exporters or banks financing such trade. For the past few years, U.S. firms have enjoyed lower export insurance rates than those available in other countries. Companies in Sweden and Germany paid 3.4 and 2.3 percent, respectively.

Medium-Term Financing Eximbank classifies terms ranging from 181 days to five years as medium-term. To serve exporters, four special programs exist: the medium-term export credit insurance (FCIA) programs, the U.S. Commercial Bank Guarantee Program, the Discount Loan Program, and the Cooperative Financing Facility.

Several insurance alternatives are available through FCIA. Provided the foreign buyer makes a cash payment of 15 percent on or before delivery, and subject to a deductible of 10 percent, Eximbank will insure each specific transaction. Through the cooperation of nearly three hundred U.S. commercial banks, Eximbank organized the U.S. Commercial Bank Guarantee Program. Under this program, Eximbank offers protection against commercial and political risks on debts acquired by U.S. banks from U.S. exporters. This coverage is now extended to more than 140 countries. Conditions for the guarantee program include a cash payment of 15 percent by the foreign buyer, a deductible of 10 percent, and passing credit checks imposed by Eximbank and the participating commercial bank. The interest rate is set by the commercial bank according to prevailing domestic market conditions.

Long-Term Financing Long-term financing by Eximbank extends from five to ten years. Under special circumstances, as in the case of conventional or nuclear power plants, financing may be arranged for longer periods. Financing may occur either by direct credit to the foreign buyer or by a guarantee of repayment of private financing arranged by the buyer. Eximbank requires a 15 percent down payment by the foreign buyer and assurance that private financing is not possible on similar terms. In the past, foreign airlines and utilities have made frequent use of such facilities to finance purchases of aircraft and power-generating equipment.

In general, Eximbank programs do not extend direct financing to the U.S. exporter. Rather, the bank closes the gap between commercial bank financing and foreign buyer needs by guarantees or financing for the foreign buyer.

The Value of Eximbank Loans to U.S. Exporters Although less than 10 percent of U.S. exports are financed through Eximbank, loans at lower than market rates are crucial to exporters of many products. In 1998, Eximbank financed $13 billion of U.S. exports.[66] President Clinton boosted funding for Eximbank in

66. "Houston Exporter Heats Up Sales to Mexico's Power Industry," Press release, Export-Import Bank of the United States, February 4, 1999; www.exim.gov.

1999 to help meet the demand for aircraft and capital equipment exports to emerging markets.[67]

Another U.S. company that relied heavily on Eximbank financing was J. I. Case. Ellen Robinson, Case Corporation's VP for communications and government affairs, identified over 235 companies in thirty states that had benefited as subsuppliers to Case on Eximbank-financed exports.[68]

Eximbank support of U.S. exporters depends on funding from the U.S. government. U.S. exporters have in the past lobbied heavily to expand Eximbank funding, hoping to receive more loans at more favorable rates. However, many critics argue that Eximbank serves large firms that are already profitable. The political debate surrounding Eximbank is expected to continue, and its lending authority will vary as Congress appropriates differing fund levels from year to year. The Office of Management and Budget (OMB) has recommended that the federal government overhaul U.S. export functions by merging the Export-Import Bank of the United States with two other agencies: the Overseas Private Investment Corp., which provides political risk insurance, and the Trade and Development Agency, which develops feasibility studies for overseas export and investment in emerging markets.[69]

Eximbank has created a program that is used by over 1,100 U.S. small business exporters per year. Small businesses can use the short-term interest rates of Eximbank (6.5 to 7.5 percent in mid-1999) to offer attractive credit terms to their overseas customers. Also, the Eximbank Insurance Program, which costs about $940 on a $100,000 order, protects the business against payment default. Eximbank will pay 95 percent of the invoice if the buyer goes bankrupt, or 100 percent if the buyer cannot pay for political reasons, such as war.[70]

Financial Engineering: A New Marketing Tool With financing costs becoming ever more important for capital goods, many companies have moved toward exploiting the best financial deal from bases around the world. A company with manufacturing bases in several countries may bid on a contract from several subsidiaries to let the client select the most advantageous package, or it may preselect the subsidiary that will bid based on available financing. Devising such financial packages is known as *financial engineering*. It is practiced by independent specialists located in leading financial centers and by international banks that have developed expertise in this field.

67. "President's Manufacturing Export Initiative Would Increase Resources for Export-Import Bank," Press release, Export-Import Bank of the United States, January 9, 1999; www.exim.gov.
68. "Ex-Im Bank, Trade Groups Work Together to Meet U.S. Export Financing Needs," Press release, Export-Import Bank of the United States, March 12, 1999; www.exim.gov.
69. David Sanger, "U.S. Backs Export Groups," *International Herald Tribune*, January 25–26, 1997, p. 10.
70. "Ex-Im Bank Support for Small Business Exporters," Press release, Export-Import Bank of the United States, May 13,1999; www.exim.gov.

Massey-Ferguson, Ltd., a Canadian farm machinery manufacturer, provides an example of financial engineering.[71] Massey-Ferguson had traditionally supplied tractors to Turkey from its U.K. plants. Turkey experienced balance-of-payments difficulty, and the company had problems obtaining credit for the country. Massey-Ferguson looked to its other manufacturing bases for new sources of financing. The best deal was offered by Brazil, a country eager to expand its exports. Brazilians helped convince the Turkish customer Mafer to buy Brazilian-made equipment in U.S. dollars.

Massey sold 7,200 tractors worth $53 million to a Brazilian agency, which in turn sold to the Turkish buyer. Massey was to be paid cash, and a Brazilian state agency guaranteed payment. Thus, Brazil was able to take business of about 20,000 tractors annually from the United Kingdom because it assumed all risk for Massey-Ferguson.

Other companies are now institutionalizing financial engineering in their global operations. Some maintain full-time specialists at their global divisions who are prepared to advise operating divisions on financial engineering opportunities in bidding. Allowing customers to select the best financing options from any factory often results in increased sales. This strategy works best if products are highly standardized and quality differences between the various plants are minimal.

Noncash Pricing: Countertrade

International marketers are likely to find many situations in which an interested customer will not be able to find any hard-currency financing at all. In such circumstances, the customer might offer a product or commodity in return. The supplier must then turn the product offered into hard currency. Such transactions, known as *countertrades*, are estimated to have accounted for an estimated 15 to 25 percent of world trade in the mid-1980s.[72]

The U.S. International Trade Commission surveyed five hundred of the largest U.S. companies, accounting for some 60 percent of U.S. exports, on their use of countertrade. For 1984, the survey found that 5.6 percent of those firms' exports, totaling U.S. $7.1 billion, were covered by some part of a countertrade arrangement. About 80 percent of this volume was accounted for by military equipment sales.[73] With the end of the geopolitical struggle against communism and the breakup of the former Soviet Union, the international demand for weapons declined from 3.6 percent of GDP in 1990 to 2.4 percent in

71. "How Massey-Ferguson Uses Brazil for Export Financing," *Business Week*, March 17, 1978, p. 86.
72. "Beleaguered Third World Leads the Barter Boom," *Financial Times*, February 28, 1984, p. 6.
73. "Countertrade Comes Out of the Closet," *Economist*, December 20, 1986, p. 89.

1995. This lead to a reduction of the need for financial engineering of defense-related expenditures.[74]

Recent political changes in the world have not eliminated the need for countertrade. The eastern European countries, including Russia, remain plagued by a scarcity of foreign exchange. For example, Bulgaria has agreed to pay for its purchase of Russian natural gas with building materials.[75] Many more private or privatized companies are now looking to help themselves through such methods. Kotva, the Czech Republic's leading department store, could not get access to sufficient western goods even after the liberalization there in late 1989. The store traded Czech paper for Lego toys and Czech cheese for Italian vermouth.[76] The world financial crisis in Asia has led many developing countries short of strong currency to use financial engineering to fund infrastructure projects, which represent approximately 4 percent of GDP.[77] Over one hundred countries have some form of countertrade requirement as part of their public procurement program. Malcolm Taylor, president of the Australian Countertrade Association, reported that in 1998, 2 percent of Southeast Asia's trade was countertrade, and it was expected to grow to 20 percent by 2001.[78](To respond to this challenge, international marketers have developed several forms of countertrade (see Figure 10.6). The following sections explain each one and then examine the problems associated with each.[79]

Barter Barter, one of the most basic types of countertrade, consists of a direct exchange of goods between two parties. In most cases, these transactions take place between two or more nations (three in cases of triangular barter). Barter involves no currency and is concluded without the help of intermediaries.

One of the largest barter deals ever, valued at about $3 billion, was signed by PepsiCo and Russia. Since 1974, PepsiCo had engaged in business with Russia, shipping soft-drink syrup, bottling it into Pepsi-Cola, and marketing it within Russia. By 1989, the business had reached some 40 million cases (each containing twenty-four 8-ounce bottles). Within Russia, PepsiCo was running some twenty-six bottling plants, all producing at full capacity. The volume amounted to about $300 million for 1989. Since hard currency was not available

74. David B. Yoffie, "Barter: Looking Beyond the Short-Term Payoffs and Long-Term Threat," *International Management*, August 1984, p. 36.
75. "Countertrade Comes Out," p. 89.
76. "Czech Retailer Leads in Effort for Western Goods," *New York Times*, November 26, 1990, p. D7.
77. Pompiliu Verzariu, "Risk Mitigating Roles for Countertrade Techniques in Project Finance," *Journal of Project Finance* (New York), Fall 1998, pp. 57–62.
78. Darren McDermott and S. Karene Witcher, "Bartering Gains Currency in Hard-Hit Southeast," *Wall Street Journal*, April 6, 1998, p. A10.
79. The terminology used in this section is based on *Barter, Compensation and Cooperation*, vol. 47 IV (Zurich: Credit Suisse, 1978).

FIGURE 10.6

Forms of Countertrade

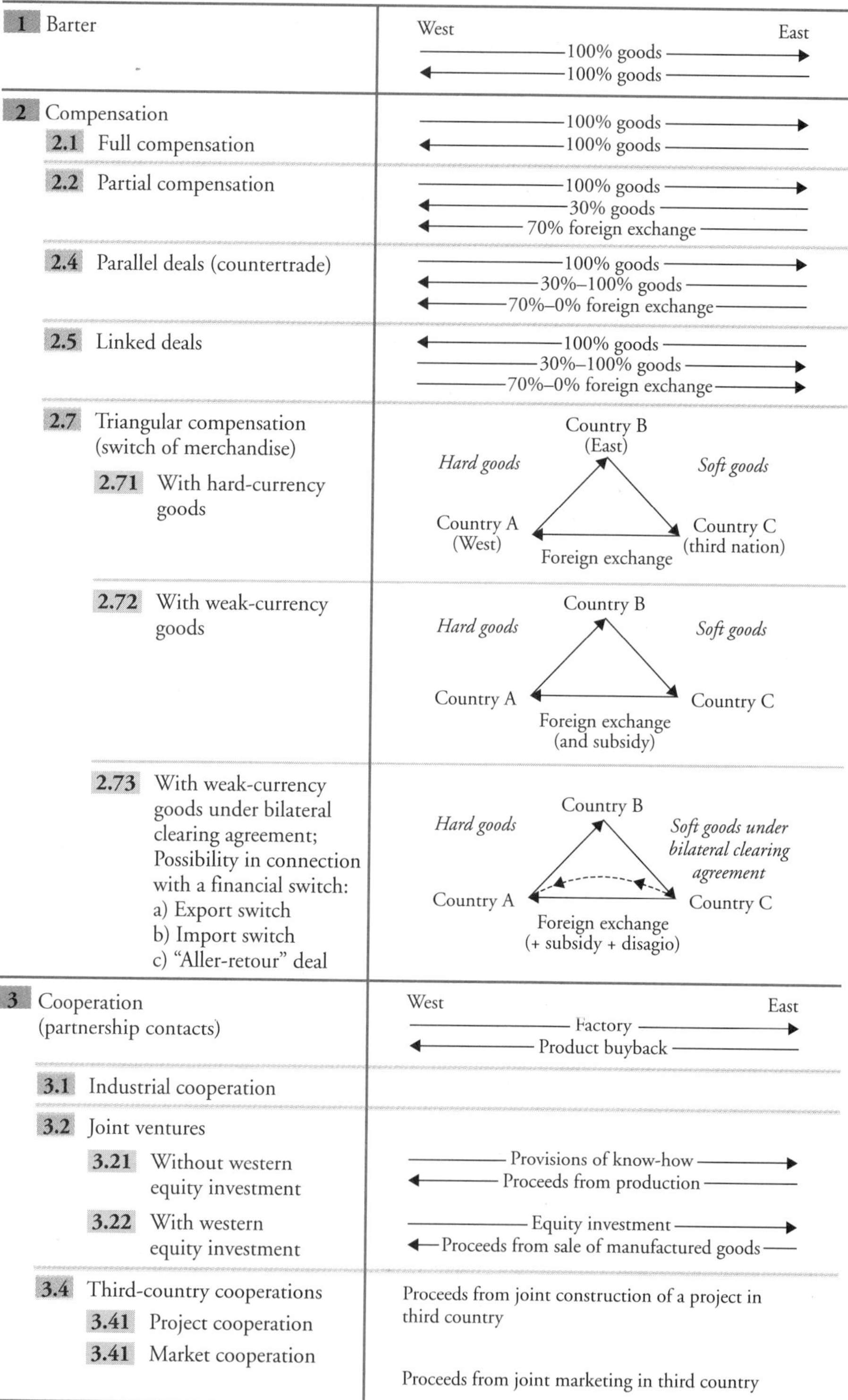

Source: Barter, Compensation and Cooperation, Credit Suisse, Zurich, Switzerland, Vol. 47, IV, 1978, pp. 8–9. Reprinted by permission.

for takeout profits, PepsiCo had entered an agreement to export Stolichnaya vodka to the United States, where it was sold through an independent liquor company. That volume had reached some 1 million cases (each containing twelve 25-ounce bottles), or about $156 million in sales. In 1990, a new deal was signed that included the sale or the lease of at least ten Russian tanker ships ranging from 28,000 to 65,000 tons. The proceeds of these transactions were to be used to expand the ongoing PepsiCo business in Russia by expanding Pepsi-Cola into national distribution and to fund the expansion of the Pizza Hut restaurant chain.[80]

Compensation Arrangements Compensation arrangements are transactions that include payment in merchandise or foreign exchange. Depending on the type of arrangement, the method or structure of the compensation transaction may change. One usually speaks of a compensation transaction when the value of an export delivery is offset by an import transaction or vice versa. Compensation transactions are typical for large governmental purchases, such as for defense, when a country wants to obtain some extra exports for the import of defense systems.[81] Compensation transactions may be classified into several categories, as described below.

Full Versus Partial Compensation. *Full* compensation is similar to barter in that a 100 percent mutual transfer of goods takes place. However, deliveries are made and paid for separately. By signing the sales agreement, the exporter commits to purchase products or services at an amount equal to that specified in the export contract. An option exists to sell such a commitment to a third party who may take over the commitment from the exporter for a fee. For example, Vietnam agreed to provide the Philippine Phosphate Corporation with fifty thousand tons of rice for an equivalent value of fertilizer.[82]

Under *partial* compensation, the exporter receives a portion of the purchase price in hard currency and the remainder in merchandise. The exporter will not be able to convert such merchandise into cash until a buyer can be found, and even then only at a discount.

A partial compensation transaction was concluded in 1998 by an Italian company building electric services in Thailand that agreed to take 30 percent of the value of the contract, or 218 million baht, in agricultural products, including rubber, rice, and tapioca.[83]

Parallel Deals. In a parallel deal, the exporter agrees to accept the merchandise equivalent of a given percentage of the export amount. Payment is received

80. "Pepsi Will Be Bartered for Ships and Vodka in Deal with Soviets," *New York Times*, April 9, 1990, p. 1.
81. "Excitement of Bartering Is Fading Away," *Financial Times*, June 1, 1989, Sec. 3, p. 111.
82. "Philippines to Swap Fertilizer for Rice with Vietnam," *World Reporter*, May 9, 1999, p. 1.
83. "Countertrade: Farm Goods Swapped for Italian Electricity, *Bangkok Post*, July 23, 1998, p. 1.

on delivery. This arrangement is intended to offset the outflow of wealth from the country when a very large purchase has been made. Within a given amount of time, the exporter searches for a specific amount of merchandise that can be bought from the country or company that purchased the products originally. Eastern European countries often include a penalty fee in case the western exporter defaults on the countertrade portion of the arrangement. Boeing agreed to increase its purchases of titanium from Russia's Verhnyaya Salda metallurgical plant from 2,000 to 2,200 tons in a deal that secured Boeing's sale of ten 737-400s to Aeroflot Russian International Airlines. Offset arrangements are a type of parallel deal gaining popularity today.[84]

Linked Deals. Linked deals, sometimes called junctions, are a form of countertrade not frequently used. A western importer finds a western exporter willing to deliver merchandise to a country in eastern Europe or to a developing nation. At the same time, the importer is released from a counterpurchase agreement by paying a premium to the exporter, which in turn organizes the counterpurchase. This transaction requires agreement of the state-controlled trading nation.

Triangular Compensation. Triangular compensation arrangements, also called *switch trades*, involve three countries. The western exporter delivers hard goods (salable merchandise) to an importing country, typically in eastern Europe. As payment, the importing country may transfer hard goods (easily salable merchandise) or soft goods (heavily discounted merchandise) to a third country in the West or in eastern Europe, which then reimburses the western exporter for the goods received. Such negotiations may become complex and time consuming. Often the assistance of skilled switch traders is required to ensure profitable participation by the western exporter.

Marc Rich & Co., a Swiss commodities firm, has been very successful in the republics of the former Soviet Union with complicated triangular arrangements. For example, in one deal, the company bought 70,000 tons of raw sugar in Brazil and shipped it to Ukraine to be processed. It paid for the processing with some of the sugar, then shipped 30,000 tons of the refined sugar six thousand miles to several huge Siberian oil refineries, which needed the sugar for their work force. Strapped for hard currency, the oil refineries paid with 130,000 tons of low-grade A-76 gasoline, which was shipped to Mongolia. The Mongolians paid for the gasoline with 35,000 tons of copper concentrate, which was shipped across the border to Kazakhstan, where it was refined to copper metal and shipped to a Baltic port. Marc Rich then sold the copper on the world market for hard currency and a profit.[85]

84. Jonathon Bell, "Plane Trading," *Airfinance Journal*, June 1998, pp. 34-36.

85. "Commodity Grant: Marc Rich & Co. Does Big Deals at Big Risk in the Former USSR," *Wall Street Journal*, May 13, 1993, pp. 1, A6.

Offset Deals. One of the fastest-growing types of countertrade is offset. In an offset transaction, the selling company guarantees to use some products or services from the buying country in the final product. These transactions are particularly common when large purchases from government-type agencies are involved, such as public utilities or defense-related equipment. The South African government has used offset deals very effectively to stimulate local industrial development in exchange for purchasing military equipment. In 1998, Saab and British Aerospace landed the sale of twenty-eight Gripen fighter planes by agreeing to industrial purchasing and investment in South Africa valued at 480 percent of the contract value.[86]

Cooperation Agreements. Cooperation agreements are special types of compensation deals extending over longer periods of time. They may be called product purchase transactions, buyback deals, or pay-as-you-earn deals. Compensation usually refers to an exchange of unrelated merchandise, such as coal for machine tools. Cooperation usually involves related goods, such as payment for new textile machinery by the output produced by these machines.

Although sale of large equipment or of a whole factory can sometimes only be clinched by a cooperation agreement involving buyback of plant output, long-term negative effects must be considered before any deal is concluded. In industries such as steel or chemicals, the effect of high-volume buyback arrangements between western exporters of manufacturing technology and eastern European importers has been devastating. Western countries, especially Europe, have been flooded with surplus products. European Union members established a general policy on cooperation arrangements to avoid further disruption of their domestic industries.

International Harvester is one U.S. company with experience in buyback arrangements.[87] In 1973, the company sold the basic design and technology for a tractor crawler to Poland. At the same time, International Harvester agreed to buy back tractor components manufactured by the Polish plant. These components were shipped to a subassembly plant in the United Kingdom that served the European market. In 1976, the company sold Hungary the design for an axle. To offset this sale, the company agreed to purchase complete axles for highway trucks.

Dangers in Compensation Deals. The greatest danger in compensation arrangements stems from the difficulty of finding a buyer of the merchandise accepted as part of the transaction. Often such transactions are concluded with organizations of countries in which industry is under government control. Since prices for goods in these countries are not determined by the supply-and-

86. Robert Koch, "Saab-British Aerospace Take Big Step Ahead of Competitors," *Agence France-Presse*, November 18, 1998, p. 1.

87. "Countertrade," *Commerce America*, June 19, 1978, p. 1.

demand forces of a free-market economy, merchandise transferred under compensation arrangements is often overvalued compared to open-market products. In addition, such merchandise, obviously not salable on its own, may be of low quality. As a result, the exporter may be able to sell the merchandise only at a discount. The size of these discounts may vary considerably, ranging from 10 percent to 33 percent of product value.[88] The astute exporter will raise the price of the export contract to cover such potential discounts on the compensating transaction.

The experience of a multinational chemical company serves as a good example of the difficulties encountered in barter deals. The company had sold $8 million worth of chemicals to Zimbabwe and agreed to take payment in tobacco, which was sold to Egypt along with another $12 million worth of chemicals to that country in the process. To pay for this transaction, Egypt was offering a whole range of basic commodities and materials as payment in lieu of the $20 million cash price. A specialty company was engaged that selected appropriate products and found buyers elsewhere in the world, collecting the cash. All told, the $20 million deal with Egypt involved ten different countries and six different product categories (see Figure 10.7).[89]

Precautions for Countertrade. A study of fifty-seven British companies involved in countertrade reported that the most difficult problems with countertrade were that there was no in-house use for the goods offered and the negotiations were complex and time consuming.[90]

At the conclusion of the sales agreement, the exporter should obtain a clear notion of the merchandise offered for countertrade. The description, origin, quality, quantity, delivery schedules, price, and purchasing currency in local or hard currency should be determined. With a detailed description given to a specialized trader, an estimate on the applicable discount may be rendered. The sale price of merchandise offered may be structured to include the difference between purchase amount and actual cash value. It is paramount that the western exporter not agree on any price before these other items are determined. Maintaining flexibility in negotiation requires skill and patience.

Organizing for Countertrade.[91] International companies are moving toward organizing countertrade for higher leverage. Many larger firms have established specialized units whose single purpose is to engage in countertrade. Many inde-

88. "Algeria: When Barter Is Battery," *Economist*, October 3, 1981, p. 80.
89. "Barter Is His Stock in Trade," *New York Times*, September 25, 1988, Special Business Supplement, pp. 32–36.
90. David Shipley and Bill Neale, "Industrial Barter and Countertrade," *Industrial Marketing Management*, February 1987, p. 6.
91. See also Christopher M. Korth, *International Countertrade* (Westport, Conn.: Quorum Books, 1987).

FIGURE 10.7

Countertrade with International Chemical Company

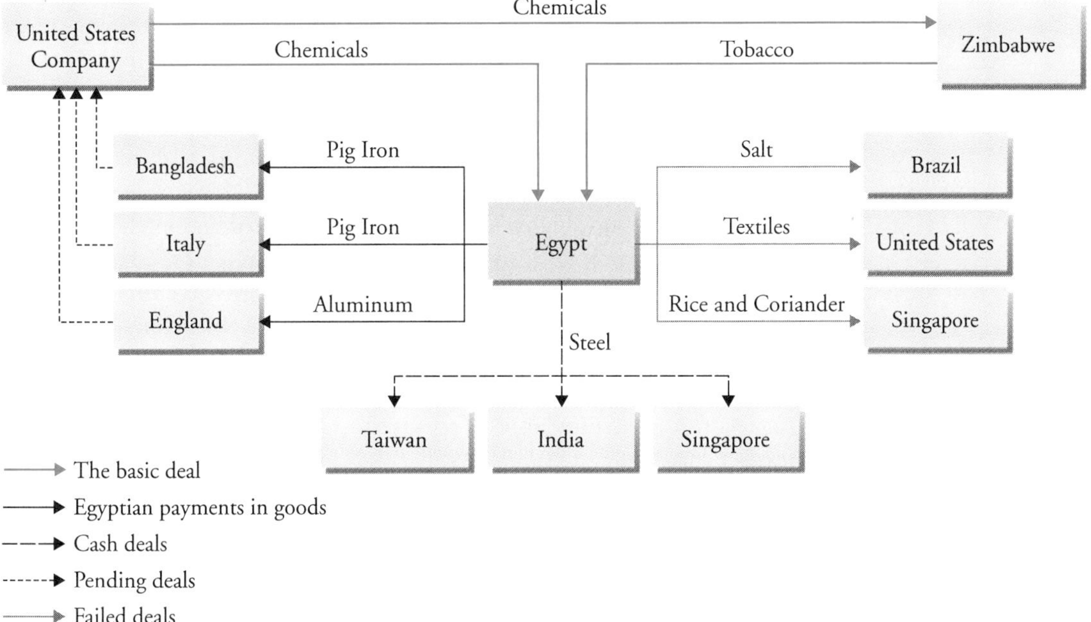

Source: New York Times, Special Business Supplement, September 25, 1988, p. 34.

pendent trading companies offer countertrading services. Several large U.S. banks have formed their own countertrade units.

Daihatsu, a Japanese automobile manufacturer, offers a good example of how a willingness to engage in countertrade can lead to a competitive advantage. Although the company was the smallest Japanese automobile manufacturer, Daihatsu managed to become the market leader for imported cars in eastern European countries such as Poland or Hungary. In Hungary, the company went as far as to schedule its parties for retiring Japanese workers through Hungary, allowing that country to earn additional foreign exchange, which resulted in the sale of another forty cars.[92]

92. "Daihatsu Sets Sights on Europe," *Financial Times*, March 5, 1986, p. 4.

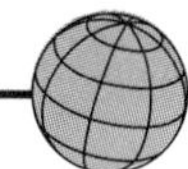

Conclusions

Managing pricing policies for an global firm is an especially challenging task. The global marketer is confronted with a number of uncontrollable factors deriving from the economic, legal, and regulatory environment, all of which have an impact on how prices are established in various countries. Though these influences are usually quite manageable in any given country, pricing across many markets means coping with price differentials that evolve out of environmental factors working in various combinations in different countries. Managing these price differentials and keeping them within tolerable limits are major tasks in global pricing.

One of the most critical values affecting price levels is foreign exchange rates. Today, managers find currencies moving both up and down, and the swings have assumed magnitudes that may substantially affect the competitiveness of a company. Understanding the factors that shape the directions of the foreign exchange market and mastering the technical tools that protect firms against large swings have become required skills for the global marketer. To the extent that a company can make itself less vulnerable to exchange rate movements, compared to its competitors, it may gain additional competitive advantage.

Because the relevant factors that affect price levels on an international scale are always fluctuating, the global pricing task is a never-ending process in which each day may bring new problems to be resolved. Whenever a company is slow to adapt or makes a wrong judgment, the market is very quick at adapting and at exploiting any weaknesses. As long as uncontrollable factors such as currency rates and inflation are subject to considerable fluctuations, the pricing strategies of international companies will have to remain under constant review. The ultimate goal is to minimize the gap between the price levels of various markets.

In this chapter, we have also examined the rather technical aspects of trade financing and countertrade. Many executives have realized that they cannot leave these trade forms to the occasional specialist but must use them proficiently as a competitive weapon in the aggressive global arena. If knowledge of financial engineering and countertrade is to become a competitive advantage, marketing executives negotiating such transactions must master these techniques. Global companies will be forced to expose and train their executives in these aspects of trade. We can expect an increasing world trade to be attached to one or the other of these techniques.

As competition in many industries increases, companies that have maintained a policy of "cash or no deal" often face a situation of "countertrade or no deal." Companies established in industrialized countries have seen that expansion into state-controlled economies or Third World countries and the hard-currency poor countries of eastern Europe requires a willingness to engage in countertrade. Understanding countertrade has become a prerequisite for an international marketing executive.

QUESTIONS FOR DISCUSSION

1. Discuss the difficulty or desirability of having a standardized price for a company's products across all countries.
2. Why should a company not go ahead and price its products in each market according to local factors?
3. How will the establishment of the euro affect consumer pricing in Europe?
4. You are an exporter of industrial installations and have received a $100,000 order from a Japanese customer. The job will take six months to complete and will be paid in full at that time. Now your Japanese customer has called you to request a price quote in yen. What will you quote him?
5. What factors may influence McDonald's to price its Big Mac differently throughout Latin America?
6. What strategies, other than through pricing, do companies have for combating parallel imports?
7. What should be the government's position on the issue of parallel imports? Should the government take any particular actions?
8. What is meant by the term *financial engineering*?
9. How should a firm approach the decision on whether to insure its exports?
10. Explain the major forms of countertrade. Under what circumstances should a company enter into such transactions?
11. What are the major risks to a firm engaging in countertrade?

FOR FURTHER READING

Assmus, Gert, and Carsten Wiese. "How to Address the Gray Market Threat Using Price Coordination." *Sloan Management Review*, 1995, vol. 36, no. 3, pp. 31-42.

Baker, James C., and John K. Ryans Jr. "International Pricing Policies of Industrial Product Manufacturers." *Journal of International Marketing*, 1982, vol. 1, no. 3, pp. 127-133.

Cavusgil, S. Tamer. "Pricing for Global Markets." *Columbia Journal of World Business*, Winter 1996, pp. 66-78.

Cavusgil, S. Tamer, and Ed Sikora. "How Multinationals Can Counter Gray Market Imports." *Columbia Journal of World Business*, Winter 1988, pp. 75-85.

Davis, H. Thomas Jr. "Transfer Prices in the Real World—10 Steps Companies Should Take Before It Is Too Late." *CPA Journal*, vol. 64, no. 10 (October 1994), pp. 82-83.

Dolan, Robert J., and Hermann Simon. *Power Pricing*. New York: The Free Press, 1996.

Dunhan, Dale F., and Mary Jane Sheffet. "Gray Markets and the Legal Status of Parallel Importation." *Journal of Marketing*, vol. 52 (July 1988), pp. 75-83.

Elderkin, Kenton W., and W. E. Norquist. *Creative Countertrade: A Guide to Doing Business Worldwide*. Cambridge: Ballinger, 1987.

Frazer, Jill Andresky. "Controlling Global Taxes." *Inc.*, August 1993, p. 35.

"Global Networks, Global Pricing." *Data Communications*, July 1993, p. 18.

Glowacki, Roman, and Leon Zurawicki. "Marketing for Hard Currency in Polish Domestic Markets." *Journal of Global Marketing*, 1991, vol. 4, no. 4, p. 85.

Horlick, Gary N., and Eleanor C. Shea. "The World Trade Organization Antidumping Agreement." *Journal of World Trade*, vol. 29, no. 1 (February 1995), pp. 5-31.

Huddleson, Patricia, and Linda K. Good. "The Price-Quality Relationship: Does It Hold True for Russian and Polish Consumers?" *International Review of Retail, Distribution and Consumer Research*, 1998, vol. 8, no. 1, pp. 35-51.

Korth, Christopher M. *International Countertrade*. Westport, Conn.: Quorum Books, 1987.

McGowan, Karen M., and Brenda J. Sternquist. "Dimensions of Price as a Marketing Universal: A Comparison of Japanese and U.S. Consumers." *Journal of*

International Marketing, vol. 6, no. 4 (November 1998), pp. 77-83.

Royal, Weld, and Allison Lucas. "Global Pricing and Other Hazards." *Sales & Marketing Management*, vol. 147, no. 8 (August 1995), pp. 80-83.

Samiee, Saeed, Patrick Anckar, and Abo Akademi. "Currency Choice in Industrial Pricing: A Cross-National Evaluation." *Journal of Marketing*, vol. 62, no. 3 (July 1998), pp. 112-128.

Simon, Hermann, and Eckhard Kucher. "The European Pricing Time Bomb: And How to Cope With It." *European Management Journal*, June 1992, pp. 136-144.

Sinclair, Stuart. "A Guide to Global Pricing." *Journal of Business Strategy*, May-June 1993, pp. 16-19.

Sweeny, Paul. "The Transfer Price Bomb." *Global Finance*, December 1992, pp. 32-33.

Weekly, James K. "Pricing in Foreign Markets." *Industrial Marketing Management*, May 1992, pp. 173-179.

Wrappe, Steven C., and George H. Soba. "A Practical Guide to the U.S. Advance Pricing Agreement Process." *Tax Executive*, Nov/Dec 1998.

11

Global Promotion Strategies

MANAGING THE COMMUNICATIONS PROCESS FOR A SINGLE MARKET IS NO EASY task. However, the task is even more difficult for global marketers, who must communicate to prospective customers in many markets. In the process, they struggle with different cultures, habits, and languages.

In this chapter, we describe the communications process when more than one country is involved and explore how a company structures its global promotion mix. (Advertising, a key element of the promotional mix, will be covered in detail in Chapter 12.) After a closer look at the differences between single-country and multi-country communications processes, we will turn to the challenge of developing a personal selling effort on a global level. Various methods of sales promotion are analyzed, and special problems involving the selling of industrial goods are highlighted, including the effects of the Internet and the World Wide Web on global marketing operations.

The Single-Country Promotion Process

Before discussing the various tools available to firms in the global promotion area, we first need to discuss the country-to-country dimension of the communications process. From studying basic marketing, you are familiar with the generalized single-country communications process. Communications flow from a source, in this case the company, through several types of channels to the receiver, in this case the customer. Channels are the mass media, both print and electronic, and the company's sales force. Communication takes place when intended content is received as the perceived content by the receiver or customer. Through a feedback mechanism, the communication sender verifies that the intended and perceived content are in fact identical.

This communications process typically is hindered by three potentially critical variables. A *source effect* exists when the receiver evaluates the received messages based on the status or image of the sender. Second, the *level of noise* caused by other messages being transmitted simultaneously tends to reduce the chances of effective communication. Finally, the messages have to pass through the receiver's, or target's, *perceptional filter*, which keeps out any messages that are not relevant to or consistent with the receiver's experience. Consequently, effective communications require that the source, or sender, overcome the source effect, noise level, and perceptional filter. This is the communications process familiar to most marketers in a domestic, or single-country, situation.

The Multicountry Communications Process

Research evidence and experience have demonstrated that the single-country/domestic communications model is applied to consumers in other countries as well. What we also find, however, are some additional barriers to overcome: the cultural barrier, different source effects, and various noise levels. Figure 11.1 presents a multicountry communications model with the cultural barrier arising at different times in the process.

What is a cultural barrier? In any multicountry communications flow, the source and the receiver are often located in different countries and thus have different cultural environments. The kind of influence that culture can have on the marketing environment has already been discussed at length in Chapter 3. The difficulty of communicating across cultural barriers, however, lies in the danger

FIGURE 11.1

Barriers in the Multicountry Communications Process

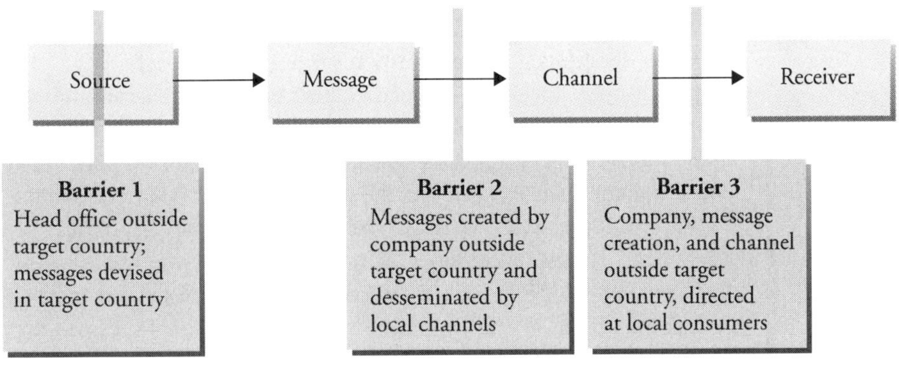

of substituting, or falling back on, one's own self-reference criteria in situations in which no particular information exists. This danger is particularly acute for executives who are physically removed from the target country. By moving additional decision-making responsibility into the local market, the cultural barrier may be overcome at a point closer to the source.

Even when a local subsidiary has substantial decision-making authority, some input comes from a regional or corporate head office operation. For most firms, then, some effort to overcome this cultural barrier will have to be made. In virtually all cases, certain executives are charged with bridging two cultures. The consequences of not successfully bridging this gap can be corporate failure and substantial losses.

For example, when Sara Lee's Hosiery Division was working with the retailer Marks & Spencer in the United Kingdom to introduce Hanes and L'eggs, it found significant differences between U.S. and British management. Pantyhose, which the English call tights, are a major product for Marks & Spencer, which has 20 percent of the U.K. hosiery market. Every product sold in Marks & Spencer is sold under the St. Michael brand name. After a long period of negotiations and market research, Sara Lee convinced Lord Rayner, the chairman, to use the L'eggs name with an addendum, "for St. Michael." The key reason Sara Lee was successful is that it respected Marks & Spencer's expertise and tradition and focused on collaboration rather than the typical approach of "Everything you people are doing is wrong; adopt our recommendations and your sales will double."[1]

1. "Pushing Yankee Products in Lord Rayner's Court," *Brandweek*, July 12, 1993, pp. 26–29.

Multicountry communications may also have an impact on the source effect. A foreign company's communications may trigger different reactions than do the communications of a local firm. In cases in which a positive reference group effect exists, an international company may want to exploit the situation. Frequently, however, the reaction to international firms is negative, forcing companies to deemphasize their foreign origins.

The noise level may differ because of different economic and competitive circumstances. In highly developed countries, noise from companies competing for the attention of target customers is extremely high. In some developing countries, fewer companies may vie for the attention of prospective clients. With media availability differing widely from country to country, the nature of channels used to reach target customers tends to vary. And finally, the feedback mechanisms may be subject to additional delays because of the distances involved. A concern in Moscow about all the foreign advertising and signs sapping the capital city of its "Russianness" led to a new requirement that all business and store displays be in Russian. This local requirement has created some additional noise and confusion for companies such as Puma, McDonald's, Benetton, Baskin & Robbins, and Reebok.[2]

Consequently, we can characterize the multicountry communications process as similar to the single-country process, though subject to considerable additional difficulties that make it a highly challenging task. The purpose of this chapter is to suggest strategies that global companies can employ to overcome these additional difficulties and barriers. Therefore, we begin our analysis by concentrating first on the different elements of the communications mix.

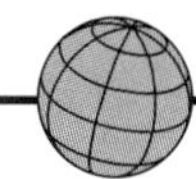

Global Promotion Strategies

How to manage the promotion mix globally is a critical question for many companies. Most firms do business in a certain way and do not rethink their promotion mix regularly. However, global marketers cannot take the full availability of all promotion elements for granted. As a result, many companies find themselves in countries or situations that require an adjustment or a substantial change in their promotion mix. This section and the ones that follow are devoted to understanding how different international environments affect promotion mix decisions.

In a domestic, or single-country, environment, companies achieve a balance in their promotion mix on the basis of experience, costs, and effectiveness. For most companies, communications mix decisions require the selection of an appropriate balance between advertising and personal selling. This translates into a push-versus-pull strategy decision (see Figure 11.2). How different is the company's approach to marketing its products globally?

2. "The Latest Signs of Change: Russify That Name!" *New York Times*, May 25, 1993, p. A4.

FIGURE 11.2

Global Promotion Strategies

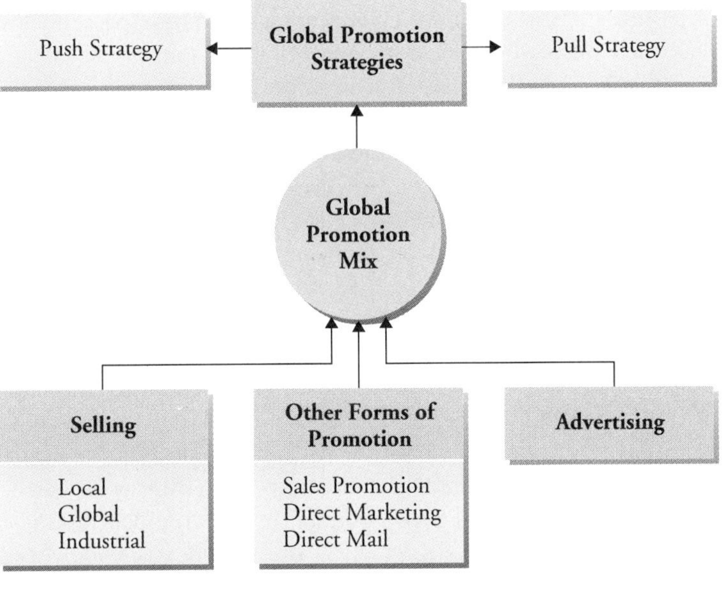

Push-Oriented Strategy

In a domestic setting, *push-oriented marketing strategies* emphasize personal selling rather that advertising in their promotion mix. Although very effective as a promotion tool, personal selling, which requires intensive use of a sales force, is costly. Companies marketing industrial or other complex products to other firms or governmental agencies have relied on personal selling. Personal selling is usually more effective when a company is faced with a short channel. Global marketers basically look at the personal selling requirements in the same way that marketers do in a domestic situation. However, some of the key inputs into the decision-making process need to be reviewed.

The complexity of a product usually influences how extensively personal selling is used. The level of complexity has to be compared with the product knowledge of the clients. A company selling the same products abroad as those sold domestically may therefore find that more personal selling may be necessary abroad because some foreign clients are less sophisticated than domestic clients. A U.S. company may use the same amount of personal selling in Europe as it does in the

United States but may need to put forth a greater personal selling effort in developing countries, where the product may not be well understood.

Though they may prefer personal selling as a promotion mix, many companies increasingly are using advertising to avoid the high cost of maintaining a personal sales force. These costs, which are estimated to have passed $300 for a typical sales call, have motivated some companies to shift a part of the selling job to advertising.

Channel length can also be an important factor in determining the amount of personal selling or push strategy to be used. To the extent that a company faces the same channel length abroad as it does in the domestic market, no change is needed in the push strategy. However, when a company does face a longer channel because other intermediaries such as local distributors are added, the firm may be better off shifting to a pull campaign.

Pull-Oriented Strategy

Pull strategy is characterized by a relatively greater dependence on advertising directed at the end user for a product or service. Pull campaigns are typical for consumer goods firms that need to approach a large segment of the market. For such companies, the economies of using mass communications such as advertising dictate a reliance on pulling the product through the distribution channel. Pull campaigns are usually advisable when the product is widely used by consumers, when the channel is long, when the product is not very complex, and when self-service is the predominant shopping behavior.

Increased or decreased reliance on pull campaigns for global markets depends on a number of factors. Most important are access to advertising media, channel length, and the leverage the company has with the distribution channel.

Marketers accustomed to having a large number of media available may find the choices limited in overseas markets. For many products, pull campaigns work only if access to electronic media, particularly TV, is available. This is the case in Japan and in some developing countries, where radio and TV stations tend to be commercially operated. In other areas, such as some European countries, liberalization of the media and full commercial access are relatively new. This trend was sparked by the advent of satellite radio and television in Europe and Asia, allowing commercial operators to beam signals into countries where commercial media were previously nonexistent. As a result, most areas of the world are now accessible to both electronic and print media advertising.

In some other countries, access to those media is restricted through time limits imposed by governments. Consequently, companies will find it difficult to duplicate their promotional strategies when moving from an unregulated environment to more restricted environments. Although in many countries a company may be able to shift advertising from one medium into another, it is nevertheless true that the unfolding of a full-blown pull campaign is usually more difficult to do in many countries.

Channel length is another major determinant of the feasibility of a pull campaign. Companies in complex consumer markets often face long channels and thus try to overcome channel inertia by directing their advertising directly to end users. When a company markets in other markets, it may face an even longer channel because local distribution arrangements are different. In Japan, for example, channels tend to be much longer than those in the United States. As a result, a greater reliance on a pull strategy may be advisable or necessary.

Distribution leverage is also different for each company from market to market. Getting cooperation from local selling points, particularly in the retail sector, is often more difficult than in the domestic market. The fight for shelf space may be very intensive; shelf space in most markets is limited, where carrying several competing brands of a product category is not customary. Under these more competitive situations, the reliance on a pull campaign becomes more important. If consumers are demanding the company's product, retailers will make every effort to carry it.

Push Versus Pull Strategies

In selecting the best balance between advertising and personal selling for the pull versus push decision, companies have to analyze the markets to determine the relative need for these two major communications mix elements. However, as we have seen, the availability of or access to any one of them may be limited. This is particularly the case for firms depending a great deal on pull policies. Many such companies find themselves limited in the use of the most powerful communications tools. How must a company adjust its communications policy under such circumstances?

When lack of access to advertising media makes the pull strategy less effective, a company may have to resort to more of a push strategy, making a greater use of personal selling. In some instances, this may already be the case when limited access to television advertising forces a company to use less effective media forms such as print advertising. In such circumstances, a company will employ a larger sales force to compensate for the reduced efficiency of consumer-directed promotions.

Limited ability to unfold a pull strategy from a company's home market has other effects on the company's marketing strategy. Reduced advertising tends to slow the product adoption process in new markets, thus forcing the firm to accept slower growth. In markets crowded with existing competitors, newcomers will find it difficult to establish themselves when avenues for pull campaigns are blocked.

Consequently, a company entering a new market may want to consider such situations for its planning and adjust expected results accordingly. A company accustomed to a given type of communications mix usually develops an expertise or a distinctive competence in the media commonly used. When suddenly faced with a situation in which that competence cannot be fully applied, the risk of failure or underachievement multiplies. Such constraints can even affect entry strategies or the market selection process.

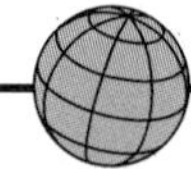

Personal Selling

Personal selling takes place whenever a customer is met in person by a representative of the marketing company. When doing business globally, companies must meet customers from different countries. These customers may be accustomed to different business customs and may speak a different language. That is why personal selling in an individual context is extremely complex and requires some very special skills on the part of the salesperson.

In this section, we differentiate between global selling and local selling. When a company's sales force travels across countries and meets directly with clients abroad, it is practicing *global selling*. This type of selling requires the special skill of being able to manage across several cultures. Much more often, however, companies engage in *local selling:* they organize and staff a local sales force made up of local nationals to do the selling in only one country. Managing and operating a local sales force involves different problems from those encountered by managing multicountry salespersons.

Global Selling (Multicountry Sales Force)

The job of the global salesperson seems glamorous. One imagines a professional who frequently travels abroad, visiting a large number of countries and meeting a large number of different businesspeople with various backgrounds. However, this type of work is quite demanding and requires a special set of skills.

Global salespeople are needed only when companies deal directly with their clients abroad. This is usually the case for industrial equipment or business services, rarely for consumer products or services. Consequently, for our purposes, global sales will be described in the context of industrial selling.

Purchasing Behavior In industrial (business-to-business) selling, one of the most important parts of the job is finding the right decision maker in the client company. The seller must locate the key decision makers, who may hold different positions from company to company or from country to country. In some countries, the purchasing manager may have different responsibilities, or the engineers may play a greater role. The global salesperson must be able to identify and deal effectively with buying units that differ by country. For example, when selling in Japan, the salesperson must recognize that the decision process will be slower than in other countries, as the members of the buying unit will want to explore and debate alternatives, while striving for unity and collegiality among the players. The Japanese buying behavior will require a different set of sales skills tailored to the culture.[3]

Buying Criteria In addition to different purchasing patterns, the global salesperson may have to deal with different decision criteria or objectives on the part of the purchaser. Buyers or users of industrial products in different countries may expect to maximize different goals. However, it should be pointed out that for standardized uses for specific industries, relatively little difference between countries applies. Particularly for high-technology products, such as production equipment for semiconductor components used in the electronics industry, the applications are virtually identical regardless of whether the factory is located in Korea or in the United States.

Language Overcoming the language barrier is an especially difficult task for the global salesperson. The personal selling effort is markedly enhanced if the salesperson speaks the language of the customer.

For some of the products marketed by a global sales force today, two trends have emerged. First, the dependency on the local language for many industries is not as strong today as it was just one or two decades ago. For many new and highly sophisticated products (e.g., electronics, aerospace), English is the business language spoken by most customers. Consequently, with more and more executives speaking English in many countries, more firms have been in a position to actually market their products directly, without local intermediaries. English is widely spoken in Scandinavia and in Europe, just as it is the leading second language in Asia and Latin America. Consequently, we now see that the ability to speak a number of foreign languages is less of a necessity. However, learning a foreign language can be an excellent way to understand a foreign culture. Also, language proficiency continues to have a very favorable impact on the sales process.

In industries in which knowledge of the local language is important, companies tend to assign sales territories to salespersons on the basis of language skills. A European multinational manufacturer of textile equipment assigns countries to its sales staff according to the languages they speak. This is more important in the traditional industries such as textile manufacturing, in which businesses are more local in orientation and in which English is not spoken that well by management.

Even executives who speak fairly good English may not understand all the details of product descriptions or specifications. As a result, a company can make an excellent impression by having its sales brochures translated into some of the key languages. European companies routinely produce company publications in

3. Paul Romani, "Selling in the Global Community: The Japanese Model," *American Salesman*, October 1998, pp. 21–25.

several languages. Such translations may not be needed for Scandinavia but may go a long way in other parts of the world where the level of English language skills is not that high.

Business Etiquette Global marketers selling to many markets are likely to encounter a diverse set of business practices as they move from one country to another. Since interpersonal behavior is intensely culture-bound, this part of the salesperson's job will vary by country. Many differences exist for how an appointment is made, how (and whether) an introduction is made, and how much lead time is needed for making appointments. The salesperson must also know whether or not gifts are expected or desired. When a salesperson travels to the same area repeatedly, familiarity with local customs can be expected. But for newcomers or experienced executives traveling to a new area, finding out the correct cultural information is necessary.

For example, visiting businesspeople must attend long banquets when engaging in negotiations with the Chinese. These banquets may start in the late morning or early in the evening. Sitting mostly at a round table, the visitors will normally be seated next to the host, who is expected to fill the visitor's plate at regular intervals. Foreigners are cautioned that frequent toasts are the norm and that many Chinese business hosts expect that the guest should become drunk; otherwise, the guest is believed not to have had a good time.[4] Also, business etiquette can differ from one country to another. Although it is acceptable for visitors to arrive late in China, India, or Indonesia, arriving late in Hong Kong is not acceptable. Lateness causes the visitor to "lose face," which is an extremely serious matter among Hong Kong businesspeople.[5]

Since no manager can be expected to know the business customs of every country, important information can be obtained from special sources. For one, the company's own foreign market representatives or sales subsidiary can provide important information or suggestions. Also, when such access is not available, governments tend to collect data on business practices through their commercial officers posted abroad. For example, the U.S. Department of Commerce publishes a regular series entitled *Doing Business in . . .*, which offers a wealth of helpful suggestions. Some business service companies, such as global accounting firms or global banks, also provide customers with profiles of business practices in foreign countries.

Foreign businesspersons receiving visitors from other foreign countries rarely expect the foreign visitor to be familiar with all local customs. However, it is always appreciated when the visitor can indicate familiarity with the most common practices and some willingness to try to conform. Learning some foreign customs

4. "Chemicals in China: Capacity for Enjoyment," *Financial Times*, September 30, 1986, p. VI.
5. "Hong Kong: Executive Guide to the Territory," *Financial Times*, June 27, 1986, p. XV.

helps to generate goodwill toward the company and therefore can enhance the chance of doing business.

Negotiations Strategies Negotiations in the global arena are complicated because the negotiating partners frequently come from different cultural backgrounds. As a result, misunderstandings or misjudgments can occur that will lead to failure. To maximize the outcome in the often difficult and protracted negotiations, global sales personnel must be in tune with the cultural differences.

A common approach to cross-cultural negotiations relies on the old proverb "When in Rome, do as the Romans do." This approach, which assumes that the visitor will follow local customs and use the local language, has two problems. First, many non-Romans may be unable to act Roman beyond the normal greeting protocol. Second, most Romans will probably not act Roman themselves with a non-Roman in Rome.[6]

Although a myriad of negotiation strategies exist, concentrating on mutual needs rather than the issues is a much practiced approach. In global marketing, the salesperson, or negotiator, must first determine the true objectives and needs of the other party. When negotiating within an unknown cultural setting, this is often a challenging task. However, careful assessment of the negotiating party's needs can enhance the chance for success.

For successful negotiation, understanding the *mindscape* of the counterpart can be very important.[7] Wenlee Ting, a noted anthropologist, defined the mindscape as "a structure of reasoning, cognition, perception, design, planning, and decision making that may vary from individual to individual and from culture to culture." Ting developed mindscape models based on the earlier work of another anthropologist, Magorah Maruyama. Building on Maruyama's work, Ting identified three common mindscapes for Hong Kong executives. Executives with an H-type mindscape tended to be interested in structured competition and the scientific organization of business. The tendency of executives with the I-type mindscape was to see separation of individual efforts as a key to higher efficiency. The G-type mindscape considered heterogeneity as a basis for mutually beneficial competition and tended to encourage differences among units. I-type mindscapes were said to be predominant among players in international finance or real estate; H-type mindscapes were predominant in family businesses; and G-type mindscapes were typical in international trading and business.[8]

6. Stephen E. Weiss, "Negotiating with Romans," *Sloan Management Review*, Winter 1994, pp. 51–61.
7. Alf H. Walle, "Conceptualizing Personal Selling for International Business: A Continuum of Exchange Perspective," *Journal of Personal Selling and Sales Management*, November 1986, pp. 9–17.
8. Wenlee Ting, *Business and Technological Dynamics in Newly Industrialized Asia* (Westport, Conn.: Greenwood, 1985); Magorah Maruyama, "Mindscapes and Social Theories," *Current Anthropology*, 1980, pp. 589–608.

The evidence further indicated that Hong Kong businesspeople negotiate well in eastern and western cultures. Skilled Hong Kong negotiators are able to engage in reasoning with western counterparts while simultaneously employing other reasoning and negotiation techniques when dealing with local groups, family members, and other business associates.[9] This suggests that successful negotiation may depend on the foreign businessperson's ability to scout out the foreign counterpart's mindscape. Careful background preparation on the cultural norms prevalent in the foreign country is the starting point to successful negotiations and selling. A fifteen-year study of negotiation styles of seventeen cultures found significant differences from culture to culture. For example, the Japanese were the least aggressive, with few threats or warnings, whereas the French and Brazilians were aggressive, using warnings, threats, and interruptions frequently. The research found that cultural differences caused misunderstandings, which could be reduced with cross-cultural awareness.[10]

Timing is also an important aspect for negotiating abroad. In some countries, such as China, negotiations tend to take much more time than in the United States or some other western countries. One European company that operated a joint venture in China observed that during one annual meeting, two weeks were spent in a discussion that elsewhere might have only taken a few hours. In this situation, however, much of the time was used for interdepartmental negotiations among various Chinese agencies rather than for face-to-face negotiations with the European company.

In another instance, a European firm negotiated with a Middle Eastern company over several months for the delivery of several hundred machines. When the company representatives went into that country for the final round of negotiations, they found that the competing firm had already been there several weeks before their arrival. The European firm's representatives decided to prepare themselves for long negotiations and refused to make concessions, figuring that the competitor had most likely been worn out in the prior weeks. As it turned out, that assessment was correct, and the European company won the order by outstaying its competitor in a rather difficult negotiating environment. Obviously, unprepared sales executives may lose out to competitors if they do not understand the negotiation customs of a foreign country as they relate to the amount of time necessary to conclude a deal.

Global Selling at Soudronic The sales function at Soudronic AG, a medium-sized manufacturer of welding equipment used primarily in the can-making industry, offers a good example of how a global sales force is organized and operated.[11]

9. Walle, "Conceptualizing Personal Selling," pp. 9–17.
10. William Briggs, "Next for Communicators: Global Negotiation," *Communication World*, December 1, 1998, pp. 1–3.
11. Jean-Pierre Jeannet, *Soudronic AG*, Case (Lausanne: IMD, International Management Development Institute, 1983).

Located in Switzerland, where all of its machines were produced, the company sold to can makers in some eighty countries. The selling of these machines, which welded the bodies of metal cans at very high speeds, rested with a small sales force of seven sales managers. These managers reported to two regional sales managers, who in turn reported to the manager for sales and marketing. The entire world territory was divided into seven parts in such a way that made travel schedules more efficient, maximized the language competency of the sales force, and balanced overall workloads.

Each sales manager was responsible for all client contact in his territory. In their assigned countries, sales managers usually worked with local agents who indicated when a prospective client needed to be visited. When a client needed to be visited, the sales manager would schedule a visit on the next trip to the country and visit the client along with the local agent. The sales managers were technically trained to the extent that they could answer most questions on the spot. They also negotiated with clients for delivery and for price terms within limits. Once a contract had been negotiated, the sales manager would turn the client contact over to a service technician, although in many cases the sales manager would remain in contact with the client, who preferred to deal primarily with one person.

Sales managers were expected to spend 50 percent of their time with clients in the form of either local contact, telephone contact, or correspondence. As a result, the Soudronic sales staff traveled a good percentage of the time. The availability of candidates for such positions was limited. The company preferred to hire people who had a technical or engineering background together with several years of sales experience in the capital goods sector, not necessarily in the can-making industry. Prospective sales managers were also expected to have good firsthand knowledge of their assigned region, preferably through one or more years of work experience, and to have acquired the language locally. Compensation was base salary plus a commission based on sales.

Local Selling (Single-Country Sales Force)

When a company is able to maintain a local sales force in the countries where it does business, many of the difficulties of bridging the cultural gap with clients are minimized. The local sales force can be expected to understand the local customs, which helps the global company gain additional acceptance in the market. This is primarily because local sales forces are usually staffed with local nationals. However, many challenges remain, and the management of a local sales force often requires different strategies from those used in running a sales force in the company's domestic market.

Role of Local Sales Force and Control When a company has decided to build a local sales force, the decision has already been made for forward integration in its distribution effort. As we learned in Chapter 9, establishing a sales force means that the company has moved to assume the full role of a local sales subsidiary, sidestepping the independent distributor. Depending on the distribution strategy adopted, the company may sell directly, as often is the case for many industrial products or business services, or indirectly through local wholesalers, as is the case for many consumer products and services. Although global companies will not make such a move unless present business volume justifies it, there are substantial benefits associated with having one's own sales force.

Control over a firm's sales activities is a frequently cited advantage for operating a company-owned local sales force. With its own sales force, the company can emphasize the products it wants to market at any time, and the company has better control over the way it is represented. In many cases, price negotiations, in the form of discounts or rebates, are handled uniformly rather than leaving these decisions to an independent distributor with different interests. Having a company sales force also ensures that the personnel are of the necessary level and qualification. Control over all of these parameters usually means higher sales compared with using a distributor sales force.

Also, the local sales force can represent an important bridge with the local business community. For industries in which the buying process is local rather than global, the sales force speaks the language of the local customer, can be expected to understand the local business customs, and thus can bring the global firm closer to its end users. In many instances, local customers, though not objecting to buying from a foreign firm, may prefer to deal with local representatives of that firm. As a result, the ability of the global company to make its case heard with prospective customers is substantially enhanced.

However, local sales forces are single-country, or single-culture, by nature. Although they speak the language of the local customers, they may not speak any other language. The local sales force may have a very limited understanding of the head-office language that is, in general, not sufficient to conduct business in that language. Furthermore, a local sales force cannot be expected to speak the languages of the neighboring countries sufficiently to deal directly with such customers. In Europe, where this problem is particularly acute, language competency usually precludes a German firm from sending its sales force into France or a French firm from sending its sales force into Italy or Spain. In some countries, such as the Netherlands, Switzerland, and Belgium, several different languages are spoken, and this tends to further enhance the mobility of a sales force serving these countries from adjoining countries.

Local Sales Job The type and extent of local sales effort a company will need are dependent on its own distribution effort and the relationship of distribution to the other communications mix elements. For firms that still use distributor sales forces to a large extent, a missionary sales force with limited responsibilities may suffice. This missionary sales force would concentrate on visiting clients together with the local distributor's sales force. If the global company's sales force needs to do the entire job, a much larger sales force will be necessary. As for the global firm's domestic market, the size of the local sales force depends to a large extent on the number of clients and the desired frequency of visits. This frequency may differ from country to country, which means that the size of the sales force will differ from country to country.

The role of the local sales force needs to be coordinated with the promotion mix selected for each market. As many companies have learned, advertising and other forms of promotion can be used to make the function of the sales force more efficient. In many consumer goods industries, companies prefer a pull strategy, concentrating their promotion budget on the final consumer. In such cases, the role of the sales force is restricted to gaining distribution access. However, as we have mentioned previously, in some countries, access to communications media is severely restricted. As a result, companies may place greater emphasis on a push strategy utilizing the local sales force, which affects both role definition and size.

Foreign Sales Practices Although sales forces are employed virtually everywhere, the nature of their interaction with the local customer is unique to each market and may affect local sales operations. For most westerners, Japanese practices seem substantially different. The following example was reported by Masaaki Imai, president of Cambridge Corporation, a Tokyo management consulting and recruiting firm.

When Bausch & Lomb Japan introduced its then new soft-lens line into Japan, the company targeted influential eye doctors in each sales territory for its introductory launch. The assumption was that once these leading practitioners signed up for the new product, marketing to the majority of eye doctors would be easier. One salesperson was quickly dismissed by a key customer. The doctor said that he thought very highly of Bausch & Lomb equipment but preferred regular lenses for his patients. The salesperson did not even have a chance to respond; but he decided, since it was his first visit to this clinic, to stay around for awhile. He talked to several assistants at the clinic and to the doctor's wife, who was, as is typical for Japan, handling the administration of the practice.

The next morning, the salesperson returned to the clinic and observed that the doctor was very busy. He talked again with the assistants and joined the doctor's wife when she was cooking and talked with her about food. When the couple's young son returned from kindergarten, the salesperson played with him and even went out to buy him a toy. The wife was very pleased with the well-intentioned babysitter. She later explained to the salesperson that her husband had very little time to listen to any sales presentations during the day, so she invited him to come to their home in the evening. The doctor, obviously primed by his wife, received the man very warmly, and they enjoyed *sake* together. The doctor listened patiently to the sales presentation and responded that he did not want to use the soft lenses on his patients right away. However, he suggested that the salesperson try them on his assistants the next day. So on the third day, the salesperson returned to the clinic and fitted soft lenses on several of the clinic's assistants. The reaction was very favorable, and the doctor placed an order on the third day of the sales call.[12]

It is probably fair to say that salespeople in many countries would have taken the initial negative response as the final answer from the doctor and would have tried elsewhere for success. In Japan, however, the customer expects a different reaction. Japanese customers often judge from the frequency of the sales calls they receive whether the company really wants to do business. Salespeople who make more frequent calls to a potential customer than the competition does may be regarded as more sincere.

This also means that companies doing business in Japan have to make frequent sales calls to their top customers, often only for courtesy reasons. Customers get visited twice a year, usually in June and December, without necessarily discussing any business. Although this may occasionally be only a telephone call, the high frequency of visits significantly affects the staffing levels of the company-owned sales force.

Recruiting Companies have often found recruiting sales professionals quite challenging in many global markets. Although the availability of qualified sales personnel is a problem even in developed countries, the scarcity of skilled personnel is even more acute in developing countries. Global companies, accustomed to having sales staff with certain standard qualifications, may not find it easy to locate the necessary salespeople in a short period of time. One factor limiting their availability in many countries is the local economic situation. Depending on the economic cycle, the level of unemployment may be an excellent indicator as to the difficulty of finding prospects. This will limit the number of people a company can expect to hire away from existing firms unless a substantial increase over present compensation is offered.

More important, sales positions don't enjoy uniformly high esteem from country to country. Typically, sales as an occupation or career has a relatively high image in the United States. This allows companies to recruit excellent talent, usually fresh from universities, for sales careers. These university recruits can usually consider sales as a career path toward middle-management positions. Such an image of selling is rare elsewhere in the world. In Europe, many companies continue to find it difficult to recruit university graduates into their sales forces, except in such highly technical fields as computers, where the recruits are typically engineers. When sales is a less desirable occupation, the quality of the sales force

12. "Salesmen Need to Make More Calls Than Competitors to Be Accepted," *Japan Economic Journal*, June 26, 1979, p. 30.

may suffer. If the company wants to insist on top quality, the time it will take to fill sales positions can be expected to increase dramatically.

Compensation In their home markets, where they usually employ large sales forces, global companies become accustomed to handling and motivating their sales forces in a given way. In the United States, typical motivation programs include some form of commission or bonus for meeting volume or budget projections, as well as vacation prizes for top performers. When a global company manages local sales forces in various countries, the company is challenged to determine the best way to motivate them. Not all cultures may respond the same way, and motivating practices may differ from country to country.

One of the frequently discussed topics in motivating salespeople is the value of the commission or bonus structure. U.S. companies in particular have tended to use some form of commission structure for their sales force. Although this may fluctuate from industry to industry, U.S. firms tend to use more of a flexible and volume-dependent compensation structure than European firms do. Japanese firms more often use a straight salary type of compensation. To motivate the sales force to achieve superior performance, the global company may be faced with using different compensation practices, depending on the local customs.

Local Sales Force Examples Managing a local sales force tends to be different according to the requirements of any given country. Local selling is one of the marketing elements that displays relatively great variety and is frequently adjusted for local customs, even for companies in which other marketing elements are standardized, such as advertising. The following examples are intended to give the reader some background on local sales force issues and practices.

Ericsson do Brasil. Ericsson do Brasil was the Brazilian affiliate of L. M. Ericsson, a Swedish multinational firm with a strong position in the telecommunications industry.[13] The company marketed both central switching equipment for telephone companies and private exchanges (PBXs) for individual firms. The sales force for the PBX business numbered about one hundred persons and was organized geographically.

In the southern sector of Brazil, where industry is concentrated, the sales force was divided into specialists either for large PBXs, with up to two hundred external lines and several thousand internal lines, or for smaller systems, called key systems, that could accommodate up to twenty-five incoming lines or up to fifty internal lines. In the northern, more rural part of Brazil, fewer accounts made

13. Jean-Pierre Jeannet, *Ericsson Do Brasil: Ericall System*, Case M-296 (Lausanne: IMD, International Management Development Institute, 1983).

this customer-size specialization impractical. As a result, the northern sales offices had sales representatives that sold both large and small systems.

Ericsson's sales force was compensated partially with a fixed salary and partially with commissions. Fixed monthly salaries amounted to about $400. A good salesperson could earn about $2,000 a month when the 4 percent sales commission was added to the base salary. Special government regulations required that each salesperson be assigned an exclusive territory. If a salesperson was reassigned, the company was then liable to maintain his or her income for another twelve months. As a result, changes in sales territory had to be considered carefully. When Ericsson do Brasil was faced with the introduction of a new paging system that was to be sold to corporate clients, most of whom also bought telephone equipment, the company found it difficult to assign territories to each of its current salespersons. If it wanted to reassign territories later on, once it became clear who was good at selling paging systems over and above the telephone systems, the company would not be able to easily reassign territories without incurring compensation costs. In the end, Ericsson decided to assign the new paging system to its salespersons on a temporary basis only, thus preserving the chance to make other assignments later on without extra costs.

Wiltech India. Selling in India is very different from selling in other countries.[14] India, with the second largest population in the world, is an example of a developing country. Wiltech, a joint venture between the British company Wilkinson and a large Indian conglomerate, was founded to market Wilkinson technology-based razor blades in India. Founded in the early 1980s, the company needed to build up its sales force to compete against local competition. In India, there are more than 400,000 retailers or distributors of razor blades, and about 20 percent of them carry Wiltech blades.

The sales force of sixty persons concentrated primarily on urban markets. The sales representative working in a big metropolitan city directly handled one distributor and about 600 to 700 retail outlets. He or she was expected to visit the distributor every day and to make another forty to sixty calls per day. The sales representative accomplished this largely on foot because the sales outlets were relatively small and clustered close to each other. The goal was to see important retailers at least twice per month and smaller retailers once a month. The sales representative working in smaller cities covered about a dozen distributors and some 800 to 1,000 outlets. He or she saw distributors once or twice per month and saw from thirty-five to forty outlets per day. Travel was by railway or by bus, whichever is more convenient.

Wiltech sales representatives were paid a fixed salary of 800 to 1,200 rupees per month (about U.S. $70 to $100). Sales representatives that achieve their quo-

14. Jean-Pierre Jeannet, *Wiltech India*, Case M-336 (Lausanne: IMD, International Management Development Institute, 1988).

tas and productivity targets could earn another 400 to 500 rupees per month in a bonus. Expenses were paid on the basis of daily allowances for transportation, lunch, and hotel stays when necessary. For sales representatives selling from a fixed location, this daily allowance amounted to 30 rupees per day. When traveling away from home, the daily allowance amounted to 50 rupees plus the actual transportation costs for first-class train or bus fare. Although these costs appear minimal compared with typical salaries and travel expenses paid in a developed country, they nevertheless represent an enviable income in India, where the cost of living is very low by western standards.

Alternatives to a Local Sales Force Because building up a local sales force is both costly and time consuming, some companies have looked for alternatives without necessarily falling back on independent distributors. When competitive pressures require a rapid access to a sales force, piggybacking (as described in Chapter 15) has been practiced by some companies.

Recently, companies have entered into a wide variety of international distribution alliances. The sales alliance format differs from other ventures because the two firms that join forces do so as independent firms and not necessarily in the form of a limited joint venture. In an alliance, two companies may swap products, with one company carrying the other firm's products in one market and vice versa. Such swaps have been used extensively in the pharmaceutical industry. The short period of time left for marketing once the products have been approved and before the patents expire calls for a very rapid product rollout in as many countries as possible.

Business-to-Business Selling

Many of the promotion strategies discussed so far are geared toward the marketing of typical consumer goods and industrial goods. However, some specific promotion methods oriented largely toward the business-to-business market play an important role in the global marketing of such products. The use of global trade fairs, bidding procedures for global projects, and consortium selling all have to be understood if an investment or industrial products company wants to succeed in international markets.

Global Trade Fairs

Participation in global trade fairs has become an important aspect of marketing industrial products abroad. Trade fairs are ideal for exposing new customers and potential distributors to a company's product range and have been used extensively by both newcomers and established firms. In the United States, business-to-business customers can be reached through a wide range of media, such as specialized magazines with a particular industry focus. In many overseas countries, the markets are too small to allow for the publication of such trade magazines in only one country. As a result, prospective customers usually attend these trade fairs on a regular basis. Trade fairs also offer companies a chance to meet with prospective customers in a less formal atmosphere. For a company that is new to a certain market and does not yet have any established contacts, participation in a trade fair may be the only way to reach potential customers. There are an estimated six hundred trade shows in 70 countries every year. For example, the Cologne Trade Fair brings together 28,000 exhibitors from 100 countries with 1.8 million buyers from 150 countries. The Hanover Fair is considered the largest industrial fair in the world. With over 7,100 exhibitors in engineering and technology from over 70 countries, the fair attracts 330,000 visitors.[15] Other large general fairs include the Canton Fair in China and the Milan Fair in Italy.

Specialized trade fairs concentrate on a certain segment of the industry or user group. Such fairs usually attract limited participation in terms of both exhibitors and visitors. Typically, they are more technical in nature. Some of the specialized trade fairs may not take place every year. One of the leading specialized fairs is the Achema for the chemical industry in Germany, held every three years. Annual fairs having an international reputation include the air shows of Farnborough (England) and Paris, where aerospace products are displayed. The Comdex computer trade show, running annually since 1979, attracts 2,400 exhibitors and 220,000 visitors each year. The show has become so big that some exhibitors, such as Intel, IBM, and Compaq, have decided not to participate.[16]

Participation in trade fairs can save both time and effort for a company that wants to break into a new market and does not yet have any contacts. For new-product announcements or demonstrations, the trade fair offers an ideal forum for display. Trade fairs are also used by competitors to check on one another's most recent developments. They can give a newcomer an idea of the potential competition in some foreign markets before actual market entry. Consequently, trade fairs are a means of both selling products and gathering important and useful market intelligence. Therefore, marketers with global aspirations will do well to search out the relevant trade fairs directed at their industry or customer segment and to schedule regular attendance. Global exhibiting may require additional planning over domestic shows. First, planning should begin twelve to eighteen months in advance, since international shipping may involve delays. Second, show attendance should be checked, as it is common for many shows to allow the public to visit; marketers may therefore want to plan a separate private area for viable prospects. Third, in the United States, a show may be staffed by sales-

15. "Welcome to Europe's Biggest Industrial Fair: Hannover Messe 1998," *Modern Materials Handling*, March 1998, p. E3.

16. Jim Carlton, "Comdex Loses Appeal to Industry Players," *Wall Street Journal*, November 16, 1998, p. B6.

people and middle managers. At many global shows, customers expect to see the CEO and senior management. Finally, a local distributor, consultant, or sales representative should be used to help with the local logistics and culture.

Selling Through a Bidding Process

The bidding process for industrial products is more complicated than for consumer products, particularly when major industrial equipment is involved. Companies competing for such major projects have to pass a number of stages before negotiations for a specific purchase can ever take place. Typically, companies go through a search process for new projects, then move on to prequalify for the particular project before a formal project bid or tender is submitted. Each phase requires careful management and the appropriate allocation of resources.

During the search phase, companies want to make sure that they are informed of any project worth their interest that is related to their product lines. For particularly large projects that are government sponsored, full-page advertisements may appear in leading international newspapers. More likely, companies have to have a network of agents, contacts, or former customers who will inform them of any project being considered.

In the prequalifying phase, the purchaser will frequently ask for documentation from interested companies that would like to make a formal tender. At this phase, no formal bidding or tender documents are submitted. Instead, more general company background will be required that may describe other or similar projects the company has finished in the past. At this stage, the company will have to sell itself and its capabilities. A large number of companies can be expected to pursue prequalification.

In the next phase, the customer will select the companies—usually only three or four—to be invited to submit a formal bid. Formal bids consist of a proposal of how to solve the specific client problem at hand. For industrial equipment, this usually requires personal visits on location, special design of some components, and the preparation of full documentation, including engineering drawings for the client.[17] The bid preparation costs can be enormous, even up to several million dollars for some very large projects. The customer will select the winner from among those submitting formal proposals. Normally, it is not simply the lowest bidder who will obtain the order. Technology, the type of solution proposed, and the financing arrangements all play a role (see Chapter 10).

Once an order is obtained, the supplying company may be expected to insure its own performance. For that purpose, the company may be asked to post a performance bond, which is a guarantee that the company will pay certain specified

17. Iris Kapustein, "Selling and Exhibiting Across the Globe," *Doors and Hardware*, September 1, 1998, p. 34.

damages to the customer if the job is not completed within the preagreed specifications. Performance bonds are usually issued by banks on behalf of the supplier. The entire process, from finding out about a new prospect until the order is actually received in hand, may take from several months to several years, depending on the project size or industry.

Consortium Selling

Because of the high stakes involved in marketing equipment or *turnkey* projects (a plant, system, or project in which the buyer acquires a complete solution so that the entire operation can commence at the turn of a key), companies frequently band together to form a consortium. A *consortium* is a group of firms that share in a certain contract or project on a preagreed basis but act almost as one company toward the customers. Joining together in a consortium can help companies share the risk in some very large projects. A consortium can enhance the competitiveness of the members by offering a turnkey solution to the customer.

Most consortiums are formed on an ad hoc basis. For the supply of a major steel mill, for example, companies supplying individual components may combine into a group and offer a single tender to the customer. The consortium members have agreed to share all marketing costs and can help one another with design and engineering questions. The customer gets a chance to deal with one supplier only, which substantially simplifies the process. Ad hoc consortiums can be found for some very large projects that require unique skills from their members. The consortium members frequently come from the same country and, thus, expect to have a greater chance to get the contract than if they operated on their own. In situations in which the same set of skills or products is in frequent demand, companies may form a permanent consortium. Whenever a chance for a deal arises, the consortium members will immediately prepare to qualify for the bidding.

Consortium selling is frequently practiced by companies banding together to obtain telecommunications licenses in foreign countries. The consortium members might include a local firm with its local connections, combined with one or two international telephone operating companies with expertise in running a network. On occasion, such a consortium may include equipment suppliers that join to ensure their equipment will be included in any eventual contract.

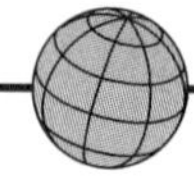

Global Account Management

Traditionally, account management has been performed on a country-by-country basis. This practice invariably led to a country-specific sales force, which was typical even for large global firms. Over the last few years, an emerging trend has seen companies organize their sales force into global account teams. The global team would service an entire customer globally, or in all countries where a customer relationship exists. Global account teams may comprise members in different parts of the world, all serving segments of a global account and coordinated through a global account management structure.

The trend toward global account management is rooted in ever-increasing global purchasing logic (see Chapter 7) among customers, primarily industrial ones. Companies who purchase similar, or the same, components, raw materials, or services in many parts of the world realize that by combining the purchasing function and managing it more centrally, they can obtain substantial savings. Companies are scanning the global market for the best buy, and in the process they want to deal with the most advantageous source.

Siemens's Automotive Systems Division, producing electronic components for automotive firms, has tailored its sales structure to these requirements. The company maintains global account teams for key customers, such as Volkswagen and Ford; the teams are in charge of the firm's entire business, regardless of where the components are sourced or used. From the customer's perspective, the advantage stems from the clear designation of a counterpart who will handle all business aspects.[18] The system of global account management is also practiced widely in the professional service sectors. Globally active banks like Citibank have maintained global account structures for years. Likewise, advertising agencies offer global clients global account management with seamless coordination across many countries. And finally, the world's leading accounting firms, such as Deloitte Touche Tohmatsu International, have long-standing traditions of leading their engagements for international clients from one single place. At Deloitte, the system of lead client service partners (LCSPs) is well developed. The LCSP is empowered, for example, to direct a global audit for a large multinational account across all countries where the work must be performed.[19]

Global account management is greatly enhanced by sophisticated information technology. With members of the team dispersed around the globe, it becomes essential to coordinate all actions meticulously. The development and rapid spread of such tools as videoconferencing, electronic mail, and groupware applications have greatly extended the reach of a management team beyond the typical one-location office. Many customers who are ambitious to do business across the world but who prefer to deal with fewer suppliers will demand this new sales approach more and more. Many of the national selling organizations now maintained by international firms will inevitably be transferred, or transformed, into smaller, but globally acting, account teams.

18. Jean-Pierre Jeannet, *Siemens Automotive Systems: Brazil Strategy*, Case (Lausanne: IMD, 1993).
19. Jean-Pierre Jeannet and Robert Collins, *Deloitte Touche Tohmatsu International Europe*, Case (Lausanne: IMD, 1993).

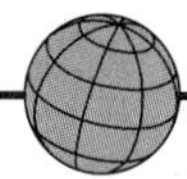

Other Forms of Promotion

So far, our discussion has been concentrated on personal and industrial selling as key elements of the communications mix. However, besides advertising, various other forms of promotion play a key role in marketing. Usually combined under the generic title of global promotions, they may include such elements as in-store retail promotions and coupons. Many of these tools are consumer goods oriented and are used less often in industrial goods marketing. In this section, we look at sales promotion activities, as well as sports promotions and sponsorships.

Sales Promotion

The area of sales promotion has a largely local focus. Although some forms of promotions, such as coupons, gifts, and various types of reduced-priced labels, are in use in most countries, strict government regulations and different retailing practices tend to limit the options for global firms, as shown in Table 11.1.

In the United States, coupons are the leading form of sales promotion. Consumers bring product coupons to the retail store and obtain a reduced price for the product. Second in importance are refund offers. Consumers who send a proof of purchase to the manufacturer will receive a refund in the form of a check. Also used, but less frequently, are cents-off labels or factory-bonus packs, which induce customers to buy large quantities because of the price incentive. Marketers of consumer goods in the United States, the primary users of these types of sales promotion, find a full array of services available to run their promotions. Companies such as ACNielsen specialize in managing coupon redemption centers centrally, so that all handling of promotions can be turned over to an outside contractor.

Couponing varies significantly from country to country. Coupon distribution is popular and growing in Italy. In the United Kingdom and Spain, couponing is declining. Couponing is in its infancy in Japan, with restrictions on newspaper coupons lifted in 1991. Couponing is limited in Germany, Holland, Switzerland, and Greece. The European Commission is working toward a policy of allowing pan-European sales promotion as long as the practices are legal in the country of origin, therefore requiring each country to mutually recognize the laws of the other countries. This new policy if approved will significantly increase sales promotion across Europe.[20] Couponing is also now available on the Internet; for example, in South Africa, electronic coupons can be found at coupons.co.za.[21]

In most overseas markets, price reductions in the store are usually the most important promotional tool, followed by reductions to the trade, such as whole-

20. David Murphy, "Sales Promotion: Cross-Border Conflicts," *Marketing*, February 11, 1999, p. 30.
21. Anne Stephens and Andy Rice, "Digital Discounting Arrives," *Finance Week*, July 23, 1998, p. 33.

TABLE 11.1

Concise Guide to Promotion Techniques and Restrictions

Country	Top Three Sales Promotion Techniques	Restrictions on Sales Promotion Techniques
Argentina	Reduced price in store Trade discounts In-store displays, promotions	Rules on lotteries, special prizes Products such as pharmaceuticals cannot be promoted through prices
Australia	Reduced price in store Trade discounts Promotional pack sizes with extra free product	Individual state coupon restrictions Promotions and trade support must be available for all stores Lotteries and games of chance subject to government authorization Some restrictions on proof of purchase
Austria	Reduced price in store Open competitions Trade discounts	No coupons Restrictions for on-pack deals
Belgium	Reduced price in store Trade discounts Extra product free	No free draws No sweepstakes
Brazil	Gift-banded packs Reduced price in store	Distribution of prizes via vouchers, contests, etc., is subject to government authorization
Canada	Reduced price in store Trade discounts Coupons	Ethical products, alcoholic beverages, cigarettes, cigars not permitted any type of sale promotion
France	Reduced price in store Trade discounts Coupons	Games of chance are usually forbidden Premiums and gifts are limited to 5% of product value and no more than 1% off
Germany	Reduced price in store Displays Trade discounts	No coupons Free goods restricted to value of about DM 0.10 No in-pack premium or cross-product offers No free-draws or money-off vouchers
Great Britain	Reduced price in store Trade discounts Coupons	Legislation on bargain offers, lotteries, sweepstakes Competitions must include a degree of skill No price promotion on categories such as pharmaceuticals

TABLE 11.1

Concise Guide to Promotion Techniques and Restrictions (cont.)

Country	*Top Three Sales Promotion Techniques*	*Restrictions on Sales Promotion Techniques*
Greece	Trade discounts Special offers Reduced price in store	No coupons Gifts limited to 5% of product value
Ireland	Reduced price in store Trade discounts Extra product free	Below-cost selling License required for competitions, which must require a degree of skill
Italy	Reduced price in store Banded packs Coupons	No coupons on butter, oil, coffee No self-liquidating offer or contest or gifts Gifts limited to 8% of product value
Japan	Reduced price in store Trade discounts Premiums	Some regulations regarding lotteries Some regulations on excessive gifts or premiums
Mexico	Reduced price in store Bonus packs On-pack premiums	Government authorization required No promotions based on collecting a series of labels, etc. No promotions of alcohol, tobacco products
Netherlands	Trade discounts Reduced price in store Display promotions, premiums	Legislation on gift schemes, pharmaceuticals, tobacco, games of chance
New Zealand	Reduced price in store Banded packs Coupons	No pyramid selling or trading stamps Coupons redeemable for cash only Competitions require a degree of skill Legislation on Christmas Club funds
Portugal	Trade discounts Reduced price in store Competitions	Some rules regarding lotteries and sweepstakes
South Africa	Reduced price in store Trade discounts In-store coupons, promotions	No lotteries or games of chance Restrictions on coupons, especially no conditional purchase No comparative advertising
Spain	Coupons Free goods Reduced price in store	None

TABLE 11.1

Concise Guide to Promotion Techniques and Restrictions (cont.)

Country	Top Three Sales Promotion Techniques	Restrictions on Sales Promotion Techniques
Sweden	Co-op advertising and money off Local activities Coupons	No premium redemption plans Competitions must include a degree of skill Mixed offers are restricted In-pack or on-pack cross-coupons not allowed
Switzerland	Reduced price in store Trade discounts Merchandising contribution to manufacturers to trade	Laws against unfair competition No competition, free draws, sweepstakes, money-off vouchers, or money off next purchase
United States	Coupons Refund offers Cents-off label, factory packs, and bonus packs	All promotion and trade support must include a degree of skill Mixed offers are restricted In-pack or on-pack cross-coupons not allowed

Source: From William J. Hawkes's presentation of ACNielsen Company material to the International Marketing Workshop. AMA/MSI, March 1983. Reprinted by permission of ACNielsen Company. Updated December 1990.

salers and retailers. Also of importance in some countries are free goods, double-pack promotions, and in-store displays.

Japan, for instance, restricts the value of a promotional gift to a maximum of 10 percent of the value of the accompanying merchandise. In addition, the value of the free merchandise cannot exceed 50,000 yen, or about $425. Even the value of prizes awarded through lotteries is regulated to a maximum of ¥1 million for an open lottery available to everyone, and ¥50,000 for lotteries that are attached to the purchase of specific products. For global firms such as American Express, these limits cause difficulties. In the United States, American Express offers free trips from New York to London as prizes to qualifying customers. The company would like to offer similar promotions to its Japanese customers, but the limitation of ¥50,000 allows for only a three-day package tour from Tokyo to Seoul.[22]

Most countries have restrictions on some forms of promotions. Frequently regulated are any games of chance, but games in which some type of skill is required are usually allowed. When reductions are made available, they often are

22. "U.S. Urges Easing of Product-Promotion Rules," *Nikkei Weekly*, November 6, 1995, p. 3.

not allowed to exceed a certain percentage of the product's purchase price. Because global firms will encounter a series of regulations and restrictions on promotions that differ among countries, there is little opportunity to standardize sales promotion techniques across many markets. This has caused most companies to make sales promotions the responsibility of local managers, who are expected to understand the local preferences and restrictions. Sales promotion can also be influenced by local culture. A study of consumer attitudes regarding sales promotion found significant differences between Taiwan, Thailand, and Malaysia. The Taiwanese consumer preferred coupons over sweepstakes and had a low fear of embarrassment when using coupons. The Malaysians and Thais both preferred sweepstakes over coupons, and although they were generally price conscious, this did not influence their sales promotion attitudes.[23]

Sports Promotions and Sponsorships

With major sports events increasingly being covered by the mass media, television in particular, the commercial value of these events has increased tremendously over the last decade. Today, large sports events, such as the Olympics or world championships in specific sports, cannot exist in their present form without funding by companies, which do this either through advertising or through different types of sponsorships.

In the United States, companies have for some time purchased TV advertising space for such events as regularly broadcasted baseball, basketball, and American football events. Gillette is one company that regularly uses sponsorship of the World Series to introduce new products. This is just another extension of the company's media strategy to air television and radio commercials at times when its prime target group can be found in large numbers watching TV or listening to the radio. More recently, companies have purchased similar time slots for the Olympics when they are broadcast in the United States.

The cost of purchasing the rights to broadcast the Olympics on television in the United States continues to escalate. NBC acquired the TV rights for the United States in a long-term contract with the International Olympic Committee (IOC) through the 2008 Olympic Games for a total of $2.3 billion. The summer 2000 (Australia) and winter 2002 (Salt Lake City, Utah) games went for $1.25 billion. For the 2008 games, NBC agreed to pay $894 million and 50 percent of the advertising revenue. As a result, the typical thirty-second television spot for U.S. broadcasting was expected to increase from $380,000 for the 1996 Atlanta games to $445,000 for the 2000 games and to $608,000 to the 2008 games.[24] Similarly, the rights to broadcast the Olympics elsewhere were sold to the European Broadcast-

23. Lenard C. Huff and Dana L. Alden, "An Investigation of Consumer Response to Sales Promotion in Developing Markets," *Journal of Advertising Research*, May/June 1998, pp. 47–57.
24. "NBC, IOC Chase Long-Term Deals," *Advertising Age*, December 18, 1995, p. 3.

ing Union, which covers Europe, North Africa, and the Middle East, through the 2008 games for a reported $1.44 billion.[25] General Motors, a sponsor of the summer 2000 games, began running advertisements fifteen months before the games to break through the clutter of all the advertisements leading up to the games.[26] The scandal surrounding the International Olympic Committee's site selection caused John Hancock to back away from buying advertisements for the summer 2000 Olympic Games in Sydney.[27]

To circumvent restrictions on commercial television during sports programs, companies have purchased space for signs along the stadiums or the arenas where sports events take place. When the event is covered on television, the cameras will automatically take in the signs as part of the regular coverage. No mention of the company's product is made in any way, either by the announcer or in the form of commercials. It is the visual identification that the firms are looking for.

Aside from purchasing advertising spots or signage space in broadcast programs, individual companies can also engage in sponsorship. Main sponsors for the Olympic games pay a fee of $40 million to the IOC. Coca-Cola, one of the companies that became a sponsor for the 1996 summer games in Atlanta, spent another estimated $100 million on purchasing commercial time slots from NBC, the owner of the U.S. broadcast rights. Coca-Cola also sponsors many other sports events, such as the European football (soccer) championship, and the Tour de France, the famous multistage bicycle race. In an average year, Coca-Cola spends about 20 percent of its entire consumer marketing budget on sports-related sponsorships, or about $300 million.[28]

To take advantage of global sports events, a company should have a logo or brand name that is worth exposing to a global audience. It is not surprising to find that the most common sponsors are companies producing consumer goods with a global appeal, such as soft-drink manufacturers, consumer electronics producers, and film companies. To purchase sign space, a firm must take into consideration the popularity of certain sports. Few sports have global appeal. Football (soccer) is the number one spectator sport in much of the world. MasterCard International has renewed its official sponsorship of the World Cup football games, to be held in 2002 in Japan and South Korea. Between 1999 and 2002, MasterCard will have been the sponsor at four hundred championship matches, with a projected cumulative television audience of 50 billion people.[29] The World Cup football tournament was in the United States in 1994 for the first time. In

25. "Murdoch Loses Bidding for Olympic Television Rights," *Financial Times*, January 31, 1996, p. 1.
26. Sally Beatty, "GM Gets Unusually Early Start, Bragging About Sydney Olympics," *Wall Street Journal*, June 18, 1999, p. B2.
27. "Insurers to Fill John Hancock's Olympic Advertising Space," *Best's Insurance News*, June 4, 1999, pp. 1–3.
28. "Coca-Cola's Return of Serve," *Financial Times*, July 26, 1996, p. 14.
29. "MasterCard Renews Commitments with FICA World Cup Through 2002," *Comline Pacific Research Consulting*, March 19, 1999, pp. 1–2.

contrast, baseball and American football have little appeal in Europe or parts of Asia and Africa. Many other sports also have only local or regional character, which requires a company to know its market and the interests—even the athletic interests—of its target audience very well.

In 1996 in China, Philip Morris sponsored the newly formed football (soccer) league, which it named the Marlboro League, for $2 million annually. Within a short period of time, the league teams increased their per game revenue to $150,000. In 1999, Pepsi beat out Coca-Cola for the sponsorship of the fourteen-team China football league. Pepsi paid a reported $11 million for exposure to the 400 million football fans in China.[30]

A Japanese financial services company, Orient Leasing, purchased one of Japan's twelve professional baseball teams, the Braves. As a result, the company was allowed to call the team by the company's name and promptly changed its name to the shorter Orix. Within a short time, the national awareness of the company rose from 25 to 85 percent. This recognition was aided not only through the team name but also by placing the Orix name on the players' uniforms.[31]

Korean global firms have used sports sponsorship abroad extensively. Typically, Korean firms have underwritten individual teams overseas. Samsung is sponsoring ten sports teams or events in eastern Europe, eight in Latin America, and two each in Asia and the Middle East. The company increased its $2.8 million budget in 1996 to $4 million in 1997. Among the Samsung-sponsored teams are twelve foreign football (soccer) teams, whom the company plans to invite to Korea for a Samsung tournament. Other Korean firms are active too. Hyundai supports eastern European and African football (soccer) teams, and the LG Group has been very active in sponsoring local sports teams. In 2002, Korea and Japan will jointly host the world football championship. These Korean firms consider sports sponsorship a cost-effective way to boost their brand or company recognition in emerging or untapped markets.[32]

Aside from sponsoring sporting events, companies have also moved more aggressively into sponsoring direct competitors or teams. Manufacturers of sports equipment have for some time concentrated on getting leading athletes to use their equipment. For sports that have achieved even global reach, such as tennis, skiing, or football, an endorsement of sports products by leading athletes can be a key to success. This is why manufacturers of sports equipment have always attempted to get world-class athletes to use their equipment. As part of its aggressive plan to raise its profits in sports sponsorship, the U.S. firm Nike has moved

30. "Pepsi Scores over Coke in China Battle," *Stadium and Arena Financing News*, February 22, 1999, p. 1.
31. "Sponsorship in Japan: Benefits of Keeping an Eye on the Ball," *Financial Times*, May 25, 1989, p. 16.
32. "Chaebol Takes a Sporting Chance, Raises Spending on Advertising," *Nikkei Weekly*, January 27, 1997, p. 26.

beyond the sponsorship of individual superstars, such as basketball's Michael Jordan and golf's Tiger Woods, to sponsor entire teams. For a sum of $200 million, Nike obtained sole sponsorship of the Brazilian national teams at all levels for ten years, including football (soccer) world championships and Olympic games.[33] Since Nike already sponsors the national football (soccer) teams of the United States, the Netherlands, Italy, and Russia, the company is considering Nike-sponsored matches among those teams outside the regular championship schedule.[34] With football (soccer) the most popular sport worldwide, Nike aims to increase its competitiveness against major rivals like Reebok and Adidas.

To exploit the media coverage of spectator sports, many non-sporting goods manufacturers have joined the sponsoring of specific athletes or teams. These are firms that intend to exploit the visual identification created by the media coverage. Many will remember the pictures of winning racecar drivers with all the various corporation names or logos on their uniforms. Although these promotions once tended to be mostly related to sports products, sponsors increasingly have no relationship to the sports. Sponsoring a team for competition in the sixteen Grand Prix races all over the world is estimated to cost about $45 to $60 million for one year. The main sponsor is expected to carry about one-half to two-thirds of the cost and gets to paint the cars in its colors with its logo. The expenses are substantial because the winners do not get very high purses; yet leading racecar drivers are reported to get salaries as high as $9 million for one year. In 1988, the races were broadcast in eighty-one countries over 100,000 minutes and attracted 3.3 billion viewers, resulting in some 17 billion "viewings." Major sponsors were tobacco companies (Marlboro, Camel, John Player, Gitanes/Loto) and other consumer goods firms (Benetton).[35]

Through the intensive coverage of sports in the news media all over the world, many companies continue to use the sponsorship of sporting events as an important element in their global communications programs. Successful companies have to track the interest of various countries in the many types of sports and to exhibit both flexibility and ingenuity in the selection of available events or participants. In many parts of the world, sports sponsorship may continue to be the only available way to reach large numbers of prospective customers.

Direct Marketing

Direct marketing includes a number of marketing approaches that involve direct access to the customer. Direct mail, door-to-door selling, telemarketing, and the Internet are the primary direct marketing tools used around the world. Some

33. "Nike Puts Its Hands on Ultimate Trophy," *Financial Times*, December 14/15, 1996, p. 5.
34. "The Game's the Thing at Nike Now," *Business Week*, January 27, 1997, p. 88.
35. "Motor Sport Industry," *Financial Times*, January 26, 1990, Section 3, p. 1.

companies have achieved considerable success in their fields through aggressive direct marketing. Many of these firms realize that not all markets respond equally well to direct marketing.

The development of the global versus U.S. business of the leading direct marketing agencies serves as a good indicator of how fast this type of selling has grown globally. Three of the four leading agencies practicing direct marketing now generate more than half their revenue from overseas. This is the case for Rapp Collins, Wunderman Cato Johnson, and Ogilvy & Mather Direct. The top five global home shopping markets are the United States (44 percent), Germany (19 percent), Japan (13 percent), the United Kingdom (5 percent), and France (5 percent).[36]

Regionally, Europe claims the largest portion of direct marketing volume outside the United States. However, Asia and Latin America are growing rapidly. Asia is benefiting from a new and advanced telecommunications infrastructure with modern postal, telecommunications, cellular, and interactive capabilities.[37] In Latin America, many global firms have begun to use direct marketing. Both Nestlé and IBM did so in Brazil, where seventy-two direct marketing agencies operate, as did American Express in Argentina, where some ten agencies are active. Direct marketing volume is expected to grow 30 percent annually and is especially useful in overcoming large distances and compensating for less developed traditional physical distribution capabilities.[38]

Direct Mail

Direct mail, largely pioneered in the United States, is being used extensively in many countries. Successful mail-order sales require an efficient postal system and an effective delivery system for the shipped products. In countries where these preconditions exist, direct mail is being used extensively by retail organizations and other service organizations, such as *Reader's Digest* and credit card suppliers.

The U.S.-based catalog house Lands' End entered the German market in 1996 with a German-language version of its catalog, including prices in local currency. The company was attracted to Germany as one of the top three mail-order countries, next to Japan and the United States. German consumers were known to purchase more apparel per person through mail order than any other buyers. To support its operation, Lands' End established a fifty-person telephone/customer service facility near the borders of France, Luxembourg, and Germany where customers may order toll-free on a twenty-four-hour basis. All merchandise is shipped from a Lands' End European distribution center in Oakham, United Kingdom, and reaches German customers in four to five days. Lands' End has also maintained local-language catalogs for France and the Netherlands since 1994.[39]

36. Tony Stockil, "East of West," *Catalog Age*, February 1, 1998, p. 69.
37. "Rapp Collins Zips into Worldwide Direct-Shop Lead," *Advertising Age*, August 5, 1996, p. 56.
38. "New Ways to Reach Customers," *Ad Age International*, March 11, 1996, p. 130.
39. "Lands' End Debuts German Catalog," *DM News*, August 26, 1996, p. 4.

Global mail-order companies have also begun to target Japan. Japanese consumers were estimated to have ordered $750 million worth of merchandise in 1995 alone. Japanese consumers covet the American look, take advantage of lower U.S. prices for imported merchandise, and profit from an efficient postal system. The Japanese post office, which handled some four hundred mail sacks a day in 1994, saw the volume increase to nine hundred sacks per day in 1995, or the equivalent of about 3 million packages annually. L. L. Bean, the ultimate outfitter headquartered in Freeport, Maine, mails thousands of catalogs to Japan. Sales reached U.S. $100 million in Japan in 1995, up 66 percent from the previous year, and made Japan the company's largest market after the United States.[40]

Companies that may want to engage in direct mail will have to ensure that their mail pieces or catalogs are translated into the respective foreign language. There is a great variety of mailing lists in both the United States and Europe. There are also list brokers and lists available in most markets. For example, in Brazil DataListas has over 10 million names, with extensive segmentation options.[41] Direct mail offers an opportunity for companies that want to extend their business beyond a limited location and even into foreign countries. In general, however, shipping packages abroad always involves the receiver country's customs system, which tends to delay parcels.

Door-to-Door Sales

Avon, a leader in the field of door-to-door retailing, has long emphasized international markets. In 1998, the company's revenue in international markets was $3.15 billion, exceeding U.S. revenues by $2.06 billion. Avon has been able to employ its selling concept successfully in most markets, having built up operations in some 135 countries. Avon has encountered some difficulties because its brand name is less well known than local brands. In Russia, the company even tried to do without door-to-door selling, using wholesalers instead. After disappointing sales, Avon began to hire its own door-to-door sales force after all. In 1998, Avon's direct sales force abroad amounted to 2.8 million salespeople compared to 465,000 in the United States.[42] In April 1998, Avon, Amway, and Mary Kay Cosmetics were thrown out of China. The door-to-door selling efforts of all three companies had been very successful in China; however, the Chinese government questioned their sales practices. Having renegotiated deals with the Chinese government, all three have returned to China, but with limitations on door-to-door selling efforts.[43]

40. "Japanese Takes to Package Deals," *Herald Tribune*, July 4, 1995, p. 11.
41. Peter J. Rosenwald, "Pointed Advise for Direct Marketers in Brazil," *Advertising Age International*, October 5, 1998, p. 6.
42. 1998 Annual Report, Avon Company, pp. 8–10.
43. Melinda Ligos, "Direct Sales Dies in China," *Sales and Marketing Management*, August 1, 1998, p. 14.

The concept of door-to-door selling is not equally accepted in all countries. Moreover, it is not equally accepted everywhere to make a profit from selling to a friend, colleague at work, or neighbors. The willingness to find suitable salespeople on a part-time basis may also be limited because in some countries women or even students are not necessarily expected to work. As a result, the type of door-to-door selling may not be limited only to the cultural background of the United States, but likewise may not be warmly welcomed universally.

Telemarketing

To make telephone sales effective, an efficient telephone system is a requirement. Telephone sales for individual households may become practical when a larger number of subscribers exist and when their telephone numbers can be easily obtained. However, not all countries accept the practice of soliciting business directly at home. Yet in western Europe, where the economic pressures on selling are the same as they are in the United States, companies can expect gains from effective use of telemarketing. Because of the language problems involved, companies must make sure their telemarketing sales forces not only speak the language of the local customer but do so fluently and with the correct local or regional accent.

Telemarketing is already a big business in Europe, where total full-time employment in the field is estimated at 1.5 million. In the United Kingdom, telemarketing volume was believed to have reached $16.2 billion in 1995.[44] European Union telemarketing directives allow consumers to place their name on a telephone preference service to eliminate telemarketing calls. Any firm that continues to call can be fined £5,000.[45] Lands' End, the U.S.-based catalog house, opened its European call center at the junction of the French, German, and Luxembourg borders. Employing fifty people, the call center operates twenty-four hours a day and was established to offer support to shoppers and to answer questions. Elsewhere, telemarketing has been intensifying also. In Latin America, growth has been substantial, with thirty-six telemarketing firms reported active in Brazil, twenty-five in Argentina, and fifteen in Chile. Call centers have grown very fast in Brazil, where the market for telemarketing center software and hardware exceeds $500 million per year.[46]

On a global level, telephone sales may be helpful for business-to-business marketing when decision makers can be contacted quickly and when they can be identified from available directories. Since costs for overseas travel are considerable and direct dialing is now possible for international calls in many countries, telemarketing on a cross-country or global basis may be possible.

44. "Eurotelemarketing in Trouble," *Advertising Age*, November 27, 1995, p. 4.
45. Paul Sade, "Hang Up and Hit Telesales in the Pocket: New EU Directives Make It Harder for Telemarketing Companies," *The Independent*, June 5, 1999, p. 1.
46. "Brazil: Boom in the Call Centers Market," *Gazeta Mercantil*, May 31, 1999, p. 1.

Global Marketing via Internet and World Wide Web

The emergence of the commercial use of the Internet, along with the rapid expansion of World Wide Web applications, has been one of the most important developments affecting global marketing in this decade.[47] In 1999, ACNielsen estimated there were 200 million Internet users, of which 42 percent were outside the United States[48] It is expected that 250 million will be online by 2003.[49] The Internet offers companies an entirely new vehicle to communicate and interact with current and potential customers.

The availability of Internet technology is of particular importance to global marketers. Firms are able to eliminate the time and distance gaps that hinder many international dealings, using the most interactive of all direct marketing tools. A company anywhere in the world can establish a web site on the Internet and be instantly available to potential customers from anywhere in the world. This immediate availability, of great importance to all firms, gives a particularly valuable opportunity to smaller firms that lack established international sales channels.[50]

Internet advertising has been growing rapidly, from $340 million in 1995 to $3.4 billion in 1999, and is estimated by Forrester Research to grow to $33 billion in 2004.[51] This acceleration of Internet advertising expenditures worldwide illustrates the global potential of this new communications tool. Advertisers are awakening to the potential of the Web, hoping to build brand awareness early before the explosion of available sites. ACNielsen and NetRatings have formed a joint venture called ACNielsen eRatings.com, which will provide data to global marketers on Internet advertising effectiveness and e-commerce sales.[52]

The potential power of the Internet is demonstrated by both large- and small-sized companies. DSM, the Dutch chemicals group announced in early 2000 that within three years 100 percent of their purchases and 50 percent of their sales would be via the Internet. Peter Elverding, DSM chairman, said the Internet would increase sales and reduce costs. DSM will increase its Internet-based dealings with customers and suppliers. Also, they will be trading through ChemConnect, an Internet exchange for chemicals in which DSM has equity ownership. According to Elverding, "if you don't go down this road, you will be out of business."[53]

47. Philip Kotler, *Kotler on Marketing: How to Create, Win, and Dominate Markets,* Boston: Free Press, 1999, p. 205.
48. Juliana Koranteng, "ACNielsen to Offer Data on Net Ad Effectiveness," *Ad Age International*, October 1999, p. 44.
49. "Advertising That Clicks," *Economist*, October 6, 1999, p. 71.
50. Jean-Pierre Jeannet, "Interactive Marketing: A Revolution in the Making," *Perspectives for Managers*, vol. 19, no. 3 (April 1996); reprinted in *Financial Times*, Mastering Management series, April 19, 1996, p. 13.
51. "Advertising That Clicks."
52. Ibid.
53. Ian Bickerton, "DSM Set to Expand Web-based Dealings," *Financial Times*, February 24, 2000, p. 17.

Levenger's, the Florida-based catalog for readers, has built a large global business through their web site. Historically, Levenger's translated and mailed catalogs to Japanese consumers. However, when the Japanese market declined, Levenger's stopped mailing catalogs but used the Web to serve customers. Currently in English, like 82 percent of all web sites, Levenger's was planning to offer multilingual sites in 2000.[54]

Although initial interest in the Internet has focused on advertising to potential consumers, the most potent quality of the Internet may be its interactive nature. Companies are able to communicate directly with potential customers and measure what actually interests customers. Click-through rates on banners and web sites measure interest. Purchases measure behavior, and illustrate the real potential benefit of the Internet. Although it may not be economically viable to sell cornflakes or hambugers over the Net, it is economical to sell many consumer and business products via the web.

Another major impact of the Internet will be market harmonization. By creating a common trading channel with broad reach, real time information and new revenue opportunities, Forrester Research predicts that Europe will become a single market more quickly with the Internet and expects a European eZone to be created that will support cross-border commerce.[55]

The impact of the Internet on global marketing will be pervasive. Small and large companies alike will be able to reach customers across the world almost instantly, and vice versa. Answers to questions, transmitted via email, will arrive in seconds. Small firms that previously had little chance to reach into global markets will be able to do so. Electronic commerce will of course bring global competition to small or domestic firms, which will suddenly see their markets invaded. The result will be pressures on prices where margins are high. The ultimate winner may be the world's large number of consumers, who will suddenly have an astonishing array of purchasing options.

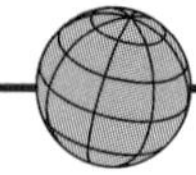

Conclusions

Communications in a global context are particularly challenging because managers are constantly faced with communicating to customers with different cultural backgrounds. This tends to add to the complexity of the communications task, which demands a particular sensitivity to culture, habits, and at times even different types of rational reasoning.

54. Kelly J. Andrews, "The World Wide Web Lives Up to Its Name," *Target Marketing*, June 1999, p. 48.
55. Robert F. Randall, "Internet Will Speed European Market Harmonization," *Strategic Finance*, May 1999, p. 20.

Aside from the cultural differences that largely affect the content and form of the communications, global firms also encounter a different set of cost constraints for the principal communications mix elements, such as selling or advertising. Given such diversity from country to country with respect to sales force costs or media costs, global firms have to carefully design their communications mix to fit each individual market. Furthermore, the availability of any one individual communications mix element cannot be taken for granted. The absence of one or the other, due to either legal or economic development considerations, will force the global firm to compensate with a greater reliance on other mix elements.

When designing effective sales forces for local markets, global marketers need to take into consideration the challenge of global sales and the requirements for doing well. Such global sales efforts can usually be maintained for companies selling highly differentiated and complex products to a clearly defined target market. In most other situations, ones in which the products are targeted at a broader type of industrial or consumer customer group, global firms will typically have to engage a local sales force for each market. Local sales forces are usually very effective in reaching their own market or country, but they are not always able to transfer to another country because of language limitations. Building up and managing a local sales force are challenging tasks in most foreign markets and require managers with a special sensitivity to local laws, regulations, and trade practices.

All forms of direct and interactive marketing apply to the global market as well. As we have seen, many firms have succeeded by adopting U.S.-based or U.S.-originated direct marketing ideas and using them skillfully abroad. With the global telecommunications infrastructure developing rapidly, the applications for the World Wide Web and Internet-based interactive marketing will continue to expand and will undoubtedly become ever more important communications mix elements for globally active firms, large or small.

QUESTIONS FOR DISCUSSION

1. What factors appear to affect the extension of push or pull policies in global markets?
2. Under what circumstances should a company pursue a global versus a local selling effort?
3. What factors most often appear to make local selling different from country to country?
4. What patterns can you detect in the use of sales promotion tools across many countries?
5. To what types of companies would you suggest sponsorship in the next Olympic Games, and which sports would you recommend to them? How would such firms profit from their association with the Olympic Games?
6. What role will the Internet play in global promotion?

FOR FURTHER READING

Batista, Michael J. "Recruit an International Sales Force." *Global Trade and Transportation*, August 1993, p. 32.

Cook, Roy A., and Joel Herche. "Assessment Centers: An Untapped Resource for Global Sales Management." *Journal of Personal Selling and Sales Management*, Summer 1992, pp. 31–38.

Corcoran, Kevin J., et al. *High Performance Sales Organizations: Achieving Competitive Performance in the Global Marketplace*. New York: McGraw-Hill, 1995.

Deighton, John. "Interactive Marketing." *Harvard Business Review*, November-December 1996, p. 151.

Federation of European Direct Marketing Associations. *The Handbook of International Direct Marketing*, 4th ed. Kogan Page, 1999.

Hoke, Peter, "Wunderman's View of Global Direct Marketing." *Direct Marketing*, vol. 48 (March 1986), pp. 76-88, 153.

Kamins, Michael A., Wesley J. Johnston, and John L. Graham. "A Multi-Method Examination of Buyer-Seller Interactions Among Japanese and American Businesspeople." *Journal of International Marketing*, Spring 1998, pp. 27-38.

Kashani, Kamran, and John A. Quelch. "Can Sales Promotion Go Global?" *Business Horizons*, vol. 33, no. 3 (May/June 1990), pp. 37-43.

McDonald, William J. "International Direct Marketing." *Direct Marketing*, March 3, 1999, pp. 44-450.

McMahon, Timothy J. "Sales Automation: For Many Companies a Final Link in Global Management." *Business Marketing*, May 1993, p. 56.

Miller, Russell R. *Selling to Newly Emerging Markets*. Westport, Conn.: Quorum Books. April 1998.

Simintiras, Antonis C., and Andrew H. Thomas. "Cross-Cultural Sales Negotiations: A Literature Review and Research Propositions." *International Marketing Review*, 1998, vol. 16, no. 1, pp. 10-28.

Still, Richard R. "Sales Management: Some Cross-Cultural Aspects." *Journal of Personal Selling and Sales Management*, Spring-Summer 1981, pp. 6-9.

Weser, Robert E. *The Marketer's Guide to Selling Products Abroad*. Westport, Conn.: Quorum Books, 1989.

12

Managing Global Advertising

AT THE BEGINNING OF THIS BOOK, WE DEFINED GLOBAL MARKETING AS THOSE marketing activities that applied simultaneously to more than one country. In the case of advertising, the volume of activity directed simultaneously toward targets in several countries is actually small. The majority of advertising activity tends to be directed toward one country only. Despite the "local" nature of global advertising, it is important to recognize that the initial input, in terms of either the product idea or the basic communications strategy, largely originates in another country. Consequently, although there is a largely local aspect to most global advertising, there is also a global country-to-country aspect to consider.

FIGURE 12.1

Global Advertising

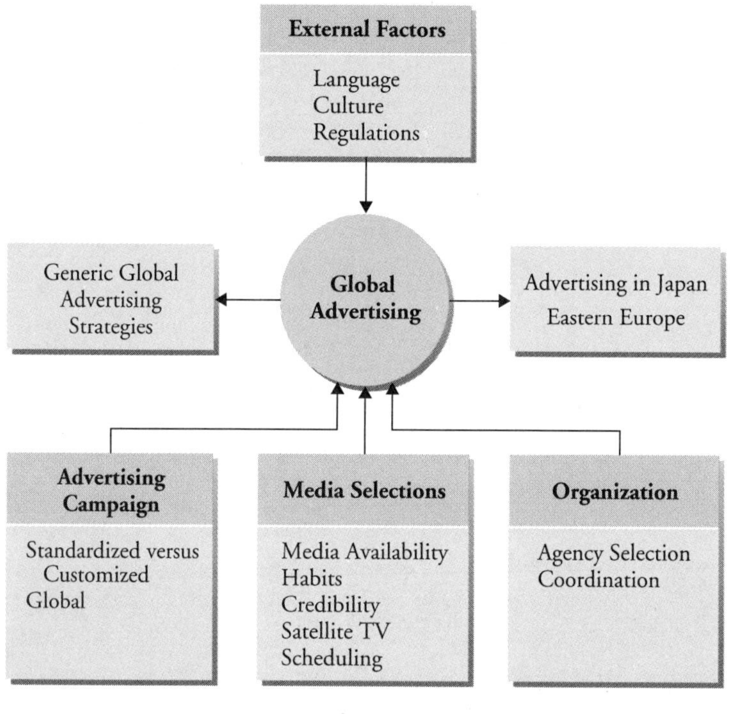

Two important questions must be answered in global advertising: (1) How much of a local versus a global emphasis should there be? (2) What should be the nature and content of the advertising itself? The first part of the chapter (see Figure 12.1) is organized around the explanation of key external factors and their influence on global advertising. The rest of the chapter focuses on the major advertising decisions and helps to explain how external factors affect specific advertising areas.

Challenges in Global Advertising

Probably no other aspect of global marketing has received as much attention as advertising. Many mistakes have been made in translating advertising copy from one language into another. Most, however, occurred in the 1960s, when global advertising was in its infancy. Today, most companies and advertising agencies have reached a level of sophistication that reduces the chance of translation error. This does not mean that language is not a factor to consider in today's global communications strategy. However, the industry has moved from a primary concern about translation to concerns about ways to be more efficient.

A second major cause of global advertising mistakes has traditionally been the neglect of cultural attitudes of consumers in foreign countries. Benetton, the Italian clothing manufacturer selling through stores all over the world, was one example of a company that ran into cultural problems with its advertising. The company launched a campaign under the theme "United Colors of Benetton," which had won awards in France. One of its ads featured a black woman breast-feeding a white baby; another had a black and a white man locked together in handcuffs. The ads came under protest from U.S. civil rights groups and had to be withdrawn. Benetton also fired its advertising agency, Eldorado of France, the creator of the ads.[1] In another case, Nike found that its flame logo on shoes offended Islamic followers as the flame was similar to the Arabic symbol for Allah, whereas in Islam the feet are seen as unclean. Nike has now withdrawn the use of the flame symbol.[2]

Such examples show that, even when the language or translation hurdle is correctly cleared, firms still need to consider the cultural and social background of the target market. Mistakes based on a misinterpretation of cultural habits are more difficult to avoid, though substantial progress has been made by global marketers to steer clear of the most obvious violations. However, merely avoiding translation or cultural errors does not guarantee an effective advertising campaign. Although we initially concentrate on ways to overcome cultural difficulties, later in the chapter we cover the critical issues related to organizing effective global advertising campaigns.

Overcoming the Language Barrier

Most of the translation blunders that plagued global advertising in the past were the result of literal translations performed outside the target country. The translators, not always in contact with the culture of the target country, were unable to judge the actual meaning of the translated copy for the target audience. Furthermore, the faulty translation could not be checked by the executives involved because they too were from a different culture and did not possess the necessary language skills.

Today, the traps of faulty translations can be avoided through the involvement of local nationals or language experts. Typically, global marketers have translations checked by either a local advertising agency, their own local subsidiary,

1. International Advertising Supplement, *Financial Times*, December 7, 1989, p. 3.
2. Allyson L. Stewart-Allen, "Cultural Quandaries Can Lead to Misnomers," *Marketing News*, November 23, 1998, p. 9.

or an independent distributor located in the target country. Because firms are active in a large number of countries and thus require the use of many languages, today's global marketers can find an organizational solution to most translation errors of the past.

In the European Union (EU), nine official languages are spoken. As a result, much advertising puts a special emphasis on communicating visually rather than through the various languages. Graphics are used more effectively in print media, too. Even the satellite TV service Sky Channel has discovered that not everyone in Europe speaks English well enough to understand English commercials and that, if given a chance, most people like to watch programs in their own language. Super Channel, the other satellite channel, moved to trilingual program service, and rather than offer pan-European programs, the operators of satellite channels in Europe are moving toward multiregional programming.[3] There are economies-of-scale benefits if a campaign can be run across a number of countries with a multilanguage approach. For example, Pepsi ran a multilanguage campaign on pack promotion for exclusive Spice Girl prizes in nine countries, with a menu of redemption options tailored to the market needs and legal requirements of each country.[4]

Adjusting to a local language often requires changes in the product name or positioning. For example, Coca-Cola was first rendered as *Ke-kou-ke-la* in Chinese, which meant "bite the wax tadpole" or "female horse stuffed with wax," depending on the dialect. After the problem was discovered, Coke researched 40,000 Chinese characters and found *Ko-kou-ko-le* a close phonetic for Coca-Cola, meaning "happiness in the mouth."[5]

Overcoming the Cultural Barrier

When global marketers fail because of misinterpretation of the local culture, they usually do so because they advocated an action inconsistent with the local culture or because they chose an appeal inconsistent with the motivational pattern of the target culture. Advocating the purchase of a product whose use is inconsistent with the local culture will result in failure, even if the appeal itself does not violate that culture per se. Similarly, companies can also fail if the appeal, or message employed, is inconsistent with the local culture, even if the action promoted is not. Consequently, a foreign company entering a new market has to be aware of both cultural aspects: the product's use and the message employed.

Sara Lee, the U.S.-based global firm that owns such lingerie brands as Playtex, Cacharel, and Wonderbra, faced intensive opposition to a series of billboards in Mexico. The company launched a global Wonderbra campaign that featured a

3. "Reaching United Europe Won't Be a Simple Task," *Advertising Age*, April 9, 1990, p. 31.
4. Allyson L. Stewart-Allen, "Cross-Border Conflicts of European Sales Promotions," *Marketing News*, April 26, 1999, p. 10.
5. "Getting Lost in the Translation," *Computer Dealers News*, April 6, 1998, p. 56.

Czech model posing in the bra on all of its outdoor advertising. In Mexican cities, citizens protested the ads as offensive, and pressured by the public, the company redesigned its billboards; for Mexico, the model wore a suit. Sara Lee learned that in some countries it had to change the visual of the global campaign on a case-by-case basis.[6]

To ensure that a message is in line with the existing cultural beliefs of the target market, companies can use resources similar to those used to overcome the translation barriers. Local subsidiary personnel or local distributors can judge the cultural content of the message. Also helpful are advertising agencies with local offices. Global marketers cannot possibly know enough about all the cultures they will come into contact with to assess the appropriateness of appeals. However, it is the responsibility of the international executive to make sure that knowledgeable local nationals have given enough input so that the mistake of using an inappropriate appeal in any given culture will be avoided.

For successful advertising in Nigeria, Africa's largest and most populous nation, the standard advertising patterns used in other countries will not necessarily work.[7] Gulda beer ads showed a large, rough-hewn man in a blue-jeans jacket based on the American movie character Shaft. The person was shown holding a mug, and the brown glass bottle of Gulda beer rested on the table. The slogan "Gulda man, Gulda man, sure of his taste, proud to be different" was used. However, this ad did not appear to promote the brand. Research showed that Nigerian consumers of beer felt that good beer came only in green bottles. They also noted that the person in the Gulda ad was always drinking alone; for many Nigerians, drinking beer is a social activity. The ad was finally changed. Gulda was presented in a green bottle, the theme was changed to "Gulda makes you feel real fine," and the setting was changed to show elegant people drinking together. Sales volume increased dramatically.

Leo Burnett Bangkok Advertising launched a local campaign in Thailand for Brand "X" potato chips. The advertisement depicted Hitler addressing an audience with a swastika in the background. It then switched to a Thai sorceress performing voodoo on a Hitler doll, which transfomed the dictator into a break-dancer and the swastika into a giant X. The campaign meant to communicate that the world would be a better place if happiness ruled; however, it was quickly pulled by the local Thai agency as it offended westerners in Thailand.[8]

Procter & Gamble was pleased by the initial success of its Vidal Sassoon Wash & Go shampoo in Poland. The company launched the shampoo in August 1991 with a major advertising campaign and whistle-stop tour by Vidal Sassoon, the British-born hairdresser. It captured 30 percent of the market. Unfortunately,

6. "Mexico Forces a Wonderbra Cover-Up," *Financial Times*, August 19, 1996, p. 4.
7. "Of Ads and Elders: Selling to Nigerians," *New York Times*, April 20, 1987, p. D10.
8. "Thai Ad Agency Drops Offending Hitler Advertisement," *Deutsche Presse-Agentur*, June 3, 1998, p. 1.

sales plummeted as rumors began that Wash & Go caused dandruff and hair loss. P&G had tried to use its U.S. commercials in Poland. They seemed to be too brash, causing 75 percent of the Poles to dislike the ads. Also, some believe the rumors were started by the numerous entrepreneurial hairdressers who felt Vidal Sassoon would open shops in Poland and threaten their business.[9]

Judging the appropriateness of a product or service for a culture is substantially more difficult than making a judgment only on the type of advertising to be employed. In Chapter 3 we discussed the nature of cultural and social forces, and in Chapter 6 we covered the evaluation of market potential for products. Here, we restrict ourselves to a discussion of the advertising aspects of cultural analysis.

The Impact of Regulations on Global Advertising

Although there are numerous situations in which differing customer needs require tailor-made advertising campaigns, in many instances the particular regulations of a country prevent firms from using standardized approaches, even when they would appear desirable. In countries such as Malaysia, regulations are a direct outgrowth of changing political circumstances. Following the influence of Islam in many parts of the world, Malaysia, a country with a large Muslim population, outlawed ads showing women in sleeveless dresses and pictures showing underarms. Given the strict rules in Malaysia governing the production and screening of commercials, Unilever found it best to film its Lipton Yellow Label Tea commercial in Malaysia. Using local talent and internationally acceptable scenery, Unilever was able to shoot three versions of the commercial on the same storyline for fifteen European and Asian countries at a substantial savings over doing local commercials in each market.[10]

Advertising for cigarettes and tobacco products is under strict regulation in many countries. In France, R.J. Reynolds, the manufacturer of Camel cigarettes, was prohibited from showing humans smoking cigarettes. The company finally overcame the restrictions by showing a smiling cartoon camel smoking a Camel cigarette.[11] The European Union has banned all tobacco billboards as of August 2001 and tobacco print advertising as of May 2000.[12] The 191 members of the World Health Organization are negotiating a treaty that will establish global regulations on cigarette advertising; limits will be set as to where smoking will be allowed, and cigarette taxation will be raised in all countries. The treaty will be the

9. "Wash & Get into a Lather in Poland," *Financial Times*, May 28, 1992, p. 10.
10. Eirmalasare Bani, "Lipton Shoots Its Latest Commercial in Malaysia," *Business Times* (Malaysia), June 9, 1999, p. 15.
11. "Defending the Rights of Marlboro Man," *Economist*, April 21, 1990, p. 84.
12. Vincent Moss, "Blair Speeds Up Total Ban on Tobacco Adverts," *Mail on Sunday*, May 23, 1999, p. 7.

first binding global treaty on social behavior and is scheduled to be implemented in 2003.[13]

One of the few areas in which cigarette and tobacco advertising is still relatively restriction-free is Central Asia and the Caucasus, formerly part of the Soviet Union. Most of these countries permit cigarette advertising in radio and television, although some relegate it to late-night slots. Such freedoms, however, are rare, and global marketers are well advised to check the local regulations carefully before launching any type of advertising campaign. Even in Russia, where 77 percent of men, 27 percent of women, and 42 percent of teenagers smoke, legislation is being considered that would ban smoking in hospitals, schools, and government offices.[14]

Advertising directed at children is also facing considerable regulation. Any toy company intending to launch a pan-European advertising campaign will run into a range of obstacles of differing rules and regulations even within the EU. In Sweden and Norway, all advertising aimed at children under the age of twelve is forbidden. In Greece, TV toy advertising is banned between 7:00 in the morning and 10:00 in the evening. Regulations in Europe are also affecting the confectionery industry, as some countries require that such advertising show a toothbrush symbol. Similarly, differing national rules govern the advertising of pharmaceuticals, alcohol, tobacco, and financial services.[15]

The European Union is debating a series of rulings that could have great impact on advertising in Europe. The discussions involve efforts toward both greater harmonization and the extent of regulation. Greater harmonization is generally viewed as desirable throughout Europe and potentially would result in uniform regulations for advertising. This would greatly enhance the potential for pan-European marketing campaigns and bring greater advertising efficiency. When Sweden takes over the presidency of the EU in 2001, it is expected to harmonize advertising regulations in the EU, pushing for the most restrictive national regulations on pharmaceuticals, food, and advertising to children.[16]

Other regulations companies may encounter cover the production of advertising material. Some countries require all advertising, particularly television and radio, to be produced locally. As a result, it has become a real challenge for global advertisers to find campaigns that can be used in as many countries as possible to save on the production costs. Such campaigns are, however, possible only if a

13. Frances Williams, "Curbs on Tobacco: WHO to Launch Talks on Treaty," *Financial Times*, October 26, 1999, p. 6.
14. Melissa Akin, "Duma Smoking Bill Proves Nothing Is Sacred," *Moscow Times*, June 11, 1999, p. 1.
15. "Campaigns sans Frontières," *Financial Times*, May 31, 1996, p. 10.
16. Harriet Green, "Cam Campaign International: Issue Marketing to Children," *Campaign*, May 7, 1999, p. 34.

marketer has sufficient input from the very beginning on the applicable legislation so as to take all regulations into account.

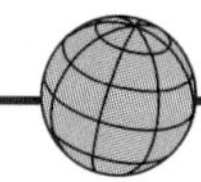

Selecting an Advertising Theme

Standardization Versus Customization

For marketers with products sold in many countries, the basic decision tends to center around the appropriate level of standardization for the advertising theme and its creative execution. As a result of early failures by inexperienced companies that employed a totally standardized approach, companies shifted to the other extreme by allowing each market to design its own campaign. In the mid-1960s, European-based advertising executives started to discuss the possibility of greater standardization. Erik Elinder was among the first to advocate the benefits of a more standardized approach.[17] Elinder argued that European consumers were increasingly "living under similar conditions although they read and speak different languages."[18]

A study by BBDO of the "Eurowoman," which included a thousand interviews with women from twenty-six countries, found there is a consistent profile of the Eurowoman. The study reported that communications to European women often depend on stereotypes of either the sexy bimbo or the veteran housewife, ignoring the working female. The research identified an opportunity to improve European advertising with women through the use of the workingwoman image and the recognition that today's woman has humor, confidence, and individuality.[19]

Advantages of Standardizing Global Advertising First, because *creative* talent is scarce, one effort to develop a campaign will likely produce better results than forty or fifty efforts. This particularly applies to countries for which the marketing or advertising experience is limited. A second advantage centers around the economics of a global campaign. To develop an individual campaign in many countries creates costs for photographs, layouts, and the production of television commercials. In a standardized approach, these production costs can be reduced, and more funds can be spent on purchasing space in the media. Unilever paid $700,000 for one series of TV commercials to be used in eighteen Asian and European countries. By reusing its commercials in many countries, the company saved in production costs. Furthermore, the company was able to

17. Erik Elinder, "How International Can Advertising Be?" *International Adviser*, December 1961, pp. 12–16; ibid., "How International Can European Advertising Be?" *Journal of Marketing*, April 1965, pp. 7–11.
18. "How International Can European Advertising Be?" *Journal of Marketing*, April 1965, p. 9.
19. "Advertisers Glimpse Their Dream Woman," *International Management*, March 1993, p. 21.

spend more on the original version and thus produce a better advertisement.[20] A third reason for a standardized approach is found in global brand names. Many companies market products under a single brand name in several countries within the same region. With the substantial amount of international travel occurring today and the considerable overlap in media across national borders, companies are interested in creating a single image to avoid any confusion caused through local campaigns that may be in conflict with each other.

One of the best examples of a successful standardized campaign was Philip Morris's Marlboro campaign in Europe. Marlboro's success as a leading brand began in the 1950s, when the brand was repositioned to assure smokers that the flavor would be unchanged by the effect of the filter. The theme "*Come to where the flavor is. Come to Marlboro country*" became an immediate success in the United States and abroad.[21] In all overseas markets, the advertising theme makes use of the same type of ad used in the United States. The cowboy has become a symbol of freedom and evokes the same feeling among Americans, Brazilians, and Germans. (This phenomenon was discussed in Chapter 3 under the subject of reference groups.) Consequently, the cowboy is a relevant reference group for the German smoker, invoking a positive identification. Patek Philippe, the prestige watchmaker has supported its brand with a global print and TV campaign using the theme "You never actually own a Patek Philippe. You merely look after it for the next generation." The campaign has been successful in the United States, Europe, China, Japan, Singapore and Tiawan.[22]

Procter & Gamble launched Pringles potato chips in the 1970s and existed for fifteen years without any significant penetration in the salty-snack market, dominated by Frito-Lay. However, between 1995 and 1999, P&G doubled the sales of Pringles to $1.0 billion. Now one of P&G's top three global brands, Pringles are in over forty countries. P&G attributes the global success of Pringles to a uniform package, product, and advertising message aimed at young children (six to eleven) and teens (twelve to seventeen). The message used around the world is "once you pop, you can't stop."Although P&G allows some local tactical differences market to market, including some flavor variations, the bulk of the advertising and merchandising is global.[23]

Warner Lambert Co. is developing a revitalized image for Chiclets gum. Whereas advertisements in the past were created on a country-by-country basis with no central theme, research showed that Chiclets faced low visibility across many countries. The new positioning and campaign are targeted to the eighteen- to

20. "Ads Astride the World," *Financial Times*, April 13, 1989, p. 16.
21. "Defending the Rights of Marlboro Man," *Economist*, April 21, 1990, p. 84.
22. "Patek Philippe: Tradition Anyone?" *Ad Age International*, January 11, 1999, p. 9.
23. Judann Pollack, "Pringles Wins Worldwide with One Message," *Ad Age International*, January 11, 1999, p. 14.

twenty-four-year-old consumer. The commercial, shot in the sand dunes of northern Brazil, includes a desert shack occupied by a young man and a monkey. By rattling a Chiclets box they summon an international audience ranging from Japanese geishas to English schoolboys. The tag line in English is "Chiclets make cool things happen." Hoping to use the ad worldwide, Warner Lambert wanted to maximize the impact of its advertising expenditures.[24]

China is another country that makes standardized approaches difficult. Research has shown that Chinese display sharply different attitudes in three areas. First, Chinese consumers emphasize respect and harmony more than U.S. consumers do. Second, the Chinese view health in broader terms than Americans, including sleeping well and peace. Third, the Chinese place a higher priority on family life within the home.[25] The experience of TCBY frozen yogurt in China indicates that an even more specific approach is necessary. The company maintains that each city is different, and that *even within China* a single commercial was not feasible. Thus TCBY advertisements try to address the interests of Chinese consumers in each city or province separately.[26]

Taco Bell, a U.S.-based chain with seven thousand restaurants, found that Gidget the talking chihuahua dog used in advertisments in the United States could not be used in Asia, where many consider dogs a delicacy, or in Muslium countries, where it is taboo to even touch a dog.[27] As these examples show, specific factors will either allow or prevent standardization of some parts of an advertising campaign. The nature of these factors is the topic of the following section.

Requirements for Standardized Campaigns For a company to launch a worldwide standardized campaign, some requirements first have to be met with regard to the product name, packaging, awareness, competitive situation, and consumer or customer attitudes.

The need for a standardized brand name or trademark is viewed by many companies as a prerequisite to a standardized campaign. Not only should the name always be written in identical format, but it should be pronounced identically. Trademarks or corporate logos can also help in achieving greater standardization of corporate campaigns. Such well-known logos as Kodak's, Sony's, and General Electric's are used the world over. The power of a company's brand name has a considerable influence on whether the company can use a standardized campaign. Few brand names are universally known. A research firm reviewed some of

24. "Chiclets Tries New Language," *Advertising Age International*, April 19, 1993, p. I-1.
25. "Burnett Tracks Shifts in Norms Shaping China," *Advertising Age International*, March 1997, p. I-32.
26. "Frozen Assets: TCBY Takes a Scoop Out of the China Market," *Far Eastern Economic Review*, November 14, 1996, p. 68.
27. Normandy Madden and Andrew Hornery, "As Taco Bell Enters Singapore, Gidget Avoids the Ad Limelight," *Ad Age International*, January 11, 1999, p. 13.

TABLE 12.1

The World's Top Ten Brands

Rank	1990	1996	1999
1	Coca-Cola	McDonald's	Coca-Cola
2	Kellogg	Coca-Cola	Microsoft
3	McDonald's	Disney	IBM
4	Kodak	Kodak	General Electric
5	Marlboro	Sony	Ford
6	IBM	Gillette	Disney
7	American Express	Mercedes-Benz	Intel
8	Sony	Levi's	McDonald's
9	Mercedes-Benz	Microsoft	AT&T
10	Nescafé	Marlboro	Marlboro

Source: From "The World's Biggest Brands," *Economist*, November 16, 1996, p. 75.

the best-known brands and rated them on market share within category, breadth of global brand appeal, depth of brand loyalty, and stretching ability beyond the original product category. The results, and the change in ranking from 1990 to 1996, are shown in Table 12.1

When Whirlpool acquired the Philips business in 1989, the firm became the world's largest appliance maker, overtaking Electrolux of Sweden. The joint venture resulted in a market share of 12 percent in Europe, compared with European leader Electrolux's 22 percent. In the U.S. market, the positions were reversed, with Whirlpool taking a 30 percent and Electrolux a 15 percent market share.[28] Since Whirlpool was largely unknown to European consumers, the company undertook a pan-European advertising campaign costing some $110 million over several years. The advertising was the result of some exhaustive testing of housewives in the United Kingdom, France, Spain, and Austria. Two test campaigns

28. "Whirlpool Striving to Clean Up Europe," *Advertising Age*, March 5, 1990, p. 30.

were not universally accepted, forcing Whirlpool to develop yet a third campaign that was based on features that had tested positive in both test campaigns.[29] The introductory TV spot featured a woman and her son moving through an ultramodern, computer-animated house from one electric appliance to another while a voice-over described the economic and ecological advantages of using Philips Whirlpool and its reliability. The TV campaign was to use the same ads in eleven countries. The strategy was to combine Philips's reputation for reliability with the U.S. firm's image of innovation and eventually to create a pan-European brand recognition that would completely phase out the Philips name. The phase-out was planned to take place country by country, depending on how fast Whirlpool could establish its own brand identity.[30] Whirlpool maintained a 12 percent share of the European market, not expanding to 20 percent as was forecast by its CEO, David Whitwam. The major appliance companies in Europe, such as Electrolux and Bosch-Siemens, restructured and cut costs to be more competitive. Also, Whirlpool focused most of its advertising efforts on promoting the Whirlpool brand names but neglected some of the original brand names like Bauknecht in Germany, which was a strong brand.[31]

To aid the prospective customer in identifying the advertised product with the actual one placed in retail stores, consumer products manufacturers in particular aim at packages that are of standardized appearance. Despite differences in sizes, these packages carry the same design in terms of color, layout, and name. Nonstandardized packages cannot be featured in a standardized campaign. Naturally, this concern is of interest to consumer products companies because the package has to double both as a protective and as a promotional device.

Because products may be at different stages of their product life cycles in different countries, different types of advertising may be required to appeal to the various levels of customer awareness. Typically, a campaign during the earlier stages of the product life cycle concentrates on the product category since many prospective customers may not have heard about it. In later stages, with more intensive competition, the campaign tends to shift toward emphasizing the product's advantages over competitive products.

Consider the experience of Procter & Gamble when advertising first became available in former East Germany. P&G developed a series of advertisements for TV that featured specific information on a product's function rather than the typical ads situated in lifestyle situations aired for West German consumers. The company found that consumer products such as fabric softeners, liquid detergents, and household cleaners were misused and that the reusable containers, intended to cut down on garbage, were given to children as toys. The company expected

29. "Women of Europe Put Whirlpool in a Spin," *Financial Times*, March 1, 1990, p. 11a.
30. "Whirlpool Seeks European Identity," *Financial Times*, January 13, 1990, p. 10.
31. Greg Steinmetz and Carl Quintanilla, "The New Europe: Whirlpool's European Sales Short-Circuit," *Asian Wall Street Journal*, April 15, 1998, p. 1.

that in time it would be able to air the same TV commercials throughout reunited Germany.[32]

As companies enter new markets, they can expect to find different competitive situations that require an adjustment in the advertising campaign. Competing with a different group of companies and being placed in the position of an outsider often demand a change from the advertising policy used in the domestic market, where these firms might well have a strong position. Perrier entered the U.S. market using a snob appeal. Emphasizing the product's noncaloric attributes, Perrier was positioned as an alternative to soft drinks and alcoholic beverages. With a premium price, Perrier was geared toward more affluent adults.[33] In European markets, where Perrier was well entrenched and the drinking of mineral water accepted by a vast number of consumers, such an approach would not have yielded the same results.

These examples show companies with solid leadership positions at home entering foreign markets as outsiders. They were forced by this circumstance to develop advertising programs substantially different from those used in their home markets.

Land of the Soft Sell: Advertising in the Japanese Market

Japan is the world's second-largest advertising market after the United States.[34] In 1998, Japan's advertising spending was $38 billion, still behind the $112 billion spent by the United States.[35] The dominant style of advertising in Japan uses an image-oriented approach, or "soft sell," compared with the more factual or "hard sell" typical in the United States, or the "wit" prevalent in the United Kingdom.[36]

Because different cultural backgrounds produce varying consumer attitudes, it is quite normal to expect differences in advertising appeals. Japan offers several examples that contrast with experiences in the United States or Europe. In Japan, consumers tend to be moved more by emotion than by logic, in contrast to North Americans or Europeans.[37] According to Gregory Clark, a European teaching at Sophia University in Tokyo, the Japanese are culturally oriented to consider the mood, style,

32. "Lifestyle Ads Irk East Europeans," *Advertising Age*, October 8, 1990, p. 56.
33. "Perrier: The Astonishing Success of an Appeal to Affluent Adults," *Business Week*, January 22, 1979, p. 64.
34. Alexandra Harney, "Interest in Japan Surges as Agencies Begin to Think Globally," *Campaign*, September 11, 1998, p. 23.
35. Juliana Koranteng, "Top Global Ad Markets," *Ad Age International*, May 11, 1998, p. 15.
36. Gregory M. Rose, Victoria D. Bush, and Lynn Kahle, "The Influence of Family Communication Patterns on Parental Reactions Toward Advertising: A Cross-National Examination," *Journal of Advertising*, January 1, 1998, p. 71.
37. "Emotion, Not Logic, Sways the Japanese Consumer," *Japan Economic Journal*, April 22, 1980, p. 24.

and sincerity demonstrated by a deed more important than its content. Consequently, consumers are searching for ways to be emotionally convinced about a product. This leads to advertising that rarely mentions price, occasionally even omits the distinctive features or qualities of a product, and shies away from competitive advertising aimed at competing firms. This type of advertising is further supported by the Japanese language, which even has a verb (*kawasarern*) to describe the process of being convinced to buy a product contrary to one's own rational judgment.

Some differences were further elaborated by an American executive working for one of the largest Japanese advertising agencies:[38] Japanese advertising has a strong nonverbal component; uses a contemporary Japanese language; frequently shows man-woman, mother-child, or even father-daughter relationships; demonstrates Japanese humor; and above all stresses long-term relationships. There is also some evidence of the individual's place in Japanese society in the use of evocative pictures or events to indicate individual values. With respect to the emotional tendency, the use of nonverbal communication and inference seems to prevail. Also important is the product origin and the need to present the product as being right for the Japanese. This requires a strong corporate identity program to establish a firm's credibility in the Japanese market.

Research conducted for the Nikkei Advertising Research Institute in Japan on advertising expressions used in Japan, South Korea, Taiwan, the United States, and France demonstrated statistically this high degree of nonverbal communication in Asia.[39] The study found that sentences of less than four phrases or words appeared in 50.1 percent of Japanese ads, 81.6 percent in Korea, and 80.6 percent in Taiwan, but only in 22.6 percent in the United States and 21.3 percent in France. The same study also compared the number of foreign words appearing in advertising headlines. Japan, with 39.2 percent, used the highest number of foreign words, followed by Taiwan with 32.1 percent, Korea with 15.7 percent, and France with 9.1 percent. The United States used foreign words in only 1.8 percent of the headlines investigated. This underlines the strong Japanese interest in foreign countries and words, particularly those of the English language. A later study confirmed the Japanese preference for less wordy advertising copy and a greater reliance on mood or symbolism.[40]

Although one may conclude that U.S. products do not sell in Japan, reality shows that this is not necessarily so. Japanese television commercials are full of U.S. themes, use many U.S. stars or heroes, and frequently have U.S. landscapes or backgrounds. By using U.S. stars in their commercials, Japanese companies give the impression that these products are very popular in the United States.

38. James Herendeen, "How to Japanize Your Creative," *International Advertiser*, September–October 1980, p. 22.
39. *Japan Economic Journal*, December 23, 1980, p. 33.
40. Jae W. Hong, Aydin Muderrisoglu, and George M. Zinkhan, "Cultural Differences and Advertising Expression: A Comparative Content Analysis of Japanese and U.S. Magazine Advertising," *Journal of Advertising*, vol. 16, no. 1 (1987), pp. 55–62.

Given the Japanese interest in and positive attitudes toward many U.S. cultural themes, such strategies have worked out well for Japanese advertisers. This is why Nissan asked Paul Newman to drive the new Skyline model in its ads and why John Travolta was asked to appear in an ad sipping semialcoholic fruit juice.[41] When Mitsubishi Electric paid rock singer Madonna a reported $650,000 for the right to use fragments of a rock tour, the company's VCR sales doubled in three months, whereas competitors experienced only a 15 percent increase.[42] In contrast to U.S. testimonials, however, Japanese advertisers tend to use foreign stars as actors using the product but not openly endorsing it.

A more recent development is the use of Japanese in an international setting. This leads to the use of Japanese models or businesspeople in foreign settings, such as in Matsushita's ad depicting a jazz-loving employee visiting the United States, where he is given a welcoming embrace by his friend, who happens to be a black New Orleans saxophone player. Asahi, a successful Japanese brewery that launched the dry beer, used actual Japanese professionals working in the United States in a series of ads in Japan to show that "the brains created in Japan are becoming successful abroad."[43] It is part of a Japanese tendency to strive for product awareness only; advertisements are devoid of any mention of the product itself. As a result, comparative advertising rarely exists in Japan; before-and-after claims are also seldom used. According to some experts, western advertising is designed to make the product look superior, whereas Japanese advertising is aimed at making it desirable.[44]

Using a new approach in Japan, Sega was able to recover from losses of market share to Sony's PlayStation and Nintendo 64. The first in a series of commercials played on the poor performance of Sega. The commercial began with one junior school boy saying to another, "Sega sucks. Let's go play with PlayStation," as a senior Sega executive, Hidekazu Yukawa, overhears the conversation.[45] Mr. Yukawa then goes on to losing battles with disheartening workers, a bottle of booze, and tough guys on the street before stumbling home to his wife. Later commercials went on to show that Sega was able to challenge Playstation with the launch of Dreamcast. According to Yasumichi Oka, the creative director at the ad agency Dentsu, if the commercials had started by saying everything was good at Sega, no one would believe it. The seven commercial series successfully launched Dreamcast with sales of 3 million units in the first month, compared with only 5 million units of Sega's previous product, Saturn, over forty months.[46]

41. "U.S. Sets the Pace Despite Growing Pride in Things Japanese," *International Herald Tribune*, October 1, 1984, p. 12.
42. "Madonna In Japan," *Fortune*, September 15, 1986, p. 9.
43. "Tokyo TV Ads Portray Japanese as the Savvy International Type," *Wall Street Journal*, October 11, 1990, p. B6.
44. "Advertising: Upping a Youthful Image," *Financial Times*, October 22, 1986, p. VI.
45. Jon Herskovitz, "Sega's Sales Rise as Ads Play on Woes," *Ad Age International*, February 8, 1999, p. 1.
46. Ibid.

Advertising in Japan also differs from western practice in its management and structure. In Japan, the conflict-of-interest rules do not apply, and competing brands can be handled by the same agency. The market is dominated by Dentsu, by far Japan's largest advertising agency and one of the world's as well. Dentsu is the Japanese media's biggest single customer, accounting for some 20 percent of all billings in Japan and 50 percent of prime-time television. As such, Dentsu usually commands the best price and the best space in the press.[47] None of the other major advertising markets in the world is so dominated by a single local agency.

The Impact of Recent Changes in Eastern Europe

With the political changes in eastern Europe, advertising suddenly became available to foreign companies and is developing as an acceptable economic activity. It has been hampered by the fact that commercial advertising as known in the open economies had been used largely for political purposes and to advertise excess goods. In Hungary, Procter & Gamble replaced its campaign for Blend-a-Med toothpaste because the claim "Reduces cavities by 80 percent" reminded consumers of the false statements used by the Communists of the former political situation.[48] When the markets in eastern Europe opened up, changes had to come both in the media policy of these countries and in the acceptability of advertising.

According to one expert, "The last hundred years of western advertising [experience] have been compressed into just four years for us."[49] The differences between Czech consumers and western consumers are said to be the smallest among eastern European countries, but significant differences persist elsewhere. When an international soft-drink company wanted to bring its brand to Bulgaria with advertising emphasizing health-minded young people, the local agency recommended instead a focus on glitzy night clubs and bars, since many young Bulgarian consumers were starved for such images after decades of Communist rule. In another example, a western food company wanted to introduce bouillon cubes to Romania in advertising featuring a happy family gathered around the dinner table. The campaign had to be changed because Romanian consumers were not familiar with the family dinner concept at all.[50]

In other eastern European nations, advertising is likewise in the early phases of development. The present infrastructure is radically different from what global firms are used to. Few full-service advertising agencies existed. Many western agencies are now establishing local offices, some as joint ventures with local account

47. Alexandra Harney, "The Dentsu Story," *Campaign*, April 9, 1999, p. 38.
48. "Road to E. Europe Paved with Marketing Mistakes," *Advertising Age International*, October 26, 1992, p. I-21.
49. "Full of Eastern Promise," *Financial Times*, June 8, 1995, p. 13.
50. Ibid.

managers. The many western agency networks attracted to eastern Europe collectively reported gross income of about $180 million in 1995, covering total billings of about $1 billion (see Table 12.2). The majority of their business was concentrated in four countries: Poland, the Czech Republic, Hungary, and Russia.[51] Table 12.2 shows the top European firms, most of which operate in Eastern Europe.

A study of 12,000 consumers in central and eastern Europe by the Leo Burnett ad agency revealed three general mindsets of the consumers: (1) optimists—not afraid of change, enjoy life, usually opinion leaders; (2) engaged—hopeful, early adoptors of new ideas; and (3) defeatist—lacking financial security, believe lives are changing for the worst, prefer communism.[52] Each eastern European country had 40 to 50 percent optimists and engaged, who together are the most willing to buy new products, with the greatest percentage of optimists being in Russia and the Ukraine.[53]

Following perestroika in 1985 and the breakup of the former Soviet Union, consumers were anxious to have more choice of products. A survey of Ukrainian consumers found that across all ages, consumers desired quality products, both foreign and domestic. Further, the study revealed that 98 percent of Ukranians were more aware of advertising after perestroika, especially on television and billboards.[54] In Russia, outside posters and neon signs were among the first signs of advertising to appear, with Samsung and Goldstar, both of South Korea, being among the first firms to pay the $200,000 in annual fees for two spots in Moscow or St. Petersburg.[55]

As eastern European markets make the transition to market economies, western firms have significant opportunities to build brand awareness quickly. For example, only 5 percent of Russians could name Snickers as a candy bar in 1992. One year later, after a campaign featuring the Rolling Stones' "(I Can't Get No) Satisfaction," 82 percent could name Snickers.[56] As Russia's population of 218 million citizens grows more prosperous, the opportunities for marketing consumer products will grow.

Procter & Gamble is exporting several brands to Russia, among them Crest toothpaste and Camay soap. Colgate Palmolive, one of the world leaders in toothpaste, is importing Colgate toothpaste from an Indian company. Both companies can sell whatever they can ship.[57] Colgate had previously given away hundreds of

51. "Agencies Expanding Eastern European Penetration," *Advertising Age International*, October 1996, p. I-8.
52. "European Consumers Studied by Burnett," *Direct Marketing*, August 1998, pp. 14–15.
53. "Polish Advertising Most Effective Outside Media," *Polish Press Agency*, May 14, 1998, p. 1.
54. Jean Grow vonDorn and Irina Akimova, "Advertising in the Ukraine: Cultural Perspectives, *International Journal of Advertising*, May 1, 1998, p. 189.
55. "UK Helps to Make Advertising and Promotion a Priority," *Financial Times*, December 8, 1988, p. 12.
56. "In Moscow, the Attack of the Killer Brands," *Business Week*, January 10, 1994, p. 40.
57. "Colgate, P&G Pack for Road to Russia," *Advertising Age*, March 12, 1990, p. 56.

TABLE 12.2

Top 25 Networks in Europe

Agency (Multinational Network)	*1998 Gross Income*	*Percent Change from 1997*	*1998 Billings*
Euro RSCG Worldwide	$647.4	8.7	$4,109.1
BBDO Worldwide	634.8	53.1	4,742.7
McCann-Erickson Worldwide	627.5	16.2	5,473.9
Publicis Worldwide	586.8	36.6	3,726.2
Young & Rubicam	516.3	11.0	4,686.6
Ogilvy & Mather Worldwide	498.1	9.7	4,753.5
DDB Needham Worldwide	480.4	8.0	3,421.4
Grey Advertising	433.1	6.6	3,055.9
J. Walter Thompson Co.	431.7	9.0	3,102.3
TBWA International	357.9	17.7	2,441.0
Ammirati Puris Lintas	334.0	6.8	2,445.5
D'Arcy Masius Benton & Bowles	301.3	−4.5	2,784.4
Bates Worldwide	272.7	7.4	3,208.5
Leo Burnett Co.	257.5	15.2	2,119.1
Lowe & Partners Worldwide	212.3	9.0	1,475.5
Saatchi & Saatchi	154.4	2.2	1,979.7
Brann Worldwide	148.1	37.9	987.8
Rapp Collins Worldwide	116.0	NA	773.4
Foote, Cone & Belding	104.8	NA	758.3
TMP Worldwide	89.1	33.0	593.8
Bozell Worldwide	78.9	4.4	521.3
Campus	72.5	59.9	594.4
FCA/BMZ	69.5	3.2	457.6
Carlson Marketing	44.5	25.9	519.2
Draft Worldwide	44.4	61.6	554.6

Note: All figures are in millions of dollars.
Source: Reprinted with permission from Advertising Age International. Copyright, Crain Communications, Inc. 1999.

thousands of toothpaste samples. When the company exhibited in a trade show in Moscow and gave away free samples, local residents stood in line for two hours. Many were reported to have returned to the end of the line for another sample. With strong interest among global firms to eventually be present in the large Russian consumer market, several global advertising agencies have set up shop in Moscow.

Global Advertising

Global advertising received a considerable amount of attention in the 1980s and is now considered the most controversial topic in global marketing. The debate was triggered by Professor Theodore Levitt, who argues in an article and in his book *The Marketing Imagination* that markets are becoming increasingly alike worldwide and that the trend is toward a global approach to marketing.[58]

Interestingly, a study of European consumers found that, although there was a strong preference for global products, consumers preferred advertising for local products. In many cases, the most memorable ads were of local brands, but the preferred product was a foreign brand! This indicates that more than advertising is needed to influence consumer behavior.[59]

Levitt's ideas were applied to the field of global advertising by Saatchi & Saatchi, a British advertising agency that rose to prominence on the basis of its global campaigns.[60] Saatchi & Saatchi claimed that worldwide brands would soon become the norm and that such an advertising challenge could only be handled by worldwide agencies. Saatchi & Saatchi purchased a number of privately held agencies, including Ted Bates, in 1986. In response, the industry began a period of consolidations that resulted in large global agencies, including WPP Group, Omnicom, Interpublic, and Saatchi & Saatchi. Saatchi & Saatchi has had financial difficulty because of its large debt, but its actions led to the development of a number of global advertising firms.[61]

Consumer tastes, needs, and purchasing patterns are said to be converging. This can be supported by the converging trends in demographics across many countries. At the forefront of these trends has been the decline of the nuclear family, both in North America and in many countries around the globe. In most countries, more women are working. Similarly, divorce trends are increasingly pointing in the same direction in North America, Europe, and other developed

58. Theodore Levitt, "The Globalization of Markets," *Harvard Business Review*, May-June 1983, p. 92; *The Marketing Imagination* (New York: Free Press, 1983); *International Herald Tribune*, October 1, 1984, p. 7 (interview with Theodore Levitt).
59. Nancy Giges, "Europeans Buy Outside Goods, but Like Local Ads," *Advertising Age International*, April 27, 1992, p. I-1.
60. "Saatchi & Saatchi Will Keep Gobbling," *Fortune*, June 23, 1986, p. 36.
61. Noreen O'Leary and Greg Farrell, "British Invasion," *Adweek*, November 9, 1998, pp. 31–41.

countries. This has changed the role of women in society almost everywhere. Standards of living have risen in many countries, and earlier differences among nations have been reduced. In addition to these demographic trends, common media such as films, television, and music are creating cultural convergence as well. These developments are said to reduce cultural barriers among countries; such barriers are expected to diminish even further through satellite television networks covering many countries with identical programs.

One of the stronger believers in global advertising, British Airways, broke new ground in its industry by airing the well-known "Manhattan" TV commercial in 1983. Designed by Saatchi & Saatchi, the spot showed the flight across the Atlantic and the landing on the island of Manhattan as an expression of British Airways flying as many passengers annually across the Atlantic as people lived in Manhattan. In 1989, the same advertising agency designed a new global campaign for British Airways, featuring some four thousand people greeting each other and interspersed with the creation of a smiling face when viewed from the air. The commercial was produced in the U.S. Midwest and directed by a well-known movie director. The company believes that the strong visual value allows it to use the production everywhere, resulting in a global campaign production cost of about half the traditional cost of creating advertising for each market.[62] Its recent campaign continued British Airways' global advertising approach. The company split the emphasis, however, between business and leisure travel, launching the new advertising simultaneously in 133 countries. The company moved from a single global campaign for this overall image to two global campaigns directed at two separate types of air traveler.[63]

Researchers who have studied global advertisements have found that visual ads were more universally understood. Visuals have the obvious advantage of not being culturally specific. The researchers also found that most global ads are linked to the brand, with the visual image helping to register the brand in the consumer's mind.[64] Cartier, the French luxury products firm, launched a global campaign in 123 countries with multinational positioning. The 1996 campaign featured minimal copy language and emphasized dramatic photography so that the same message could be conveyed in Brazil, Japan, Russia, and dozens of other countries. The campaign used magazines only. Although designed and executed centrally, the campaign budgets were dispersed at Cartier's twenty-five subsidiaries.[65]

62. "BA's Warm Approach," *Financial Times*, December 28, 1989, p. 8.
63. "BA's $150 Million Campaign Makes Worldwide Debut," *Advertising Age*, January 8, 1996, p. 33.
64. M. Roland Jeannet, "Global Advertising," presentation made at 1988 Annual Conference of U.K. Advertising Agency Planners, London, 1988.
65. "Cartier Softens French Accent in International Campaign," *Advertising Age*, October 7, 1996, p. 12.

For a global strategy to be successful, experience indicates that four requirements must be fulfilled. First, the product must be able to deliver the same benefit in each market. Second, the market or the product category development in each market must be at the same level in terms of product life cycle, penetration, and usage. Third, the competitive environment—that is, the type of competition and the nature of the competitive products encountered—must be similar in each market. And fourth, the heritage of the brand must not be restricted to particular countries, and the brand history must be similar in the various markets.[66]

Many marketing executives remain skeptical about the value of global advertising campaigns. Global campaigns do appear to work, however, if the target market is relatively narrowly defined. Take Sprite, for example. The Coca-Cola Company owns Sprite, the number-three soft drink worldwide. Central to the brand's global advertising strategy is the fact that the meaning of Sprite as a brand—what it stands for in the eyes of consumers—is exactly the same globally. Many Sprite ads are run worldwide unchanged, while others are tailored locally. All share the same basic theme of self-reliance and trusting one's instincts. The company found that despite cultural differences in different markets around the world, there was strong global similarity among teenagers no matter which country was involved. The entire global campaign was thus built on the apparently universal teenage sentiment toward soft drinks and similar products, and toward what Sprite "symbolizes."[67]

In 1999, the value of Coca-Cola declined as the company became over-centralized, slow-moving, and insensitive to local needs. Douglas Daft, the new chairman and chief executive officer of Coca-Cola, reported that while Coke is a brand with global relevance, "that global success of Coca-Cola is the direct result of people drinking one bottle at a time in their own local communities. So we are placing responsibility and accountability in the land of our colleagues who are closest to those billions of individual sales."[68]

The sales of Levi's, the global producers of 501 jeans, have fallen from $7.1 billion in 1996 to $5.1 billion in 1999. Sales were lost to more fashionable Tommy Hilfiger and Calvin Klein and to less expensive products in discount stores. According to Philip Marineau, the new chief executive hired from PepsiCo, Levi's advertising focused too much on being "hip and cool" and not on having a great product and wrapping it with an attitude of youthfulness and sexiness."[69] Both Coca-Cola and Levi's examples illustrate the potential fragility of global brands.

66. Jerome B. Kernan and Teresa J. Domzal, "International Advertising: To Globalize, Visualize," *Journal of International Consumer Marketing,* 1993, vol. 5, no. 4, pp. 51–71.
67. "Sprite Is Riding Global Ad Effort to No. 4 Status," *Advertising Age*, November 18, 1996, p. 30.
68. "Back to Classic Coke," *Financial Times*, March 27, 2000, p. 16.
69. Andrew Edgecliffe-Johnson, "Tightening Levi's Belt," *Financial Times*, February 28, 2000, p. 8.

A number of companies have begun the process of developing regional or global brands:

- L'Oréal, the French cosmetics company, has grown sales to $12.4 billion based on its global campaigns for Maybelline, Ralph Lauren perfumes, Helena Rubinstein cosmetics, and Redken hair care.[70]
- H.J. Heinz has launched a global campaign for Heinz ketchup to develop consistency in its brand image and advertising worldwide. CEO William Johnson sees the global approach as a way to shore up the brand in Heinz's biggest markets—the United States, the United Kingdom, and Germany—and to build sales in eastern Europe and South America.[71]
- Hewlett-Packard will spend $100 to $150 million to unify its corporate computer and services offering, moving them from a box provider to a strong business partner.[72]
- Volvo launched a $98 million campaign to add styling and design to its long-standing safety image worldwide.[73]
- "More power. more life" will be Duracell's new tag line in its campiagn that helps support the company's 42 percent share of the battery business over rival Energizer's 38 percent.[74]
- Jaguar found that its new S-type model would appeal to similar customers around the world, so the company has launched the same campaign from "Chicago to Riyadh, Tokyo, and Berlin," therefore having a consistent image worldwide and saving money by not having to develop different themes for each market.[75]
- Sony launched a massive global image, dubbed the Millennium Project, to position its electronics, music, and software empire as the leading lifestyle and technology brand for the twenty-first century.[76]

What may be more likely to happen is a modularized approach to global advertising. A company may select some features as standard for all its advertising

70. Gail Edmondson et al., "The Beauty of Global Branding," *Business Week*, June 28, 1999, p. 70.
71. Patricia Sabatini, "Heinz Re-enlists Leo Burnett for Global Campaign," *Pittsburgh Post-Gazette*, March 27, 1999, p. C1.
72. Bradley Johnson, "HP Sets $150 Million Global Ad Effort," *Advertising Age*, February 8, 1999, p. 76.
73. Jean Haliday, "European Automakers Plan Global Advertising Campaigns," *Automotive News Europe*, Sepetember 28, 1998, p. 6.
74. "Duracell Given More Life Is Launching $50 million Global Campaign," *Adweek*, June 15, 1998, p. 84.
75. Bradford Wernie, "Jaguar Goes Global," *Automotive News Europe*, April 12, 1999, p. V.
76. Andrew McMains and Tobi Elkin, "Sony Eyes Massive 2000 Image Effort," *Adweek*, July 27, 1998, p. 3.

while localizing some others. Pepsi-Cola chose this approach in its 1986 global campaign. The company wanted to use modern music in connection with its products while still using some local identification. As a result, with the assistance of Ogilvy & Mather, its advertising agency, Pepsi-Cola hired the U.S. singer Tina Turner, who teamed up in a big concert setting with local rock stars from six countries singing and performing the Pepsi-Cola theme song. In the commercials, the local rock stars are shown together with Tina Turner. Except for the footage of the local stars, all the commercials were identical. For other countries, local rock stars were spliced into the footage so that they also appear to be onstage with Tina Turner. By shooting the commercials all at once, the company saved in production costs. The overall concept of the campaign was extended to some thirty countries without forcing local subsidiaries or bottlers to come up with their own campaigns.[77]

Global companies are finding that advertising jingles that become hit singles in the United States often become popular in other countries, therefore providing support for the brand. For example, the Coke theme song "First Time" became popular in the United States and then Europe, helping to boost global sales.[78]

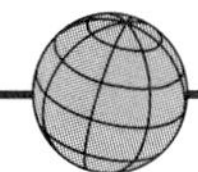

Global Media Strategy

The global marketer is faced with a variety of media across the world. Difficulties arise because not all media are available in all countries; if they are available, their technical capability to deliver to the required audience may be limited. Therefore, aside from the considerations that concern domestic operations, global media decisions are influenced by the availability or accessibility of various media for advertisers and the media habits of the target country.

Media Availability

Advertisers in the United States and many European countries have become accustomed to the availability of a full range of media for advertising purposes. Aside from the traditional print media, consisting of newspapers and magazines, the U.S. advertiser has access to radio, television, billboards, cinemas, and the Internet. In addition, direct mail is available to most prospective client groups. This complete choice of media is not available in every country, so a company marketing its products in several countries may find itself unable to apply the same media mix in all markets. Even when some media are available, access may

77. "Advertising: Tina Turner Helping Pepsi's Global Effort," *New York Times*, March 10, 1986, p. D13.
78. "It's Got a Good Beat, You Can Dance to It and It Sells Coke," *Wall Street Journal*, August 20, 1993, p. A7B.

be partially restricted. The use of commercials interspersed throughout programs on radio or television is common in North America, Japan, and Latin America, among others, but is less so in Europe. The global print media include mostly magazines targeted toward business executives, such as ***Business Week***, *The Economist*, *Fortune*, and *Time*, with a few consumer magazines like *Reader's Digest* and *Elle*. Global television includes news networks, such as BBC World and CNN and consumer channels such as Animal Planet, Discovery, ESPN, and MTV.[79]

Advertising on the Czech Republic's, two local channels is limited to 1 percent of total air time per channel, although the allowance is sometimes combined into 2 percent for the more popular first channel, or up to 6 minutes per hour of programming. Additional revenue is raised by charging each Czech household a viewing fee of $1.85 per month. On the other hand, the competing private network, TV Nova, which is owned by Ronald Lauder's Central European Media Enterprises, has an advertising ceiling of 10 percent of total air time. However, the private channel depends entirely on its advertising revenue. In Poland, the public channel also operates under a limit of 10 percent advertising on air time, the same as for the private channels.[80]

In some countries, the available time for commercials is allocated for various product groups, often regardless of the number of competitors or products on the market. For some competitive product categories, new products may only be launched by reallocating a company's television time among its existing products. This lack of flexibility inhibits new-product introduction in some consumer product categories for which television would be the most efficient advertising medium.

Existing government regulations have also had a substantial impact on how much television advertising is used. In Europe, television time is freely available only in the United Kingdom, Greece, Ireland, Portugal, Spain, and Italy.[81] In Italy, the breakup of the state monopoly resulted in the creation of several hundred commercial television stations alone.[82] In those countries, television advertising equals 30 to 50 percent of the print advertising volume. In European countries with restricted or limited access, television advertising amounts to 5 to 20 percent of the total amount spent on print advertising.

The European market has changed significantly with the advent of satellite and cable TV, which offers significant competition to the two or three state-controlled stations in each country. In 1980, there were approximately 40 channels throughout the European Union; by 1993, there were 150 channels. The televi-

79. Juliana Koranteng, "Global Media," *Ad Age International*, February 8, 1999, p. 23.
80. "Czech Government Targets Public Television Network," *Advertising Age International*, January 1997, p. I-6.
81. "European Ads' Potential 'Vast,'" *Financial Times*, March 24, 1983, p. 10.
82. "U.S. Style TV Turns on Europe," *Fortune*, April 13, 1987, p. 95.

sion advertising market has grown from $3.0 billion, or 15 percent of total advertising, in 1980 to $25.0 billion, or 29 percent of total advertising, in 1993.[83]

The growth of Asian economies and the opening of the eastern bloc have rapidly increased the size of the global television market. The breakdown of the 1 billion televisions in use in 1994 was as follows:[84]

Europe and former Soviet Union	350,000,000
Asia	320,000,000
North America and Caribbean	200,000,000
Latin America	80,000,000
Middle East	40,000,000
Africa	10,000,000

These examples demonstrate that, on an international basis, companies have to remain flexible with respect to their media plans. A company cannot expect to be able to use its preferred medium to the fullest extent everywhere. Consequently, global advertising campaigns will have to be designed with delivery over several media in mind.

Credibility of Advertising

Countries view the value of advertising in very different ways. A 1995 survey conducted by the marketing research company Roper Starch investigated advertising credibility in forty countries.[85] In the United States, 86 percent of consumers were eager to criticize marketing practices, particularly those aimed at children, whereas 75 percent of consumers praised its creativity. In Asia, consumers were more positive, with 47 percent indicating that advertisers provided good product information and 40 percent saying that advertisers respected consumers' intelligence. Globally, the results were 38 percent and 30 percent, respectively. The former Soviet Union bucks the trend: among consumers there, only 9 percent considered advertising to provide good information, and only 10 percent said it respected consumers' intelligence. Although globally 61 percent of consumers appreciated advertising for both its creativity and entertainment value, the same was true for only 23 percent of consumers living in the former Soviet Union.

Differences in the credibility of advertising in general, and some media in particular, will have to be taken into consideration by the international firm. Companies may want to place a greater reliance on advertising in countries where its credibility is very high. In other countries, the marketer should think seriously about using alternative forms of communication.

83. "Wired Planet," *Economist*, February 12, 1994, p. 12, Special section, "A Survey of Television."
84. "Television—What If They're Right?" *Economist*, February 12, 1994, p. 4, Special section, "A Survey of Television."
85. "Ex-Soviet States Lead World in Ad Cynicism," *Advertising Age*, June 5, 1995, p. 3.

Media Habits

As the experienced media buyer for any domestic market knows, the media habits of the target market are a major factor in deciding which media to use. The same applies on the international level. However, substantial differences in media habits exist because of a number of factors that are of little importance to the domestic or single-country operation. First of all, the penetration of various media differs substantially from one country to another. Second, advertisers encounter radically different literacy rates in many parts of the world. And finally, they may find different cultural habits or traits that favor one medium over another regardless of the penetration ratios or literacy rates.

Ownership or usage of television, radio, newspapers, and magazines varies considerably from one country to another. Whereas the developed industrial nations show high penetration ratios for all three major media carriers, developing countries have few radio and television receivers and low newspaper circulation. In general, the use of penetration of all of these media increases with the average income of a country. In most countries, the higher-income classes avail themselves first of the electronic media and newspapers. International marketers have to be aware that some media, though generally accessible for the advertiser, may be only of limited use since they reach only a small part of the country's target population.

The literacy of a country's population is an important factor influencing media decisions. Though this is less of a concern for companies in the industrial products market, it is a crucial factor in consumer goods advertising. In countries where large portions of the population are illiterate, the use of print media is of limited value. (See Table 3.2 for literacy rates of selected countries.) Both radio and television have been used by companies to circumvent the literacy problem. Other media that are occasionally used for this purpose are billboards and cinemas. The absence of a high level of literacy has forced consumer goods companies to translate their advertising campaigns into media and messages that communicate strictly by sound or demonstration. Television and radio have been used most successfully to overcome this problem, but they cannot be used in areas where the penetration of such receivers is limited. Frequently, this applies particularly to countries that have low electronic media penetration and low literacy rates.

Global advertising spending reflects different media availability. In 1998, ad spending reached $417 billion worldwide and was estimated to increase 4.6 percent to $436 in 1999.[86] Because of the limited accessibility of commercial TV in Europe, TV advertising amounted to 30 percent of the total spent in Europe, compared with 40 percent in North America and Asia. The biggest boom was forecast

86. Eric R. Quinones, "Ad Spending Growth May Cool After a Strong 1998," *Marketing News*, January 1, 1999, p. 43.

for Latin America, where advertising had reached a level of 1.3 percent of gross domestic product (GDP), higher than in any other region.[87]

Satellite Television

Satellite television channels, which are not subject to government regulations, have revolutionized television in many parts of the world. The impact of satellite television channels is nowhere felt more directly than in Europe.

The leader in this field of privately owned channels is Sky Channel, owned by Rupert Murdoch, who controls vast media interests in many countries. In 1993, Murdoch purchased the Star Satellite System, serving 45 million people from Egypt to Mongolia.[88] The Star System relies heavily on advertising revenue, which could reach $72 million with full use (it operated at 10 percent of full use in 1992). Star's advertisers include Nike and Coca-Cola.[89]

Originally only available as English-speaking television, satellite channels are now available in several European languages, such as German, French, and Swedish. Some 42.9 million viewers tuned into satellite TV in Europe in 1989, a 70 percent increase over 1988.[90] The average weekly viewing almost doubled to seven hours. One of the largest winners was CNN, with an increase of almost 184 percent.

With the advent of local-language satellite TV, more attractive than the traditional national TV channels, many viewers left the English-speaking Sky and Super Channel.[91] Furthermore, satellite TV has not attracted as much advertising expenditures as first anticipated, with major advertisers only scheduling a small percentage of their budgets on satellite TV.[92]

One of the most successful global satellite TV ventures is MTV. This music channel, launched in 1981 in the United States, by 1995 reached 250 million homes in more than sixty countries (see Figure 12.2).[93] The Murdoch group is eyeing expansion in Asia, where the multichannel market was already twice the size of western Europe's. By 2005, Murdoch expects 178 million cable and satellite homes for Asia, about 150 million of those in China, India, and Japan.[94]

For satellite-shown commercials to be effective, companies have to be able to profit from a global brand name and a uniform logo. Also, language remains a

87. "Advertising," *Economist*, January 18, 1997, p. 104.
88. "Wired Planet."
89. "A Minefield of Uncertainty," *Financial Times—Cable and Satellite Broadcasting*, October 6, 1992, p. V, Special section.
90. "Europe's Satellite TV Viewers Soar," *Advertising Age*, September 24, 1990, p. 39.
91. "Auf Wiedersehen, Roops," *Economist*, September 17, 1988, p. 80.
92. "Satellite Broadcasting: Healthy Long-Term Outlook," *Financial Times*, March 14, 1989, p. V.
93. "MTV Makes the Big Record Groups Dance to Its Tune," *Financial Times*, July 4, 1995, p. 17.
94. "Rival Media Scions Plot Growth in Asia-Pacific," *Advertising Age*, September 19, 1996, p. 46.

FIGURE 12.2

MTV Home Coverage Worldwide (in Millions of Homes)

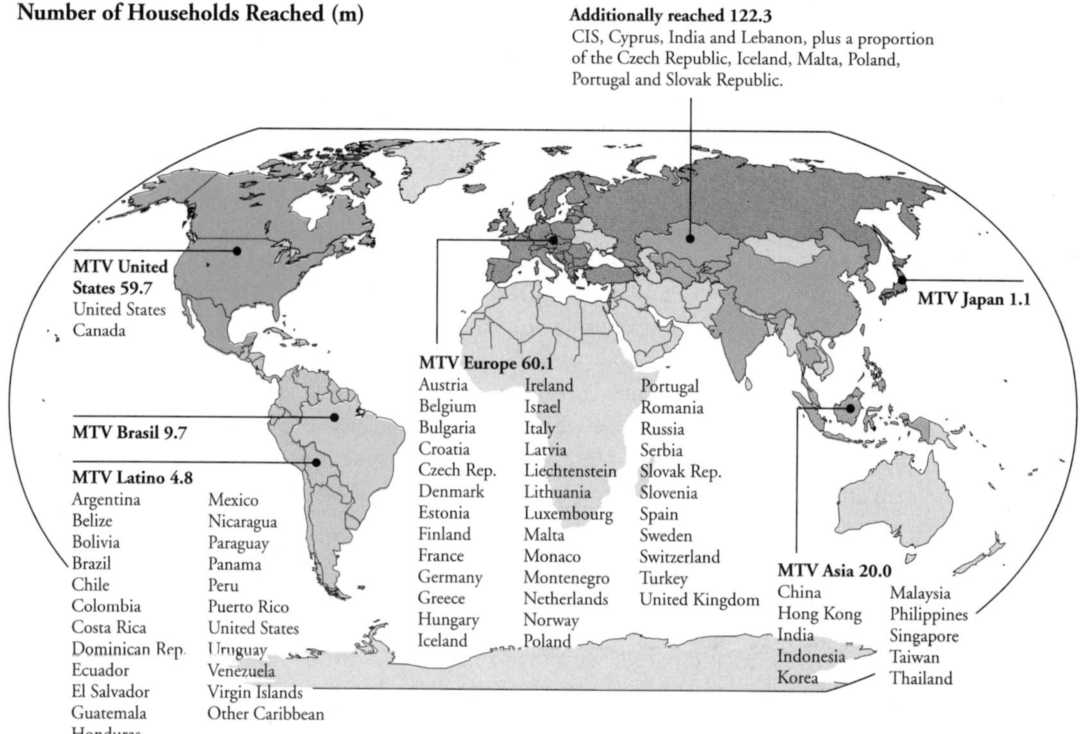

Source: Financial Times, July 4, 1995, p. 17. Reprinted by permission.

problem. English is the common language of the majority of satellite channels; however, there is a trend toward local-language satellites.

Most observers admit that the availability of satellite commercial networks has already had an impact on the national regulatory boards of countries that tended to restrict or limit commercial air time. Most predict that, even in Scandinavia, commercial television will become the norm. In other parts of Europe, existing commercial television time is not expected to lose out to other channels. This may substantially enlarge the TV advertising market in Europe.

The growth of mobile handheld devices with Internet capabilities is opening a new market for delivering entertainment, information, and advertising. Nokia, the largest manufacturer of mobile devices, has had discussions with both AOL and

News Corporation about providing content for these devices.[95] The new use of mobile devices provides potential global advertising opportunities.

Scheduling Global Advertising

The general rule in scheduling advertising suggests that the company more or less duplicates the sales curve or seasonality of its product. Furthermore, depending on the complexity of the buying decision or the deliberation time, the media expenditures tend to peak before the actual sales peak. This practice, though somewhat generalized here, applies as well to global markets as to domestic. Differences may exist, however, due to different sales peaks in the year, vacations or religious holidays, and differences in the deliberation time with regard to purchases.

Sales peaks are influenced both by climatic seasons and by customs and traditions. Winter months in North America and Europe are summer months in some countries of the Southern Hemisphere, namely Australia, New Zealand, South Africa, and Argentina. This substantially influences the purchase of many consumer goods, such as clothing, vacation services, and travel. Vacations are particularly important for some European countries. In Europe, school summer vacations tend to be shorter than in the United States, but employees typically are granted four to five weeks, which is more than those granted to the average U.S. employee. Religious holidays may also affect the placement or timing of advertising. During the Islamic Ramadan, usually celebrated over a month during July, many Muslim countries do not allow the placement of any advertising.

For industrial products, the timing of advertising in support of sales efforts may be affected by the budgetary cycles prevailing in a given country. For countries with large state-controlled sectors, heavy emphasis needs to be placed on the period before a new national or sector plan is developed. Private-sector companies tend to be more influenced by their own budgetary cycles, usually coinciding with their fiscal years. In Japan, many companies begin their fiscal year in June rather than January. To the extent that capital budgets are completed before the new fiscal year commences, products that require budgetary approval will need advertising support in advance of the budget completion.

The time needed to think about a purchase has been cited as a primary factor in deciding on the appropriate time by which the advertising peak is to precede the sales peak. In its domestic market, a company may have become accustomed to a given purchase deliberation time by its customers. Since the deliberation may be determined by income levels or other environmental factors, other markets

95. James Harding, "Nokia in 'Exploratory Talks' with News Corp. about Internet Tie-Up," *Financial Times*, February 2, 2000, p. 13.

may show different patterns. The purchase or replacement of a small electrical household appliance may be a routine decision for a North American household, and the purchase may occur whenever the need arises. In a country with lower income levels, such a purchase may be planned several weeks or even months ahead. Consequently, a company engaged in international advertising needs to carefully evaluate the underlying assumptions of its domestic advertising policies and not automatically assume that they apply elsewhere.

Organizing the Global Advertising Effort

A major concern for global marketing executives centers around the organization of their company's global advertising effort. Key concerns are the role of centralization at the head office versus the roles that subsidiaries and the advertising agency should play. Marketers are aware that a more harmonious approach to the global advertising effort may enhance both the quality and efficiency of the total effort. Thus, organizing the effort deserves as much time as individual advertising decisions about individual products or campaigns. Thus, in this section, we look in greater detail at advertising agency selection and the managerial issues of running a global advertising effort in a multinational corporation.

Advertising Agency Selection

Global companies face a number of options with respect to working with a given advertising agency. Many companies first develop an agency relationship domestically and have to decide at one point if they expect their domestic agency to handle their global advertising business as well. In some foreign markets, companies need to select foreign agencies to work with them—a decision that may be left to the local subsidiaries or may be made by the head office alone. Recently, some agencies have banded together to form international networks to attract more global business.

Working with Domestic Agencies When a company starts to grow internationally, it is not unusual for the domestic advertising agency to handle the international business as well. However, this is only possible when the domestic agency has global experience and capability. Many smaller domestic agencies do not have global experience. Thus, companies are forced to make other arrangements. Frequently, the global company starts to appoint individual agencies in each of the various foreign markets where it is operating. This may be done with the help of the local subsidiaries or through the company's head-office staff. Before long, the company will end up with a series of agency relationships that may make global coordination very difficult.

Working with Local Agencies The local-agency relationship offers some specific advantages. First of all, the local advertising agency is expected to fully understand the local environment and is in a position to create advertising targeted to the local market. However, many firms question the expertise and professionalism of local agencies, particularly in countries where advertising is not as developed as in the major markets of North America and Europe.

Jaguar had some interesting experiences in penetrating the Saudi Arabian market.[96] Jaguar had its own advertising in the Middle East handled through a British agency. The Saudi audience reacted negatively to the Lebanese Arabic used in the copy. They also noticed that the visuals had been shot in the United Arab Emirates, because the drivers in the pictures were wearing black bands with long black strings at the back that weighted down the Arabian headdress. Though this type of headdress was typical for that part of the Arabian Gulf region, it was not typical for Saudi Arabia. When the Jaguar importer in Saudi Arabia complained about the advertising, Jaguar looked for a local agency run by U.S. and British expatriates. However, this attempt was also a failure, and the account was finally shifted to a local agency run largely by Saudi managers. This agency relied heavily on high-quality visuals from Jaguar in the United Kingdom but wrote all of its own copy.[97]

Although one of the world's best-known brands, Mercedes-Benz has a strategy of utilizing many local agencies. Its $400 million worldwide advertising budget is spread among about two hundred local agencies. The company follows a policy of engaging the most creative shop in each country. Prior to 1980, the company did engage heavily in global advertising using the Ogilvy & Mather Worldwide agency. But Ogilvy & Mather pitched for the Ford Motor Company business, and Mercedes fired the agency. Mercedes, although known the world over, does vary its brand image from country to country and is thus not in a position to use global advertising campaigns at this time. The company's versatile advertising effort is supervised by a small staff of six at the head office in Germany.[98]

Working with Global Affiliates in Local Markets Increasingly, global companies have the option of working with local affiliates of global agencies. Often these agencies were locally founded and at some time sold a minority stake to larger foreign agencies. More recently, global agencies have acquired majority stakes or started new branches from scratch. The capabilities of these agencies depend on the extent to which they can be supported by the owner's network. However, this trend has brought new sophistication and expertise to countries where little existed.

96. "The Sleek Cat Springs into the Saudi Market," *Financial Times*, November 2, 1985, p. 14.
97. Ibid.
98. "Luxury Loves Company," *Advertising Age International*, March 1997, p. I-34.

Global agencies are favored in eastern Europe, where in some markets up to 90 percent of the advertising is handled by affiliates of global firms. In those countries, which suffer from very little local expertise in advertising, global agencies become a repository of advertising knowledge. These affiliates can rely on the skills of their global networks and can therefore leverage on their vast knowledge and transfer much-needed skills. McCann-Erickson has become the primary global agency network operating in eastern Europe and has attracted business from such leading firms as Coca-Cola, Nestlé, and Unilever.[99]

Working with Global Advertising Networks Many companies with extensive global operations find it too difficult and cumbersome to deal simultaneously with a large number of agencies, both domestic and global. For that reason, multinational firms have tended to concentrate their accounts with some large advertising agencies that operate their own global networks. Among the leaders are McCann-Erickson (Inter-Public Group), Young & Rubicam, J. Walter Thompson and Ogilvy & Mather (WPF Group), and BBDO (Omnicon Group).[100] Table 12.3 lists several leading global firms and their main agency relationships.

As companies develop global business, they are likely to change agencies. In 1995 Colgate-Palmolive became the first packaged goods company to consolidate its entire worldwide $500 million advertising accounts in the hands of a single agency. For the monumental task, it appointed Young & Rubicam, an agency it had worked with for some twelve years. The move was further aided by the fact that Colgate spent all but $82 million of its advertising outside the United States, where it also generates two-thirds of its sales. In return for a single, huge account, the company expected more creative effectiveness for its fifteen global campaigns. Y&R would set up several centers of excellence, spread throughout the world, that would assemble global teams to handle the many Colgate campaigns.[101]

Other companies that have reduced their advertising rosters include Dow, which concentrated its global $100 million billings spread across ten agencies into a single effort in November 1994. In a similar vein, IBM selected Ogilvy & Mather to control its $450 million in billings, previously scattered among forty different agencies. Procter & Gamble used nine core agencies for its U.S. business but focused its global advertising thrust on three major urgency networks. Kraft Foods also used three networks for its advertising in more than thirty countries.[102]

99. "Agencies Expanding E. European Penetration," *Advertising Age International*, October 1996, p. I-8.
100. "World's Top 50 Advertising Organizations," *Advertising Age International*, November 1996, p. I-15.
101. "$500 Million in Colgate Eggs in One Y&R Basket," *Advertising Age*, December 4, 1995, p. 1.
102. Ibid.

TABLE 12.3

Major International Firm/Agency Relationships

Agency	Bayer Corp.	Braun	Bristol-Meyers Squibb Co.	British American Tobacco Co.	Coca-Cola Co.	Ford Motor Co.	Gillette Co.	Groupe Danone	Henkel	Hewlett-Packard Co.	IBM Corp.	Johnson & Johnson	Kellogg Co.	Kimberly-Clark Corp.	Kraft Foods Inc.	L'Oreal	Mars Inc.	Nestlé	Novartis	Philip Morris Cos. Inc.	Procter & Gamble Co.	Royal Dutch/Shell Corp.	Smithkline Beecham Corp.	Unilever	Warner-Lambert Co.
Ammirati Puris Lintas					●							●						●	●					●	
Bates Worldwide				●						●									●		●				●
BBDO Worldwide	●	●					●		●								●								
Bozell Worldwide			●																						
D'Arcy Masius Benton & Bowles			●		●												●				●				
DDB Needham Worldwide	●							●	●			●						●							
Dentsu																									
Dentsu Young & Rubicam																				●					
EURO RSCG Worldwide								●							●	●		●			●				
FCA! BMZ International									●																
FCB Worldwide			●											●				●							
Grey Advertising	●		●	●				●			●	●					●		●		●		●		
Hakuhodo																									
Leo Burnett Co.					●								●		●			●		●	●				
Lowe & Partners Worldwide		●			●				●																
McCann-Erickson Worldwide		●			●		●			●		●				●		●						●	
Ogilvy & Mather Worldwide			●	●		●	●				●			●				●		●		●	●	●	
Publicis Communication					●					●								●						●	
Saatchi & Saatchi							●			●		●						●			●				
TBWA Worldwide								●	●										●						
J. Walter Thompson Co.			●			●							●	●	●			●	●			●		●	●
Y&R Advertising						●		●											●	●					

Source: Reprinted with permission from Ad Age International. Copyright, Crain Communications, Inc. 1998.

The first generation of global networks was created by U.S.-based advertising agencies in the 1950s and 1960s. The major driving forces were clients, who encouraged their U.S. agencies to move into local markets where the advertising agencies were weak. Leaders in this process were J. Walter Thompson, Oglivy & Mather, BBDO, and Young & Rubicam. The second wave of global networks was dominated by British entrepreneurs Saatchi & Saatchi and WPP, which assembled a series of global agency networks under one corporate name. Saatchi & Saatchi has two major global networks, Saatchi & Saatchi Advertising and BSB Worldwide. Other networks are being built by some of the French agencies, and the Japanese agencies are now also building their own networks through acquisition.[103]

International advertising networks are sought after because of their ability to quickly spread around the globe with one single campaign. Usually, only one set of advertisements will be made and then circulated among the local agencies. Working within the same agency guarantees consistency and a certain willingness to accept direction from a central location. If a company tries to coordinate a global effort alone, without the help of an international network, the burden of coordination largely rests with the company itself. Not all firms are geared toward or equipped for such an effort. Therefore, the international network is a convenience to multinational firms. Apple Computer, after years of letting international divisions handle all its own advertising, decided to centralize management of worldwide communications in its Cupertino, California, headquarters. Using BBDO Worldwide as its advertising agent, Apple wants to have the same brand identity and same campaigns globally.[104] Table 12.4 provides a list of leading world advertising agencies. Table 12.5 provides a list of leading advertising agency brands.

Not all companies find a network a necessity. Some advertisers argue that a company may profit from a single strategy but that the execution of this strategy in the various markets should be left to local agencies that are willing to work in an ad hoc network responsive only to the company's needs. A company that does not subscribe to global advertising to the same extent as other global firms is Visa International. For its international advertising promoting the Visa credit card, the firm believes that no two markets are alike, and thus no single global advertising campaign makes sense for Visa. This attitude is in contrast to that of American Express, which launched a global campaign. However, according to a company spokesperson, "Visa will emphasize a single brand identity that it intends to communicate in various relevant advertising forms, tailored to each market."[105]

103. Andreas Grein and Robert Ducoffe, "Strategic Responses to Market Globalisation Among Advertising Agencies," *International Journal of Advertising*, August 1, 1998, p. 301.

104. "Apple Wants United Worldwide Image," *Advertising Age*, April 12, 1993, p. 2.

105. "Visa's Global Strategies to Go Under Microscope," *Advertising Age*, October 14, 1996, p. 55.

TABLE 12.4

World's Top Fifty Advertising Organizations (in Millions of Dollars)

Rank 1998	Rank 1997	Ad Organization	Headquarters	Worldwide Gross Income 1998	Worldwide Gross Income 1997	% change
1	1	Omnicom Group	New York	$4,812.0	$4,295.7	12.0
2	2	Interpublic Group of Cos.	New York	4,304.5	3,806.1	13.1
3	3	WPP Group	London	4,156.8	3,616.9	14.9
4	4	Dentsu	Tokyo	1,786.0	1,987.8	−10.2
5	5	Young & Rubicam	New York	1,659.9	1,497.9	10.8
6	7	Havas Advertising	Paris	1,297.9	1,183.6	9.7
7	6	True North Communications	Chicago	1,242.3	1,204.9	3.1
8	8	Grey Advertising	New York	1,240.4	1,143.0	8.5
9	9	Leo Burnett Co.	Chicago	949.8	878.0	8.2
10	12	Publicis	New York	930.0	721.8	28.8
11	13	Snyder Communications	Bethesda, Md.	904.2	700.6	29.1
12	11	MacManus Group	New York	859.2	842.6	2.0
13	10	Hakuhodo	Tokyo	734.8	848.0	−13.4
14	14	Saatchi & Saatchi	New York	682.1	634.6	7.5
15	15	Cordiant Communications Group	London	603.2	597.3	1.0
16	17	TMP Worldwide	New York	347.4	305.4	13.7
17	16	Asatsu-DK	Tokyo	343.4	392.5	−12.5

(continued)

TABLE 12.4

World's Top Fifty Advertising Organizations (in Millions of Dollars) (cont.)

Rank 1998	Rank 1997	Ad Organization	Headquarters	Worldwide Gross Income 1998	Worldwide Gross Income 1997	% change
18	18	Carlson Marketing Group	Plymouth, Minn.	326.8	283.8	15.2
19	26	USWeb/CKS	Santa Clara	228.6	114.3	100.0
20	21	HA-LO	Niles, Ill.	224.0	163.0	37.4
21	20	Daiko Advertising	Tokyo	168.7	204.4	−17.5
22	19	Tokyu Agency	Tokyo	167.1	204.5	−18.3
23	22	Dentsu, Young & Rubicam Partnerships	Singapore	145.5	162.8	−10.6
24	28	Cyrk-Simon	Gloucester, Mass.	137.9	103.1	33.7
25	27	Nelson Communications	New York	130.8	107.1	22.1
26	29	Bronner Slosberg Humphrey	Boston	124.2	101.2	22.7
27	23	Cheil Communications	Seoul	106.0	154.1	−31.2
28	24	Yomiko Advertising	Tokyo	102.8	119.4	−13.9
29	31	Clemenger BBDO	Melbourne	101.8	94.1	8.2
30	44	Healthworld Corp.	New York	99.6	62.9	58.3
31	33	EPB Partners	New York	93.7	81.2	15.4
32	35	Harte-Hanks/DiMark	Langhorne, Pa.	90.5	75.6	19.8
33	25	I&S/BBDO	Tokyo	89.5	117.5	−23.9

34	34	Frankel	Chicago	87.9	77.7	13.1
35	48	IXL Enterprises	Atlanta	87.2	55.3	57.6
36	51	Deutsch	New York	86.9	53.3	63.2
37	30	Wieden & Kennedy	Portland, Ore.	86.9	96.3	−9.7
38	40	Doner	Southfield, Mich.	85.7	68.5	25.0
39	38	Incepta Group	London	78.2	70.3	11.2
40	43	Spar Group	Tarrytown, N.Y.	74.8	63.6	17.6
41	32	Asahi Advertising	Tokyo	74.6	85.6	−12.8
42	41	MDC Communications Corp.	Toronto	74.2	67.9	9.3
43	NR	Agency.com	New York	72.0	NA	NA
44	39	Duailibi Petit Zaragoza Propaganda	Sao Paulo	71.2	69.4	2.6
45	55	HMG Worldwide Corp.	New York	70.0	46.3	51.2
46	42	Fallon McElligott	Minneapolis	68.5	64.0	7.0
47	46	Fischer America Comunicacao Total	Sao Paulo	66.9	59.3	12.8
48	36	Oricom Co.	Tokyo	64.1	75.3	−14.8
49	52	Gage Marketing Group	Minneapolis	63.8	51.4	24.1
50	47	Springer & Jacoby Werbung	Hamburg, Germany	61.4	56.8	8.0

Source: Reprinted with permission from Advertising Age International. Copyright, Crain Communications, Inc. 1999.

TABLE 12.5

World's Top Twenty-five Advertising Agency Brands

Rank 1998	Rank 1997	Agency	Worldwide Gross Income 1998	Worldwide Gross Income 1997	'98–'97 % Change	Worldwide Volume 1998	Worldwide Volume 1997	% Change
1	1	Dentsu	$1,786.0	$1,987.8	−10.2	$13,032.9	$14,473.3	−10.0
2	2	McCann-Erickson Worldwide	1,640.1	1,414.8	15.9	13,610.5	10,880.0	25.1
3	3	BBDO Worldwide	1,304.2	1,193.0	9.3	10,910.1	9,640.2	13.2
4	4	J. Walter Thompson Co.	1,176.6	1,115.9	5.4	8,077.4	7,638.3	5.7
5	5	Euro RSCG Worldwide	1,018.7	938.1	8.6	7,340.9	7,069.1	3.8
6	6	DDB Needham Worldwide	1,007.1	928.0	8.5	7,800.5	6,999.0	11.5
7	7	Grey Advertising	942.8	918.3	2.7	6,289.0	6,431.6	−2.2
8	8	Leo Burnett Co.	933.7	867.8	7.6	6,708.0	5,908.8	13.5
9	11	Young & Rubicam	878.7	780.8	12.5	9,308.6	8,004.0	16.3
10	10	Ogilvy & Mather Worldwide	860.5	816.8	5.3	7,984.9	7,256.3	10.0
11	12	TBWA Worldwide	781.8	714.4	9.4	5,530.2	5,029.6	10.0
12	15	Publicis	764.7	570.3	34.1	5,105.9	3,742.9	36.4

13	9	Hakuhodo	734.8	848.0	−13.4	5,663.7	6,475.6	−12.5
14	13	Ammirati Puris Lintas	655.6	616.7	6.3	4,826.3	4,420.4	9.2
15	14	D'Arcy Masius Benton & Bowles	616.7	606.8	1.6	5,791.8	5,806.6	−0.3
16	16	Foote, Cone & Belding	510.0	481.0	6.0	5,645.4	5,509.6	2.5
17	18	Saatchi & Saatchi	444.8	416.1	6.9	5,727.9	5,358.5	6.9
18	22	Brann Worldwide	435.7	322.6	35.1	2,906.0	2,151.6	35.1
19	17	Bates Worldwide	431.0	439.2	−1.9	5,044.3	4,749.6	6.2
20	20	Bozell Worldwide	371.9	365.4	1.8	3,055.0	2,971.0	2.8
21	21	Lowe & Partners Worldwide	368.5	339.0	8.7	2,772.6	2,478.5	11.9
22	23	TMP Worldwide	349.3	298.4	17.1	3,328.7	2,664.9	24.9
23	19	Asatsu-DK	343.4	392.5	−12.5	2,726.6	3,097.2	−12.0
24	24	Carlson Marketing Group	326.8	283.8	15.2	2,591.8	2,244.8	15.5
25	25	Wunderman Cato Johnson	323.0	280.5	15.2	2,414.7	2,032.3	18.8

Source: Reprinted with permission from Advertising Age International. Copyright, Crain Communications, Inc. 1999.

Coordinating Global Advertising

The role the global marketing executive plays in a company's global advertising effort may differ from firm to firm and depend on several factors. Outside factors, such as the nature of the market or competition, and company internal factors, such as company culture or philosophy, may lead some firms to adopt a more centralized approach in global advertising. Other firms, for different reasons, may prefer to delegate more authority to local subsidiaries and local agencies. Key factors that may cause a firm to either centralize or decentralize decision making for global advertising will be reviewed in the sections that follow.

External Factors Affecting Advertising Coordination One of the most important factors influencing how companies allocate decision making for global advertising is market diversity. For products or services for which customer needs and interests are homogeneous across many countries, greater opportunities for standardization exist. For companies with relatively standardized products, pressures also point in the direction of centralized decision making. Consequently, companies that face markets with very different customer needs or market systems and structures will work more toward decentralizing their global advertising decision making. Local knowledge would be more important to the success of these firms.

The nature of the competition can also affect the way a global firm plans for advertising decision making. Firms that essentially face local competition or different sets of competitors from country to country will find it more logical to delegate global advertising to local subsidiaries. On the other hand, if a company is competing everywhere with a few sets of firms, which are essentially global firms using a similar type of advertising, the need to centralize will be apparent.

Internal Factors Affecting Advertising Coordination A company's own internal structure and organization can also greatly influence its options of either centralizing or decentralizing global advertising decision making. The opportunities for centralizing are few when a company follows an approach of customizing advertising for each local market. However, when a company follows a standardized advertising format, a more centralized approach will be possible and probably even desirable.

Skill levels and efficiency concerns can also determine the level of centralization. Decentralization requires that the advertising skills of local subsidiaries and local agencies be sufficient to perform successfully. On the other hand, global advertising may not be centralized successfully in companies in which the head-office staff does not possess a full appreciation of the global dimension of the firm's business. Decentralization is often believed to result in inefficiencies or decreased quality because a firm's budget may be spread over too many individual agencies. Instead of having a large budget in one agency, the firm has created minibudgets that may not be sufficient to obtain the best creative talent to work on its products. Centralization will often give access to better talent, though knowledge of the local markets may be sacrificed.

The managerial style of the global company may affect the centralization decision in advertising as well. Some companies pride themselves on giving a considerable amount of freedom to local subsidiary managers. Under such circumstances, centralizing advertising decisions will only be counterproductive. It has been observed with many multinational firms that the general approach taken by the company's top management toward global markets relates closely to its desire to centralize or decentralize global advertising. However, since the company's internal and external factors are subject to change over time, it can be expected that the decision to centralize or decentralize will never be a permanent one.

Generic Global Advertising Strategies

You are now familiar with the concept of generic global marketing strategies introduced in Chapter 8. For our purposes, it is important to recognize that global firms likewise can select from a series of generic global advertising strategies. Table 12.6 shows the top 100 global marketers based on their advertising expenditures outside the United States.

A company can adopt a single *global advertising campaign*, which would consist of essentially equal execution across the globe. Although this type of single global campaign is not likely to be the rule, other options exist.

Alternatively, a company may select a *global brand* approach, using essentially the same brand name, logo, and so on, but otherwise engaging different advertising apparatuses by country. This is the type of approach utilized by Mercedes-Benz, as described earlier.

Companies using a *global theme* employ a more coordinated approach, using the same advertising theme around the world but varying it with local execution. The localization typically involves the visuals, chosen specifically to suit each country or region.

Finally, companies need to adopt a strategy on *global coordination*. Global advertising coordination, usually done through a global advertising agency network, gives companies acceptable control and yet allows them to rely on the agency for the detailed coordination work. Table 12.7 shows how companies used Saatchi & Saatchi to coordinate their advertising. Some companies, as we have seen in the case of Levi Strauss, prefer to do their own coordination. Should a company adopt a largely local advertising approach, the coordination requirement would be minimized, or even redundant.

Companies involved in global advertising will have to determine which type of generic global advertising strategy to employ. It is important to recognize that the choice is not simply between global or local advertising, but rather that different aspects of a communications campaign may be globalized. This modular approach requires companies to select carefully which aspects of their communications to globalize and which to localize.

TABLE 12.6

Top 100 Global Marketers by Media Ad Spending Outside the United States

Rank 1998	Rank 1997	Advertiser	Headquarters	1998 Media Spending Outside U.S.	1997 Media Spending Outside U.S.	% Change	Country Count
1	1	Procter & Gamble Co,	Cincinnati	$3,018.2	$2,879.3	4.8	68
2	2	Unilever	Rotterdam/London	2,737.3	2,510.5	9.0	67
3	3	Nestle	Vevey, Switzerland	1,559.3	1,355.9	15.0	65
4	7	Volkswagen	Wolfsburg, Germany	1,070.4	916.8	16.8	37
5	6	Ford Motor Co.	Dearborn, Mich.	1,049.5	960.5	9.3	45
6	8	General Motors Corp.	Detroit	1,039.3	915.8	13.5	39
7	4	Toyota Motor Corp.	Toyota City, Japan	1,034.9	1,127.7	−8.2	41
8	5	Coca-Cola Co.	Atlanta	1,011.5	980.1	3.2	69
9	9	Peugeot Citroen	Paris	854.9	835.1	2.4	37
10	13	L'Oreal	Paris	840.9	677.8	24.1	42
11	11	Mars Inc.	McLean, Va	793.0	783.3	1.2	33
12	12	Sony Corp.	Tokyo	775.1	718.9	7.8	52
13	15	Philip Morris Cos.	New York	715.8	634.4	12.8	51
14	14	Henkel	Ducesseldorf	699.2	669.6	4.4	31
15	17	Renault	Paris	688.2	590.1	16.6	23
16	10	Nissan Motor Co.	Tokyo	663.6	814.0	−18.5	33
17	18	Fiat	Turin, Italy	628.3	587.6	6.9	19
18	16	Honda Motor Co.	Tokyo	603.2	612.4	−1.5	29

19	22	Colgate-Palmolive Co.	New York	596.9	516.7	15.5	54
20	20	McDonald's Corp.	Oak Brook, Ill.	592.3	545.8	8.5	49
21	21	Ferrero	Perugia, Italy	558.7	531.3	5.2	31
22	23	Danone Group	Levallois-Perret, France	550.0	507.2	8.4	23
23	25	DaimlerChrysler	Stuttgart, Germany/ Auburn Hill, Mich.	522.4	458.7	13.9	35
24	19	Kao Corp.	Tokyo	511.8	567.4	−9.8	4
25	24	BMW	Munich	455.9	463.0	−1.5	25
26	26	Johnson & Johnson	New Brunswick, N.J.	446.5	447.9	−0.3	53
27	28	Joh. A. Benckiser	Ludwigshafen, Germany	385.8	375.7	2.7	29
28	29	Kellogg Co.	Battle Creek, Mich.	381.5	360.3	5.9	25
29	27	Mitsubishi Motor Co.	Tokyo	374.8	429.5	−12.7	27
30	30	Philips Electronics	Eindhoven, The Netherlands	372.6	317.8	17.2	50
31	34	PepsiCo	Purchase, N.Y.	365.9	285.4	28.2	47
32	32	Beiersdorf	Hamburg	324.3	316.3	2.6	41
33	40	Bertelsmann	Guetersloh, Germany	296.0	256.3	15.5	22
34	38	SmithKline Beecham	London	289.3	260.4	11.1	40
35	36	IBM Corp.	Armonk, N.Y.	286.1	268.4	6.6	21
36	50	News Corp.	Sydney	279.1	190.6	46.4	14
37	42	Seagram Co.	Montreal	276.7	234.1	18.2	16
38	33	Mattel	El Segundo, Calif.	272.1	290.4	−6.3	21
39	35	Matsushita Electric Industrial Co.	Osaka	268.7	278.3	−3.5	27

(continued)

TABLE 12.6

Top 100 Global Marketers by Media Ad Spending Outside the United States

Rank 1998	Rank 1997	Advertiser	Headquarters	1998 Media Spending Outside U.S.	1997 Media Spending Outside U.S.	% Change	Country Count
40	39	Walt Disney Co.	Burbank, Calif.	262.8	258.3	1.8	14
41	31	Shiseido Co.	Tokyo	261.2	316.8	−17.6	4
42	47	Diageo	London	254.0	214.0	18.7	29
43	41	Mazda Motor Corp.	Hiroshima	250.3	245.7	1.9	30
44	46	Gillette Co.	Boston	245.8	214.0	14.9	48
45	43	B.A.T. Industries	London	235.2	232.0	1.3	38
46	37	Daewoo Corp.	Seoul	230.7	266.1	−13.3	34
47	53	Time Warner	New York	226.4	184.1	22.9	20
48	49	Warner-Lambert Co.	Morris Plains, N.J.	212.9	194.6	9.4	30
49	69	Carrefour Group	Paris	212.8	139.4	52.7	5
50	59	Bacardi-Martini Co.	Hamilton, Bermuda	203.2	166.0	22.4	15
51	63	Bayer	Leverkusen, Germany	198.4	151.6	30.8	27
52	61	Japan Tobacco Co.	Tokyo	194.8	154.2	26.3	17
53	56	Suzuki Motor Co.	Hamamatsu, Japan	191.2	170.3	12.3	24
54	70	C&A Breninkmeyer	Amsterdam	190.6	138.4	37.7	5
55	51	EMI Group	London	188.1	187.1	0.5	13
56	58	Sara Lee Corp.	Chicago	183.4	168.6	8.8	10
57	67	Wm. Wrigley Jr. Co.	Chicago	180.3	148.0	21.8	35

58	52	Ajinomoto	Tokyo	179.8	184.8	−2.7	5
59	54	Hasbro	Pawtucket, R.I.	179.0	183.5	−2.5	12
60	71	S.C. Johnson & Son	Racine, Wis.	174.6	135.6	28.8	31
61	62	Ericsson	Stockholm	162.9	153.2	6.3	46
62	45	Hyundai Group	Seoul	157.3	216.1	−27.2	26
63	57	Toshiba Corp.	Tokyo	153.1	169.1	−9.4	13
64	55	Kimberly-Clark Corp.	Irving, Texas	151.2	181.2	−16.5	18
65	60	Bestfoods	Englewood Cliffs, N.J.	149.2	158.1	−5.7	24
66	99	United International Pictures	Amsterdam	144.7	79.5	81.9	11
67	91	Nokia	Helsinki	144.2	99.3	45.2	35
68	78	Reckitt & Colman	London	143.6	116.3	23.5	14
69	64	Barilla	Parma, Italy	141.3	151.2	−6.6	4
70	87	Nintendo Co.	Kyoto, Japan	140.7	101.5	38.6	5
71	68	LVMH Moet Hennessy Louis	Paris	137.6	141.8	−3.0	11
72	66	Tricon Global Restaurants	Louisville, Kentucky	134.4	148.7	−9.6	23
73	72	Cadbury Schweppes	London	128.3	131.5	−2.5	19
74	44	LG Group	Seoul	127.5	223.1	−42.9	21
75	74	Boots Co.	Nottingham, U.K.	127.3	125.7	1.3	13
76	65	Canon	Tokyo	126.1	149.2	−15.5	23
77	81	Siemens	Munich	115.0	111.4	3.2	28
78	75	Novartis	Basel, Switzerland	113.8	125.2	−9.1	13

(continued)

TABLE 12.6

Top 100 Global Marketers by Media Ad Spending Outside the United States

Rank 1998	Rank 1997	Advertiser	Headquarters	1998 Media Spending Outside U.S.	1997 Media Spending Outside U.S.	% Change	Country Count
79	76	Microsoft Corp.	Redmond, Wash.	113.2	124.8	−9.3	15
80	93	Compaq Computer Corp.	Houston	112.3	98.3	14.3	18
81	84	Axa Group	Paris	111.5	104.9	6.3	6
82	82	American Home Products Corp.	New York	106.1	109.0	−2.6	14
83	48	Samsung Group	Seoul	105.2	204.3	−48.5	25
84	80	Roche Holdings	Basel, Switzerland	103.4	113.4	−8.8	25
85	83	SCA Molnlycke	Goteborg, Sweden	103.4	107.0	−3.4	23
86	90	Heineken	Amsterdam	103.2	99.6	3.6	13
87	101	Bristol-Meyers Squibb Co.	New York	102.9	77.5	32.7	18

88	102	Seiko Epson Corp.	Nagano, Japan	101.8	75.2	35.2	10
89	89	Ingka Holdings	Humlebaek, Denmark	89.4	100.5	−11.0	13
90	73	Royal Dutch Shell	The Hague	89.3	129.6	−31.1	41
91	86	Daihatsu	Osaka	89.1	102.5	−13.0	4
92	79	Tchibo	Hamburg, Germany	85.9	114.3	−24.9	4
93	92	Hitachi	Tokyo	84.6	99.0	−14.5	10
94	77	Fujitsu	Tokyo	84.3	116.5	−27.6	5
95	94	American Express Co.	New York	82.5	97.6	−15.5	12
96	107	Eastman Kodak Co.	Rochester, N.Y.	81.5	72.3	12.7	22
97	96	Fuji Photo Film Co.	Tokyo	78.2	86.9	−10.1	9
98	104	Interbrew	Leuven, Belgium	73.6	73.9	−0.4	5
99	126	Allianz	Munich	73.4	55.9	31.2	8
100	112	Bass	London	72.5	62.9	15.3	7

Notes: Figures are in millions of U.S. dollars. 1997 rankings reflect data collected in 1999. Country count is the number of countries where spending was reported in 1998.
Source: Reprinted with permission from Advertising Age International.

TABLE 12.7

Saatchi & Saatchi Advertising Worldwide Client Assignments by Country

	The Americas																						Europe																					
Clients served multinationally:	*U.S.*	*Canada*	*Argentina**	*Barbados**	*Bermuda**	*Brazil*	*Chile**	*Colombia**	*Costa Rica**	*Dom. Republic**	*Ecuador**	*El Salvador**	*Guatemala**	*Honduras**	*Jamaica**	*Mexico*	*Panama**	*Peru**	*Puerto Rico*	*Trinidad**	*Uruguay**	*Venezuela*	*Austria*	*Belgium*	*Bulgaria**	*Croatia**	*Czech Republic*	*Denmark*	*Estonia**	*Finland*	*France*	*Germany*	*Greece*	*Hungary*	*Ireland*	*Italy*	*Latvia**	*Lithuania**	*Macedonia**	*Netherlands*	*Norway*	*Poland*	*Portugal*	*Romania**
Alcatel Alsthom			•			•			•				•			•								•							•	•								•				
Allied Domecq	•										•																						•		•									
Asia Pacific Breweries																																												
Bonduelle																								•							•											•	•	
Borden																				•																								
Bristol-Myers Squibb																											•				•										•		•	
CPC International					•						•													•	•				•	•	•			•			•	•						•
Cadbury Schweppes																	•											•														•		
Carlsberg																												•			•													
Danone Groupe																							•								•					•	•							
Duracell				•					•	•	•	•	•	•	•		•		•	•		•																						
Du Pont	•												•																		•	•		•						•		•		
Eastman Kodak	•	•	•			•	•									•			•	•	•										•	•												
Electrolux																												•			•	•						•		•				
Essilor																							•								•	•											•	
G-Tech																•						•																						
Grand Metropolitan			•								•	•							•		•	•										•		•										
Guess Inc.	•																																											
Hewlett-Packard	•	•	•			•	•	•								•						•	•	•			•	•	•		•	•		•		•	•	•		•	•	•	•	
Johnson & Johnson	•	•	•	•		•		•		•	•				•	•	•		•	•	•			•							•							•					•	
Lion Nathan	•																																											
LYMH																													•		•	•				•	•							
Matsushita											•				•																													
NetHold (Multichoice)																																											•	
NZ Dairy Board				•											•					•																								
Novartis		•			•																		•					•			•				•	•								
PepsiCo				•						•									•	•		•							•								•	•				•		
Pfizer																															•				•						•			
Pozuelo (Riviana Foods)									•			•	•	•			•																											
Procter & Gamble	•	•		•											•					•			•	•	•	•	•	•	•	•	•	•	•	•	•	•	•	•	•	•	•	•	•	•
Ralston Purina																				•					•	•	•		•		•			•		•	•	•				•		•
Samsung	•																			•												•		•									•	
Sara Lee	•												•	•					•					•							•	•	•			•						•		
Seiko																							•					•		•					•						•		•	
Shell					•										•					•											•													
Singapore Tourist Board																																												
Sony			•						•					•							•																							
Tenneco (Monroe)																								•		•	•	•		•	•	•	•			•					•	•	•	
Tetra Laval Group																													•					•			•	•						•
Toyota	•	•		•															•				•	•	•				•				•											
Visa												•		•									•	•			•						•	•		•					•		•	
Walt Disney Co.		•				•										•																•				•								
Weetabix																														•	•	•	•							•	•		•	
Whirlpool																																												

*Nonequity affiliation. **Also covers Albania.

Source: Reprinted with permission from Advertising Age International. Copyright, Crain Communications, Inc. 1996.

Europe									Middle East										Africa															Asia/Pacific														
Russia	Slovenia*	Spain	Sweden*	Switzerland	Turkey	U.K.	Ukraine*	Yugoslavia*	Bahrain	Egypt*	Israel*	Jordan*	Kuwait	Lebanon*	Oman*	Qatar*	Saudi Arabia	U.A.E.	Botswana*	Cameroon*	Ghana*	Cote d'Ivoire*	Kenya*	Malawi*	Mauritius*	Mozambique*	Namibia*	Nigeria*	South Africa*	Tanzania*	Uganda*	Zambia*	Zimbabwe*	Australia	China	Hong Kong	India	Indonesia	Japan	Malaysia	New Zealand	Pakistan*	Philippines	Singapore	South Korea*	Taiwan	Thailand	Vietnam
		●			●	●																																										
●	●					●																																										
																																			●	●								●		●	●	
		●																																														
																			●																	●		●		●				●		●	●	
										●																									●	●												
●											●								●																													
●						●															●											●				●		●		●	●			●				
					●	●					●																																					
●		●		●							●																	●													●							
●				●	●	●																							●						●		●	●	●	●				●	●	●	●	
						●					●																							●	●	●	●		●				●	●		●		
						●																																										
		●				●																																										
						●																							●																	●		
																							●		●										●	●			●		●		●	●	●			
																																				●		●		●				●		●	●	
●			●	●	●	●		●		●		●											●											●	●	●		●	●	●	●			●			●	
●					●	●	●										●	●								●			●			●		●	●										●			
						●																												●		●					●							
		●		●		●																														●												
																		●					●																			●						
																		●	●	●	●	●	●	●		●	●	●	●	●	●	●	●															
●						●				●																			●												●							
						●																												●												●		
●											●							●										●	●																			
					●																													●														
●	●	●	●	●	●	●		●	●	●	●		●	●	●	●	●	●										●	●						●	●	●	●	●	●	●		●	●	●	●	●	●
●	●	●				●	●	●																																								
		●				●												●																●				●		●				●		●	●	
		●				●																							●					●		●					●							
																													●						●				●									
																			●																													
																		●																	●		●		●			●		●	●	●		
						●						●																											●		●							
		●				●																																										
																																														●		
						●				●											●			●					●					●	●	●			●		●		●	●			●	●
		●	●	●	●	●											●												●									●	●		●						●	
						●																																										
		●		●																					●																							
																																							●						●	●		

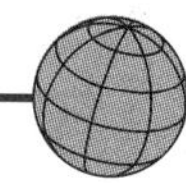

Conclusions

Few areas of global marketing are subject to hotter debate than global advertising. The complexity of dealing simultaneously with a large number of different customers in many countries, all speaking their own languages and subject to their own cultural heritage, offers a real challenge to the global marketer. Global executives must find the common ground within these diverse influences to that coherent campaigns can still be possible.

The debate in the field has recently shifted from one of standardization versus customization to one of global versus nonglobal advertising. Proponents of global advertising point to the convergence of customer needs and the emergence of the "world consumer," a person who is becoming ever more homogeneous whether he or she lives in Paris, London, New York, or Tokyo. However, many aspects of the advertising environment remain considerably diverse. Although English is rapidly becoming a global language, most messages still have to be translated into local languages. Diverse regulations in many countries on the execution, content, and format of advertisements still make it very difficult to offer standardized solutions to advertising problems. Also, media availability to advertisers is substantially different in many parts of the world, so many companies still have to adapt their media mix to the local situation. Thus, many executives believe that much local content is necessary; therefore, they will give the local country organizations substantial responsibility for input and decision making.

Most marketers realize that total customization is not desirable because it would require that each market create and implement its own advertising strategies. Top creative talent is scarce everywhere, and better creative solutions tend to be costlier ones. As a result, companies appear to be moving toward modularization, in which some elements of the advertising message are common to all advertisements while other elements are tailored to local requirements. To make customization work, however, companies cannot simply design one set of advertisements and later expect to adapt the content. Successful modularization requires that companies, from the very outset, plan for such a process by including and considering the full range of possibilities and requirements to be satisfied. This offers a considerable challenge to global marketing executives and their advertising partners.

QUESTIONS FOR DISCUSSION

1. What major factors affect the extension of a domestic advertising campaign into several other countries?
2. How do you explain that some companies appear to be successful with very similar campaigns worldwide whereas others fail with the same strategy?
3. What advice will you give to a U.S. firm interested in advertising in Japan, and what will you suggest to a Japanese firm interested in advertising in the United States?
4. What future do you see for global advertising?

5. What will be the impact of increased commercial satellite television on global advertising, both in the United States and abroad?
6. How will the advertising industry need to react to the new trends in global marketing?

FOR FURTHER READING

Alden, Dana L., Jan-Benedict E. M. Steenkamp, and Rajeev Batra. "Brand Positioning Through Advertising in Asia, North America, and Europe: The Role of Global Consumer Culture," *Journal of Marketing*, January 1999, pp. 75–87.

Alden, Dana L., Wayne D. Hoeyer, and Chol Lee. "Identifying Global and Culture-Specific Dimensions of Humor in Advertising," *Journal of Marketing*, April 1993, pp. 64–75.

De Pelsmacker, Patrick, and M. Geuens. "Reactions to Different Types of Ads in Belgium and Poland," *International Marketing Review*, 1998, vol. 15, no. 4, pp. 277–290.

Harker, Debra. "Achieving Acceptable Advertising: An Analysis of Advertising Regulation in Five Countries," *International Marketing Review*, 1998, vol. 15, no. 2, pp. 101–118.

Jo, Myung-Soo. "Contingency and Contextual Issues of Ethnocentrism-Pitched Advertisements: A Cross-National Comparison," *International Marketing Review*, 1998, vol. 15, no. 6, pp. 447–457.

Kanso, Ali. "International Advertising Strategies: Global Commitment to Local Vision," *Journal of Advertising Research*, January–February 1992, pp. 10–14.

Keillor, Bruce D., Stephen Parker, and T. Bettina Cornwell. "Using Advertising to Manage Consumer Satisfaction in an International Market," *Journal of Global Marketing*, 1998, vol. 12, no. 1 pp. 27–46.

Melewar, T. C., and John Saunders. "Global Corporate Visual Identity Systems: Standardization, Control and Benefits," *International Marketing Review*, 1998, vol. 15, no. 4, pp. 291–308.

Milavsky, J. Ronald. "Recent Journal and Trade Publication Treatments of Globalization in Mass Media Marketing and Social Change," *International Journal of Advertising*, 1993, vol. 12, no. 1, pp. 45–56.

Roth, Martin S. "Depth Versus Breadth Strategies for Global Brand Image Management," *Journal of Advertising*, June 1992, pp. 25–36.

Sandler, Dennis M., and David Shani. "Brand Globally but Advertise Locally: An Empirical Investigation," *International Marketing Review*, 1992, vol. 9, no. 4, pp. 18–31.

Shao, Alan T., and John S. Hill. "Executing Transitional Advertising Campaigns: Do U.S. Agencies Have the Overseas Talent?" *Journal of Advertising Research*, January–February 1992, pp. 49–58.

Whitelock, Jeryl, and Jean-Christophe Rey. "Cross-Cultural Advertising in Europe: An Empirical Survey of Television Advertising in France and the UK," *International Marketing Review*, 1998, vol. 15, no. 4, pp. 257–276.

Witkowski T. H., and J. Kellner. "Convergent, Contrasting and Country-Specific Attitudes Towards Television Advertising in Germany and the United States," *Journal of Business Research* (USA), 1998, vol. 42, no. 2 (June).

13

Global Product and Service Strategies

Product Design in a Global Environment

Branding Decisions

Packaging for Global Markets

Managing a Global Product Line

Global Warranty and Service Policies

Marketing Services Globally

THIS CHAPTER LOOKS AT THE STRATEGIES COMPANIES CAN PURSUE TO ADAPT their products and services to global markets. Figure 13.1 highlights the elements involved in product strategy decisions. The chapter discussion first centers on the many environmental factors that tend to prevent the marketing of uniform and standardized products across a multitude of markets. Attention then shifts to the various implications of selecting brand names for global markets. International firms are concerned not only with determining appropriate brand names but also with protecting those names against abuse and piracy. Subsequent sections focus on packaging and managing product lines and support services. The chapter concludes with a section on the marketing of services on a global scale.

FIGURE 13.1

Global Product Strategies

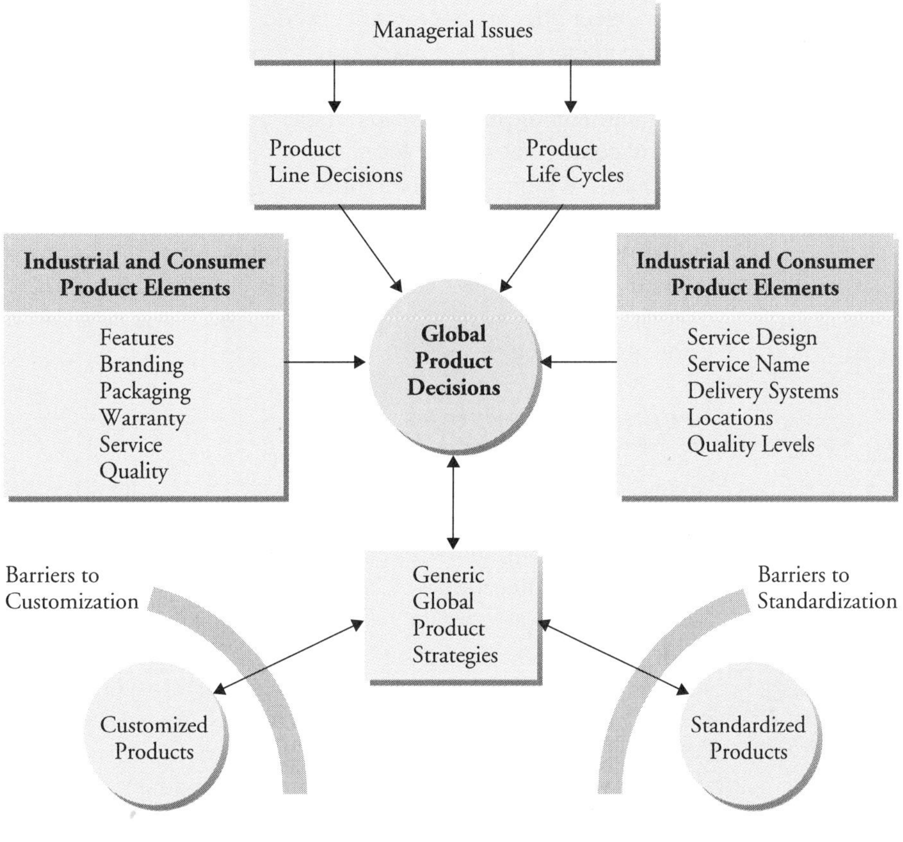

We also highlight the enormous opportunities in the service industry and explain how various companies are pursuing them globally.

Product Design in a Global Environment

One of the principal questions in global marketing concerns the types of products that can be sold in different markets. The international firm will want to know whether existing products have to be adapted to certain global requirements or whether they can be shipped in their present form. For new products, the firm will have to select the particular features its products should incorporate and to determine the desired function and performance of these features. The major elements of product design are explained in the following sections, with an emphasis on the effect of global complexities.

To select the most desirable product features is an involved decision for global marketers. The approach taken should include a thorough review of all the environmental factors that may affect product use, such as the level of literacy, income, and technical skills of potential customers. Also to be considered are the climatic conditions, power level, and availability and quality of maintenance support, all of which will affect product performance. Furthermore, a thorough analysis should include a review of the physical environment, described in detail in Chapter 6. In all cases, however, a firm will have to picture its products in the targeted market and ask the question, How would our product be used in that country? In some situations, it may be necessary to send some units to the various markets for testing purposes.

Product Dimensions

Dimensions as expressed by size, capacity, or volume are subject to market and environmental influences that often require different approaches to any given market. One important factor, particularly for U.S. firms, is the selection of a metric versus a nonmetric scale. The firm must go beyond a single translation of nonmetric into metric sizes to help users or consumers understand the design of products and meet legal requirements. Simple translations do not lead to round standardized numbers, forcing companies actually to change the physical sizes of their products to conform to new standards. With Europe (the only exception being the United Kingdom) and Japan operating on the metric standard, the United States is one of the few remaining major nonmetric markets. Translation of product dimensions is therefore less of an issue for non-U.S. firms than for U.S.-based companies that normally operate on a nonmetric basis at home.

The different physical characteristics of consumers often influence product design. Swiss watch manufacturers have learned over the years to adapt their watchbands to different wrist sizes. The Japanese have smaller wrists than Americans; thus, design changes are required that do not necessarily change the function or look of the watch. A leading Italian shoe manufacturer has had a similar experience exporting shoes to the United States. Research revealed that feet were not the same in every country. Americans were found to have longer toes than Italians and smaller insteps,[1] as well as thicker ankles and narrower, flatter feet.

1. "Three Scientists Seek U.S. Data on Genetic Engineering," *New York Times*, March 8, 1978, p. A-19.

To produce a properly fitting shoe, the Italian company decided to make appropriate changes in its design to achieve the necessary comfort for U.S. customers. Ansell Edmont asked Japanese factory workers to test their new work gloves. They found that Japanese workers have smaller hands and shorter fingers than their counterparts in Europe and the United States and therefore require different gloves.[2] Domino's Pizza found that one size pizza did not fit all appetites. In Germany, consumers preferred a smaller individual pizza. By tailoring to local sizes and tastes, Domino's overseas sales increased from $16 million in 1986 to $503 million in 1996.[3]

Although product characteristics may vary from market to market, companies also look for similarities across geographic boundaries. If market segments can be identified with similar product needs that cut across geographic products, the company can reduce the number of product variations needed to serve the global marketplace. For example, in one study of four different cultural and geographic markets, researchers identified three distinct segments of fruit-flavored-soda drinkers. The segments were based on sensory preferences: (1) weak aroma, light color, low sweetness, and low flavor; (2) stronger aroma, medium color, medium sweetness, and stronger flavor; (3) strongest aroma, darkest color, high sweetness, and strongest flavor.[4] Although products often must be tailored to the needs of different markets, more and more companies are looking for similarities across markets.

Size is often affected by the physical surroundings of product use or space. In some countries, limited living space necessitates home appliances that are substantially smaller than those found in a country such as the United States, where people live in larger dwellings. Recently, U.S.-made major appliances have been imported into Japan by some discount chains. Although the volume is still small by international standards, some wealthier Japanese consumers favor these large appliances. Some of the customers have had to return them after purchase, however, because they could not get the refrigerators through their own apartment doors. Chrysler found it needed to make numerous changes to its Jeep to be successful in Japan. Underhood wiring was changed to meet Japanese standards, the owner's manual had to be revised to include big diagrams and cartoons, and each Japan-bound Jeep had to receive special quality checks to meet the standards of Japanese consumers.[5] For the latest models, Chrysler added automatic side mirrors just the for Japanese market.[6] In many countries, customers have come to

2. Robert Thomas, vice president, Ansell Edmont, in a discussion with authors on July 13, 1987.
3. "Think Globally, Bake Locally," *Fortune*, October 14, 1996, p. 205.
4. Howard R. Moskowitz and Samuel Rubino, "Sensory Segmentation: An Organizing Principle for International Product Concept Generation," unpublished article.
5. "The Man Who's Selling Japan on Jeeps," *Business Week*, July 19, 1993, pp. 56–57.
6. "New Grand Cherokee to Hit Japanese Market," *Jiji Press English Service*, May 11, 1999.

expect certain products in certain sizes; thus, international firms are forced to adapt to meet these expectations.

Design Features

Invariably, international firms find they must alter some components or parts of a product because of local circumstances. One worldwide manufacturer of industrial abrasives has had to adjust to different raw material supply situations by varying the raw material input according to country while still maintaining abrasive performance standards. Paint is another product that requires adaptation to climatic and surface circumstances. As a result, paint will differ from region to region even though the particular application may be identical.[7]

Procter & Gamble, the large U.S.-based consumer products company, found it had to adapt the formulation of its Cheer laundry detergent to fit Japanese market requirements. Cheer, initially promoted as an all-temperature product, ran into trouble because many Japanese consumers washed their clothes in cold tap water or used leftover bath water. The Japanese also liked to add fabric softeners, which tend to cut down on the suds produced by the detergent. P&G reformulated the product to work effectively in cold water with fabric softeners added and changed the positioning to superior cleaning in cold water. The brand is now one of P&G's best-selling products in Japan.[8]

Researchers have long considered the U.S. customer to be particularly feature-conscious.[9] Consequently, features considered necessary in the United States may not be required abroad, although others may be in greater demand. Adding the desired features can strengthen a company's marketing effort and offset the added engineering and production costs. In some local markets, customers may even expect a product to perform a function different from the one originally intended. One U.S. exporter of gardening tools found that its battery-operated trimmers were used by the Japanese as lawn mowers on their small lawns. As a result, the batteries and motors did not last as long as they would have under the intended use. Because of the different function desired by Japanese customers, a design change eventually was required.

Adapting Products to Cultural Preferences To the extent that fashion and tastes differ by country, companies often change their styling. Color, for example,

7. Robert Howard and Jean-Pierre Jeannet, *The World Paint Industry Note (1992)*, case, (Lausanne: IMD Institute, 1993).
8. "After Early Stumbles, P&G Is Making Inroads Overseas," *Wall Street Journal*, February 6, 1989, p. B1.
9. Montrose Sommers and Jerome Kernan, "Why Products Flourish Here, Fizzle There," *Columbia Journal of World Business*, March–April 1967, pp. 89–97.

should reflect the values of each country.[10] For Japan, red and white have happy associations, whereas black and white indicate mourning. Green is an unpopular color in Malaysia, where it is associated with the jungle and illness. Green is the national color of Egypt and therefore should not be used for packaging purposes there. Textile manufacturers in the United States who have started to expand their export businesses have consciously used color to suit local needs.[11] For example, the Lowenstein Corporation has successfully used brighter colors for fabrics exported to Africa.

Scent is also subject to change from one country to another. S. C. Johnson & Son, a manufacturer of furniture polish products, encountered resistance to its Lemon Pledge furniture polish among older consumers in Japan. Careful market research revealed that the polish smelled similar to a latrine disinfectant used widely in Japan in the 1940s. Sales rose sharply after the scent was adjusted.[12]

Food is one of the most culturally distinct product areas. Pizza is a western product introduced in Japan in 1986 by Domino's; the original cheese and pepperoni was quickly adapted to suit Japanese tastes. Today, a variety of ingredients are available on pizza in Japan, including curry, squid, spinach, corn, tuna, teriyaki, barbecued beef, burdock root, shrimp, seaweed, apples, and rice.[13] Eventually, Domino's carved out a niche in high-end pizzas, such as its twelve-inch, thin-crust mille-feuille pizza with Camembert and cheddar cheeses, priced at $29.92 in local currency equivalents.[14] Of course, adaptation is not always necessary. Kentucky Fried Chicken is doing very well in Pakistan, where chicken is a preferred meat. The menu is not substantially different than elsewhere, and in the two years following its initial market entry in 1997, KFC quickly grew to ten restaurants in two major cities.[15]

Adapting Performance Standards Manufacturers typically design products to meet domestic performance standards. As we have already seen, such standards do not always apply in other countries, and product changes are required in some circumstances. Products designed in highly developed countries often exceed the performance needed in developing nations. These customers prefer

10. Michael J. Thomas, ed., *International Marketing Management* (Boston: Houghton Mifflin, 1969), p. 35.
11. Herbert E. Meyer, "How U.S. Textiles Got to Be Winners in the Export Game," *Fortune*, May 5, 1980, p. 260.
12. Vernon R. Alden, "Who Says You Can't Crack Japanese Markets?" *Harvard Business Review*, January–February 1987, pp. 52–56.
13. "Pizza in Japan Is Adapted tzo Local Tastes," *Wall Street Journal*, June 4, 1993, p. B1.
14. "Japan's Deep Recession Spells Big Change for Branches of US Brands," *Nation's Restaurant News*, February 15, 1999.
15. "Foreign Fast Food Firms Flourish in Pakistan," *AFP*, March 22, 1999.

products of greater simplicity, not only to save costs but to ensure better service over a product lifetime. Companies have been criticized for selling excess performance where simpler products will do. Stepping into this market gap are companies from some of the less developed countries whose present technology levels are more in line with the consumer's needs.

The need for different product standards was behind a foreign acquisition by GE. The U.S.-based company acquired the low-voltage business of GEC-Alsthom in the United Kingdom with the strategic intent to position itself better for competition under the International Electric Committee (IEC) electrical standard. Standards for electrical equipment in the United States differed from those adopted by many foreign countries; relevant standards abroad were often set by the IEC. Rather than rebuilding the U.S.-made controls, GE decided to acquire a European firm specializing in IEC standard controls for use in its equipment.[16]

Of course, manufacturers from developing countries face the opposite challenge; companies must increase the performance of their products to meet the standards of industrialized countries. In general, the necessity to increase performance tends to be more apparent as the need arises, whereas opportunities for product simplification are frequently less obvious to the observer.

Sometimes manufacturers have to build design changes into products for overseas sales, changes that are not apparent to the buyer. These internal design changes can increase product use or performance or adapt it to a new environment. In the mobile phone market, different standards prevail in various regions or countries. The first generation of mobile phones had to be built to country-specific standards, forcing low volumes. In Europe, there were two analog standards (TACS and NMT), whereas in the United States there was a single analog standard (AMPS). The second and digital generation was dominated by the GSM standard in Europe and different standards in the United States (TDNA, DCNA, and some GSM). Eventually, some companies began to offer dual-standard phones. The challenge of multiple standards continues, however, and forces companies such as Motorola, Ericsson, and Nokia to decide how many different standards they want or can serve effectively.[17]

Adapting High-Technology Products Technology-intensive and industrial products frequently find that standards for product performance differ from one country to the next. In telecommunications, the signaling standards used for U.S. switching systems differ from those used in Europe. As a result, significant barriers exist when a company wants to become an exporter. In effect, the exporter often faces the decision to become a multistandard firm. Designing and manufacturing such systems to several standards, or languages, adds to the total cost, and

16. "GEC Deal Boosts Power Control LV Market Share," *Electrical Review*, March 17, 1999, p. 1.
17. Jean-Pierre Jeannet, *Managing with a Global Mindset* (Financial Times Prentice Hall, 2000), p. 99.

without minimum volume a company may have to forgo export opportunities if the adaptation costs outweigh the business opportunity. 3Com, the U.S.-based maker of Palm Computing products and related devices, distributes its products to thirty-five different countries and supports many languages, including English, French, German, and Spanish. To continue to build its global leadership, the company also entered an alliance to offer Japanese language support for its Palm Computing products. In Japan, the company will offer Japanese language software, as well as dictionaries covering the Japanese and English languages.[18] Likewise, Accrue Software, Inc., a leading provider of enterprise e-business analysis and software and services, entered the Japanese market with Sumitomo Electronics in order to localize its software and offer it in the Japanese language.[19] Both 3Com and Accrue believed they needed to enter the large Japanese market and yet also understood that such entry would not be successful unless their complicated software products were localized for Japanese customers.

Computer manufacturers also need to consider adapting products to different technologies. Apple Computer adapted its operating system and software for Office 98 to include Japan-specific features, including the direct entry of hiragana text and support for vertical text in documents. Help characters were also localized for Japanese users. Although Apple's overall market share in personal computers is small, the entire Asia Pacific region accounted for 20 percent of the company's corporate sales. In some specific applications, such as for graphics, architecture, or medicine, Apple had a leading share, with up to a 70 percent market share in selected segments.[20] To protect that share, the company was eager to adjust and adapt its products.

Changing Proven Products to Meet Foreign Requirements One of the most difficult decisions for international companies to make is whether or not to change a proven product that has sold well in the past. Sometimes, a company may be in a position to change a proven design to gain a competitive advantage because other, more tradition-bound firms declined.

To meet European Union (EU)–imposed noise standards, Murray Ohio Manufacturing, a manufacturer of lawn mowers, incurred significant production cost increases. To reduce noise, Murray had to slow down the blade speed, which in turn necessitated changes to the exhaust and bagging system. In spite of the increased costs, Murray made these changes because the EU is a large and growing market that it cannot afford to ignore.[21]

18. "3Com Delivers Japanese Language Support for World-Leading Palm Computing Platform Products," *Business Wire*, February 3, 1999.
19. "Accrue Software Expands into Japan Market," *Business Wire*, June 8, 1999.
20. "Microsoft, Apple Court Macworld Tokyo Crowds," *MacWeek*, February 23, 1998, p. 1.
21. Michael R. Czinkota and Ilkka A. Ronkainen, "European Product Standards: Headache or Headache Relief?" in *International Marketing*, 4th ed. (Fort Worth: Harcourt Brace, 1995), p. 261.

Sometimes different standards are mandated by governments, leaving international marketers to scramble for compliance. In the United Kingdom, Caterpillar manufactured a backhoe/loader type of construction machinery for all of Europe. These machines are tractors with a bucket up front and a digger at the back. All tractors destined for Germany required a separate brake with an anti-drive-through mechanism attached to the rear axle. The operating valve for the backhoe required a special locking capability, the steering system needed to be equipped with specially positioned valves, and the bucket had to be equipped with a lock for traveling. The cost of these "extras" amounted to about 5 percent of total cost. In process was the establishment of pan-European standards for construction machinery. By avoiding such country-specific standards, the EU expected savings for industry and more competitiveness.[22]

Quality

The quality of a product reflects the intended function and the circumstances of product use. Consequently, as these circumstances change, it is sometimes necessary to adjust quality accordingly. Products that receive less service or care in a given country have to be reengineered to live up to the added stress. At times, there may be an opportunity to lower product cost by reducing the built-in quality and, in turn, to reduce the price to the customary purchase levels of the local market. However, such reductions may be dangerous if the company reputation suffers in the process. Not marketing a product at all may be preferable.

Some companies go to great lengths to live up to different quality standards in foreign markets. The experience of BMW, the German automaker exporting to Japan, serves as an excellent example of the extra efforts frequently involved. BMW found that its customers in Japan expected the very finest quality. Typically, cars shipped to Japan had to be completely repainted. Even very small mistakes were not tolerated by customers. When a service call was made, the car was picked up at the customer's home and returned when completed.

Global Standards[23]

Most countries have some type of organization that sets standards for business processes and practices. Groups such as the Canadian Standards Association, the British Standards Institute (BSI), and the American National Standards Institute (ANSI) all formulate standards for product design and testing. If products adhere to the standards, buyers are assured of a stated level of product quality.

Given the growth in global commerce, there are benefits to having global standards for items such as credit cards, speed codes for 35 mm film, paper sizes,

22. "A Bumpy Ride over Europe's Traditions," *Financial Times*, October 31, 1988, p. 5.
23. Charles Batchelor, "International Standards," *Financial Times*, October 14, 1993, pp. 23–25.

screw threads, and car tires. Although the national standards institutes ensure consistency within countries, an international agency is required to coordinate across countries. The country-to-country differences become immediately obvious when you try to plug in your hair dryer in various different countries.

The International Standards Organization (ISO), located in Geneva, coordinates the setting of global standards. To set a global standard, representatives from various countries meet and attempt to agree on a common standard. Sometimes they adopt the standard set by a country. For example, the British standard for quality assurance (BS5750) was adopted internationally as ISO 9000. Initially a European standard, ISO 9000 is becoming recognized globally.

The unification of Europe has forced the Europeans to recognize the need for multicountry standards. In areas where a European standard has been developed, manufacturers who meet the standard are allowed to include the EU certification symbol, "CE." Firms both in and out of the EU are eligible to use the CE symbol, but they must be able to verify compliance with the standards.[24] If Europe continues to dominate the creation of global standards through ISO, the United States and Japan will be under pressure to conform. The U.S. standard-setting process is much more fragmented than Europe's. In the United States, there are over 450 different standard-setting groups, loosely coordinated by ANSI. After a standard is set by one of the 450 groups, ANSI certifies that it is an "American National Standard," of which there were 11,000 on the books in 1993.[25]

ISO 9000 is one of the most widely recognized standards. As the global quality standard, ISO 9000 ensures that an organization can consistently deliver a product or service that satisfies the customer's requirements. The number of global standards has grown from 4,917 in 1982 to 8,651 in 1992.

The "standards wars" will have great impact on the operation of global marketing for firms regardless of their home base. Regional standards, such as those put forth by the European Commission (EC) can become effective standards for firms in Asia or Latin America aspiring to export to Europe. Particularly for international firms based in emerging markets, meeting those newly emerging de facto global standards will become the basic requirement to secure export orders.

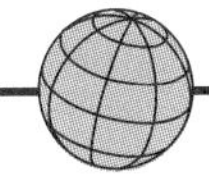

Branding Decisions

Selecting appropriate brand names on a global basis is substantially more complex than deciding on a brand name for just one country. Typically, a brand name

24. Tom Reilly, "The Harmonization of Standards in the European Union and the Impact on U.S. Businesses," *Business Horizons*, March/April 1995, pp. 28–34.
25. For more details, see Raymond G. Krammer, "Technical Barriers to Free Trade," Congressional Testimony by Federal Document Clearing House, April 28, 1998 (Testimony by R. G. Krammer, director of National Institute of Standards and Technology, before the House Committee on Science Subcommittee on Technology).

is rooted in a given language and, if used elsewhere, may have either a different meaning or none at all. Ideally, marketers look for brand names that evoke similar emotions or images around the world. By past learning experience, people worldwide have come to expect the same thing from such brand names as Coca-Cola, IBM, Minolta, and Mercedes-Benz. However, it has become increasingly difficult for new entrants to become recognized unless the name has some meaning for the prospective customer. Language problems are particularly difficult to overcome. Colgate-Palmolive, the large U.S.-based toiletries manufacturer, purchased the leading toothpaste brand in Southeast Asia, "Darkie." With a minstrel in blackface as its logo, the product had been marketed by a local company since 1920. After the acquisition in 1985, Colgate-Palmolive came under pressure from many groups in the United States to use a less offensive brand name. The company undertook a large amount of research to find both a brand name and logo that were racially inoffensive and yet close enough to be quickly recognized by consumers. The company changed the name to Darlie after an exhaustive search. In some markets where the Darkie brand had as much as 50 percent market share, the marketing challenge was substantial to migrate brand loyalty from the old to the new name.[26]

Selection Procedures

Brand name selection is critical. Global marketers must carefully evaluate the meanings and word references in the languages of their target audiences. Can the name be easily pronounced, or will it be distorted in the local language? Branding in Asia, and especially in China, is based on visual appeal, whereas speakers of English tend to judge a brand name on its sound. Asian firms spend extraordinary time and resources selecting brand names. Western firms will benefit from such extensive research. Good examples are Coca-Cola, which means "tasty and happy" in Chinese. Mercedes-Benz's Chinese name means "striving forward fast," and Sharp's means "the treasure of sound." The visual image of the logo is also important to Chinese consumers. The simple graphic logos of Volkswagen, Mercedes-Benz, and Lexus are rated high, but the icons of Cadillac, General Motors, and Fiat are less appealing.[27]

Given almost unlimited possibilities for names and the restricted opportunities to find and register a desirable one, international companies spend considerable effort on the selection procedure. One consulting company specializes in finding brand names with worldwide application. The company brings citizens of many countries together in Paris where, under the guidance of a specialist, they are asked to state names in their particular language that would combine well with

26. "Darkie No, Darlie Yes," *South China Morning Post*, May 16, 1999, p. 2.

27. Bernd Schmitt, "Language and Visual Imagery: Issues of Corporate Identity in East Asia," *Columbia Journal of World Business*, Winter 1995, pp. 28–36.

the product to be named.[28] Speakers of other languages can immediately react if a name comes up that sounds unpleasant or has distasteful connotations in their language. After a few such sessions, the company may accumulate as many as one thousand names, which will later be reduced to five hundred by a company linguist. The client company then is asked to select fifty to one hundred names for further consideration. At this point, the names are subjected to a search procedure to determine which ones have not been registered in any of the countries under consideration. In the end, only about ten names may survive this process; from these, the company will have to make the final selection. Although this process may be expensive, the cost is generally considered negligible compared with the advertising expenditures invested in the brand name over many years.

When confronted with the need to search for a brand name with global applications, a company may consider the following:

1. An arbitrary or invented word not to be found in any standard English (or other language) dictionary, such as Toyota's Lexus.
2. A recognizable English (or foreign-language) word, but one totally unrelated to the product in question, such as the detergent Cheer.
3. An English (or other language) word that merely suggests some characteristic or purpose of the product, such as Mr. Clean.
4. A word that is evidently descriptive of the product, although the word may have no meaning to persons unacquainted with English (or the other language), such as the diaper brand Pampers.
5. Within one or more of these categories, a geographical place or a common surname, such as Kentucky Fried Chicken.
6. A device, design, number, or some other element that is not a word or a combination of words, such as 3M Company.[29]

Selection of a brand name based on these six approaches is closely related to another key issue in global branding: should the company use one brand name worldwide or should it use different names in different countries?

Selection of Internet Domain Names

Selection of an Internet domain name poses even more problems. With already more than 2 million names registered, companies are hard pressed to find suitable

28. "Trademarks Are a Global Business These Days, but Finding Registrable Ones Is a Big Problem," *Wall Street Journal*, September 4, 1975, p. 28.
29. George W. Cooper, "On Your 'Mark,'" *Columbia Journal of World Business*, March–April 1970, pp. 67–76.

names not already used by some other business.[30] As registration of Internet domain names has become open to all users worldwide, and since the cost of a registration is less than $100 for the first two years, many individuals and firms have begun registering names regardless of prior or intended use. A company starting with a new product or company name is thus challenged to register its Internet domain name at the same time as its legal papers registering the company. Trade name registration and protection alone does not guarantee access to an Internet domain name. As a result, initial Internet domain name registration is fast becoming the first step before either a product or a company may want to go public.

Single-Country Versus Global Brand Names

Global marketers are constantly confronted with the decision of whether the brand name needs to be universal. Brands such as Coca-Cola and Kodak have universal use and lend themselves to an integrated global marketing strategy. With worldwide travel a common occurrence, many companies do not think they should accept a brand name unless it can be used universally.

Brands provide a badge, emblem, or symbol that gives the product credibility and helps the consumer identify products and make choices. A brand that consumers know and trust helps them make choices faster and more easily.[31] Companies are investing into their brands, both in brand identity and in product quality. One of the biggest success stories is Intel. After losing a trademark case to protect the "386" name, Intel launched the "Intel Inside" campaign through cooperative advertising. Awareness of the company's chip went from 22 percent to 80 percent in two years.[32] Since then, Intel has been able to migrate the brand equity into its Pentium processor brands and a whole list of licensing requirements that the company imposes on its chip clients for use in PCs.[33] A global brand name can be a huge asset as a firm enters new markets. For example, when McDonald's opened its doors in Johannesburg, South Africa, thousands of people stood in line. In another example, when Coke entered Poland, its red-and-white delivery trucks drew applause at traffic lights.[34]

Of course, using the same name elsewhere is not always possible, and a change in the home market may jeopardize the positive feelings for the original name gained after years of marketing efforts. In such instances, different names have to be found. Procter & Gamble had successfully marketed its household cleaner, Mr. Clean, in the United States for some time. This name, however, had

30. "Losing the Name Game," *Newsweek*, June 8, 1998, p. 44.
31. "The Brand's the Thing," *Fortune*, March 4, 1996, p. 75.
32. Ibid.
33. "Inside intel: Chip Maker's Restrictive Marketing Program and Millions in Subsidies Shackel PC Makers," *PC Week*, April 5, 1999.
34. "The Brand's the Thing," *Fortune*, March 4, 1996, p. 75.

no meaning except in countries using the English language. This prompted the company to arrive at several adaptations abroad, such as Monsieur Propre in France and Meister Proper in Germany. In all cases, however, the symbol of the genie with gleaming eyes was retained because it evoked responses abroad that were similar to those in the United States.

Private Branding Strategies

The practice of private branding, or supplying products to a third party for sale under its brand name, has become quite common in many domestic markets. Similar opportunities exist on a global scale and may be used to the manufacturer's advantage. Private branding offers particular advantages to a company with strong manufacturing skills but little access to foreign markets. Arranging for distribution of the firm's product through local distributors or companies with already existing distribution networks reduces the risk of failure and provides for rapid volume growth via instant market access. Some Japanese companies have used the private branding approach to gain market access in Europe and the United States. Ricoh of Japan, originally known as a manufacturer of cameras, entered the market for small plain paper copiers (PPCs) in the early 1970s. Private branding supply contracts were signed with several U.S.-based and European firms. Ricoh used this strategy to enter when not yet well known but later on switched its brands to its own name and acquired many of its initial partners. The company is now a global leader for both small personal copiers and fax machines.[35]

These private branding arrangements are also called OEM (original equipment manufacturer) contracts, in which the foreign manufacturer assumes the role of the OEM. As the market grows, these arrangements become difficult to manage from the manufacturer's point of view. Nevertheless, they have opened markets more quickly and at much lower investment cost than would have been required to develop these markets on their own. LG, an international Korea-based firm that used to operate under the brand name Goldstar has used various OEM relationships to help it expand into established markets. In the United States, the company acquired Zenith and is now supplying TVs under that brand name.[36] To build up the European market for its home appliances, TVs, and microwave ovens, the company relied on private branding. For its more recent products, such as digital TVs and DVDs, the company will use the LG brand name.[37] In entering Romania, where there was not a strong local producer, LG entered the market directly under its own brand name.[38]

35. "Ricoh Distributes Whistle Communications' Award Winning Internet Solutions in Japan," *PR Newswire*, March 23, 1998.
36. "LG Starts Digital TV Exports to US," *Comline Business News*, July 15, 1999.
37. "LGE Reacts to Integration in Europe, Strengthens Own Brand Name Sales," *Korea Herald*, June 15, 1999.
38. "LG Becomes Household Name Among Romanian Consumers," *Korea Herald*, June 25, 1999.

Private branding or OEM contracts are not without drawbacks for the manufacturer. With control over marketing in the hands of the distributor, the manufacturer remains dependent and can only indirectly influence marketing. For long-term profitability, companies often find that they need to sell products under their own names, even where the OEM has achieved substantial marketing success. Such partnerships often end because of conflicting interests. Ricoh, which successfully used OEM arrangements to carve out a large market share in the United States for its copiers, reportedly paid Savin $14.5 million in compensatory royalties to obtain the right to sell copiers under its own name, Ricoh.[39]

Global Brands

Experts disagree on what makes a global brand. However, few brands are marketed in the same way, with the same strategy, and as identical products worldwide. Furthermore, many that are actually marketed as global brands with a largely identical strategy still have not yet received major recognition beyond their own home regions. For example, Federal Express launched its courier business in the United States in the 1970s. The Federal Express name reflected the U.S. overnight delivery service. As Federal Express opened its international operations, however, the name was a problem. In Latin America, *federal* connoted corrupt police, and in Europe the name was linked to the former Federal Republic of Germany. In 1994, Federal Express changed its name to FedEx, which in some cases is used as a verb meaning "to ship overnight."[40]

Although a number of Japanese companies like Toyota, Panasonic, and Sony have built strong global brands, few other Asian companies have achieved such status. Acer Corp., the Taiwanese PC maker, has begun to build a global brand, followed by LG, formerly known under Lucky-Gold Star, the Korean electronics company. LG Group, the $40 billion Korean conglomerate, hired Landor Associates to build its global image.[41] Samsung, the South Korean electronics manufacturing company, retained Vogt-Wein of Westport, Connecticut, to build its global brand image to cover VCRs, satellite dishes, personal computers, cameras, and automobiles.[42]

Global brands have been very successful in China. In the cities of Beijing, Shanghai, Guangzhou, and Chengdu, foreign brands control 85 percent of the shampoo market, 72 percent of the chocolate market, and 81 percent of the carbonated soft-drink market. Although global brands control 40 percent of the laundry detergent sales in the top four Chinese cities, the local state-owned enterprise—Shanghai's White Cat—is putting up a fight. White Cat copied Unilever's

39. "PPC Marketers Take Over American Distribution," *Japan Economic Journal*, May 22, 1979, p. 7.
40. "Landor: Experts on Identity Crisis," *Ad Age International*, March 1997, p. I-44.
41. Ibid.
42. "Gaining Recognition for Asian Brands," *Ad Age International*, June 1996, p. I-36.

Omo brand detergent right down to the red, blue, and yellow cardboard packaging.[43] White Cat is the Chinese market leader for detergents, with about 19 percent share, well ahead of leading global brands such as Ariel, Tide, and Omo.[44]

The opportunity for global branding is partially driven by the presence of a strong global information logic, as explained in detail in Chapter 7. Customers who do not scan the world for brands are much less aware of globally launched brands. Increasingly, however, customers look elsewhere for products and are becoming more aware of brands offered internationally, even globally. As this awareness continues to expand, the payoff for global brands, with their strong appeal for perceived quality, will outweigh the difficulties of launching them.

Panregional Brands

Brands actively marketed in a geographic region, such as Europe, are considered panregional. (In the case of Europe, they are also called pan-European brands, or Eurobrands for short.) In the strictest sense, packaged goods marketed across Europe with the same formula, the same brand name, and the same positioning strategy, package, and advertising are still said to amount for a small portion of total volume in Europe. Examples of such products include P&G's Pampers and Head & Shoulders, Michelin tires, and Rolex watches. Experts expect Eurobrands' share of all brands to rise, however. Another group of products, marketed with semistandardized strategies but with changes in one or more of the marketing variables, is estimated to account for as much as 40 percent of the European consumer goods business. Consequently, purely national brands may decline in share from more than 50 percent today to about one-third in the next decade. In Latin America, Brazil's Varig Airlines has undertaken a design and logo change to broaden its regional appeal. The revamped Varig logo is modern and warm looking, which supports the company's advertising program of well-rested passengers getting off their flights.[45] In Asia, the Shangri-La hotel chain, with thirty-four hotels, has built a strong regional brand. Shangri-La offers all the amenities of a luxury hotel, along with Asian hospitality. The staff uniforms reflect the local costumes. Shangri-La also uses its advertising to appeal to executives in Asia, who are judged by the hotels they choose. The tag line on Shangri-La ads is "It must be Shangri-La."[46]

Electrolux, the Swedish white goods (household appliances) company, made more than one hundred acquisitions between 1975 and 1985, which left the company with more than twenty brands sold in forty countries. Large markets such as

43. "China's Brand-Name Cat," *Far Eastern Economic Review*, April 18, 1996, p. 70.
44. "China's Detergent Market Expands in 1998," *Asia Pulse*, January 25, 1999.
45. "Regional Brands: Varig Eyes the Skies Outside of Brazil," *Advertising Age International*, March 1997, p. I-19.
46. "Shangri-La on Earth," *Advertising Age International*, March 1997, p. I-24.

the United Kingdom and Germany had as many as six major Electrolux brands. A study by Electrolux found a convergence of market segments across Europe, with the consumers' need for "localness" being primarily in terms of distribution channels, promotion in local media, and use of local names instead of product design and features. From this analysis, Electrolux developed a strategy with two pan-European brands and one or two local brands in each market. The Electrolux brand was targeted to the high-prestige, conservative consumers, and the Zanussi brand was targeted to the innovative, trend-setter consumers. The local brands were targeted to the young, aggressive urban professionals and the warm and friendly, value-oriented consumers.[47] In a survey of more than two hundred European brand managers in thirteen countries, 81 percent indicated they were aiming for standardization and homogenization, whereas only 13 percent said they were leaving each country free to decide its own strategy.[48] The survey clearly indicates a strong preference for a Eurobrand strategy for most companies.

As BSN, the third-largest food group in Europe, has grown beyond its base in France to become a pan-European company with global aspirations, it has found its name to be a weakness. BSN, which stands for the two former companies of Boussois and Souchon-Neuvesel, which merged in 1966, was recognized by 93 percent of people in France, but by only 7 percent in Italy and 5 percent in Spain. To support its global image, BSN changed its name to Danone, after its dairy and yogurt brand.[49] Danone developed into one of the world's top ten brand names.[50]

Trademarks

Because brand names or trademarks are usually backed with substantial advertising funds, it makes sense to register such brands for the exclusive use of the sponsoring firm. However, registration abroad is often hampered by a number of factors. Trademarks still have to be registered one country at a time.

Different interpretations exist in different countries and may affect filing. In some countries, registration authorities may object that the name lacks the inherent distinctiveness needed for registration or that the chosen word is too common to be essential to the promotion of the product, thus allowing other firms to continue to use the name in a descriptive manner. Other countries allow registration of trademarks and renewals for actual or intended use, thus increasing the possibility that some other firm may already have registered the name. In countries where the first applicant always obtains exclusive rights, companies risk the

47. Christopher A. Bartlett and Sumantra Ghosal, "What Is a Global Manager?" *Harvard Business Review*, September–October 1992, p. 125.
48. "Who Favors Branding with Euro Approach?" *Advertising Age International*, May 25, 1992, p. I-16.
49. "BSN Puts New Name on the Table," *Financial Times*, May 11, 1994, p. 18.
50. "Danone Hits Its Stride," *Business Week International*, February 1, 1999, p. 18.

possibility of having their brand names pirated by outsiders who apply for a new name first. The foreign company is then forced to buy back its own trademark. When a country does not allow registrations until all objections are settled, registration may be postponed for years.

Maintaining the Budweiser trademark has been an interesting saga for Anheuser Busch. In 1911, Anheuser Busch gave Budvar, a Czech brewery in Ceske Budejovice, a Czech town also known as Budweis, the rights to the Budweiser name in continental Europe. When Anheuser Busch decided to enter Europe, it tried to renegotiate with Budvar. When this failed, Anheuser Busch took Budvar to court, winning in many European courts.[51] Although it seems Budvar may lose access to the Budweiser name in Europe, it still owns the name in Vietnam, causing Anheuser Busch to pull out of a $145 million join venture, and in the Czech Republic.[52] Budweiser's attempt at acquiring the Czech brewery outright was thwarted. In the continuing fight, Budweiser's legal strategy was to block any export shipments of its Czech rival whenever they appeared in its own legal territory.[53]

Trademark and Brand Protection

Violations of trademarks have been an inescapable problem for global marketers. Many companies have found themselves subject to violations by people who use either the protected name or a very similar one. Deliberate violations can usually be fought in court, though often at great expense. Violations of trademarks, or counterfeit products, are estimated to account for 3 percent of world trade according to the International Chamber of Commerce. The U.S. Department of Commerce estimated that some 750,000 U.S. jobs were lost because of foreign forgeries of U.S. products.[54] Some sources estimated the annual trade in counterfeit products at $250 billion on a global scale.[55]

Recorded music has long suffered from pirating, with global sales of such products estimated at $4.5 billion worldwide, consisting of about 400 million CDs and 1.6 billion cassettes. In 1998, pirated music was believed to outsell legitimate music in twenty countries, including Hong Kong, Malaysia, Ukraine, Israel, Estonia, and Latvia, up from fourteen countries a year earlier. The Ukraine has assumed the position of music counterfeit capital of Europe; legislation is inadequate and the Ukrainian authorities lack commitment to clamp down on the problem.[56] Other sectors affected by counterfeiting are toys and sporting goods,

51. "U.S. Brewer Loses Budvar Fighting for Identity," *Financial Times*, November 1, 1996, p. 20.
52. "Anheuser Ends Czech Talks over the Budweiser Name," *New York Times*, September 24, 1996, p. D6.
53. "Budweiser Takes on the World," *New York Times*, June 24, 1999, p. C16.
54. "Stop, Thief," *International Management*, September 1990, p. 48.
55. "Sleaze E-Commerce," *Wall Street Journal*, May 14, 1999, p. W1.
56. "Music Piracy Remains Headache for Big Labels," *Wall Street Journal Europe*, June 11, 1999, p. UK16.

with an estimated loss of 13 percent of sales; perfumes and toiletries, with a 10 percent loss; and clothing and footwear, with 4 percent of total sales lost to pirated products.[57]

Any kind of computer software is also battling piracy. Surveys conducted in 1999 indicated that about 40 percent of all new business software applications are pirated, resulting in a revenue loss of $11 billion. The biggest offenders were Vietnam with 97 percent, China with 95 percent, and Indonesia with 92 percent of all installed new software pirated. Even in the United States, the piracy rate was estimated at 25 percent, resulting in some $2.9 billion revenue loss. The problem was estimated to be far greater for consumer applications produced by Microsoft or Norton Utilities, for which illegal copies outsold legal copies.[58]

Counterfeiting injures both businesses and consumers. In some cases, trademark violations can result in potential harm to the customer. In India, some counterfeit pharmaceutical drugs were not only copies but were also made of different chemical compounds, thereby posing serious threats to patients.[59] Glaxo Wellcome, a leading U.K. pharmaceutical company, worked on making its products and packaging unique so that it could not be copied by counterfeiters. Zantac, its leading ulcer drug, was made as a five-sided peach-colored pill for the U.S. market. Prescribing doctors could look the drug up in the *Physicians' Desk Reference* to verify its looks.[60] U.K. sources estimated that the world pharmaceutical industry lost about 6 percent of sales to counterfeit products.[61]

Piracy of trademark-protected products flourishes in countries where legal protection of such trademarks is weak. In Vietnam, the nature of copyright infringement is open to interpretation. Furthermore, enforcement is weak as the government does not have resources to effectively enforce existing laws or to control the borders. Some international consumer good companies doing business in Vietnam claim that their sales are reduced by as much as 50 percent because of illegal, and cheaper, products. Procter & Gamble is believed to have lost sales of up to 25 percent as illegal operators collected its containers and refilled them with counterfeit products. The same happened to brand name cognac and whiskies. Reused bottles have been known to be filled with sugar rum.[62]

Finally, the emergence of e-business has contributed to the further growth of counterfeit global trade. Online counterfeit business volume was estimated at $25 billion, a tenth of the total counterfeit volume. Internet counterfeiters are scattered around an estimated five thousand web sites and include shady overseas op-

57. "Counterfeits Costs Pounds 8 Billion a Year," *Times of London*, June 14, 1999, p. 48.
58. "Software Piracy Costs Billions in Revenue," *Baltimore Sun*, June 13, 1999, p. 2D.
59. "Fake Drugs Numb Profits of Indian Pharmaceutical Industry," *Agence France-Presse*, July 16, 1999.
60. "Businesses Battle Bogus Products," *AP Online*, January 26, 1999.
61. "Counterfeits Costs Pounds 8 Billion a Year."
62. "Vietnam's Prolific Counterfeiters Take a Walk on 'LaVile' Slide," *Asian Wall Street Journal*, June 4, 1998, p. 1.

erators to local school kids operating out of a basement. Rolex, the Swiss-based luxury watch producer regularly checks eBay auctions, where on any given day several hundred of these watches may be up for bids. Many of these are counterfeit. The same applies to manufacturers of many other luxury items. Louis Vuitton regularly checks eBay and acts on counterfeit products.[63]

International companies have gone on the offensive to defend themselves against counterfeiting. The United States passed the Trademark Counterfeiting Act of 1984, which makes counterfeiting punishable by fines of up to $250,000 and prison terms of up to five years. International companies are increasingly focusing on methods to stop counterfeiting. Many firms find that subcontractors, who know manufacturing processes, are becoming a problem. These companies may fulfill their regular contracts to an international company while selling extra volume on the black market. To stop such practices, new marketing systems are being developed to allow companies to monitor abuses and customers to spot counterfeit products. Polaproof by Polaroid is one tamper-proof label, holograms are another, and many invisible marketing devices or inks exist. However, given the difficulty of tracking counterfeiters and the obvious opportunities for making quick profits, counterfeiting is a problem that international companies will have to deal with for some time to come.

Packaging for Global Markets

Differences in the marketing environment may require special adaptation in product packaging. Changed climatic conditions often demand a change in the package to ensure sufficient protection or shelf life. The role a package assumes in promotion also depends on the market retailing structure. In countries with a substantial degree of self-service merchandising, a package with strong promotional appeal is desirable for consumer products; these requirements may be substantially scaled down in areas where over-the-counter service still dominates. In addition, distribution handling requirements are not identical the world over. In high-wage countries of the developed world, products tend to be packaged to reduce further handling by retailing employees. For consumer products, all mass merchandisers have to do is place products on shelves. In countries with lower wages and less-developed retailing structures, individual orders may be filled from larger packaged units, entailing extra labor by the retailer.

R.J. Reynolds of Winston-Salem, North Carolina, exported cigarettes to 170 countries and territories.[64] The company observed more than 1,400 different product codes covering its various brands in all markets. For its leading brand,

63. "Sleaze E-Commerce."
64. "RJR—A Truly Global Company in a Global Market," *World Tobacco*, September 1, 1998, p. S12.

Winston, the company needed more than 250 different packages to satisfy different brand styles and foreign government requirements. The U.S. package design was used for fewer than six markets. Differences were due to various regulations on health warnings. In Australia, the number of cigarettes contained in a package had to be printed on the package front. Some countries, such as Canada, require bilingual text. To avoid errors in the printing process when working with alphabets as diverse as Greek, Arabic, or Japanese, replicas of the original package were prepared in the foreign market and forwarded for production to the United States.[65]

Specific packaging decisions affected by the particular foreign market for which the product is designated are size, shape, materials, color, and text. Size may differ by custom or by existing standards such as metric and nonmetric requirements. Higher-income countries tend to require larger unit sizes, since these populations shop less frequently and can afford to buy larger quantities each time. In countries with lower income levels, consumers buy in smaller quantities and more often. Gillette, the world's largest producer of razor blades, sells products in packages of five or ten in the United States and Europe, whereas singles are sold in some emerging markets.

Packages can assume almost any shape, largely depending on the customs and traditions of each market. Materials used for packaging can also differ widely. Whereas Americans prefer to buy mayonnaise and mustard in glass containers, consumers in Germany and Switzerland buy these same products in tubes. Cans are the customary material to package beer in the United States, whereas most European countries prefer glass bottles. The package color and text have to be integrated into a company's promotional strategy and therefore may be subject to specific tailoring by country. The promotional effect is of great importance for consumer goods and has led some companies to attempt to standardize their packaging in color and layout. In areas such as Europe or Latin America, where the consumers frequently travel to other countries, standardized colors help identify a product quickly. This strategy depends on devising a set of colors or a layout with an appeal beyond one single culture or market. An example of a company pursuing a standardized package color is Procter & Gamble, the U.S. manufacturer of the leading detergent, Tide. The orange-and-white box familiar to millions of U.S. consumers can be found in many foreign markets, even though the package text may appear in the language or print of the given country.

As consumers and governments become more concerned about the environmental consequences of excess or inappropriate packaging, companies are expected to develop packaging that is environmentally friendly. Responding to con-

65. "Tobacco Companies Face Special International Packaging Obstacles," *Marketing News*, February 4, 1984, p. 20.

sumer concern, the U.K. retailer Sainsbury examines every product it sells to ensure each uses only the minimum packaging necessary.[66]

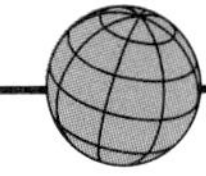

Managing a Global Product Line

In early sections of this chapter, we covered decisions about individual products in detail. Most companies, however, manufacture or sell a multitude of products; some, such as General Electric, produce as many as 200,000 different items. To facilitate marketing operations, companies group these items into product groups consisting of several product lines. Each product line is made up of several individual items of close similarity. Quaker Oats organized its European operation into four pan-European business groups: pet food, cereals, Gatorade, and corn oil. The pan-European approach was designed to increase efficiency and take advantage of the single European market.[67]

A company with several product lines is faced with the decision to select those most appropriate for global marketing. As with each individual product or decision, the firm can either offer an identical line in its home market and abroad or, if circumstances demand, make appropriate changes. In most cases, a firm would look at the individual items within a product line and assess marketability on a product-by-product basis. As a result, the product lines abroad are frequently characterized by a narrower width than those found in a company's domestic market.

The circumstances for deletions from product lines vary, but some reasons dominate. Lack of sufficient market size is a frequently mentioned reason. Companies with their home base in large markets such as the United States, Japan, or Germany will find sufficient demand in their home markets for even the smallest market segments, justifying additional product variations and greater depth in their lines. Abroad, opportunities for such segmentation strategies may not exist because the individual segments may be too small to warrant commercial exploitation. Lack of market sophistication is another factor in product line variation. Aside from the top twenty developed markets, many markets are less sophisticated and their stage of development may not demand some of the most advanced items in a product line. And finally, new-product introduction strategies can impact product lines abroad. For most companies, new products are first introduced in their home markets and introduced abroad only after the product has been successful at home. As a result, the lag in extending new products to foreign markets also contributes toward a product line configuration that differs from that of the firm's domestic market.

66. "Keeping It to a Minimum," *Financial Times*, May 28, 1992, Special section: Packaging and the Environment, p. 5.
67. "Quaker as a Europhile," *Advertising Age*, August 26, 1991, p. 26.

Firms confronted with deletions in their product lines somctimcs add specialized offerings to fill the gap in the line, either by producing a more suitable product or by developing an entirely new product that may not have any application outside a specific market. Such a strategy can only be pursued by a firm with adequate research and development strength in its foreign subsidiaries.

Exploiting Product Life Cycles

The existence of product life cycles immediately opens opportunities to the international firm but, on the other hand, poses additional hurdles that may complicate product strategy. Experience has shown that products do not always occupy the same position on the product life cycle curve in different countries.

New products receiving initial introduction in the world's developed markets tend to move into later life cycle stages before those in countries that receive the product at a later date. As shown in Figure 13.2, it is possible for a product to be in different stages of the product life cycle in different countries. Other countries follow, usually each according to its own stage of economic development. Consequently, although a product may be offered and produced worldwide, it is common for it to range over several stages in the product life cycle at any point in time. The principal opportunity offered to the firm is the chance to extend product growth by expanding into new markets to compensate for declining growth rates in mature markets. A risk arises when a company enters new markets or countries too fast, before the local market is ready to absorb the new product. To avoid such pitfalls and to take advantage of long-term opportunities, international companies may follow several strategies.

During the introductory phase, a product may have to be debugged and refined. This job can best be handled in the originating market or in a country close to company research and development centers. Also, the marketing approach will have to be refined. At this stage, the market in even the more advanced countries is relatively small, and demand in countries with lower levels of economic development will hardly be commercially exploitable. Therefore, the introductory stage will be limited to the advanced markets, often the company's domestic market.

Once the product has been fully developed and a larger group of buyers has become interested, volume will increase substantially. Domestic marketing policies foresee price decreases due to volume gains and to the entry of new competitors, with an expansion of the entire market. At this stage, many firms start to investigate opportunities elsewhere by introducing the product in selective markets, where it would be in the introductory phase. This requires some adaptation of communication strategy to parallel earlier efforts in the home market, as the approach designed for the second phase, the growth stage, cannot be used. In the late 1980s and early 1990s, U.S. white goods manufacturers faced a

FIGURE 13.2

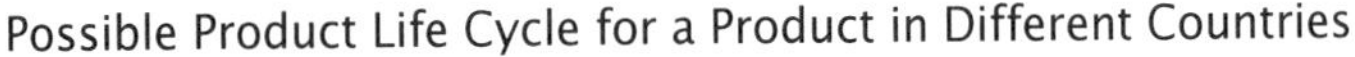

Possible Product Life Cycle for a Product in Different Countries

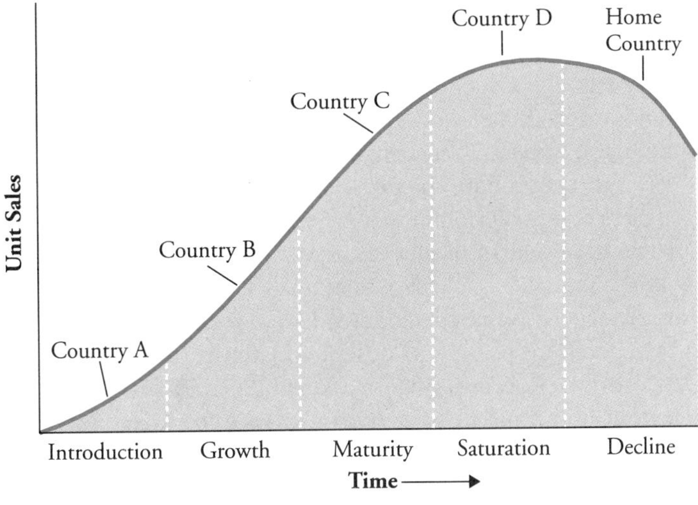

mature market in the United States, with a decline in total volume. This led Whirlpool, GE, Hoover, and Maytag to enter the European market, which is expected to grow with the European Union and the economic liberalization of eastern Europe.[68]

A product facing life cycle decline may be withdrawn in stages, similar to its introduction. The most advanced countries will see such a withdrawal earlier than some of the less developed markets. Volkswagen, the German automaker, offers an example of how an old design may still sell in some countries while being long gone in others. Its famous Beetle car, originally introduced in the 1930s, was withdrawn from production everywhere but Mexico. There the Beetle remains the best-selling car and helps make VW a leading car producer. The model has been adapted for modern environmental requirements but comes only in a simple version without extras or options. In 1990, the car was priced at $5,300, and the company has pledged to keep the price pegged to rises in the minimum wage. As a result, VW obtained some important tax relief,[69] and in 1990, Beetles accounted

68. "The Deal Steps Up the U.S. Group's Drive into Europe, the Final Link in Whirlpool's Global Circle," *Financial Times*, June 7, 1991, p. 12.
69. "Miss the VW Bug? It Lives Beyond the Rio Grande," *New York Times*, October 20, 1990, p. 2.

for two-thirds of VW's Mexican output.[70] More recently, VW has begun to export a totally redesigned Beetle from Mexico into the U.S. market. However, this new model is destined largely for export markets and less so for local consumers.[71]

Exploiting product life cycles was a profitable strategy for Samsun Electronics, a Korea-based international firm. In the 1970s, Samsun deliberately targeted to produce products that had reached the declining stage of the product life cycle in developed markets such as the United States. Samsun was easily able to obtain technology for those products. As the company successfully assimilated new technologies, Samsun increasingly entered product segments with younger product life cycle stages until the firm reached the point where it could compete with world-class companies on new, emerging products.[72]

As we have seen, a product cannot automatically be assumed to reach the various stages in its life cycle simultaneously in all countries; thus, flexibility in marketing strategy is required. To introduce a product abroad in stages represents a strategic decision in itself, as described later in this chapter. Though typical, the phased introduction to foreign markets may not always be in the best interest of the firm, as it may offer competitors a chance to expand locally.

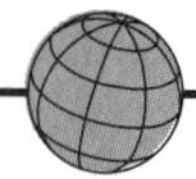

Global Warranty and Service Policies

Buyers around the world, as do domestic consumers, expect more than just the physical benefits of a product. Clients purchase products with certain performance expectations and in their purchase choice will consider company policies for backing promises. As a result, warranties and service policies have to be considered as an integral aspect of a company's global product strategy. Companies interested in doing business abroad frequently find themselves at a disadvantage with local competitors in the area of warranties and service. With the supplier's plant often thousands of miles away, foreign buyers sometimes want extra assurance that the supplier will back the product. Thus, a comprehensive warranty and service policy can become a very important marketing tool for global companies.

Product Warranties

A company must address its warranty policy for global markets either by declaring its domestic warranty valid worldwide or by tailoring to specific countries or

70. "VW's Humble Hunch-back Makes a Comeback in Mexico," *Financial Times*, October 23, 1990, p. 8.
71. "Beetlemania to the Rescue," *Business Week*, January 12, 1998, p. 46
72. Seongjae Yu, "The Growth Pattern of Samsung Electronics: A Strategy Perspective," *International Studies of Management Organization*, January 1, 1998, vol. 28, no. 4, p. 57–72.

markets. Although declaring worldwide warranty with uniform performance standards would be administratively simple, local market conditions often dictate a differentiated approach. In the United States, most computer manufacturers sell their equipment with a thirty- or sixty-day warranty, whereas twelve months is more typical in Europe or Japan.

Aside from the two technical decisions as to what standards should be covered under a warranty and for how long, a company would be well advised to consider the type of actual product use. If buyers in a foreign market subject the product to more stress or abuse, some shortening of the warranty period may become necessary. A company may be able to change product design to allow for different standard performance requirements. In developing countries, where technical sophistication is below North American or European standards, maintenance may not be adequate, causing more frequent equipment breakdowns. Another important factor is local competition. Since an attractive warranty policy can be helpful in obtaining sales, a firm's warranty policy should be in line with that of other firms competing in the local market.

Just how important global product warranty expectations have become is demonstrated by the experience of Perrier, the French bottled water company. In February 1990, the company had to withdraw its Perrier water from U.S. retail stores after the product was found to contain benzine in concentrations above the legal limit. This U.S. test result triggered similar tests by health authorities in other countries. Soon Perrier had to withdraw its products in other countries, eventually resulting in a worldwide brand recall. This illustrates the interdependence of many products in today's open and accessible markets. Failure to maintain quality, service, or performance in one country can rapidly have a negative impact in other areas.[73] Coca-Cola experienced a similar problem with bottling plants in Belgium, which led to a recall of many products, not only in Belgium but also in France. Some two hundred consumers had complained of illness after drinking Coca-Cola products, leading to the largest product recall in Coca-Cola's history. Inadequate sanitation procedures resulted in recalls in Poland as well.[74]

Global Product Service

No warranty will be believable unless backed with an effective service organization. Although important to the consumer, service is even more crucial to the industrial buyer, since any breakdown of equipment or product is apt to cause substantial economic loss. This risk has led industrial buyers to be conservative in their choice of products, always carefully analyzing the supplier's ability to provide service in case of need.

73. "Brit Helps Perrier Move Beyond the Recall Crisis," *Advertising Age*, November 12, 1990.
74. "Coca-Cola Poland Details Scope of Product Recalls," *Wall Street Journal*, July 14, 1999, p. A17.

To provide the required level of service outside the company's home base poses special problems for global marketers. The selection of an organization to perform the service is an important decision. Ideally, company personnel are preferable since they tend to be better trained. However, use of company personnel is only feasible economically if the installed base of the market is large enough to justify such an investment. In cases in which a company does not maintain its own sales subsidiary, it is generally more efficient to turn to an independent service company or to a local distributor. To have adequate services via independent distributors requires extra training for the service technician, usually at the manufacturer's expense. In any case, the selection of an appropriate service organization should be made so that fully trained service personnel are readily available within the customary time frame for the particular market.

Closely related to any satisfactory service policy is an adequate inventory for spare parts. Because service often means replacing some parts, the company must place sufficient inventory of spare parts within reach of its markets. Whether this inventory is maintained in regional warehouses or through sales subsidiaries and distributors depends on the volume and the required reaction time for service calls. Buyers will generally want to know how the manufacturer plans to organize service before making substantial commitments.

Firms that demonstrate serious interest in a market by committing to their own sales subsidiaries are often at an advantage over firms using distributors. One German truck manufacturer that entered the U.S. market advertised the fact that "97 percent of all spare parts are kept in local inventory," thus assuring prospective buyers that they can get spares readily. In some instances, the difficulty with service outlets may even influence a company's market entry strategy. This was the case with Fujitsu, a Japanese manufacturer of electronic office equipment. By combining forces with TRW Inc., a U.S.-based company, Fujitsu was able to sell its office equipment in the U.S. market with the extensive service organization of TRW.

Since the guarantee of reliable and efficient service is such an important aspect of a firm's entire product strategy, investment in service centers at times must be made before any sales can take place. In this case, service costs must be viewed as an investment in future volume rather than as a recurring expense.

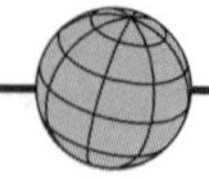

Marketing Services Globally

In 1998, global trade in services reached $1,290 billion worldwide. Services included business services, travel, transportation, and government services. One of the largest categoies of service exports was business services. Export services included communications, financial services, software development, database management, construction, computer, accounting, advertising, consulting, and legal services. The export of business services took place primarily from developed economies such as the United States, the Netherlands, France, Japan, the United Kingdom, Germany, and Italy. The U.S. share of global service import trade amounted to about 12 percent, with 18 percent for service exports.[75]

Decisions about marketing services are related to the structure of the service itself. A firm has to decide which service to sell or offer and how the service should be designed. Again, the issue of standardization needs to be addressed, although there are fewer opportunities for economies of scale by standardizing services worldwide. A company needs to decide on the content of the service it wants to offer and the manner in which the service is to be performed or consumed. Business services tend to be more standardized, and more in demand worldwide, because the needs of companies are more uniform than those of individual consumers. To a much greater degree, personal services are subject to cultural and social influences and exhibit a greater need for tailoring to local circumstances.

Business Services

The services aimed at business buyers that are most likely to be exported are those that have already met with success. The experience of U.S.-based service companies can be used as an example. Some of the services most successfully marketed abroad include financial services. Commercial banks such as Citibank, Chase, and BankAmerica built extensive branch networks around the world, to the extent that foreign deposits and profits make up nearly half of business volume. Advertising agencies have also expanded overseas, either by building branch networks or by merging with local agencies. Similar strategies were followed by accounting and management consulting firms. More recently, many U.S.-based marketing research firms have expanded into foreign countries.

Opportunities for New Service Firms

Just as the U.S. economy is slowly moving to become a service economy, similar trends can be found in the economies of other developed countries in western Europe and Japan. Many types of services are in great demand abroad. For example, the global courier service is an area in which several companies are vying for global positions. U.S.-based Federal Express built up its overseas business by buying Flying Tiger, the largest international cargo airline, and merging it with FedEx's international small-documents and parcel service.[76] However, building up its courier service worldwide initially resulted in tremendous losses. The company scaled back its European operations in 1991 but in 1996 committed to a

75. "World Trade in Commercial Services by Selected Region and Economy," *World Trade Organization*, Trade in Services Section of the Statistics Division, March 1999.
76. "A Fragile Air Freight Strategy," *New York Times*, September 6, 1989, p. D1.

major European hub, to become operational in 1999.[77] In 1998, FedEx connected areas that accounted for 90 percent of global gross national product with its twenty-four- to forty-eight-hour door-to-door service. Shipping more than 3 million items to 211 countries each working day, the company employed more than 142,000 employees, 615 aircraft, and 40,900 vehicles, with an annual revenue of $13.3 billion.[78]

Another major company in the small-parcels business with global ambitions is United Parcel Service (UPS), which is using its considerable cash flow from U.S. operations to build its global network. It took UPS some twelve years to build its German operation to 6,000 employees. To help its overseas strategy, UPS acquired several local courier companies in various countries. UPS, however, grew its business in Europe more slowly than did FedEx and was able to learn in the process. UPS is now pushing beyond Europe into Latin America and Asia and is scheduling its own overseas flights.[79]

International accounting and consulting services are an area that saw tremendous growth in the 1980s. Major firms started to think in global terms and to expand their operations into many markets. Among the leading accounting firms, international revenue typically was larger than domestic (or U.S.) revenue. Several firms merged, so the former "Big Eight" are now down to five. Ernst & Whitney merged with Arthur Young because of the latter firm's strong international network. Peat Marwick merged with KMG, a company that was traditionally strong in Europe. Price Waterhouse merged with Coopers and Lybrand to form PricewaterhouseCoopers.[80] Overseas expansion is important to these U.S.-based firms because revenue is growing faster abroad and margins are also better for international business. Furthermore, many of the firms' accounting clients have recently gone through globalization themselves and demand different services. Finally, the liberalization of trade in Europe has also boosted cross-national business and mergers.

Big British and U.S. law firms are also finding numerous opportunities overseas. The unification of Europe has accelerated cross-border mergers and acquisitions. The growth of the European Union in Brussels has created a demand for lawyers to lobby the EU, and privatization of many businesses in eastern Europe has created a legal gold mine. Although France and Japan have established local requirements to slow down the growth of British and U.S. firms in their countries, the legal profession has become another global service industry. Many U.S. law firms are opening up overseas branch locations, primarily in London, to capture business from investment banks and other financial services

77. "FedEx Rebuilds Operations," *Journal of Commerce*, March 23, 1999, p. 6A.
78. "FedEx to Deliver New Level of International Service," *Business Wire*, August 12, 1998.
79. "UPS Adjusts International Plans," *American Shipper*, December 1, 1998.
80. "Big Five Accounting Firms Unlikely to Shrink, but the Possibility Exists," *Pittsburgh Business Times & Journal*, May 28, 1999, p. 33.

firms that require presence in both New York and London, major capital market centers.[81]

Services for Consumers and Individual Households

Marketing services to consumers turns out to be more difficult than selling to industrial users. Since consumer purchasing and usage patterns between countries differ to a greater degree than industry usage patterns do, many services have to be adapted to local conditions to make them successful. The U.S.-based fast-food chains were some of the first consumer service companies to pursue foreign opportunities. McDonald's, Kentucky Fried Chicken, Dairy Queen, and many others opened restaurants in Europe and Asia in large numbers.

Though success came eventually, initial results were disappointing for McDonald's in Europe. The company had anticipated differences in taste by serving wine in France, beer in Munich and Stockholm, and tea in England, where the company also lowered the sugar content of its buns by 4 percent. But McDonald's based its first store locations on U.S. criteria and moved into the suburbs and along highways. When volume did not develop according to expectations, McDonald's quickly moved into the inner cities. Once this initial problem had been overcome, McDonald's grew very quickly abroad. In 1985, international revenue accounted for 24 percent of revenue, but by 1992 it had grown to almost 50 percent.[82] Although some local food variations have been allowed, the company operates using the same standardized manual worldwide, indoctrinating all of its franchise operations abroad with the same type of operating culture.

Insurance companies have found significant opportunities in emerging markets. For example, in Shanghai, China, the American International Group (AIG) sold more than twelve thousand policies in eight months. Although it took AIG over ten years to get licensed in China, the company believes that opportunities there are tremendous.[83] AIG was one of only six foreign insurance firms licensed in China and the first foreign firm ever to gain a license in 1992.[84]

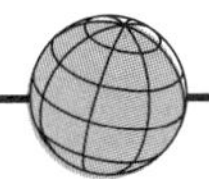

Conclusions

To be successful in global markets, companies need to be flexible in product and service offerings. Although a given product may have been very successful in a

81. "US Law Firms Are on the Prowl in London," *Wall Street Journal Europe*, June 1, 1999, p. 4.
82. "Overseas Sizzle for McDonald's," *New York Times*, April 17, 1992, p. D1.
83. "AIG Sells Insurance in Shanghai, Testing Service Firms' Role," *Wall Street Journal*, July 21, 1993, pp. 1, A-9.
84. "China Shows Promise for Foreign Entrants," *Life Insurance International*, November 1, 1998, p. 14.

firm's home market, environmental differences can often force the company to make unexpected or costly changes. Although a small group of products may be marketed worldwide without significant changes, most companies will find that global success depends on a willingness to adapt to local market requirements. Additional efforts are frequently required in product support services to assure foreign clients that the company will stand behind its products. For companies that successfully master the additional international difficulties while showing a commitment to foreign clients, global success can lead to increased profits and more secure market positions domestically.

QUESTIONS FOR DISCUSSION

1. Generalize about the overall need for product adaptations for consumer products versus high-technology industrial products. What differences exist? Why?
2. American fast food, music, and movies have become popular around the world, with little adaptation, whereas U.S. retailers, banks, and beer companies have had slower progress in global markets. Why?
3. What are the major reasons for a company to choose a worldwide brand name for its product?
4. Under what circumstances would using different brand names in different countries be advisable?
5. Are there any differences between the international marketing of services and the international marketing of products?

FOR FURTHER READING

Ayal, Igal. "International Product Life Cycle: A Reassessment and Product Implications," *Journal of Marketing*, Fall 1981, pp. 91-96.

Davidson, William H., and Richard Harrigan. "Key Decisions in International Marketing: Introducing New Products Abroad," *Columbia Journal of World Business*, Winter 1977, pp. 15-23.

Hill, John S., and Richard R. Still. "Adapting Products to LDC Tastes," *Harvard Business Review*, March-April 1984, pp. 92-101.

Jones, Barry, and Roger Ramsden. "The Global Brand Age," *Management Today*, September 1991, pp. 78-80.

Kelz, Andreas, and Brian Block. "Global Branding: Why and How?" *Industrial Management & Data Systems*, 1993, vol. 93, no. 4, pp. 11-17.

Levitt, Theodore. "Globalization of Markets," *Harvard Business Review*, May-June 1983, pp. 92-102.

Samiee, Saeed, and Kendall Roth. "The Influence of Global Marketing Standardization on Performance," *Journal of Marketing*, April 1992, pp. 1-17.

Sorenson, Ralph Z., and Ulrich E. Wiechmann. "How Multinationals View Marketing Standardization," *Harvard Business Review*, May-June 1975.

Wilson, Steven R. "The Impact of Standards on Industrial Development and Trade," *Quality Progress*, vol. 32, no. 7 (July 1, 1999), p. 71.

14

Developing New Products for Global Markets

Global Product Strategies

New-Product Development Processes for Global Markets

Globalization of the Product Development Process

Introducing New Products to Global Markets

IN CHAPTER 13, WE FOCUSED ON INDIVIDUAL PRODUCT DECISIONS. HERE WE concentrate on the strategic issues of product design and development for global markets (see Figure 14.1). Following an analysis of the standardization versus adaptation issue, the first part of this chapter covers a series of alternatives involving product extension, adaptation, and innovation strategies. Included is a segment on global products that deals with the complexities of designing products for many markets simultaneously. The second part of the chapter is devoted to product development strategies for international companies. Emphasis is on organizational issues, sources, and approaches that will enhance a firm's ability to innovate in a changing

FIGURE 14.1

Global Product Development Strategies

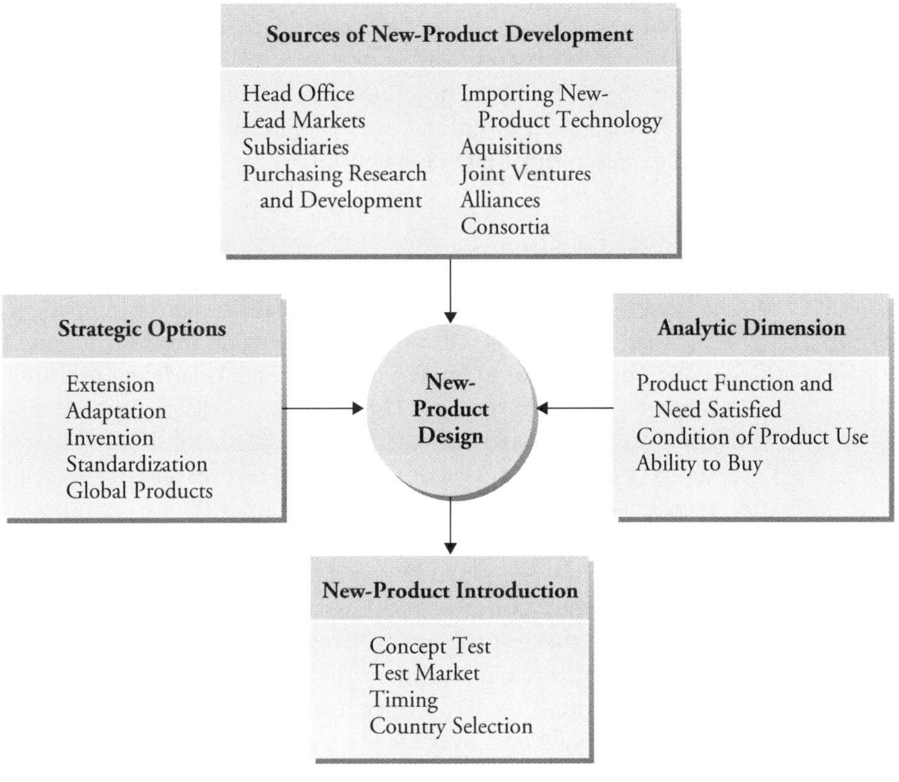

marketplace. We conclude the chapter with a discussion of new-product launch issues.

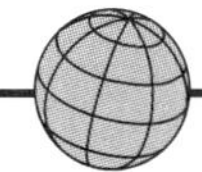

Global Product Strategies

The purpose of this section is to outline the basic product strategies a firm may select and to demonstrate their close relationship with a company's communication policy, particularly with respect to advertising.[1]

1. This section is based on Warren J. Keegan, *Global Marketing Management*, 5th ed.: 1995, pp. 489–495.

Analytic Issues: Standardization Versus Adaptation

A company's decision to pursue a specific product strategy primarily depends on three factors: (1) whether the product function or the need satisfied is the same or different in a new market, (2) whether particular conditions surrounding product use can affect company strategy, and (3) whether target market customers are financially able to buy the product. Because these three factors greatly influence the product strategy chosen, we examine each one here before turning our attention to a company's strategic options.

Product Function, or the Need Satisfied The key to the product function factor is the role the product plays in a given market. Although certain types of products may be consumed by individuals in many countries, a company cannot automatically assume that the underlying motivation to purchase is identical. Take, for example, the difference between Americans and Russians with respect to purchasing and wearing T-shirts and blue jeans. In the United States, T-shirts and jeans convey an informal attitude toward clothing and a lack of interest in any status that clothing may convey. In fact, by dressing this way, Americans give the appearance of wanting to be ordinary rather than to stand out. In Russia the opposite is true. Because real blue jeans and T-shirts are in short supply, those who wear such clothing signal to society that they are aware of current fashions and are highly status-conscious. In Russia, jeans and T-shirts clearly separate the individual from the rest of society. Thus, the rationale for buying them is different and contradictory in these two countries.

On the other hand, products for industrial use, such as plant machinery, are purchased the world over for the same intention or reason. Therefore, very little difference in product function or satisfied need is expected. Also, many examples of consumer goods can be pointed to for which the need to be satisfied is identical. For one, the motivation behind the purchase of razor blades is homogeneous across countries and cultures.

Differences in product function or satisfied need, even when present, do not necessarily call for a change in product design or features. The primary focus here is on the buyer and the motivation that triggers a purchase. As a psychological concept, motivation requires a corresponding response. Therefore, dissimilar purchasing motives require unique communications responses, or a change in a firm's advertising, to relate the product to these different motives.

Conditions of Product Use Physical environmental variables combine into a physical event that determines the salient factors surrounding a product's actual use. To the extent that these events are identical within any two countries, a product may be marketed without any changes or alterations. The conditions of product use reflect the actual use or consumption of a product regardless of the motivation that triggered its purchase. In seeking opportunities for product standardization, marketers must consider the physical events surrounding product use that substantially determine the viability of the strategy.

Ability to Buy Although purchasing power is generally not an issue in developed economies, there are, nevertheless, hundreds of millions of potential customers in countries that simply do not have the economic resources found in more affluent markets. In such countries, the motivation to purchase a product and actual use conditions may be identical to those in affluent societies, but the products used to satisfy these demands are beyond the price that buyers can afford. Such situations may require an entirely different strategy. For example, the product can be changed so that it can be made available at a much lower price. Thus, substantial differences in the nature of the economic event can have a significant influence on global product strategy. As Unilever expects revenues from developing and emerging markets to approach 50 percent of company sales in the next decade, it has developed smaller packages to appeal to lower-income consumers. The small packages reduced unit price to low-income consumers in Asia. The company has also introduced alternative packaging to bring the overall costs down. Unilever is recognized in Asia for its "mulitilocal, multinational" approach and in 1999 was among the top ten international firms operating throughout the Asia Pacific area.[2] In India, Unilever offers its detergent Wheel, Sunsilk shampoo, and A1 tea in small packets. The promising results in India led Unilever to try the same approach in Brazil with its laundry powder Ala. Test marketing has been successful, and Unilever plans to use the scaled-down size strategy in Egypt and Pakistan as well.[3]

Advantages of Product Standardization Complete standardization of product design results in a substantial saving of production and research and development costs and allows a company to take advantage of economies of scale. Often, several markets can be supplied from a regional or central manufacturing plant with efficient and long production runs. Aside from these obvious advantages, production sharing and simultaneously supplying markets from several plants are important factors that support standardized output. Managers in the U.S. subsidiary of Liebherr, a large German company producing construction machinery, decided to make some changes in the basic design of an excavator that was built to identical specifications elsewhere in Europe and Latin America. To

2. "Unilever Among Asia's 10 Most Admired," *Manila Standard*, June 13, 1999.
3. "Unilever Tests Small Sizes," *Ad Age International*, March 1997, pp. I-3, I-36.

make the excavator more acceptable to U.S. customers, the Virginia-based subsidiary enlarged the fuel tank and strengthened the undercarriage. When U.S. sales dropped as a result of a recession, the company accumulated a substantial inventory of excavators. However, it could not help its European plants, plagued with back orders, because of the difference in design.[4] Obviously, the advantages gained from adaptation have to be compared with the overall loss in manufacturing flexibility.

Despite the advantages of economies of scale, few companies can fully standardize their products for the many markets they serve. To bridge the gap between various local adaptations and the need to standardize some components, some international firms have moved to a new breed of products, the global product, which we discuss later in the chapter.

Three Strategic Choices: Extension, Adaptation, Invention

A company can follow one of three basic strategies when moving into a foreign market. With respect to both its product and its communications policy, the firm can opt for an *extension* strategy, basically adopting the same approach as in its home market. The strategy of *adaptation* requires some changes to fit the new market requirements. When an entirely new approach is required, the company can adopt the strategy of *invention*. These three basic strategies can be further refined into the five strategies shown in Table 14.1 and are explained in the following sections.

Strategy One: Product Extension—Communications Extension One extension strategy calls for marketing a standardized product with the same communications strategy across the globe. Although this strategy has considerable attraction because of its cost effectiveness, it is rarely feasible for consumer products. The few exceptions include companies in the soft-drink industry and some luxury goods firms. Industrial products, with a greater homogeneity of buyers internationally, offer a somewhat greater opportunity for this strategy, but again the extension strategy is far from the norm.

The cost effectiveness of this strategy should not be underestimated. Product adaptations entail additional research and development expenses and tooling costs, and they do not allow economies of scale to the extent possible under an extension strategy. Though less substantial, savings from the creation of only one communications strategy should also be considered. In any case, decision makers should consider the anticipated impact on demand in the foreign market if the

4. "It's Tough Digging in the U.S.," *Fortune*, August 11, 1980, p. 146.

TABLE 14.1

Global Product Strategies

Strategy	Product Function or Need Satisfied	Conditions of Product Use	Ability to Buy Product	Recommended Product Strategy	Recommended Communications Strategy	Rank Order from Least to Most Expensive	Product Examples
1	Same	Same	Yes	Extension	Extension	1	Soft drinks
2	Different	Same	Yes	Extension	Adaptation	2	Bicycles, motor-scooters
3	Same	Different	Yes	Adaptation	Extension	3	Gasoline, detergents
4	Different	Different	Yes	Adaptation	Adaptation	4	Clothing, greeting cards
5	Same	—	No	Invention	Develop new communications	5	Hand-powered washing machines

Source: From Warren J. Keegan, "Multinational Product Planning: Strategic Alternatives." Reprinted from *Journal of Marketing*, vol. 33, January 1969, pp. 58–62, published by the American Marketing Association. Reprinted by permission.

product is not fully suited to local tastes or preferences, as well as the potential savings. Past experience shows that rigidly enforcing a product and communications extension policy can lead to disaster and therefore should be adopted only if all requirements with respect to product function, satisfied need, use conditions, and ability to buy are met.

Strategy Two: Product Extension—Communications Adaptations When the sociocultural event surrounding product consumption differs from country to country but the use conditions as part of the physical event are identical, the same product can be marketed with a change in the communications strategy. Examples can be found among bicycle and motorcycle manufacturers. In developing countries, a bicycle or motorcycle is primarily a means of transportation, whereas the same products are used in sports or for recreation purposes in a developed market. This strategy is still quite cost-effective, since communications adaptation represents a lower cost than tailoring a product to a local market. In eastern Europe, tobacco companies have had great success developing local brands that appeal to national pride. The product is basically the same, but the brand and communications are adapted to each local market. BAT captured a significant share of the Polish market with its brand JanIII Sobieski, named for the popular Polish figure.[5] Similarly, R.J. Reynolds was successful with its new Peter I brand in Russia, which captured 18 percent of the local market.[6]

Strategy Three: Product Adaptation—Communications Extension Strategy three is appropriate when the physical event surrounding product use varies but the sociocultural event is the same as in the company's home market. Although changes in a product are substantially more costly than changes in the communications approach, a company will follow this course when the product otherwise may not sell in a foreign market. In some cases, product formulations may be changed without the consumer knowing it, as with detergents and gasoline, so that the product can function under different environmental circumstances.

Strategy Four: Product Adaptation—Communications Adaptation When both the physical and sociocultural events vary, a strategy of dual adaptation is generally favored. To make this strategy profitable, however, the foreign market or markets need to be of sufficient volume to justify the costs of dual adaptation. As Campbell Soup entered overseas markets, it found that tastes differed from market to market. Although U.S. products such as cream of mushroom and cream of chicken soup were successful in some markets, watercress and duck gizzard soup was successful in China.[7]

Strategy Five: Product Invention When the ability to purchase a product is generally missing, some companies have elected to invent an entirely new product, usually by redesigning the original product to a lower level of complexity. The resulting, substantially cheaper, product leads to more purchases. An example was the strategy followed by Philips, the Dutch multinational corporation. In response to the desire of many developing countries to own their own television manufacturing plants, the Dutch company redesigned its equipment and tools to suit the volume requirements of some of the world's poorest countries. Compa-

5. "BAT–Rothmans Merger to Affect Polish Operations," *Polish News Bulletin*, June 16, 1999.
6. "Japan Tobacco Wins RJR's Russia Unit," *Moscow Times*, March 11, 1999, p. 11.
7. "Campbell: Now It's M-M-Global," *Business Week*, March 15, 1993, p. 53.

nies also can develop or invent entirely new products. For example, trumpet players in Japan had difficulty practicing as most Japanese houses have thin walls and brass playing is banned in most parks. Yamaha seized the opportunity and developed an electronic mute that deadened the sound to the outside world while allowing the player to listen through headphones. In the first four months, Yamaha sold thirteen thousand units.[8]

Global Products

In response to the pressure for cost reduction and considering the relatively few opportunities for producing completely standardized products, many firms have moved to the creation of a *global product*. The global product, based on the acknowledged fact that only a portion of the final design can be standardized, builds on flexibility to tailor the end product to the needs of individual markets. This represents a move to standardize as much as possible those areas involving common components or parts. This modularized approach has become of particular importance in the automobile industry, in which both U.S. and European manufacturers are moving toward the creation of world components to combat growing Japanese competitiveness.

One of the first world cars was introduced by Ford during the 1981 model year. Ford's Escort model was simultaneously assembled in the United States, Great Britain, and Germany from parts produced in ten countries. The U.S.-assembled Escort contained parts made in Japan, Spain, Brazil, Britain, Italy, France, Mexico, Taiwan, and West Germany.[9] The European assembly plants, in return, bought automatic transmissions from a U.S. plant. Ford was estimated to have saved engineering and development costs amounting to hundreds of millions of dollars because the design standardized engines, transmissions, and ancillary systems for heating, air conditioning, wheels, and seats.[10] Still, the U.S. and European Escorts were two distinctly different cars.

The second generation of global products was started in 1981, the year the first original Escort rolled off the line, to be ready for production in 1991. With a budget of some $2 billion, Ford designed its second-generation Escort with Mazda, the Japanese car manufacturer partly owned by Ford. The design was done by Ford engineers in the United States, with the engineering and manufacturing planning performed by the Japanese engineers at Mazda. This new model was planned for assembly in twelve different locations where Ford sold the car under its Escort name, although Mazda used various different brand names (the 323, Protégé, or Familia). Ford's strategy was driven by the fact that product development duplication was a very costly process. By pooling development

8. "Yamaha: Perfect Pitch?" *Economist*, February 17, 1996, p. 62.
9. *New York Times*, November 9, 1980.
10. "Ford's Financial Hurdle," *Business Week*, February 2, 1981, p. 66.

resources, Ford was estimated to have saved as much as $1 billion in development costs.[11]

Ford's global car, the Mondeo (called the Contour in the United States), was launched in 1993 in Europe and in 1994 in the United States. Ford invested $6 billion in the development of the new model, which included research and development as well as two new assembly plants and four new engine plants. Ford expected to gain significant economies of scale by selling 700,000 cars a year.[12] Although sales in Europe were strong, the Mondeo-derived U.S. models did not do very well. Although well designed for Europe, these models turned out to be too expensive for their segments in the U.S. market.[13]

For its latest version of "world cars," Ford has changed its strategy. Instead of trying to build like models in multiple markets, the company has moved toward building and launching different versions of cars on the same identical chassis (underpinning), giving a greater variety of car models while saving on the critical components and developments of the drive train, transmissions, and so forth. As part of this new strategy, Ford launched a new Escort as part of its 1999 model range, with European and U.S. versions.[14]

As Ford was moving toward common designs for markets on three continents, some Japanese car companies were moving in the opposite direction. Honda has steadily added to its development and design function in North America. In 1996, Honda made more cars overseas than in Japan. The company launched a number of new models with simplified assembly. For example, Honda has built its new RVs from Civic and Accord platforms in as little as eighteen months from design to production.[15]

Toyota launched its popular Camry in 1991. Three inches wider than its Japanese version, the Camry was intended to be better able to challenge the standard North American sedans of Ford and General Motors. Toyota also developed a new large pickup truck that was unsuitable for Japan's much narrower roads. The strategy pursued by some Japanese companies has been called a "tripolar strategy." It allows them to spread the expensive research and development costs across a worldwide production system; the regions can help each other when demand shifts or shortages occur. Furthermore, it allows the companies to put design teams closest to the markets, thus ensuring maximum acceptance of the models.[16]

11. "How Ford and Mazda Shared the Driver's Seat," *Business Week*, March 26, 1990, p. 94.
12. "Ford Mondaine or Mundane," *Economist*, January 8, 1993, pp. 92–94.
13. "The Revolution at Ford," *Economist*, August 7, 1999, p. 51.
14. "Ford Motor Unveils Replacement of Ford Escort," *Knight-Ridder Tribune Business News*, March 3, 1998.
15. "The Man Who Put Honda Back on Track," *Fortune*, September 9, 1996, p. 92.
16. "Japan's New U.S. Car Strategy," *Fortune*, September 10, 1990, p. 65.

One of the most significant changes in product development strategy in the 1990s has been modularity. This process involves the development of standard modules that can easily be connected with other standard modules to increase the variety of products. For example, General Motors has established a modular product architecture for all its global automobile projects. Future GM cars will be designed using combinations of components from seventy different body modules and about one hundred major mechanical components such as engines, power trains, and suspension systems. The new approach requires standardized interface points between all the different modules.[17]

The challenge faced by Ford and other automobile manufacturers is similar to that faced by manufacturers and marketers of both industrial and consumer products all over the world. Cost pressures force them to standardize, whereas market pressures require more customization. Conceptually, these companies will gain from increasing the standardized components in their products while maintaining the ability to customize the product at the end for each market segment. International firms will have to respond by achieving economies of scale on the core of their products—the key portion offered as a standard across all markets—by building on a series of standardized components. Different firms will have different levels of standardization, but rarely will one be able to standardize the product 100 percent. For one company, even moving from a global core representing 15 percent of the total product to 20 percent of the total product may result in a considerable cost improvement, and this may be the maximum level of standardization desirable. For another firm, the core may have to represent some 80 percent of the total product to achieve the same effect. These levels will depend on the market characteristics faced by the company or industry. The limits to possible standardization were explained in the previous chapter.

The experience of many firms has led to the concept of building new products for global markets on the basis of "platforms" and "derivatives." The product core might be the same for all products in all regions. An extended core might only apply for each region but differ across regions. Each region might support one or more basic platforms based on the extended-core concept. And finally, each region might launch product derivatives specific to the regional conditions. This "platform" strategy allows for maximim different configurations while maintaining a stable product base, thus reducing basic development costs. However, such a global product strategy would only be possible if a company had a coherent, well-planned global product development concept.[18] See Figure 14.2.

17. "Strategic Product Creation," *European Management Journal*, 1996, vol. 14, no. 2, p. 127.
18. Based upon conceptual work by Jean-Philippe Deschamps, IMD, Lausanne, Switzerland.

FIGURE 14.2

Selecting Opportunities for Global Products

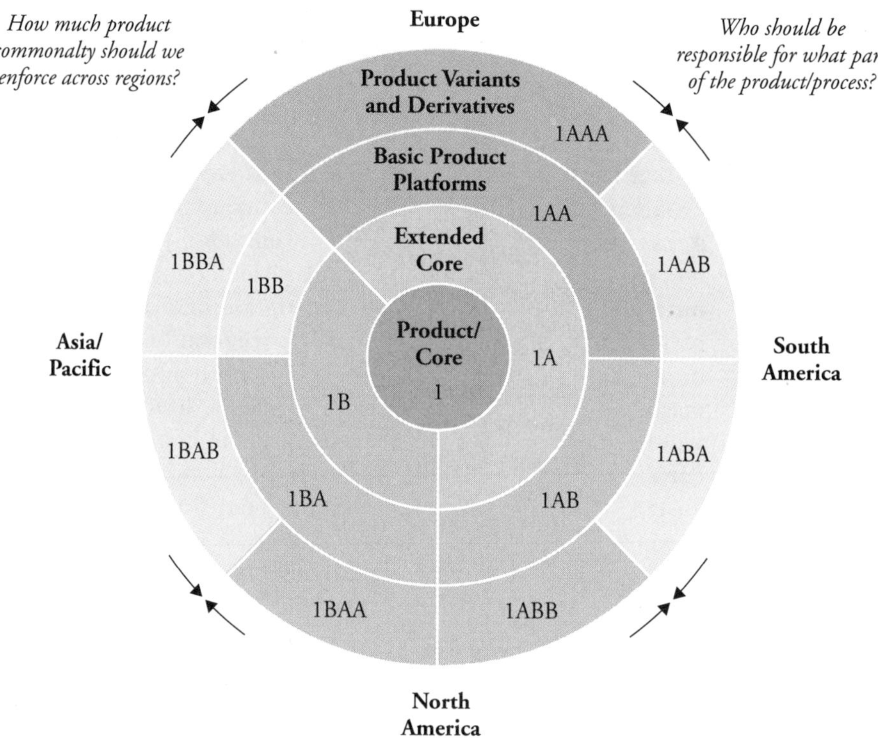

Source: Reprinted with permission from the IMD Presentation, "Formulating a Product Strategy," February, 1997.

New-Product Development Processes for Global Markets

Developing new products or services for global markets offers unique challenges to a firm. In contrast to the strictly domestic company, international firms must assign development responsibilities to any one of their often numerous international subsidiaries. Aside from the question of who should perform development work, there are organizational problems to overcome that pertain to participation by experts in many subsidiaries. No doubt, the future success of international firms will depend to a substantial degree on how well firms marshal their resources on a global scale to develop new products for foreign markets.

The Organization of Head Office–Sponsored Research and Development

Most companies currently engaging in research and development on a global scale originally conducted their development efforts strictly in centralized facilities in the firm's domestic market. Even today, the largest portion of research and development monies spent by international firms is for efforts in domestically located facilities. As a result, new-product ideas are first developed in the context of the domestic market, with initial introduction at home followed by a phase-in introduction to the company's foreign markets.

There are several reasons for this traditional centralized approach. First, research and development must be integrated into a firm's overall marketing strategy. Such integration requires frequent contacts and interfacing between research and development facilities and the company's main offices. Such contacts are maintained more easily with close proximity. The argument for centralization of research and development is based on the concern that duplication of efforts will result if this responsibility is spread over several subsidiaries; centralized research and development is thought to maximize results from scarce research funds. A final important reason for centralization is the company's experience in its home, or domestic, market. Typically, the domestic market is very important to the company and, in the case of international companies based in the United States, Germany, and Japan, is often the largest market as well. As a result, new products are developed with special emphasis on the domestic market, and research and development facilities, therefore, should be close by. For example, Gillette's global success is unquestionably the result of a hefty R&D investment. According to its CEO, "Good products come out of market research. Great products come out of R&D."[19] Between 1992 and 1998, Gillette introduced twenty new products per year, most of which were successful. Its Mach 3 shaving system cost $750 million to research and develop.[20]

Traditionally, the level of R&D spent in a company or country was considered one of the best indicators of long-term growth. An Organization for Economic Cooperation and Development (OECD) study found that although the investments in science and engineering were important, equally important was the diffusion of the new technology.[21]

19. "Gillette Knows Shaving—How to Turn Out Hot New Products," *Fortune*, October 14, 1996, pp. 207–210.
20. "New Razor Hype Boosts Gillette's Shares" (A Barron's Feature), *Dow Jones News Service*, July 11, 1998.
21. "Playing Godmother to Invention," *Economist*, May 24, 1997, p. 76.

Although there are many good reasons for centralizing product development at the company's head office, it will remain a challenge for the engineering and development staff of the firm to keep in mind all relevant product modifications before the design is frozen. Experience shows that later changes or modifications can be expensive. To keep a product acceptable in many or all relevant markets from the outset requires the product development staff to become globalized early in the creation process. Only a globally thinking product development staff will ensure the global acceptability of a product by incorporating the maximum possible number of variations in the original product.

International Lead Markets and Research and Development

Prior to 1960, new developments in industry, marketing, and management tended to emerge primarily in the United States.[22] Such developments, once accepted in the United States, were apt to be adopted later in other countries. As a result, the U.S. market served as the lead market for much of the rest of the world. In general, a *lead market* is a market whose level of development exceeds that of the market in other countries worldwide and whose developments tend to set a pattern for other countries.

Lead markets are not restricted to technological developments as embodied in product hardware. The concept covers developments in design, production processes, patterns in consumer demand, and methods of marketing. Therefore, virtually every phase of a company's operation is subject to lead market influences, although those focusing on technological developments are of special importance.

During the first half of the twentieth century, the United States achieved a position of virtual dominance as a lead market. Not only were U.S. products the most advanced with respect to features, function, and quality, but they also tended to be marketed to the most sophisticated and advanced consumers and industrial buyers. This U.S. advantage was partially based on superior production methods, with the pioneering of mass production in the form of the assembly line. The U.S. advantage extended to management methods in general, and particularly to access to new consumers. The rapid development of U.S.-based international firms was to a considerable degree based on the exploitation of these advantages in applying new U.S. developments abroad and in creating extensive networks of subsidiaries across a large number of countries.

22. This section is based on Jean-Pierre Jeannet, "Lead Markets: A Concept for Designing Global Business Strategies," working paper, International Institute for Management Development (IMD), May 1986.

But the total U.S. lead over other countries did not last. Foreign competitors from Europe and Japan eroded the U.S. firms' advantages; as a result, no single country or market now unilaterally dominates the world economy. Though the United States may have lost its lead in steel, television, radios, shoes, textiles, and automobiles, it still leads the world in electronics, the biosciences, computers, and aerospace (see Figure 14.3). One area in which the United States has maintained supremacy is the Internet router market. Cisco Systems dominates the market with an 85 percent share worldwide. Given the universal standards of the Internet, Cisco does not have a monopoly position. Cisco has maintained its position and doubled in size every year through constant innovation. By listening to the customer and constantly developing new and faster products, Cisco has outdistanced all its smaller competitors.[23] Although the company is courted by governments everywhere, it decided to build its new-capacity expansion in California's Silicon Valley, the heart of the Internet revolution.[24]

Although the general-purpose computer industry is still dominated by mostly U.S. companies, with the United States still serving as the lead market, there are many signs that this position may be challenged in the future. In 1983, U.S. companies had an 81 percent share of computer sales, which had decreased to 61 percent by 1989. Over the same period, the share of Japanese companies rose from 8 percent to 22 percent. Although the United States once dominated the Japanese personal computer (PC) market, U.S. manufacturers in 1992 only had 15 percent of the market, while NEC had 53 percent. However, U.S. manufacturers have rebounded with high-quality graphics, software modified for Japan, and low prices. Apple, IBM, Compaq, and Dell now are the main U.S. PC suppliers in Japan.[25] The leading Japanese suppliers, NEC and Fujitsu, were down to 30 percent and 24 percent, respectively, in 1998.[26]

The fragmentation of lead markets led to a proliferation of centers, substantially complicating the task of keeping abreast of the latest developments in market demands, product design, and production techniques. Even formerly developing countries, such as South Korea, have reached lead market status in some categories. It was the Korean company Samsun that created the world's first next-generation 1-gigabyte computer chip, a major development that is bound to change the nature of the industry.[27]

23. "The Other Technopolists: Bigger, Faster, Better Ears," *Economist*, December 7, 1996, pp. 59–60.
24. "Cisco Systems Plans Expansion to Allow Work Force to Double," *Knight-Ridder Tribune Business News, Mercury News* (San Jose, Calif.), March 2, 1999.
25. "U.S. PC's Invade Japan," *Fortune*, July 12, 1993, pp. 68–73.
26. "Japan's PC Shipments Seen to Rise 7.3 Percent in 1998," *Agence France-Presse*, March 6, 1998.
27. "South Korea's Samsun Announces Next-Generation Computer Chip," *Agence France-Presse*, June 28, 1999.

FIGURE 14.3

How the United States Stacks Up in a Dozen Emerging Technologies

Technology	Compared to Japan				Compared to Europe			
	R & D		New Products		R & D		New Products	
	Status	Trend	Status	Trend	Status	Trend	Status	Trend
Advanced Material	↔	↓	↓	↓	↑	↔	↔	↔
Advanced Semiconductor Devices	↔	↔	↓	↓	↑	↔	↔	↔
Artificial Intelligence	↑	↔	↑	↔	↑	↑	↑	↔
Biotechnology	↑	↓	↓	↓	↑	↑	↑	↔
Digital Imaging Technology	↔	↓	↓	↓	↔	↓	↓	↓
Flexible Computer-Integrated Manufacturing	↑	↔	↔	↔	↑	↓	↓	↓
High-Density Data Storage	↔	↔	↓	↓	↑	↔	↔	↔
High-Performance Computing	↑	↔	↑	↓	↑	↑	↑	↑
Medical Devices and Diagnostics	↑	↔	↑	↓	↑	↔	↑	↓
Optoelectronics	↔	↔	↓	↓	↔	↔	↑	↔
Sensor Technology	↑	↓	↔	↔	↑	↔	↔	↔
Superconductors	↔	↓	↔	↓	↔	↔	↔	↔

United States Status: ↑ Ahead ↔ Even ↓ Behind

United States Trend: ↑ Gaining ↔ Holding ↓ Losing

Source: U.S. Commerce Dept. Reprinted from the June 15, 1990 issue of *Business Week* by special permission, copyright © 1990 by The McGraw-Hill Companies, Inc.

To prosper in today's increasingly internationalized business climate, corporations must keep track of evolving lead markets as major sources for new product ideas and production techniques. New product ideas can stem from influences in demand, processes of manufacture, and scientific discoveries; no single country should expect to play a lead role in all facets of a firm's business. This means any corporate research and development effort must look for new developments abroad rather than solely in the domestic market. Because tire makers Kumho of East Asia and Hankook of South Korea have become very competitive in Europe, with prices sometimes half that of premium brands, the European manufacturers have responded. Pirelli, the Italian tire company, increased its launch of new products sixfold and expected that over half of its 1997 sales would be from new products. Pirelli planned to focus on the market for luxury and speed, offering "good products at good prices to good people," who were likely to be brand-loyal.[28]

The rapid international expansion of U.S.-based firms depends to a large extent on their capacity to take advantage of lessons learned in the U.S. market. This strategy is characterized by centralized research and development functions and initial product introductions in the United States. Naturally, to a large degree, the success of this strategy depends on the inputs the central research and development staff derives from its own market environment. Should any part of a company's market become subject to foreign lead market influences, the organization of a firm's research and development function will have to be adjusted. Steel companies in the United States and manufacturers of automobiles, shoes, and textiles cannot disregard developments elsewhere in the world, since the lead market for these industries is no longer the United States. To expose itself to lead market developments, Kodak invested in a research and development center in Japan. The company hired about one hundred professional researchers and directed the lab to concentrate on electronic imaging technology.[29] Other U.S. companies have built up their own R&D facilities in Japan, including Corning, Texas Instruments, IBM, Digital Equipment, Procter & Gamble, and several chemical and pharmaceutical companies such as Upjohn, Pfizer, DuPont, and Monsanto. In 1990, U.S. companies spent $491 million to license technology from Japan, compared with just $89 million eight years earlier. This speaks for the fact that Japan is increasingly becoming a lead market for many technology areas.[30]

Japanese firms have also seen the need to locate research and development facilities in lead markets. For example, Nissan set up an R&D center in Detroit. Recognizing that Detroit is an important part of the automotive industry, Nissan wanted to be there to maintain a solid global position.[31]

28. "Tyres in Europe: A Bumpy Ride," *Economist*, February 17, 1996, p. 61.
29. "When the Corporate Lab Goes to Japan," *New York Times*, April 28, 1991, sec. 3, p. 1.
30. "Picking Japan's Research Brain," *Fortune*, March 25, 1991, p. 84.
31. "Companies Set Up Overseas R&D Bases," *Nikkei Weekly*, November 9, 1992, p. 13.

The Role of Foreign Subsidiaries in Research and Development

Foreign subsidiaries of international firms rarely play an active role in research and development unless they have manufacturing responsibilities. Sales subsidiaries may provide the central organization with feedback on product adjustments or adaptation, but generally this participation does not go beyond the generation of ideas. Past research has shown that subsidiaries may assume some research and development functions if the products require some adaptation to the local market.[32] The ensuing research and development capability is often extended to other applications unique to the local market. In many instances, however, the new product may prove to have potential in other markets, and as a result these developments get transferred to other subsidiaries and to the central research and development staff.

International subsidiaries assume special positions when lead markets change from one country to another. Countries that can assume lead market status tend to be among the most advanced industrial nations of North America, Europe, and Asia. Larger international firms quite often have subsidiaries in all these markets. A subsidiary located in a lead market is usually in a better position to observe developments and to accommodate new demands. Consequently, international firms with subsidiaries in lead markets are in a unique position to turn such units into effective "listening posts." Unilever found that some countries of the world were very good at innovation in research and marketing, so it set up a global network of innovation centers. These centers were directed to expand their in-depth experience in research and marketing for Unilever's four categories of personal care products: dental, hair, deodorant, and skin. This expertise was then shared around the world.[33]

In the future, international companies will have to make better use of the talents of local subsidiaries in the development of new products. Increasingly, the role of the subsidiary as a selling or production arm of the company will have to be abandoned, and companies will have to find innovative ways to involve their foreign affiliates into the product development process. This involvement can be patterned around several role models. The *strategic leader* role for developing a new range of products to be used by the entire company may be assigned to a highly competent subsidiary in a market of strategic importance. Another subsidiary with competence in a distinct area may be assigned the role of *contributor*, adapting some products in smaller but nevertheless important markets. Most

32. Jean-Pierre Jeannet, *Transfer of Technology Within Multinational Corporations* (New York: Arno Press, 1980).

33. "Fanning Unilever's Flame of Innovation," *Advertising Age International*, November 23, 1992, p. I-3.

subsidiaries, being of smaller size and located in less strategic markets, will be expected to be *implementers* of the overall strategy and contribute less either technologically or strategically.

Some subsidiaries may become less desirable. For example, Piramal Enterprises, an Indian company, has successfully acquired the Indian operations of foreign pharmaceutical companies such as Aspro Nicholas, Hoffman-LaRoche, and Boehringer Mannheim. The multinationals, hampered in their operations by government price controls, weak patent protection, and restrictions on foreign companies' activities, are happy to sell off their Indian subsidiaries. Piramal slims down management, increases sales, and boosts prices. While the multinational gets royalties, Piramal gets a steady stream of new technologies.[34]

Purchasing Research and Development from Foreign Countries

Instead of developing new products through its own research and development personnel, a company may acquire such material or information from independent outside sources. These sources are usually located in foreign countries that have acquired lead market status. Managers commonly read literature published by lead markets. Also, through regular visits to foreign countries and trade fairs, managers maintain close contact with lead markets. Increasingly, however, these ad hoc measures are becoming insufficient for maintaining the necessary flow of information in rapidly changing markets.

For companies without immediate access to new technology embodied in new products, the licensing avenue has been the traditional approach to gain new developments from lead markets. U.S. technology has been tapped through many independent licensing arrangements. Japanese companies have made extensive use of the licensing alternative to acquire technologies developed in countries that were lead markets from Japan's point of view. In the 1960s, several Japanese manufacturers of earthmoving equipment signed licensing agreements with the U.S. manufacturers to obtain expertise in hydraulic power shovels. Though some Japanese companies attempted to develop a new product line from their own internal resources, it was Komatsu that, based on a licensing agreement with a U.S. company, achieved leadership in Japan. By 1989, Japanese companies manufacturing earthmoving equipment owned twenty-one facilities abroad, some partly owned and others fully owned. Many firms that were originally licensers to those Japanese firms are no longer independent or have even become Japanese partners, joint ventures, or subsidiaries.[35] Though the advantage of licensing lies

34. "Pharmaceuticals in India: Best of Both Worlds," *Economist*, December 7, 1996, p. 6.
35. "Japan's Earth Movers Look Abroad," *Financial Times*, April 11, 1989, p. 25.

in its potential to teach new product technologies, there are typically some restrictions attached, such as limiting the sale of such products to specific geographic regions or countries.

The Korean firm LG is an example of a company that aggressively buys technology abroad to assist in the development of its technologically advanced products. Over the years, the company has formed some twenty joint ventures and maintained technology cooperation agreements with more than fifty foreign firms. LG linked up with U.S.-based AT&T to manufacture electronic telephone switching gear, fiberoptic cables, and semiconductors. Entering such agreements gave the Korean firm quick access to modern technologies while allowing AT&T to build contacts within a new market.[36]

Importing as a Source of New-Product Technology

Some corporations decide to forgo internally sponsored research and development, importing finished products directly from a foreign firm. Sometimes the importer assumes the role of an original equipment manufacturer (OEM) by marketing products under its own name. Two agreements made between Japanese suppliers and U.S. manufacturers serve to illustrate this strategy.

Though the importing method gives a firm quick access to new products without incurring any research and development expenditures, a company could become dependent and lose the capacity to innovate on its own in the future. As was the case with General Electric's color TV production, economic changes can lead to reversals later on. GE had stopped production of color TV sets in the United States in the mid-1970s and sourced all such products from Matsushita in Japan. When the value of the yen rose to record levels in 1986, GE switched back to U.S. sourcing. This move was made possible because the company had earlier acquired RCA, which still operated a color TV plant in the United States.[37] The strategy of importing new products should be pursued with great care and possibly only in areas that do not represent the core of the firm's business and technology.

Acquisitions as a Route to New Products

Acquiring a company for its new technology or products is a strategy many firms have followed in domestic markets. To make international acquisitions for the purpose of gaining a window on emerging technologies or products is becoming an acceptable strategy for many firms. Robert Bosch, a German firm,

36. "Lucky-Gold Star: Using Joint Ventures to Sprint Ahead in the High-Tech Race," *Business Week*, July 9, 1984, p. 94.

37. "GE Will Resume Some U.S. Production of Color TVs Instead of Buying Abroad," *Wall Street Journal*, February 13, 1987, p. 6.

acquired an interest in American Microsystems, and Philips of the Netherlands purchased Signetics. In both cases, the foreign firms had to pay substantial premiums over the market value of the stock as a price for an inside look at new-product development.

Japanese companies illustrate how the acquisition strategy can be used to get access to new products and technologies. Japanese firms are reported to have invested about $350 million in some 60 deals for a wide range of minority positions in U.S.-based high-technology firms through either joint ventures, licensing, or direct investments as minority shareholders. In 1989, Chugai Pharmaceutical acquired Gen-Probe of San Diego to get access to the firm's products, including test kits for the detection of cancer and viral infections. Gen-Probe has since become a recognized world leader in the development, manufacture, and commercialization of diagnostic products based on its patented genetic probe technologies.[38]

The Joint Venture Route to New-Product Development

Forming a joint venture with a technologically advanced foreign company can also lead to new-product development, often at lower costs. In the 1960s and 1970s, it was largely Japanese companies that sought to attract foreign technology for the manufacture of advanced products in Japan. Today, many of these Japanese companies can be found in the front ranks of their industries. Typically, these joint ventures were set up as separate entities, with their own manufacturing and marketing functions.

Joint ventures are concluded today by firms from many different countries. GM operates a JV in Japan with Suzuki, a company in which it has a 10 percent share participation, and with Isuzu, a truck producer in which GM owns 49 percent. GM jointly develops cars with those firms for local markets.[39] GM is not a newcomer to JVs with Japanese car makers. It has operated a JV production unit in California with Toyota (NUMMI) since 1984.[40] GM also signed an agreement to purchase low-emission engines from Honda Motors. In return, the Japanese firm will purchase diesel engines from Isuzu, a GM affiliate.[41] And Ford uses a joint venture in Taiwan to build a new development center to develop products specifically for the Taiwanese market.[42]

38. "Gen-Probe Expands with a New State of the Art Manufacturing Facility," *Chemical Business NewsBase*: Press Release, May 17, 1999.
39. "GM Says Auto Plant in Japan Is Part of Long-Term Strategy," *Agence France-Presse*, August 6, 1999.
40. "General Motors–Toyota Plant in Fremont, Calif. Thrives," *Knight-Ridder Tribune Business News* (Contra Costa Times, Walnut Creek, Calif.), July 20, 1999.
41. "Stand-Alone Honda Strikes a Deal," *Nikkei Weekly*, December 6, 1999, p. 8.
42. "Ford Joint Venture in Taiwan to Invest in New Product Development," *AFX News*, May 5, 1999.

In Europe, joint ventures between different international firms are also common. Toyoda Automatic Loom works operates a joint venture for forklifts in France.[43] Denso is planning to set up a joint venture in Germany with Toyota to make compressors.[44] Even e-business calls for joint ventures. Softbank of Japan established joint ventures in Europe with Vivendi of France to provide services for e-business firms.[45]

Alliances for New-Product Development

Many companies are finding alliances a way to share technology and research and development for competitive advantage. Alliances are not as structured as a joint venture but include some type of mutually beneficial management. For example, Electrolux, the Swedish appliance manufacturer, has concluded a broad-based alliance with Toshiba of Japan. The two firms plan to cooperate in household appliances through the exchange of technology, product sourcing, and purchasing. Some fifteen projects are being undertaken covering technology development, procurement, environmental issues, and cooperation for the Japanese market. This alliance helps both companies get access to what they individually would not have been able to undertake.[46]

Sun Microsystem's alliance with Fujitsu Ltd. was critical to Sun's success in the workstations market. Fujitsu developed the 32-bit processor based on Sun's proprietary SPARC (scalable processor architecture).[47] The Sun-Fujitsu alliance demonstrates how companies can leverage their individual capabilities for competitive advantage through an alliance. More recently, Fujitsu signed another alliance with Siemens of Germany involving that company's computer interest. Siemens gets access to the SPARC technology that was part of the earlier Sun-Fujitsu deal.[48]

Alliances can sometimes be formed by firms for some part of their business although they remain competitors in other segments. Olivetti of Italy and Canon of Japan decided to join forces to develop and market office equipment in Europe. The companies created a new joint company in Italy consisting of Olivetti production and research facilities for copiers and an infusion of capital and technology from Canon. With access to Canon's latest technology, particu-

43. "French Region Invites Japanese Companies," *Japan Economic Newswire*, June 20, 1998.
44. "Japan's Auto Equipment Maker Denso to Set Up Joint Venture in Germany," *Agence France-Presse*, August 31, 1998.
45. "Softbank to Set Up Joint Ventures in Britain, France," *Japan Computer Industry Scan*, July 5, 1999.
46. "Toshiba, Electrolux Ink Alliance," *National Post*, May 27, 1999, p. C12.
47. Fumio Kodama, "Innovation Forged by Technology Fusion," *Nikkei Weekly*, March 1, 1993, p. 6.
48. "Fujitsu-Siemens Alliance to Leverage Sun for Global Push," *Computergram International*, July 7, 1999.

larly in the laser printing and electronic publishing area, Olivetti managers hoped that the new company would triple present volume—supplying both Olivetti and Canon distribution channels in Europe. Despite this cooperation, the two firms were to remain competitors in the typewriter market.[49] Not to be deterred, Olivetti entered into a different alliance with Xerox to strengthen and modernize its range of office equipment while maintaining its other alliance with Canon.[50]

The Consortium Approach

To share the huge cost of developing new products, some companies have established or joined consortia to share in new-product development. Under the consortium approach, member firms join in a working relationship without forming a new entity. On completion of the assigned task, member firms are free to seek other relationships with different firms. Consortia have been used for some time in marketing entire factories or plants or in the banking industry, but they are a relatively new approach to new product research and development.

Since the development of new aircraft is particularly cost-intensive, the aircraft industry offers several examples of the consortium approach to product development. The high development costs require that large passenger aircraft must be built in series of two hundred or three hundred units just to break even. Under these circumstances, several companies form a consortium to share the risk. One of the first highly successful efforts was the European Airbus, developed and produced by French, British, and German manufacturers.

For its latest generation of long-range aircraft, the 777, Boeing was facing development and launch costs of some $4 billion. Such programs could not be justified unless several airlines, including foreign ones, could be involved from the outset with large capital commitments. To reduce the risk, Boeing offered a 25 percent share in the project to three Japanese companies: Mitsubishi Heavy Industries, Fuji Heavy Industries, and Kawasaki Heavy Industries. These companies had been major suppliers of subassemblies for the 767 model range. It is believed that such Japanese participation was invited not only to share development costs but to help in the marketing of the planes. The fact that All Nippon Airlines was the largest operator of Boeing 767 planes outside the United States was linked to the strong participation of Japanese firms in the production of the plane. Both Japan Airlines and All Nippon Airlines were among the key accounts sought for the launch of the Boeing 777 model range.[51] Japan Airlines

49. "Olivetti and Canon Form Venture for Office Equipment Production," *Financial Times*, January 20, 1987, p. 1.
50. "Olivetti Set for Partnership with Xerox," *Financial Times*, March 17, 1998, p. 36.
51. "How Boeing Does It," *Business Week*, July 9, 1990, p. 46.

was already the world's largest operator of Boeing 747s. The fact that Japanese airlines are the largest buyers of long-range planes underscores the need to bring in Japanese partners in the early stages of any long-range passenger plane project.

Responding to the same pressures as those faced by the airplane manufacturers, the major jet engine companies have also engaged in a number of consortia. U.S.-based General Electric has had a long-term agreement with Snecma of France. The alliance has been highly successful, capturing a majority of large aircraft engine orders and producing its ten-thousandth engine in 1999.[52] Pratt & Whitney, the other leading U.S. jet engine firm, joined a partnership with MTU, a subsidiary of the German firm Daimler-Benz. MTU has taken successive participations in a series of P&W engines over the years and has expanded its own alliances to Rolls-Royce (now BMW).[53]

British Rolls-Royce, the smallest of the major jet engine firms, made a series of collaborative ventures with different firms. Rolls-Royce's strategy has been to make project-specific ventures (see Figure 14.4). Rolls-Royce also made a deal with BMW of Germany for the production of jet engines for the civil aviation market.[54] GE, United Technologies (Pratt & Whitney), Rolls-Royce, and Snecma were in return invited by three Japanese engine producers, Mitsubishi Heavy Industries, Ishikawajima-Harima, and Kawasaki Heavy Industries, to help build new engines for supersonic planes. The four European and U.S. companies would provide technology assistance to the Japanese partners, thus saving development costs and time.[55]

Another advantage of a consortium approach lies in sales. The widespread participation of companies from the United States, Europe, and Japan gives partial reassurance for future sales, thus further reducing the risk to each participating company. Airbus, a rival consortium competing with Boeing, was trying to enter the Japanese market for wide-bodied planes. The absence of strong consortium partners in the Japanese aircraft industry was viewed as a handicap for Airbus in signing major contracts. Airbus was thus starting to grant subcontracting work to selected Japanese firms.[56]

The consortium approach is becoming increasingly popular in several technology-intensive industries. Companies in the automobile, computer, and biotechnology industries have formed cooperative agreements to share in the development and exploitation of technology. What is new to this trend is that

52. "GE French Alliance Pays Off: CFMI Will Build Its 10,000th Engine," *Cincinnati Post*, March 10, 1999, p. 5C.
53. "Growing Friction May Thwart MTU," *Aviation Week & Space Technology*, June 28, 1999, p. 68.
54. "Modest Alliance Between Two Pioneers," *Financial Times*, May 4, 1990, p. 21.
55. "GE Rolls Royce, Snecma Reportedly Join Japan Jet Engine Project," *AFX News*, April 19, 1999.
56. "Airbus Plans Based On Asia's Leadership," *Aviation Week & Space Technology*, July 26, 1999, p. 59.

FIGURE 14.4

Rolls-Royce's Main Collaborative Relationships, 1990

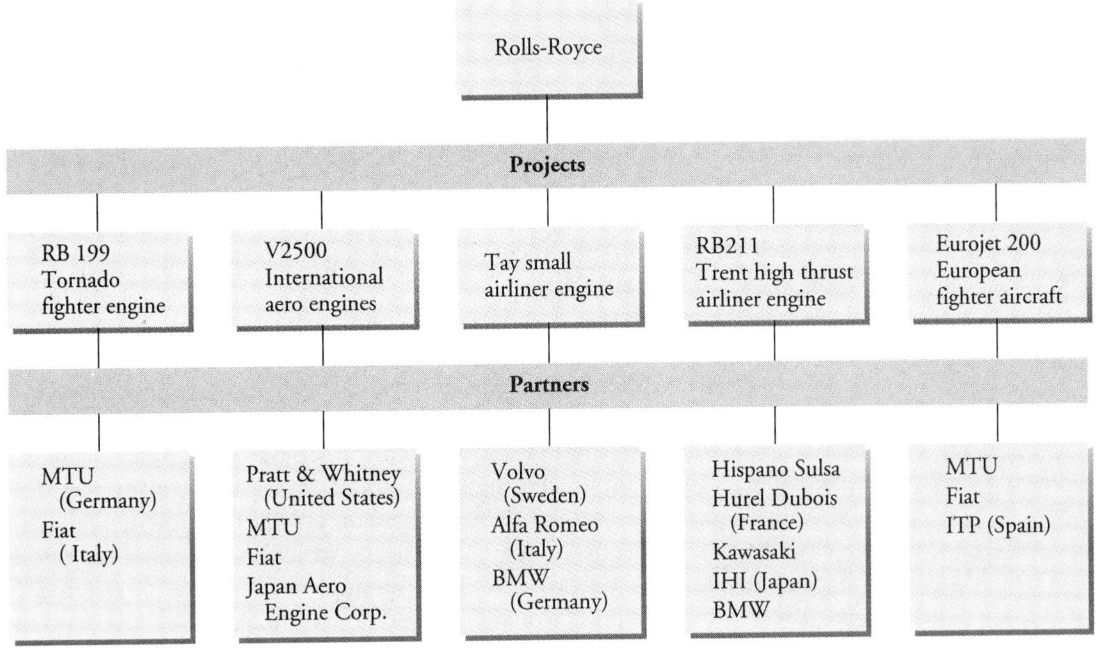

Source: *Financial Times*, May 4, 1990, p. 2. Reprinted by permission.

sometimes competitors will become partners, whereas previously such cooperation was unthinkable.

Globalization of the Product Development Process

The previous section dealt primarily with the sources of product development. To bring about a total integration of the product development process for a multinational enterprise often requires the adoption of new organizational forms and the restructuring of the development process as a whole. The challenge in multinational product development is finding a way to combine domestic and foreign expertise so that truly global products can result.

The global approach to new-product development was described by an executive of Fiat, the Italian car manufacturer, in 1978: "Fifteen years ago we designed cars for the Italian market. Ten years ago we began designing 'European' cars. Now we develop them for the country with the biggest market—the United States—and scale them down for the others."[57] This shift from local to global development requires that the unique or special concerns for major markets be considered from the outset of the process, rather than a company attempting to make various adaptations on the initial model or prototype. This early introduction of global considerations not only ensures that the product will achieve wide acceptance but also aims at maximizing the commonality of models to achieve economies in component manufacturing. A global product, then, is not identical in all countries. Instead, a world product is engineered from the outset with the goal of maximizing the percentage of identical components, design, and parts to the point where local needs can be met with a minimum of additional costs in tooling, engineering, and development.

To globalize their own research, Japanese companies have made heavy investments in U.S.-based research facilities. Hundreds of Japanese scientists already work side by side with Americans in research laboratories on exchange programs. This investment aims at getting access to scientific talent in other countries. Companies chasing such talent around the world are opening development centers where the talent can be found. One such country is China, where many western firms have opened development facilities to obtain access to Chinese scientific talent. Among those firms are Intel and Microsoft, which have opened research centers near Beijing, where many of China's leading universities are clustered.[58] In 1998, Microsoft indicated it would spend some $80 million over six years to expand its new research center, which is to house one hundred employees. One of the main tasks of the lab is to find ways to make software more useful to Chinese computer users.[59]

The research and development process is stimulated by ideas for new products. Global companies must identify sources of new ideas from potential markets. Microsoft sponsored a nationwide contest in Russia to develop a Russian version of Microsoft Windows. Microsoft hopes to generate an attractive product for the Russian market as well as to stimulate product development.[60] In some markets, local competitors may be the best source of product ideas. For example, in India, McDonald's needed to adapt to the Hindu custom of not eating beef. Nirula's, a fast-growing fast-food outlet in India, was offering burgers with lamb and mixed vegetables as an alternative to beef.[61] McDonald's developed the Maharajah Mac, made of lamb, and also offers its only vegetarian menu, for which a sepa-

57. "To a Global Car," *Business Week*, November 20, 1978, p. 102.
58. "China: Back to the Future," *Far Eastern Economic Review*, March 11, 1999, p. 10.
59. "Microsoft Lab in China, *Wall Street Journal*, November 6, 1998.
60. "Microsoft Urges Russian Software Bootleggers: Join Us," *Wall Street Journal*, May 18, 1993, p. B4.
61. "Where Is the Beef?" *Fortune*, January 24, 1994, p. 16.

rate kitchen is used. McDonald's also finds it a challenge to operate in a country where electricity, gas, and filtered fresh water have to be procured at high prices.[62]

To develop a global product also requires a different organizational setup. Changes instituted by General Motors reflect moves made by other international firms. With the advent of world cars, GM realized that the company needed closer coordination between its domestic units and its overseas subsidiaries. It therefore moved its overseas staff from New York to Detroit in order to speed up communication between domestic and international staffs and adopted the "project center" concept to manage its engineering effort. Each division or subsidiary involved in a new car design lends engineers to a centrally organized project center, which designs, develops, and introduces the new model. Upon introduction of the model, the project center is disbanded. Of course, not every firm will find a project center approach feasible. Other alternatives include assigning primary responsibility to a subsidiary with special capability in the new-product field.

Introducing New Products to Global Markets

Once a product has been developed for commercial introduction, a number of complex decisions still need to be made. Aside from the question of whether to introduce the product abroad, the firm has to decide on a desirable test-marketing procedure, select target countries for introduction, and determine the timing or sequence of the introduction. Given the large number of alternatives inherent in numerous possible markets, decisions surrounding new-product introduction often attain strategic significance.

Determining which product to introduce abroad depends of course on sales potential. Following a careful analysis, a marketer develops a list of target countries. A company then can choose from among several paths leading to actual introduction in the target countries.

Concept Tests

Once a prototype or sample product has been developed, a company may decide to subject its new creation to a series of tests to determine commercial feasibility. It is particularly important to subject a new product to actual use conditions. When the development process takes place outside the country of actual use, a practical field test can be crucial. The test must include all necessary usage steps to provide complete information. For example, in testing the U.S. market for dehydrated soups made by its newly acquired Knorr subsidiary, CPC International

62. "McDonald's to Expand Indian Operation," *Economic Times*, November 6, 1998, p. 4.

concentrated primarily on taste tests to ensure that the final product suited U.S. consumers. Extensive testing led to soups different in formulation from those sold in Europe. CPC, however, had neglected to have consumers actually try out the product at home as part of their regular cooking activities. Such a test would have revealed consumers' discontent with the relatively long cooking time—up to twenty minutes, compared to three minutes for comparable canned soups. The company realized these difficulties only after a national introduction had been completed and sales fell short of original expectations.

The concept-testing stage would be incomplete if the products were tested only in the company's domestic market. A full test in several major markets is essential so that any shortcomings can be alleviated at an early stage before costly adaptations for individual countries are made. Such an approach is particularly important in cases in which product development is occurring on a multinational basis, with simultaneous inputs from several foreign subsidiaries. When Volkswagen tested its original Rabbit models, test vehicles were made available to all principal subsidiaries in order to ensure that each market's requirements were met by the otherwise standardized car.

There may be some differences between concept testing for consumer products and concept testing for industrial products. Industrial products tend to be used worldwide for the same purposes under very similar circumstances. Factories using textile machinery are relatively standardized across the world so that a machinery test in one country may be quite adequate for most others. As a result, single-country market testing may be more appropriate for industrial products.

Test Marketing

Just as there are good reasons to test-market a product in a domestic market, an international test can give the firm valuable insights into potential future success. A key question is where the market test should be held. Companies in the United States have largely pioneered test-marketing procedures because it has been possible to isolate a given market in terms of media and distribution. Such market isolation may not always be possible in smaller countries and even less so in countries where most of the media are national rather than local. If a market test were considered in a country with national TV only and if print media were substituted for TV for the purpose of the test, the test would not be a true replication of the actual full-scale introduction. As a result, the opportunities for small local market tests are substantially reduced outside the United States.

To overcome the shortage of test-market possibilities, international firms often substitute the experience in one country for a market test in another. Although market tests were typical for many U.S.-based firms before full-scale introduction in the U.S. market, subsidiaries tended to use these early U.S. results as a basis for analysis. Such a strategy requires that at least one subsidiary of an international firm have actual commercial experience with a product or any given aspect of the marketing strategy before introducing the product elsewhere.

Use of the U.S. market as a test market depends on the market situation and the degree to which results can be extrapolated to other countries. Since circumstances are rarely exactly the same, early U.S. results must be regarded with caution. Also, extrapolation may only be appropriate for other advanced countries in Europe and Asia. See also our explanation of the comparative analytic approach in Chapter 6.

For firms with extensive foreign networks of subsidiaries, market tests can be used beyond the traditional mode. Another approach to test marketing is to use a foreign country as a first introduction and proving ground before other markets are entered. In Europe, smaller markets such as the Netherlands, Belgium, Austria, and Switzerland may be used to launch a new product. Because of their size, a test would include national introduction with results applicable in other countries.

Special attention should be given to the lead market as a potential test market. Any new product that succeeds in its lead market can be judged to have good potential elsewhere as other markets mature.

Timing of New-Product Introductions

Very early in the introduction process, a company will be faced with establishing the timing and sequence of its introduction. Timing determines when a product should be introduced in a foreign market. Sequencing becomes an issue when a firm deals with several countries and must decide on a phased or simultaneous entry approach. Traditionally, firms have introduced new products first in their domestic markets to gain experience in production, marketing, and service. Foreign market introductions are attempted only after a product has proven itself in the domestic market. Research has revealed, however, a steadily shortening time lag between domestic and initial foreign market introduction.[63] From 1945 to 1950, only 5.6 percent of investigated firms introduced new products abroad within one year. By 1975, the percentage had increased to 38.7 percent, and about two-thirds were introduced abroad within five years. This time lag reduction reflects the increased capability by U.S. firms to introduce products abroad rapidly. It also reflects the rapid economic development of many advanced countries, to the point where the United States no longer leads in a number of fields. The average time lag can safely be assumed to continue to decline. Procter & Gamble is one firm that does not believe it can compete with long product introduction times. Having been confronted with an average of five years for global product rollouts, the

63. William H. Davidson and Richard Harrigan, "Key Decisions in International Marketing: Introducing New Products Abroad," *Columbia Journal of World Business*, Winter 1977, p. 15.

company is reducing test marketing in multiple areas to eighteen months, followed by rollout of the product globally in key markets in another eighteen months. P & G's first use of this new timetable was to be with its new Dryel home dry-cleaning kit and Swiffer, a sweeper system.[64]

Some companies are now in a position to introduce products simultaneously in several countries. When Apple revamped its product line in 1990, the launch of the Macintosh Classic line was communicated via television broadcasts to 121 countries in a total campaign costing $45 million worldwide. Previously, Apple had introduced products in the United States first, announcing shipping dates weeks or months later for its other markets. For its new line, most European countries were shipped localized versions of the original product the same week as the selling started in the United States. Japan and other Asian countries were expected to follow within just a few weeks with localized versions.[65] Simultaneous introduction depends on the company's foreign market development stage and its ability to satisfy demand. When the primary function of foreign subsidiaries is the sale of products shipped from one or a small number of central manufacturing centers, simultaneous introduction is possible as long as marketing efforts can be coordinated. This structure is typical for electronics firms. Other companies produce in many markets; thus, the manufacturing function would be strained if simultaneous introduction were attempted.

Increasingly, companies have to invest ever larger amounts for developing new technologies or products. As these investments rise, the time requirement to bring new generations of products on the market has increased, leaving less time for the commercialization of products until patent protections run out or until new competitors come out with similar products. As a result, companies have been forced to move into a rapid introduction of new products, so that we can now often talk of a *global product rollout*. Global rollout was practiced by Gillette with the introduction of its new Sensor and Mach 3 razors, with simultaneous introduction in both Europe and North America.

Country Selection

Although international firms have subsidiaries in numerous countries, initial product introductions have always been limited to the industrialized nations. In one study of forty-four U.S.-based firms, 83.5 percent of first introductions took place in developed countries for the 1945–1976 time period. Leading target countries for the 1965–1975 period were the United Kingdom, Japan, Australia, France, and West Germany.[66]

64. "P&G Puts Two Cleaning Products on Its New Marketing Fast Track," *Wall Street Journal*, May 18, 1999, p. B6.
65. "Fruits of Flexibility," *Financial Times*, October 17, 1990, p. 17.
66. William H. Davidson and Richard Harrigan, "Key Decisions in International Marketing: Introducing New Products Abroad," *Columbia Journal of World Business*, Winter 1977, p. 15.

Other research has shown that some companies use a two-step approach to new-product introduction. At first, products are introduced in the most advanced markets, with developing countries following in a second stage.[67] Many U.S.-based international firms have used their European subsidiaries as stepping stones to Latin America or eastern Europe. One electronics manufacturer transferred an innovation first to its Italian subsidiary; the Italian subsidiary then introduced it in Spain through another subsidiary there. The same company has also used its Dutch subsidiary to transfer innovations to Poland.

The selection of countries for new-product launches is increasingly based on one single test market in possibly one or two countries, with a rapid move toward a global rollout. Most importantly, the test market may not even be the place of initial launch. IBM tested a new branding campaign for its Global Services line in Canada but launched it in the United States. Heinz also tested its new teenager-oriented ketchup campaign in Canada, rolling it out worldwide with minor creative modifications. Testing overseas prior to U.S. launch may even be cheaper but requires a better understanding of how to translate foreign results in likely U.S. market realities. Clearly, global marketing is moving rapidly in a direction where testing and test interpretations will be made on the basis of data from different markets; the time when each local market tested locally before launch is rapidly passing.[68]

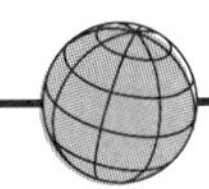

Conclusions

When companies search for new markets for their products, they face the difficult task of adapting those products to new environments. Such adaptations are frequently expensive when done after the fact. In the future, companies will increasingly consider international opportunities early in the development cycle of a new product. Incorporating international requirements and standards early will allow new products to be immediately usable in many markets. Such a move toward internationalization of the product development cycle will result in the development of more global products. These products will be produced in modularized forms to include as many global components as possible, and they will incorporate a set of unique components to fit the product needs of individual markets. The challenge for global marketers is to find the best tradeoffs between the standardized global components of a product and the tailor-made components designed for specific markets.

Another, increasingly influential, factor in new-product development processes is speed. For competitive reasons, companies want to be among the

67. Jeannet, *Transfer of Technology*.
68. "Test It in Paris, France, Launch It in Paris, Texas," *Advertising Age*, May 31, 1999, p. 28.

first to enter with a new product or service because early entrants tend to obtain the biggest market share. To increase speed, companies work on collaborative development processes. Furthermore, they will shrink the time it will take from first domestic introduction until worldwide launch. In the end, many firms will undertake multicountry launches or simultaneous global product rollouts. The risk increases with such global launches because less time is available to test the product, ensure that it meets the market performance needs, and sufficiently tailor it to a given country.

QUESTIONS FOR DISCUSSION

1. Analyze three different products (freezers, compact discs, and contact eye lenses) according to Table 14.1. What general marketing strategy recommendations do you arrive at?
2. What, in your opinion, is the future for global products?
3. How should international firms organize their new-product development efforts today and in the future?
4. What is the impact of a loss of lead market position in several industries for U.S.-based corporations?
5. If you were to test-market a new consumer product today for worldwide introduction, how would you select test countries for Europe, Asia, and Latin America?

FOR FURTHER READING

Afriyie, Koti. "International Technology Transfers." In *Cooperative Strategies in International Business*, ed. Farok Contractor and Peter Lorange. Lexington, Mass.: D. C. Heath, 1987.

Behrman, J. N., and W. A. Fischer. "Transnational Corporation: Market Orientations and R&D Abroad," *Columbia Journal of World Business*, Fall 1980, pp. 55–60.

Cheng, Joseph L. C., and Douglas J. Bolon. "The Management of Multinational R&D: A Neglected Topic in International Business Research," *Journal of International Business Studies*, 1st Quarter 1993, pp. 1–18.

Crawford, Merle C. *New Products Management*. Homewood, Ill.: Irwin, 1983.

Hill, John S., and Richard R. Still. "Cultural Effects of Technology Transfer by Multinational Corporations in Lesser Developed Countries," *Columbia Journal of World Business*, Summer 1980, pp. 40–50.

Kaikati, Jack G. "Domestically Banned Products: For Export Only," *Journal of Public Policy and Marketing*, 1984, vol. 3, pp. 125–133.

Leroy, Georges. *Multinational Product Strategy*. New York: Praeger, 1976.

Mabert, Vincent A., John F. Muth, and Robert W. Schmennor. "Collapsing New Product Development Time," *Journal of Product Innovation Management*, September 1992, pp. 200–212.

Manu, Franklyn A. "Innovation, Orientation, Environment and Performance: A Comparison of U.S. and European Markets," *Journal of International Business Studies*, 2nd Quarter 1992, p. 333.

Ogbuehi, Alphonso O., and Ralph A. Bellis Jr. "Decent Sized R&D for Global Development: Strategic Implications for the Multinational Corporation," *International Marketing Review*, 1992, vol. 19, no. 5, pp. 60–70.

Ohmae, Kenichi. *Triad Power: The Coming Shape of Global Competition*, New York: Free Press, 1985.

Ronstadt, Robert. "The Establishment and Evolution of R&D Abroad," *Journal of International Business Studies*, Spring–Summer 1978, pp. 7–24.

Wind, Yoram, and Vigay Mahajan. "New Product Development Process: A Perspective for Reexamination," *Journal of Product Innovation Management*, 1998, vol. 5, no. 4, pp. 304–310.

15

Managing Global Distribution Channels

Global Marketing Distribution decisions are similar to those in a domestic setting. What differs, of course, are the environmental influences that, in the end, may lead to substantially different policies and channel options. Global marketers need to understand how environmental influences may affect these distribution policies and options. Using this knowledge, they must structure efficient channels for products on a country-by-country basis.

In this chapter we discuss the structure of global distribution systems; the process of developing a distribution strategy; and methods for selecting, locating, and managing channel members (see Figure 15.1). We also explain the issues of gaining access to channels, global supply chain management, and global trends in distribution.

FIGURE 15.1

Global Distribution

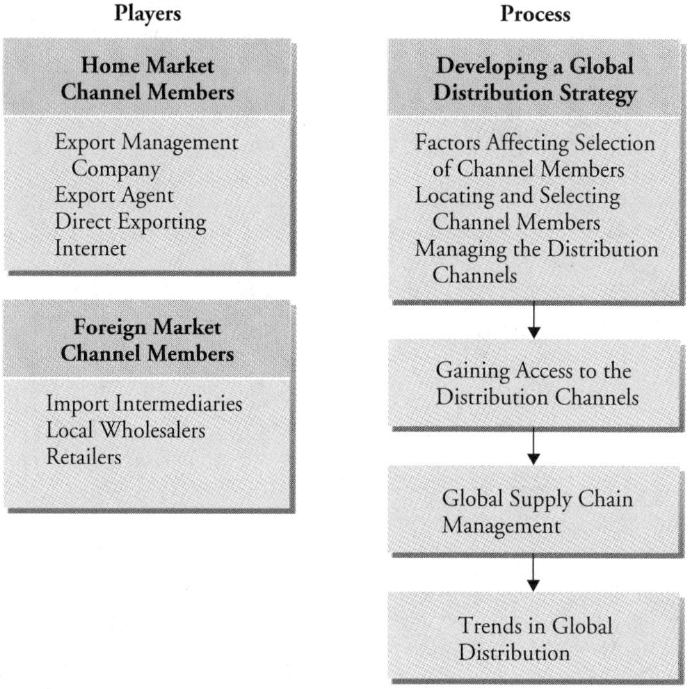

Players

Home Market Channel Members

- Export Management Company
- Export Agent
- Direct Exporting
- Internet

Foreign Market Channel Members

- Import Intermediaries
- Local Wholesalers
- Retailers

Process

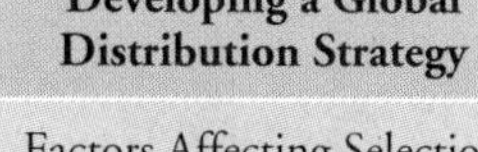

- Factors Affecting Selection of Channel Members
- Locating and Selecting Channel Members
- Managing the Distribution Channels

↓

Gaining Access to the Distribution Channels

↓

Global Supply Chain Management

↓

Trends in Global Distribution

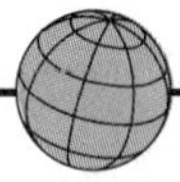

The Structure of the Global Distribution System

The structure of the distribution systems available in a country is affected by the level of economic development, the personal disposable income of consumers, and the quality of the infrastructure, as well as environmental factors such as culture, physical environment, and the legal/political system. Marketers who develop a distribution strategy must decide how to transport the products from the manufacturing locations to the consumer. Although distribution can be handled completely by the manufacturer, often products are moved through intermediaries, such as agents, wholesalers, distributors, and retailers. An understanding of the structure of available distribution systems is extremely important in the development of a strategy. The various global distribution channels available to a manufacturer are shown in Figure 15.2.

There are two major categories of potential channel members: (1) those located in the home country and (2) those located abroad. In the home country, a

FIGURE 15.2

Global Marketing Channel Alternatives

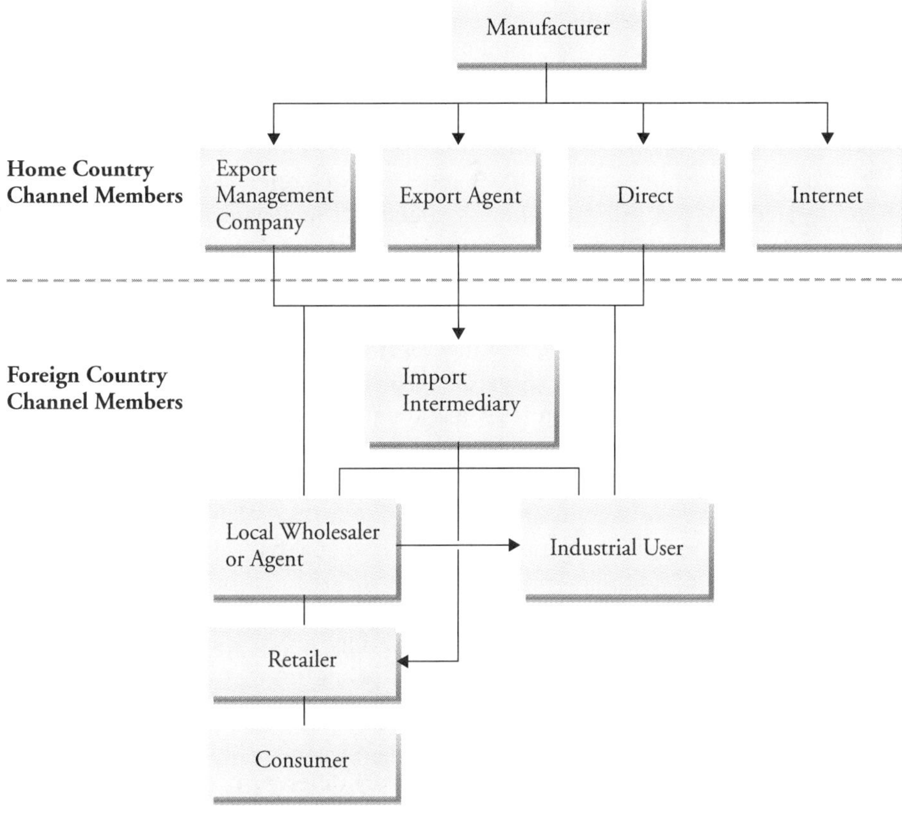

manufacturer can utilize the services of an export management company or an export agent, or it can use company personnel to export products directly. In Chapter 9, we discussed whether or not any of these channel members should be used. In this chapter, our focus is on how to locate, select, use, and manage both home country and foreign channel members.

Home Market Channel Members

Within a manufacturer's home market, a number of different types of export-related channel members can help with the export process. The most common types are export management companies and export agents. Alternatively, a firm can bypass the help of these specialists and use internal company expertise to export or engage in e-commerce.

Export Management Company The export management company (EMC) is a firm that handles all aspects of export operations under a contractual agreement. The EMC will normally take responsibility for the promotion of products, marketing research, credit, physical handling or logistics, patents, and licensing. The population of EMCs in 1994 was estimated to be 1,200 firms, representing some 10,000 manufacturers and accounting for 10 percent of U.S.-manufactured exports.[1] Arrangements between an EMC and a manufacturer will vary, depending on the services offered and the volume expected. The advantages of an EMC are that (1) little or no investment is required to enter the global marketplace, (2) no company personnel are required, and (3) the EMC will have an established network of sales offices and international marketing and distribution knowledge.[2] The main disadvantage is that the manufacturer gives up direct control of the international sales and marketing effort. Also, if the product has a long purchase cycle and requires a large amount of market development and education, the EMC may not expend the necessary effort to penetrate a new market.

Export Agents Export agents are individuals or firms that assist manufacturers in exporting goods. They are similar to EMCs, except that they tend to provide more-limited services and focus on one country or one part of the world. Export agents understand all the requirements for moving goods through the customs process, but they do not provide the marketing skills that an EMC provides; these agents focus more on the sale and handling of goods. The advantage of using an export agent is that the manufacturer does not need to have an export manager to handle all the documentation and shipping tasks. The main disadvantage is the export agent's limited market coverage; to cover different parts of the world, a firm would need the services of numerous export agents.

Direct Exporting Instead of using an EMC or export agent, a firm can export its goods directly, through in-house company personnel or an in-house export department. Because of the complexity of trade regulations, customs documentation, insurance requirements, and worldwide transportation alternatives, people with special training and experience must be hired to handle these tasks. Also, the current or expected volume must be sufficient to support the in-house staff.

Internet In the United States, many smaller manufacturers have been opening up their own web presence. This presence allows foreign clients easier access to

1. Franklin R. Root, *Entry Strategies for International Markets* (Lexington, Mass.: D. C. Heath, 1994), p. 81.
2. "Get Ready, Export Intermediaries Use Internet to Prepare for 21st Century," *Journal of Commerce*, August 19, 1998, p. 5.

smaller firms and tends to mitigate the need to use some form of agent. To enable the web presence to really pay off, the site needs to be constructed in such a way that a foreign buyer can easily access information, obtain order forms, and drop email questions. Experts also recommend that a web site needs to be marketed appropriately to search engines so that it shows up well placed under certain key search words. Although a web presence goes a long way toward reaching and communicating with foreign markets, the export-willing manufacturer still needs to deal with the entire logistics area and credit information. For logistics, companies such as FedEx, UPS, and Emery provide considerable online help, which is of great use to smaller companies without that particular expertise.[3]

Foreign Market Channel Members

As shown in Figure 15.2, once products have left the home market, there are a variety of channel alternatives in the global marketplace: import intermediaries, local wholesalers or agents, and retailers. Even with local manufacturing, the company will still need to get its products from the factory to the consumers.

Import Intermediaries Import intermediaries identify needs in their local market and find products from the world market to satisfy these needs. They will normally purchase goods in their own name and act independently of the manufacturers. As independents, these channel members use their own marketing strategies and keep in close contact with the markets they serve. A manufacturer desiring distribution in an independent intermediary's market area should investigate this channel partner as one of the ways to get its product to wholesalers and retailers in that area.

Local Wholesalers or Agents In each country, there will be a series of possible channel members who move manufacturers' products to retailers, industrial firms, or in some cases other wholesalers. Local wholesalers will take title to the products, whereas local agents will not take title. Local wholesalers are also called distributors or dealers. In many cases, the local wholesaler has exclusive distribution rights for a specific geographic area or country.

The structure of wholesale distribution varies greatly from country to country. The number of wholesalers and the number of retailers per wholesaler vary according to the distribution structure and wholesale pattern of the country. For example, although Denmark and Portugal have approximately the same number of wholesalers, the Denmark wholesaler will indirectly serve 1.3 retailers, whereas in Portugal a wholesaler will serve 5.5 retailers.[4] Wholesale channels in Japan are very complex, with most products moving through as many as six intermediaries.

3. Ibid.
4. *Retailing in the European Single Market 1993*, Table EUR1a.

This lengthy distribution channel causes Japan to have elevated prices—$20 for a bottle of aspirin, or $72 for a package of golf balls costing $26.80 in U.S. stores.[5]

The functions of wholesalers can vary by country. In some countries, wholesalers provide a warehouse function, taking orders from retailers and shipping them appropriate quantities. Wholesalers in Japan provide the basic wholesale functions but also share risk with retailers by providing financing, product development, and even occasional managerial and marketing skills.[6]

Retailers Retailers, the final members of the consumer distribution channel, purchase products for resale to consumers. The size and accessibility of retail channels vary greatly by country. In 1997, the population per retailer in Europe varied from a low of only 48 people per retailer in Poland to 564 people in Russia.[7] Japan has a large number of retailers, with 13 per 1,000 inhabitants, versus 6 in Europe or the United States. For example, in Japan, Shiseido, a maker of cosmetics, has 25,000 outlets selling only their products, and Matsushita has 19,000 electrical appliance stores.[8] Until recently, all retailing in China was through state-owned stores. However, since China's economic liberalization, the number of retail outlets has grown from 1.4 million in 1980 to 10 million in 1996. The ratio of state-owned to private or collective-owned stores has gone from 92:8 percent to 40:60 percent.[9] The global marketer must evaluate the available retailers in a country and develop a strategy around the existing structure.

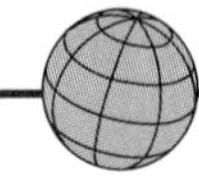

Developing a Global Distribution Strategy

The environmental forces of culture, physical environment, and the legal/political system, combined with the unique structure of wholesale and retail distribution systems, complicate the development of a global distribution strategy. A distribution strategy is one part of the marketing mix, and it needs to be consistent with other aspects of the marketing strategy: product policies, pricing strategy, and communications strategy (see Figure 15.3).

Within the structure of the marketing mix, the global marketer makes distribution decisions about each of the following variables:

1. *Distribution density*. Density refers to the amount of exposure or coverage desired for a product, particularly the number of sales outlets required to provide for adequate coverage of the entire market.

5. "Revolution in Japanese Retailing," *Fortune*, February 7, 1994, pp. 143, 146.
6. "Why Japanese Shoppers Are Lost in a Maze," *Economist*, January 31, 1987, p. 62.
7. *European Marketing Data and Statistics*, 32nd ed. (Euromonitor Publications, 1997), Table 1203.
8. "Marketing in Japan—Taking Aim," *Economist*, April 24, 1993, p. 74.
9. *International Marketing Data & Statistics, Euromonitor Publications*, 1996, Table 1201.

2. *Channel length*. The concept of channel length involves the number of intermediaries involved in bringing a given product to the market.
3. *Channel alignment and leadership*. The area of alignment deals with the structure of the chosen channel members to achieve a unified strategy.
4. *Distribution logistics*. Logistics involves the physical flow of products as they move through the channel.

These four decision areas cannot be approached independently. The decisions are interrelated, and they need to be consistent with other aspects of the marketing strategy. Although it is important to evaluate the distribution strategy logically, marketing managers often must work with an international distribution structure held over from previous managers. That existing system may limit the flexibility of a company to change and grow; nevertheless, a creative marketer can usually find opportunities for circumventing the current arrangement.

FIGURE 15.3

Distribution Strategy

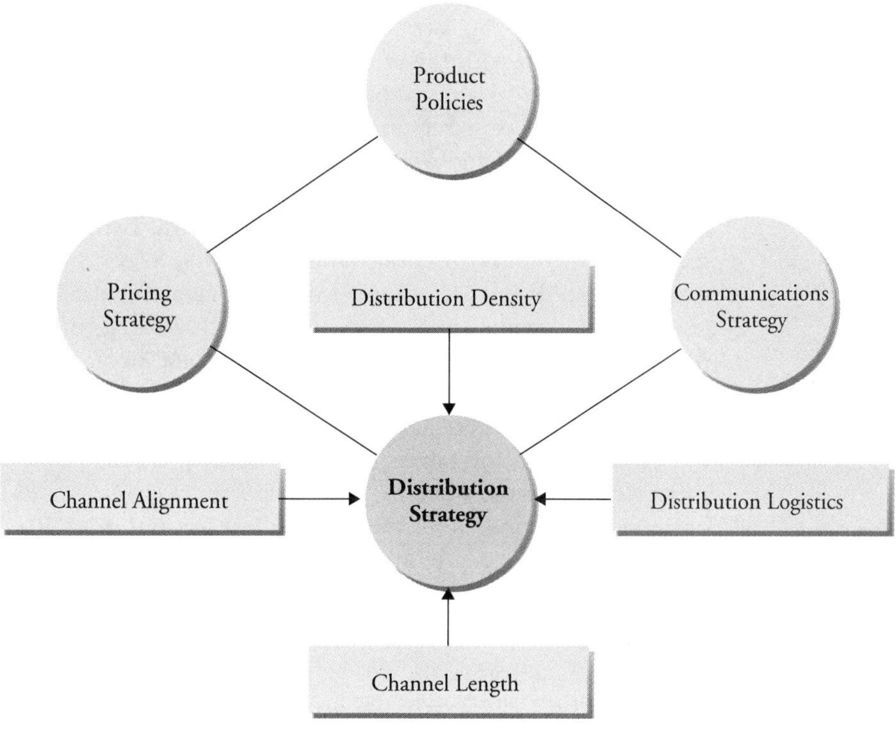

For example, Nordica of Italy had been selling in Japan since 1960. In 1985, the company decided it needed to change its distribution system from its exclusive distributor, Daiwa Sports. Nordica reached a financial agreement with Daiwa Sports and hired the eighty-five employees who had been handling its line. These employees made up most of Nordica Japan, the company-owned sales organization in Japan, which had been very successful.[10] The following sections deal primarily with a company's distribution policies, dependence on distribution-specific variables, and its relationship to the other elements of the marketing strategy.

Distribution Density

The number of sales outlets or distribution points required for the efficient marketing of a firm's products is referred to as the *density of distribution*. The density is dependent on the shopping or buying habits of the average customer. An optimum distribution network requires the marketer to examine how customers select dealers and retail outlets by segment.[11] For consumer goods, an *extensive*, or wide, distribution is required if the consumer is not likely to exert much shopping effort. Such products, also called convenience goods, are bought frequently and in nearby outlets. Other products, such as appliances or clothing, are shopped for by visiting two or more stores; these require a more limited, or *selective*, distribution, with fewer outlets per market area. For products that inspire consumer loyalty to specific brands, called specialty goods, a very limited, or *exclusive*, distribution is required. It is assumed that the customer will search for the desired product and will not accept substitutes.

The key to distribution density, then, is the consumer's shopping behavior, the effort expended to locate a desired item. This behavior, however, may vary greatly from country to country. In the United States, for example, where per capita income is high, consumers shop for many regular-use items in supermarkets and other widely accessible outlets, such as drugstores. In other countries, particularly some with a much lower per capita income, the purchase of such items is likely to be a less routine affair, causing consumers to exert more effort to locate such items. This allows a less extensive distribution of products. It is therefore necessary for the international marketer to assess the shopping behavior of various countries' consumers. Yaohan, a large Japanese retailer, planned to open one thousand stores in China by 2005 but has put growth plans on hold as it seems most shoppers are only window shopping. Although China has 1.2 billion potential customers, only 120 million urban Chinese have sufficient income (over

10. "Nordica and Salomon Put the Boots In," *Financial Times*, August 30, 1990, p. 12.
11. Allan J. Magrath and Kenneth G. Hardy, "How Much Distribution Coverage Is Enough?" *Business Horizons*, June 1989, p. 20.

$1,000/year) to afford the packaged soap or prepared foods on Yaohan's shelves.[12] Where consumers buy certain products also varies a great deal from country to country. In Germany, contact lens solution is found only in stores that sell eyeglasses, but in France it is also found in most drugstores. Although magazines are sold in many grocery stores in the United States, in the United Kingdom they are sold almost exclusively through news agents. It is important for marketers to find out where consumers buy the types of products the firm plans to market early in the distribution analysis.

Retailing is exploding in many parts of Asia, where a large portion of the population is crossing the income threshold at which they start to buy entirely new categories of goods, such as packaged foods, televisions, or mopeds. This phenomenon, called "magic moments," has hit Taiwan, Indonesia, Thailand, Malaysia, and China. When a country crosses the magic-moments threshold, distribution systems start to improve with modern stores. Hero Supermarkets, the local leader in Indonesia, increased sales by 18 percent in the first half of 1993. Led by the Japanese, retailers around the world are moving into Asia to acquire premium locations and take advantage of a fast-growing market.[13] Ito-Yokado, which owns 7-Eleven, has been very successful. In 1997, with ten thousand outlets and 15 percent of the convenience-store market in Japan, 7-Eleven outsold the next largest convenience retail store chain by 37 percent on a revenue-per-store basis.[14]

In the industrial sector, differences in buyer behavior or in the use of a particular product may require changes in distribution density. Since industrial products applications are more uniform around the world as a result of similar customer needs and use conditions, what constitutes capital equipment in one country typically is also classified as capital equipment in another. Differences may exist, however, among the decision makers. In the United States, for instance, radiology supply products are sold directly to hospitals and radiology departments through hospital supply distributors. However, in France, patients must pick up radiology supplies by prescription from a pharmacy before visiting the radiology department at the hospital. In this latter case, radiology supplies have to be presold to physicians and stocked with pharmacies to be successful. This is the same strategy pursued by pharmaceutical firms. Of course, when selling to both physicians and pharmacies, the necessary distribution in France is much more extensive than it is in the United States, where only hospitals are channel members.[15]

12. "Window Shopping in Shanghai," *Economist*, January 25, 1997, p. 62.
13. "Asian Retailing: Teach Me Shopping," *Economist*, December 18, 1994, p. 64.
14. "Japanese Retailing: A Matter of Convenience," *Economist*, January 25, 1997, p. 62.
15. Warren J. Keegan, *Multinational Marketing Management* (Englewood Cliffs, N.J.: Prentice Hall, 1989), p. 175.

Channel Length

The number of intermediaries directly involved in the physical or ownership path of a product from the manufacturer to the customer is indicative of the channel length. Long channels have several intermediaries, whereas short or direct channels have few or no intermediaries. Channel length is usually influenced by three factors: (1) a product's distribution density, (2) the average order quantities, and (3) the availability of channel members. Products with extensive distribution, or large numbers of final sales points, tend to have longer channels of distribution. Similarly, as the average order quantity decreases, products move through longer channels to add to the distribution efficiency.

Since distribution density does affect channel length, it is clear that the same factors that influence distribution density influence channel length—namely, the shopping behaviors of consumers. The average order quantity often depends on the purchasing power or income level of a given customer group. In countries with lower income levels, people often buy food on a daily basis at nearby small stores. This contrasts sharply with more affluent consumers, who can afford to buy food or staples for one week or even a month and who don't mind traveling some distance to do this more infrequent type of shopping. In the first case, a longer channel is required, whereas a shorter channel is adequate in the latter case. The type of distributors available in a country affects the channel length. Also, the culture may demand a specific type of channel member.

Channel length does have important cost considerations. Salomon of France originally entered the Japanese ski equipment market with the giant Mitsui trading company. Mitsui insisted on taking delivery of goods through its Paris subsidiary, then transferring them to wholesalers and then to retailers. This long channel resulted in Salomon bindings being very expensive in Japan. By the time all the intermediaries took their cut, little was left for the manufacturer. As the company entered the ski boot business in 1980, it set up its own sales company that sold directly to a new breed of sport shops. In 1982, Mitsui did not renew the distribution contract on Salomon bindings.[16]

Japan is known for its lengthy, complex channels, which increase the cost of goods to consumers. Seiko Epson bypassed Japanese channel members and began a direct sales effort to sell its NEC and IBM-compatible PCs. Following the lead of Dell Computer, Seiko Epson hoped to attract consumers by offering significant savings through its direct marketing effort.[17] Delta Computer, a local Japanese company, also did very well with a direct sales approach in Japan, moving into second place overall behind Compaq and beating larger rivals such as IBM and NEC.[18]

16. "Nordica and Salomon Put the Boots In."
17. "Seiko Epson Clones Strategy of U.S. Rival," *Nikkei Weekly*, January 17, 1994, p. 8.
18. "Global PC Shipments Rise 9.5 percent in 1998," *The Yomuri Shimbun/Daily Yomuri*, January 14, 1999.

Korean automaker Daewoo decided to sell directly to consumers rather than go through traditional dealers. It equipped its sales outlets with a multimedia touch-screen kiosk that allows consumers to "build" the car they want on the screen. This approach has positioned Daewoo as a manufacturer/dealer offering a hassle-free car buying experience. In the United Kingdom, Daewoo representatives took cars directly to consumers' homes and did the entire transaction in the customer's living room on a laptop computer.[19]

Channel Alignment

One of the most difficult tasks of marketing is to get various channel members to coordinate their actions so that a unified approach can be achieved. The longer the channel, the more difficult it becomes to maintain a coordinated and integrated approach. On a global level, the coordinating task is made all the more difficult because the company organizing the channel may be removed by large distances from the distribution system, with little influence over the local scene. In each country, the strongest channel member will be able to dictate policies to the other channel members, though situations will vary by country. The international company will find it much easier to control the distribution channel if a local subsidiary with a strong sales force exists. In countries where the company has no local presence and depends on independent distributors, control is likely to slip to the independent distributor. This loss of control may be further aggravated if the international company's sales volume represents only a small fraction of the local distributor's business. Of course, the opposite will be true when a high percentage of the volume consists of the international corporation's products.

To achieve maximum efficiency in a channel of distribution, one participant must emerge as the channel captain, or dominating member. Differences exist among countries as to who typically emerges as the dominating member. In the United States, for example, the once-strong wholesalers have become less influential, with manufacturers now playing the dominant role in some channels. More and more in the United States, large retailers like Home Depot or Wal-Mart have become channel captains. In Japan, on the other hand, wholesalers continue to dominate the channel structure. In many developing countries, independent distributors are very strong because they are the only authorized importers.

Some companies find it necessary to acquire the channel captain in order to further grow a market. For example, in 1994, Nike acquired Nissho Iwai Corp., the Japanese trading house that had been distributing Nike products in Japan. Nike felt that acquiring its Japanese distributor and converting Nissho Iwai to a

19. "Ding-Dong, It's Seat Calling," *The Age*, July 30, 1998, p. 9.

wholly owned subsidiary would give Nike the increased control and expertise to further penetrate the Japanese market.[20]

A different approach was chosen by Caterpillar, the large U.S. manufacturer of earthmoving equipment, for its entry into Japan. At first, the company's joint venture partner, Mitsubishi, suggested marketing equipment through existing channels. (In Japan, the manufacturers sell through large trading houses that resell and provide financing to dealers. The dealers are relatively small and leave parts inventory and service to independent repair shops.) Caterpillar preferred to market its equipment through large, independent dealers that not only sold but also serviced the equipment and maintained a sufficient parts inventory. Caterpillar recognized that its distribution strategy was a critical global strength difficult for competitors to match, so it invested heavily in building and training its dealers. Thus, Caterpillar successfully implemented its traditional strategy in Japan and emerged as one of the leading earthmoving equipment manufacturers in Japan.[21]

Distribution Logistics

Distribution logistics focuses on the physical movement of goods through the channels. An extremely important part of the distribution system, logistics is discussed in detail later in this chapter (see "Global Supply Chain Management") and in Chapter 18.

Factors Influencing the Selection of Channel Members

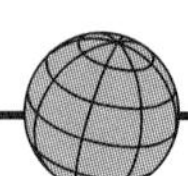

After developing a distribution strategy, a marketer then needs to identify and select appropriate distribution partners to support the overall distribution strategy. This selection of distribution partners is an extremely important decision because often the partner will assume a portion of or the entire marketing responsibility for a set of markets. The distribution partner decision is one of the most important elements of the entry strategy. A poor decision will often lead to lackluster performance. Because of local laws, it is often expensive or sometimes impossible to change a distribution partner. For example, in 1992, PepsiCo went through a year-long court battle to terminate its twenty-two-year contract with Perrier to bottle and distribute Pepsi in France. PepsiCo contended that Perrier had underperformed and had let Pepsi-Cola's share decline from 17 percent to 7 percent over the previous ten years.[22] Also, the distribution partner usually is involved in

20. "Nike 'Just Does it' Alone with Buyout of Japan Partner," *Nikkei Weekly*, January 17, 1994, p. 10.
21. S. Tamer Cavusgil, "The Importance of Distributor Training at Caterpillar," *Industrial Marketing Management*, 1990, vol. 19, pp. 1–9.
22. "Pepsi Wins Its Battle with Perrier over Marketing, *Financial Times*, December 18, 1992, p. 18.

the physical movement (logistics) of products to the customers. Therefore, the success of a firm's international efforts depends on the partners it selects. A number of factors influence the selection of distribution partners. Those that have significant effect are

1. Cost
2. Capital requirement
3. Product and product line
4. Control
5. Coverage
6. Synergy

Cost

Channel costs fall into three categories: initial costs, maintenance costs, and logistics costs. The *initial costs* include all the costs of locating and setting up the channel, such as executive time and travel to locate and select channel members, cost of negotiating an agreement with channel members, and the capital cost of setting up the channel. The capital cost is discussed separately in the next segment of this chapter. The *maintenance costs* of the channel include the cost of the company's salespeople, sales managers, travel expenses, and the cost of auditing and controlling channel operations, local advertising expenses, and the profit margin of the intermediaries. The *logistical costs* comprise the transportation expenses, storage costs, the cost of breaking bulk shipments into smaller lot sizes, and the cost for customs paperwork.

Although predicting all of these various costs when selecting different channel members is often difficult, it is necessary to estimate the cost of various alternatives. High distribution costs usually result in higher prices at the consumer level, which may hamper entry into a new market. Companies often will establish direct channels, hoping to reduce distribution cost. Unfortunately, most of the functions of the channel cannot be eliminated, so these costs eventually show up anyway. A study of five different international channels of distribution found that the least profitable is exporting directly to the retailers in the host country. The most profitable channel is selling to a distributor in a country that has its own marketing channels.[23]

Capital Requirement

The capital cost of different channel alternatives can be very high. The capital cost includes the cost for inventories, the cost of goods in transit, accounts receivable, and inventories on consignment. The capital cost is offset by the cash-flow patterns from a channel alternative. For example, an import distributor will

23. Warren J. Bilkey, "Variables Associated with Export Profitability," paper presented at the 1980 Academy of International Business Conference, New Orleans, October 23, 1980.

often pay for the goods when they are received, before they are sold to the retailer or industrial firm. On the other hand, an agent may not receive payment until the goods reach the industrial customer or retailer. This is also true of direct sales efforts. The establishment of a direct sales channel often requires the maximum investment, whereas use of distributors often reduces the investment required. The capital cost of various distribution channels affects the company's return on investment. In the early stages of the life cycle of organizations (see Chapter 16), companies often export through a distributor or agent because they cannot afford the capital cost of setting up a direct sales effort.

Product and Product Line

The nature of a product can affect channel selection. If the product is perishable or has a short shelf life, then the manufacturer is forced to use shorter channels to get the product to the consumer faster. Delta Dairy, a Greek producer of dairy products and chilled fruit juices, was faced with increased transportation costs of shipping from Greece to France when the United Nations banned transit across the former Yugoslavia. In addition to a 25 percent increase in production costs, Delta lost five days of product shelf life, so it set up production in Switzerland to shorten the distance to the French market.[24]

A technical product often requires direct sales or highly technical channel partners. For example, Index Technology of Cambridge, Massachusetts, sells a sophisticated software product, called computer-aided systems engineering, which automates the development of software systems. The company entered the United Kingdom and Australia with a direct sales effort, but to avoid start-up costs it used distributors in France, Germany, and Scandinavia. Insufficient revenues from distributors led the company to set up its own sales efforts in France and Germany and to purchase the distributor in Scandinavia. The highly sophisticated nature of the product required a direct sales effort. Nonperishable or generic, unsophisticated products, such as batteries, that are available in many types of retail stores may be distributed through a long channel that reaches many different types of retailers.

The size of the product line also affects selection of channel members. A broader product line is more desirable for channel members. A distributor or dealer is more likely to stock a broad product line than a single item. Limited product lines often must be sold through agents. If a manufacturer has a very broad, complete line, it is easier to justify the cost of a more direct channel. With more products to sell, it is easier to generate a high average order on each sales call. With a limited product line, an agent or distributor will group one firm's

24. "Delta Dairy Streamlined Food Producer," *Financial Times*, July 8, 1993, p. 11.

products together with products from other companies to increase the average order size.

Control

Each type of channel arrangement offers a different level of control by the manufacturer. With a direct sales force, a manufacturer can control price, promotion, amount of effort, and type of retail outlet used. If these are important, the increased level of control may offset the increased cost of a direct sales force. Longer channels, particularly with distributors who take title to goods, often result in little or no control. In many cases, a company may not know who is ultimately buying the product.

Limited control is not necessarily bad, however. If the volume of sales is adequate, the manufacturer may not necessarily care where the product is being used. Also, a manufacturer can increase its level of market knowledge, its influence on channel members, and its channel control by increasing its presence in the market. For example, the manager of international sales and marketing may be located in Europe and spend all of his or her time traveling with distributor salespeople.

Coverage

Coverage refers to the geographic coverage that a manufacturer desires. Though coverage is usually easy to get in major metropolitan areas, gaining adequate coverage in smaller cities or sparsely populated areas can be difficult. Selection of one channel member over another may be influenced by the respective market coverage. To determine an agent's, broker's, or distributor's coverage, the following must be determined: (1) location of sales offices, (2) salesperson's home base, and (3) previous year's sales by geographic location. The location of sales offices indicates where efforts are focused. Salespeople generally have the best penetration near their homes. Past sales clearly indicate the channel member's success in each geographic area.

Synergy

The choice of channel members or partners can sometimes be influenced by the existence of complementary skills that can increase the total output of the distribution system. This normally occurs where the potential distributor partner has some skill or expertise that will allow quicker access to the market. For example, when Compaq entered the international personal computer market, it decided to sell only through a network of strong authorized dealers. While Compaq focused on developing market applications such as sales force automation, computer-aided design, and office productivity, it used the dealers to penetrate the marketplace. Compaq's international sales grew from $20 million in 1984 to $5 billion in 1996 through the combination of marketing and technical expertise from Compaq and sales and implementation expertise from the authorized dealers.

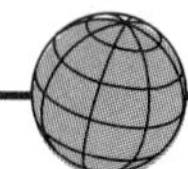

Locating and Selecting Global Channel Partners

Building a global distribution system normally takes one to three years. The process involves a series of steps that are shown in Table 15.1. The critical aspect of developing a successful system is locating and selecting channel partners.

The development of a global distribution strategy in terms of distribution density, channel length, channel alignment, and distribution logistics will establish a framework for the "ideal" distribution partners. The company's preference regarding key factors that influence selection of channel partners (cost, capital requirements, product, control, coverage, and synergy) will be used with the distribution strategy to establish criteria for the selection of partners. The strategy normally focuses the selection on one or two types of channel partners—for example, export manager's company and import distributors.

Selection criteria include geographic coverage, managerial ability, financial stability, annual volume, reputation, and so on. The following sources are useful in locating possible distribution partners:

1. *U.S. Department of Commerce.* The Agent Distributor Service is a customized service of the Department of Commerce that locates distributors and agents in-

TABLE 15.1

Process of Establishing a Global Distribution System

1. Develop a distribution strategy
2. Establish criteria for selecting distribution partners
3. Locate potential distribution partners
4. Solicit the interest of distributors
5. Screen and select distribution partners
6. Negotiate agreements

terested in a certain product line. Also, the department's Export Marketing Service can be used to locate distribution partners.

2. *Banks*. If the firm's bank has foreign branches, they may be happy to help locate distributors.
3. *Directories*. Country directories of distributors or specialized directories, such as those listing computer distributors, can be helpful.
4. *Trade shows*. Exhibiting at an international trade show, or just attending, exposes managers to a large number of distributors and their salespeople.
5. *Competitor's distribution partners*. Sometimes a competitor's distributor may be interested in switching product lines.
6. *Consultants*. Some international marketing consultants specialize in locating distributors.
7. *Associations*. There are associations of international intermediaries or country associations of intermediaries; for example, Japan has numerous industry associations.
8. *Foreign consulates*. Most countries post commercial attachés at their embassies or at separate consulates; these individuals are helpful in locating agents/distributors in their country.

After compiling a list of possible distribution partners, the firm may send each a letter with product literature and distribution requirements. The prospective distributors who have an interest in the firm's product line can be asked to supply relevant information, such as lines currently carried, annual volume, number of salespeople, geographic territory covered, credit and bank references, physical facilities, relationship with local government, and knowledge of English or other relevant languages. Firms that respond should be checked against the selection criteria. Before making a final decision, a manufacturer's representative should go to the country and talk to the industrial end users or retailers to narrow the field to the strongest two or three contenders. While in the country, the manufacturer's representative should meet and evaluate the distribution partner candidates before making a final decision.

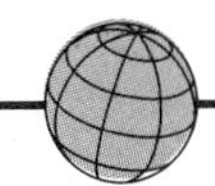

Managing Global Distribution

Selecting the most suitable channel participants and gaining access to the market are extremely important steps in achieving an integrated and responsive distribution channel. However, without proper motivation of and control over channel participants, sales may remain unsatisfactory to the foreign marketer.

This section discusses the steps that must be taken to ensure the flow of the firm's products through the channel by gaining the full cooperation of all channel members.

Motivating Channel Participants

Keeping channel participants motivated is an important aspect of global distribution policies. Financial incentives in the form of higher than average gross margins can be a very powerful inducement, particularly for the management of independent distributors, wholesalers, and retailers. The expected gross margins are influenced by the cultural history of that channel. For example, if a certain type of retailer usually gets a 50 percent margin and the firm offers 40 percent, the effort may be less than expected. Inviting channel members to annual conferences and introductions of new products is also effective. By extending help to the management of distributorships in areas such as inventory control, collections, advertising, and so on, goodwill can be gained that later will be of advantage to the international firm. Special programs may also be instituted to train or motivate the channel members' sales forces.

Programs to motivate foreign independent intermediaries are likely to succeed if monetary incentives are considered along with efforts that help make the channel members more efficient and competitive. To have prosperous intermediaries is, of course, also in the interest of the international firm. These programs or policies are particularly important in the case of independents who distribute products on a nonexclusive basis. Often they are beleaguered by the principals of other products they carry; each is attempting to get the greatest possible attention from the distributor for its own purposes. Therefore, the international firm must have policies that make sure the channel members devote sufficient effort to its products.

The motivation of channel partners and the amount of effort devoted to the firm's product line are enhanced by a continuous flow of two-way information between manufacturer and distributor. The amount of effort an international firm needs to expend depends on the marketing strategy for that market. For example, if the firm is using extensive advertising to pull products through a channel, the intermediary may be expected only to take orders and deliver the product with no real sales effort. If the marketing strategy depends on the channel member's developing the market or pushing the product through the channel, then a significant sales effort will be required. As much as possible, the manufacturer should send letters, public relations releases, product news, and so on to encourage attention to its product line and reduce conflict. More intense contact between the export manufacturer and the distributor is expected to resulted in better performance by the distributor.

In addition to telephone and mail communication, periodic visits to distribution partners can have a positive effect on their motivation and control. Visits can provide other benefits as well. By visiting the distribution partner, the firm can resolve any difficulties. Also, sales volumes can be reviewed and emphasis placed on the most important products or types of customers. Often it is helpful to travel with a channel member salesperson to gain knowledge of the marketplace and to evaluate the skills of the salesperson. The most important benefit of a visit to the channel member is that it gives a clear message that the member's performance is important to the firm. Visits strengthen the personal relationship between the manufacturer and the channel member.

During these personal visits, the manufacturer can identify other ways to help and support the channel member. Strong advertising support through either national advertising or cooperative advertising can help strengthen the manufacturer's consumer franchise. Effective advertising makes it easier for the channel member to sell the manufacturer's products, which leads to increased sales and often more attention devoted to the product line.

Beware of strategies that cause conflict between manufacturers and channel members. The most common causes of channel conflict are (1) bypassing channels to sell directly to large customers, (2) oversaturating a market with too many dealers/distributors, (3) establishing too many levels in the distribution system (that is, requiring smaller distributors to buy from large ones), and (4) opening new discount channels that offer the same goods at lower prices.[25] Research has shown that efforts by manufacturers to train and educate dealers in developing countries lead to increased revenue.[26] Caterpillar has faced the strong Japanese competitor Komatsu in the earthmoving equipment world market. Caterpillar found that dealer training could develop a strong competitive advantage difficult for Komatsu to copy. In fact, during the pilot of the dealer sales training program, participating dealers increased revenue by 102 percent.[27]

Controlling Channel Participants

Although motivated intermediaries will expend the necessary effort on an international company's products, there is generally no assurance that these efforts will be channeled in the right direction. Therefore, the company will want to exert enough control over channel members to help guarantee that they interpret and execute the company's marketing strategies. The firm wants to be sure that the local intermediaries price the products according to the company's policies. The same could be said for sales, advertising, and service policies. Since the company's

25. Allan J. Magrath and Kenneth G. Hardy, "Avoiding the Pitfalls in Managing Distribution Channels," *Business Horizons*, September–October 1987, p. 31.
26. Gary L. Frazier, James D. Gill, and Sudhir H. Hale, "Dealer Dependence Levels and Reciprocal Actions in a Channel of Distribution in a Developing Country," *Journal of Marketing*, January 1989, pp. 50–69.
27. Cavusgil, "Importance of Distributor Training," p. 5.

reputation in a local market can be tarnished when independent intermediaries handle local distribution ineffectively or inefficiently, international companies closely monitor the performance of local channel members. After the takeover of United Distillers by Guinness, the company reorganized to become a worldwide marketer of high-quality branded alcoholic drinks. In 1986, 75 percent of United Distillers' volume was sold through 1,304 distributors; the company had very little control over the distribution. By 1990, the number of distributors was reduced to 470, and through acquisition or joint ventures, United Distillers had gained direct control over 80 percent of its distribution.[28] In Japan, in 1998, the company further consolidated its distributors to one, closing one unit and moving the business into a joint venture that had been set up in 1987 with the equity participation of Moet of France and Jardine of Hong Kong.[29]

One way to exert influence over international channel members is to spell out the specific responsibilities of each, including minimum annual sales, in the distribution agreement. Attainment of the sales goal can be required for renewal of the contract. Also, the awarding of exclusive distribution rights can be used to increase control. Typically, business is channeled through one intermediary in a given geographic area only, raising the firm's importance to the intermediary.

Frequently, exclusive rights are coupled with a prohibition against carrying directly competing products. When the small British company Filofax (maker of binders containing customized inserts such as calendars and diaries) entered the Japanese market in 1984, it decided to use Apex Inc. as its exclusive distributor. The exclusive distributorship gave Apex the incentive to push Filofax and was successful in getting the product into three hundred outlets, including sixty in Tokyo, supported by heavy advertising showing Diane Keaton and Steven Spielberg using their Filofaxes. Although there were thirty makers of imitation products, Filofax sold at a 50 percent price premium, with high-quality packaging and a leather binder. The relationship became very profitable for both Filofax and Apex.[30] The exclusive distributor's leverage is knowledge and expertise in the market. The leverage of the manufacturer is the patent on the product, the brand name, and possible economies of scale. Of course, the exclusive distributor can become too powerful and even evolve from a collaborator into a competitor. Many international companies limit the distribution rights to short time periods with periodic renewal. Caution is advised, however, since cancellation of distribution rights is frequently subject to local laws that prohibit a sudden termination.

Although termination of a distributor or agent for nonperformance is a relatively simple action in the United States, termination of international channel members can be very costly in many parts of the world. In some countries, the termination of an agent may cost a multiple of the annual gross profits plus the

28. "Re-shaping United Distillers," *Financial Times*, June 13, 1990, p. 12.
29. "UK Distillers to Unify Japan Whiskey Sales," *Dow Jones International News*, January 19, 1998.
30. "Organized, but Not Personally," *Economist*, November 12, 1988, pp. 82–83.

value of the agent's investment, plus all kinds of additional payments. In other countries, termination compensation for agents and distributors can include the value of any goodwill plus expenses in developing the business plus the amount of compensation claimed by discharged employees who worked on the product line. The minimum termination notices are frequently inforced. As a result, termination of a channel member can be a costly, painful process governed in almost all cases by local laws that tend to protect and compensate the channel member. Nissan of Japan was involved in a legal battle with its exclusive U.K. distributorship of twenty-one years when the company sent a fax to terminate the agreement at the end of 1990 and opened its own dealerships. Nissan-U.K., owned by a British entrepreneur, oversaw a network of four hundred Nissan dealers who sold 138,000 cars in the United Kingdom in 1989.[31]

Gaining Access to Distribution Channels

To actually gain access to distribution channels may well be the most formidable challenge in global marketing. Decisions on product designs, communications strategies, and pricing can be very complex and pose difficult choices, but once a company has made the choices, the implementation requires significant management expertise and resources. The distribution system is critical to implementing the marketing strategy.

Entry into a market can be accomplished through a variety of channel members described earlier in the chapter (see Figure 15.1). Often, however, the most logical channel member already has a relationship with one of a firm's competitors, thereby limiting the firm's access and posing special challenges to the global marketer. This section illustrates alternatives available to companies that encounter difficulties in convincing channel members to carry their products.

The "Locked-Up" Channel

A channel is considered locked up when a newcomer cannot easily convince any channel member to participate despite the fact that both market and economic reasons suggest otherwise. Channel members customarily decide on a case-by-case basis what products they should add to or drop from their line. Retailers typically select products that they expect to sell easily and in volume, and they can be expected to switch sources when better opportunities arise. Similarly, wholesalers and distributors compete for retail accounts or industrial users on economic terms. They can expect to entice a prospective client to switch by buying from a new source that can offer a better deal. Likewise, manufacturers compete

31. "Nissan to Split with U.K. Dealer After Row," *Financial Times*, December 28, 1990, p. 1.

for wholesale accounts with the expectation that channel members can be convinced to purchase from any given manufacturer if the offer exceeds those made by competitors.

Often there are barriers that limit a wholesaler's flexibility to add or drop a particular line. The distributor may have an agreement not to sell competitive products, or its business may include a significant volume from one manufacturer, which it does not want to risk upsetting. In Japan, relationships between manufacturers, wholesalers, and retailers are long-standing in nature and do not allow channel participants to change allegiance quickly to another source because of a superior product or price. Japanese channel members develop strong personal ties, and a sense of economic dependence develops. These close ties make it very difficult for any participant to break a long-standing relationship. In some cases, most existing wholesale or retail outlets may be committed in such a way that a newcomer to the market may not find qualified channel participants.

Cultural forces may not be the only influence in blocking a channel of distribution. Competitors, domestic or foreign, may try to obstruct the entry of a new company; or the members of a channel may not be willing to take any risks by pioneering unknown products. In all of these instances, the result is a locked-up channel that virtually stifles access to markets. Trade friction between the United States and Japan led to a bilateral accord on opening Japan's market for foreign cars and parts. Nissan started selling Ford cars through Tokyo Nissan, its largest dealer. The bottom line so far has not been pretty: Nissan has only sold four hundred Ford models and has accumulated debts of $2.8 million. Sales of foreign cars in Japan doubled from 5 percent to 10 percent between 1990 and 1995. However, Japanese dealers worried that their brand-conscious consumers would not purchase Ford or GM cars, which are not as well known in Japan as other foreign cars like Mercedes and BMW.[32] When American Standard, the world's largest supplier of plumbing fixtures, tried to enter the Korean market, it found itself locked out of the normal distributors, who were controlled by local manufacturers. American Standard looked for an alternative distribution channel that served the building trade. It found Home Center, one of the largest suppliers of home building materials and appliances. With a local factory, American Standard successfully circumvented the locked channels.[33]

Manufacturers in the United States are not entirely novices at dealing with the locked-up channel. Marketers of consumer goods developed the pull-type communications strategy to sidestep nonresponsive channel members by concentrating advertising directly on consumers. Manufacturers of industrial products usually can make use of independent manufacturers' representatives or agents to

32. "Selling U.S. Cars in Japan: More Than a Matter of Trade Policy," *Financial Times*, September 19, 1996, p. 6.

33. "American Standard Succeeds in Korea by Outflanking Local Firms' Lockout," *Financial Times*, August 26, 1993, p. A6.

gain quick access to users. To use the same strategies abroad requires equally free access to communications channels in other countries. However, this access is restricted in some countries (see Chapter 12) by government regulations that forbid TV or radio advertising or allow only limited availability of these media. In the case of industrial markets, the frequent entry of new entrepreneurs as independent agents is also considerably less prevalent.

Alternative Entry Approaches

With fewer chances to outflank nonresponsive channels abroad, global marketers have developed new approaches to the difficult situation of gaining access to distribution channels.

Piggybacking When a company does not find any channel partners with sufficient interest to pioneer new products, the practice of piggybacking may offer a way out of the situation. *Piggybacking* is an arrangement with another company that sells to the same customer segment to take on the new products as if it were the manufacturer. The products retain the name of the manufacturer, and both partners normally sign a multiyear contract to provide for continuity. The new company is, in essence, "piggybacking" its products on the shoulders of the established company's sales force.

Under a piggyback arrangement, the manufacturer retains control over marketing strategy, particularly pricing, positioning, and advertising. The partner acts as a "rented" sales force only. Of course, this is quite different from the private-label strategy, whereby the manufacturer supplies a marketer that places its own brand name on the product. This approach has become quite common in the pharmaceutical industry, in which at times rival companies get other firms involved for the launch of a particular new drug. Warner-Lambert, one of the leading pharmaceutical companies, launched its leading cholesterol-lowering drug Lipitor in the United States with the help of Pfizer. The drug was one of the most successful introductions ever, reaching sales of $3.5 billion in 1999 and expected to reach $5 billion in the year 2000.[34]

Joint Ventures As discussed in Chapter 9, when two companies agree jointly to form a new legal entity, it is called a *joint venture*. Such operations have been quite common in the area of joint production. Our interest here is restricted to joint ventures in which distribution is the primary objective. Normally, such companies are formed between a local firm with existing market access and a foreign firm that would like to market its products in a country where it has no existing

34. "Two Drug Giants Are Expected to Set $70 Billion Merger," *New York Times*, November 4, 1999, p. C10.

market access. One of the best ways to enter the Japanese market is a joint venture with a Japanese partner that is in a similar but not competitive field. Many such joint ventures have been signed between Japanese firms and foreign companies eager to enter the Japanese market. Through access to the distribution channel, the Japanese partner either acts as a sales agent or opens the doors for the joint venture's sales force.

Many such joint ventures expand into production, though the original intention of the foreign partner clearly was to gain access to the distribution system. Kodak began selling in Japan in the 1980s but found itself in a weak position in the mid-1980s with only fifteen people in its Tokyo office selling through four distributors. Kodak had 1 percent of the market, whereas Fuji had 70 percent and was attacking Kodak in the United States and Europe. Kodak formed a joint venture with Nagase Sangyo, an Osaka-based trading company specializing in chemicals, to attack Fuji in its home market. With heavy investment in plant, promotion, and distribution, by 1990 Kodak had 4,500 employees in Japan and 15 percent of the market.[35] To enter the Brazilian appliance market, Whirlpool formed a partnership with Brasmotor, a local manufacturer in São Paulo, purchasing 31 percent of the company. The partnership paid off, with Whirlpool reaching 39 percent of the white goods market in Brazil in 1996.[36]

The Mexican beer market is controlled by two companies—Femsa with a 49 percent share and Modelo with 51 percent. These two domestic producers had tied up the retail outlets with exclusivity constraints, which explains why Anheuser-Busch decided to enter Mexico through a joint venture with Modelo rather than trying to build a distribution system from scratch. Positioned as the market leader, Anheuser-Busch continues to rely on this joint venture for Mexico.[37] In another beer example, foreign beers have made little headway into the Japanese beer market, which is controlled by four domestic producers: Kirin, Asahi, Sapporo, and Suntory. In 1993, these four producers had a 98 percent share of the Japanese market. To enter these locked channels, in 1993 Budweiser established a joint venture with Kirin, the largest domestic brewer. Budweiser hoped to grow its share of the Japanese market to 5 percent or even 10 percent.[38] Progress was slow, however, so in 1998 the U.S. firm decided to ask its distribution partner to produce canned beer locally to assure freshness in the Japanese market.[39] In a reverse example, Asahi of Japan turned to Miller Brewing to form a joint venture in the United States to obtain quick distribution for its Super Dry beer, hoping to reach a volume of 1 million cases a year. The two companies had

35. "The Revenge of Big Yellow," *Economist*, November 10, 1990, p. 103.
36. "Brasmotor's Success Draws Competitors," *Wall Street Journal*, July 11, 1997, p. A10.
37. "The Lure of Mass Markets," *Prepared Foods*, July 1, 1998, p. 33.
38. "Anheuser-Busch's Defection Looks Set to Shake Up Japan's Beer Market," *Financial Times*, July 30, 1993, p. 21.
39. "Kirin Produces Bud in Cans'" Comline Pacific Research Consulting, August 11, 1998.

collaborated before: in Japan, Asahi has the exclusive right to brew and distribute Miller beer for the Japanese market.[40]

Roche, a Swiss drug company, had used Procter & Gamble to market its over-the-counter (OTC) products such as Aleve and Femstat-3 yeast infection treatment in the United States. Unhappy with the results, Roche formed a joint venture with Bayer, the Germany chemicals company, to market and sell OTC painkiller and gynecological products. Roche and Bayer wanted to receive the wider market penetration they are confident will come from the joint venture.[41]

To build one's own distribution system is not only costly but also requires patience and time. Until recently, the Japanese retail market was highly regulated, with new stores over 500 square meters needing permission from local store owners to open. Although now weakened, the Large-Scale Retail Stores Law remains an important element for foreign marketers. To overcome local hurdles, the U.S. retailer Toys 'R' Us started a completely new joint venture with Den Fujita, the founder of the McDonald's chain in Japan. The joint venture prospered, and by 1998 Toys 'R' Us had sixty-four stores in Japan.[42] Through the joint venture, Toys 'R' Us ceded some equity to its local partner. On the other hand, it obtained invaluable help in navigating the complex Japanese retail legislation.

Original Equipment Manufacturers (OEMs) In a situation in which the international manufacturer signs a supply agreement with a domestic or local firm to sell the international manufacturer's products but under the established brand name of the local firm, the arrangement is termed an *OEM agreement*, or *private labeling* (for consumer products). The foreign company uses the already existing distribution network of the local company, whereas the local company gains a chance to broaden its product lines.

Japanese companies have been particularly adept at using the OEM strategy to build whole alliances of captive markets. In the computer field, Japanese companies have adopted strategies that differ from those customarily chosen by U.S. computer manufacturers. Hewlett-Packard (HP), a leader in the server market used for Internet applications, has had a long-standing OEM relationship with NEC, a major Japanese computer company. Under this arrangement, NEC is able to purchase HP servers and related technology to resell them under the NEC name in Japan.[43] This relationship allows HP to sell in the vast Japanese market at a higher volume than it could on its own, while NEC gets access to more-superior products than it might be able to develop alone.

40. "Miller, Japan's Asahi Form Joint Venture," March 31, 1998, p. 2.
41. "Bayer and Roche in U.S. OTC Tie-Up," *Financial Times*, September 17, 1996, p. 20.
42. "U.S. Retailers Surmount Japanese Protectionism," *Arizona Republic*, February 1, 1998, p. D1.
43. "HP, NEC to Team on Next-Gen Internet Protocol Servers in Japan," *Electronic Engineering Times*, July 5, 1999, p. 14.

Distributing in foreign markets under OEM agreements has its pitfalls as well. Since the local OEM will put its own label on the imported product, the international company does not get any access to local customers and therefore will find it difficult to achieve a strong identity in the market. This reliance on the local OEM can also pose problems when the local company's performance declines. An excellent example is the situation faced by Mitsubishi International Corporation, a large Japanese automobile manufacturer that supplied Chrysler Corporation with small cars under an OEM agreement. With Chrysler's weak financial situation from 1983 to 1985, Mitsubishi would have preferred to sell its cars directly to the U.S. market under Mitsubishi's brand name. As long as the agreement was in effect, Mitsubishi was prohibited from doing that, and its fortune in the U.S. market continued to depend on Chrysler's efforts. The OEM tie-up allows a company to reach a high volume more quickly by sacrificing independence and control over its own distribution system. Of course, a company selecting this route is partially motivated by the corresponding savings of expenses by not building its own distribution system.

Acquisitions Acquiring an existing company can give a foreign entrant immediate access to a distribution system. Although it requires a substantial amount of capital, operating results tend to be better than those after starting a new venture, which often brings initial losses. It is often less important to find an acquisition candidate with a healthy financial outlook or top products than one with a good relationship to wholesale and retail outlets. A good example of the acquisition strategy to gain access to distribution channels was Merck's purchase of 51 percent of Japan's Banyu pharmaceutical company in 1990.[44] Merck has since been able to expand its Japanese staff to four hundred.[45]

The Japanese car market had been difficult to enter because of the stiff tax on big cars and limited distribution access. After the tax was dropped, Ford acquired a stake in Autorama, a nationwide distributorship, to expand its sales. As a result, Autorama sold 44,000 cars in 1993. As Japanese car dealers were no longer limited to selling just Japanese cars, the exclusive arrangements were eliminated, opening up the dealer sales networks to foreign manufacturers. In addition to a joint venture with Mazda, Ford broke new ground in 1994 by forming alliances with Nissan and Toyota dealers to sell Ford cars in Japan.[46] To assist its market development further, in 1999 Ford announced that it wanted to acquire the outstanding shares of Autorama from Mazda, thus giving it more complete control over its marketing operations in that country.[47]

44. "You Can Make Money in Japan," *Fortune*, February 12, 1990, p. 45.
45. "Banyu to Build Up Research and Development Activities as Merck's Foothold in Japan," Chemical Business NewsBase: *Japan Chemical Week*, July 22, 1999, p. 8.
46. "Nissan Affiliate to Sell Ford Cars; Toyota Dealership Follows with Negotiations," *Nikkei Weekly*, January 17, 1994, pp. 1, 23.
47. "Ford Japan to Bring Sales Subsidiary Totally Under Its Wings," *Comline PacificResearch Consulting*, March 26, 1999.

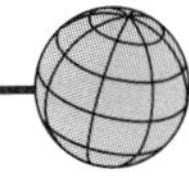

Global Supply Chain Management

The logistics system, including physical distribution of manufactured products, involves planning, implementing, and controlling the physical flow of materials and finished products from points of origin to points of use. On a global scale, the task becomes more complex because so many external variables have an impact on that flow of materials or products. As geographical distances to foreign markets grow, competitive advantages are often derived from a more effective structuring of the logistics system, by either saving time or costs or increasing a firm's reliability. The emergence of logistics as a means of competitive advantage is leading companies to focus increased attention on this vital area. Many manufacturers and retailers are restructuring their logistics efforts and divesting their in-house distribution divisions in favor of outside logistics specialists.

A capital- and labor-intensive function outside of the core business of most companies, logistics has become increasingly complex. For many concerns, it represents 16 to 35 percent of total revenues. Marks & Spencer, a U.K. retailer that operates in eight countries, found it could increase its sales per square foot and eliminate the need for most stockrooms by increasing the frequency of delivery. To guarantee delivery reliability, the company used outside contractors. The company spun off its entire logistics system into a partnership with a logistics firm with the expectation to save a substantial part of its £300 million annual distribution bill.[48]

Logistics Decision Areas

In this section, we describe the objectives of a global logistics system and the individual organizational operations that have to be managed and integrated into an efficient system. The total task of logistics management consists of five separate though interrelated jobs:

1. Traffic or transportation management
2. Inventory control
3. Order processing
4. Materials handling and warehousing
5. Fixed facilities location management

Each of these five jobs, or decision areas, offers unique challenges to the international marketer and is described below in more detail.

Traffic or Transportation Management Traffic management deals primarily with the mode of transportation. Principal choices are air, sea, rail, and truck, or

48. "M&S Distribution Deal Could Cut Costs by 20 Percent," *Supply Management*, June 24, 1999, p. 12.

some combination thereof. Since transportation expenses contribute substantially to the costs of marketing products globally, special attention has to be given to the selection of the transportation mode. Such choices are made by considering three principal factors: lead-time, transit time, and cost. Companies operating with long lead-times tend to use slower and therefore lower-cost transportation modes such as sea and freight. For short lead-time situations, faster modes of transportation such as air and truck are used. Also important are transit times. Long transit times require higher financial costs since payments arrive later, and normally higher average inventories are stocked at either the point of origin or the destination. Modes of transportation with long transit times are sea or rail, whereas air or truck transportation results in much shorter transit times. Costs are the third factor considered when selecting a mode of transport. Typically, air or truck transportation is more expensive than either sea or rail for any given distance.

Local laws and restrictions can have a significant impact on transport costs. For example, France restricted foreign truck drivers from traveling on Sundays. The Dutch Transport Association reports these bans are costing $60 million in Holland and billions across Europe. The Dutch have asked the European Union (EU) to investigate the forty-seven different bans in Europe regarding transport on holidays, Sundays, and summer holiday.[49]

Rank Xerox found by centralizing inbound deliveries from fifteen different trucking companies to one, it reduced transport costs by 40 percent in its Holland plant. Through this and further moves to centralize logistics, it expected to save $200,000 a year, reducing transport cost, inventories, and warehouse costs while at the same time improving the management and control of the logistics system.[50] Some companies have found they can reduce logistics costs by cooperating with competitors. For example, Toyota and Nissan deliver each other's cars to avoid empty return trips.[51]

Inventory Control The level of inventory on hand significantly affects the service level of a firm's logistics system. To avoid the substantial costs of tied-up capital, inventory is ideally reduced to the minimum level needed. In global operations, adequate inventories are needed as insurance against unexpected breakdowns in the logistics system. To reduce inventory levels, a number of companies have adopted the Japanese system of just-in-time (JIT) deliveries of parts and components. Also, companies are developing regional manufacturing strategies to minimize cost. For example, Rank Xerox produces its models for the entire world market (except the U.S. market) in four European plants. Prior to adopting a just-in-time system, the company kept buffer stocks of ten to forty days and an inventory of finished goods of ninety days. Now there is no stock for just-

49. "Hauliers Urge Brussels to Curb Lorry Bans," *Financial Times*, July 16, 1997, p. 4.
50. Ibid.
51. "Rivals Draw Distribution Truce to Cut Costs," *Nikkei Weekly*, January 31, 1994, p. 10.

in-time parts and components, and an inventory of finished goods of only fifteen days. The improvements are the result of a just-in-time strategy: a reduced number of suppliers, improved quality control, and a more efficient logistics system.[52]

Order Processing Since rapid processing of orders shortens the order cycle and allows for lower safety stocks on the part of the client, this area is a central concern for logistics management. The available communications technology greatly influences the time it takes to process an order. Managers cannot expect to find perfectly working mail, telephone, or fax systems everywhere. To offer an efficient order-processing system worldwide represents a considerable challenge to any company today. However, being able to offer efficient order processing is a competitive advantage since customers reap added benefits from such a system, and satisfied customers mean repeat business.

Toshiba Semiconductors, a major chip supplier based in Japan with global operations, is revamping its global supply chain network to obtain faster deliveries and to ship its products on the shortest possible notice from any supply point in the world. Its OEM customers require this level of service for just-in-time delivery. To obtain these benefits, the company is also using a third-party logistics provider in Europe.[53]

Materials Handling and Warehousing Throughout the logistics cycle, materials and products will have to be stored and prepared for moving or transportation. How products are stored or moved is the principal concern of materials handling management. For international shipments, the shipping technology or quantities may be different, causing firms to adjust domestic policies to the circumstances. Warehousing in foreign countries involves dealing with different climatic situations, and longer average storage periods may require changing warehousing practices. In general, international shipments often move through different transportation modes from those of domestic shipments. Substantial logistics costs can be saved if the firm adjusts shipping arrangements according to the prevalent handling procedures abroad.

Automated warehousing is a relatively new concept for the handling, storage, and shipping of goods. Warehouses are often adjacent to the factory, and all goods are stored automatically in bins up to twelve stories high. The delivery and retrieval of all goods are controlled by a computer system. Although automated warehouses require significant up-front capital and technology, they ultimately reduce warehousing costs significantly.

Fixed Facilities Location Management The facilities crucial to the logistics flow are, of course, production facilities and warehouses. To serve customers

52. Ibid.
53. "Toshiba Sets Fast-Forward System," *Electronic Buyer's News*, August 2, 1999, p. 10.

worldwide and to maximize the efficiency of the total logistics system, production facilities may have to be placed in several countries. In doing so, there is a tradeoff between economies of scale and savings in logistics costs.

At times, an advantage can be gained from shipping raw materials or semi-processed products to a market for further processing and manufacture instead of supplying the finished product. These advantages arise from varying transportation costs for given freight modes or from different rates for each product category. Some companies compare the costs for several operational alternatives before making a final decision. The location of warehousing facilities greatly affects the company's ability to respond to orders once they are received or processed. A company with warehouses in every country where it does business would have a natural advantage in delivery, but such a system greatly increases the costs of warehousing and, most likely, the required level of inventory systemwide. Thus, a balance is sought that satisfies the customer's requirements on delivery and at the same time reduces overall logistics costs. Microsoft opened a single warehouse and distribution center in Dublin, Ireland, to serve all of Europe. The distribution center removes the need for Microsoft to keep a warehouse and inventory in each country.[54]

Managing the Global Logistics System

The objective of a firm's global logistics system is to meet the company's service levels at the lowest cost. Costs are understood as total costs covering all five decision areas. Consequently,. a company has to combine cost information into one overall budget typically involving many departments from several countries. The key to effective management is coordination. A situation in which managers all try to reduce costs in their individual areas either will reduce the service levels provided or force other areas to make up for the initial reduction by possibly spending more than the original savings. Consequently, companies have to look carefully at opportunities to save in one area by comparing additional costs accruing in another. This process of comparison has caused some managers to refer to the logistics system as tradeoff management.

High-quality logistics does pay off. With 50 percent of all customer complaints to manufacturers being the result of poor logistics, there are substantial rewards for well-managed logistics that result in better service. Research by the Strategic Planning Institute revealed that companies with superior service received 7 percent higher prices and grew 8 percent faster than low-service companies. Also, on average they were twelve times more profitable.[55]

With markets becoming more scattered and dispersed over numerous countries, the opportunities for competitive advantages in global logistics grow.

54. "Microsoft Alters Distribution Chain for Europe," *Financial Times*, November 12, 1993, p. 20.
55. Neil S. Novich, "Leading-Edge Distribution Strategies," *Journal of Business Strategy*, November–December 1990, p. 49.

The firms that are able to combine the various logistics areas under the responsibility of one manager have a chance at achieving either substantial cost savings or enhanced market positions by increasing service levels at minimum costs.

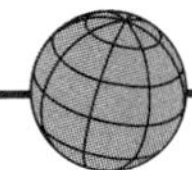

Trends in Global Distribution

Distribution systems throughout the world are continually evolving in response to economic and social changes. A manager developing a worldwide distribution strategy must consider not only the state of distribution today but also the expected state of distribution systems in the future. Five major trends are currently prevailing throughout the world: (1) the growth of larger-scale retailers, (2) an increased number of international retailers, (3) the proliferation of direct marketing, (4) the spread of online retailing, and (5) the dominant role of information technology to support a distribution strategy.

Larger-Scale Retailers

There is a trend toward fewer but larger-scale retailers. As countries become more economically developed, they seem to follow a pattern of fewer, larger stores. Three factors contribute toward this trend: an increase in car ownership, an increase in the number of households with refrigerators and freezers, and an increase in the number of working wives. Although the European housewife twenty years ago may have shopped two or three times a day in local stores, the increase in transportation capacity, refrigerator capacity, and cash flow and the reduction of available shopping time have increased the practice of one-stop shopping in supermarkets.

In the United Kingdom, the most striking change in the retail marketplace has been the opening of warehouse clubs. With six clubs opening in 1993 and 1994, U.K. consumers were able to buy merchandise at 25 to 30 percent less than at the typical retailer.[56] This trend, along with the growth of superstores, has significantly reduced the number of medium-sized and small stores in other parts of Europe as well. For example, the number of food stores in the Netherlands fell by 22.1 percent from 1982 to 1992, but the number of superstores increased 33.3 percent.[57]

IKEA, the Scandinavian retailer, has been very successful in Europe, Asia, and the United States in luring customers into its 200,000-square-foot stores. The IKEA strategy of offering a narrow range of low-cost furniture that the customer

56. "Silent Enemy Stalks the Aisles," *Financial Times*, November 30, 1993, p. 15.
57. "Europe's Smaller Shops Face Finis," *Wall Street Journal*, May 12, 1993, p. B1.

self-selects, carries away, and assembles results in a lower price to the consumer.[58] Once in the store, customers are given tape measures, catalogs, paper, and pencils. Child-care strollers are available, as well as free diapers. Each store has a restaurant with Scandinavian delicacies such as smoked salmon and Swedish meatballs. Customers can also borrow roof racks to help bring furniture home. IKEA has created a fun shopping experience that encourages people to enjoy themselves and make purchases. Sales per square foot are three times higher than in traditional furniture stores. IKEA's most recent stores were opened in Shanghai and Beijing, and the company harbors plans to expand in Russia and other Asian countries as well.[59] With its strong influence on furniture retailing, the company is likely to influence the general retailing scene in the markets where it opens new stores.

Globally Active Retailers

The number of globally active retailers is rising.[60] Most originate in advanced industrial countries and spread to the developed countries of the world. For example, Sears is now in Mexico, South America, Spain, and Japan; Walgreen's is in Mexico; Tandy is in Belgium, the Netherlands, Germany, the United Kingdom, and France. The globalization of retailing includes firms originating in the United States, Canada, France, Germany, and Japan. The wave was started by a number of large retailers in mature domestic markets that saw limited growth opportunities at home compared with the potential opportunities overseas. This principal reason for the trend toward global retailing has led Wal-Mart, IKEA, McDonald's, Pizza Hut, KFC, Carrefour, Marks & Spencer, Laura Ashley, and many others to seek opportunities in Europe, the United States, and Japan. The path toward an international presence has been made smoother by a number of facilitating factors, such as enhanced data communications, new forms of international financing, and lower barriers to entry. The single European market has also motivated retailers to expand overseas as they see a number of new global retailers entering their domestic markets.[61] The trend toward global retailing allows manufacturers to build relationships with retailers who are active in a number of markets. Retailers are also expanding their global umbrellas through acquisition.

The Asian markets have also been particularly attractive to global retailers. Unfortunately, some have found the Asian market problematic. Lane Crawford, a

58. Michael Porter, "What Is Strategy?" *Harvard Business Review*, November/December 1996, p. 65.
59. "IKEA," *The Times of London*, January 14, 1999, p. 26.
60. "Shopping All Over the World," *Economist*, June 19, 1999, p. 59.
61. Alan D. Treadgold, "The Developing Internationalization of Retailing," *International Journal of Retail and Distribution Management*, 1990, vol. 18, no. 2, p. 5.

Hong Kong retailer, U.S.-based Kmart, and the French group Galeries Lafayette have withdrawn from Singapore. Wal-Mart also experienced difficulty in Asia. The two discount stores Wal-Mart opened in Hong Kong with the Thai conglomerate Charoen Pokphand failed, and the partnership was dissolved. Apparently Wal-Mart assumed its winning formula in the United States could be easily transferred to Asia. However, the small homes of the people living in apartment blocks did not have room for the bulk purchases that Americans found so alluring. Wal-Mart is making a second attempt by opening two stores in Schezhen with a pair of mainland Chinese partners that are performing well.

Despite some difficulties, U.S.-based retailers are continuing to expand in Asia. Toys 'R' Us is favoring Asia because of saturation of its domestic market in the United States. In 1998, the toy retailer operated twelve stores in Japan, its largest non-U.S. market, with intentions to expand to seventy-six stores, and it had another twenty-three stores in Hong Kong, Indonesia, Malaysia, Singapore, and Taiwan. Starbucks, the specialty coffee firm, has opened stores in Malaysia, Thailand, and South Korea and intends to be present in every major urban Asian market by 2003. The Gap intends to double its Japan store chain from fourteen to thirty.[62]

European retailers have found it essential to establish a unique selling position. C&A, the privately owned Dutch chain of clothing stores; the Body Shop, the U.K. natural cosmetics group; Benetton, the Italian fashion chain; IKEA, the Swedish furniture store; and Aldi, the low-priced German food retailer, are all successful international retailers that have developed a distinctive style. Each has a clearly defined trading format and product range that enable it to distinguish itself in every European market. Retailing formats can be translated into other countries as long as the message is clear enough in the first place.

Direct Marketing

There has been a concomitant growth of direct marketing around the world. The complex multilayered Japanese distribution system has encouraged some foreign companies to skip the stores and go directly to consumers. The growth in direct marketing in Japan is supported by a number of demographic and technical factors. The dramatic increase in employed women from 50 percent to 75 percent resulted in fewer available shopping hours. The introduction of toll-free telephones, cable TV, videotext, and smart cards has also made it easier to shop at home. But U.S.-type mail-order companies have had their share of difficulties in penetrating the Japanese market. Paul Fredrick Menswear, a small U.S.-based catalog of men's shirts and ties, was able to expand to $8 million of

62. "Retailers See Asia Crisis as Expansion Opportunity," *USA Today*, June 4, 1998, p. 1B.

sales in Japan in 1997, a considerable volume by comparison with other, much larger U.S. mail-order houses. The company adapted its products to the Japanese market, offering sleeve lengths of 30 and 31 inches instead of the U.S. standard of 32 inches. The company also found out that Japanese men have different color preferences, requiring a different catalog. The catalog was also translated into Japanese, resulting in an immediate sales increase. Larger U.S. firms, such as Brooks Brothers, were unwilling to make similar changes in their merchandise or approach.[63] One of the most successful direct marketing companies in Japan is Amway. With sales of $1.5 billion in 1999, the company employees approximately 1.1 million independent distributors, using a direct sales model.[64]

Although the United States is the global leader in direct marketing, with $230 billion in sales in 1996, the market is also growing elsewhere. France is comparably smaller, with sales of $8.15 billion in 1996. Whereas in the United States the direct marketing segment is dominated by specialty catalogs, in France as in other European countries the market is dominated by general merchandise catalogs. But U.S. direct marketing companies can do well in foreign markets such as France. Reader's Digest ($136 million in 1997) and Inmac ($52 million in 1995) are two typical examples. In 1998, U.S. mail-order firms accounted for 25 percent of French foreign direct marketing sales, second behind German companies, which took the largest share with 50 percent.[65]

Direct marketing is beginning to play a role in emerging markets as well. In Russia, direct marketing is a new concept and tends to be viewed negatively as one of those new western business ideas. The Russian infrastructure in terms of delivery and telecommunications is also lagging behind other markets and tends to hold back progress. In Brazil, direct marketing has begun to take off, with consumers in cities receiving an average of ten pieces a month. Telemarketing is hampered by a lack of phones (only one in ten Brazilians has a phone). Brazil is nevertheless a large market and tends to be ahead of the rest of Latin America in direct marketing. India is also only at the beginning of developing a direct marketing community. Bertelsmann, the German-based media company, put its planned Book Club India project on hold after realizing that a segmentation exercise on India's twenty-three largest urban markets had yielded a total of only 297,000 potential club members, too few to pursue the opportunity.[66]

63. "Competing in Japan's Catalog Market," *Target Marketing,* April 1, 1998, p. 30.
64. "Amway Japan Announces Fiscal 1999 First Quarter," *PR Newswire*, July 14, 1999.
65. "France: Catalog Sales Market," U.S. Department of State, U.S. and Foreign Commercial Service, April 1998.
66. "International Direct Marketing in a Rapidly Changing World," *Direct Marketing*, March 1, 1999, p. 44.

In China, direct marketing is also a new phenomenon, and the lack of a sophisticated infrastructure poses big problems for direct marketing firms. Amway, a U.S.-based company, had begun to build a major operation there, investing as much as $100 million into a direct selling organization. However, the Chinese authorities denied the right to sell door-to-door, and the only way for Amway to salvage its investment was to agree to market its products through regular retail stores.[67]

For direct marketing to be effective, a company needs to be able to rely on a specific infrastructure that supports it. Basic requirements are a reliable telecommunications system, access to good mailing lists and a variety of those, a target market with wide ownership of credit cards, an efficient postal or package delivery system, and telemarketing facilities such as call centers. In developed countries such as the United States, these requirements can easily be met. In many other markets, particularly emerging ones, the infrastructure is still lacking. As developing countries expand and improve their general communications infrastructure, direct marketing can be expected to expand.

Online Retailing

The Internet has opened an entirely new channel through which retailers and manufacturers can sell their products. The United States is the undisputed leader in online retailing, or e-commerce, with estimates of about $36 billion in 1999 sales. However, this amount represents only about 1 percent of total retail sales.[68] E-commerce is, nevertheless, a fast-growing segment. U.S.-based online retailers such as Amazon.com have expanded abroad, with specific "stores" in the United Kingdom and Germany. Most online retailing, however, crosses borders, since through the Internet consumers can reach any store anywhere with a legitimate Internet address.

In other countries, online retailing continues to expand as well. The second largest e-commerce market after the United States, is Japan, with an estimated revenue for 2001 of $8 billion.[69] Germany is also showing rapid growth, with Europe's highest number of households online, estimated at 6.4 million as of 1999. Other large online groups are in the United Kingdom (3.6 million) and France (1.7 million). These numbers were expected to grow quickly, fueling online retail growth. In Germany, surveys found that some 27 percent of all Internet users had ordered or purchased a product online.[70] Online retailing will

67. "Amway Gets Okay to Operate in China," *Grand Rapids Press*, July 21, 1998, p. A1.
68. "Boom in E-Commerce," *Il Sole*, vol. 24, August 11, 1999, p. 12.
69. "Japan's Retail E-Commerce," *U.S. Newswire*, June 22, 1999.
70. "Germany: Europe's On-Line Front Runner," *Communications Week International*, March 15, 1999, p. 6.

begin to expand even more rapidly as the perceived security problems are resolved and more consumers feel secure in using credit cards over the Internet. But other infrastructure issues remain. Online retailing requires a solid Internet network available at low prices. The United States still leads the world in low-cost Internet connections, and phone service in the United States is unmeasured for local calls. In many other countries, this is not the case, and a lengthy Internet connection can turn into an expensive shopping foray, particularly if nothing is purchased.

Finally, online retailing requires a large connected population. As many e-commerce executives know, online retailing also depends on a solid fulfillment cycle that gets the ordered merchandise quickly into the hands of the consumer. When transport must take place across borders, issues of taxation and duty remain, slowing down delivery systems. Many foreign markets do not yet offer reliable fulfillment centers for use by small online retailers. However, the trend is clearly in the direction of resolving this issue over time. Once the problem is solved, many more consumers will reach into online stores in faraway places, potentially turning every online marketer into a global retailer.

Information Technology

The worldwide retail industry is moving fast toward the use of electronic checkouts that scan the bar codes on products, speeding up the checkout, reducing errors, and eliminating the need to put a price label on each item. Electronic checkouts also improve the stores' ability to keep track of inventory and purchase behavior. As retailers and manufacturers begin to share consumer scanner data, opportunities exist to improve profitability.[71] Procter & Gamble, which had 53 percent of the U.K. detergent market in 1997, plans to reduce its product range by 40 percent, and to increase profits by 40 percent.[72] More and more companies are developing global networks to assist with their global business. The networks improve communication, coordination, and sharing of best business practices. An additional benefit for many users of global networks is the recovery of value-added taxes (VATs) paid in multiple countries.[73]

Computerized retail systems have led to better monitoring of consumer purchases, lower inventories, quicker stock turns, better assessment of product profitability, and the possibility of just-in-time retailing. Retailers are beginning to link the electronic point-of-sale terminals with input on promotion and marketing

71. "Industry Analysts Predict Technology Driven Changes for Grocery Shopping," *Knight-Ridder Tribune Business News* (Miami Herald), February 18, 1999.
72. Marcia MacLeod, "A Complex Route to Customised Solutions," *Financial Times IT: Networking*, July 3, 1996, p. 5.
73. Ibid.

plans to generate more accurate orders. In 1995, Somerfield, a U.K.-based retailer, was experimenting with a system that would link terminals directly with suppliers.[74] Technology is one of the keys to the success of 7-Eleven in Japan, owned by Ito-Yokado Company, Japan's most profitable retailer. Store clerks keep track of customer preferences and inventory through a sophisticated tracking system. The clerk enters the consumer's sex and approximate age, as well as the items purchased. 7-Eleven-Japan posted a pretax profit of $680 million on $1.44 billion in 1992.[75]

Some stores are experimenting with self-scanning as a way to speed up checkout and reduce costs. Royal Ahold of Holland, the parent company of Stop & Shop in the United States, introduced self-scanning in Europe and is now experimenting in the United States. The same applies to Shaw's, another U.S.-based supermarket chain with a European parent, J. Sainsbury of the United Kingdom.[76] Modern retailing systems are clearly developed in many parts of the world and their diffusion takes place much more rapidly. This changes the retailing environment in many countries toward a "world standard" that is best in class wherever it takes place.

Conclusions

To be successful in the global marketplace, a company needs market acceptance among buyers and market access via distribution channels. Companies entering foreign markets often do so initially without noteworthy acceptance. Consequently, the company must guarantee some degree of market access through either effective marketing programs or sheer financial strength. To achieve access, the firm must select the most suitable members, or actors, of a channel, keeping in mind that substantial differences exist among countries on both the wholesale and the retail levels. There are major differences in distribution country to country. Local habits and cultures, planning restrictions, and infrastructure can all affect success in a new country.

Proper distribution policies have to allow for the local market's buying or shopping habits. A company should not expect to be able to use the same distribution density, channel alignment, or channel length in all its markets. The logistics system must reflect both local market situations and additional difficulties inherent in longer distances. To actually find willing and suitable channel members may

74. George Black, "Microsoft Sets the Pace," *Financial Times IT Focus: Computers in Retail*, October 4, 1995, p. 5.
75. "Listening to Shoppers' Voices," *Business Week/Reinventing America 1992*, p. 69.
76. "New Concepts Check Out: Self-Scanning Reduces Lines, Personal Scanning Checks Out," *Boston Herald*, January 25, 1999, p. O27.

be extremely difficult; access may only be achieved by forging special alliances with present channel members or local companies with access to them. Once the distribution system has been designed, participants still have to be motivated and controlled to ensure that the firm's marketing strategy is properly executed.

A major technological revolution is taking place with the emergence of the Internet, online retailing, and the widespread use of the Internet by consumers. These trends are likely to reshape the global distribution system and the way companies tap into markets all over the world. The easy access to the Internet makes it easier for business or household customers to reach into faraway markets, thus raising the global purchasing logic for all players. This has far-reaching consequences for all global marketers and needs to be taken into consideration as the new world economy adapts to the Internet challenge over the next few years.

QUESTIONS FOR DISCUSSION

1. Your firm is just beginning to export printing equipment. How would you assess the decision to use an export management company or an export agent versus direct exporting?
2. What are the key elements of a distribution strategy?
3. If you enter a new marketplace and decide to distribute the product directly to the consumer, what types of costs will you incur?
4. You have been assigned the task of selecting distributors to handle your firm's line of car batteries. What criteria will you use to select among the twenty possible distributors?
5. The performance of your agents and distributors in South America has been poor over the past three years. How will you improve the management of these agents and distributors?
6. What are the elements of an international logistics system, and how will they differ from a domestic logistics system?
7. Your firm has just entered the South Korean market for automobile parts; the major distributor is owned by a competitive manufacturer of automobile parts. What strategies can you use to gain access to this market?
8. Given the trends in distribution, what distribution strategies should a worldwide manufacturer of women's clothing consider?
9. What impact do you see on global marketing from the development of e-business?

FOR FURTHER READING

Bello, Daniel C., David J. Urban, and Bronislaw J. Verhage. "Evaluating Export Middlemen in Alternative Channel Structures," *International Marketing Review*, 1991, vol. 8, no. 5, pp. 49–64.

Cooper, James C. "Logistics Strategies for Global Business," *International Journal of Physical Distribution and Logistics Management*, 1993, vol. 23, no. 4, pp. 12–23.

Czinkota, Michael R. "Distribution of Consumer Products in Japan," *International Marketing Review*, Autumn 1985, pp. 39–51.

Czinkota, Michael R., and Masaaki Kotabe. *The Japanese Distribution System*. Chicago: American Marketing Association, 1993.

Foster, Thomas. "Global Logistics Benetton Style," *Distribution*, 1993, vol. 92, no. 10, pp. 62–66.

Govindarajan, Vijay, and Anil K. Gupta. "Taking Wal-Mart Global: Lessons from Retailing's Giant," *Strategy & Business*, no. 17, 4th quarter 1999, p. 14.

"How Levi's Works with Retailers," *Business Europe*, July 19, 1993, p. 24.

Johnson, Gregory S. "Survey: Companies Consider Logistics a Key to Profits," *Journal of Commerce*, May 31, 1995, p. 2B.

Kale, Sudhir H., and Roger P. McIntyre. "Distribution Channel Relationships in Diverse Cultures," *International Marketing Review*, 1991, vol. 8, pp. 31-45.

Klein, Saul. "Selection of International Marketing Channels," *Journal of Global Marketing*, 1991, vol. 4, no. 4, pp. 21-37.

McDonald, William J. "International Direct Marketing in a Rapidly Changing World," *Direct Marketing*, March 1, 1999, p. 44.

Munns, Peter J. S. "Marketing and Distribution in Japan Today." Master's thesis, Graduate School of Management, International University of Japan, 1994.

Price, Retha. "Channel Leadership Behavior: A Framework for Improving Channel Leadership Effectiveness," *Journal of Marketing Channels*, 1991, no. 1, pp. 87-93.

Rapoport, Carla, with Justin Martin. "Retailers Go Global," *Fortune*, February 20, 1995, pp. 102-108.

"SKF to Centralize Distribution," *Business Europe*, April 12, 1993, p. 7.

Williams, David E. "Differential Firm Advantages and Retailer," *International Journal Internationalization of Retail and Distribution Management*, 1991, vol. 19, no. 4, pp. 3-12.

V Managing the Global Marketing Effort

COMPETENCE LEVEL	GLOBAL ENVIRONMENT	
ENVIRONMENTAL COMPETENCE	*Understanding the Global Marketing Environment*	2 3 4
ANALYTIC COMPETENCE	*Analyzing Global Marketing Opportunities*	5 6
STRATEGIC COMPETENCE	*Developing Global Marketing Strategies*	7 8 9
FUNCTIONAL COMPETENCE	*Designing Global Marketing Programs*	10 11 12 13 14 15
MANAGERIAL COMPETENCE	*Managing the Global Marketing Effort*	16 17 18

To be successful at global marketing, a company must do more than analyze markets and devise marketing programs. Increasingly, international companies run complex organizations with operating units in many different countries. The managerial challenges of running such diverse organizations are substantial and require skills that are different form those required by single-country organizations.

This final part of our text is devoted to issues involving the managerial competence of international and global marketing managers. Our goal is to show how managers can guide their operations more effectively in this very competitive global marketplace. In Chapter 16, we concentrate on organizational design issues for global firms and look at where the decision-making process should be concentrated. Chapter 17 focuses on how global firms should control their operations and marketing programs. The final chapter, Chapter 18, covers the various exporting and importing procedures faced by global marketing managers.

16

Organizing for Global Marketing

AN IMPORTANT ASPECT OF GLOBAL MARKETING IS THE ESTABLISHMENT OF AN appropriate organization. The organization must be able to formulate and implement strategies for each local market and for the global market as well. The objective is to develop a structure that will allow the firm to respond to distinct variations in each market while utilizing the company's relevant experience from other markets and products. The key issue in establishing a global organization is deciding where to locate the global responsibility in the firm. The major dilemma facing global marketers involves the tradeoff between the need for an individual response to the local environment and the value of centralized knowledge and control. To be successful, companies need to find a proper balance between these two extremes.

A number of organizational structures are suitable for different internal and external environmental factors. No one structure is best. In this chapter, we examine the elements that affect the global marketing organization, several types of global organizational structures, recent trends in global organization design, common stages through which organizations evolve, and locations of corporate global mandates in an organization.

Organizing: The Key to Strategy Implementation

The global marketplace offers numerous opportunities for astute marketers. To take advantage of these opportunities, they will develop strategies to fit the needs of diverse markets while capitalizing on economies of scale in centralized operations, centralized control, and experience in other markets. These strategies will be adapted to the internal and external environment so that they will prevail over the competition.[1] The final success of the strategy will be influenced by the selection of an appropriate organizational structure to implement that strategy.

The structure of a global organization should be congruent with the tasks to be performed, the need for product knowledge, and the need for market knowledge. It is difficult to select an organizational structure that can effectively and efficiently implement a marketing strategy while responding to the diverse needs of customers and the corporate staff. Chapter 17, "Planning and Controlling Global Marketing," examines the simultaneous pressures for greater integration and greater diversity, which act to create a significant tension in the development and control of an ideal organizational structure.

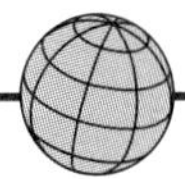

Elements Affecting a Global Marketing Organization

The ideal structure of an organization should be a function of the products or services to be sold in the marketplace and the external and internal environments. Theoretically, the approach to developing such an organization is to analyze the specific tasks to be accomplished within an environment and then to design a structure that will complete these tasks most effectively. A number of other factors complicate the selection of an appropriate organization. In most cases, a company already has an existing organizational structure. As the internal and external environments change, companies will often change that structure. The search for an appropriate organizational structure must balance the forces for local responsiveness against the forces for global integration.[2]

1. Alfred D. Chandler, *Strategy and Structure* (Cambridge, Mass.: MIT Press, 1962).
2. Sumantra Ghoshal and Nitin Nohria, "Horses for Courses: Organizational Forms for Multinational Corporations," *Sloan Management Review*, Winter 1993, p. 27.

FIGURE 16.1

Factors Affecting Organizational Design

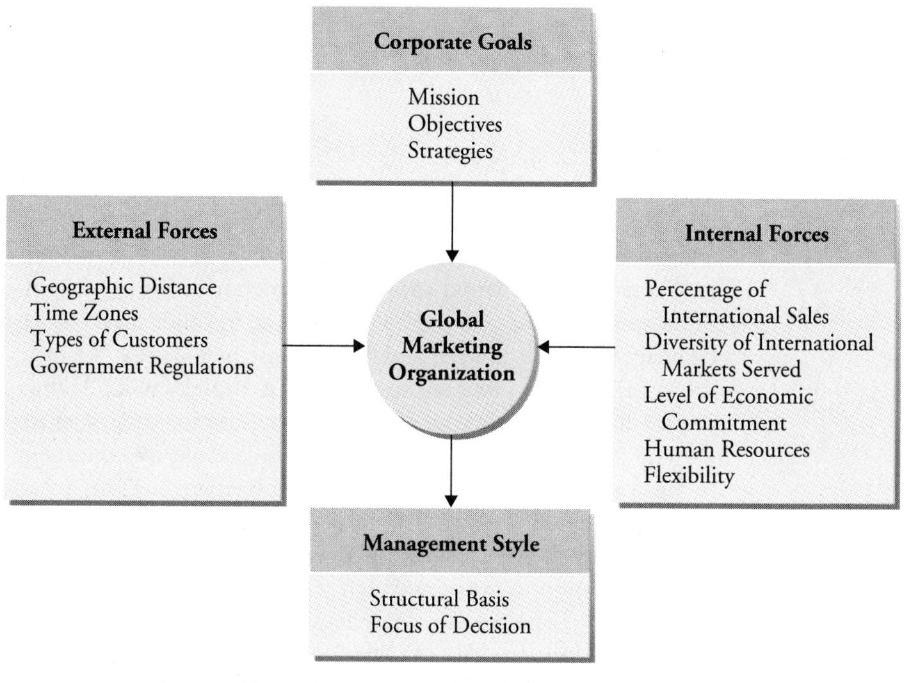

It is important to understand the strengths and weaknesses of different organizational structures as well as the factors that usually lead to change in the structure. The diagram in Figure 16.1 reflects the elements that affect organizational design. In the following paragraphs, we discuss each of these elements individually.

External Forces

The most important external factors are geographic distance, time zone differences, types of customers, and government regulations. In the international environment, each issue should be examined to determine its effect on the organization.

Geographic Distance Technological innovations have somewhat eased the problems associated with physical distance. Companies, primarily in the United

States and other developed countries, enjoy such conveniences as next-day mail and email, facsimile machines, videoconferencing, mobile phones, mobile data transmissions, and rapid transportation. However, these benefits cannot be taken for granted. Distance becomes a distinct barrier when operations are established in developing countries, where the telecommunications infrastructure is less developed. Moreover, companies invariably find it necessary to have key personnel make trips to engage in face-to-face conversations. In order to save on travel cost and time, organizations in regional proximity are often grouped together to allow for a minimization of travel time for senior executives. Technology has thus shortened, but not eliminated, the distance gap.

Time Zones One problem even high technology cannot solve is time differentials (see Figure 16.2). Managers in New York who reach an agreement over lunch

FIGURE 16.2

Time Zones of the World

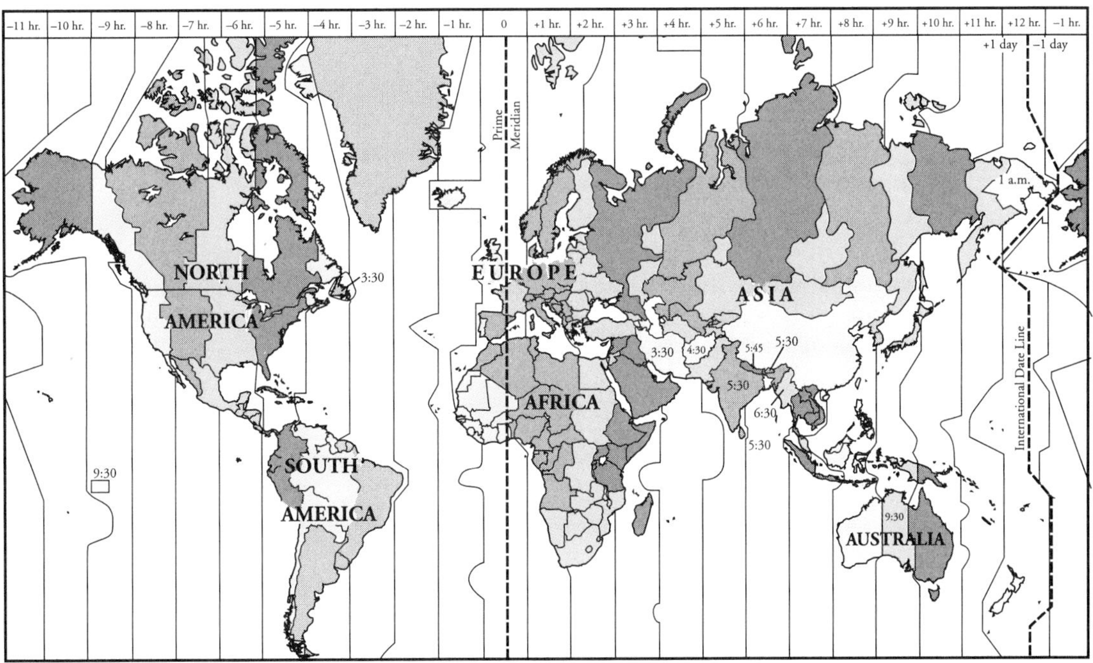

Source: From *The 1996 Information Please® Almanac.*

will have a hard time finalizing the deal with their headquarters in London until the following day, as most executives in England will be on their way home for the evening. The five-hour difference results in lost communication time, which impedes rapid results in a divisional structure. If regular face-to-face meetings are required, different time zones affect the relationship between a subsidiary and its headquarters. Electronic mail has contributed substantially to overcoming time zone differences and facilitating interactions among far-flung units.

Types of Customers Depending on their types of customers, companies may need to structure their global marketing organization differently. Companies facing very few, concentrated global customers will organize their global marketing efforts differently from firms that face a large number of small customers in country after country. In the former instance, when faced with extensive global customer or purchasing logic (see Chapter 7), firms tend to adjust their organizations and select their office locations according to where their customers are located. Many companies selling equipment or parts to automotive firms maintain marketing units near major concentrations of automotive activity, such as in Detroit or in Stuttgart, Germany. On the other hand, companies that face large numbers of customers with little global logic tend to maintain diverse organizations catering to different type of regions.

Global Logic. Companies that face very little global logic in terms of industry, competition, or size will find considerably less need to integrate any international operations they may have. This leads to a more regional, or even country-specific, organization, with relatively less structure. Firms facing considerable global logic and a strong need to respond to that logic are typically forced to use different organizational forms leading to more integration.

Government Regulations How various countries attract or repel foreign operations affects the structure of the organization. Laws involving imports, exports, taxes, hiring, and so on differ from country to country. Local taxes, statutory holidays, and political risk can deter a company from establishing a subsidiary or management center in a country. Some countries require a firm that establishes plants on their territory to hire, train, and develop local employees and to share ownership with the government or local citizens. These requirements for local investment and ownership may demand an organization with a local decision-making group.

Internal Forces

Internal factors often impact the global organization. In this section, we examine these factors, including volume of international business, diversity of the markets being served, economic commitment to international business, available human resources, and flexibility within the company.

Percentage of International Sales If only a small percentage of sales (1 to 10 percent) is international, a company will tend to have a simple organization with an export department. As the proportion of international sales increases relative to total sales, a company is more likely to change from an export department to an international division and then to a worldwide organization.

Diversity of International Markets Served As the number and diversity of international markets increase, the organization necessary to manage the marketing effort becomes more complex and requires a larger number of people to understand the markets and implement the strategies.

Level of Economic Commitment A company unwilling or unable to allocate adequate financial resources to its international efforts will not be able to sustain a complex or costly international structure. The less expensive organizational approaches to global marketing usually result in less control by the company on the local level. It is extremely important to build an organization that will provide the flexibility and resources to achieve the corporation's long-term goals for global markets.

Human Resources Available and capable personnel are just as vital to a firm as financial resources. Some companies send top domestic executives to foreign operations and then find that these exported executives do not understand the nation's culture. The hiring of local executives is also difficult because competition for such people is extremely intense in many countries. When Panasonic U.K. began to build up its U.K. organization, the company recruited graduates from British universities. The graduate trainees were then sent to Japan for one year to absorb Japanese culture and discipline. The program was extremely popular. With a long-term approach to developing local talent, Panasonic preferred "to grow its own."[3] Archrival Sony used executive search firms extensively to recruit local managers.[4] Because people are such an important resource in global organizations, many companies structure their organizations based on the availability of globally trained executive talent. Also, many companies are developing cross-cultural training programs to help prepare executives for new environments.

Flexibility Although a rigid structure gives a firm more control over operations, it also restricts adaptability. When a company devises an organization structure, it must build in some flexibility, especially in the event of the need for future reorganization. A study of the implementation of a global strategy for seventeen products found that organizational flexibility was one of the key success factors.

3. "A Tortoise That Stays Within Its Shell," *Financial Times*, October 30, 1989, p. 13.
4. Ibid.

The structure needs to be flexible enough to respond to the needs of the consumers.[5] Companies that establish a perfect design for the present find themselves in trouble later on if the firm grows or declines.

Management Style

The management style of a company can be described in terms of its structure and its decision-making processes. These factors influence the type of international organization the company adopts.

Structural Basis There are three basic options for the managerial structure of an organization: functional, market-based, or matrix. These options provide the foundation on which to design an organization. Figure 16.3 depicts the options a company has once it decides on the basic framework.

FIGURE 16.3

Basis for Organizational Design

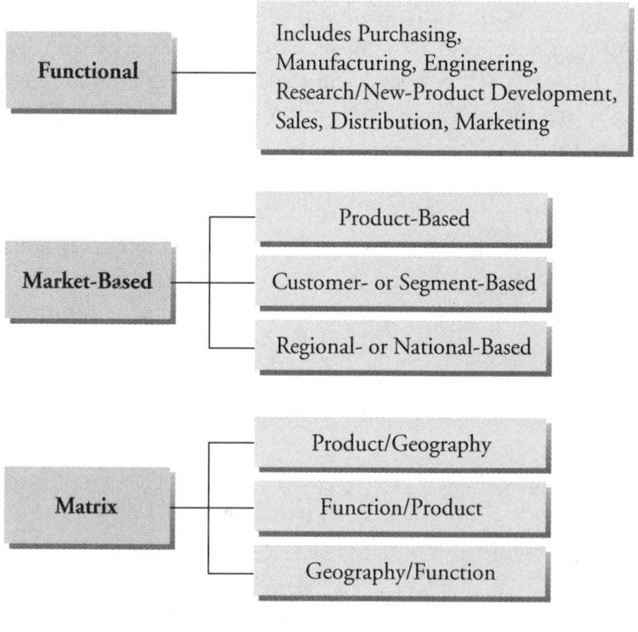

5. Kamran Kashani, "Why Does Global Marketing Work—or Not Work?" *European Management Journal*, June 1990, p. 154.

When American Standard restructured its company from a geographic organization to a product-based organization, it did so to encourage cross-fertilization of management skills and technology. Additionally, American Standard's corporate philosophy was to promote the best person. This policy meant that non-Americans not only ran most of the overseas divisions but also were moving into senior U.S. and global jobs. This philosophy enabled American Standard to shed its reputation as a U.S.-oriented company.[6]

The prospect of an integrated Europe gave a number of firms the impetus to change their organizational structures. ICI, British Petroleum (BP), Unilever, Procter & Gamble, Electrolux, Philips, United Distillers, and many others reorganized to improve their abilities to respond to the needs of the European markets. In 1987, United Distillers was still largely a loose federation of twelve brand-owning groups that included Johnnie Walker, Dewar, and Haig. Each distilled its own whiskies and sold them around the world through third-party distribution. There was a great deal of interbrand competition. The company decided to abolish the old product-based structure and introduce a simple regional structure that would place operational management into the markets: Europe, North America, Asia Pacific, and international (South America, the Middle East, and Africa). A central strategic unit was established to research and produce individual brand marketing plans and portfolio strategies and to handle new-product development in a liaison with regional managers. United's new organization focused on the needs of each market without cannibalizing its own brands.[7]

Locus of Decision Who makes what decision guides the organizational design. If all decision-making responsibility is in the hands of headquarters, then the global operations should reflect this. There are many layers, or types, of decisions to be made, from the purchasing of paper clips to the acquisition of a product line or a company.

Over a ten-year period, Electrolux made over one hundred acquisitions to become one of the leading manufacturers of large appliances, vacuum cleaners, chain saws, and garden appliances. Because the company grew very rapidly, there was pressure to develop a more formalized and centralized decision-making process. Electrolux adopted a multifaceted organization that both preserved local decision making where it was needed and still allowed for global control of key product lines. At the Electrolux head office in Stockholm, Sweden, several product categories were created covering major appliance areas—"Hot" (cookers, ranges), "Cold" (refrigerators, freezers), and "Wet" (washers, dryers). The product category managers maintained control over design and coordinated local plant networks. Separate marketing groups coordinated the marketing activities

6. "Happy Days at American Standard," *Fortune*, September 22, 1980, p. 136.
7. "Re-shaping United Distillers," *Financial Times*, June 13, 1990, p. 12.

for Europe and overseas. And local country mangers were in charge of coordinating product divisions (plants) and local marketing sales companies. No single locus of decision was selected.[8]

Corporate Goals

Every company needs a mission. The mission is the business's framework: the values that drive the company and the belief the company has for itself. The glue that holds the company together, the mission statement answers four questions: (1) Why do we exist? (2) Where are we going? (3) What do we believe in? (4) What is our distinctive competence?[9]

After reviewing its mission, no company should begin establishing a global organization until it has reviewed and established its strategies and objectives. If the company anticipates future growth in global markets, it must establish a structure that can evolve effectively and efficiently into a large operation. Too often, shortsighted executives establish international operations that do not enable the managers to grow with the company when markets begin to expand. These managers are not equipped to take on any added responsibility. Additionally, headquarters can fail to communicate short-term goals, long-range objectives, and sometimes even the total mission of the company. Inadequate communications result in an ambiguous corporate image and the inability to facilitate coordination of all marketing elements.

Recent authors go beyond the need for goals and objectives and call for "strategic intent." They argue that some companies that have risen to global leadership did so with a ten- to twenty-year quest for winning. Corporate leaders developed a strategic intent with such slogans as "Encircle Caterpillar" for Komatsu and "Beat Xerox" for Canon. If the head of a company can develop this sense of winning throughout the company, it will stretch the organization to excel and achieve far greater goals.[10]

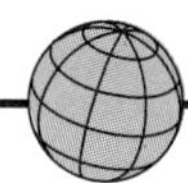

Types of Global Organizations

The global marketplace offers many opportunities. To take advantage of these opportunities, a company must evaluate the options, develop a strategy, and establish an organization to implement the strategy. The organization should take into account all the factors affecting organizational design shown in Figure 16.1. In

8. Christopher Lorenz, "The Birth of a Transnational," *McKinsey Quarterly*, Autumn 1989, p. 72.
9. Andrew Campbell, Marion Devine, and David Young, *A Sense of Mission* (London: Economist Books, 1990), pp. 19–41.
10. Gary Hamel and C. K. Prahalad, "Strategic Intent," *Harvard Business Review*, May–June 1989, pp. 63–68.

this section, we review the various types of international and global organizational structure.

Companies Without International Specialists

Many companies, when they begin selling products to foreign markets, are without a separate international organization or an international specialist. A domestically oriented company may begin to receive inquiries from foreign buyers who saw an advertisement in a trade magazine or attended a domestic trade show. The domestic staff will respond to the inquiry in the same fashion as it does other inquiries. Product brochures will be sent to the potential buyer for review. If sufficient interest exists on the part of both buyer and seller, then more communication (email, airmail, faxes, telephone calls, personal visits) may transpire. With no specific individual designated to handle international business, it may be directed to a sales manager, an inside salesperson, a product manager, or an outside salesperson.

Companies without an international organization will obviously have limited costs. Of course, with no one responsible for international business, it will probably provide little or no sales and profit. Also, when the firm attempts to respond to the occasional inquiry, no one will understand the difficulties of translation into another language, the particular needs of the customer, the transfer of funds, fluctuating exchange rates, shipping, legal liabilities, or the other many differences between domestic and international business. As the number of international inquiries grows or management recognizes the potential in global markets, global specialists will be added to the domestic organization.

International Specialists and Export Departments

The complexities of selling a product to a variety of different countries prompt most domestically oriented firms to establish a global expertise. This can vary from retaining a part-time global specialist to having a full staff of specialists organized into an export department or international department. Figure 16.4 illustrates an organization operating with a global specialist.

Global specialists and export departments are primarily a sales function. They will respond to inquiries, exhibit at international trade shows, and handle export documentation, shipping, insurance, and financial matters. Also, the global specialist(s) will maintain contact with embassies, export financing agencies, and the Department of Commerce. All of these groups regularly publish requests for bid quotations from other countries. The global specialist or export department may use the services of an export agent, an export management company, or import intermediaries to assist in the process (see Chapter 15).

Hiring global specialists gives firms the ability to respond to, bid for, and process foreign business. The size of this type of organization will be directly

FIGURE 16.4

Organization with an International Specialist

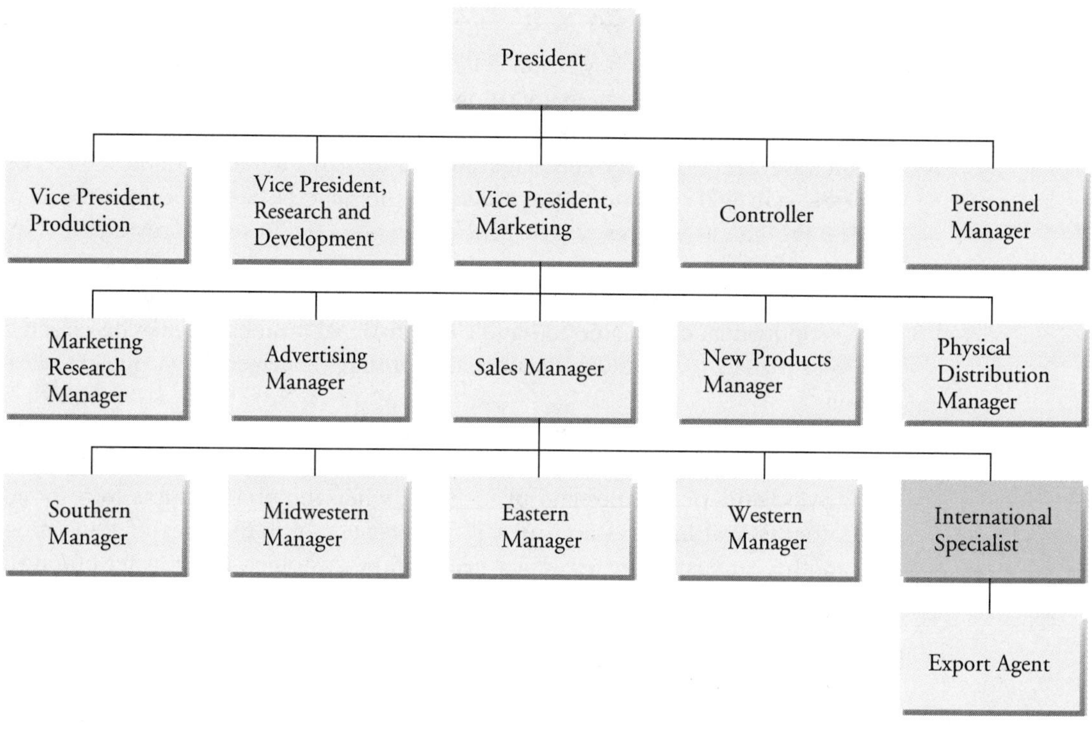

related to the amount of international business handled. The costs should be minor when compared with the potential.

Global specialist/export departments are often reactive rather than proactive in nature. These specialists do not usually evaluate the worldwide demand for a product or service, identify pockets of opportunities, develop a strategy to infiltrate these opportunities, or reap the rewards; they usually respond to inquiries. Also, because international sales are so small, the global specialist may have little opportunity to modify the current products or services to meet global market needs. In most cases, the products are sold as is, with no modification.

International Division

As sales to foreign markets become more important to the company and the complexity of coordinating the global effort extends beyond a specialist or a single department, a company may establish an international division. The international division normally will report to the president, thus having an equal status with other functions such as marketing, finance, and production. Figure 16.5 illustrates the organizational design of a firm using an international division.

The international division will be directly involved in the development and implementation of a global strategy. Heads of the international divisions will have marketing, sales, and possibly production managers reporting to them. These individuals focus their entire efforts on the global markets. It has been suggested that the international division is the best organizational alternative when international business represents a small percentage of the total business.

An international division focuses on the global market at a high enough level in the organization to directly influence strategy. Also, the international division will begin actively to seek out market opportunities in foreign companies. The sales

FIGURE 16.5

Organization with an International Division

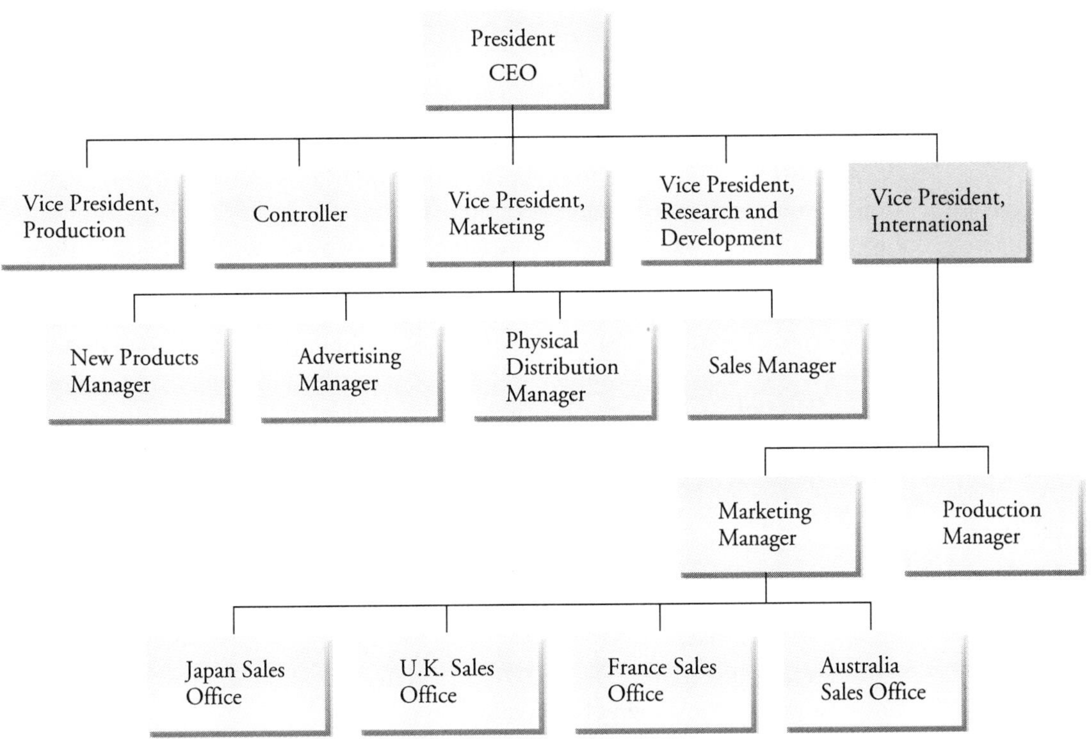

and marketing efforts in each country will be supported through a regional or local office. These offices will be able to understand the local environment, including legal requirements, customer needs, competition, and so on. This close contact with the market improves the organization's ability to perform successfully.

The use of international divisions is most common among large multinational corporations (MNCs) with many different product lines or businesses. This has been very typical in the United States, where many MNCs operate several separate product divisions for the large domestic market. Because none of the divisions has extensive global experience, all international business is often combined into the international division, responsible for marketing in all overseas markets. IBM created its separate IBM World Trade organization that became the focus for its global operations and control of international country subsidiaries. Alcon, a $1.5 billion U.S.-based company owned by Nestlé of Switzerland and active in the ophthalmic area, operated four major domestic divisions for equipment, pharmaceuticals, professional materials for surgeons, and over-the-counter eye-care products. Its international business was combined under an international division with operating responsibility for carrying out its foreign business through its many subsidiaries.

Worldwide or Global Organizations

As a firm recognizes the potential size of the global market, it begins to change from a domestic company doing some business overseas to a worldwide company doing business in a number of countries. A worldwide focus will normally result in a worldwide organizational design.

A company can choose to organize around four dimensions: geography, function, product, and strategic business unit. The matrix organization, another possible type of worldwide organization, combines two or more of the four dimensions. We will discuss and illustrate each organizational alternative.

Geographic Organizational Structures Geographic organizational designs focus on the need for an intimate knowledge of the company's customers and their environment. A geographic organization will allow a company the opportunity to understand local culture, economy, politics, law, and the competitive situation. There are two general types of geographic organizations: a regional management center and a country-based organization. In many cases, the regional management center and country-based organizations are combined.

Regional Management Centers. Regional management centers form a worldwide organization that focuses on one or more particular regions of the world, such as Europe, the Middle East, Latin America, North America, the Caribbean, or the Far East. Figure 16.6 illustrates the regional management structure of a worldwide geographic organization.

The reasons for using a regional geographic approach to organizational design are twofold. First, there is the pressure of size. Once a market reaches a certain

FIGURE 16.6

Geographic Organization by Regional Management Centers

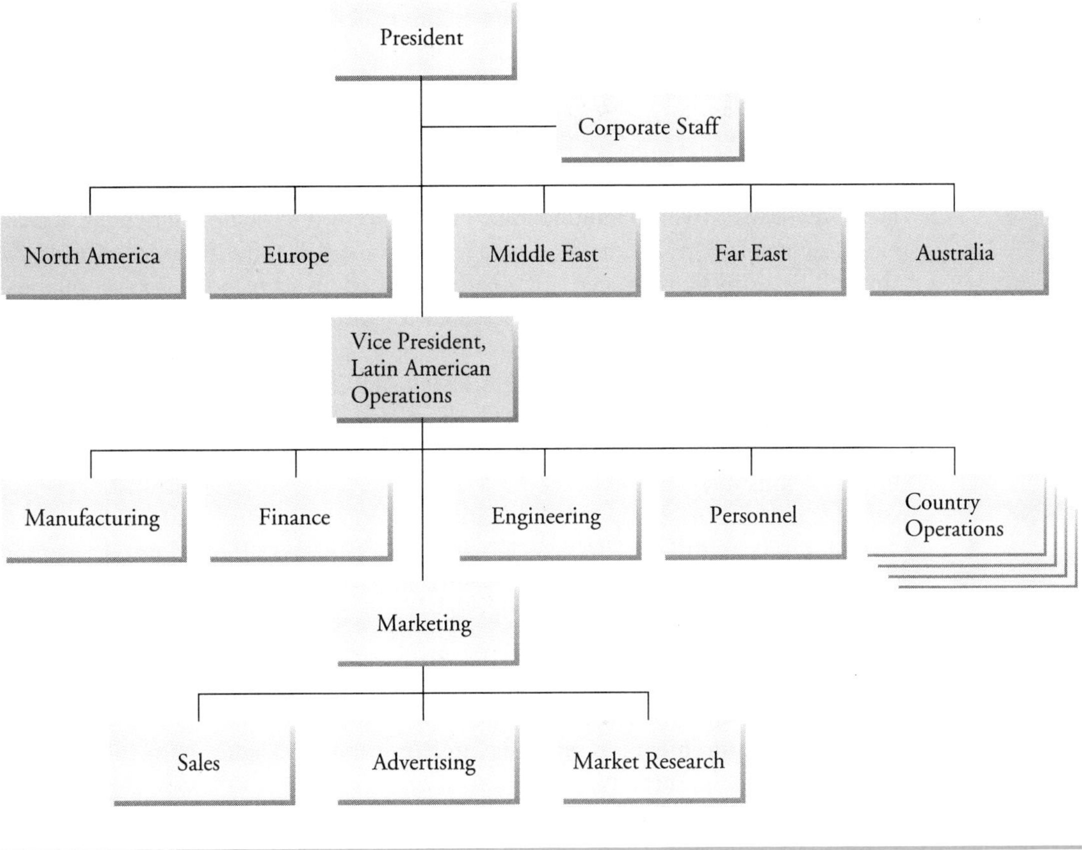

size, the firm must have a staff focused on that region to maximize revenues from that area of the world and to protect the firm's assets there. The second reason for a regional focus is the regional nature of markets. A group of countries located close together, and having similar social and cultural histories, climates, resources, and often languages, will have many similar needs for products. Often, these regional country groups have unified themselves for political and economic reasons; for example, the European Union (EU) is such a regional grouping.

The regional approach to a worldwide organization has a number of benefits. It allows a company to locate marketing and manufacturing efforts to take advantage of regional agreements such as the EU or the North American Free Trade

Agreement (NAFTA). Also, the regional approach puts the company in close contact with distributors, customers, and subsidiaries. Regional management will be able to respond to local conditions and react faster than a totally centralized organization in which all decisions are made at the headquarters.

In Europe, many large international companies were organized on a national basis. The national organizations, including those in France, Germany, Italy, and the United Kingdom, often were coordinated through a regional management center, or the European headquarters. The development of a single European market caused companies to rethink their European organization, often reducing the role of the national organization in favor of a stronger pan-European management. A study of twenty multinational companies found that a big benefit of a regional or pan-European structure was reduced finance function costs. The study showed that, by sharing accounting services such as accounts payables, billings, accounts receivables, and general ledger accounting, firms could save 35 to 45 percent of finance function costs.[11]

Restructuring of manufacturing and logistics in Europe is proceeding at a rapid pace as companies centralize production to lower costs and increase flexibility.[12] For example, Anglo-Dutch Unilever, one of the world's largest manufacturers of consumer products, set up a new organization in 1990 called Lever Europe. This was a change for Unilever, a company that had always been decentralized, with each national organization having full autonomy to modify and market products as dictated by local conditions. This decentralization had led to a hodgepodge of brands, resulting in the same liquid abrasive cleaner being called Cif, Jif, Vif, or Viss, depending on the country. Unilever, by centralizing both marketing and manufacturing, ended up reducing the decision-making authority of its country managers.[13] Unilever was attempting to balance the need for centralized requirements in research, finance, and packaging with the need to stay close to the markets.[14]

Regional organizations have their disadvantages, too. First, regional organization implies that many functions are duplicated, either at regional head offices or in the countries. Such duplication, together with the need to rent offices, tends to add significantly to costs. A second, and more serious, disadvantage is that regional organizations inherently divide global authority. In a purely regionally organized company, only the CEO has true global responsibility. Developing global marketing strategies for products or services is difficult because the key drivers

11. "European Study Finds Companies Can Save 35–45% by Moving to Financial Shared Services," A. T. Kearney news release, December 16, 1993, p. 1.
12. George Taucher, "1992: The End to European National Organizations?" *International Business Communications*, 2, no. 3 (1990), pp. 4–7.
13. Ian Fraser, "Now Only the Name's Not the Same." *Eurobusiness*, April 1990, pp. 22–25.
14. Floris A. Maljers, "Inside Unilever: The Evolving Transnational Company," *Harvard Business Review*, September–October 1992, p. 48.

FIGURE 16.7

Country-Based Geographic Organization

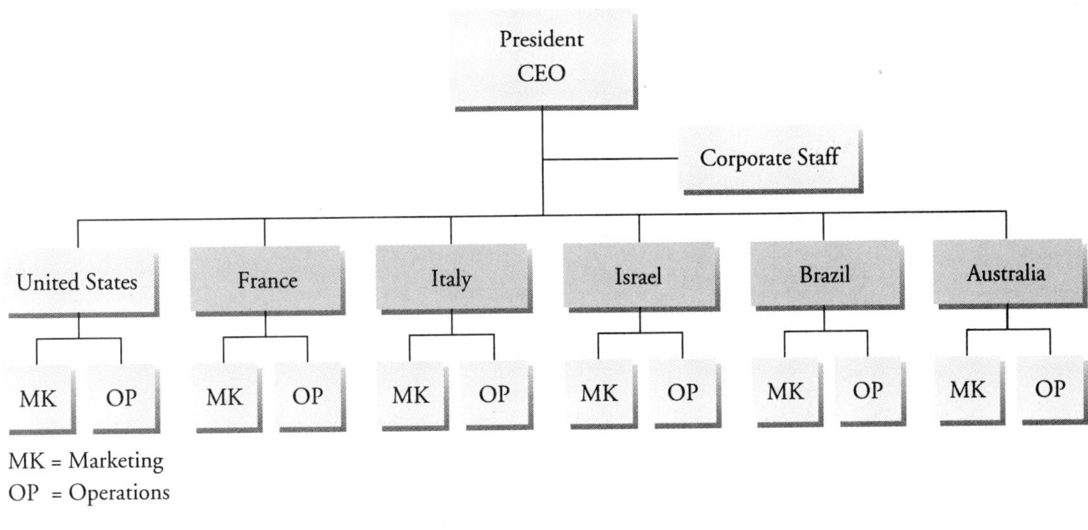

are regional executives who tend to see most initiatives primarily from their limited regional perspective.

Country-Based Organizations. The second type of geographic organization is the country-based organization, which utilizes a separate unit for each country. Figure 16.7 illustrates a simple country-based geographic organization.

A country-based organization resembles a regional management center, except that the focus is on a single country rather than a group of countries. For example, instead of having a regional management center in Brussels overseeing all European sales and operations, the company has an organizational unit in each country. The country-based organization can be extremely sensitive to local customs, laws, and needs, which may be different even though the countries participate in a regional organization, such as the EU. With the integration of Europe came the acceptance of European-wide product standards, the elimination of border restrictions, and the moves to financial unity. These have caused many companies to look at Europe as a single market.

Country organizations are being phased out or reduced as pan-European organizations emerge.[15] Reckitt and Colman, the U.K.-based toiletries and household

15. George Taucher, "1992: The End to European National Organizations?"

FIGURE 16.8

Organization Using Both Country-Based Units and Regional Management Centers

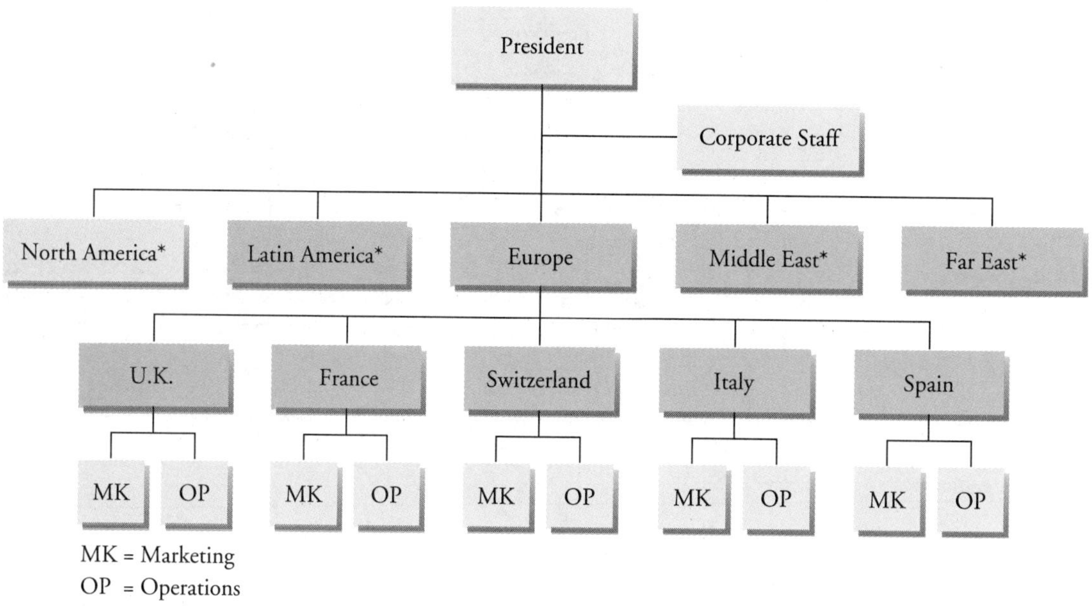

*Under these regional offices would be country organizations similar to those shown for the European center.

goods company, reorganized its corporate structure in response to the European integration. Manufacturing operations were consolidated so one or two factories will be making products for all of Europe, rather than having factories in each country making most products. Product marketing was also reorganized into Eurobrand groups rather than by country.[16]

In response to the signing of NAFTA, many firms began to integrate their separate organizations for Canada, the United States, and Mexico. Among those was Lego, the Danish toymaker with major U.S. operations. Lego reduced the responsibility of its Canadian operation and combined some executive positions at its Enfield, Connecticut, operation. At the same time, it decided to build up its Mexican operation from the U.S. location. Other firms have chosen the same path of integrating their Canadian subsidiaries with their U.S. company and, instead of building a separate Mexican company as they might have done in the past, developing the Mexican market from a U.S. base.

16. "Reckitt to Cut About 500 Jobs over Two Years," *Financial Times*, July 1, 1989, p. 22.

One of the difficulties of a country-based organization is its higher costs. Therefore, the benefit of a local organization must offset its cost. The second difficulty involves the coordination with headquarters. If a company is involved in forty countries, it is difficult and cumbersome to have all forty country-based organizational units reporting to one or more people in the company's headquarters. The third problem of a country-based unit is that it may not take advantage of regional groupings of countries (Chapter 5). Regional trading agreements, such as the EU, make it valuable to coordinate activities in involved countries. Also, regional media, such as television and print media, often transcend country boundaries and require coordination.

To deal with the shortcomings of a country-based organization, many firms combine the concepts of a regional management center and a country-based unit, as shown in Figure 16.8. Combining regional and country approaches minimizes many of the limitations of both designs, but it also adds an additional layer of management. Some executives think that the regional headquarters' additional layer reduces the country-level implementation of strategy rather than improves it. In order to receive benefits from a regional center in such a combined approach, there must be a value in a regional strategy. Each company must reach its own decision regarding the organization design, its cost, and its benefits.

Functional Organizational Structures A second way of organizing a worldwide business is by function. In such an organization, the top executives in marketing, finance, production, accounting, and research and development all have worldwide responsibilities. For international companies, this type of organization is best for narrow or homogeneous product lines, with little variation between products or geographic markets. As shown in Figure 16.9, the functional organization is a simple structure. Each functional manager has worldwide responsibility for that function. Usually, the manager supervises people responsible for the function in regions or countries around the world.

Coca-Cola Company reorganized its marketing function from a country-focused organization to a worldwide functional organization. In the transition, market research and marketing operations that previously reported to the senior vice president of marketing U.S.A. were transferred to the newly formed global marketing division. With the majority of its earnings growth coming from overseas markets, Coca-Cola decided to shift the focus away from a U.S.-dominated structure to a global one.[17] Ford likewise went to a global functional organization, to eliminate the duplication of functions among regional organizations in the United States, Europe, Asia, and Latin America. Ford was expected to save $2 to $3 billion per year by 2000, as well as to speed up development of new models.[18]

17. "Coke's Zyman Fires Marketing Blitzkrieg," *Advertising Age*, August 30, 1993, p. 1.
18. "A Global Tune-up for Ford," *Business Week*, May 2, 1994, p. 38.

FIGURE 16.9

Functional Global Organization

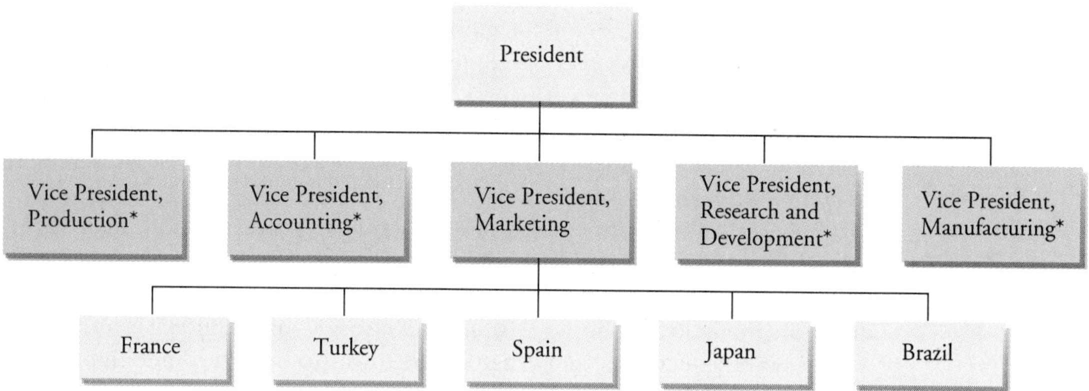

*Each functional vice president has managers of that function in the countries served reporting to him or her, as illustrated with the vice president, marketing.

Product Organizational Structures A third type of worldwide marketing organization is based on product line rather than on function or geographic area. The product group, which incorporates marketing, sales, planning, and in some cases production, becomes responsible for the performance of the organizational units. Other functions, such as legal, accounting, and finance, can be included in the product group or be performed by the corporate staff.

Structuring by product line is common for companies with several unrelated product lines. The rationale for selecting a product versus a regional focus is that the differences between the marketing of the products is greater than the differences between the geographic markets. In the 1970s and 1980s, many global companies used a dual structure referred to as a matrix, which we discuss below. During the 1990s, a number of companies, such as Philips and ICI, switched away from their geographic and product matrix to strong product divisions.[19] Typically, the end users for a product organization will vary by product line, so there is no advantage to having the marketing for the different product lines done by the same group. The product is the focus of the organizational structure shown in Figure 16.10.

A product organization concentrates management on the product line, which is an advantage when the product line constantly changes because of ad-

19. "ICI Proffers More Corporate Clout to Its Customers," *Financial Times*, September 7, 1990, p. 12.

FIGURE 16.10

Global Product Organization

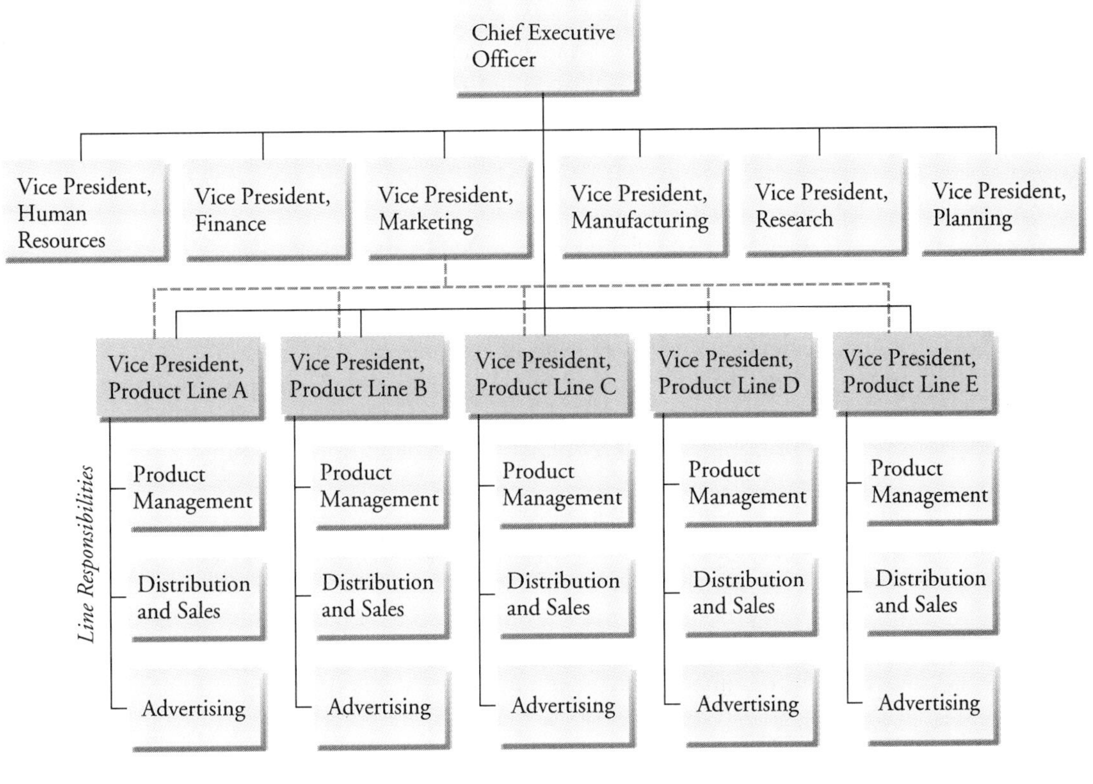

vances in technology. The product focus also gives the organization excellent flexibility. Within a product group, management can control the product life cycle, adding and deleting products with a marginal effect on overall operations. Also, the firm can add new product groups as it adds new, unrelated products through acquisition.

Monsanto adopted a global product organization. The transition was accompanied by a shift of the resins staff from St. Louis to Brussels. The previous organization forced the company to focus primarily on North America—at the expense of product and market opportunities elsewhere.[20]

20. "When Head Office Goes Native," *Financial Times*, December 2, 1992, p. 11.

The product organization has its limitations. Knowledge of specific areas may be limited, since each product group cannot afford a local organization. This lack of knowledge may cause the company to miss market opportunities. The managers of international product divisions can also be a problem. They can be ethnocentric and relatively disinterested in or uneasy with the international side of the business. Another limitation of a product organization is the lack of coordination in international markets. If each product group goes its own way, the company's global development may result in inefficiencies. For example, two product divisions separately may be purchasing advertising space in the same magazine, which will be more expensive than if the purchases are combined.

To offset the inefficiencies of a worldwide product organization, some companies provide for global coordination of activities such as advertising, customer service, and government relations. In Europe, 3M shifted most strategic and operational responsibilities away from its national subsidiaries and into nineteen centralized product divisions, each with pan-European responsibility. The European business centers were quickly accepted because managers saw the need for pricing coordination, faster development and launch of new products, and better coordination of large customers in multiple countries.[21]

Matrix Organizational Structures Some companies have become frustrated with the limitations of the one-dimensional geographic, product, and functional organization structures. To overcome these drawbacks, the matrix organization was developed. As shown in Figure 16.11, the matrix organization allows for two dimensions of equal weight (here, geographic and product dimensions) in the organization structure and in decision-making responsibility. A matrix organization structure has a dual rather than a single chain of command, which means that many individuals will have two superiors. Firms tend to adopt matrix organizations when they need to be highly responsive to two dimensions (for example, product and geography), when there are stringent constraints on financial or human resources, and when uncertainties generate very high information processing requirements. In the early 1990s, Procter & Gamble strengthened its global management matrix of product and geography for two reasons. First, the matrix organization was able to handle twice the volume of business with the same staff. Second, the matrix allowed much quicker rollout of a product worldwide than was the case in the past with a country-based organization.[22]

A matrix organization can include both product and geographic management components. Product management has worldwide responsibility for a specific

21. "Facing Up to Responsibility," *Financial Times*, December 13, 1993, p. 10.
22. "Behind the Tumult at P&G," *Fortune*, March 7, 1994, p. 82.

FIGURE 16.11

Matrix Organization

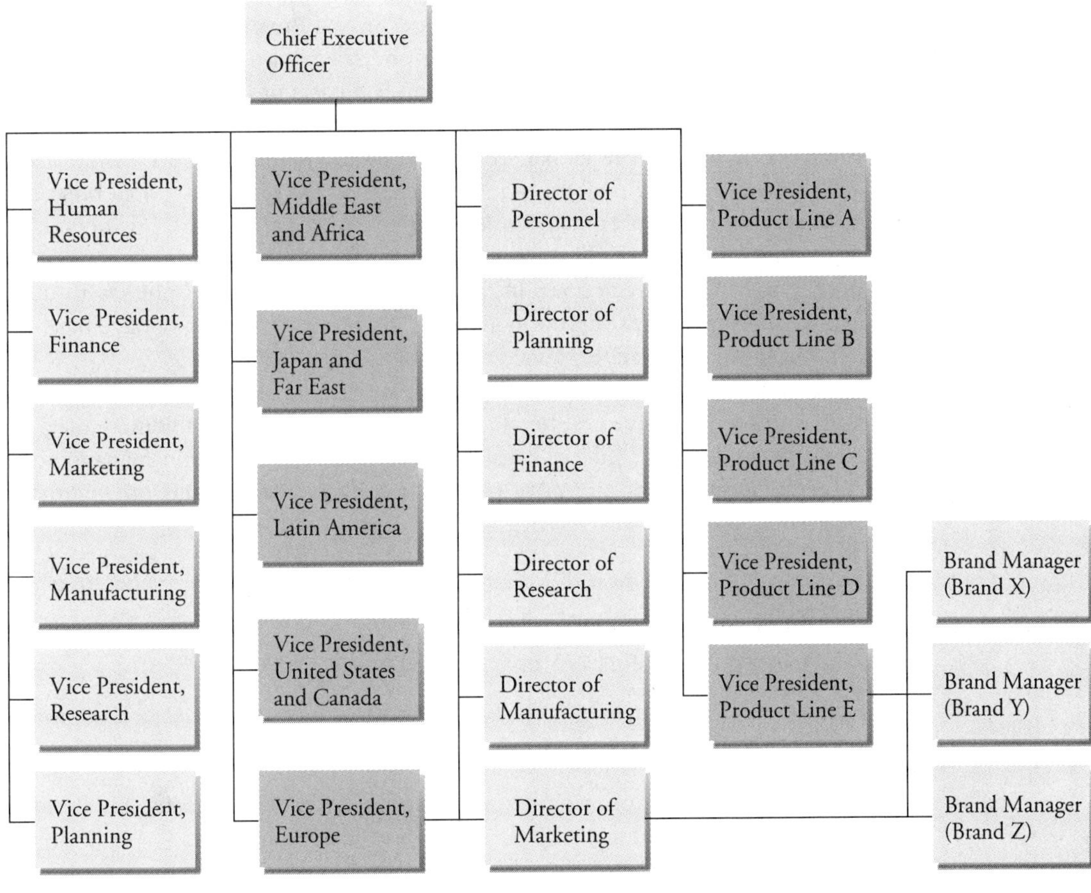

product line, whereas geographic management is responsible for all product lines in a specific geographic area. These management structures overlap at the national product/market level.

The combination of different organizational objectives and dual reporting relationships fosters conflict and complexity. Power struggles are a common problem when a matrix organization is first established. The power struggle is the result of the dual reporting relationship. The power limits of the two relationships are tested as each side attempts to identify its place in the organization. One of the most extensive global matrix organizations is employed by ABB, a Swedish-Swiss company with several major businesses in electric power generation, railways, industry automation, and environmental equipment. Formed in 1987 as a merger between Swedish-based Asea and Swiss-based Brown Boveri, the company operated worldwide around some sixty business areas. Each business area had global responsibility for strategy and is measured on the basis of its own profit-and-loss account. On the other side of the matrix are numerous country organizations responsible for delivering the global strategy in their assigned territory. Each local manager reports to a regional manager as well as to the assigned global business area manager. For the matrix to work, both the regional and the business area manager must jointly agree on the local strategy, budget, and business approach. The company has been structured into more than three thousand units with dual reporting. ABB has also promoted behavioral patterns among its management to make the best of the matrix organization.[23]

The key to successful matrix management is the degree to which managers in an organization can resolve conflict and achieve the successful implementation of plans and programs. The matrix organization requires a change in management behavior from traditional authority to an influence system based on technical competence, interpersonal sensitivity, and leadership.

- It permits an organization to function better in an uncertain and changing environment.
- It increases potential for control and coordination.
- It gives more individuals the chance to develop from technical or functional specialists to generalists.

The matrix organization requires a substantial investment in dual budgeting, accounting, transfer pricing, and personnel evaluation systems. The additional complexity and cost of a matrix organization should be offset, however, by the benefits of the dual focus, increased flexibility and sales, and economies of scale.

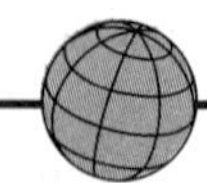

New Trends in Global Organizations

International companies are continually challenged by the need to adapt their organizations to the needs of the marketplace. Three major challenges confront them: the need for efficiency, the need for responsiveness, and the need for learning.[24]

23. Christopher A. Bartlett, "ABB's Relays Business: Building and Managing a Global Matrix," Harvard Business School Case, 1993.
24. Christopher A. Bartlett and Sumantra Ghoshal, *Managing Across Borders* (London: Hutchinson Business Books, 1989), pp. 3–17.

As companies compete on a worldwide basis, they need to develop global economies of scale. Instead of supporting manufacturing plants in each major market, products or components are standardized. Electrolux, Black & Decker, Unilever, and many other firms have rationalized their manufacturing to yield economies of scale. Although the washing machine or power tool may vary from country to country, the motors can be standardized and manufactured in large volumes to reduce costs. The organizational structure needs to encourage this trend toward efficiency, which is why, as part of its complex matrix organization, Electrolux has three senior-level executives—"Mr. Hot," responsible for stoves and cookers; "Mr. Cold," responsible for refrigerators and freezers; and "Mr. Wet," responsible for washers and dryers—who coordinate the manufacturing and marketing of their product lines across all markets.[25]

The increased cost of R&D, shortened product life cycles, and consumer demand for the latest technology have increased the need for development and diffusion of worldwide learning. This learning is often related to R&D but can also include marketing or manufacturing learning. ITT's strategy of individually developing its telecommunication switch technology for each country without gaining any global expertise was one of the factors leading to the company's exit from that business. On the other hand, P&G's seven years of research to develop a heavy-duty liquid laundry detergent in Europe was quickly and successfully transferred to the United States in the form of Liquid Tide.

Bartlett and Ghoshal interviewed 236 managers in diverse groups of nine companies—P&G, Kao, Unilever, ITT, Ericsson, NEC, GE, Philips, and Matsushita. Based on their research, they suggest that the challenges of global efficiency, local responsiveness, and global learning have become so strong that the future global organization must contend with all these challenges simultaneously.[26]

Much of this chapter has focused on the company's formal structure, which establishes lines of authority and responsibility. In global organizations, the formal structure, while important, is only one part of the organizational challenge. The interpersonal relationships, decision-making process, and individual behavior of managers must also be responsive to the needs of the market. Bartlett and Ghoshal argue that *people* are the key to managing complex strategies and organizations.

Global Product Divisions

There has been a shift away from the geographic/divisional matrix toward global divisions. These global divisions have responsibility for a set of products world-

25. "An Impossible Organization, but the Only One That Works," *Financial Times*, June 21, 1989, p. 14.
26. Bartlett and Ghoshal, *Managing Across Borders*, pp. 16–17.

wide. The shift has been part of the multinationals' quest for simple structures, faster decision making, and greater global effectiveness.[27] Philips, Citibank, Novartis, Texas Instruments, BP, and General Electric have all switched from matrix organizations to worldwide product divisions. The main problem with the matrix organization is that it assumes that product and geographic consideration are evenly balanced; in reality, few large, diversified companies have such a balance.

Companies adopting the global product division structure want to make sure that each product division gets a chance to fully develop the international side of its business on its own. When combined in a heterogeneous international division responsible for the international marketing of many (domestic) product divisions, the unavoidable tradeoffs often favor large, established product lines.

When a company adopts the global product division structure, it usually leads to the dissolution of its international division, or at least to the downgrading of its strategic role. Furthermore, when each division obtains global responsibility for its business, the divisions require direct control of the local business. Heterogeneous, multiproduct local subsidiaries are split up to grant each division its own local arm, severely affecting the local organizations and their traditional management structure. IBM, long operating under an international division structure, moved toward an organization with some fourteen major industry sectors. Assigning these divisions international and global responsibility led to some discussions within the firm as to the role of its local subsidiary managers, and the role of IBM World Trade.[28] American Standard, one of the world's largest plumbing product manufacturers, moved toward a global product organization by combining both the U.S. and the international part of its business into the Worldwide Fittings Group. The Fittings Group was asked to develop its business on a global scale.[29]

Global Mandates

As companies are concerned with globalizing their marketing organizations, the issue of who, or which units, should receive global mandates will become an important aspect of the discussion. Under global mandate we understand the expressed assignment to carry out a task on a global scale. Global mandates might be assigned to individual managers, such as a global brand manager, or to company teams, such as a global brand team. In both cases, the responsibility would be executed across all geographies, and the teams or marketing managers would

27. "Re-appraising the Power Base of Regional Barons," *Financial Times*, March 26, 1990, p. 12.
28. "Big Blue Wants the World to Know Who's the Boss," *Business Week*, September 26, 1994, p. 78.
29. "American Standard Reorganizes Global Fittings Organization," *PR Newswire*, December 2, 1998.

be able to make decisions for all geographies. Global mandates might also be of a temporary nature, such as when executives are named to a task force that might deal with a particular global marketing issue and after conclusion be dissolved. The decision as to who should receive a global mandate is an important one for all globally active firms. It would be difficult to act on a required global marketing strategy if the company did not endow key marketing executives with global mandates.[30] We will describe several forms of global mandates below and describe the type of organizations in more detail.

Strategic Business Units with Global Responsibilities One of the most recent forms of organizational design is the *strategic business unit* (SBU). The SBU is an organizational group supporting products and technologies that serve an identified market and compete with identified competitors. The SBU may either be a separate organizational design, similar to a product organization, or it can be an organizational unit used only for the purpose of developing a business strategy for many products in a geographic area.

The increased penetration of global competition has forced many firms to set up SBUs to address the global markets and assess competition in developing a global business strategy. The SBU structure goes beyond the divisional structure. An SBU is organized as a self-contained unit, typically with its own associated production and technological resources. In some of the newer types of organizations, SBUs have been set up as legally incorporated firms, with the parent organization adopting the role of the key strategist, owning all the shares of its SBUs, and intimately involved in their strategy formulation.

Certain Scandinavian firms pioneered this type of organizational structure—Atlas-Copco, producer of compressors, and Alfa-Laval, manufacturer of industrial equipment, among them. The establishment of SBUs as separate legal units has also been adopted by ABB and Novartis, a Swiss-based pharmaceutical firm.

For SBU structures to be successful, the individual business units must operate in a self-contained way with different customer groups and different technologies and production units, sharing relatively little of daily operations. Critics of this type of organization charge that the resulting small units, each trying to build its own global structure in major global markets, can often be under critical mass.

Global Segment Organizations Within individual product divisions or newly formed SBUs, companies often find different types of customer groups. In order to treat these groups with the required focus, global segment units are formed, charged with marketing toward one particular segment only. Global segment

30. Jean-Pierre Jeannet, *Managing with a Global Mindset*, (London: Financial Times Pitman, 2000), Chapter 13, p. 171.

units were formed by a number of ICI SBUs. ICI Explosives, marketing explosives to various types of mining firms, created segment teams for different mining situations, such as deep mines, quarries, or surface mines.[31] ICI's Polyurethane Unit created segment teams for marketing to, among others, athletic shoe firms and major appliance manufacturers. In both situations, the segment units were responsible for marketing a full product line with respect to a homogeneous customer segment.[32] These units were not full-fledged SBUs since they shared the same production units all over the world. Global segment organizations are of particular importance to firms pursing global strategies from the same asset base but serving market segments with substantially different customer needs.

Global Category Organizations Firms with a number of different but related products often find it advantageous to create category units that allow them to organize and coordinate global marketing. Many of the world's best-known consumer goods firms, such as Colgate, Nestlé, Procter & Gamble, and Unilever, have recently moved toward the adoption of global product categories. Nestlé has several such units, such as for beverage, dairy, and similar categories. Each category contains a number of brands or products, making loose coordination across customer groups or technologies possible. Global categories typically contain separate global brand units with their own separate manufacturing units and facilitate the coordination of new technologies. The global category organization allows for better transfer of learning across countries. Procter & Gamble adopted a global category organization along seven product-related groups, ranging from baby care (Pampers and related products) to food (Pringles potato chips and other products). This organization was expected to allow P&G to move faster overseas and introduce new products more quickly than with a regionally focused organization.[33]

Global Customer Organizations As we have seen in Chapter 11, some firms are creating global customer organizations intended to coordinate a firm's business with individual worldwide customers. Such organizations are useful if a company has a substantial amount of business distributed all over the world with one worldwide account. Typically, these units are part of either a global business structure or SBUs and do not have full independence with respect to production or technology.

Over the past few years, companies have developed a number of different ways to organize their business globally. The trend has been toward the cre-

31. ICI has since sold off its explosive unit.
32. ICI sold its PU unit to Huntsman Chemicals in 1999.
33. "Can Procter & Gamble Make the Tide Turn?" *Los Angeles Times*, June 13, 1999, p. C1.

ation of increasingly global forms of organizations, and away from the traditional approach of divided responsibility for domestic and international business. This has created many opportunities for executives with global mindsets at ever lower levels of organizational management. Which type of organization a company selects should also reflect the type of global logic (Chapter 7) the company faces.

Ford: The Transformation into a Global Organization Ford Motor Company is a firm that has undergone a major transformation in its organization. Operating on a more or less regional structure, Ford had created major operating units in North America, Europe, Latin America, Africa, and Asia. Each regional unit tended to be responsible for its own operations, developing and producing cars for its regional markets. Faced with strong competition from its bigger rival, General Motors, and the more efficient Japanese companies, especially Toyota, Ford realized that under the regional setup it incurred a massive penalty for unnecessary duplication of key functions and efforts. Even though it served what amounted to almost identical customer needs in many countries, the company was developing separate power trains and engines and was purchasing different component parts at a cost of $3 billion, astronomical compared with what an integrated operation would spend.[34]

Ford had tried global integration before, but usually on a project basis, not by integrating the entire organization. In the late 1970s, Ford created a subcompact car (Fiesta) that it hoped would be marketed in Europe and the United States. The resulting infighting prevented a true world car from being developed, and the company ended up with two similar cars that were developed separately in Europe and North America. In the 1990s, Ford spent about $6 billion to develop midsize cars for both Europe and North America. Successful in Europe, the cars did not fare well in the United States, where they were launched late.[35]

Ford began its reorganization by merging its North American organization with its European car operation, creating an integrated firm under the "Ford 2000" banner.[36] The new organization of Ford Automotive called for four major functions to each be headed by one executive with global responsibility. The most important function was vehicle development, structured around five vehicle centers in the United States and in Europe. The other global functions were marketing and sales, manufacturing, and purchasing.[37] The development center for small cars was in Europe, with locations in both Germany and the United

34. "Ford Maps Out a Global Ambition," *Financial Times*, April 3, 1995, p. 9.
35. "Ford's Really Big Leap at the Future," *Fortune*, September 18, 1995, p. 134.
36. "Ford: Alex Trotman's Daring Global Strategy," *Business Week*, April 3, 1995, p. 94.
37. "The World That Changed the Machine," *Economist*, March 30, 1996, p. 63.

Kingdom. In the United States were the development centers for rear-wheel-drive cars and commercial trucks, all with global development responsibility.[38] The company hoped to cut development costs by using fewer components, fewer engines, and fewer power trains, as well as by speeding up development cycles. As a result of this reorganization, some 25,000 Ford managers were believed to have either moved locations or to have been reassigned to report to new supervisors. Ford continues to pursue a very aggressive marketing strategy, both at home and abroad, capped by the acquisition of Volvo Cars.[39]

The Development Cycle of Global Marketing Organizations

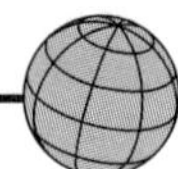

Companies evolve as organizations over time. As their international involvement expands, the degree of organizational complexity increases, and firms reorganize accordingly. As a firm moves from exporting a few goods to being a worldwide organization, it finds itself going through organizational changes with differing structures and focus. Organizations change to reflect the importance of different markets and the needs of the customer. As the amount of international business increases and the needs of the customers become more complex, the organization will change to reflect the market. Figure 16.12 depicts the typical progression of the global organization's life cycle. Because this is a dynamic and integrative process, most companies do not follow this life cycle exactly, but the framework does provide a method by which to evaluate the degree of focus and responsibility.

Export

When the domestic market becomes saturated or a need is identified in foreign markets, companies begin exporting their product or services. The export department is still a function of and normally reports to the company and follows company procedures and strategies. Often, companies will first begin to receive inquiries from foreign companies about their products. At that point, an export person or department is established to process and respond to the foreign inquiries.

Foreign Sales Office

If the demand for the product increases and there appears to be a need to establish an office either to ease administrative procedures or to investigate new mar-

38. "Ford: Alex Trotman's Daring Global Strategy."
39. Christopher A. Bartlett and Sumantra Ghoshal, "Matrix Management: Not a Structure, a Frame of Mind," *Harvard Business Review*, July–August 1990, pp. 138–145.

FIGURE 16.12

Development Cycle of International Organizations

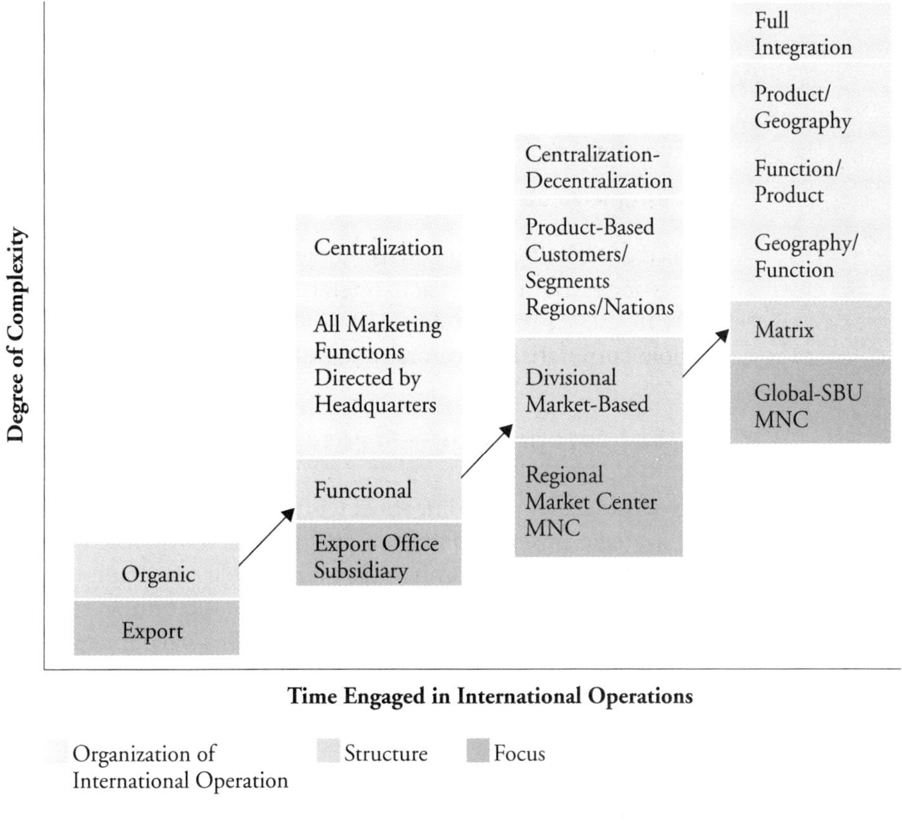

kets or refine old markets, a company will normally establish an office in a foreign country. Usually, this office is under headquarters' control and acts according to home office directions.

Regional Market Center

Regional market centers act as filters between the headquarters and various country organizations. Regional market centers coordinate the marketing function of the branches so that they remain in line with corporate objectives. Regional market centers are normally organized along geographic lines; however, they may be organized along product groups or similar target markets.

Matrix Organizations

The matrix organization is the most complex and sophisticated structure. It requires a firm to be fully competent in the following areas:

1. Geographic knowledge
2. Product knowledge
3. Functional aspects, such as finance, production, and marketing
4. Customer/industry knowledge

Instead of focusing in one area—geographic or product organization—the matrix incorporates both, and each operates as a profit center. Matrix organizations allow low levels to have substantial authority; however, they require an open and flexible corporate culture/orientation for successful implementation.

Global Integration—Strategic Business Units

Fully advanced global companies with complete integration have begun to establish strategic business units. An SBU acts as a separate business and contains a group of products or technologies directed at a specific target market. SBUs are part of a formal structure but act primarily to determine strategies. As mentioned earlier in the chapter, a number of companies have moved from the geography/product division matrix to a global product division structure.

Conclusions

Organizing the marketing efforts of a company across a number of countries is a difficult process. As the scope of a company's global business changes, its organizational structure must be modified in accordance with the internal and external environments. As the number of countries in which a company is marketing increases, as product lines expand, and as objectives change, so will the organization. In this chapter, we have reviewed the various organizations commonly used, showing the benefits of each. The dynamic nature of business requires a constant reevaluation of organizational structure with necessary modifications to meet the objectives of the firm.

The task of molding an organization to respond to the needs of a global marketplace involves building a shared vision and developing human resources. A clear vision of the purpose of the company that is shared by everyone gives meaning and direction to each manager.

Managers are a company's scarcest resource. The process of recruiting, selecting, training, and managing the human resources must help build a common vision and values. Matsushita (Panasonic) gives new white-collar workers six months of cultural and spiritual training; Philips has organization cohesion training; and Unilever's new hires go through indoctrination. Such initiation programs help to build vision and shared values. Managers also receive ongoing training. For example, Unilever brings four hundred to five hundred international managers from around the world to its international management training center. Unilever spends as much on training as it does on R&D, not only to upgrade skills but also to indoctrinate managers into the Unilever club and help build personal relationships and informal contacts that are more powerful than the formal systems or structures.

QUESTIONS FOR DISCUSSION

1. What aspects of the external environment cause structures of multicountry marketing organizations to be different from those of single-country marketing organizations?
2. What effect will the marketing strategy have on an international marketing organization? For example, if the key aspect of a computer manufacturer's strategy is to focus on three industries worldwide—banks, stockbrokers, and educational institutions—will the organization be different from that of another company that decides to focus on end users who require mainframe computers?
3. How does a single-country organization evolve into an international organization? What type of international organization is likely to develop first? Second? Why?
4. What actions will cause a company to develop an international marketing organization?
5. What are the pros and cons of a regional management center versus a product organization?
6. A country-based geographic structure responds well to the local culture and marketing. What will cause a company to switch from a country structure to a worldwide product organization?
7. Matrix organizations can be very costly and complex. What advantages do they offer to offset these problems?
8. In addition to the formal organization structure, how does the global company ensure that it is responding to the market and achieving efficiency, local responsiveness, and global learning?

FOR FURTHER READING

Bartlett, Christopher A. "MNCs: Get Off the Reorganization Merry-Go-Round," *Harvard Business Review*, March–April 1983, pp. 138–146.

Bartlett, Christopher A., and Sumantra Ghoshal. *Managing Across Borders: The Transnational Solution.* Boston: Harvard Business School Press, 1989.

Doyle, Peter, John Saunders, and Veronica Wong. "Competition in Global Markets: A Case Study of American and Japanese Competition in the British Market," *Journal of International Business Studies*, 3rd Quarter 1992, pp. 419–426.

Handy, Charles. *The Age of Unreason.* London: Hutchinson, 1989.

———. *Inside Organizations.* London: BBC Books, 1990.

Howard, Robert. "The Designer Organization: Italy's GFT Goes Global," *Harvard Business Review*, September–October 1991, pp. 28–44.

Kets de Vries, Manfred F. R. "Charisma in Action: The Transformation Abilities of Virgin's Richard Branson and ABB's Percy Barnevik," *Organizational Dynamics*, vol. 26, no. 3, January 1, 1998.

Laabs, Jennifer. "Building a Global Management Team," *Personnel Journal*, 1993, vol. 72, no. 8 p. 75.

Lei, David, John W. Slocum, and Robert A. Pitts. "Designing Organizations for Competitive Advantage: The Power of Unlearning and Learning," *Organizational Dynamics*, vol. 27, no. 3, January 1, 1999, pp. 24–28.

Maruca, Regina Fazio. "The Right Way to Go Global: An Interview with Whirlpool CEO David Whitwam," *Harvard Business Review*, March–April 1994, pp. 135–145.

Ohmae, Kenichi. *The Borderless World.* London: Collins, 1990.

17

Planning and Controlling Global Marketing

THE PROCESS OF GLOBAL MARKETING WOULD NOT BE ABLE TO FUNCTION IN A complex organization without the necessary attention to planning and controlling. In this chapter we focus on the particular challenges faced by the planning process when carried out in the global environment. Beginning with some of the traditional strategic planning approaches, we point out the difficulties entailed in stretching them into the global environment. In particular, we argue that planning needs to occur with the full global opportunity in view, and that global marketing is difficult, if not impossible, to plan on a country-by-country basis only. Making the distinction between corporate and business unit planning, the chapter also covers the necessary control processes and revisits the perennial debate between

FIGURE 17.1

Planning and Controlling Global Marketing

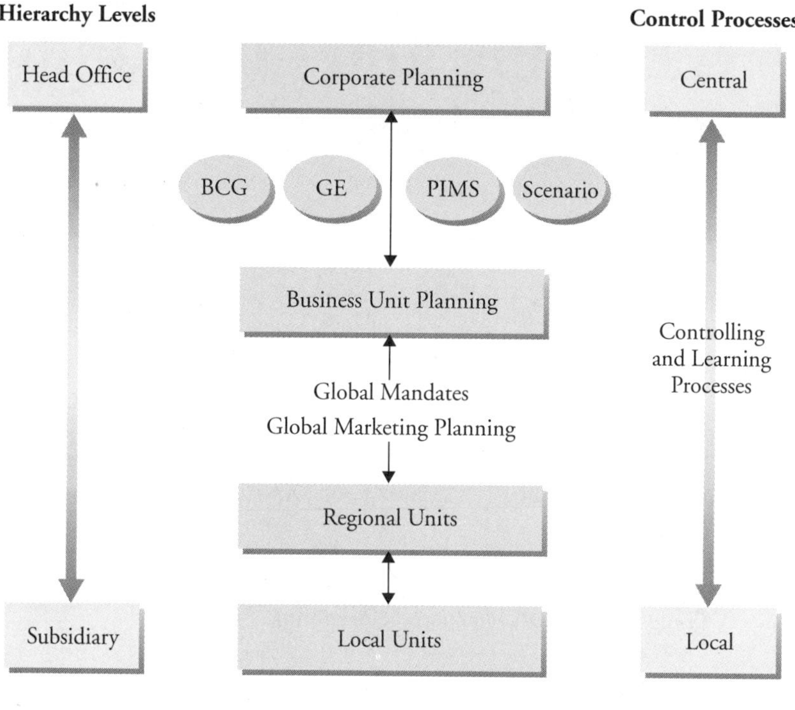

central versus local control. The chapter introduces the reader to the new developments of assigning global mandates to separate business units, and the challenge to make organizations learn globally rather than just locally. An overview of the chapter topics is provided in Figure 17.1.

The Global Planning Process

Planning in the global environment is difficult because of the number of extraneous elements involved. Table 17.1 illustrates the differences between planning in a domestic setting and planning in a global one.

As shown in Table 17.1, numerous factors, such as language, political differences, currency fluctuations, and insufficient market data, increase the complexity of global planning. These differences make developing and implementing global plans more difficult.

TABLE 17.1

Domestic Versus International Planning Factors

Domestic Planning	*International Planning*
1. Single language and nationality	1. Multilingual/multinational/multicultural factors
2. Relatively homogeneous market	2. Fragmented and diverse markets
3. Data available, usually accurate, and collection easy	3. Data collection a formidable task, requiring significantly higher budgets and personnel allocation
4. Political factors relatively unimportant	4. Political factors frequently vital
5. Relative freedom from government interference	5. Involvement in national economic plans; government influences affect business decisions
6. Individual corporation has little effect on environment	6. "Gravitational" distortion by large companies
7. Chauvinism helps	7. Chauvinism hinders
8. Relatively stable business environment	8. Multiple environments, many of which are highly unstable (but may be highly profitable)
9. Uniform financial climate	9. Variety of financial climates ranging from overconservative to wildly inflationary
10. Single currency	10. Currencies differing in stability and real value
11. Business "rules of the game" mature and understood	11. Rules diverse, changeable, and unclear
12. Management generally accustomed to sharing responsibilities and using financial controls	12. Management frequently autonomous and unfamiliar with budgets and controls

Source: William W. Cain, "International Planning: Mission Impossible?" *Columbia Journal of World Business*, July–August 1970, p. 58. Reprinted by permission.

Strategic planning is a widely accepted practice of corporate business. The issue of globalization demands strategic research and thought in addressing increasingly complex and competitive world markets.[1] Often, global strategic planning takes place at the highest levels of a company. Relatively young, well-trained executives commonly provide the information and analysis for these high-level discussions and decisions. It is important to understand the process that the board or executive committee takes to make a strategic decision, as you may be the marketing manager implementing that decision.

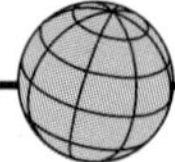

Corporate Versus Business Planning

Global planning may take place at two levels. First, at the corporate level, a company decides which businesses it wants to be in. This choice between different businesses has traditionally been the occupation of corporate planners. At a lower level, planning is undertaken to determine resource allocations and strategies within a given business. Here, the issue is how to distribute resources across functional activities, product lines, segments, or geographic markets.

For the purpose of this text, we are more interested in the business level planning and less so in the corporate planning activities. We cover some of the approaches for corporate level planning, because they are frequently practiced at international firms, at the same time pointing out the weaknesses of those approaches when it comes to planning business activities, such as marketing, on a global basis within a given business.

Traditional Corporate Planning Models

In this section we review the various types of planning processes currently being used, their application to the global market environment, and the advantages and disadvantages of each procedure when used for planning the global marketing effort. The most widely used approaches to planning are the following:

Boston Consulting Group (BCG) approach
General Electric/McKinsey (GE) approach
Profit impact of market strategy (PIMS)
Scenario planning[2]

Numerous articles and papers review and compare the various planning models as they apply to domestic markets. Using these domestic systems as a base, each approach will be examined as it is used for global markets.

1. George Rabstejnek, "Let's Get Back to the Basics of Global Strategy," *Journal of Business Strategy*, September–October 1989, p. 34.
2. Richard G. Hamermesh, "Making Planning Strategy," *Harvard Business Review*, July–August 1986, p. 115.

A firm frequently consists of a number of businesses. When established, each of these businesses was expected to grow. The firm would encourage growth by expanding research and development, advertising, and promotional budgets for all but the declining products. In recent years, the cost and availability of capital have caused corporations to be much more selective in the financing of their businesses. The tendency has been for a firm to look at its individual businesses and decide which ones to build, maintain, phase down, or close down. Therefore, the job of planning has become one of evaluating current businesses and searching out new opportunities so that the mixture of businesses within the firm will provide the necessary growth and cash flow for growth. Once the firm is broken down into strategic business units (SBUs), planning must classify them based on expected future potential. Although the concept of an SBU is widely accepted, it does have limitations. For example, because vertically integrated businesses share facilities and their performances are interrelated, it may not be easy to neatly sort out business units.[3]

The Boston Consulting Group Approach The Boston Consulting Group (BCG) approach classifies all current strategic business units into a business portfolio matrix, shown in Figure 17.2. The matrix includes both current SBUs and potential or proposed opportunities. The proposed opportunities are normally an extension of the current business via expansion into a new country or new product. BCG's methodology classifies these businesses by market growth rate and market share. The market growth rate is the expected total market demand growth on an annualized basis. The market share is the company's relative share compared with that of the largest competitor. For example, a rate of 1.0 means the SBU has the same share as the next competitor, a 0.5 means it has one-half the share of the competitor ahead of it, and a 3.0 means it has a three times larger share than the next-largest competitor.[4]

A firm's SBUs are evaluated and classified based on this approach. Market growth rate relates to the stage of the product life cycle, and relative market share is based on the concept of market dominance. To survive in the long term, a firm needs the proper balance of business in each area of the matrix—dubbed stars, cash cows, dogs, and problem children.

Over time, businesses will change their positions. Many SBUs start as problem children, then become stars, then cash cows, and finally dogs. The corporate planning function must work with the managers of each SBU to forecast the future mix of businesses in each area. Then resources must be allocated based on this forecast as well as on the corporate objectives.

3. Rael T. Hussein, "A Critical Review of Strategic Planning Models," *Quarterly Review of Marketing*, Spring–Summer 1987, p. 17.
4. Bruce D. Henderson, "The Experience Curve Reviewed: IV. The Growth Share Matrix of the Product Portfolio," *Perspectives*, no. 135 (Boston: Boston Consulting Group, 1973).

FIGURE 17.2

Boston Consulting Group Matrix

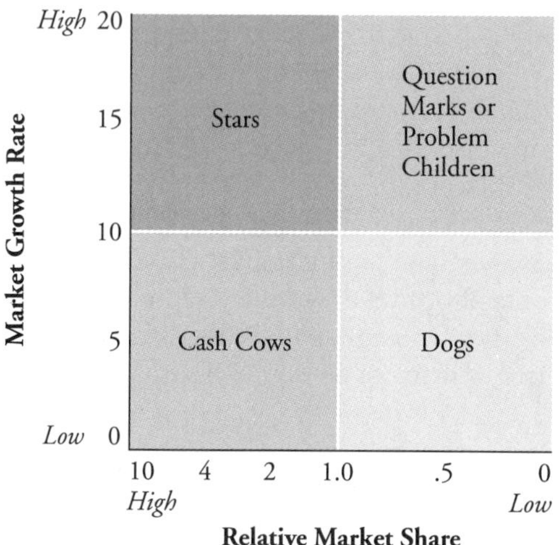

Source: PERSPECTIVES, no. 135, "The Experience Curve-Reviewed, IV. The Growth Share Matrix or The Product Portfolio." Adapted by permission from The Boston Consulting Group, Inc., 1973.

The BCG approach in global planning has the following major advantages:

- Requires a global view of the firm's business and its competition
- Provides a framework for analysis and comparison of business
- Is a good basis for the formulation of marketing objectives for specific international markets
- Allows a convenient graphic form that is easily understood by executives

Keep in mind that the individual firm may have other objectives besides the generation of cash, such as gaining technical information, preventing competition, or establishing good relations with a local government. For example, Philips, the Dutch electronics giant, has argued that it must keep its semiconductor business, which is a money-losing business. Philips executives maintain that without proprietory access to semiconductor know-how, the company's ability to compete with the Japanese in consumer electronics would be fatally undermined.[5]

5. "The Powerhouse That Blew a Fuse," *Sunday New York Times*, May 20, 1990, p. D9.

The General Electric/McKinsey Approach General Electric and McKinsey management consultants worked together to develop the GE business screen, a multifactor assessment based on an analysis of factors relating to profitability. The approach is an extension of the BCG approach.[6]

The GE screen uses the following factors to evaluate SBUs:

Industry attractiveness	*Business strength*
Market size	Relative market share
Market growth	Price competitiveness
Market diversity	Size, growth
Profit margins	Product quality
Competitive structure	Profitability
Technical role	Technological position
Cyclicality	Strengths and weaknesses
Environment	Knowledge of customers/market
Legal, human, social	Image, pollution, people

The GE approach rates each SBU, on the basis of these factors, for industry attractiveness and business strength. Each factor is given a certain weight. A procedure of aggregating various executives' opinions on these weights results in high, medium, or low attractiveness and business strength ratings.[7] Each SBU is then located on GE's nine-cell business screen, shown in Figure 17.3.

The principles of the GE approach have been modified and used in the global environment. As we mentioned in Chapter 6, Ford Motor Co.'s Tractor Division developed a strategic market portfolio evaluation system that focused on country attractiveness and competitive strengths.[8]

The GE approach has the same limitations as the BCG method. However, the GE method is more adaptable to global markets. Each firm can determine which factors are important to its success in a global market and can evaluate SBUs

6. Information in this section is drawn from *Managing Strategies for the Future Through Current Crises* (Fairfield, Conn.: General Electric Company, 1975).
7. Peter Turnbull, "A Review of Portfolio Planning Models for Industrial Marketing and Purchasing Management," *European Journal of Marketing*, 1990, vol. 24, no. 3, pp. 7–10.
8. Gilbert D. Harrell and Richard O'Kiefer, "Multinational Strategic Market Portfolios," *MSU Business Topics*, Winter 1981, p. 12.

FIGURE 17.3

GE's Business Screen for Evaluating SBUs

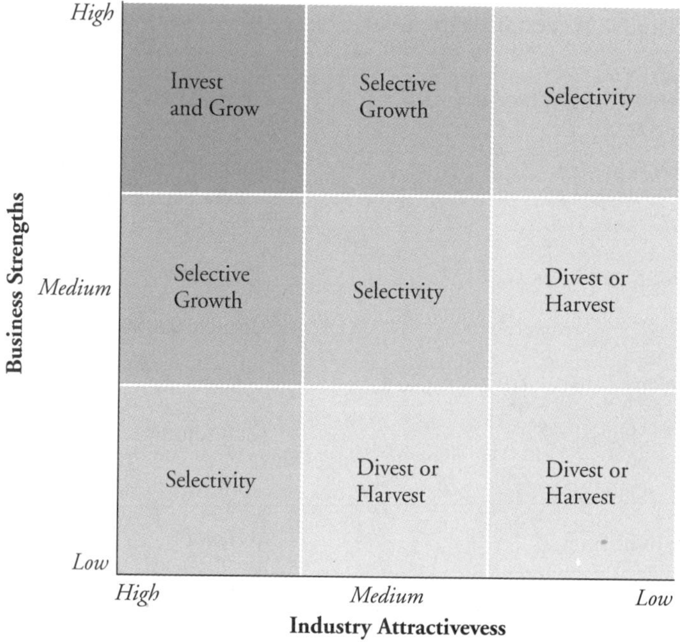

based on these factors. Unfortunately, little empirical work has been done on either approach in the global market. The GE approach is still two dimensional, using only the factors of industry attractiveness and business strength. This ignores the form of entry. For example, the importance of political stability varies greatly, depending on whether a firm is exporting or involved in direct foreign investment.

In conclusion, the GE approach is useful for international companies. It provides more flexibility than the BCG approach, but its limitations should not be ignored.

Profit Impact of Marketing Strategy (PIMS) The PIMS project was started in 1960 at General Electric. Over the years, the model was developed at the Harvard Business School, the Marketing Science Institute, and finally at the Strategic

Planning Institute. The PIMS model database includes the history and performance of over 450 companies and 3,000 businesses. The model includes a computer-based regression model that utilizes the experience of the database to determine what explains (or drives) profitability.[9]

Each business is described in terms of thirty-seven factors, such as growth rate, market share, product quality, and investment intensity. The PIMS model uses multivariate regression equations to establish relationships between these different factors and two separate measures of performance, specifically return on investment (ROI) and cash flow. PIMS research indicates that these performance measures are explained by general factors such as the following:

Market growth rate
Market share of business
Market share divided by share of three largest competitors
Degree of vertical integration
Working capital requirements per dollars of sales
Plant and equipment requirements per dollars of sales
Relative product quality

The PIMS model uses many more variables than either the BCG or GE approach. Using the thirty-seven factors, the model explains over 80 percent of the observed variation in profitability of the three thousand businesses in the database.

The PIMS model may become one of the key strategic planning models in the future. With the utilization of a multinational database, the PIMS model will be able to assist planners in deciding how to allocate resources to meet corporate objectives.[10]

Scenario Planning The three strategic planning models discussed so far are referred to as portfolio models. These models do not take into consideration the impact of various external factors such as economic growth, energy costs, inflation, international relations, war, and economic fluctuations.[11] Scenario planning is a unique approach to strategic planning. With scenario planning, the multinational's business is broken down into business/country segments. A central or most probable scenario is developed regarding significant external variables such as energy costs, world politics, and inflation. Possible variants of this

9. Robert D. Buzzell and Bradley T. Gale, *The PIMS Principles: Linking Strategy to Performance* (New York: Free Press, 1987).
10. Mark Drexler, and Thomas Reedy, "Managing Customers Profitably," *Canadian Insurance*, July 1, 1999, vol. 104, no. 8, p. 26.
11. Kerry Tucker, "Scenario Planning," *Association Management*, April 1, 1999, vol. 51, no. 4, p. 70.

central scenario are also developed. Then the business/country segments are evaluated based on the central scenario and the variant scenarios. Ideally, investment decisions can be based on this analysis.

Scenario planning has limitations. First, the development of a central scenario and variants will be difficult. There will be many inputs to this scenario, with limited agreement. Second, analysis of the effect of each scenario will also be complex. For example, if a firm is selling pipe to the United Kingdom and the central scenario predicts oil prices will go up 10 percent per year, how will the firm evaluate the U.K. pipe market? Increased oil prices mean more tax revenues from North Sea oil, an increase in exports, a favorable impact on the balance of trade, the strengthening of the pound sterling, an increase in imports, and a decrease in the ability of the remaining U.K. industries to export.

Although scenario planning and contingency planning are useful techniques, they are best used to augment the portfolio methods—BCG, GE, and PIMS.

Limitations to Traditional Corporate Planning Approaches

The traditional approaches described in the previous sections were all conceived in the United States and originally applied to multiproduct companies doing mostly domestic business. Although they did help managers understand which businesses might be emphasized over others in terms of resource allocations, they did not help in allocating resources within a business once it was selected for further investment.

To overcome the limitations of the data, some companies have traditionally treated each country, or market, as a distinctly different business and analyzed each foreign market in the same way as the domestic division. The disadvantage of this approach stems from the fact that the firm would be treating each country as a separate investment decision, selecting those that "fit the approach" and eliminating others that did not look good in the databank. However, as we have pointed out earlier (Chapters 7 and 8), a firm must take into account the entire set of data of its chessboard on a global basis, and not evaluate opportunities on a country-by-country basis only. Doing so would preclude a firm from treating each country as a separate entry decision. Rather, the company would have to support an entire business, with all of its implications, and only later determine resource allocations within the business.

To make these approaches more helpful in planning at the corporate, multiproduct level, the entire data set needs to consist of global data, not just U.S. or single-country data. Whether using a BCG, GE, or PIMS approach, the data must be drawn from the entire global market of each business. That is, only if a company were to do a BCG analysis across all of its separate SBUs, each based on a complete and globalized data set, would the allocation or priority-setting process be relevant for the planning of global operations.

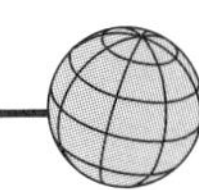

Corporate Planning in the Global Age: Assigning Global Mandates

Companies looking at the entire global opportunity frequently observe that they must look at their business in a global context. Achieving global leadership is therefore considered a prize, a first competitive priority. With this in mind, global market share in a sector, segment, or business is viewed as the ultimate aim. Business units, divisions, or SBUs are thus asked, even instructed, to maximize their opportunity globally. This we call *receiving a global mandate*. (See Chapter 16 for definition.)

A major decision at the corporate level must therefore be, "Who should receive a global mandate?" Businesses that develop on a global basis typically need a larger resource base than those competing on a domestic basis only. Greater claims for resources make it more difficult for corporations to support all of their businesses in the drive to achieve global leadership status. Corporate planning will thus have to assist in the selection and resource allocation process.

First, corporate planners will initiate a thorough analysis of the need to assign SBUs' global mandates. Using our language developed in Chapter 7, it is clear that only businesses that face significant global logic should receive such global mandates. However, for many firms, that criterion applies to a number of businesses. In the case of General Electric, in fact, global mandates apply to *all* of its major businesses, ranging from plastics to transportation, energy generation, medical technology, and more. At Siemens of Germany, all of its more than two hundred separate strategic planning units have essentially global mandates. The same is true for the independent chemical businesses of ICI and the United Kingdom.

The resources required to make a global business out of a not-yet-globalized one are considerable. At one large European firm, the corporate planning staff determined that the company's cash-generating resources would never suffice to feed all the needs of the globalizing SBUs. Consequently, companies have to make resource allocations and set priorities.

At ICI, the company was faced with enormous resource demands from both its chemical fibers and acrylics divisions. Neither had achieved global leadership status, and both were thus competitively weak. And yet, to move them to global leadership status would have required substantial investments across the world. Rather than maintain two subcritical businesses, or to attempt to expand both of them but neither quite enough, the company found a partner to trade. ICI divested its fibers business, selling it to DuPont of the United States. In return,

DuPont sold its acrylics business to ICI. This trade allowed ICI to become the global leader in the acrylics category. DuPont, in return, strengthened its presence in the European fibers business and in the textile sector. Both parties gained, and both ended up with a global leader.

Another firm that has made substantial resource allocation by focusing on a few global opportunities is Nokia of Finland. Originally a company active in forestry and paper production, the company successfully diversified into machinery, electronics, and telecommunications in the 1980s. However, the demands of its growing telecommunications businesses became so important that Nokia began to divest itself of a number of its original businesses, including the paper business, the computer business, and the consumer electronics business. This left Nokia with essentially two businesses: cellular infrastructure and cellular handsets. Both are now in a leading position in the race for global market dominance. For Nokia, fewer but globally well-positioned businesses were far preferable to a wide range of regional businesses.

The substantial resource commitments demanded of companies that want to expand their SBUs globally has also taken its toll among large U.S.-based multinational firms. PepsiCo, involved in a very difficult fight with Coca-Cola Co. for global market leadership in the soft-drink sector, has had to contend with a competitor that has *only* a soft-drink business. In contrast, PepsiCo has, in addition to soft drinks, a large snacks business (Frito-Lay) and several large internationally active fast-food restaurant chains (Pizza Hut, Taco Bell, KFC). The company has thus announced its intention to divest itself of the restaurant business and to reinvest the proceeds into the soft-drink business, particularly for market expansion in countries such as China, India, and eastern Europe, where the Coke position is not yet entrenched. Pepsi will avoid Japan and Germany, where it sees little chance to dethrone Coke.[12]

It appears that the main efforts in the areas of global corporate planning lie in selecting, supporting, and guiding businesses that deserve a global mandate and have a realistic chance to achieve global leadership in selective niches.

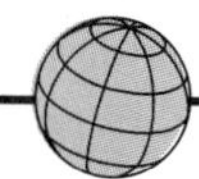

Global Business Strategy Planning

When planning at the business unit level, the issues are different from those raised at the corporate level. In particular, when a business has been assigned a global mandate from its head office organization, the planning focus must turn toward the approach to be taken to build a globally competitive business that can climb to a leading position.

12. "PepsiCo Loses Its Taste for Fast Food Chains," *Financial Times*, January 27, 1997, p. 19. "PepsiCo's New Formula," *Business Week*, April 10, 2000, p.172.

The germane questions turn from which business to support to which actions the business must undertake to achieve the required competitive position. The starting point again is the entire global opportunity for the business, or the relevant global chessboard that best depicts the potential across the world. In business planning, the business must allocate resources across various functions, marketing being only one among such others as research and development (R&D) and production. Furthermore, the business unit needs to plan these resource allocations across the relevant geography and determine the nature of business focus, whether narrow or broad.

The following questions need to be addressed in global business planning:

1. What is the relevant global opportunity for the business?
   Description of the global chessboard, determination of the relevant metrics that describe the opportunity set worldwide, and so on.

2. What are the developments of the global chessboard?
   Determination of trends in volume, future volumes, and so forth.

3. What are the relevant global logics facing the business?
   Clear understanding of global logics as described in Chapter 7 (customer, purchasing, industry, competitor, size or scale, regulatory, competitive).

4. What are the imperatives of the global logics?
   Refers to the markets or countries where a company with a global mandate has to compete, markets it must win, segments to be in, and the like. All of these elements are required on the way to gain a global competitive position that could lead to market leadership.

5. How are resources to be allocated?
   Resource allocations occur across a wide geography, segments, and several business functions. Marketing is but one core function, although in global battles it is a key weapon.

6. What are the business objectives for functions and segments?
   Setting measurable objectives, such as market shares, volume, or profitability, that become guideposts for the business and the individual functions, such as marketing, in their own planning cycles.

For a business or business unit that operates under a global mandate or that has decided to operate in such a way, these planning questions are different than for a domestic unit. The approach we advocate is to answer these planning questions *first* from a global point of view. If a business is planning from the bottom up, asking each country operation to submit plans to be later integrated, it is questionable if that business could ever achieve a single, unified global strategy. However, local country or regional units would be required to plan their activities in line with an overall global business strategy.

The Global Marketing Planning Process

The complexity of global markets requires a structured approach to the planning process. Research into the practices of multinational companies has revealed a number of problems regarding the planning process, among them the following:

- Too much information of the wrong kind and a lack of useful information for planning
- A neglect of strategic or long-term planning
- Overemphasis on the plan as a control device instead of as a means to achieving the objectives
- A belief that forecasting and budgeting were market planning
- A separation of long-term and short-term plans, which precluded operational management from considering more desirable alternatives.[13]

The heterogeneous nature of global markets and the difficulty of data collection require that the marketer take an organized approach to evaluating opportunities and preparing plans. Figure 17.4 illustrates a global marketing planning matrix.

The planning matrix is an organized approach to evaluating global opportunities. The matrix requires that the marketer evaluate the marketing planning variables at each level of decision making. Levels of decision making, which are located on the vertical axis, begin with the commitment decision. This first decision, whether or not to enter foreign markets, is based on the firm's objectives, its resources, and the opportunities available in international versus domestic markets. After making the commitment decision, a company will select the country it wishes to enter. The country decision is based on evaluation of the environment, the demand, the corporate resources, and the financial projections. The mode of entering the selected country will be based on the firm's commitment decision, the country selection, and the cost/benefit evaluation of different modes of entry.

As discussed in Chapter 9, the mode of entry will also be affected by a variety of other factors, such as risk assessment and laws of foreign ownership. The marketing strategy will flow logically from the firm's objective in a market, which will include the marketing mix required to differentiate products in that environment. The market organization decision is related to the objective and strategy for each market. The organization structure will determine which people will be where, how decisions will be made, what information and services will go back and forth between the organizational unit and headquarters, and the budgeting control

13. Tom Griffin, "Marketing Planning: Observations on Current Practices and Recent Studies," *European Journal of Marketing*, 1989, vol. 24, no. 12, pp. 21–22.

FIGURE 17.4

Global Marketing Planning Matrix

Global Decisions	Marketing Planning Variables					
	Situation Analysis	Problems-Opportunity Analysis	Objectives	Marketing Program	Marketing Budgets	Sales Volume Cost/Profit Estimate
A. Committment Decisions						
B. Country Selection						
C. Mode of Entry						
D. Marketing Strategy						
E. Marketing Organization						

Source: Reprinted with permission from Helmut Becker and Hans B. Thorelli: *International Marketing Strategy*, Copyright © 1980, Pergamon Press PLC.

process. A recent study of seventy-nine businesses from twenty countries found that all companies prepared some type of marketing plan.

Coordinating the Global Planning Process

Coordinating the strategic planning process between the product marketing functions and the country managers is a challenging process. A natural tendency to emphasize the product element shortchanges the geographic element. To improve coordination of product management and country management while utilizing the expertise of each, General Electric has each *country* executive develop a comprehensive country opportunity plan that covers all products and strategies. The country executive's plan is compared to the plans of GE's individual strategic business units for that market. The combination of the two different organizations provides a rich pool of information on tactics and opportunities. The final plan integrates the product and country points of view, with conflicts identified and solutions proposed.[14]

Hoechst, a leading global chemical company based in Germany, used a multilevel planning system to coordinate the different layers of management, as well as to get the full benefit of its knowledge and coordinate strategy from different parts of the company. The Hoechst planning system is illustrated in Figure 17.5. The top layer is strategic planning covering a ten-year horizon for products and regions. For example, what is Hoechst planning over the next ten years for agricultural operations and pharmaceuticals? In addition, what are the plans for Japan or France? Care is taken to ensure that the strategic goals match for products and regions. Strategic planning at Hoechst involves the following four steps:

1. Gathering internal data about markets, competitors, and capacities
2. Gathering and analyzing external data on world economics, industry dynamics, market trends, and key success factors
3. Developing strategic options and selecting a preferred solution
4. Developing an implementation plan with milestones identified and target dates set

The middle layer of Hoechst's system is operational planning. This process covers the next four years on a rolling forecast, which is revised each year. The first year is in detail, and the second to fourth years are in rougher outline. The bottom layer is a control system for following up and monitoring, on a quarterly basis, the progress of the operational plans. This allows deviations to be tracked and plans adjusted to deal with shocks, such as currency fluctuations. The planning system has proved successful, with Hoechst achieving a 1988 profit of 2.0 billion deutsche marks, the largest in its 125-year history.[15]

Siemens, one of the world's largest electrical and electronics equipment manufacturers, has a formalized communication phase between the product groups and the geographic structures; during this formal communication phase of the planning process, the product and country management meet to establish an understanding of each other's position. Eaton Corporation, organized around a worldwide product structure, found it necessary to inform managers of methods to respond to common environmental issues such as political conditions, taxes, inflation, and joint ownership.

14. "Many Subs in One Country? Getting More Coordination Without Stifling Initiative," *Business International*, January 15, 1982, pp. 17–19.
15. Carol Kennedy, "Hoechst: Re-positioning for a Global Market," *Long Range Planning*, 1990, vol. 23, no. 3, pp. 16–22.

FIGURE 17.5

Hoechst Planning System

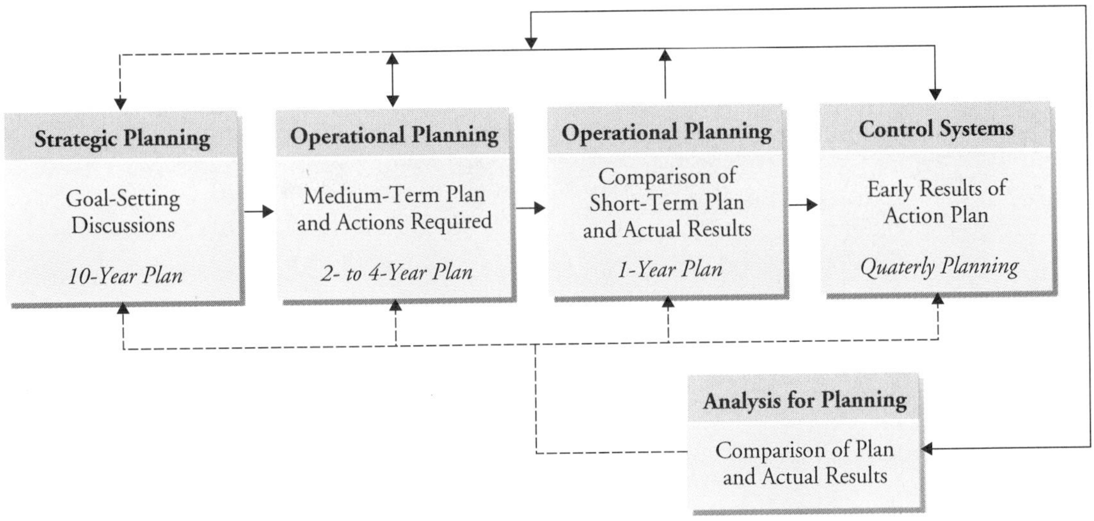

Source: Reprinted from *Long Range Planning*, vol. 23, no. 3, p. 18. Copyright 1990, with kind permission from Elsevier Science Ltd., The Boulevard, Langford Lane, Kidlington, OX5 1GB, UK.

Centralized Versus Localized Marketing

The arguments about centralized versus localized decision making in planning have been around for a long time. Although differences exist between companies and industries, some widespread trends have emerged. Originally, when international firms had little experience with planning, much of the planning and decision making was centralized around headquarters. As companies became more mature and hired more managers with planning experience, and as managers around the world became more familiar with modern planning approaches, companies began to decentralize the process. Nevertheless, each company has to find the appropriate equilibrium between a desire to plan locally and the desire to retain home office control.

The central versus local argument coalesces around two separate decision areas. First, there is the location issue, ranging from head office, to regional office if applicable, to local subsidiary. Secondly, there are the decision areas themselves—such issues as segmentation, positioning, distribution, pricing, and other crucial marketing decisions. Who should make these decisions, and who should

FIGURE 17.6

Global Marketing Responsibility Matrix

Marketing Decision Area	Head Office Control	Regional Control	Local Control
Marketing Planning			
Marketing Strategy			
Segment Selection			
Product Development			
Positioning			
Communications			
Pricing			
Sales Management			
Distribution Channel			

be responsible for planning them? (See Figure 17.6 for a decision making responsibility grid.)

The type of global marketing strategy selected by a firm greatly influences the type of organizational charter awarded to individual units. Companies subscribing to a multidomestic strategy (see Chapter 8) are more likely to favor local decision making because their business thinking rewards such an approach. Companies with a global marketing mix strategy, in which much of the marketing strategy is part of an integrated global marketing plan, are not inclined to let local affiliates make many decisions. Likewise, a company that practices a global segment strategy would not be in a position to let local management select target segments according to local requirements. As a result, the responsibility allocation matrix will have to be consistent with the type of global marketing strategy adopted.

Ford Motor Company, in its transition to a stronger articulated global strategy, changed its marketing planning approach in Europe. Traditionally, each individual country devised its own marketing plan. When Ford reorganized and began to market car models and brands on a pan-European basis, the company moved marketing strategy planning into a central unit in the United Kingdom. Eventually, Ford will market its various brands across units according to a strategy determined centrally.[16]

When prospective markets can be grouped together as a result of homogeneous characteristics, marketing decisions can often be standardized and applied to the markets.

A study of seventeen attempts of standardization of marketing functions at U.S. and European multinationals in 1989 found that half of the attempts failed. The researcher recommended: (1) more uniform market research to determine the similarities and differences from country to country; (2) use of local initiative and decision making while implementing the strategy; (3) improved follow-up to identify and solve local implementation problems; (4) active participation from subsidiaries in the development of the strategy; and (5) increased flexibility to allow global standards to be modified or developed when dictated by local conditions.[17]

The single European market offers a new opportunity for companies to standardize. A survey of forty companies inside the European Union (EU) and forty companies outside the EU, from the European Free Trade Association (EFTA), North America, Australasia, and the Far East, revealed their views about the opportunities that an integrated Europe presented. Both insiders and outsiders reported that a unified Europe would encourage them to centralize strategic market decision making and advertising and promotion. Particularly the insiders thought that marketing operations should be decentralized to get close to the customer and delivery quality by the account management staff.[18] Others have argued that the global product and centralized approach will only apply to cosmopolitan products such as expensive watches and perfume, so marketers should continue to adapt products to meet local consumers' preferences.[19]

The annual operating plan is the most widely used process in most international firms. Most firms combine their annual operating plan with a five-year plan. The planning process should be a major force for increasing the degree of

16. "EuroMarketing," *Advertising Age International*, March 1997, p. 126.
17. Kamran Kashani, "Beware the Pitfalls of Global Marketing," *Harvard Business Review*, September-October 1989, pp. 91–98.
18. Sandra Vandermerwe, "Strategies for a Pan European Market," *Long Range Planning*, 1989, vol. 22, no. 3, pp. 50–51.
19. Jurgen Reichel, "How Can Marketing Be Successfully Standardized for the European Market?" *European Journal of Marketing*, 1989, vol. 23, no. 7, pp. 60–67.

integration and coordination between different entities of a global enterprise. According to Lovering,

> Planning is very simple. It is deciding what to do, and making it happen. In my experience the second is much harder than the first. It is doomed to failure unless the necessary organizational steps are taken, and the use of strategic controls and reinforcing incentive and reward systems are central to this task.[20]

Controlling Global Marketing Operations

Maintaining control of global operations is a growing concern in light of the increasing trend toward global companies. As a company becomes larger, it faces more critical decisions, and control over operations tends to dissipate. A company's planning process is usually based on a number of assumptions about country environments, competitors, pricing, government regulations, and so on. As a plan is implemented, the company must monitor its success, as well as the variables that were used to develop the plan. As the environment changes, so will the plan; therefore, a critical part of planning is control. Establishment of a system to control marketing activities in numerous markets is not an easy job. But if companies expect to achieve the goals they have set, they must establish a control system to regulate the activities for achieving the desired goals.

Variables That Affect Control

Several variables affect the degree and effectiveness of a control system for global operations. A number of these are described in the following sections.

Communication Systems Effective communication systems facilitate control. Physical communication methods, such as the telephone, mail, and personal visits, are greatly affected by both distance and location. The more sophisticated a country's telecommunications are, the easier the communication process is. Telecommunications technology greatly improved in the 1980s with global optical fibers and satellite networks. Global voice mail, facsimile transmissions, and telephone communications have greatly enhanced communication and reporting.

Likewise, the closer the subdivision is to headquarters, the less chance there is to lose control. As physical distances separating headquarters and operating divisions increase, the time, expense, and potential for error increase. Physical dis-

20. John Lovering, "Brief Case: Developing a Strategic Planning and Control Process," *Long Range Planning*, 1990, vol. 23, no. 2, pp. 112–114.

tance also affects the speed with which changes can be implemented and problems can be detected.

Global information networks are becoming available that allow improved communication around the world. For example, the Internet links millions of computer users, who have access to information, research, and services. These information superhighways are reducing many of the constraints of geography. Long-term, these inexpensive global networks will allow for better control.

Adequacy of Data The accuracy and completeness of economic, industrial, and consumer data affect control. If the marketing plan and the goals for a particular country are based on inadequate data, then the ability to control and modify the marketing activities will be affected. For example, consider the goal of selling washing machines to Malaysia, maybe to achieve a 30 percent share of last year's market, which was estimated at 100,000 units. Therefore, the goal would be 30,000 units. But if the actual sales last year were only 70,000 units because the government had exaggerated its report to indicate economic prosperity, then the goal of 30,000 units would be too high. It may also be difficult to get timely and accurate statistics, such as the level of inflation and disposable income, which will influence the marketing strategy.

Diversity of Environments Currency values, legal structures, political systems, advertising options, number and type of public holidays, and cultural factors all influence the task of developing and controlling a marketing program. Because of this diversity of the local environments, there are continuous conflicts between the needs of the local situation and overall corporate goals. The issue of diversity must be reflected in the control system.

Management Philosophy Management philosophy about whether the company should be centralized or localized will affect the development of a control system. A highly centralized management control system will require an effective communication system so that the headquarters staff has timely and accurate local input that may affect decision making. The communication system must also allow decisions to be made quickly and transmitted to the local management for quick implementation. A localized management control system may not require the same type of communication system for day-to-day decision making, but it will require a well-documented and fully communicated set of objectives for each autonomous unit. These objectives will help guide local decision making and control so that the corporate goals are achieved.

Size of International Operations As the size of the international operation increases as a percentage of total sales, top management becomes more active in decision making. One author found that as the size of a local affiliate grew, the frequency of decisions imposed by headquarters declined and the frequency of decisions shared with headquarters increased.[21]

Elements of a Control Strategy

Control is the cornerstone of management. Control provides the means to direct, regulate, and manage business operations. The implementation of a marketing program requires a significant amount of interaction among the individual areas of marketing (product development, advertising, sales), as well as the other functional areas (production, research and development, finance). The control system is used to measure these business activities, competitive reaction, and market reaction. Deviations from the planned activities and results are analyzed and reported so that corrective action can be taken.

Many companies need to improve their control process. Without some type of control system, strategies that look good on paper never get implemented. Most strategies are long-term in nature and can often take a back seat to the short-term tactical decisions needed for quarterly results. Through interviews with over fifty companies regarding their control systems, Goold assessed control systems on two dimensions: number of performance criteria and formality of the strategic control process. Figure 17.7 summarizes the control systems of eighteen multinational companies. The research on these companies found that strategic control systems add value in the following ways:

- Forcing greater clarity and realism in planning
- Encouraging higher standards of performance
- Providing more motivation for business managers
- Permitting timely intervention by corporate management
- Ensuring that financial objectives do not overwhelm strategic objectives
- Defining responsibilities more clearly, making decentralization work better[22]

A control system has three basic elements: (1) the establishment of standards, (2) the measurement of performance against standards, and (3) the analysis and correction of any deviations from the standards. Although control seemingly is a conceptually simple aspect of the management process, a wide variety of problems arise in international situations, resulting in inefficiencies and intracompany conflicts.

21. R. J. Aylmer, "Who Makes the Decisions in the Multinational Firm?" *Journal of Marketing*, October 1970, p. 26.
22. Michael Goold, *Strategic Control* (London: Economist Books, 1990), p. 125.

FIGURE 17.7

Strategic Control Processes of 18 Multinationals

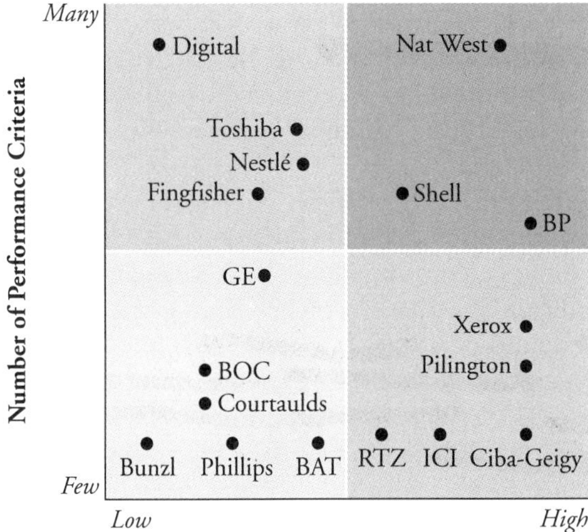

Source: Michael Goold, *Strategic Control* (London: Economist Books, 1990), p. 33. Reprinted by permission.

Companies have found many inefficiencies and redundancies in the way business is done. Thus, many are looking for ways to radically improve performance as well as reduce costs. "Business process reengineering is the fundamental rethinking and radical design of business processes to achieve dramatic improvements in critical, contemporary measures of performance, such as costs, quality service and speed."[23] Rank Xerox developed a set of seven uniform basic processes to be used across all functional departments in Europe. The company expected to cut overheads by $200 million per year and to improve productivity.[24]

Developing Standards Setting standards is an extremely important part of the control process because standards will direct the efforts of individual managers.

23. Michael Hammer and James Champy, *Reengineering the Corporation* (New York: HarperCollins, 1993), p. 32.
24. "Time to Get Serious," *Financial Times*, June 25, 1993, p. 9.

To effectively influence the behavior of the managers who direct the global marketing programs, the standards must be clearly defined, accepted, and understood by these managers. Standard setting is driven by the corporate goals. Corporate goals are achieved through the effective and efficient implementation of a marketing strategy on a local-country level. The standards should be related to the sources of long-term competitive advantage. In companies in which the strategies are decentralized to a business, it is recommended that there be only four to six key objectives. Fewer objectives focus management's efforts without causing confusion about priorities.[25]

Control standards must be specifically tied to the strategy and based on the desired behavior of the local marketing people. The desired behavior should reflect the actions to be taken to implement the strategy, as well as performance standards that indicate the success of the strategy, such as increased market share or sales. Examples of *behavioral standards* include the type and amount of advertising, the distribution coverage, market research to be performed, and expected price levels. *Performance standards* can include trial rates by customers or sales by product line. In the 1990s, there has been a trend to broaden the measures of business performance beyond financial data. More and more companies are measuring quality, customer satisfaction, innovation, and market share.[26]

The standards should be set through a joint process with corporate headquarters personnel and the local marketing organization. Normally the standard setting will be done annually, when the operational business plan is established.

Management systems need to be somewhat consistent for comparability. For example, James River, the papermaking company, had a European joint venture with Nokia of Finland and Cragnotti & Partners, an Italian merchant bank. The joint venture organization acquired thirteen companies in ten countries. When comparing plant utilization, the company found that some companies operated 330 days per year, allowing for holidays and maintenance, whereas other companies operated 350 days. To accurately measure results, the company found it needed to develop uniform standards and measurement systems.[27]

Measuring and Evaluating Performance After standards are set, a process is required for monitoring performance. In order to monitor performance against standards, management must be able to observe current performance. Observa-

25. Goold, *Strategic Control*, p. 120.
26. Ibid.
27. Janet Guyon, "A Joint-Venture Papermaker Casts Net Across Europe," *Wall Street Journal*, December 7, 1992, p. B4.

tion in the international environment is often impersonal through mail, cable, or fax, but it also can be personal through telephone, travel, or meetings. Much of the numerical information, such as sales and expenses, will be reported through the accounting system. Other items, such as the implementation of an advertising program, will be communicated through a report. The reporting system may be weekly, monthly, or quarterly. Motorola has found that a hybrid organization best suits the semiconductor business. Production and finance are directed from the center, and marketing and distribution are done locally, by geography. To measure this hybrid organization, the factories are evaluated on costs, quality, and timeliness of production, whereas the geographic territories are judged on sales, profit, and market share.[28]

Analyzing and Correcting Deviations from the Standards The purpose of establishing standards and reporting performance is to ensure achievement of the corporate goals. To achieve these goals, management must evaluate performance versus standards and initiate actions where performance is below the standards set. Because of distance, communication, and cultural difference issues, the control process can be difficult in the international setting.

Control strategy can be related to the principle of the carrot and the stick, using both positive and negative incentives. On the positive side, outstanding performance may result in increased independence, more marketing dollars, and salary increases or bonuses for the managers. On the negative side, unsatisfactory performance can lead to the reduction of all the items associated with a satisfactory performance, as well as the threat of firing the managers responsible. The key to correcting deviations is to get the managers to understand and agree with the standards, then give them the ability to correct the deficiencies. This will often mean that the managers will be given some flexibility with resources. For example, if sales are down 10 percent, managers may need the authority to increase advertising or reduce prices to offset the sales decline.

Making Strategic Control Work Most companies do not have a formal strategic control system. Few define and monitor their strategic objectives as systematically as they monitor their budgets. Although most managers can tell you within pennies how much the advertising expenditures are over or under the plan, few will be able to tell you the six milestones to implementing the 1998 strategy and the company's progress on each. To establish and get full value from a formal strategic control system, Goold offers several practical recommendations, summarized in Table 17.2.

28. "Asia Beckons," *Economist*, May 30, 1992, p. 64.

TABLE 17.2

Making Formal Strategic Control Work

Issues	*Recommendations*
Selecting the right objectives	Based on analysis of competitive advantage
	Few in number
	Milestones that measure short-term progress
	Leading indicators of future performance
	Projects or action programs only if important for competitive advantage
Setting suitable targets	Precise and objectively measurable, if possible
	Proposed by business managers but stretched by the center
	Competitively benchmarked
	Consistent with budget targets: tradeoffs openly confronted and resolved
Creating pressure for strategic performance	Systematic progress monitoring and reviews
	Personal rewards indirectly tied to achievement of strategic targets
	Performance against strategic targets matters to top management and is the basis for corporate interventions
Strategic planning and strategic control	High-quality strategic planning needed as basis for strategic controls
	Strategic planning process used to review strategic progress
Formality without bureaucracy	Avoid large staff departments and lengthy reports
	Avoid specially gathered data
	Conduct reviews face to face
	Supplement formal reviews with informal contacts
	Be prepared to short-circuit formal process if necessary

Source: Michael Goold, *Strategic Control* (London: Economist Books, 1990), p. 199. Reprinted by permission.

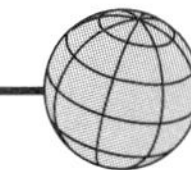

Conflict Between Headquarters and Subsidiaries

A universal problem facing global marketers executives is internal conflict between headquarters and subsidiaries. A study of 109 large U.S. and European multinationals and their worldwide subsidiaries found that this conflict was a bigger problem than competition, political instability, or any of the other challenges of global marketing. Table 17.3 summarizes the results of the study.

Conflicts between two parts of a corporation are inevitable given the natural differences in orientation and perception between the two groups. The subsidiary manager usually wants less control, more authority, and more local differentiation, whereas headquarters wants more detailed reporting and greater unification of geographically dispersed operations. This expected conflict is not

TABLE 17.3

Key Problems Identified by Large U.S. and European Multinationals

KEY PROBLEMS IDENTIFIED BY HEADQUARTERS EXECUTIVES
Lack of qualified personnel
Lack of strategic thinking and long-range planning at subsidiary level
Lack of marketing expertise at the subsidiary level
Too little relevant communication between headquarters and subsidiaries
Insufficient utilization of multinational marketing experience
Restricted headquarters control of the subsidiaries
KEY PROBLEMS IDENTIFIED BY SUBSIDIARY EXECUTIVES
Excessive headquarters control procedures
Excessive financial and marketing constraints
Insufficient participation of subsidiaries in product decisions
Insensitivity of headquarters to local market differences
Shortage of useful information from headquarters
Lack of multinational orientation at headquarters

Source: Adapted and reprinted by permission of the *Harvard Business Review*, "Problems That Plague Multinational Marketers" by Ulrich E. Wiechmann and Lewis G. Pringle (July–August 1979).

bad. In fact, the conflict causes constant dialogue between different organizational levels during the planning and implementation of strategies. This dialogue will result in a balance between headquarters and subsidiary authority, global and local perspective, and standardization and differentiation of the global marketing mix.

Some of the problems in planning and controlling global marketing operations can be reduced or eliminated. Common problems, such as deficiencies in the communications process, overemphasis on short-term issues, and failure to take full advantage of an organization's global experience, require open discussions between headquarters and subsidiary executives.

Creating a Global Learning Organization

Global companies with operations in many countries need to move beyond the traditional planning and controlling processes. One of the major problems companies face is to assure that relevant knowledge learned from experience in one part of the world is either transferred directly and put to use elsewhere or, at the very least, learned in some other parts of the world.

In conventional marketing responsibility, local managers accumulate local experiences and mature on a local learning curve. On that local learning curve, they accumulate new trends spotted locally, create ways to compete against other firms, and might even develop particular approaches to marketing practices.

In the globally learning company, all of these events would be accumulated on a single learning curve, relevant for all local operations, thus allowing the firm to learn more quickly and to move along this experience curve more rapidly than if each local unit relied only on its own narrow experience (see Figure 17.8). A firm that accomplishes this can truly be called global, and its managers will develop global mindsets as a result. To achieve such global learning, both the planning and control processes will have to be shaped in such a way that they facilitate cross-border learning.

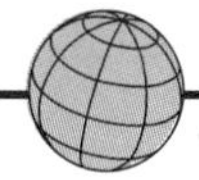

Conclusions

The processes of planning marketing programs and controlling their implementation are the first and last steps in global marketing. Marketers must first evaluate the global environment and select opportunities, using one of several planning approaches. This process will lead to a strategy, which is implemented by the organization. Sometimes, the organization's structure will be changed in order to effectively implement the strategy. Finally, a system must be put in place to evaluate the implementation and measure progress toward the desired effect of the strategy.

The planning and controlling processes are critical parts of the marketing process that require communication and agreement from different parts of the

FIGURE 17.8

Global Learning on a Cross-Border Basis

Company Learning on a Per-Country Basis:

Product Line	Country 1	Country 2	Country 3	Country 4	Country 5
Product Line A					
Product Line B					
Product Line C					
Product Line D					

Company Pooling Learning on One Single Learning Curve:

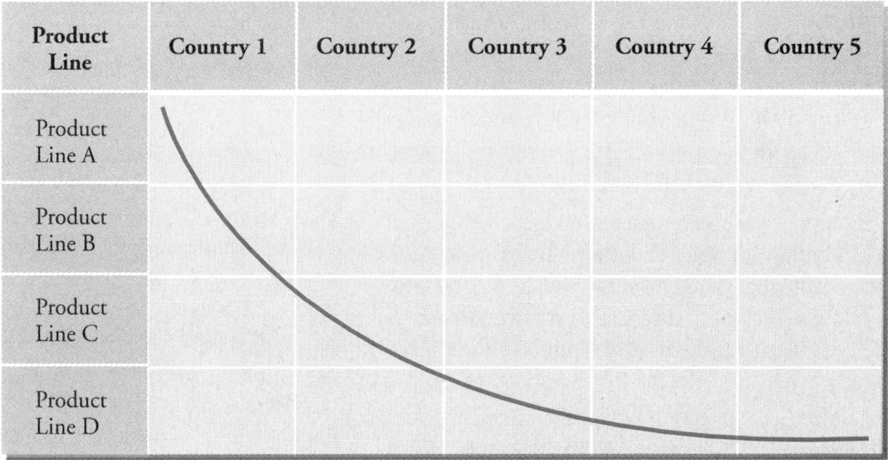

organization. This is difficult. It is no surprise that the planning and controlling processes lead to conflict. However, they also promote a firm's understanding of the world market, its development of effective strategies, and its successful implementation of those strategies with excellent results.

QUESTIONS FOR DISCUSSION

1. You have recently been transferred from a domestic marketing division to the international marketing staff. Part of your new job is to review the planning process of each geographic marketing group—Europe, Asia, and South America. What differences can you expect from domestic planning?
2. What are the advantages and disadvantages of the Boston Consulting Group planning method when applied to global markets?
3. What are the advantages and disadvantages of the PIMS model over other planning methods that can be used for global planning?
4. What types of marketing decisions are usually left to the local management? Why?
5. What is the purpose of a control system? How do you differentiate a good control system from a poor one?
6. Recent feedback for sales, profit, and market share indicates that your subsidiary in Japan has not implemented the strategy that was developed. How will you influence the management to focus more effort on successful strategy implementation?
7. Recently, you have lost four key international marketing people to other companies. You suspect that these losses indicate that the morale of your international executives is poor. What can be done to improve morale?

FOR FURTHER READING

Ansoff, H. Igor, and Edward J. McDonnell. *Implanting Strategic Management.* 2nd ed. Englewood Cliffs, N.J.: Prentice Hall, 1990.

Axton, David J. "Refining Approaches for Better Decision-Making Through Performance." *Strategy & Leadership*, May 1, 1999, vol. 27, no. 3, p. 6.

Bartness, Andrew, and Keith Cerny. "Building Competitive Advantage Through a Global Network of Capabilities." *California Management Review*, Winter 1993, pp. 78–103.

Campbell, Andrew, Marion Devine, and David Young. *A Sense of Mission.* London: Economist Books, 1990.

Cerny, Keith. "Making Local Knowledge Global." *Harvard Business Review*, May-June 1996, p. 22.

Chakravarthy, Balaji S., and Howard V. Perlmutter. "Strategic Planning for a Global Business." *Columbia Journal of World Business*, Summer 1985, pp. 3–10.

Day, George S. *Market Driven Strategy.* New York: Free Press, 1990.

Gale, Bradley T., and Ben Branch. "Allocating Capital More Effectively." *Sloan Management Review*, Fall 1987, p. 21.

Goold, Michael, and Andrew Campbell. *Strategies and Styles: The Role of the Centre in Managing Diversified Corporations.* Oxford: Basil Blackwell, 1987.

Hamel, Gary. "Strategy as Revolution." *Harvard Business Review*, July-August 1996, p. 69.

Hamel, Gary, and C. K. Prahalad. "Strategic Intent." *Harvard Business Review*, May-June 1989, pp. 63–76.

Marchand, Donald. "Balancing Business Flexibility and Global IT." *Australian Financial Review*, September 30, 1998, p. 6.

Pink, Alan I. H. "Strategic Leadership Through Corporate Planning at ICI." *Long Range Planning*, 1988, vol. 21, no. 1, pp. 18–25.

Porter, Michael E. "What Is Strategy?" *Harvard Business Review*, November-December 1996, p. 61.

———, ed. *Competition in Global Industries.* Boston: Harvard Business School Press, 1986.

Roth, Kendall, and Allen J. Morrison. "Implementing Global Strategy: Characteristics of Global Subsidiary Mandates." *Journal of International Business Studies*, 4th quarter 1992, pp. 715–735.

Strebel, Paul. *Breakpoints.* Boston: Harvard Business School Press, 1992.

18

The Export and Import Trade Process

THROUGHOUT PREVIOUS CHAPTERS, WE HAVE MAINTAINED THAT EXPORTING and importing are subsets of global marketing. We have also indicated that global marketing may take place without any physical movement of products across country borders, thereby taking an even broader view of global marketing. However, most companies will, as part of their global marketing activities, engage in some form of exporting or importing. This can take place in the form of shipments from the headquarters location to a foreign market or through cross-shipments among various subsidiaries. Invariably, such export or import shipments cause specific problems that we have not yet discussed and that can best be handled in a separate chapter such as this one.

FIGURE 18.1

Export and Import Trading Process

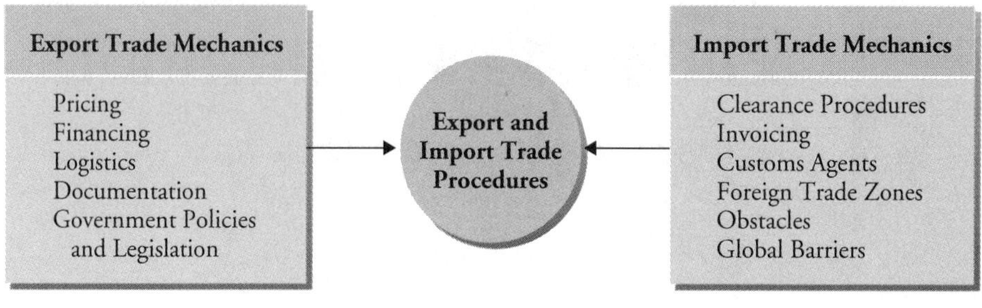

To deal with all the specific rules and regulations that characterize today's complex global business environments is not possible—or necessary for our purposes. In this chapter, we will view the export and import mechanics from the point of view of a U.S.-based firm. However, many aspects of the export section, such as those related to pricing, are of universal application and would be of interest to all readers. The structure and components of the chapter are depicted in Figure 18.1.

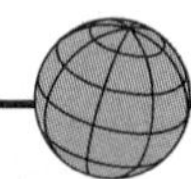

Export Trade Mechanics

As we pointed out in Chapter 1, exporting is a foundational activity in global marketing.[1] All global firms export for part of their volume because virtually no such companies produce locally all the products they sell. The growth in world exports peaked in 1997 with a 10.5 percent growth over 1996. The growth rate declined to only 3.5 percent in 1998, largely because of the contraction of much of Asia. The World Trade Organization (WTO) predicted world export growth of only 3.5 percent in 1999.[2]

Any successful export activity of a firm should be based on a careful analysis of a company's export potential, as was discussed in Chapter 9. Techniques and approaches for such an analysis were covered in Chapters 5 and 6. Consequently, we start our discussion of export trade mechanics with the assumption that a potential market has been defined, measured, and located and that the company has made the

1. This section has been adapted and based on *A Basic Guide to Exporting* (Washington, D.C.: U.S. Department of Commerce, International Trade Administration, 1994). Available from NTC Business Books, Lincolnwood, Illinois.
2. Narendra Aggarwal, "Growth in World Trade Slows to 3.5%," *Straits Times*, April 23, 1999, p. 74.

decision to exploit the opportunity through exporting. Our focus is on the execution of a U.S. firm's export operation, paying special attention to pricing, financing, logistics, documentation, and government policies that affect the individual firm.

Pricing for Exports

In Chapter 10, we described in detail the process by which companies determine prices for products to be shipped abroad. These methods of internal costing, profit analyses, and demand analyses can be applied to the export process. Peculiar to exporting, however, is the method of quoting prices. Foreign buyers need to know precisely where they will take over responsibility for the product—or what shipping costs the exporter is willing to assume. In the United States, it is customary to ship f.o.b. factory, (see below), freight collect, prepaid, charge, or COD (collect on delivery). However, in export marketing, different terms are used worldwide.

Figure 18.2 contains commonly used export quotations. In international trade, nearly twenty different alternatives exist for quoting the price of the merchandise, all indicating different responsibilities for the U.S. company or its foreign client. The terms most commonly used in quoting prices in international trade are these:

c.i.f.: Cost, insurance, freight, to a named port of import. Under this term, the seller quotes a price that includes the product, all transportation, and insurance to the point of unloading from the vessel or aircraft at the named destination.

c.f.: Cost and freight, similar to c.i.f. except that insurance of the shipment is not included.

f.a.s.: Free alongside ship, at a named port in the exporter's country. Under this term, the exporter quotes a price that includes the goods and any service and delivery charges to get the shipment alongside the vessel used for further transportation, but now at the buyer's expense.

f.o.b.: Free on board. Includes the price of placing the shipment onto a specified vessel or aircraft, but further transportation will be the buyer's responsibility.

ex (named point of origin): Applies to a price for products at the point of origin and requires that the buyer assume all transportation charges.

The incorrect use of a delivery term can cause significant problems between the exporter and the buyer.[3]

3. *Incoterms* is a booklet of terms and their definitions. These are the internationally agreed-on terms used by international freight forwarders all over the world. *Incoterms* can be obtained from the International Chamber of Commerce, 801 Second Avenue, Suite 1204, New York, NY 10017: telephone (212) 206-1150. The U.S. Customs Department can be found at *www.customs.ustreas.gov.*

FIGURE 18.2A

Export Price Quotations and Terms

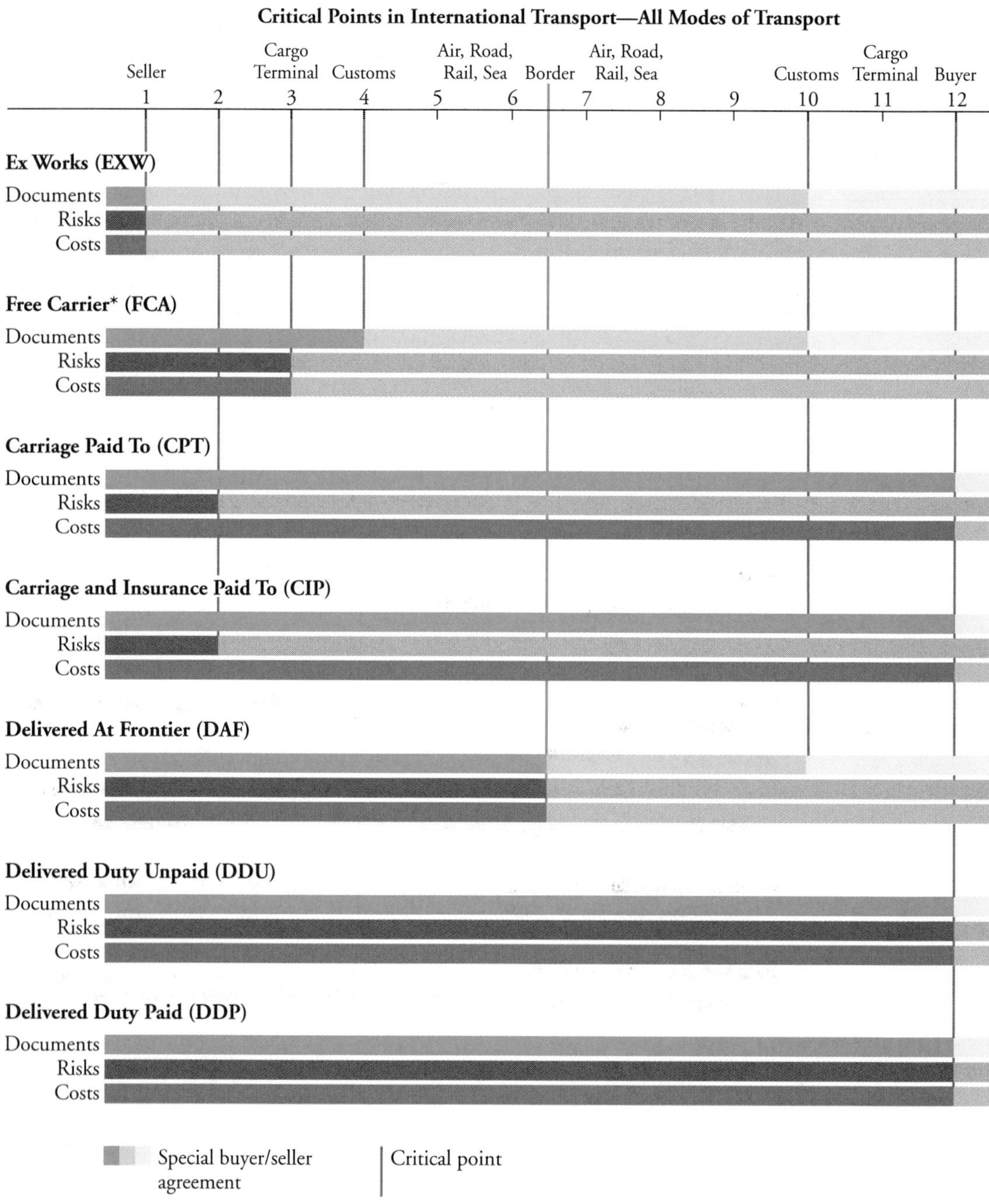

*Reprinted courtesy of Philips.

FIGURE 18.2B

Export Price Quotations and Terms

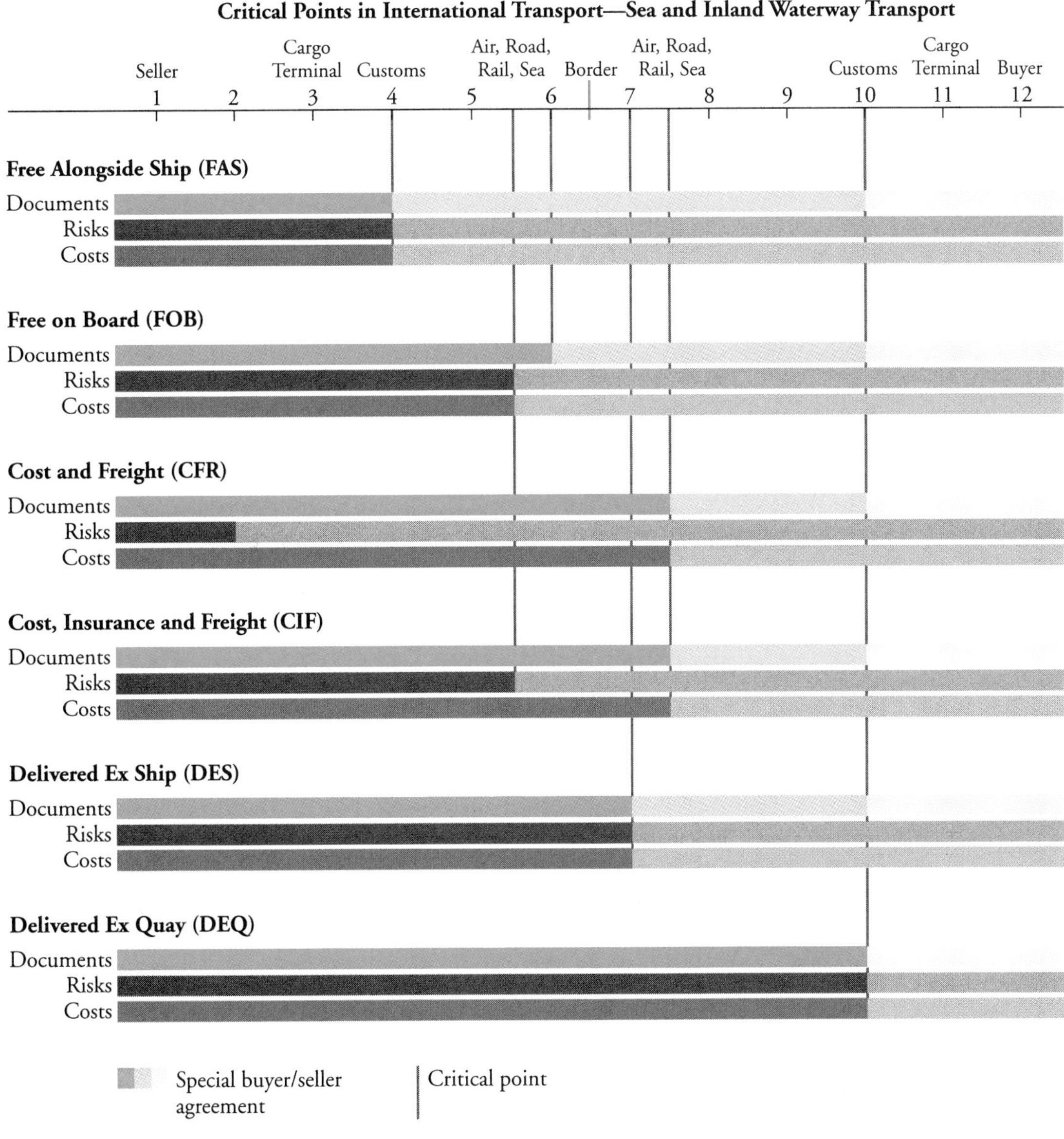

When asked by a foreign buyer to quote a price, the exporter will have to quote a price that takes into consideration the methods of freight payment. In quoting a price, the company is advised to stipulate a price that easily allows the buyer to figure out total costs for the shipment. Usually, this means quoting a price c.i.f. foreign port. The foreign buyer can then estimate additional transportation charges for the final distance under known circumstances.

The most meaningful quote for the foreign buyer is c.i.f. foreign destination. Quoting a price ex factory places the burden of estimating transportation entirely on the foreign buyer. But, as one may imagine, estimation of costs can be quite difficult to do from abroad. An exporter can do a great service to the buyer by quoting prices that reflect the final destination charges based on information from freight forwarders with experience in shipping to the foreign country. It also makes it easier for the buyer to compare prices from different companies if they are all quoted to one point. Sometimes the buyer will request a specific type of price. For example, a foreign buyer who regularly imports from New York may request all prices be quoted f.o.b. New York.

The freight, transportation, and insurance charges may also depend on the leverage the exporter or importer has with freight forwarders. The exporter may have only one shipment going to a certain foreign destination. Therefore, shipping costs will be relatively high. Should the importer have several shipments that could be combined, average freight costs may be less. The exporter can facilitate the process by quoting several prices at various points along the shipment route and then leaving the choice to the buyer, who will select the best method.

Exporters should not underestimate the possibility of using the export pricing process as a selling tool, particularly when similar products are available from other manufacturers. Also, different pricing strategies present obvious risks. For example, if you quote in a foreign currency rather than dollars, you assume the risk of exchange rate fluctuation. As the dollar ran up huge gains against other currencies in early 1997 (up 47 percent since 1995 against the Japanese yen and 19 percent against the German DM), some exporters quoting in U.S. dollars immediately felt the market reaction. Computer Network Technology of Minneapolis witnessed an immediate decline in sales of its networking systems to Japan. AlliedSignal, a major U.S.-based firm producing automotive components, lost a $13 million contract to supply air-bag modules to Suzuki Motor of Japan to a non-U.S. rival.[4]

Even insurance costs can fluctuate: insurance rates doubled for goods being shipped to the Persian Gulf after Iraq's invasion of Kuwait on August 2, 1990.[5]

4. "Strong Dollar Creates Winners and Losers," *Wall Street Journal*, February 6, 1997, p. A2.
5. "Ship Insurance Rates Soar in Some Areas of Persian Gulf as Jan. 15 Deadline Nears," *Wall Street Journal*, January 10, 1991, p. A16.

Pricing for export involves many variables that require close examination. A miscalculation or misjudgment can often turn a profitable order to a losing order.

Financing Export Operations

Chapter 10 contained several sections on financing international marketing operations through, among others, export banks of various countries. Also discussed were noncash transactions such as barter and countertrade. These types of arrangements are not repeated in this chapter. This section focuses on various arrangements exporters can make to ensure payment for their merchandise and on credit options that can be offered to foreign clients.

Although cash transactions can be desirable, this form of payment is rarely used. The shipment may be in transit for weeks or even months at a time, thus tying up the importer's capital. Also, the importer does not really know what was shipped until the products are in its possession. Consequently, most forms of payment are designed to protect both parties. When an exporter knows the foreign clients and fully trusts their financial integrity, shipments on *open account* may be arranged. Usually, the terms are arranged such that the foreign client can wait to make payment until the goods have arrived at their final destination. However, in this case, the exporter will have risked capital in the transaction.

Consignment sales is the method whereby credit is extended by the exporter. The exporter is not compensated until the products are physically sold by the importer. The consignment goods are often held in free trade zones (discussed later in the chapter) or in a bonded warehouse until sold by an agent or needed by the buyer. With appropriate payment, the consigned goods will be released to the buyer. This approach increases the exporter's capital costs because no funds are received until the goods are collected by the buyer.

To control both ownership and payment terms for international shipments, traders have developed the *draft* or *bill of exchange.* The draft is a formal order the exporter issues to the importer, specifying when the sum is to be paid to the third party, usually the exporter's bank. A triangular relationship is established with the issuer of the draft, the exporter, as drawer; the importer as drawee; and the payee as the recipient of the payment. Since the draft is a negotiable instrument, it can be sold, transferred, and discounted, and the exporter can use it to finance the shipment.

Exporters may use either a *sight draft* or a *time draft.* Sight drafts are used when the exporter desires to control the shipment beyond the point of original shipment, usually to ensure payment. In practice, the exporter endorses the bill of lading (B/L) and adds a sight draft on the correspondent bank of the exporter's bank. Along with the bill of lading and sight draft, other documents will be provided such as the packing list, invoice, consular invoices, and certificate of insurance. Once the documents have arrived, a transfer by way of endorsement to the importer will be made on payment in full at that bank. Consequently, the importer cannot take possession of the goods until payment has been made (on sight of documents). Yet, the importer is assured that the goods have actually been shipped as indicated by the accompanying documents.

Alternatively, transactions can be made in time drafts. This method specifies the period in which the payment is to be made. The payment period beginning on receiving the documents may be thirty, sixty, or ninety days or longer. Not only will drafts allow the exporter to control the shipment until proper payment occurs, but they also allow further financing by having the properly signed draft discounted with a bank before the agreed-upon payment term expires. In such a case, the banking system assumes the role of the creditor, thus reducing the capital risks of the exporter.

Also used quite frequently is a financial instrument called a *letter of credit*. With a letter of credit, the importer, or foreign buyer, finances the transaction, thus alleviating the credit burden on the exporter. With a letter of credit, the responsibility is in the hands of the importer. Once informed that the exporter will ship with a letter of credit (L/C), the importer will ask the bank to write an irrevocable L/C with a bank specified by the exporter on the latter's behalf. The importer will usually instruct the bank on the conditions of payment, typically against submission of all necessary documents, including a bill of lading. When the exporter has placed the shipment on the appropriate vessel, the company will go to the bank and turn over all documents associated with the transaction. When satisfied, the exporter's bank will pay out the funds and debit the importer's bank, which will in turn debit the importing company.

Overall, the irrevocable L/C has distinct advantages for the exporter because it represents a firm order that, once issued by the bank, cannot be canceled or revoked. For example, a company that sells machinery built to order can use the irrevocable L/C to guarantee that payment will be made. Time limits are placed on the L/C that protect the importer against an open-ended transaction. Should the exporter fail to ship and submit documents before the expiration date, the L/C would expire without any further responsibility on the part of the importer to finance the transaction. Any bank charges associated with the transaction are usually paid by the buyer. Letters of credit are normally prepared at commercial banks by a staff of back-office clerks. The paperwork required for each letter of credit, as well as the possibility of typing errors, can make the issuing of these instruments slow. Pressure from exports has motivated many banks to automate this process with computer technology to speed up the process so payments can be processed quickly.[6]

6. Jon Marks, "Letters of Credit Are Beginning to Change, a Rich Link with the Past," *Financial Times*, June 1, 1989, Export Finance Section 7.

Letters of credit are a widely used instrument that has developed into several specialized forms over and above the standard irrevocable L/C described above. The following additional forms exist:

Revolving or *periodic letters of credit* allow for a repetition of the same transaction as soon as the previous amount has been paid by the bank that originated the L/C.

Cumulative letters of credit are opened to cover payments of partial shipments and/or the use of the unused portion of the L/C for another transaction between the same parties.

Red clause letters of credit are used to permit partial cash payments to the beneficiary, or exporter, as an advance on the shipment without any documentation. Final payments are made only against full documentation, however.

Back-to-back letters of credit are issued based on an earlier L/C. This may be done if an exporter, in whose favor an L/C was opened by a foreign client, will use the original L/C as a basis or security to issue a second L/C in favor of a supplier for materials connected with that particular transaction.

Circular letters of credit are issued without designating any particular bank. The exporter may send documents to the issuing bank or present them to any bank that will send them on for collection.

Performance letters of credit are used to guarantee the completion of a contract undertaken abroad. They can be drawn upon if the exporter fails to meet performance requirements and are therefore also known under the term *performance bonds.*[7]

Letters of credit can be a costly and time-consuming way to do business. The World Trade Centers Association, a not-for-profit group that provides trade-related services to 500,000 companies through a network of 327 centers in ninety-seven countries, has developed an electronic letter of credit alternative. The new approach, called TradeCard, reduces paperwork by 80 percent and shortens processing time by 60 percent. The product is available through *www.tradecard.bm.*[8] In addition to TradeCard, a number of banks now allow customers to initiate, amend, and track letters of credit through the bank web site on the Internet.[9] It is expected that export documentation, financing, and insurance will all eventually be done via the Internet.

7. Endel J. Kolde, *International Business Enterprise*, 2nd ed. (Englewood Cliffs, N.J.: Prentice Hall, 1973), p. 294.
8. David Bieederman, "Here Comes TradeCard," *Traffic World*, March 8, 1999, p. 25.
9. Robb Evans, "Best Practices in Global Payments and Collections," *TMA Journal*, January 1, 1999, pp. 51–52.

When a company exports to a politically volatile area or to a new customer, guaranteeing payment of invoices is always a concern. A letter of credit is a relatively safe instrument to guarantee payment. In some cases, letters of credit may not be acceptable to the buyer, or they may not be practical. In the United States, exporters can turn to the Foreign Credit Insurance Association (FCIA) for assistance. The FCIA is an association of fifty marine and insurance casualty companies created in 1961 to insure U.S. exporters of goods and services against commercial and political risks. There are numerous risks with any foreign buyer. Exporters increasingly see late payments and collection delays, as illustrated in Table 18.1 and Figure 18.3. The firm can go out of business. The local government can change standards. Natural disasters such as floods or earthquakes can eliminate the buyer's ability to pay. FCIA offers insurance to protect against a buyer's failure to pay. Most developed countries have some type of export insurance program similar to FCIA.

Some companies who market major infrastructure projects, such as roads, airports, telecommunication systems, and ports, find that few companies or customers can go directly to capital markets for financing. In 2000, in Latin America, for example, only Chile was still considered investment-grade risks by U.S. rating agencies. In February 2000, Moody's Investor Service announced it might grant Mexico investment-grade status.[10] For most other projects, customers or suppliers will have to find loans from international commercial banks. Helping customers gain access to international financing can often be the key to clinching a major project or deal.

As we have seen, numerous options are available to arrange for payment in export transactions. The exporting company can, of course, select the particular type of transaction, always keeping in mind the needs and requirements of the buyer—who may, if offered better credit terms elsewhere, decide to place an order with a different company. The payment process is an important part of the transaction between the buyer and seller in an export situation; it can minimize the risks of exchange rate fluctuations and the process of dealing with a distant buyer or seller. Experienced exporters study government assistance and financing programs looking for creative ways to use these programs for the benefit of the buyer. Australian companies can rely on a government-owned Export Finance and Insurance Corporation (EFIC) to assist in both the financing of exporters' capital needs and the financing of customers' purchases. EFIC underwrites some $6 billion of exports annually. Australian exporters of ferries were able to avail themselves of EFIC finance and compete effectively with competitors elsewhere to secure several contracts in Asia. Without the creative use of EFIC, these contracts would not have been concluded.[11]

10. Geri Smith, "Mexico Isn't Investment Grade Yet," *Business Week*, March 13, 2000, p. 140.
11. "EFIC Eases Risk Burden," *International Business Asia*, April 19, 1996, p. 7.

TABLE 18.1

Export and Debt Collection Survey

Country	Exchange Delays (months)	Collection Experience	Most Liberal Suggested Terms
Australia	2	good-fair	OA
Brazil	4	fair	ULC
Canada	2	good-fair	OA
Chile	3	good-fair	SD
Egypt	3	fair-good	ULC
Ghana	4	fair	SD
Hong Kong	2	good-fair	SD
India	2	fair-good	SD
Indonesia	3	fair-good	SD
Israel	3	fair	ULC
Jamaica	3	fair	ULC
Japan	1	good	60/SD
Kenya	3	fair-poor	ULC
South Korea	3	fair-good	SD
Kuwait	2	fair-good	SD
Malaysia	3	good-fair	SD
Mexico	3	fair-good	SD
New Zealand	2	good-fair	30/SD
Nigeria	4	fair	ULC
Oman	3	good-fair	SD
Pakistan	3	fair-good	ULC
Philippines	3	fair	ULC
Saudi Arabia	3	fair	SD

TABLE 18.1

Export and Debt Collection Survey (cont.)

Country	Exchange Delays (months)	Collection Experience	Most Liberal Suggested Terms
Singapore	2	good-fair	30/SD
South Africa	3	good-fair	SD
Thailand	3	good-fair	SD
Trin. & Tobago	3	fair-good	ULC
Turkey	3	fair	ULC
UAE	3	fair-good	SD
US	2	good-fair	60/SD
Venezuela	3	fair	ULC
Vietnam	5	mostly l/c	ULC

Footnotes: 1. OA: unopened account; ULC: unconfirmed letter of credit; SD: sighted draft; 30/SD: 30 days sight draft. 2. Exchange delays refer to the time taken from the due date for the importer to deposit local currency with the central bank or other authorizing body and for foreign currency to be deposited with the exporter. 3. Collection experience refers to the risk attached to exchange delays. 4. Individual experiences can vary considerably, depending on the relationship with the buyers, the type of goods involved, etc. 5. All of the above countries appear in the UK Department of Trade and Industry's List of Target Markets.
Source: FT Reporter, *Financial Times,* May 5, 1994, p. 26. Reprinted by permission.

The Multilateral Investment Guarantee Agency (MIGA), a World Bank affiliate, was founded in 1987 to provide investment protection to companies in the 149 member countries that are doing direct foreign investment in any of 127 developing countries. MIGA will complement private insurance and national insurance like FICA and EFIC.[12]

Export Logistics

The requirements of export logistics differ substantially from domestic operations, calling for special care on the part of the exporting firm. Practices must ensure that the shipment arrives in the best possible condition and at the lowest

12. "Australian Firms Seem Keen on Political Risk Insurance," *Asia Pulse*, May 18, 1999, p. 1.

FIGURE 18.3

Average Collection Periods in Europe

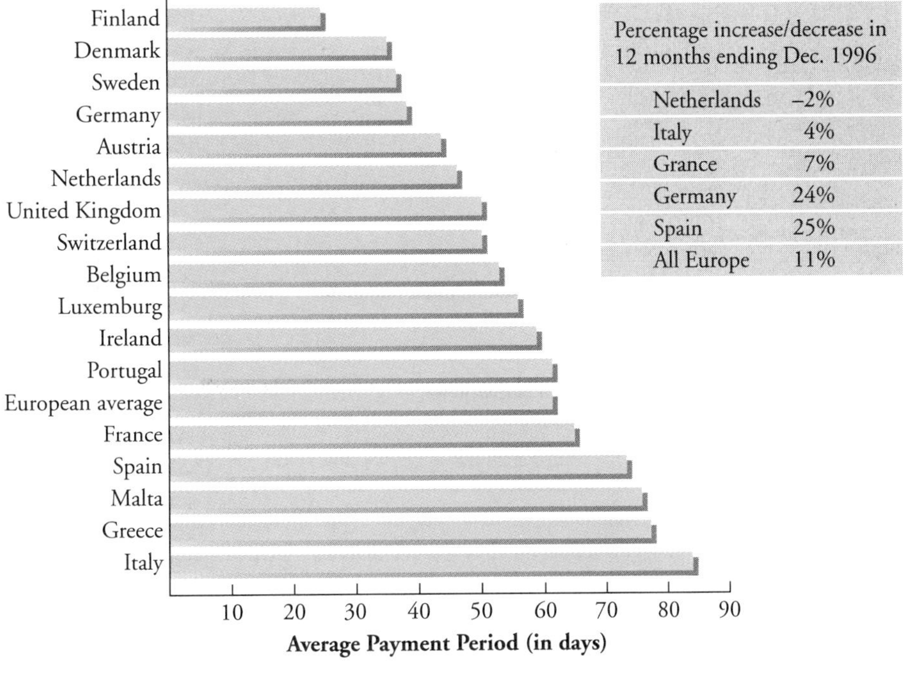

Percentage increase/decrease in 12 months ending Dec. 1996	
Netherlands	–2%
Italy	4%
Grance	7%
Germany	24%
Spain	25%
All Europe	11%

Source: Financial Times, January 28, 1997, p. 10. Reprinted by permission.

possible cost. To ensure that the products arrive in usable condition, export packages have to be prepared to avoid four typical problems: breakage, weight, moisture, and pilferage.

Export shipments often are subject to additional handling procedures, including the use of a sling for loading onto a vessel, nets to combine various items for loading, or conveyors, chutes, and other methods that put added stress and strain on the shipment and are frequently the cause of breakage. Once on board a vessel, the weight of other cargo placed on top of the shipment can also be hazardous. At the overseas destination, handling facilities are sometimes unsophisticated. Consequently, the cargo may even be dragged, pushed, or rolled during unloading, causing damage to the goods.

While packages are on a voyage, moisture due to condensation in the hold of a ship is a constant problem. This may even be so for vessels equipped with air conditioning and dehumidifiers. At the point of arrival, unloading may take place in the rain, and many foreign ports lack covered storage facilities. Furthermore, without adequate protection, theft and pilferage are common.

To avoid these problems, exporters are encouraged to add extra packaging to protect their cargo. However, overpacking should be avoided because both freight and customs are frequently assessed on the gross weight of the merchandise, resulting in unneeded charges for extra packaging. Airfreight usually requires less packaging than ocean freight, and container shipments can be used to provide added protection for the goods. Exporters are encouraged to check with carriers or marine insurance companies for advice on proper packaging. For companies that are not equipped to do export packaging, professional companies provide this service for a moderate fee.

Equally important is the proper marking of the shipment. Although the destination should be marked clearly and in large stenciled letters of black waterproof ink, experienced exporters advise that, to avoid pilferage or theft, no additional facts be provided on the content of the packages. Where necessary, special handling instructions should be added in the language of the port of destination.

Arrangements for the actual shipping of a company's products can be made through the services of an international freight forwarder. In general, a freight forwarder licensed by the Federal Maritime Administration should be used because these agents are familiar with foreign import regulations, methods of shipping, and the requirements of U.S. export documentation. Not only will freight forwarders advise on freight costs and other related fees, they can also make recommendations on packaging. Since the cost for their services is a legitimate export cost, exporters can add such costs to their prices charged to foreign customers. Aside from advising exporters, forwarders also make the necessary arrangements to clear shipments through customs, arrange for the actual shipping, and check for the necessary documents as described in the section below.

In many parts of the world, exporters have to overcome considerable logistical barriers to meet delivery expectations. For sea shipments to Russia, several ports can be used, some of them in the Baltic countries that were part of the former Soviet Union. Exporters need to overcome shipment delays and potential documentation problems when using ports such as Tallin (Estonia), Rīga (Latvia), or Klaipėda (Lithuania), as compared with facilities in St. Petersburg or Kaliningrad (Russia). Privatization of the ports and state shipping companies have led to ambitious expansions in the ports of Tallin, Rīga, and Klaipėda that will turn the Baltic ports into a major transit hub for Europe.[13] Truck shipments customary between some Latin American countries invariably face long delays. The MERCOSUR trade pact (see Chapter 5) has brought increased trade between Brazil and Argentina; unfortunately, much of it is

13. Rajesh Joshi, "Trading Hub on the New Europe," *Lloyds List*, June 25, 1999, pp. 1–2.

trucked along a single road through Paraguay, where border crossings can consume as much as three days.[14]

The emergence of the international courier services (Federal Express, UPS, DHL, TNT) has given many firms a chance to review and reengineer export logistics. Life Services International, a U.K.-based supplier of laboratory equipment for hospitals and universities, has begun to closely coordinate its own logistics due to the availability of international courier services, using them for both planned and emergency shipments. The company has found that delivery reliability was a key to its export performance.[15]

Export Documentation

To facilitate the transfer of goods out of the United States and through a foreign country's procedures, a series of export documents have to be prepared. Exporters prepare such documents with care, since export documents frequently have been used as a basis for obtaining trade credit from banks or collection from the buyer.

One requirement is a detailed export packing list, usually containing substantially more details about weight and volume than those used for domestic commerce. This packing list is used by shippers to reserve or book the necessary space on the vessel. Furthermore, port officials at the dock use this list to determine whether the correct cargo has been received. In addition, customs officials both in the United States and abroad use the packing list, and ultimately the buyer will want to check the goods against the list to verify that the entire shipment was received. To satisfy all these users, the packing list must contain not only a detailed description of the products for each packaging unit but also weights, volume, and dimensions in both metric and nonmetric terms.

Most countries have specific requirements for the marking and labeling of imports. Failure to comply can result in severe penalties. For example, Peru requires that all imports be labeled with the brand name, country of origin, and an expiration date on the product. Customs officials will refuse clearance of any imports not complying with the regulations. The importer must ship the goods out of Peru within sixty days, or they are seized and auctioned as abandoned goods. A basic guide published by the Department of Commerce for U.S. exporters will describe the required export documents and pertinent regulations for labeling, marking, and packing products for import. The pamphlet series entitled "Preparing Shipment to (Country)" helps exporters avoid delays and penalties.[16]

The U.S. government requires that all export shipments be subject to a licensing procedure. Basically, there exist two types of export licenses. The *validated*

14. "Mercosur: Trade Pact Sets Pace for Integration," *Financial Times*, February 4, 1997, p. 12.
15. "When Precision Is Everything," *FT Exporter, Financial Times*, May 5, 1994, p. 15.
16. "Tools of the Export Trade," *Business America*, October 28, 1988, pp. 2–5.

export license must be secured for each individual order from the Bureau of Export Administration in Washington, D.C. Several types of products and commodities may fall into this category, including chemicals, special types of plastic, advanced electronic and communications equipment, and scarce materials, including petroleum. For defense products, licenses are issued by the Department of State. The requirement for a validated export license may apply for shipments of certain commodities to all countries or only to a limited number of countries. The entire mechanism was instituted to protect the United States' strategic position for reasons of foreign policy or national security or to regulate supply for select scarce products. Regulations are also subject to frequent changes depending on the political or economic climate prevailing at the time of decision.

All other products are subject to several types of *general licenses*. These are published general authorizations, each with a specific license symbol that is dependent on product category. Exporters must inquire at the Bureau of Export Administration of the Department of Commerce to obtain the correct general license symbol. Exporters usually check with the Department of Commerce before an order is accepted to determine the type of license required. Obtaining export licenses from the government has often been a slow process that can cause delays for the exporter. To reduce the paperwork and speed up the process, the Department of Commerce introduced two new systems. The Export License Application and Information Network (ELAIN) allows exporters to submit license applications electronically for all free world applications. When approved, the license is conveyed back to the exporter electronically. The ELAIN allows companies to use the Internet to process export license applications. In 1997, twelve thousand applications were filed, of which 40 percent were done electronically.[17] The System for Tracking Export License Applications (STELA) is a voice-answering service that allows exporters to check the status of their license application. The new systems drastically cut processing time from an average of forty-six days in 1984 to fourteen days. The Simplified Network Application Process (SNAP) is a web-based system that enables exporters to submit export-license applications directly to the Bureau of Export Administration in a secure environment. In many cases, processing time has been reduced to less than three days.[18]

The exporter's *shipper's export declaration* has to be added to all shipments. It requires a declaration of the products in terms of the U.S. Customs Service definitions and classifications. In this form, the exporter must note the applicable license for the shipment.

17. "BXA Accepts Export Applications Over Net," *New Technology Week*, July 13, 1998, vol. 12, no. 28. "Fact Sheet BXA's Automated Services," The Bureau of Export Administration website.
18. "The Electronic Age of Export Licensing in ELAIN Joins STELA to Cut Processing Time," *Business America*, February 29, 1988, pp. 7–11.

Most exporters also submit a series of documents to their customers to facilitate additional financing or handling at the point of destination. These documents may vary by country, method of payment, mode of transportation, and even by customer. The following documents may be required:

Commercial invoice. In addition to the customary content, the invoice should indicate the origin of the products and export marks. Also needed is an antidiversion clause, such as "United States law prohibits disposition of these commodities to North Korea, Cambodia, or Cuba." When payment is against a letter of credit, the invoice should contain all necessary numbers and bank names. Some countries even require special certification, at times in the language of that country, and a few countries may need signed invoices with notarization. The Commerce Department keeps a current list of all requirements by country.

Consular invoice. Some countries, particularly in Latin America, require a special invoice in addition to the commercial invoice prepared in the language of the country and issued on official forms by the consulate. The forms are typically prepared by the forwarding agent.

Certificate of origin. Some countries may require a specific and separate statement that is normally countersigned by a recognized chamber of commerce. Based on this statement, import duties are assessed; if preferential rates are claimed, the inclusion of the certificate of origin is often necessary.

Inspection certificate. A foreign buyer may request that the products be inspected, typically by an independent inspection firm, with respect to quality, quantity, and conformity of goods as stated in the order and invoice.

Bill of lading. Bills of lading (B/L) are issued in various forms, depending on the mode of transportation. The exporter endorses the B/L in favor of either the buyer or the bank financing the transaction. The B/L identifies the owner of the shipment and is needed to claim the products at the point of destination. The bill of lading provides three functions: (1) receipt for goods, (2) content for shipment, and (3) title to the goods, if consigned "to the order of."

Dock receipts or warehouse receipts. In cases in which the shipper or exporter is responsible for moving the goods not to the foreign destination but only to the U.S. port, a dock or warehouse receipt is usually required confirming that the shipment was actually received at the port for further shipment.

Certificate of manufacture. Such a certificate may be issued for cases in which the buyer intends to pay for the order before shipment. The certificate, combined with a commercial invoice, may be presented to a bank appointed by the buyer for early payment. More typical is to pay only against a B/L indicating that the merchandise has actually been shipped.

Insurance certificates. Particularly where the exporter is required to arrange for insurance, such certificates are usually necessary. They are negotiable instruments and must be endorsed accordingly.

Exporters pay careful attention to the specifications attached to letters of credit with respect to the required set of documents. The paying bank will effect payment only if all submitted documents fully conform to the specifications determined by the buyer. Mistakes can cause lengthy delays that can be costly to the exporter.

Government Export Policies and Legislation

There is no doubt that exports can greatly enhance the economy of any nation. The U.S. Department of Commerce reported in 1999 that exports accounted for one-third of the U.S. economic growth and that export-related jobs pay 13 to 16 percent higher than other sectors.[19] Thus, governments everywhere frequently try to influence their country's export volume through legislation or direct government supports. To outline the export policies of all major countries is too difficult. Consequently, this section concentrates on the United States. Though the respective export policies of other countries may vary by specific objective or by approach, understanding the U.S. export policies will provide some conceptual background for the understanding of the policies of all countries and an appreciation for the important role governments can play.

Shaping U.S. Export Policies The execution of the U.S. government's export policies lies with the Department of Commerce, whereas negotiations and policy advisement to the president are the responsibilities of the trade representative, a cabinet position. Also part of the U.S. export policymaking is the Export-Import Bank, an independent agency whose activities were described in Chapter 10. The bank makes loans, guarantees, and export credit insurance available. For 1998, the total volume of Eximbank financing to U.S. exporters amounted to $13 billion, which helped 2,060 companies export to developing countries.[20]

The U.S. Department of Commerce coordinates the activities of 162 commercial attachés in sixty-five countries. Involved with U.S. embassies abroad, these attachés provide U.S. business with support at the local level. Also available are about 150 international trade specialists in thirty-two U.S. cities. An important aspect of the Commerce Department's activities is trade promotion programs that include permanent overseas trade fairs and seminars on exporting for U.S. businesspeople in the United States.

19. David L. Aaron, "International Trade and Development," *Congressional Testimony: Federal Documents Clearing House*, June 6, 1999, pp. 1–12.

20. Nan Smith, "Ex-Im Bank Officials Pitches to Local Business," *Birmingham Business Journal*, March 15, 1999, p. 7.

Through the Trade Information Center (1-800-USA-TRAD[E]), the Department of Commerce received 475,000 inquires for export information and assistance in 1998. Twenty-five thousand requests were via fax, and 364,000 were through the Trade Information Center web site.[21]

Most governments have some type of agency or program to support exporting initiatives. These programs are often targeted to the smaller company that does not have export experience. For example, Rieke, a small Indiana manufacturer of specialized bulk packaging products, was shut out of the European market because a competitor was able to have product standards changed to exclude the Rieke design. The Market Access and Compliance Unit of the International Trade Administration was able to have European governments remove the discrimination, which saved three hundred Indiana jobs.[22]

In addition to federal government programs, many states have established organizations and agencies to assist U.S. companies in their exporting efforts. In 1987, thirty-six states maintained offices abroad and programs at home to encourage export trade, particularly with smaller companies.[23] For example, C. M. Magnetics, a three-year-old company in Santa Fe Springs, California, received a $2.7 million order from China. This order was the direct result of efforts by the state of California's World Trade Commission. "Without their help," company president J. Carlos Macrel said of the agency, "we probably wouldn't be in business today."[24]

Though the resources committed on behalf of U.S. exports may appear substantial, the amount spent on the export development program was substantially less than the corresponding budget of the Japan External Trade Organization (JETRO). For many U.S. businesspeople, this difference in funding of export programs is symbolic of a lack of interest on the part of many government officials and legislators, who have accumulated a substantial amount of legislation that actually hinders U.S. exports. In the following section, we explore the various legislative and regulative disincentives that the United States and some other countries have accumulated.

Obstacles to U.S. Exports The U.S. International Trade Commission conducted a study on U.S. economic sanctions for the U.S. House of Representatives in 1999. The commission found forty-two separate laws that restricted economic activity with another country by U.S. firms. These laws limit the exports, imports, investment, and therefore jobs, so they are considered a hindrance to trade. The sanctions are the result of terrorism, nuclear and other arms proliferation, national

21. David L. Aaron, "International Trade and Development," *Congressional Testimony: Federal Documents Clearing House*, June 6, 1999, pp. 1–12.
22. Ibid.
23. "Big Plans for Small Business: Firms Try to Boost Exports," *Insight*, July 13, 1987, p. 40.
24. "States Launch Efforts to Make Small Firms Better Exporters," *Wall Street Journal*, February 2, 1987, p. 25.

security, narcotics, expropriation, human rights, and environmental concerns.[25] These sanctions affect thirty-five countries, or 42 percent of the world population, and a potential of $800 billion of exports for U.S. firms.[26]

The Foreign Corrupt Practices Act of 1977 was enacted as a result of published reports on corporate bribery of foreign nationals, initially triggered by the "United Brands affair" in Honduras. The company reportedly paid funds to that country's president to get favorable tax treatment on banana exports. Subsequent investigations by the Securities and Exchange Commission (SEC) and the U.S. government found scores of other U.S. companies guilty of the same practices. The resulting 1977 act places stringent restrictions on the type of payments that third-party agents can receive. Consequently, some U.S. companies have the expense accounts of their foreign representatives certified by U.S. consular officers. However, competitors from other major trading nations are not subject to such legislation, a fact that many U.S. businesspeople consider a disadvantage. A study of 207 U.S. exporters found that the most difficult aspect of global marketing in terms of ethical and moral problems is bribery. Thirty-four percent of the companies cited bribery as a problem, followed by 15 percent reporting government interference and 7 percent citing customs clearance.[27]

The policy on nuclear power plant exports illustrates the effect of a political decision on foreign trade. The United States passed the Nuclear Non-Proliferation Act of 1978 requiring all governments that use enriched uranium from U.S. sources to obtain the U.S. government's permission in advance if the uranium is to be sent anywhere for reprocessing.[28] The retroactive law applied to most of the United States' twenty-six loyal and trusted foreign customers, who would face a cutoff in supplies if this new feature was not approved by them.

The U.S. Nuclear Non-Proliferation Act was intended to enhance existing controls administered by the International Atomic Energy Agency (IAEA), based in Vienna, Austria. An international nonproliferation treaty, in effect since 1970, had been signed by over one hundred governments, including those who had purchased uranium under U.S. contracts. The act reflects the U.S. government's position that existing controls were not strict enough to prevent further proliferation of atomic weapons to nations that were on the verge of attaining such capabilities (Brazil, Argentina, Iran, North Korea, Pakistan, and India among them).

The U.S. government has also affected exports through politically motivated actions. Unilaterally, the United States has employed trade embargoes against

25. Robert A. Rogowsky, "Effect of Unilateral Trade Sanctions," *Congressional Testimony: Federal Document Clearing House*, May 27, 1999, pp. 1–7.
26. Donald L. Losman, "Economic Sanctions: An Emerging Menace," *Business Economics*, April 1, 1998, p. 37.
27. Robert Armstrong, Bruce W. Stening, John K. Ryans, Larry Marks, and Michael Mayo, "International Marketing Ethics," *European Journal of Marketing*, 1990, vol. 24, no. 10, p. 10.
28. "How Carter's Nuclear Policy Backfired Abroad," *Fortune*, October 23, 1978, p. 124.

Cuba, Vietnam, Libya, and Burma (Myanmar). Most of these actions were imposed by the U.S. government alone and were not followed by other nations, thus giving the clear advantage to foreign countries. The cutoff of Soviet aid and the U.S. embargo devastated the Cuban economy. In 1996, the U.S. export embargo toward Cuba was further tightened with the passage of the Helms-Burton Act. As part of this legislation, individuals with claims for property confiscated by Cuba can sue in U.S. courts to collect damages. Moreover, the targets of such suits may be foreign firms who have profited from dealings with Cuba. This provision has created thorny difficulties between the U.S. and European trading partners. The EU complained to the WTO that the Helm-Burton Act applied U.S. domestic law to foreign companies operating in a foreign country and therefore violated international trade rules. However, the EU let its complaint lapse after one year as both sides preferred not to involve the WTO.[29]

The 1994 lifting of the nineteen-year trade embargo on Vietnam opened this fast-growing market to U.S. companies. Within months of the embargo being lifted, Coke, Pepsi, IBM, Kodak, GE, Citibank, Boeing, and many others were doing business in Vietnam, hoping to tap a market of some million consumers in one of the fastest-growing Asian countries. However, as of 1999, Coca-Cola and Procter & Gamble had yet to turn a profit there.[30]

Sometimes, local authorities can establish their own boycotts. In 1996, the city of San Francisco passed a law prohibiting the city from doing business with or granting contracts to firms that engaged in business in Burma (Myanmar), a country under military rule. When the city needed to acquire a new emergency radio system, Motorola of the United States was competing against Ericsson of Sweden. Since Ericsson had not stopped its operations in Burma, the $40 million contract was awarded to Motorola.[31]

The Institute for International Economics (IIE) found that only 20 percent of the economic sanctions imposed by the United States between 1914 and 1998 achieved their stated objectives. The IIE concluded that the sanctions eliminated more than 200,000 jobs and cost the U.S. economy $15 to 19 billion in 1995.[32]

Many business and political leaders have recognized the considerable negative effect of such rules for U.S. exports. Lucio A. Noto, chairman of Mobil Corp., stated in a letter to President Clinton, "We will lose strategically and economically if the U.S. embargo on trade with Iran limits the ability of American firms to explore for oil in the Persian Gulf and Caspian Sea while competitors have free

29. Robert S. Greenberger, "EU Lets Deadline Lapse on Challenge to Helms-Burton," *Wall Street Journal*, April 4, 1998, p. A10.
30. "Last Chance for Vietnam-U.S. Trade Accord ," *Agence France-Presse*, June 6, 1999, p. 1.
31. "American Boycotts Start to Bite," *Financial Times*, February 6, 1997, p. 10.
32. Brian Morrissey, "Dealing with Sanctions Fever," *Journal of Commerce*, October 22, 1998, p. 8A.

rein."[33] There are efforts by the administration and legislators in the United States to increase the effectiveness of sanctions, giving the president power to grant waivers when necessary. If legislation is enacted, it would also force all sanctions to be tied to specific foreign policy objectives and require periodic reporting by the president on the cost and effect of sanctions. An example of a harmful sanction is the supercomputer rules, which limit export of supercomputers without special licenses to countries such as China, Russia, India, and Israel, giving the sales benefit to foreign competitors.[34]

Occasionally, U.S. companies have diverted export orders to foreign subsidiaries where such restrictions do not apply. In general, however, any company that depends on exports as a source of income is well advised to carefully monitor government legislations and acts, both domestically and abroad, since the potential effect can be either to create new opportunities or to prevent the exploitation of existing ones.

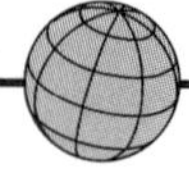

Import Trade Mechanics

In many ways, the importer is concerned with the same trade mechanics as the exporter.[35] Communications with foreign suppliers can be difficult because of distances involved, time changes, and cultural differences. Import trade makes use of the same price-quoting vocabulary as exporting does, and the payment mechanism is the same with respect to the use of letters of credit or open accounts. Finally, the logistic concerns of the importer are identical to those of the exporter, so that many of the points covered in the earlier portion of this chapter need not be repeated.

A substantial amount of effort is expended by importers to bring products through local customs. Not surprisingly, import requirements vary by nation and are numerous. In this section, we concentrate solely on the major import procedures as they apply to the United States. However, these procedures are indicative of the type of procedures employed in other countries. The Department of Commerce has a staff of specialists to help companies export. These specialists can explain the customs clearance procedures for most countries. Also, freight forwarders are very knowledgeable about customers' requirements and will assist in preparing the necessary documents.

33. Thomas W. Lippman, "U.S. Rethinking Trade Sanctions," *Washington Post*, January 26, 1998, p. A06.
34. Craig Stedman, "White House to Ease Computer Export Rules," *Computerworld*, February 7, 2000, p. 8.
35. The section on import trade mechanics is based on *Importing into the United States* (Washington, D.C.: Department of the Treasury, U.S. Customs Service, January 1989). Since these regulations are subject to frequent revisions, the interested reader is advised to obtain the latest information directly from the Customs Service.

Import Clearance Procedures

Whenever a shipment reaches the United States, the recipient, or consignee, must file an entry for the products or goods with U.S. Customs. The importer has the choice of filing for consumption or filing for storage. Under the second alternative, imported products may be stored for some time before they are officially entered for consumption in the United States, or they may be reexported.

Since the proper declaration of imported products requires some specific knowledge, many importers use the services of licensed customs brokers. A broker is empowered by the firm to act on its behalf at customs and file the necessary forms. To determine the customs status of a shipment, an examination is typically performed to check the following:

1. The value of the shipment to assess customs
2. The verification of required marking and labeling
3. Shipment of prohibited merchandise
4. Verification of invoicing and determination of either shortages or excess compared to the invoice

The importer will have to prepare all necessary forms to allow the U.S. Customs officials to make these determinations. Failure to meet these requirements may result in lengthy delays in clearing any shipment, unnecessary expenses on behalf of the importer, and higher fees charged by customs brokers.

Valuation of Shipments U.S. Customs officers are required by law to find the value of the imported merchandise. Basically, customs value is determined by selecting the higher of either foreign value or export value. *Foreign value* is based on the prices at which the imported merchandise is freely placed for sale in the country of origin in the usual wholesale quantities. The *export value* is the price at which the merchandise is freely offered for sale as an export to the United States in the major markets of the country of origin. When neither a foreign value nor an export value can be found, the merchandise may be entered at the corresponding U.S. value at which such or similar merchandise is freely offered in the United States less the necessary allowance for bringing the products into the country. If a corresponding U.S. value does not exist, valuation can be based on the cost of production. In a few cases, valuation can be based on the U.S. selling price, which is based on the typical price for the same product offered in the United States.

Products that are subject to duty are assessed either *ad valorem* (a percentage of the established value), with a *specific duty* (a specific amount per unit of measurement), or with a *compound duty* (combination of ad valorem and specific duty). Though the U.S. Customs Office publishes a list of the various duties by type of product, an importer can find out by contacting the U.S. Customs Office with the following information:

- Complete description of the imported item
- Method of manufacture
- Specifications and analyses
- Quantities and costs of component materials
- Commercial designation of the product in the United States and identification of the primary use of the product

Given sufficient material as described above, the U.S. Customs Service can provide importers with a binding assessment on import duties that makes it possible to assess the entire landed cost for the importer for later use in pricing. No binding information is available via telephone or based on incomplete information.

Marking and Labeling Unless otherwise stated, each product or article imported into the United States must be legibly marked in a conspicuous place with the name of the country of origin stated in English so that the U.S. purchaser can easily determine the country of origin. In some cases, markings may be made on the containers rather than the articles themselves. Importers are advised to obtain the particular regulations or exemptions from the U.S. Customs Service. In case of a lack of proper markings, the U.S. Customs Service can assess a special marking duty unless the imported products are marked under customs supervision. In either case, the absence of the required markings can cause costly delays to the importer.

Prohibited or Restricted Merchandise The importation of certain articles is either prohibited or restricted. It is impractical to list all the prohibited or restricted items here. However, the major classes of items are shown in Table 18.2. Restricted items can be imported with proper clearance.

Invoicing Procedures For some special categories of merchandise, only a commercial invoice prepared in the same manner typical for commercial transactions is sufficient for U.S. Customs clearance. Quite frequently, either a special invoice or a commercial invoice is not available at the time of entry. In such instances, the importer can prepare a pro forma invoice by promising to deliver final invoices within six months of the date of entry. Also, a bond must usually be posted to cover the value of the estimated duties.

Inaccurate information can cause costly delays to both the importer and exporter. To provide for smooth clearance through customs, the U.S. importer should assume the responsibility of properly informing the foreign supplier. The Journal of Commerce, a private company, offers a service called PIERS, which is a

TABLE 18.2

Classes of Products That Are Prohibited or Restricted for Import into the United States

Alcoholic beverages: Require a permit from Bureau of Alcohol, Tobacco and Firearms

Arms, ammunition, explosives: Require a permit from Bureau of Alcohol, Tobacco and Firearms

Automobiles: Must conform to federal motor vehicle safety standards

Coins, currencies, and stamps: No replicas of U.S. or foreign items permitted

Eggs and egg products: Subject to the Egg Products Inspection Act

Animals and plants: Subject to regulations of the Animal or Plant Health Inspection Service

Electronic products: Subject to the Radiation Control Act

Food, drugs, devices, cosmetics: Subject to the federal Food, Drug and Cosmetics Act

Narcotic drugs: Prohibited

Nuclear reactors and radioactive material: Subject to the U.S. Atomic Energy Commission

Obscene, immoral, seditious matter: Prohibited

Pesticides: Subject to the federal Environmental Control Act

Wool, fur, textiles, and fabric products: Subject to the Wool Products Labeling Act, the Textile Fiber Products Identification Act, the Flammable Fabrics Act, and the Fur Products Labeling Act

database of all imports and exports reported to the U.S. Customs in the forty-seven largest U.S. ports. The data are helpful for competitive and market research analysis.

Goods can be delayed at the port, waiting for the necessary paperwork before being shipped. There is a trend toward the use of electronic transmission of customers' documentation. TRADANET is a global electronic service that allows companies to send the commercial invoice and customs clearance document to the importer while the goods are in transit. With these documents, the importer can clear the goods through customs and speed up the distribution process at lower costs.[36]

36. "Data Exchange System to Benefit Firms, New Technology to Cut Costs and Boost Efficiency," *Financial Gazette*, May 28, 1998, p. 1.

The Role of the Customs Agent

Since the handling of shipments through customs requires specialized knowledge, most companies employ outside specialized firms that are registered with U.S. Customs. Not only will these agents prepare the necessary invoices from information supplied by the importer, they will also arrange for clearance through customs, inspection where necessary, payment of duties, and transport to the final destination. Frequently, such customs agents are also international freight forwarders, or freight-forwarding firms with a specialized customs section. To allow the customs agent to act on behalf of the importer, a special power of attorney is granted that identifies the customs agent as a legally empowered actor.

Free Trade Zones or Foreign Trade Zones

Free trade zones (FTZs) are industrial parks with a unique tax and legal status. These zones have been established where merchandise can be placed for unlimited time periods without the payment of duties. Duty will be assessed, however, as soon as the merchandise is transferred from the free trade zone to a country. In 1998, more than $800 billion worth of goods were handled in FTZs.[37]

Such zones offer many advantages to both exporters or importers. For one, duty payable can tie up a substantial amount of working capital. The use of a free trade zone allows a firm to keep an inventory close by without prepaying duty. In addition, many importers may later want to reexport products to other countries and thus prefer to store the merchandise temporarily in a place where no duties have to be paid until the final destination is determined. For example, almost two-thirds of the cars assembled in the BMW Spartenburg, North Carolina, FTZ are exported to other countries. According to Donnie Turbeville, customs coordinator at BMW, "BMW would not have come to the United States if there was not a FTZ program."[38]

Free trade zones are also valuable as manufacturing sites. Any merchandise brought into such zones may be broken up, repackaged, assembled, sorted, graded, cleaned, or used in the manufacturing process with domestic material. The latter can be brought duty-free into trade zones and reimported, again duty-free, into the United States. Duty will have to be paid only on components or parts subject to duty rather than on the entire value.

Free trade zones exist in most countries and are typically attached to ports or airports. In some countries with low labor costs, free trade zones were established to allow for the further processing of semimanufactured goods originating from developed countries.[39] These goods are later reexported into the country of

37. Josh Martin, "Gateways for the Global Economy," *Management Review*, December 1998, pp. 22–26.
38. "Auto Boss Wants Free Trade Zones," *Winnipeg Free Press*, June 25, 1999, p. 2.
39. Martin.

origin. Malaysia is one country that has allowed many foreign electronics companies to bring components for further assembly to Malaysian foreign trade zones. As a result, the foreign trade zones have ceased as a strictly distribution- or transportation-related phenomenon and are now incorporated by many international companies in their production or sourcing strategy.

Obstacles to Foreign Imports

Recently, there has been extensive political debate over protectionist measures for certain key U.S. industries. Although President Clinton failed to get support for "fast-track presidential authority" in 1997, it continued to be discussed in Congress. The fast-track authority would let the president negotiate trade deals with foreign countries and impose sanctions and incentives on short notice.[40]

Nowhere have imports made a bigger impression than in the steel industry. In 1999, the U.S. steel industry lobbied heavily for Congress to set steel import quotas. Although the proposed bill passed the House, it was defeated in the Senate.[41] U.S. companies claim that the steel is being "dumped" in our country at artificially low costs.. Hence, steelworkers and their companies were pushing government to protect U.S. markets against unreasonable foreign competition.

Consumers are the main beneficiaries of these imports. They are able to purchase quality at low cost. Economists argue that protecting the 150,000 U.S. steelworkers would significantly hurt all the other industries that benefit from lower-priced steel imports. The Ad Hoc Coalition Against Steel quotas, representing U.S. companies that use steel, estimated that in 1998 the United States exported $222 billion of products manufactured with steel. Steel quotas would raise the price of steel, making exports more expensive and less competitive in foreign markets. The Institute for International Economics estimated that the proposed legislation in 1999 would save only 1,700 steel jobs, at a cost of $800,000 per job, paid by higher prices to the consumers.[42] The conflict boils down to lower prices versus jobs.

Global Import Barriers

Goods do not flow freely from country to country. There are a host of impediments to the smooth flow of trade, such as import taxes, tariffs, quotas, and nontariff barriers (discussed in Chapters 2 and 4). The importing country can take a number of actions to slow down, block, or make importing unprofitable. In 1995,

40. "United States: Trade," *Cambridge International Forecasts Country Reports*, April 1, 1999, p. 1.
41. Helene Cooper, "Senate Thwarts Bill to Curb Steel Imports," *Wall Street Journal*, June 23, 1999, p. A2.
42. Helene Cooper, "Steel-Quota Bill Poses Dilemma for Clinton and Gore," *Wall Street Journal*, June 22, 1999, p. A24.

TABLE 18.3

Export Barriers the United States Hates Most

Product	*Countries*	*Barrier*	*Sales Lost by U.S.*[a]
Grain	European Union	Price supports, variable duties	$2.0 billion
Soybeans	European Union	Price supports	$1.4 billion
Rice	Japan	Ban	$300 million
Beef	European Union	Ban on growth hormones in livestock	$100 million
Commercial aircraft	Britain, France, Germany, Spain	Subsidies to Airbus Industrie	Over $850 million
Telecommunications equipment	European Union, South Korea	Standards stacked against imports	No estimate
Telecommunications satellites	Japan	Ban on import by government agencies	No estimate
Pharmaceuticals	Argentina, Brazil	No patent protection	Over $110 million
Videocassettes, films	Brazil	Requirements to subsidize and market local films	Over $40 million
Computer software	Thailand	Poor patent protection	No estimate

[a]Annual, estimated.
Source: Rahul Jacob, "Export Barriers the U.S. Hates Most," *Fortune*, February 27, 1989, p. 89.

China imposed a number of taxes on imports that substantially increased the cost of competitive imports versus locally produced products. However, in 1999, as China negotiated to obtain entry into the WTO, it reduced the duty on 1,014 items in the area of textiles, toys, and forestry products. Both of these changes in China caught many foreign companies by surprise; however, they reflect an overall desire of China to cautiously open its markets.[43]

As the European Union standardizes products for sale across Europe, it has developed the CE marking system to identify products that conform to EU direc-

43. "China to Cut Import Duty for 1,014 Items," *BBC Worldwide Monitoring*, January 6, 1999.

tives. The CE (Conformité Européene) marking is a passport for machinery, telecommunications equipment, and most electronic products. Stacy Brovitz, CEO of Dormont Manufacturing, reported to Congress that his firm had spent over $1 million on obtaining the CE mark, with limited success. After Dormont received approval for its flexible gas connectors, it was told that gas connectors did not fall under the Gas Appliance Directive. Mr. Brovitz suspects the European competition is using the EC standards to keep out foreign competitors.[44]

The manufacturers and farmers of the United States face a number of export barriers, which are being discussed through international trade negotiations, trade talks, and meetings of heads of state. The top ten barriers to trade are shown in Table 18.3.

Japan has received a great deal of pressure to open its markets. The U.S. government has often used its international trade office to push for the removal of perceived import barriers in Japan, with whom the United States has a trade deficit that reached $64 billion in 1998. AT&T and other telecommunications companies reported that Nippon Telegraph & Telephone Co. were charging foreign telecom companies very high interconnection charges to limit competition. Here, the dispute was much less over explicit trade restrictions, such as tariffs or duties, but more over hidden regulations that prevented foreign companies from competing openly.[45]

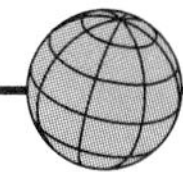

Global Trade Negotiations

The most often used forum for discussing trade disputes has been the World Trade Organization (WTO). The WTO will continue to be the primary vehicle that countries will use to encourage free trade while limiting harmful unfair trade. The next round of trade negotiations will focus on trade in services and electronic commerce.[46]

At the WTO, founded in 1995, the United States accounted for about one-third of the approximately sixty antidumping cases (1995 through 1998). Many foreign countries would prefer that the United States stop using countermeasures in trade and rely more on WTO rulings before taking unilateral action.[47] Free trade benefits both the exporter and importer. A study by the Federal Reserve of St. Louis found that U.S. exports would have been 26.2 percent higher if all countries practiced free trade. Also, U.S. protectionism was costing U.S. consumers more than $100 billion in higher prices. The Australian Department of Foreign Affairs and

44. Stacy Brovitz, "Technical Barriers to Free Trade," *Congressional Testimony: Federal Document Clearing House*, April 28, 1998, pp. 1–6.
45. "Barshefsky Threatens to Bring Telecom Reform Dispute with Japan to WTO," *Dow Jones Business News*, June 4, 1999.
46. "WTO Group Opens Talks on Trade: Services," *Associated Press Newswires*, June 17, 1999.
47. "WTO Urges US to Stop Going It Alone," *Financial Times*, November 13, 1996, p. 6.

Trade reported in a new study that if tariffs worldwide were reduced by 50 percent, global trade would increase by $400 billion, and if by 100 percent, trade would rise by $750 billion.[48]

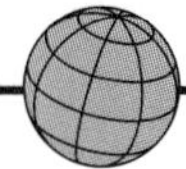

Conclusions

This chapter has explained some of the procedural aspects of global marketing, specifically exporting and importing. Thorough knowledge of these trade mechanics is often a prerequisite for global marketers. All too frequently, a global strategy fails because some of these mechanics have been neglected.

However, this text cannot and does not specify all the regulations in force for any particular product category or country. We have provided a general background, listing the factors that may have to be investigated before a strategy can be implemented. The regulations described are also subject to change. Consequently, we suggest that close contact with specialists in this area be maintained so that executives responsible for global marketing activities can keep themselves abreast of new developments.

There is a trend around the world toward reducing barriers and opening markets. The rapid growth in global trade has made more countries interdependent. If Japan continues to protect its $6 billion rice market, the United States can limit the importation of Japanese cars. World leaders are working hard to open all markets, although it will take years to remove all the barriers. Close contact with your trade association will keep your firm up-to-date on the latest agreements between governments and the trade.

QUESTIONS FOR DISCUSSION

1. Your company manufactures telephones at your plant in Scranton, Pennsylvania. South Korea wants a quote on ten thousand telephones. How should you quote so that it is convenient for the buyer?
2. Irrevocable letters of credit have become very popular. How do they protect the buyer and the seller?
3. When calculating the cost of a shipment of machinery for export, what additional costs will the exporter be faced with in addition to shipping and insurance?
4. Explain the possible uses of export documentation on a shipment of pipe from Los Angeles to Bolivia?
5. What are the critical elements of the export planning process? If you were asked to develop a plan for exporting gloves to South America, how would you do it?
6. What are the advantages and disadvantages of import limits in the United States? Use, for example, the import quotas on Japanese automobiles into the United States.
7. How can U.S. manufacturers use free trade zones?

48. Bruce Bartlett, "Market Power: The Paradox of Protectionism," *National Center for Policy Analysis*, June 15, 1999, p. C07.

FOR FURTHER READING

Albaum, Gerald, Jesper Strandskov, Edwin Duerr, and Laurence Dowd. *International Marketing and Export Management.* Wokingham, England: Addison-Wesley, 1989.

Attiyeh, Robert S., and David L. Wenner. "Critical Mass: Key to Exports." *Business Horizons*, December 1979, pp. 28-38.

Ayal, Igal. "Industry Export Performance: Assessment and Prediction." *Journal of Marketing*, Summer 1982, pp. 54-61.

Brasch, J. "Using Export Specialists to Develop Overseas Sales." *Harvard Business Review*, May-June 1981, pp. 6-8.

Dollar, David. "Import Quotas and the Product Cycle." *Quarterly Journal of Economics*, August 1987, pp. 615-632.

Filbert, William B. "The Licensing Process: Getting the Export License." *Export Today*, February 1984, pp. 60-63.

Fitzpatrick, Peter B., and Alan S. Zimmerman. *Essentials of Export Marketing.* New York: American Management Association, 1985.

Hayes, John. "Who Sets the Standards?" *Forbes*, April 17, 1989, pp. 110-112.

Johnson, Thomas E., *Export/Import Procedures and Documentation*. Saratoga Springs: AMACON, 1997.

Katsikeas, Constantine S., Shengliang L. Deng, and Lawrence H. Wortzel. "Perceived Export Success Factors of Small- and Medium-Sized Canadian Firms. *Journal of International Marketing*, vol. 5, no. 4, Winter 1997.

McGuinness, Norman W., and Blair Little. "The Influence of Product Characteristics on the Export Performance of New Industrial Products." *Journal of Marketing*, Spring 1981, pp. 110-122.

Root, Franklin R. *Entry Strategies for International Markets*. New York: Jossey-Bass, 1998.

Samiee, Saeed. "Exporting and the Internet: A Conceptual Perspective." *International Marketing Review*, 1998, vol. 15, no. 5, pp. 413-426.

Tansuhaj, Patriya S., and James W. Gentry. "Firm Differences in Perceptions of the Facilitating Role of Foreign Trade Zones in Global Marketing and Logistics." *Journal of International Business Studies*, Spring 1987, pp. 29-33.

Weiss, Kenneth D. *Building an Import-Export Business.* New York: John Wiley & Sons, 1987.

Woznick, Alexandra, and Edward G. Hinkelman, *A Basic Guide to Exporting*, Third Edition. New York: World Trade Press, 2000.

White, Steven D., David A. Griffith, and John K. Ryans Jr. "Measuring Export Performance in Service Industries." *International Marketing Review*, vol. 15, no. 3, 1998, pp. 188-204.

Zou, Shaoming, and Simona Stan. "The Determinants of Export Performance: A Review of the Empirical Literature Between 1987 and 1997." *International Marketing Review*, 1998, vol. 15, no. 5, pp. 333-356.

Name and Company Index

Subject Index